# Criminal Investigation

## FIFTH EDITION

**Wayne W. Bennett**

Former Chief of Police
Boulder City, Nevada
Edina, Minnesota

**Kären M. Hess**

Normandale Community College
Bloomington, Minnesota

## West/Wadsworth Publishing Company

I(T)P  An International Thomson Publishing Company

Belmont, CA • Albany, NY • Bonn • Boston • Cincinnati • Detroit • Johannesburg • London • Madrid
Melbourne • Mexico City • New York • Paris • San Francisco • Singapore • Tokyo • Toronto • Washington

Criminal Justice Editor: Sabra Horne
Development Editor: Dan Alpert
Project Development Editor: Claire Masson
Editorial Assistant: Jeff Kellner
Marketing Manager: Mike Dew
Project Coordinator: Debby Kramer
Print Buyer: Karen Hunt
Permissions Editor: Veronica Oliva
Production: Electronic Publishing Services, Inc., NYC
Photo Research: Electronic Publishing Services, Inc., NYC
Copy Editor: Electronic Publishing Services, Inc., NYC
Illustrator: Electronic Publishing Services, Inc., NYC
Cover: Rob Hugel
Cover Image: © FPG International, LLC
Compositor: Electronic Publishing Services, Inc., NYC
Text Printer: R. R. Donnelly
Cover Printer: Phoenix Color Corporation
Index: Christine Orthmann

Printed in the United States of America
1  2  3  4  5  6  7  8  9  10

For more information, contact Wadsworth Publishing Company, 10 Davis Drive, Belmont, CA 94002, or electronically at http://www.thomson.com/wadsworth.html

International Thomson Publishing Europe
Berkshire House 168-173
High Holborn
London, WC1V 7AA, England

International Thomson Editores
Campos Eliseos 385, Piso 7
Col. Polanco
11560 México D.F. México

Thomas Nelson Australia
102 Dodds Street
South Melbourne 3205
Victoria, Australia

International Thomson Publishing Asia
221 Henderson Road
#05-10 Henderson Building
Singapore 0315

Nelson Canada
1120 Birchmount Road
Scarborough, Ontario
Canada M1K 5G4

International Thomson Publishing Japan
Hirakawacho Kyowa Building, 3F
2-2-1 Hirakawacho
Chiyoda-ku, Tokyo 102, Japan

International Thomson Publishing GmbH
Königswinterer Strasse 418
53227 Bonn, Germany

International Thomson Publishing Southern Africa
Building 18, Constantia Park
240 Old Pretoria Road
Halfway House, 1685 South Africa

**Library of Congress Cataloging-in-Publication Data**
Bennett, Wayne.
    Criminal investigation / Wayne W. Bennett, Kären M. Hess. —5th ed.
      p. cm.
    Includes biographical references and indexes.
    ISBN 0—534—53532—1
    1. Criminal investigation. I. Hess, Kären M.
II. Title.
HV8073.B43 1997
363.25—dc20                                    97—34881

# Contents in Brief

# Contents

**vii**

## Chapter 3    Notes and Reports, 73

## Chapter 4    Searches, 100

## Chapter 5     Physical Evidence, 135

## Chapter 6     Obtaining Information, 189

**Chapter 7        Identifying and Arresting Suspects, 230**

**Section Three   Investigating Crimes against Persons, 275**

**Chapter 8        Robbery, 278**

**Chapter 9        Assault, 306**

## Chapter 10     Sex Offenses, 333

## Chapter 11     Crimes against Children, 359

## Chapter 14      Larceny/Theft, Fraud, White-Collar and Environmental Crime, 456

## Chapter 15      Computer Crime, 490

## Chapter 16      Motor Vehicle Theft, 513

## Chapter 17    Arson, 534

## Section V    Other Challenges to the Criminal Investigator, 569

## Chapter 18    Organized Crime, Gang-Related Crime, Bias/Hate Crime and Ritualistic Crime, 570

**Chapter 19     Drug Buyers and Sellers, 617**

**Section VI     The Investigator's Role in the Judicial
Process, 659**

**Chapter 20     Preparing for and Presenting Cases in Court, 660**

# Cases

# Preface

The complex responsibilities of criminal investigation must be fulfilled under constantly changing conditions and in a way that assures the rights of all citizens. Changes in technology and society continually present new challenges to investigators, requiring them to be knowledgeable in a wide variety of areas.

This book is based on many years of practical experience. Wayne Bennett has spent nearly fifty years in law enforcement as an officer and as a popular teacher of various aspects of criminal investigation. Kären Matison Hess has been developing instructional programs for more than twenty-five years. The book itself has been reviewed by experts in criminal investigation.

*Criminal Investigation,* Fifth Edition, provides fundamental information that will serve as an overview of the entire field as well as a solid foundation for specialized course work. Although the content of each chapter could easily be expanded into an entire book or course, this book can provide only the basic concepts of each area. In Section One you will be introduced to the broad field of criminal investigation, to what constitutes effective, efficient investigation and to the equipment, technology and procedures that facilitate investigation. Important court cases and decisions are cited and explained throughout the book.

In Section Two you will learn numerous investigative techniques: photographing; sketching; taking notes; identifying, collecting, examining and processing physical evidence; obtaining information; developing, locating and identifying suspects; conducting surveillances, undercover assignments and raids. In Sections Three, Four and Five you will see how those techniques are applied in specific types of investigations. You will learn the basics of investigating *crimes against the person:* robbery, assault, rape and other sex offenses and homicide; *crimes against property:* burglary, larceny/theft, computer crime, motor vehicle theft and arson; and *other crimes* including organized crime, gang-related crime, bias/hate crime and ritualistic crime. Finally, in Section Six you

**Wayne W. Bennett**

**Kären M. Hess**

will learn how investigation relates to the criminal justice system, how to prepare a case for prosecution and how to testify in court.

## How to Use This Book

*Criminal Investigation*, Fifth Edition, is more than just a textbook; it is a planned learning experience for you. The more actively you participate in it, the better your learning will be. You will learn and remember more if you first familiarize yourself with the total scope of the subject. Read and think about the Table of Contents; it provides an outline of the many facets of criminal investigation. Then follow these steps as you study each chapter:

**1.** Read the objectives at the beginning of the chapter. These are stated as "Do You Know?" questions. Assess your current knowledge of each question. Examine any preconceptions you may hold.
**2.** Read the chapter, underlining, highlighting or taking notes if that is your preferred study style.
   **a.** Pay special attention to all information that is "highlighted."

---

A criminal investigation is a thorough, objective search for truthful information.

---

The key concepts of the chapter are presented this way.
   **b.** Look up unfamiliar words in the Glossary at the back of the book.
**3.** When you have finished reading the chapter, reread the "Do You Know" questions at the beginning of the chapter to make sure you can give an educated response to each question. If you find yourself stumped by one, find the appropriate section in the chapter and review it.
**4.** Finally, in Sections Three through Six, complete the Application exercise at the end of each chapter. These exercises ask you to apply the chapter concepts in actual or hypothetical cases. Then read the Discussion Questions and be prepared to contribute to a class discussion of the ideas presented in the chapter.

By following these steps, you will learn more information, understand it more fully and remember it longer. It's up to you. Good learning!

## Acknowledgments

A number of professionals from academia and the field reviewed our manuscript and provided us with valuable suggestions. We thank them all: *Joel J. Allen*, Western Illinois University; *Thomas Allen*, University of South Dakota; *Captain Frank Anzelmi*; *Greg Arnold*, Manatee Community College; *Robert Barthol*, Chabot College; *Walt Copley*, Metropolitan State College of Denver; *Edward Creekmore*, Northland Community College; *Stanley Cunningham*, Western Illinois University; *Andrew Dantschich*, St. Petersburg Junior College; *Wayne Dunning*, Wichita State University; *Cass Gaska*, Henry Ford Community College; *Bruce Gordon*, University of Cincinnati; *Keith Haley*, University of Cincinnati; *George Henthorn*, Central Missouri State University; *John Hicks*, Hocking Technical College; *Robert R. Ives*, Rock Valley College; *George Keefer*; *Robert A. Lorinskas*,

Southern Illinois at Carbondale; *Jane E. McClellan; Michael Myer,* University of North Dakota; *Jane Kravitz Munley,* Luzerne County Community College; *James E. Newman,* Rio Hondo Community College; *William L. Pelkey,* Eastern Kentucky University; *Ronald A. Pincom,* New Mexico State University; *Charles Quarles,* University of Mississippi; *Walter F. Ruger,* Nassau Community College; *Joseph Sandoval,* Metropolitan State University; *William Straugham,* Tift College; *Clarence R. Terrill,* Harford Community College; *Charles A. Tracy,* Portland State University; *Bob Walker,* Trinity Valley Community College; and *Richard Weber,* Jamestown Community College. We greatly appreciate the input of these individuals. Sole responsibility for any errors, however, is our own.

Thank you to A. E. "Al" Hansen and Michael Bennett for providing some of the book's sketches and to Dorothy Bennett for many of the photographs.

We extend a special thank you to Christine Hess Orthmann for her careful preparation of the index and the supplemental materials. And more special thanks go to Sabra Horne, Dan Alpert, Claire Masson and Debby Kramer, our editors at Wadsworth Publishing Company, and to Margaret Dornfeld, our production editor at Electronic Publishing Services. Finally, we thank our families and colleagues for their continuing support and encouragement throughout the development of *Criminal Investigation,* Fifth Edition.

*Wayne W. Bennett*
*Kären M. Hess*

# Introduction

Criminal investigation is a complex, sophisticated field, each aspect of which could constitute a book in itself. This text includes the most basic aspects of criminal investigation. Section One presents an overview of criminal investigation and general guidelines to follow or adapt in specific circumstances, as well as basic considerations in the preliminary investigation.

Investigators must be thoroughly familiar with crimes and their elements, modus operandi information, the major goals of investigation, the basic functions of investigating officers and the investigators' relationship with other individuals and agencies.

The most critical phase in the majority of criminal investigations is the preliminary investigation. The decisions made, the responsibilities assumed and the tasks performed apply to a wide variety of crimes and must be part of every investigator's repertoire.

Investigators do not operate in a vacuum but must relate to constitutional safeguards set forth in the U.S. Constitution's Fourth, Fifth, Sixth and Fourteenth Amendments. They must also understand case law determining the parameters within which they perform the investigative process. How these constitutional safeguards and case law specifically affect investigations is emphasized throughout the text.

# Criminal Investigation: An Overview

## DO YOU KNOW

What criminal investigation is?

What the major goals of criminal investigation are?

What basic functions are performed by investigators?

What characteristics are important in investigators?

Who usually proceeds to the crime scene first?

What res gestae statements are and their importance?

What to do if a suspect is still at a crime scene? Has recently fled the scene?

How the crime scene and evidence are protected and for how long?

What responsibilities are included in the preliminary investigation?

How to determine if a crime has been committed?

Who is responsible for solving crimes?

With whom investigators must relate?

How to avoid lawsuits?

## CAN YOU DEFINE

| | | |
|---|---|---|
| civil liability | emergencies | investigate |
| crime | fact | misdemeanor |
| criminal intent | felony | modus operandi (M.O.) |
| criminal investigation | forensic science | opinion |
| criminal statute | inference | ordinance |
| criminalistics | intuition | res gestae statements |
| elements of the crime | | |

## Introduction

CRIMINAL INVESTIGATION HAS BECOME A HIGHLY SOPHISTICATED ART requiring a coordinated effort among several specialists. Ultimately, however, the entire investigation almost always depends on police officers, be they patrol officers or detectives. The following article illustrates the highly technical nature of criminal investigation.

### Sherlock Holmes Couldn't Compete*

Sherlock Holmes would have to go back to school if he opted to become a 20th Century detective instead of a Victorian era literary hero.

The magnifying glass methods his creator, Sir Arthur Conan Doyle, gave him would hardly rate a "zounds."

---

*Las Vegas Sun*, March 28, 1977. Reprinted by permission of United Press International (UPI).

Holmes—the reader, thinker and analyzer of clues—would have to study physics, chemistry, medicine, photomicroscopy, spectrometry, chromatography, hematology, etc.

The crime-solving fields he would have to master were pointed up by the American Academy of Forensic Sciences in enacting an "update" on the Holmesian approach at its San Diego convention.

The scenario for "Popped Off in the Penthouse" required nine minds—all expert in forensic science disciplines—to solve the mystery.

The purpose was "to show the interrelation of the eight or nine disciplines" in forensic science, said Joseph F. Keefe, an attorney from Torrington, Conn. He played the role of a newly elected prosecutor.

The setting: Keefe's office after discovery of a prominent man's apparent suicide by gunshot wound to the left side of the head.

The cast: experts in criminal investigation sciences.

The problem: "The high-velocity blood spatter on the wall was inconsistent with the body position," according to Gerald J. Reichardt, police technician from the Dade County Public Safety Department in Miami.

Reichardt detailed discovery of the body of William Foster, the position of a nearby revolver, the characteristics of bloodstains on the wall, the existence of a bloody handprint on a door and the presence of a suicide note.

Actual evidence from several cases was woven into the "Popped Off" presentation. The format allowed each forensic specialist to depict his or her function in the judicial system.

Vincent J. M. DiMaio, medical examiner from Dallas, described the autopsy and body examination.

Foster's hands were swabbed with a special solution to pick up traces of burnt gunpowder and primers, he said. Test firing of the pistol by crime laboratory technicians left traces of lead, antimony and barium on their hands, but none was found on the dead man's hands, he said.

Burns to the scalp showed a "muzzle-to-head" discharge of the weapon.

DiMaio said the clincher—against suicide—was the stroke-damaged brain tissue that showed the victim had limited motor control of his left arm.

"One could be fairly certain that he could not have manipulated a weapon with his left arm, and it would be nearly impossible for him to have shot himself in the left side of the head with his right hand . . . it is a case of homicide," the pathologist said.

Evidence gleaned from the pistol—a revolver with a filed-off serial number—was presented by John F. Anderson, director of the East Washington State crime laboratory at Spokane.

Test firing and comparison of lands and grooves on test bullets and the one removed from Foster's head proved the gun was the murder weapon, he said. He also explained that swabbing the butt with acid "raised" the missing serial number.

Anderson also said legwork showed Foster, a recluse, had only a few close associates including a personal secretary or "man's man," two doctors and a chauffeur.

The secretary, a Mr. Peterson, was separated from the others by a "single human hair" found on Foster's jacket, Anderson said.

Examination of the hair under a microscope for scale count, pigment distribution and other characteristics permitted Anderson to conclude: "We have reduced the population (of possible killers) to six and have eliminated five." He also said he could testify in court that salivary secretions on cigarette butts found in Foster's bedroom yielded Peterson's blood type groupings—which matched those of the bloody handprint.

Other evidence included a broken tooth found at the scene. It was found to have come from the suspect and indicated a struggle in the penthouse.

Conflicting evidence came from Emanuel Tanay, a clinical associate professor of psychiatry at Wayne State University in Detroit.

He told the prosecutor he believed Peterson's story that the victim tried to commit suicide, a struggle ensued, Peterson grabbed the gun and it went off.

The psychiatrist's position was not accepted because of discrepancies between the story and the physical evidence.

Other evidence, including bone studies of remains found to have been those of the missing chauffeur, cleared other possible suspects.

Keefe concluded the evidence would support a murder complaint against Peterson.

Holmes had been replaced by a criminalist, a police detective, an odontologist, a pathologist, a physical anthropologist, a psychiatrist, a document examiner, a toxicologist and a crime laboratory coordinator.

This was written twenty years ago! Criminal investigation has, indeed, changed. Among the major developments of the late twentieth century, the greatest assistance to police has probably been the technological advances. Technology has advanced communications and records systems, laboratory and field-testing capabilities, and computerized networks beyond police expectations. This has helped agencies at all levels of government to provide better police services and has increased their crime-solving capabilities.

---

A **criminal investigation** is usually initiated by personal observation or information from a citizen. Patrol officers may see a suspicious action or person, or a citizen may report suspicious actions or persons. Such information is received at police headquarters by telephone, teletype, radio or when a person steps up to the police complaint desk. The police dispatcher relays the information to a patrol officer by radio or teleprint, and the officer responds.

The initial response is crucial to the success of an investigation. Although it is popularly believed that cases are won or lost in court, more cases actually are lost during the first hour of the investigation—the initial response period—than in court.

Because no two crimes are identical, even if they are committed by the same person, each investigation is unique. The great range of variables in individual crimes makes it impossible to establish fixed rules for conducting an investigation. Nevertheless, some general guidelines help to ensure that investigations are thorough and effective. Investigators modify and adapt these guidelines to fit each case.

Investigators need not have superhuman reasoning ability. They must, however, proceed in an orderly, systematic way, gathering facts to analyze and evaluate. The decisions to be made and the actions to be taken are introduced in this chapter. Each step of the preliminary investigation is explained more fully in subsequent chapters.

This chapter begins with a discussion of criminal investigation, its goals and basic functions. This is followed by an examination of the characteristics of an effective investigator who is responsible for the investigative function. Next, basic considerations in the preliminary examination are described, including who responds first, the point of arrival, setting priorities, handling emergency situations, protecting the crime scene and conducting the preliminary investigation. Then the follow-up investigation, computer-aided investigation and investigative productivity are discussed, followed by an explanation of the numerous individuals and agencies with which investigators must interact. The chapter concludes with a discussion of how to avoid civil and criminal liability.

## Criminal Investigation Defined

*Investigation* means to follow step-by-step by patient inquiry or observation; to search into; to examine and inquire into with care and accuracy; to find out by careful inquisition; the taking of evidence; a legal inquiry (*Luckert v. Elridge*). The word **investigate** is derived from the Latin word *vestigare* meaning "to track or trace," a derivation easily related to police investigation. A criminal investigation seeks all facts associated with a crime to determine the truth: what happened and who is responsible.

---

A criminal investigation is the process of discovering, collecting, preparing, identifying and presenting evidence to prove the truth or falsity of an issue in law.

---

If a crime is suspected or known to have been committed, the police conduct the investigation. They may investigate alone, or they may seek help from medical and technical specialists or specialists representing private interests or groups such as insurance claims adjustors and consumer fraud investigators. Investigators from federal, state or county police agencies may also assist.

## Other Terms Defined

The first determination in a criminal investigation is whether a crime has, in fact, been committed. Does the evidence support a specific offense? A legal arrest cannot be made for an act that is not defined by statute or ordinance as a crime.

Although everyone has a notion of what *crime* is, investigators must have a very precise understanding of what it means. Specific definitions of such terms as *crime, felony, misdemeanor, criminal statute* and *ordinance* are found in case law:

■ A *crime* is an act in violation of penal law; an offense against the state. The broader use of the term includes both felonies and misdemeanors (*People v. Williams*). A crime is a violation of a public right or law (*Commonwealth v. Smith*). A crime is an act or omission forbidden by law and punishable by a fine, imprisonment or even death. This is in contrast to torts or private harms.
■ A *felony* is a serious crime, graver than a misdemeanor; it is generally punishable by death or imprisonment of more than one year in a penitentiary (*People v. Pointer*).
■ A *misdemeanor* is a crime or offense lower than a felony and punishable by fine or imprisonment of up to one year in other than a penitentiary (*People v. Harshberger*).
■ A *criminal statute* is a legislative act relating to crime and its punishment (*Brown v. Foster*).
■ An *ordinance* is an act of the legislative body of a municipality or county relating to all the rules governing the municipality, inclusive of misdemeanor crimes (*Bills v. Goshen*).

Crimes and the penalties for each are established and defined by state and federal statutes and local ordinances.* An act that is not declared a crime by statute or ordinance is not a chargeable offense, no matter how wrong it may seem. Designated crimes and their punishments change as society's attitudes change. In the past, for example, behavior associated with alcoholism was considered criminal, but today many states regard alcoholism as an illness. However, driving while under the influence is now considered a much more serious offense than it was previously. Conversely, our society has designated as crimes some acts, such as computer fraud, that were unknown in earlier times.

Crimes are divided into two general categories—felonies and misdemeanors—depending on the severity of the act and the recommended punishment. The more serious the crime is considered by society, the more severe the penalty. Investigations involve both types of crimes. Misdemeanors are sometimes further subdivided into gross and petty misdemeanors, based on the value of the property involved.

Because definitions of crimes and their penalties vary considerably on the municipal, county, state and federal level, investigators must be familiar with their area's criminal statutes and ordinances. For example, in some states such as Michigan, shoplifting is a felony. In most states the value of the property shoplifted determines whether it is a misdemeanor or a felony.

These statutes and ordinances list specific conditions, called the **elements of the crime,** that must occur for an act to be called a specific kind of crime. For example, a state statute might define burglary as occurring when (1) an accused enters a building (2) without the consent of the rightful owner (3) with the intent to commit a crime. The investigation must prove each element, even if the suspect has confessed.

Sections Three and Four of this text discuss the elements of the major crimes. Knowing these elements is essential to gathering evidence to prove that a crime has, in fact, been committed.

In addition to proving the elements of the crime, investigators must determine who committed it. Investigation is often aided by knowing how criminals usually operate, that is, their **modus operandi,** or **M.O.**

It was formerly thought that each criminal followed a certain M.O. and rarely changed from one type of crime to another or to committing the same type of crime in a different way. For example, it was relatively easy to recognize the "work" of Jack the Ripper.

Modus operandi information can provide clues in less obvious cases as well. For example, if a series of burglaries are committed between 11 A.M. and 1 P.M. in one area of the community and all involve broken glass in a door, it might be inferred that the same individual(s) committed the crimes. A similar time, area and method of entry support this assumption. Although the burglaries may be unrelated, the probability is low. It might further be assumed that the burglar would not commit armed robbery or other types of crimes unless surprised while committing a burglary.

Such assumptions are *not certainties,* however. Some criminals commit several types of crimes, and they may change the type of crime they commit because of need, opportunity, inability to perform certain types of previously engaged in crimes or greater sophistication. For example, a narcotics user may commit larceny, burglary or robbery to obtain money for drugs. A burglar may become

---

*Some states, such as Illinois, do not consider violations of city ordinances to be crimes.

too old to commit burglaries and may turn to shoplifting. Or a burglar may first steal checks and a check writer and then turn to forgery to cash the checks. Never eliminate suspects simply because their known M.O. does not fit the crime being investigated.

Sometimes investigations are classified as follows:

■ Walk-through. The suspect is at the scene and the investigator needs to develop the case for proof of the crime.
■ Where-Are-They? The same as a walk-through case, except the whereabouts of the suspect are not known.
■ Whodunit? No identification of a suspect. These are usually the most complex cases.

## Goals of Criminal Investigations

The goal of criminal investigation would obviously seem to be to solve cases; to discover "whodunit." In reality, the goals of criminal investigation are not quite so simple.

---

The goals of criminal investigation are to:
■ Determine if a crime has been committed.
■ Legally obtain information and evidence to identify the person(s) responsible.
■ Arrest the suspect(s).
■ Recover stolen property.
■ Present the best possible case to the prosecutor.

---

While committing crimes, people may make mistakes. They almost always leave some type of evidence. They may overlook tangible evidence such as a jacket, handkerchief, pen, purse, piece of paper or card that connects them with the crime scene. Such evidence is left for many reasons: carelessness, panic at noises heard while committing the crime or at encountering unforeseen circumstances, underestimation of police capabilities, misinformation about the "target," emotional or mental instability or the influence of drugs or alcohol.

More often, however, they leave less-visible evidence such as fingerprints, blood stains, small particles of glass or dirt, a faint footprint, body hairs or clothing fibers, often called *trace evidence.*

Investigators search for evidence using methods discussed fully in Chapter 4. Sometimes, however, little or no evidence exists. Not all crimes are solvable. For example, a larceny committed by a transient who enters a house through an open door, takes food (larceny), eats it and then leaves the area unseen is a crime not likely to be solved. A burglary committed by a person wearing gloves and whose footprints are washed away by a hard rain before police arrive will be more difficult to solve than if it had not rained. Often fingerprints are found, but they cannot be matched with any prints on file. Many cases have insufficient evidence, no witnesses and no informants to provide leads.

Learn to recognize when a case is unsolvable but only after all leads are exhausted. As an FBI agent once said, "Any average person with training can pursue hot leads; it is the investigator who can develop leads when the trail grows cold who is the superior investigator."

A successful investigation is one in which:

- A logical sequence is followed.
- All available physical evidence is legally obtained.
- All witnesses are effectively interviewed.
- All suspects are legally and effectively interrogated.
- All leads are thoroughly developed.
- All details of the case are accurately and completely recorded and reported.

Investigators systematically seek evidence to identify the individual(s) who committed a crime, locate the individual(s) and obtain sufficient evidence to prove the suspect(s) guilty beyond a reasonable doubt in court. Procedures to accomplish these goals are the focus of the remainder of this book. However, determining the truth is more important than obtaining a conviction or closing a case.

Investigators seek to find the truth, not simply to prove suspects guilty. As stated in Article 10 of the *Canons of Police Ethics* (International Association of Chiefs of Police):

> The law enforcement officer shall be concerned equally in the prosecution of the wrong-doer and the defense of the innocent. He shall ascertain what constitutes evidence and shall present such evidence impartially and without malice. In so doing, he will ignore social, political, and all other distinctions among the persons involved, strengthening the tradition of the reliability and integrity of an officer's word.

## Basic Functions

Successful investigation involves a balance between scientific knowledge acquired by study and experience and the skills acquired by the artful application of learned techniques. Police portrayals in mystery stories or on radio and television seldom depict police investigations accurately.

Police investigations involve great attention to details, an exceptionally suspicious nature at the appropriate time, considerable training in the classroom and the field, an unusual ability to obtain information from diverse types of personalities under adverse circumstances and endless patience and perseverance.

---

The numerous functions performed by investigators include:
- Providing emergency assistance.
- Securing the crime scene.
- Photographing, videotaping and sketching.
- Taking notes and writing reports.
- Searching for, obtaining and processing physical evidence.
- Obtaining information from witnesses and suspects.
- Identifying suspects.
- Conducting raids, surveillances, stakeouts and undercover assignments.
- Testifying in court.

---

These basic functions are discussed in depth in Section Two. What is important at this point is to realize the complexity of and interrelationships among the various functions performed by investigators and the skills that must be developed. Investigation is both a science and an art.

Criminal investigation has become more scientific over the years, more thoroughly grounded in the laws of nature and scientific principles. Nonetheless, investigators are frequently required to practice the "art" of investigation; that is, to rely on skill acquired by experience, study and observation rather than on scientific principles. They have developed the ability to see relationships between unrelated facts and to question the apparently unquestionable.

## Characteristics of an Effective Investigator

"A good detective," says Pilant (1992, p. 33), "needs more than a badge and a gun. According to one veteran homicide detective, it takes creativity, imagination and an amazing amount of persistence, dedication and patience. These men and women work long hours in cramped quarters, live on burnt coffee and bad food and wouldn't give up the job for anything." A good investigator is also one who reads a lot about a variety of subjects. Regardless of title, pay or rank, officers performing investigative functions are more effective if they possess specific intellectual, psychological and physical characteristics.

### Intellectual Characteristics

Investigators must absorb training and apply it to their work. They must know the elements of the crime, understand and be able to apply investigative techniques and be able to work with many different types of people. Exceptional intelligence is not necessary to be an effective investigator; objectivity, logic and common sense are more important.

---

Effective investigators obtain and retain information, apply technical knowledge, remain open-minded and objective and use logic.

---

Investigators obtain vast amounts of information: knowledge and descriptions of people who commit crimes, descriptions of vehicles and knowledge of areas, buildings and many other subjects. They meet and talk to people from all walks of life—factory workers, professionals, males, females, adults, juveniles—and must adjust their approach to each. In addition, each crime scene must be absorbed and recalled, sometimes months or years later. Thus, accurate, complete, well-organized reports and records are essential.

Investigators also develop knowledge of and skill in investigative techniques such as interviewing and interrogating, photographing and sketching, searching, report writing and numerous other areas discussed in depth in Section Two. Knowledge of and skill in investigative techniques are acquired through continuous training and experience. This includes academic classroom experiences, personal experiences, street learning and learning from others in the field.

The abilities to obtain and retain information and to use investigation techniques effectively are worth little without the ability to reason through a case. The mental process involved in investigation is extremely complex. Logic is indispensible and often involves reverse thinking, that is, working the case "backward." Why did it happen? When? How? Who committed it? All possible cause-and-effect relations must be examined, links found and conclusions drawn but only after thoroughly exploring all alternatives.

Decision making is continual and, to be effective, must be based on facts. When investigators review information and evidence, they concentrate on what is known (facts) rather than on what is only probable (inferences), and they eliminate personal opinions to the extent humanly possible. With *sufficient facts,* investigators can make *valid inferences,* from which *definite conclusions* can logically be drawn.

*DNA fingerprinting. Here a geneticist uses a multi-channel pipette to prepare samples for the process in which fragments of DNA are broken into bands. The pattern of DNA bands is unique to one individual. Comparison of bands can establish conclusively if two people are related and can help identify suspects from tissues left at a crime scene.*

A **fact** is an action performed, an event, a circumstance, an actual thing done or an occurrence that has taken place, as opposed to what might have taken place (*Rost v. Kessler*). In contrast, an **inference** is a process of reasoning by which a fact may be deduced as a logical consequence from other facts or information already proven (*Joyce v. Missouri & Kansas Telephone Co.*). **Opinion** is personal belief.

For example, an investigator called to the scene of a shooting finds a dead man with a revolver in his hand (fact) and a suicide note on the table (fact). The officer might *infer* that the man committed suicide. He or she might also hold the *opinion* that people who commit suicide are cowards. This opinion has no place in the investigation. The inference, however, is critical. If the officer formulates a theory behind the death based on suicide and sets out to prove the theory correct, much information and evidence may be ignored.

Although investigators must draw inferences and form theories, they must also remain open-minded and willing to consider alternatives. Preconceived ideas hinder good investigation. Objectivity is essential in investigation.

Whenever an inference is drawn, its validity should be tested by examining the facts on which it is based. All alternatives should be considered; otherwise, valuable time may be lost, evidence may disappear or the case may simply remain unsolved.

The hazards of drawing premature conclusions are illustrated by a homicide case in which lie-detection tests were given to two main suspects. Suspect A was given two polygraph tests by separate operators. Both tests indicated that he was deceptive on critical questions concerning the case. Suspect B was given a lie-detection voice-stress test that indicated he was truthful on the same questions. Based on these results, the investigators concentrated their efforts on discovering evidence to link Suspect A to the crime, ignoring Suspect B. After six months of following up leads that turned into dead ends, the investigators resumed their investigation of Suspect B and discovered enough evidence to lead him to confess to the crime.

The point of this illustration is *not* that lie-detection tests are invalid. In fact, correlation between positive test results and suspect involvement or guilt is very high. The point is that no one fact should dominate an entire investigation. All alternatives should be considered. In our illustrative case, Suspect B had taken six tranquilizers before taking the test, which made interpretation more difficult. Suspect A may have been involved in a homicide not being investigated or may simply have been extremely nervous because he was a prime suspect. Perseverance eventually revealed the truth despite evidence apparently to the contrary.

### Psychological Characteristics

Certain psychological characteristics are indispensible to effective investigation.

---

Effective investigators are emotionally well balanced, detached, inquisitive, suspecting, discerning, humble, self-disciplined and perseverant.

---

Investigation is highly stressful and involves many decisions. Therefore, it requires emotional stability. Officers who are overly defensive or oversensitive may fall victim to stress. Investigators must also absorb abuse and at the same time show kindness and sympathy. Further, they must remain detached and uninvolved, or the problems of those with whom they are in contact will decrease their objectivity. Personal involvement with individuals associated with a case under investigation not only hinders the investigation but also poses a direct threat to the investigator's emotional well-being.

Although remaining detached and objective, effective investigators are intimately involved with every aspect of the case. They do not accept things at face value; they question what they hear and see. They use their knowledge of human nature to determine the truth of what is said. People often lie or tell half-truths, but this does not necessarily mean they are criminals. With experience, investigators develop a sense for who is telling the truth, who has information of importance, who is acting suspiciously. The ability to distinguish the ordinary from the out-of-the-ordinary, the normal from the suspicious is a hallmark of an effective investigator.

In addition, investigators must be self-disciplined and able to organize their time. Success often depends on developing efficient work habits, setting priorities and using time wisely.

Closely related to self-discipline is the willingness to persevere, to "stick with it" as long as is reasonable. Investigation often involves hours or even days of waiting and watching, of performing tedious, boring assignments that may or may not yield information or evidence helpful to the case. Nonetheless, patience and perseverance are often the key to successful investigation.

Investigators often experience cases in which facts, reason and logic seem to lead nowhere and the case is about to be closed, when, by chance, additional clues are obtained. An obscure newspaper item, an anonymous phone tip, an overheard remark at a social function or even a series of events having no apparent connection with the case may provide leads for further investigation. Many cases are solved by developing leads and pursuing the relevant and seemingly irrelevant information obtained. This is where the art of investigation supersedes the science of investigation.

Perseverance, coupled with inquisitiveness and intuition, are indispensable in difficult cases. Although some deny the existence or worth of intuition, hundreds of experienced investigators know its value. **Intuition** is the "sudden knowing" without any conscious reasoning or apparent logic. It is based on knowledge and experience or what is commonly referred to as *street sense*. It is the intangible urge to go ahead without any apparent valid reason, a "gut feeling" developed through experience.

An actual case illustrates this point. While I was director of public safety for a suburban community, we had a series of car thefts from the shopping center. One day the sergeant on patrol for the middle shift came into my office to discuss the matter. I suggested we go to a gravel pit near the shopping center for a look. We did so and, as luck would have it, several juveniles were in the gravel pit painting a car. We talked with them and then checked on the car and registration, as it had not been reported stolen. When we contacted the registered owner, he said his wife had the car at the shopping center. Because the juveniles had no logical explanation for their actions, we took them to the station for questioning. It turned out they were responsible for the theft of a dozen or so vehicles from the shopping center. The case was solved by a combination of my gut feeling and the pure happenstance that the feeling occurred at precisely the same time as one of the thefts.

Although perseverance is desirable, it should not be confused with the stubborn refusal to admit a case is not likely to be solved. Investigators must exercise good judgment as well as perseverance. This judgment incorporates a good sense of timing.

Larger departments, especially, profit by having a combination of personal attributes in their staff. Investigators must interview the whole spectrum of society, and different approaches are necessary for different types of people. Pilant (1992, p. 34) suggests:

> If the guy who runs the art museum is murdered, there are some very good, qualified, smart investigators that you wouldn't send out because of their personalities. At the same time, if I had a group of investigators who were educated at St. Johns or graduated from Princeton, I would not send them to investigate a case on the waterfront. Not because they don't have the experience or the expertise or the intelligence, but because they don't have the innate ability to go out there and not get mad when some longshoreman says something about the type of pants they're wearing.

Other desirable psychological traits of investigators include being dedicated, perceptive, observant, patient, self-motivated, empathetic toward different lifestyles and professional.

## Physical Characteristics

Age, height and weight, unless they are extreme, are not important characteristics for investigators. However, some physical characteristics are important.

Effective investigators are healthy, physically fit and have good vision and hearing.

*Most police academies teach new recruits self-defense techniques. At the Dallas Police Academy
such instruction is considered vital.*

Good health and a high energy level are beneficial because the hours spent
performing investigative duties can be long and demanding.

In addition to being physically fit, investigators are aided by keen vision
and hearing. If uncorrected, color blindness, nearsightedness, night blindness
and farsightedness may impair investigative effectiveness. Hearing is especially important during night surveillance or plants when darkness limits vision. Keen hearing helps to identify the nearness of a suspect, movement of
animals or persons, direction of gunfire or other detonations and direction of
foot sounds. In addition, investigators may have to listen to words during sob-
bing, moans and hysteria; to hear a very low voice from a seriously wounded
or dying person; to listen to more than one person talking at a time; or to
conduct interviews while planes are flying over, machinery is operating or
heavy traffic is passing by.

## The Preliminary Investigation: Basic Considerations

The investigation starts with the notification to proceed to the scene.
Department policy defines not only who is to respond but also the duties of
these individuals, as well as those of evidence technicians, investigators, supervisors and command personnel. The first officer to respond is in charge until re-
lieved by another officer. The same basic procedures are followed regardless of
whether the first officer at the scene is a patrol officer, an investigator or the
chief of police.

The initial response is usually by a patrol officer assigned to the area where the
crime has occurred.

### The Initial Response

After notification, either through direct observation or through departmental communications, officers proceed to the scene as rapidly and safely as circumstances permit. A crime response survey conducted by the Law Enforcement Assistance Administration (LEAA) revealed that a response time of one minute or less is necessary to increase the probability of arrest at the scene. Most police departments, however, cannot assure their citizens such a short response time, even for emergencies. To provide a one-minute response time, police agencies would need much smaller patrol areas, much larger staffs, computer-dispatched vehicles and personnel and, thus, much larger budgets.

It is important to arrive at a crime scene rapidly because:

- The suspect may still be at or near the scene.
- Injured persons may need emergency care.
- Witnesses may still be at the scene.
- A dying person may have a confession or other pertinent information to give.
- Weather conditions may change or destroy evidence.
- Someone may attempt to alter the crime scene.

The responding officers proceed to the scene with as much speed as safety allows. Officers who injure themselves or someone else on the way to a call may create more serious problems than exist at the crime scene. They may, in fact, open themselves, their department and even their city to a civil lawsuit.

*Dallas officers planning routes to high crime areas. Preplanning can be critical to rapid response time.*

The seriousness of the crime and whether it is in progress are important factors in the rapidity of response. The speed and use of emergency lights and siren depend on the information furnished. A siren speeds arrival, but it also alerts the criminal to flee the scene. In violent crimes against a person, the siren alerts the offender but may prevent further violence. Sometimes the victim, to avoid attracting attention, requests that no sirens and red lights be used.

The route taken is also discretionary. Officers should know which streets are under construction in their areas so they can avoid them. They must also choose between the fastest route and the route the suspect(s) might use to leave the scene. Officers should observe persons leaving the scene on the approach route and make mental descriptions of them. If two officers are in the patrol vehicle, one may write descriptions of persons and vehicles observed leaving the scene. Many officers use tape recorders to record such information and observations. This equipment permits either a lone car operator or the second person in a two-officer car to record while proceeding to the scene.

If other officers are available, they are alerted to cover escape routes rather than go directly to the scene. Officers formulate a plan of action while on the way to the scene. The plan is based on the type of crime and its location.

An immediate response may be vitally important because even if no immediate arrest is made, the amount of information that can be obtained is directly related to the speed of response. Initial information is often the most important and accurate. The need for rapid response to calls for service is being seriously reevaluated in the 1990s. Guidelines for when a rapid response is critical are being developed by many departments, replacing the assumption that all calls for service should be responded to as rapidly as possible.

Other departments are finding that sending several units to the scene of a crime may not be the most effective approach. Lesce (1992) describes a plan developed by the Phoenix Police Department for responding to crime scenes where a crime has "just occurred." Called "Operation Bullseye," the plan is based on the assumptions that (1) many suspects do not live in the area where they commit their crimes, (2) they commute back to their residences after committing the crime and (3) to avoid attracting attention, they travel about one mile every two minutes. As noted by Lesce (pp. 157–158):

> When a just occurred call goes out, only two units respond to the scene. All other units proceed to major intersections and observe traffic moving away from the direction of the scene. The location of the crime is the center of the "Bullseye," with concentric rings representing time and distance from the scene. While it's impossible to place an air-tight cordon around a place where a major crime has just occurred, major intersections often offer the key to observing fleeing suspects. Success depends on getting a description of the suspects on the air quickly, and manning enough major intersections in time to intercept the suspects.

The Phoenix Police Department found that by using Operation Bullseye, they caught the suspects about 80 percent of the time. In addition, armed robberies, a crime extremely well suited for this approach, decreased by 30 percent.

### The Point of Arrival

When the first officers arrive, the scene may be utter confusion or deserted. A robbery scene in a bank during business hours may include many confused customers. An assault scene may be in the middle of a crowded bar. A rape scene may be a vacant field with only the victim present. Regardless of the situation, the officers must take charge, establish control and leadership immediately upon arrival and formulate a plan for proceeding.

People at a crime scene are usually excited, apprehensive and perplexed. They may be cooperative or uncooperative, confused or calm. Therefore, officers must be flexible and understanding. Discretion and good judgment are essential because the greatest potential for solving the case lies with those present at the initial scene, even though many details of the crime may not be known at this stage.

More decisions are made in less time at the point of arrival than at any other point in the investigation, and this is where the majority of leads for subsequent action are obtained.

In addition, information may be volunteered by victims, witnesses or suspects at or very near to the time of the criminal actions. Unplanned statements about the "things done" by persons present are called res gestae statements. Res gestae relates to things said and done, the immediate incidents of a specific act that illustrate the act. Res gestae statements are generally an exception to the hearsay rule because they are usually very closely related to facts and are, therefore, admissible in court (*Industrial Commission of Colorado v. Fotis*).

---

**Res gestae statements** are spontaneous statements made at the time of a crime, concerning and closely related to actions involved in the crime. They are often considered more truthful than later, planned responses.

---

Record res gestae statements in your notes, and have the person making them sign or initial them so there is no question of your misunderstanding or of the person later denying having made the statement.

*A police officer waves away press and onlookers from the scene of a shooting outside the White House. A knife-wielding man had been shot by a police officer, and although President Clinton was inside the executive mansion at the time, he was not harmed.*

## Setting Priorities

Circumstances at the scene often dictate what is done first. Establish priorities:

- Handle emergencies first.
- Secure the scene.
- Investigate.

Adapt the following guidelines to fit specific circumstances.

### Handling Emergency Situations

Sometimes **emergencies** dictate procedure. Emergencies include a dangerous suspect at or near the scene or a gravely injured person. For example, if you arrive at a crime scene and the suspect begins to shoot at you, apprehending the suspect obviously becomes your first priority. In other instances, a person may be so seriously injured that without immediate care, death is probable. Such emergencies take precedence over all other procedures.

Good judgment and the number of officers available dictate what should occur first if more than one emergency exists. Sometimes the decision is difficult. For example, if a victim is drowning and the suspect is running away and only one officer is at the scene, a split-second decision must be made. Usually, saving life takes precedence. However, if the officer can do nothing to save the victim, the best alternative is to pursue the suspect. Apprehension may save other victims.

Responding to emergency situations causes anyone's adrenaline to flow. At the same time, you must be planning your approach. One officer facing a life-or-death situation said he thought of a quotation: "Death must be a beautiful moment; otherwise they wouldn't save it until last." Holding this thought, he was able to carry out his immediate responsibilities without hesitation.

You should also attempt to think like the suspect. Decide which escape routes you would use and block them. The information you have about the situation will have to suffice for deciding whether using lights and siren is advantageous to you or to the suspect. Think what you would do if you were the suspect and you were cornered at the crime scene. If it is daytime, you may be visible and the suspect not. If it is nighttime, you may be able to take advantage of a darker area for your approach.

Flexibility is essential. Assess the situation; each incident is different and requires different approaches and techniques. Be cognizant that there may be more than one suspect. Check your equipment on the way to the scene. Provide the dispatcher with all pertinent information. Maintaining some distance can facilitate observation, give you time to make decisions and enhance your personal safety.

**A Suspect at or Near the Scene.** If the call is made rapidly enough and officers can respond quickly, they may observe the crime being committed and arrest the suspect at the scene. This is another point at which officers may leave themselves open to a **civil liability** suit, either for excessive use of force or for false arrest, if proper procedures are not followed. Procedures for making an arrest are discussed fully in Chapter 7.

Any suspect at the scene should be detained, questioned and then released or arrested, depending on the circumstances.

Department policy determines whether the first officer at the scene thoroughly interrogates a suspect. Before any interrogation, the suspect must be given the Miranda warning, a legality discussed in Chapter 6. Even if the policy is that officers do not interrogate suspects, officers often use discretion. For example, they may have to take a dying declaration or a suspect's spontaneous confession. If this occurs, a statement is taken immediately because the suspect may refuse, or be unable, to cooperate later. A more formal interrogation and written confession can be obtained later at the police department.

The suspect is removed from the scene as soon as possible to lessen the chances of destruction of evidence and to make questioning easier. The sooner suspects are removed, the less they can observe of the crime scene and possible evidence against them.

**If the Suspect Has Recently Fled.**   If the suspect has just left the scene, immediate action is required. If the information is provided early enough, other units proceeding to the scene might make an arrest.

If a suspect has recently left the scene, obtain a general description of the suspect, any vehicles, direction of travel and any items taken. Dispatch the information to headquarters immediately.

As soon as practical, obtain more detailed information about the suspect's possible whereabouts, friends, descriptions of items stolen and other relevant information regarding past criminal records and modus operandi.

**If a Person Is Seriously Injured.**   Emergency first aid to victims, witnesses and suspects is often a top priority of arriving officers. Sustaining life and minimizing injuries may override all other considerations. Call for medical assistance and then do whatever is possible until help arrives. Observe and record the condition of the injured person, the type of injury, its location and the victim's general condition.

If a person is injured so severely that he or she must be removed from the scene, instruct attending medical personnel to listen to any statements or utterances and to save all clothing for evidence. If the injured person is a suspect, a police officer almost always accompanies the suspect to the hospital.

The humanitarian priority of administering first aid may have to become second priority if a dangerous suspect is still at or near the scene or others may be injured or killed.

**If a Dead Body Is at the Scene.**   A body at the crime scene may immediately become the center of attention. Even a suspect might be overlooked. If the victim is obviously dead, leave the body just as it is found, but protect it and its surroundings. Identifying the body is not an immediate concern. It is more important to preserve the scene because it may later yield clues about the dead person's identity, the cause of death and the individual(s) responsible.

## Protecting the Crime Scene

Securing the crime scene is a major responsibility of the first officers to arrive. Everything of a nonemergency nature is delayed until the scene is protected.

At outdoor scenes, weather conditions such as heat, wind, rain, snow or sleet can alter or destroy physical evidence. There is also a danger that people may accidentally or intentionally disturb the scene. Additions to the scene can be as disconcerting to later investigation as the removal of evidence.

Explain to people present that protecting the crime scene is critical and that the public must be excluded. Treat them courteously but firmly. A delicate part of public relations is dealing with the family of someone who has been killed. Explain what you are doing and why. Help them understand that certain steps must be taken to increase the chance of discovering what happened and who is responsible.

Crime scene protection can be as simple as locking a door to a room or building, or it can involve roping off a large area outdoors. Within a room, chairs or boxes can be used to cordon off an area. Many officers carry rope in their vehicle for this purpose and attach a sign that says: CRIME SCENE—DO NOT ENTER.

Station a guard to maintain security. If all officers are busy with emergency matters, ask a citizen to help protect the crime scene temporarily. In such cases, record the citizen's name, address and phone number in your notes. Give the citizen specific instructions and minimal duties. The citizen's main duty is to protect the crime scene by barring entrance and to keep passersby moving along. You might instruct the citizen: "Do not let any person into this area except police who identify themselves with a badge. Keep spectators moving away from the scene." Relieve the citizen from guard duty as soon as possible and thank him or her for the assistance.

Sometimes other officers arriving at the scene can cause problems by ignoring posted warnings and barriers. *Ironically, police officers with no assigned responsibilities at the scene are often the worst offenders.* Inform arriving officers and all persons present at the scene what has happened and what you want them to do. Ask other officers to help preserve the scene, interview witnesses or search for evidence.

---

Take all necessary measures to secure the crime scene, including locking, roping, barricading and guarding, until the preliminary investigation is completed.

---

Protect evidence from destruction or alteration by the elements by covering it until photographing and measuring can be done. Sometimes evidence must be moved before it can be examined. For example, a vehicle covered with snow, dust or other materials can be moved from outside to a garage. In one case a car used in a kidnapping was found four days later in a parking lot. Snow that had fallen since the kidnapping covered the car. To process the car's exterior for fingerprints, investigators took the car to a garage to let the snow melt and the surface dry.

## Conducting the Preliminary Investigation

After all emergency matters have been handled and the crime scene has been secured, the actual preliminary investigation can begin. This includes several steps, whose order depends on the specific crime and the types of evidence and witnesses available.

Responsibilities during the preliminary investigation include:
- Measuring, photographing, videotaping and sketching the scene.
- Searching for evidence.
- Identifying, collecting, examining and processing physical evidence.
- Questioning victims, witnesses and suspects.
- Recording all statements and observations in notes.

Each of these procedures is explained in detail in Section Two. At this point, you are concerned with the total picture, the overview of what happens during the preliminary investigation. In simple cases, one officer may perform all of these procedures; in complex cases, responsibilities may be divided among several officers. Everything that occurs at a crime scene is recorded with photographs, videotape, sketches and complete, accurate notes. This record is used not only as the basis for future reports but also for future investigation and prosecution of the case.

**Field Tests.** Numerous field tests have been developed to help investigators in the preliminary examination of crime scenes. Field tests are less expensive than full laboratory examinations. They save investigators' time by identifying evidence that may have little chance of positive results in the laboratory. These tests are intended to discover clues and are used on only a small number of specific items of evidence located at crime scenes. If a field test is affirmative, the evidence is submitted to the laboratory for a more detailed and expert examination that can then be introduced into court.

Investigators often want to know if evidence discovered is what they think it is—for example, a bloodstain or a drug. Field test kits help in this determination and eliminate sending to the laboratory evidence that may be difficult to obtain and package.

Field tests can be used to develop and lift fingerprints; to discover flammable substances through vapor and fluid examination; to detect drugs, explosive substances on hands or clothing, imprints of firearms on hands or bullet-hole residue; and to conduct many other tests. Local, state and federal police laboratories can furnish information on currently available field test kits and may also provide training in their proper use.

**Establishing that a Crime Has Been Committed and When.** As soon as possible during the preliminary investigation, it is necessary to determine if a crime has, in fact, been committed. To do so, know the elements of the various offenses and the types of evidence that support them. Individual elements of various offenses are discussed in Sections Three and Four.

Establish if a crime has been committed by knowing the elements of each major offense and ascertaining if they are present. Try to determine when the crime occurred.

Observe the condition of the scene and talk to the complainant as soon as possible. After discussing the offense with the victim or complainant, determine if a specific crime has been committed. It is common for crime victims to misclassify what has occurred. For example, they may report a burglary as a robbery or a larceny as a burglary. In addition, state statutes differ in how they define the elements of certain crimes. For example, in some states entering a motor vehicle with intent to steal is larceny. In other states it is burglary. Also try to determine when the crime was committed. This is critical for checking alibis and reconstructing the modus operandi.

If no crime has, in fact, been committed, notify the complainant of the circumstances and give an explanation. If it is a civil rather than a criminal situation, suggest to the victim where to obtain assistance.

**Establishing a Command Center.**    In some complex cases involving many officers, a command center is set up where information about the crime is gathered and reviewed. This center receives summaries of communications, police reports, autopsy results, laboratory reports, results of interviews, updates on evidence discovered and tips. Personnel at the center keep files of news releases and news articles and prepare an orderly, chronological progress report of the case for police command, staff and field personnel. If the investigation becomes lengthy, the command center can be moved to police headquarters.

**Dealing with the News Media.**    A close relationship between the police and the news media is essential, as both agencies serve a public purpose. The media serve the public's right to know within legal and reasonable standards, a right that is protected by the First Amendment. The police, on the other hand, are responsible for upholding the Sixth and Fourteenth Amendment guarantees of the right to a fair trial and the protection of the suspect's rights. This often necessitates confidentiality to protect individuals' rights. Further, making some information public would literally "blow" many investigations.

Thus the media and the police must understand and respect each other's roles and responsibilities. Citizens' First Amendment rights must be balanced against the public interest in confidentiality, safe and competent law enforcement and the individual's right to privacy. Media access to police information is not comprehensive or absolute. In general, the media have no right to enter any area to which the public does not have access, and all rules at cordoned-off crime scenes are as applicable to the media as they are to the general public. On the other hand, police may not construct a "cocoon" of secrecy. Neither should regard the other as the enemy, but a balance between absolute secrecy and absolute availability of information must be achieved.

According to Guffey (1992, p. 33):

> The police and the media are two organizations that interact regularly. The relationship can be described as symbiotic. The media need the police to supply them with information about crime and crime patterns that are of interest to their readers, listeners, or viewers. The police need the media to improve their image within the community, to publicize major crimes or crime patterns, to publicize wanted persons, and to seek witnesses from the community.

Weinblatt (1992, p. 32) stresses that:

> Police officials with an active investigation in progress are very conscious of the dichotomy which exists in their mandate. On the one hand, cases are solved with information from the public. The police need the press to get to the masses. On the other, police concerns regarding next of kin notification, family suffering and investigation impairment are also bona fide issues and need to be addressed.

*A Los Angeles police officer and a television cameraman photograph one of several police vehicles that were shot up during a botched bank robbery in the North Hollywood section of Los Angeles in February 1997.*

Guffey (p. 42) cites the following media complaints regarding the police and their code of silence:

**1.** They are not forthcoming.
**2.** They cannot accept legitimate criticism.
**3.** They withhold important information.
**4.** They hide behind the shield of the Sixth Amendment too often.
**5.** They are often uncooperative.
**6.** They cannot accept that the media are a legitimate "check" on possible abuses of authority.

The police, on the other hand, have several complaints about reporters, including their interference with cases, their lack of sensitivity, their frequently inaccurate reporting and their tendency to sensationalize. Cook (1991, p. 83) notes: "A sensitive investigation is a tough job. But often the toughest part is the confrontation from a pack of reporters bent on yanking something 'newsworthy' (i.e., 'controversial') out of your mouth." He suggests that the media will try important cases, with or without the cooperation of the police, and that it is thus to law enforcement's advantage to get its side of the story told: "The best procedure is to make yourself accessible to the press, and answer questions as completely and candidly as possible."

Most members of the media understand the restrictions at a crime scene and cooperate. It is necessary to exercise firmness with those who do not follow instructions, even to excluding them if they jeopardize the investigation. Give only facts, not opinions. Give the name of someone who has been killed *only* after a careful identity check and notification of relatives. Do not release any information on cause of death; the medical examiner determines this. Do not express legal opinions as to the specific crime or who is responsible.

Some departments use public information officers (PIOs). Other departments assign the highest-ranking officer at the time of an incident or have a policy of using written information releases.

## The Follow-Up Investigation

Preliminary investigations that satisfy all the criteria for good investigation do not necessarily yield enough information to prosecute a case. Despite a thorough preliminary investigation, many cases require a follow-up investigation. Need for a follow-up investigation does not necessarily reflect poorly on those who conducted the preliminary investigation. Factors often exist that are outside the officers' control. Weather can destroy evidence before officers arrive at the scene. Witnesses can be uncooperative. The evidence may be weak or nonexistent, even after a very thorough preliminary investigation.

The follow-up investigation builds on what was learned during the preliminary investigation. It can be conducted by the officers who responded to the original call or, most often, by detectives or investigators, depending on the seriousness and complexity of the crime. If investigators take over a case begun by patrol officers, coordination is essential.

Investigative leads that may need to be followed up include checking the victim's background; talking to informants; determining who would benefit from the crime and who had knowledge sufficient to plan the crime; tracing weapons and stolen property; and searching modus operandi, mug shot and fingerprint files. Specific follow-up procedures for given offenses are discussed in Sections Three, Four and Five.

## Computer-Aided Investigation

"Computers have had a more significant impact on police operations in the last decade than any other single factor during the past century" (Sharp, 1991, p. 41). In addition to their obvious contribution to record keeping and statistical analysis, computers are becoming increasingly important in criminal investigations. Binkley (1991, p. 142) describes how Long Beach, California, has gone "from pushpins and wall maps to a computer screen" to apprehend career criminals. Using a sophisticated computer program, Long Beach's Career Criminal Apprehension Team can focus on ideal sting locations for such crimes as street robberies and carjackings. According to Binkley (p. 143): "The Long Beach system has successfully targeted high-volume crimes typically associated with career lawbreakers, including robbery, burglary, auto theft, and auto burglary."

## Investigative Productivity

Productivity has been of interest in the police field for some time. Major opposition to a focus on productivity in police work may arise because of alleged "quota systems" in issuing traffic citations. Productivity involves considerably more than issuing citations, however. Nearly all jobs have some standard of productivity, even though the job may not involve a production line.

Productivity can often be increased by using a screening process to eliminate criminal investigations with low potential for being solved. Many police departments conduct such screening using a form that asks specific questions about the facts in the investigation. If the answers to these questions are negative, the case is given low priority for assignment or is not assigned at all.

Criminal investigation personnel have traditionally been evaluated by the number and type of cases they are assigned, the number of cases brought to a successful conclusion, their number of arrests and the amount of property they have recovered. The evaluations should also assess how well the officers use investigative resources and their overall performance within the department and in the community.

The Las Vegas Metropolitan Police Department has developed an evaluation process that takes a different approach. It uses a carefully constructed Performance Appraisal Form (PAF). According to Connor and Richards (1991, p. 51):

> The foundation of the PAF was a job analysis conducted, researched and completed by detectives and supervisors with the guidance of personnel specialists. . . .
> The job analysis identified the tasks performed by detectives, as well as the knowledge, skills, abilities and behaviors needed to perform these tasks. Over 80 tasks were identified and grouped into 15 "duty areas"—seven of which contain tasks common to every police officer's job. These seven are called "global duty areas." The other eight, referred to as "specific duty areas," contain tasks that are typically unique to the detective function.
> The specific duty areas include the following: opening investigations, case preparation, conducting investigations in the field, conducting investigations in the office, administrative duties, presentation and closing of cases, and special investigative duties.

While evaluation of officers' performances is taking place, monthly reports to federal, state and local sources can be generated simultaneously. Availability of information and compilation of reports is a substantial time savings and, consequently, a cost savings.

A further advantage of continuous evaluation of productivity is that updating case status is possible at any time. Such information is useful not only for investigative purposes but also for developing budgets, making additional case assignments, identifying modus operandi similarities among cases and even responding to inquiries from the public.

## The Investigative Function: The Responsibility of All Police Personnel

Early police organizations were one unit/one purpose departments with all personnel performing generalized functions. However, as law enforcement developed in the United States, a need was perceived for specialization. This was especially true in investigation because of the need to know about criminals and their modus operandi, the amount of training necessary for learning and developing investigative techniques, the frequency with which investigators had to leave their assigned shifts and areas during an investigation, patrol forces' heavy workloads and a general administrative philosophy that supported specialization as a means to increase efficiency and, therefore, solve more crimes.

In larger police departments, specialization developed in investigative functions before it did in other areas such as traffic, crime prevention, juveniles and community relations. In departments with specialized investigative units, the investigative and patrol functions often experienced difficulty separating their respective duties and responsibilities. Duties often overlapped, decreasing efficient coordination.

Many of these difficulties have been overcome, but many others remain. Regardless of whether a department has specialists or generalists, the goal is the same: solving committed crimes.

---

The ultimate responsibility for solving crimes lies with all police personnel. It must be a cooperative, coordinated departmental effort.

---

All levels of police administration and operations contribute to successful investigations. Administrative decisions affect the selection and assignment of personnel and the policies regulating their performance.

In most larger departments, the investigative division remains a separate unit under its own command and supervisory personnel. The officer in charge reports directly to the chief of police or a chief of operations. Department policy specifies the roles of and the relationship among the administrative, uniformed patrol and investigative divisions. When these roles are clearly defined, the common goals of the department can be better achieved, with the investigative division fulfilling its assigned responsibilities in coordination with all other departments.

Today, however, researchers are studying the extent to which specialization should remain, its effectiveness, the number of personnel that should be assigned to specialized investigative functions and the selection and training required for such specialization. Several factors appear to support training all officers to perform investigative duties and responsibilities:

- Increasing competition for the tax dollar. (Increasing governmental services plus the pressure to establish tax-ceiling limits on federal, state and municipal spending is reducing the possibility of hiring more police officers.)
- Possession of highly sophisticated equipment by some criminals. (Expensive monitors and scanning devices, high-speed drills, transistorized and miniaturized radio equipment, bulletproof vests and high-mobility vehicles make modern criminals more elusive.)
- More criminals using multiple modus operandi. (A recent trend has been for criminals to commit several different types of crimes using varying techniques.)
- Withdrawal syndrome within the general public. (The desire to remain uninvolved necessitates specialized training in interviewing techniques.)
- Overwhelming workload of cases assigned to investigative personnel. (Overspecialization, increased crime, fewer officers assigned to investigation.)
- More intelligent, better-educated police recruits. (More training in shorter periods, better able to self-train by reading materials on investigation and crimes, better able to perform multiple duties and more complex duties.)
- More police training available (at federal, state and local levels).

In addition, most police officers' daily activities are investigative, even though the matters they investigate may not involve crimes. Therefore, the trend is for a few specialists to direct an investigation and for all officers to assume a more active role in investigating crimes. This role gives patrol officers more responsibility when responding to a call to proceed to a crime scene. It also enables them to conduct as much of the follow-up investigation as their shift and assigned areas of patrol permit. The importance of the patrol officer's investigative role cannot be overemphasized. Even if the patrol officer does very little, a lack of knowledge and/or inattention can make the investigator's job very difficult later.

Traditionally, uniformed patrol has been considered the backbone of the police department and has been responsible for the initial response to a crime. Being first to arrive, patrol officers are in an ideal position to do more than conduct the preliminary investigation. Experiments have shown that initial investigations by patrol officers can be as effective as those conducted by specialists. This is partly because the officers treat the entire case rather than arriving at the scene, securing it, conducting a brief preliminary investigation and then turning the case over to detectives.

This new challenge for patrol officers—involvement in the entire investigative process—creates interest in crime prevention as well as investigation. In addition, giving patrol officers increased responsibility for investigating crimes allows detectives to concentrate on offenses that require detailed investigations and on cases that require them to leave the community to conduct special interviews or to follow up leads. The result is better investigation of the more frequent, less severe crimes by the patrol officer and of the serious, difficult crimes by investigators or detectives.

## Interrelationships with Others

Investigators do not work in a vacuum. They rely on the assistance of numerous other individuals and agencies.

---

Investigators interrelate with uniformed patrol officers, dispatchers, the prosecutor's staff, the defense counsel, supervisors, physicians, the coroner or medical examiner, laboratories and citizens, including victims.

---

### Uniformed Patrol

Patrol officers are a vital part of the investigative process because they are usually the first to arrive at a crime scene. What patrol officers do or fail to do at the scene greatly influences the outcome of the investigation. The patrol officer, as the person daily in the field, is closest to potential crime and has probably developed contacts who can provide information.

That uniformed and investigative personnel need close cooperation is no professional secret. A patrol officer can be the investigator's best ally.

The principal pitfall here is a lack of direct, personal communication between uniformed and investigative personnel that can result in attitudinal differences and divisiveness. Personnel from both divisions claim "lack of return information" or "no exchange of information." Such communication problems can be substantially reduced by using a simple checklist describing the current investigative status of any cases jointly involving patrol and investigators. The form should include information such as that illustrated in Figure 1–1.

Patrol officers want to know what happens to the cases they begin. They have a personal as well as an official interest and are entitled to know. Officers who have been informed of the status of "their" cases report a feeling of work satisfaction not previously realized, increased rapport with investigative personnel and a greater desire to make good initial reports on future cases.

Investigative personnel gain by receiving more and better information and by making more arrests. Both patrol and investigative personnel realize they are a team working together toward the same goal.

```
                              STATUS REPORT

To:
From:
Case #:
Date:

_____  Offense sent to prosecution    _____  Added offenses
_____  Cleared by arrest              _____  Not cleared by arrest
_____  Refused prosecution            _____  Unfounded
_____  Suspect developed              _____  Suspect released
_____  Suspect in custody             _____  Suspect known
_____  Property recovered             _____  No property recovered
_____  Case still open                _____  Case closed
_____  Good patrol report             _____  Incomplete patrol report
_____  Need further information; please call: _____
```

**Figure 1–1 Sample Checklist for Case Status Report**

### Dispatchers

In some instances a crime is personally observed by or directly reported to a field officer by a citizen. In most cases, however, the police dispatcher is the initial contact between the citizen and the police agency. The majority of citizens call a police agency only a few times during their lives, and their permanent impression of the police may result from this contact and their perceptions of the police agency's subsequent actions.

In addition, the information obtained by the dispatcher is often critical to the officer, the victim, other citizens and the success of the investigation. The accuracy of the information dispatched to the field officer or investigator may determine the success or failure of the case. In critical incidents, it can also make the difference between life, death or injury to the officer, the victim or other people. The responding officer needs to know the exact nature of the incident and its exact location. A direct radio, computer or phone line should be cleared until the officer arrives at the scene. All pertinent descriptions and information should be dispatched directly to the responding officer.

### Prosecutor's Staff

Cooperation between investigators and the prosecutor's staff depends on the personalities involved, the time available, a recognition that it is in everyone's best interest to work together and an acceptance of each other's investigative roles and responsibilities. Given sufficient time and a willingness to work together, better investigations and prosecutions result. When investigators have concluded an investigation, they should seek the advice of the prosecutor's office. At this point the case may be prosecuted, new leads may be developed, or the case may be dropped, with both the investigator and the prosecutor's office agreeing that it would be inefficient to pursue it further.

The prosecutor's staff can give legal advice on statements, confessions, evidence, the search and necessary legal papers and may also provide new perspectives on the facts in the case. Investigators should seek the advice of the prosecutor's office when it will assist them in solving crime. The prosecutor's office can review investigative reports, review evidence in relation to the elements of the offense, advise whether the proof is sufficient to proceed and assist in further preparation of the case.

*This dispatcher of Putnam County, Florida, Sheriff's headquarters relays messages to officers on the road.*

### Defense Counsel

Our legal system is based on the adversary system: the accused against the accusor. Although both sides seek the same goal—determining truth and obtaining justice—the adversarial nature of the system requires that contacts between the defense counsel and investigators should occur only on the advice of the prosecutor's office. Inquiries from the defense counsel should be referred to the prosecutor's office. If the court orders specific documents to be provided to the defense counsel, investigators must surrender the material, but they should seek the advice of the prosecution staff before releasing any documents or information.

### Physicians, Coroners and Medical Examiners

If a victim at a crime scene is obviously injured and a doctor is called to the scene, saving life takes precedence over all aspects of the investigation. However, the physician is there for emergency treatment, not to protect the crime scene, so investigators must take every possible precaution to protect the scene during the treatment of the victim.

Physicians and medical personnel should be directed to the victim by the route through the crime scene that is least destructive of evidence. They should be asked to listen carefully to anything the victim says and to hold all clothing as evidence for the police.

The coroner or medical examiner is called if the victim has died. Coroners or medical examiners have the authority to investigate deaths to determine whether they were natural, accidental or the result of a criminal act. They can also provide information on the time of death and the type of weapon that might have caused the death.

Depending on the individual case, investigators and the medical examiner or coroner may work as a team, with an investigator present at the autopsy. The medical examiner or coroner should obtain samples of hair, clothing, fibers, blood and body organs or fluids as needed for later laboratory examination.

### Police Laboratories

Police laboratories employ specialists trained in examining evidence scientifically. When an expert has examined the evidence and the case is assigned for trial, the laboratory is notified of the time and date when its testimony is needed. These laboratories examine many types of evidence, including documents, typewriters, paints, hairs, fibers, blood and other body fluids, safe insulation and various types of impressions. Examiners may use chemistry, radio engineering, cryptanalysis and physics. They may also use standards and reference files such as fraudulent check files and bank robbery files.

In larger cities the laboratory is usually located within the police department or in the same building. The state crime laboratory is usually located in the largest city or the state capital and can be used by all police agencies of the state. The FBI Laboratory in Washington, D.C., is also available to all law enforcement agencies.

The Forensic Science Information Resource System was established in 1985 to help the FBI Laboratory and the 300 state and local crime laboratories. This system facilitates evidence examinations as well as the research and development of forensic knowledge and techniques. The library contains more than 10,000 scientific and technical reference books and more than 350 journals. Indirectly, all law enforcement officers benefit by this increased knowledge available to crime laboratories. (Information about the vast services of this library can be obtained from: Librarian, Federal Bureau of Investigation, Room 3589, 10th and Pennsylvania Avenue, N.W., Washington, DC 20535.)

**Forensic science** or **criminalistics** applies physical and biological sciences and technology to examining physical evidence. All law enforcement agencies now have access to highly sophisticated criminalistic examinations through local, state and federal laboratories and private laboratories.

Smaller departments often use the forensic departments and crime laboratories of larger cities or the state crime lab facilities. Arrangements with larger cities are normally on a fee basis. Use of the state crime lab facilities is usually on a gratis basis. In more recent years, however, because of budget restrictions, some state laboratories also charge a fee.

Selection of a laboratory is based on its capabilities and equipment, the quality of its work, distance, cost and availability of personnel to testify in court. Investigators need to be familiar with the laboratory facilities available in the particular area and the procedures and forms they require. When no government-operated laboratories are available or they cannot perform required tests, private consultants or laboratories in the region must be used.

### Private Laboratories

Many agencies hire private laboratories to examine crime evidence. Hoffmann (1992, p. 30) gives one obvious reason: "A Midwestern state crime lab was so far behind on drug cases that misdemeanor marijuana cases were taking over a year to be tested, allowing the statue [sic] of limitations to expire."

Private laboratories can handle drug, fingerprint, toolmark, firearms, trace evidence, explosives and fire cases. Their turnaround time is usually much less than state crime labs, and their results are usually accepted by the courts.

### Citizens

Investigation involves cooperation not only with other police officers and agencies but also with numerous other individuals. It is of utmost importance to establish rapport with citizens because they frequently provide the most important information in a case.

Citizens can help or hinder an investigation. Frequently, citizens who have been arrested in the past have information about crimes and the people who commit them. The manner and attitude with which such citizens are contacted will increase or decrease their cooperation with the police, as discussed in Chapter 6.

Witnesses to a crime should be contacted immediately so as to minimize their time involved and inconvenience, and information about the general progress of the case should be relayed to those who have assisted. This will maintain their interest and increase their desire to cooperate at another time. Investigators are only as good as their sources of information. They seldom solve crimes without citizen assistance.

### Victims

Almost every crime has a victim, and in many instances the victim receives the least attention and assistance. Even so-called victimless crimes often have innocent victims who are not directly involved in the specific incident. The victim is often the reporting person and often has the most valuable information.

Police are obligated to keep victims informed of investigative progress unless release of the information would jeopardize future prosecution of the case or the information is confidential. Support groups in the community are available to assist many victims, and victims should be provided with information about how to contact such groups. For example, most communities have support groups for victims of sexual offenses—if not locally, then at the county or state level. Civic-group or foundation funds may be available.

The Federal Victimization Bill provides matching-fund assistance to states for victims of some crimes. Numerous states also have victimization funds that can be used for funeral or other expenses according to predetermined criteria. Police agencies should maintain a list of federal, state and local agencies, foundations and support groups that provide assistance to victims.

Investigating officers should also provide victims with information on future crime prevention techniques and temporary safety precautions. They should help victims understand any court procedures that involve them and inform them of any court compensation they may be granted at sentencing or from victimization grant funds. Victims should be told if local counseling services are available and if there is a safe place where they can stay if this is an immediate concern.

In larger departments, psychological response teams are available. In smaller agencies, a chaplains corps or individual clergy from the community may assist with death notifications and immediate needs of victims.

## Major Case Task Forces

A *multidisciplinary* approach to case investigation uses specialists in various fields from within a particular jurisdiction. A *multijurisdictional* investigation, in contrast, uses personnel from different police agencies. Many metropolitan areas consist of twenty or more municipalities surrounding a core city. In a number of metropolitan areas, multijurisdictional major case squads or metro crime teams have been formed, drawing the most talented investigative personnel from all jurisdictions. In addition, the services of federal, state or county police agency personnel may be used.

In some major cases—for example, homicides involving multi-jurisdictional problems, serial killers, police officer killings or multiple sex offenses—it is advisable to form a major case task force. Members of the task force are drawn from the jurisdictions that have major interests in the case. At the firstmeeting, a task force director is selected from the members to chair the meetings. Typically, each jurisdiction pays its own expenses. All evidence from the joint case is normally sent to the same laboratory to maintain continuity and consistency.

On the federal level, the Violent Criminal Apprehension Program (VICAP) has been created within the FBI to study and coordinate the relationship of crimes of interstate and national interest. INTERPOL is an international organization that coordinates information on international cases. Through INTERPOL all evidence is collected and analyzed concerning cases of mutual interest and provided to the member jurisdictions.

In other instances it is often advantageous for departments to work together. For example, if a suspect commits a crime in one jurisdiction and flees to another, the departments of both jurisdictions need to exchange information. Rachlin (1992, p. 131) suggests:

> The assistance of an outside agency is not just an expedient means to further an investigation; it is a necessary one when a suspect has fled from one jurisdiction to another. . . .
> While legal and economic factors necessitate the cooperation of different agencies, working together need not be just a perfunctory process. It can be a rewarding experience in which new aspects of police work are learned, professional relationships are cultivated, and satisfaction is derived from both helping a fellow agency and carrying out justice.

*A Fresno Violent Crime Suppression Unit (VCSU) officer detains a suspect as a Fresno police officer in traditional uniform cuffs him after an early-morning raid on a suspected drug house. The Fresno police instituted the VCSU after several years of increasing violent crime and shootings at the police.*

# Crime Analysis and Problem-Oriented Policing

Criminal investigation frequently relies on information and data collected by more than one officer and by more than one agency. As noted by Goldstein (1990, p. 37):

> Initially, it [crime analysis] consisted of a review of reports on similar crimes to identify those that may have been committed by the same individual or group, with the hope that the sum of information from a number of reports might better enable the police to identify and apprehend the offender(s). If an offender was apprehended, similar analysis might enable the police to solve other crimes for which the offender was responsible and to increase the strength of the case against him or her. As crime analysis developed, attention focused on discovering patterns of criminal activity, enabling analysts to alert patrolling police officers to individuals suspected of committing a particular type of crime and to the area in which they might commit it. Anticipating where the offender was likely to strike also enabled the police to set up surveillance and undercover operations.

Data collected during criminal investigations can be extremely valuable to the problem-oriented policing being advocated by many departments in the 1990s. The data can be analyzed to determine groups of problems rather than as isolated incidents. Once specific underlying problems are identified, alternative approaches to reducing or eliminating them can be sought in attempting to reduce the incidence of particular crimes.

The subject of problem-solving policing is beyond the scope of this text, but it is an important trend that deserves attention. The information and data obtained today during routine criminal investigations may provide the basis for vitally important new knowledge in the future.

## Avoiding Liability

According to Harr and Hess (1990, p. 76):

> Only naive or deluded police officers believe they would never be sued. The past two decades have produced an unprecedented increase in suits brought against the police. It is presently estimated that over 30,000 lawsuits are initiated against law enforcement annually (Silver, 1986, p. xi). A decrease in this figure is unlikely.

Young (1996b, p. 8) likewise notes: "It is a fact of life today that if you are an active police officer, a lawsuit with your name on it as 'defendant' is likely to be waiting for you just around the corner." Young (1996a, p. 8) suggests:

> Lately, suing a police department and local government has burgeoned into a hearty cottage industry throughout the nation, because of the obvious fact that big bucks are at stake and many prospective stakeholders are vying for profitable and highly available payoffs.
>
> Members of police departments throughout the country are so liability-conscious today that a state of 'lawsuit paranoia' hampers, constricts and otherwise handicaps the effective operation of law enforcement agencies.

And, as del Carmen (1993, p. 87) observes: "There is perhaps no sizable police department in the country that has not been sued in state or federal court for damages or injunctive relief. The trend will continue as more sensational cases, like the Rodney King incident in Los Angeles, capture headlines and continue to attract the print and electronic media."

One of the best ways to avoid lawsuits or to defend yourself against one is to keep complete, accurate records on all official actions taken. Young (1996b, pp. 8, 10) suggests eight other ways to avoid or minimize lawsuits.

---

To avoid lawsuits:
- Know the law.
- Know your department policies.
- Become the best police officer you can.
- Seek to develop and fine-tune your policing skills further through education.
- Sharpen your effectiveness in all aspects of human relations.
- Give official notice regarding understaffing and equipment or vehicle needs and malfunctions.
- Double-check a supervisor's orders and evaluate fellow officers' performance.
- Unless it's a priority, don't get involved off duty.

---

Young (1996b, p. 10) concludes: "Effecting appropriate police and public safety practices, procedures and protocol out on the mean streets is the best insurance against torts [civil lawsuits]. But it's also good advice to look into professional liability insurance for your added personal protection. . . ."

## Summary

A criminal investigation is the process of discovering, collecting, preparing, identifying and presenting evidence to prove the truth or falsity of an issue in law.

The goals of police investigation vary from department to department, but most investigations aim to:

- Determine if a crime has been committed.
- Legally obtain sufficient information and evidence to learn the identity of the individual(s) committing the crime.
- Locate and arrest the suspect(s).
- Recover stolen property.
- Present the best possible case to the prosecutor.

Among the numerous functions performed by investigators in their search for the truth are providing emergency assistance; securing the crime scene; photographing, videotaping and sketching; taking notes and writing reports; searching for, obtaining and processing physical evidence; obtaining information from witnesses and suspects; identifying suspects; conducting raids, surveillances, stakeouts and undercover assignments; and testifying in court.

All investigators, patrol officers or detectives, are more effective if they possess certain intellectual, psychological and physical characteristics. Effective investigators develop and retain information, apply technical knowledge, remain open-minded and objective and use logic. They are emotionally well balanced, detached, inquisitive, suspecting, discerning, humble, self-disciplined and perseverant. Further, they are healthy, physically fit and have good vision and hearing.

The first officer to arrive at a crime scene is usually a patrol officer assigned to the area. In any preliminary investigation, it is critical to establish priorities. Handle emergencies first; then secure the scene. Emergencies include a dangerous suspect at or near the scene or a gravely injured person. Any suspects at the scene should be detained, questioned and then either released or arrested, depending on the circumstances. If a suspect has recently left the scene, obtain a general description of the suspect, any vehicles, direction of travel and any items taken. Dispatch the information to headquarters immediately.

After emergencies are dealt with, the first and most important function is to protect the crime scene and evidence. Take all necessary measures to secure the crime scene—including locking, roping, barricading and guarding—until the preliminary investigation is completed.

Once the scene is secured, proceed with the preliminary investigation. This includes measuring, photographing, videotaping and sketching the scene; searching for evidence; identifying, collecting, examining and processing physical evidence; questioning victims, witnesses and suspects; and recording all statements and observations in notes. The crime scene is preserved through these records.

As soon as possible, establish if a crime has been committed. For this, it is necessary to know the elements of each major offense and to ascertain if they are present. Also try to determine when the crime occurred.

Even in those police departments having highly specialized investigation departments, the ultimate responsibility for solving crime lies with all police personnel. It must be a cooperative, coordinated departmental effort. Cooperation and coordination of efforts is also required outside the police department. Investigators must interrelate not only with uniformed patrol officers but also with the prosecutor's office, the defense counsel, physicians, the coroner or medical examiner and citizens. Criminal investigation is, indeed, a mutual effort.

To avoid or minimize lawsuits, (1) know the law, (2) know your department policies, (3) become the best police officer you can, (4) seek to develop and fine-tune your policing skills further through education, (5) sharpen your effectiveness in all aspects of human relations, (6) give official notice regarding understaffing and equipment or vehicle needs and malfunctions, (7) double-check a supervisor's orders and evaluate fellow officers' performance and (8) unless it's a priority, don't get involved off duty.

## Checklist

### *Preliminary Investigation*

■ Was a log kept of all actions taken by police officers?

■ Were all emergencies attended to first? (First aid; detaining suspects; broadcasting information regarding suspects?)

■ Was the crime scene secured and the evidence protected?

■ Were photographs or videotapes taken?

■ Were measurements and sketches made?

■ Was all evidence preserved?

■ Were witnesses interviewed as soon as possible and statements taken?

- How was the complaint received?
- Date and time received?
- What was the initial message received—offense and location?
- Where were you when the message was received?
- Who was with you at the time?
- Were any suspicious persons or vehicles observed while en route to the scene?
- What time did you arrive at the scene?
- How light or dark was it?
- What were the weather conditions? Temperature?
- Were there other notable crime-scene conditions at time of arrival?
- How did you first enter the scene? Describe in detail the exact position of doors or windows—open, closed, locked, glass broken, ajar, pried, smashed. Lights on or off? Shades up or down?
- Was the heating or air-conditioning on or off? Television, radio, stereo on?
- Were dead or injured persons at the scene?
- What were observable injuries to persons? Was first aid administered?
- What type of crime was committed?
- Was the time the crime occurred estimated?
- Who was the first contact at the scene? Name, address, telephone number?
- Who was the victim? Name, address, telephone number? Was the victim able to give an account of the crime?
- What witnesses were at the scene? Names, addresses, telephone numbers?
- Were unusual noises heard—shots, cars, screams, loud language, prying or breaking noises?
- Had clocks stopped?
- Were animals at the scene?
- Was an exact description of the suspect obtained? Physical description, jewelry worn, unusual voice or body odors; unusual marks, wounds, scratches, scars; nicknames used; clothing; cigarettes or cigars smoked; weapon used or carried; direction of leaving the scene?
- Was a vehicle involved? Make, model, color, direction, unusual marks?
- Were items taken from the scene? Exact description(s)?
- What was done to protect the crime scene physically?
- What officers were present during the preliminary investigation?
- Were specialists called to assist? Who?
- Was the coroner or medical examiner notified?
- What evidence was discovered at the scene? How was it collected, identified, preserved? Were field tests used?

## Discussion Questions

1. What are the advantages of assigning all investigations to specialists? What disadvantages does this pose? Which do you support?
2. Of all the suggested characteristics required for an effective investigator, which three are most critical? Are these qualifications more stringent than those required for a patrol officer?
3. Should investigators be paid more than patrol officers? Why or why not?

**4.** What misconceptions regarding investigation are conveyed by television shows and movies?

**5.** Why is investigation considered more prestigious than patrol?

**6.** What major factors must responding officers consider while proceeding to a crime scene?

**7.** How important is response time to the investigation of a crime? How is the importance affected by the type of crime?

**8.** What determines who is in charge at a crime scene? What authority does this officer have?

**9.** Controversy exists over which emergency takes precedence: an armed suspect at or near the scene or a severely injured person. Which do you think should take priority? Why?

**10.** What balance should be maintained between freedom of the media to obtain information during a crime investigation and the right to privacy of the individuals involved?

# References

Binkley, Lawrence L. "Futuristic System Helps Long Beach Corner Career Criminals." *The Police Chief,* April 1991, pp. 142–145.

Connor, Paul N., and Clinton H. Richards. "Evaluating Detectives' Performance." *The Police Chief,* September 1991, pp. 51–55.

Cook, Marshall J. "How to Handle the Press." *Law and Order.* September 1991, pp. 88–94.

del Carmen, Rolando V. "Civil Liabilities in Law Enforcement: Where Are We and Where Should We Go from Here?" *American Journal of Police*, Vol. 12, No. 4, 1993, pp. 87–99.

Goldstein, Herman. *Problem-Oriented Policing.* New York: McGraw-Hill Publishing Company, 1990.

Guffey, James E. "The Police and the Media: Proposals for Managing Conflict Productively." *American Journal of Police*, Vol. XI, No. 1, 1992, pp. 33–51.

Harr, J. Scott, and Kären M. Hess. *Criminal Procedure.* St. Paul, MN: West Publishing Company, 1990.

Hoffmann, John. "Private Labs." *Law and Order,* November 1992, pp. 30–33.

Lesce, Tony. "Operation Bullseye." *Law and Order,* October 1992, pp. 157–162.

Pilant, Lois. "Spotlight on Outfitting Your Detective Unit." *The Police Chief,* March 1992, pp. 33–41.

Rachlin, Harvey. "Working Together: Big and Small Departments Assist Each Other for More Effective Investigations." *Law and Order,* October 1992, pp. 131–137.

Sharp, Arthur G. "Computers Are a Cop's Best Friend." *Law and Order,* November 1991, pp. 41–45.

Weinblatt, Richard. "The Police and the Media." *Law and Order,* February 1992, pp. 32–38.

Young, Robert A. "The Current Police Phobia: Civil Liability." *Law Enforcement News,* February 29, 1996a, p. 8.

Young, Robert. "'Liability Blues': 8 Ways to Avoid Civil Suits." *Law Enforcement News,* March 15, 1996b, pp. 8, 10.

# Investigative Techniques

The basic investigative techniques introduced in Chapter 1 are central to successful resolution of a crime. Investigators must be skilled in taking photographs and sketching crime scenes (Chapter 2), taking notes and writing reports (Chapter 3), searching (Chapter 4), obtaining and processing physical evidence (Chapter 5), obtaining information through interviews and interrogation (Chapter 6), identifying and arresting suspects and conducting raids, surveillances, stakeouts and undercover assignments (Chapter 7).

Although these techniques are discussed separately, they actually overlap and often occur simultaneously. For example, note taking occurs at almost every phase of the investigation, as does obtaining information. Further, the techniques require modification to suit specific crimes as discussed in Sections Three, Four and Five. Nonetheless, investigation of specific crimes must proceed from a base of significant common techniques applicable to most investigations. This section provides that base.

# Chapter 2

# Investigative Photography and Crime-Scene Sketches

## DO YOU KNOW

What purposes are served by crime-scene photography?

What the advantages and disadvantages of using photography are?

What the minimum photographic equipment for the investigator is?

What errors in technique to avoid?

What to photograph at a crime scene and in what sequence?

What types of photography are used in criminal investigations?

What basic rules of evidence photographs must meet?

What purposes are served by the crime-scene sketch?

What should be sketched?

What type of materials are needed to make a rough sketch?

What steps to take in making a rough sketch?

How plotting methods are used in sketches?

When a sketch or a scale drawing is admissible in court?

## CAN YOU DEFINE

backing
baseline method
compass-point method
competent photograph
cross-projection sketch
finished scale drawing
laser-beam photography
legend
macrophotography

marker
material photograph
microphotography
mug shots
overlapping
plotting methods
rectangular-coordinate
    method
relevant photograph

rogues' gallery
rough sketch
scale drawing
sketch
trap photography
triangulation
ultraviolet-light
    photography

## Introduction

PHOTOGRAPHY PLAYS AN IMPORTANT ROLE IN DETECTING AND SOLVING crimes and presenting cases in court. It is also useful in crime-prevention and investigation training. According to the *Polaroid Guide to Instant Imaging* (1992, p. 1):

> From documenting a victim at a crime scene to revealing minute fibers linked to a homicide, photographs communicate more about crime scenes and evidence than any type of written description. They serve as both a form of documentation and a communication tool, since investigators use photographs first to record what a crime scene looked like and then to explain their findings to others.

Some departments rely almost exclusively on their own specially trained photographers. Other departments rely on their investigators to perform this function. One important means of photographing is videotaping. Often, both photographs and sketches must accompany written notes to provide a clear picture of the crime scene.

Photographs alone are insufficient for a number of reasons. They are not selective, do not show objects behind other objects, do not show measurements or true distances between objects and evidence and may distort the scene because of the camera angle. Problems such as poor lighting or incorrect film may also cause pictures to be inaccurate, and errors can occur in developing.

Not all crime scenes are photographed. Many more are sketched without photographs. Crime scene sketches are especially important in homicides, in arson cases and in reconstructing traffic accidents. They can help show the scene as the officer observed it, excluding extraneous details inevitably included in photographs.

This chapter discusses both crime-scene photography and sketching. It begins by looking at the advantages and disadvantages of photographs, the basic photographic equipment needed, training in investigative photography and errors to avoid. Next is an explanation of what to photograph or video, the role of instant photography and the use of markers. This is followed by a description of other types of investigative photography and how to identify, file and maintain continuity of the photographs or videos. The discussion on photography concludes with an explanation of the rules of evidence governing admissibility of photographic evidence in court.

The second portion of the chapter, crime-scene sketching, begins with a description of the rough crime-scene sketch and the steps involved. This is followed by an explanation of how to file the sketch and how it is used in creating the finished scale drawing. The discussion on crime-scene sketching also concludes with the legal admissibility of sketches and drawings.

## Investigative Photography: An Overview

Although the initial responsibility of the officers arriving at the scene is to handle emergency matters and then to protect the scene, one of the first investigative tasks is to take photographs or to videotape the crime scene and all evidence. Photographing usually precedes sketching, note taking and searching. Do not touch or move any evidence until pictures have been taken of the general crime scene and all evidence.

The basic purpose of crime-scene photography is to record the scene permanently. Pictures taken immediately, using proper techniques to reproduce the entire crime scene, provide a factual record of highest evidentiary value.

Photographs and videotapes reproduce the crime scene in detail for presentation to the prosecution, defense, witnesses, judge and jury in court. They are used in investigating, prosecuting and police training.

Although most crime-scene photographs are taken by investigators, they may also be acquired from commercial or amateur photographers, attorneys, news media personnel or the coroner's staff. For example, in an arson case at a church, photographs came from three outside sources. The pastor hired a photographer to take pictures for historical purposes and to assess damage, an insurance company photographer took pictures, and a television reporter had

*After a crime scene is secure, an important step is photographing the scene including any evidence that is located. Here an officer photographs confiscated drugs, money and weapons.*

in-progress movies. These pictures, along with those taken by police personnel, provided an excellent record of the fire in progress, where it was started and the resulting damage.

Videotape is now well established as an investigative tool. Lightweight, handheld video camcorders are easy to use at a crime scene. Taking videos is similar to taking still pictures. The police photographer starts at the entry, obtaining wide shots, and then records details. Zoom lenses allow close shots without disturbing the crime scene, and close-ups are possible with macro lenses. The sound capability can be used to describe the procedure being used to make the video and to explain what is being taped. Videotapes can also be made of witness testimony, depositions, evidence, lineups and even trials.

## Advantages and Disadvantages of Photographs

One advantage of photographs is that they can be taken immediately, an important factor in bad weather or when large numbers of people are present. For example, a picture of a footprint in the dirt outside a window broken during a burglary can be important if it rains before casting can be done. The same is true when a large number of people present might alter the scene.

Another obvious advantage of crime-scene photographs is that they accurately represent the crime scene in court. The effect of pictures on a jury cannot be overestimated. Photographs are highly effective visual aids to corroborate the facts presented, to create interest and to increase attention to the testimony being given.

Advantages of photographs: they can be taken immediately, accurately represent the crime scene and evidence, create interest and increase attention to testimony.

Although photographs of a crime scene accurately represent what was present, they include everything at the scene, both relevant and irrelevant. The camera is not selective. Viewers of photographs may be distracted by so much detail and fail to notice what is truly relevant.

Disadvantages of photographs: they are not selective, do not show actual distances, may be distorted and may be damaged by mechanical errors in shooting or processing.

Photographs do not show actual distances, and they may be taken at an angle that hides certain objects or distorts distances. Moreover, mechanical errors in equipment, lighting or processing of the film can damage or destroy the photographs. Therefore, accurate measurements, sketches and field notes are also needed to record the crime scene.

Despite these disadvantages, photography is a valuable investigative technique. A vast array of modern equipment has greatly enhanced its usefulness in investigation.

## Basic Photographic Equipment

Crime-scene photography uses both common and special-function cameras and equipment, depending on the crime investigated and the investigator's preferences.

At the minimum, have available and be skilled in operating a 35mm camera, an instant-print camera, a press camera, a fingerprint camera and video equipment.

Investigators commonly have individual preferences about the equipment to use in a given situation. Some have switched from 35mm and press cameras to professional roll-film cameras. Generally, equipment should meet several photographic needs.

*35mm cameras* are extremely versatile and provide excellent negatives for enlargements. Mayer (1990, pp. 62–63) suggests: "Small, entirely self-contained, auto-everything compact cameras are now so extremely easy to use that they are the major type of camera being sold. . . . For many law enforcement situations (crime scenes, accidents, documenting evidence, etc.) that require record photos as soon as possible after an officer arrives on the scene, a compact 35 should be able to handle the job."

Many models have an automatic built-in flash (which can be set on *off* if desired) and can imprint the date directly on the photo. Many also allow the film to be rewound before the entire roll is shot.

*Instant-print cameras* such as those made by Polaroid and Impulse provide low-cost-per-image pictures. Color or black-and-white film may be used. Instant photography provides immediate confirmation of the quality and accuracy of the picture at a time when it is possible to take another shot. The cameras are simple to operate, which lessens the need for training. Every officer on the force can use an instant camera.

*Press cameras* provide excellent photographs of the general scene as well as of smaller areas or small pieces of evidence. The ground glass of their lenses permits perfect focusing and shows exactly what portion of the scene will appear in the photograph. The 4" × 5" negative allows enlargement for detailed court presentation.

*Fingerprint cameras* are specially constructed to take pictures of fingerprints without distortion. They provide their own light through four bulbs, one in each corner. Removing a bulb from any corner provides slanted lighting to show fingerprint ridge detail. This camera can also be used to photograph other trace evidence such as bloodstains and toolmarks.

*Movie and videotape cameras* are used to record alleged bribery, payoffs and narcotics buys. Permanently installed units frequently photograph actual crimes being committed such as bank robberies or shoplifting. Videotaping crime scenes is now commonplace. The cameras have become much less expensive, much more portable and much easier to operate. They have the advantage of immediacy and elimination of a middle processing step in the chain of evidence. In addition, most can operate with quite limited light.

*Specialized cameras* such as binocular cameras and trip cameras (cameras that set themselves off) are helpful in surveillance.

*Film* for the various cameras may be black-and-white or color. Although more expensive, color film is often preferred because it is more realistic and accurate. Film can also be special purpose such as infrared film. Literature furnished with the camera gives detailed information about the type of film to use.

It is difficult to describe color verbally and sometimes impossible to describe varying shades of color accurately. Therefore, color film is often preferred. Objects in color photographs are more easily recognized by officers and witnesses. Color photographs can bring out faintly visible stains and preserve the original colors of objects that fade because of weather conditions or age. Color photographs are especially helpful in showing the nature and extent of physical injuries. More extensive uses of color photography in police work are being developed each year, and improved film and processing are assisting in the admissibility of color photographs in court.*

*Accessories,* depending on the cameras used, include an exposure meter, flash attachments, flood lamps and high-intensity spotlights. Lighting equipment can also assist in illuminating the scene to search for minute evidence. An adjustable tripod for mounting the camera at any angle makes for better photographs in most instances.

---

*Defense attorneys sometimes object to color photographs on the grounds that they are inflammatory. This concern is discussed later in the chapter.

**43**

**Chapter 2**

**Investigative
Photography
and
Crime-Scene
Sketches**

*A Boston police latent fingerprint examiner uses a special high-tech device, the Ramcam
Crimcon System, to lift fingerprints from evidence.*

Lenses and filters are available for different purposes. Normal lenses are best
for evidence, but sometimes special lenses are needed. For example, a telephoto
lens is used for a distant subject, whereas a wide-angle lens is used to cover an
entire room in a single shot. Various filters are used to eliminate certain colors
from the photograph.

Selection of camera(s) and accessories is determined by budget, local needs
and investigator preference. Sometimes equipment is borrowed from local high
schools, vocational schools or community organizations; or it is shared with other
agencies. In some communities, private citizens loan special-purpose equipment
to the police department.

*Darkroom facilities* are an additional consideration. Smaller departments often
share a darkroom with another agency such as a fire department. Larger departments usually have their own darkrooms. If a commercial developer is used, it
may take too long to get pictures back, confidential information may be revealed,
and the commercial developer may be required to testify in court. For all these
reasons, a police department is better served by having its own darkroom facilities or sharing them with another agency.

## Training in Investigative Photography

Most photographic equipment can be mastered by reading the accompanying manuals and practicing. Some equipment, however, requires special training.
Photographic training includes instruction in the operation of all available
photographic equipment; shooting techniques; problems to be anticipated; and
identifying, filing and maintaining continuity of photographic evidence.

Learn the nomenclature and operation of your available photographic equipment. Sometimes camera and equipment manufacturers or outlets provide such training.[†]

"The equipment is only a small part of taking good photos," according to Stockton (1996, p. 117). He suggests: "What it really takes is a photographic eye." He offers the following tips for taking effective photographs:

- Look for action and emotion.
- Look for unique perspectives.
- Get in tight and fill the frame with your subject.
- Pay attention when focusing.
- Sweep the viewfinder continuously.

Sometimes, professional commercial photographers in the community can assist in training or serve as consultants. They can provide information on photographic techniques and special problems such as lighting, close-ups, exposures and use of filters. They can demonstrate these techniques in the field.

Training programs also include instructions on identifying and filing photographs and on establishing and maintaining the continuity of the chain of evidence.

## Errors to Avoid

To obtain effective photographs, know your equipment and check it before you use it.

---

Take photographs before anything is disturbed. Avoid inaccuracies and distortions.

---

Take pictures before anything is moved so that they accurately represent the scene. If something has been moved, do *not* put it back. It is legally impossible to return an object to its original position.

Distortion can result from improper camera angle, lighting, lens selection and development. To minimize distortion or misrepresentation, maintain proper perspective and attempt to show the objects in the crime scene in their relative size and position. Take pictures from eye level, the height from which people normally observe objects in a room or area.

## What to Photograph or Videotape

Take sufficient photographs and/or videotape to reconstruct the entire scene. This usually requires a series of shots, including the entrance point, the crime commission area and the exit point. If possible, show the entire scene of the crime in a pictorial sequence. This assists in relating the crime to other crimes.

---

[†]The Polaroid Corporation provides training on law-enforcement photography and publishes a photography newsletter for law enforcement called *Instant Evidence!* In addition, Polaroid has a technical assistance hotline: 1–800–225–1618.

**45**

Chapter 2

**Investigative
Photography
and
Crime-Scene
Sketches**

Move the camera to cover the entire crime-scene area, but plan your shots so as to least disturb the scene. Lloyd (1994, p. 35) suggests:

> To increase chances of admissibility of photographs in court, the initial photographs showing the entire crime scene should be done using a technique called **overlapping.** Photograph the entire scene in a clockwise direction. The picture is taken so a specific object is on the right side of the first photograph. The second photo should have that same object on the left side of the photograph. The same technique should be used until the entire crime scene is covered. A log should be kept of all pictures taken describing what each photo represents.

---

First photograph the general area, then specific areas and finally specific objects of evidence. Take exterior shots first because they are most subject to alteration by weather and security violations.

---

This progression of shots will reconstruct the commission of a crime:

**1.** Take *long-range* pictures of the locality, point of ingress and egress, normal entry to the property and buildings, exterior of the buildings and grounds and street signs or other identifiable structures that will establish location.
**2.** Take *medium-range* pictures of the immediate crime scene and the location of objects of evidence within the area or room.
**3.** Take *close-range* pictures of specific evidence such as hairs, fibers, footprints and bloodstains. The entire surface of some objects may be photographed to show all evidence; for example, a table surface may contain bloodstains, fingerprints, hairs and fibers.

Different crimes require different types of photographs. In arson cases, photograph the point of origin and any incendiary devices. In burglaries, photograph the point of entry and exit, toolmarks, fingerprints and other trace evidence. In assaults, photograph injuries, in color if possible. In homicides or suicides, photograph the deceased, including pictures of the clothing worn; a full-length picture showing height, position of the body and all extremities; and evidence near the body. Photograph injured parts of the body to show the location and extent of injuries and any postmortem lividity (discussed in Chapter 12).

Camcorders and videotaping equipment have been used for in-station recordings of bookings and for DWI-suspect tests for some time. Use of video cameras for crime scene investigations is now prevalent. *Edwards v. State* (1977) established that sound recordings are admissible, providing the operator is competent to operate the equipment and does so within procedures established under *Pennsylvania v. Muniz* (1990). *Huffman v. State* (1988) established that the video portion of the tape may be admissible without the audio.

Many police departments have purchased video equipment to record crime scenes and other criminal acts such as vandalism, drug deals and thefts for use in court. Videotapes have become a form of crime prevention and control as well as investigative aid, as discussed later in this chapter. Some police departments have mounted video cameras on their patrol vehicles' dashboards.

In addition to providing realistic accounts of traffic violations, DUI apprehensions, felony arrests and drug buys, the videotapes can be used for training. Further, when violations and arrests are videotaped and the tapes are submitted in court as evidence, convictions have increased.

*This videorecorder can be used for taping DUIs, drug arrests and traffic stops. The tapes can also be used for training.*

Another advance is the cameras used in combination with radar to document the speed of motorists. These cameras provide a photograph of the car and the driver along with the date, time, speed and location.

## Instant Photography

Instant photography has been used in police work since the 1950s, but the cameras and film have been improved to the point where it now has broad applications in law enforcement. As noted by Schmidt (1991, p. 45): "Firmly established in the booking room and laboratory, instant photography is now reaching the patrol officer on the street. . . . Once on the scene, investigators can use instant photos as visual 'notebooks,' capturing intriguing details or photographing from different angles than those employed by the department identification officer."

Another advantage is noted by Godin (1990, p. 70): "Instant print photography is recommended for use as backup for 35mm photography. It is not unheard of for a film to be lost when developed by an outside lab, or for there to be under- or over-developed photos or out-of-focus shots by inexperienced photographers."

In addition to serving as a backup, instant photography offers many other applications; for example:

■ Taking mug shots, booking and file photos at the scene rather than at the station.
■ Documenting suspects' unusual features such as scars and tattoos.
■ Preserving crime-scene evidence immediately upon arrival by the first responders.
■ Preserving minute evidence using close-up attachments and a stand.

**47**

**Chapter 2**

**Investigative
Photography
and
Crime-Scene
Sketches**

- Documenting bruises or wounds in homicides and domestic assault cases.
- Recording vandalism evidence such as graffiti on walls so that it can be compared with other cases.

A police department in a major city used instant photography to record new and unfamiliar graffiti in the community. The photos were given to a detective with the metropolitan gang unit to determine if the graffiti was simply a prank or was evidence that gangs were defining new turf.

According to Jensen (1995, p. 104): "A heavily vandalized location, used by the most active taggers in a city, would be extremely useful to an investigator to photograph as the basis for developing multiple case files." Concurring is Detective Bailey (Morrison, 1995, p. 86): "As far as law enforcement's response [to the graffiti problem], the graffiti should be photographed for intelligence purposes and/or evidence purposes."

Further, as noted in "Documenting Foreceful Impact Blood Spatter" (1995, p. 1): "To the trained eye, bloodstain patterns found at a violent crime scene tell an important story. They can bear silent witness to the ferocity of an attack, implicate or exonerate suspects, and help investigators reconstruct the event responsible for the bloodshed." If blood spatters are found at a crime scene, they should be carefully documented. As noted in the above article (p. 3): "Perhaps the most important rule to remember when documenting blood stains is that there's no such thing as too many photographs. Comprehensive documentation from multiple distances and perspectives provides bloodstain pattern analysts with as complete a picture of the evidence as possible." Among the important determinations possible from bloodstain pattern analysis are the following (p. 1):

- Whether an apparent suicide is genuine or staged.
- Whether bloodstains on a suspect can place him or her in the immediate vicinity of a victim at the time of injury.
- The point of injury.
- The amount of force involved in an attack.
- Whether bloodstains on a person or clothing are the result of spatter or of an attempt to render aid to a victim.
- The direction of a victim's movement.
- The minimum number of blows or gunshots needed to cause a victim's injuries.

Such determinations are invaluable in a criminal investigation.

Photo documentation can reduce officers' time in court. In addition, defense attorneys are more apt to enter negotiations or pleas if photographic evidence exists. Instant photos can be used in reports to reduce the necessity of writing long descriptions; a photo may, indeed, save a thousand words. A series of pictures depicting the investigative process can illustrate the case as a visual sequence. This may result in a high-impact story for other officers, superiors and the media. It is also invaluable as a training aid.

Unsworth and Forte (1991, p. 59) report that the Waltham Police Department uses instant images to supplement conventional 35mm photography: "Instant photos document an original scene and orient department spokespeople who may not be able to visit the site, but need to provide accurate information to the media."

Instant photography not only can be invaluable in investigations, its use may even serve as a deterrent to crime. According to Schmidt (1991, p. 46):

> Certain individuals will awaken a police officer's suspicion for a variety of reasons, including clothing suggestive of gang membership, a general resemblance to someone on the department's wanted list, loitering or erratic behavior and speech. An instant portrait of a suspicious individual not only allows an officer to share his observations with the entire department—including those colleagues working different shifts—but also alerts the individual to the department's scrutiny.

## Markers

A **marker** is anything used in a picture to show accurate or relative size. It is usually a ruler, but it can be some other object of a known size, such as a coin or a hairpin.

Using a marker introduces something foreign to the crime scene. The same is true of chalk marks drawn around a body or placed on walls to illustrate bullet direction. Therefore, first take a picture of the scene or object without the marker; then add the marker and take a second photograph.

## Other Types of Investigative Photography

In addition to crime-scene photography, other types of photography play vital roles in investigation.

---

Types of investigative photography include crime-scene, surveillance, aerial, night, laboratory, lineup and mug-shot photography.

---

### Surveillance Photography

Surveillance photography establishes the identity of a subject or records criminal behavior without the photographer's presence being known to the subject. The photographs or videotapes can be used to identify a suspect's associates, to destroy an alibi, to plan a raid or to develop a surveillance plan. Banks and stores frequently use surveillance cameras to help identify robbers and burglars. Numerous bank robbers have been identified through photographs of the holdup taken by special surveillance cameras permanently installed in the bank.

Photographs taken during a stakeout are usually taken with a single-reflex camera with several telephoto lenses. Sometimes infrared film is used. It may be necessary to use a van—preferably borrowed because it is best to use a vehicle only once for such purposes. An appliance repair van or any van that would commonly be seen in the area is desirable.

Problems of surveillance photography include adverse lighting conditions, people getting in the camera view and distance. Concealing the camera can also be a problem; a bag, briefcase, suitcase or coat pocket with an opening might be used. Concealment can also be accomplished by using rooftops or windows of buildings or vehicles in the area. A camera kept away from a vehicle window is rarely seen by people outside the vehicle. The camera should be kept loaded and adjusted to the required light so that pictures can be taken instantly.

Surveillance photography is often called **trap photography** because the photos prove that the incident occurred and can assist in identifying suspects and

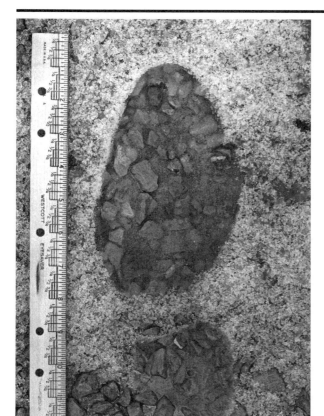

*A marker shows the accurate size of this footprint.*

**49**

**Chapter 2**

**Investigative
Photography
and
Crime-Scene
Sketches**

the weapons used. These photos corroborate witness testimony and identification. In some police departments an 85 percent conviction rate is obtained when surveillance photography is used. The fact that the photos exist often induces guilty pleas without court appearances. This saves investigators' time for other investigations.

Battery-operated cameras can be moved to different locations. The amount of film used can be reduced by using such things as bait-money pull switches or by placing activation buttons in several locations where employees can reach them easily. Lighting conditions affect whether color or black-and-white film is better to use. Hidden camcorders can be used at drug buy scenes. The use of trap cameras outdoors is restricted by weather and temperature.

Surveillance photography can also be used as a crime prevention/detection tool. For example, the Newark Police Department has video cameras mounted in six different areas of the 2-square-mile downtown area. One officer observes what is taking place in each area from a central location. Burglaries and street robberies have decreased, and the police have successfully presented the videos as evidence in court.

## Aerial Photography

Aerial photography is often used to cover extensive areas. For example, it can be used in a bank robbery to show roads leading to and from the bank. It is also useful when it is known that a crime is going to be committed but not when. Aerial photography shows routes to the scene as well as how to block escape routes, avoid detours during pursuit and set up roadblocks. It is essential in locating dead-end streets—information that can be very important in case of a chase. Aerial pictures can also help establish the location of a crime scene, especially in large rural areas or mountainous sectors.

Aerial photos can be enlarged or presented on slides to show the relationships of streets and roads. For example, in the John F. Kennedy assassination investigation, the entire area was photographed, including all points from which shots might have been fired.

Aerial photographs are often available in commercial photographers' files, engineering offices or highway planning agencies. The vast areas covered by highways and engineering projects usually require aerial mapping. Federal, state, county and municipal agencies also may have aerial photos. If none are available, a local photographer can be hired to provide them. Many larger departments and county sheriffs' offices have helicopters that might be available.

### Night Photography

Taking pictures at night presents special problems, particularly that of illuminating the scene. Adequate light can be obtained by increasing exposure time, by using a photoflash for small areas and flash series for larger areas or by using floodlights. Floodlights also aid in locating evidence and decrease the chance of evidence being accidentally destroyed.

State-of-the-art night-vision devices/cameras are dramatically better than earlier ones. They can view up to a mile. Because they are quite expensive and used infrequently, they are often shared with other federal, state or county law enforcement agencies.

### Laboratory Photography

Not all investigative photography is done in the field. Sometimes objects are photographed in the laboratory with special equipment that is too large, delicate or expensive to use in the field. For example, infrared film photographs can reveal the contents of unopened envelopes, bloodstains, alterations to documents, variations in types of ink and residue near where a bullet has passed through clothing. X-ray cameras can detect loaded dice.

**Microphotography,** taking pictures through a microscope, assists in identifying minute particles of evidence such as a hair or fiber. In contrast, **macrophotography** enlarges the subject. For example, a fingerprint or a tool-mark can be greatly enlarged to show the details of ridges or striations.

**Laser-beam photography** can reveal evidence indiscernible to the naked eye. For example, it can reveal the outline of a footprint in a carpet even though the fibers have returned to normal position.

**Ultraviolet-light photography** uses the low end of the color spectrum, which is invisible to human sight, to make visible impressions of bruises and injuries long after their actual occurrence. Bite marks, injuries due to beatings with leather belts or belt buckles, cigarette burns, neck strangulation marks and other impressions left from intentional injuries can be reproduced and used as evidence in criminal cases by scanning the presumed area of injury with a fluorescent or blue light. The damage impression left by the injury is then photographed. In addition, the type of weapon used in committing a crime can often be determined by examining its impression, developed by using ultraviolet light.

**51**

**Chapter 2**

**Investigative
Photography
and
Crime-Scene
Sketches**

*An aerial shot of the Waco aftermath provides important information to investigators, including the layout of the compound, its defenses and the extent of destruction caused by the fire.*

### Mug Shots

Although investigators seldom take **mug shots** themselves, these photographs are often significant in criminal investigations. Mug shots originated in nineteenth-century France when Alphonse Bertillon developed a method of identification using an extensive system of measurements to describe persons. The Bertillon identification system included a written description, the complete measurements of the person and a photograph. The pictures of persons in police custody were kept in department files for identification and became known as *mug shots.* Gathered in files and displayed in groups, they were called a **rogues' gallery.**

Opinions differ regarding the preferred poses for mug shots. Some agencies believe the front and profile of the head are sufficient; others prefer full-length, stand-up pictures. No matter what the pose, mug shots should include the facial features and the clothing worn at the time of arrest because a defendant's appearance may change between the time of arrest and trial (*United States v. Sherman,* 1970). Mug shots can be filed by age, sex and height to make them more readily accessible for viewing.

Mug shots can be carried in the field to identify suspicious persons or to show to crime victims to assist in identifying the attacker. They are also used for "wanted" circulars distributed to other police agencies and the public. The use of mug shots in suspect identification is discussed in Chapter 7.

Video imaging systems have greatly increased the ease of taking and using mug shots. As noted in *Law and Order* ("Video Imaging...," 1990, p. 105):

> It [a video imaging system] permits the reassignment of file clerks, and allows the accumulation and analysis of crime and criminal information that was not economically feasible before.
>
> The system also locates and prints pictures in moments and, when printed nine per page, makes a color print for $.13 each. It allows the sharing of information with other departments by modem, thereby saving travel by investigators. . . .

This source also notes that the National Crime Information Center (NCIC) began maintaining a video data base of criminals in 1992.

*Law Enforcement Technology* ("Mug Shots...," 1992, p. 34) states that video imaging systems can allow booking officers to place mug shots directly into arrest or incident files with as few as three keystrokes: "The camera and lights can be operated directly from the keyboard, the officer barely has to change his current booking procedure and the detainee can stay in one place for the whole procedure." A further advantage is that (p. 35): "The computerized mug shot system allows for faster, more accurate booking, since the officer can preview the mug before storing the shot. If the image is unacceptable, he knows immediately and can re-take it."

Another obvious advantage is that a video imaging system allows officers to sort through the data base using specific known characteristics of a suspect. They can sort by race, sex, hair color, height, age, distinguishing characteristics—in fact, by any feature that can be visually described. This capability also has greatly enhanced police departments' ability to develop photographic lineups.

### Lineup Photographs

According to *Law Enforcement Technology* ("Mug Shots...," 1992, p. 34): "The computer can sort through the data base of mug shots and bring up all the 'hits' within these physical categories. The officer-in-charge can select the six or twelve or sixteen that match, then bracket the known suspect within these lineups for presentation."

In addition, videotapes or photographs of persons included in lineups may be taken to establish the fairness of the lineup. The value of such pictures was indicated in *United States v. Branic* (1974), where a lineup picture was introduced in court and assisted the jury in determining that the persons in the lineup were similar and that the lineup was, indeed, fair. This is discussed in Chapter 7.

## Identifying, Filing and Maintaining Continuity of Evidence

Photographs must be properly identified, filed and continuously secured to be admissible as evidence.

**Identifying.** In the field notes, the photographs taken should be dated and numbered in sequence. Include the case number, type of offense and subject of the picture. To further identify the photograph with the crime scene and the subject, record the photographer's name, location and direction of the camera, lens type, approximate distance in feet to the subject, film and shutter speed, lighting, weather conditions and a brief description of the scene in the picture. According to Lloyd (1994, pp. 35–36):

> After printing, the photos should be marked like any other evidence relating to the crime scene. The procedure called **backing** includes recording on the back of the photo your initials, date photo was taken, brief description of what the photo depicts and the direction of north. This correlates the photos with the crime scene sketch, since both compliment each other. Mark on the back of the photo with a felt tip pen or use a label. For identifying small pieces of evidence on the photo, draw a circle around the evidence by holding the photo backwards so the print is toward the light. Make a circle around the evidence on the back side of the photo. Jury members also see this photo and can identify the object later in the jury deliberation room using the same technique. Do not write on the face of the picture; this destroys it as evidence.

**Filing.** File the picture and negatives for easy reference. Pictures filed in the case file are available to others. Therefore, it is usually best to put them in a special photograph file, cross-referenced by case number.

**Maintaining Security.** The chain of custody of the film and the photographs is recorded in the field notes or in a special file. Mark and identify the film as it is removed from the camera. Each time the film changes possession, record the name of the person accepting it. If a commercial firm develops the film, take it in person or send it by registered mail with a return receipt.

## Admissibility of Photographs in Court: Rules of Evidence

Photographs must be taken under certain conditions and must meet specific criteria to be admissible in court.

---

Photographs must be material, relevant, competent, accurate, free of distortion and noninflammatory.

---

A **material photograph** relates to the specific case and subject being discussed. Material evidence is relevant and forms a substantive part of the case presented or has a legitimate and effective influence on the decision of the case (*Porter v. Valentine,* 1986). A **relevant photograph** assists or explains testimony. It applies to the matter in question. It is the characteristic of the evidence that renders it applicable in determining the truth or falsity of matters in issue (*Barnett v. State,* 1922). A **competent photograph** accurately represents what it purports to represent, is properly identified and is properly placed in the chain of evidence and secured until court presentation. All competent evidence is duly qualified and answers all legal requirements (*King's Lake Drainage & Levee Dist. v. Jamison,* 1903).

Testimony is introduced regarding the exact conditions under which the photographs were taken, the equipment and type of film used and where the film was processed. Photographs must be accurate and free of distortion. If nothing has been removed from or added to the scene, the photograph will be accurate. Inaccuracies do not necessarily render the photograph inadmissible as evidence as long as any inaccuracies are fully explained and the court is not misled about what the picture represents.

Likewise, distortion may not disqualify a photograph as evidence if no attempt is made to misrepresent the photograph and the distortion is adequately explained. For example, an amateur photographer may have taken the picture from an unusual camera height to produce a dramatic effect, not knowing the picture would later be useful as evidence in a criminal investigation.

Color distortion is a frequent objection. Because most objects have color, black-and-white photographs are technically distorted. Therefore, color photographs are usually better evidence. However, color can also be distorted by inadequate lighting or faulty processing. Nevertheless, the photograph can still be useful, especially if the object's shape is more important than its color.

Although color photographs are less distorted and are usually better evidence than black-and-white photographs, they have often been objected to as being inflammatory—for example, showing in gruesome, vivid color a badly beaten body. To be ruled inadmissible, color photographs must be judged by the court to be so inflammatory that they will unduly influence the jury. The value of taking color and black-and-white pictures that might be considered inflammatory was documented in *United States v. Smith* (1974). The black-and-white pictures were introduced as evidence; the color pictures were used for investigatory purposes only.

Objections to enlargements have also been raised. Such objections can be countered by producing the original negative along with the enlargement to prove that no alterations have been made.

In addition to admissible photographs and videotapes, investigators usually must prepare a crime-scene sketch.

## Crime-Scene Sketches: An Overview

An investigator's scene **sketch** can be more descriptive than hundreds of words, and it is often an extremely important investigative aid. The crime-scene sketch:

- Accurately portrays the physical facts.
- Relates to the sequence of events at the scene.
- Establishes the precise location and relationship of objects and evidence at the scene.
- Helps to create a mental picture of the scene for those not present.
- Is a permanent record of the scene.
- Is usually admissible in court.

---

A crime-scene sketch assists in (1) interviewing and interrogating persons, (2) preparing the investigative report and (3) presenting the case in court.

---

The sketch supplements photographs, notes, plaster casts and other investigative techniques.

Artistic ability is helpful but not essential in making crime-scene sketches. Still, many police officers avoid making sketches. To overcome this hesitancy, practice by drawing familiar scenes such as your home, office or police station. Use graph paper to make sketching easier.

The most common types of sketches are those drawn at the crime scene, called *rough sketches,* and those completed later by the investigator or a drafter, called *scale* (or *finished*) *drawings.* Both describe the crime scene pictorially and show the precise location of objects and evidence.

## The Rough Sketch

The **rough sketch** is the first pencil-drawn outline of the scene and the location of objects and evidence within this outline. It is not usually drawn to scale, although distances are measured and entered in the appropriate locations.

---

Sketch all serious crime and accident scenes after photographs are taken and before anything is moved. Sketch the entire scene, the objects and the evidence.

---

It is better to include too much than too little, but do not include irrelevant objects that clutter and confuse the sketch.

The area to be sketched depends on the crime scene. If it involves a large area, make a sketch of nearby streets, vegetation and paths of entrance and exit. If the scene is inside a house or apartment building, show the scene's location in relation to the larger structure. If the scene involves only a single room, sketch only the immediate crime scene, including the outline of the room, objects and the evidence within it.

Do not overlook the possible availability of architectural drawings of the house or building. These are often on file with local engineering, assessing or building departments or with the architect who drew the original plans.

## Sketching Materials

Materials needed for rough sketches should be assembled and placed in their own kit or in the crime-scene investigation kit.

---

Materials for the rough sketch include paper, pencil, long steel measuring tape, carpenter-type ruler, straightedge, clipboard, eraser, compass, protractor and thumbtacks.

---

Paper of any type will do, but plain white or graph paper is best. No lines interfere if you use plain white. On the other hand, graph paper provides distance ratios and allows for more accurate depictions of the relationships between objects and evidence at the scene. When sketching, use a hard lead pencil to avoid smudges. Keep two or three pencils on hand.

Use a 50- to 150-foot steel measuring tape for measuring long distances. Steel is preferable because it does not stretch and is therefore more accurate than cloth tape. Use a carpenter-type ruler to take short and close-quarter measurements and a straightedge to draw straight lines. A clipboard will give a firm, level drawing surface.

*Investigators gather evidence at a crime scene where Montgomery police officers forced the car of a suspected bank robber into the side of the pickup truck during a pursuit. The suspect was then shot and killed and one officer was injured.*

Use a compass to determine true north, especially in areas and buildings laid out in other than true directions. Use a protractor to find the proper angles when determining coordinates.

Thumbtacks are helpful to hold down one end of the tape when you measure. They can also be used to fasten paper on a drawing surface if no clipboard is available.

## Steps in Sketching the Crime Scene

Once photographs have been taken and other priority steps in the preliminary investigation have been performed, you can begin sketching the crime scene. First, make an overall judgment of the scene. Remember not to move, remove, touch or pick up anything until it has been photographed, located on the rough sketch and described in detail in your notes. Then, handle objects only in accordance with the techniques for preserving evidence.

---

To sketch a crime scene:
- Observe and plan.
- Measure distances.
- Outline the area.
- Locate objects and evidence within the outline.
- Record details.
- Make notes.
- Identify the sketch with a legend and a scale.

---

**57**

Chapter 2

**Investigative
Photography
and
Crime-Scene
Sketches**

## Step One: Observe and Plan

Before starting to sketch, observe the scene as many times as you need to feel comfortable with it. Take in the entire scene mentally so that you can recall it later. Plan in advance how to proceed in an organized way to avoid destruction of evidence.

Ask yourself, "What is relevant to the crime being investigated? What should be included in the sketch?"

The size of the area determines how many sketches you make. For example, part of the crime may have taken place indoors and another part outdoors a considerable distance away. To include the entire area would make the scale too small. Therefore, make two sketches.

**Decide Where to Start.** The overview also helps you determine where to start sketching and measuring. If the scene is a room, stand in the doorway and start the sketch there. Then proceed clockwise or counterclockwise. The photographs, sketch and search are all made in the same direction to establish uniformity in procedures. Usually it does not matter which direction is selected, but try to use the direction that is least disturbing to evidence.

## Step Two: Measure and Outline the Area

All measurements must be precise and accurate. A steel tape is best for measuring because it does not stretch. Do not estimate distances or use paces or shoelength measurement. Use conventional units of measurements such as inches, feet, yards, centimeters or meters. Do not move any objects while measuring.

If another officer is helping you take measurements, reverse the ends of the tape so that both of you can observe the actual distance on the tape. Legally, it is *hearsay* for officers to testify to what they did not actually observe. If a third officer is taking notes, that officer can testify only to the measurements given to him or her unless he or she actually saw the tape measurement. However, all officers may testify from the same notes if they review and initial them as they are made.

Do not measure from movable objects. Use *fixed locations* such as walls, trees, telephone poles, building corners, curbs and the like. Measure from wall to wall, not baseboard to baseboard.

Once the outside measurements have been made, sketch the outline, maintaining some distance ratio. Use the longest measurement first and orient the sketch paper to this distance, positioning the sketch so that *north is toward the top of the paper*. Place the outside limits in the sketch using dimension lines. Dimension lines look like this:

$\vdash$————10′————$\dashv$

Determine the **scale** by taking the longest measurement at the scene and dividing it by the longest measurement of the paper used for sketching. For example, if your paper is 10" and the longest measurement at the scene is 100′, let 1 inch equal 10 feet. Use the largest, simplest scale possible.

Table 2–1 presents suggested scales for sketches. Graph paper makes it easier to draw to scale. The squares can be units of measurements. For example, each square can equal one square foot or one square inch, depending on the size of the scene. The outline sketch of a room might look like Figure 2–1, whereas the outline sketch of an outdoor scene might look like Figure 2–2.

**Table 2–1 Suggested Scales for Sketches**

| Indoor Areas | Outdoor Areas |
|---|---|
| 1/2" = 1' (small rooms)<br>1/4" = 1' (large rooms)<br>1/8" = 1' (very large rooms) | 1/2" = 10' (large buildings and grounds)<br>1/8" = 10' (large land areas) |

Next, measure and sketch the doors and windows. Record their measurements and indicate whether the doors open in or out. To measure windows, use the width and height of the actual window opening; do not include the window frame. The outline of a room with doors and windows added might look like Figure 2–3.

Sketch the location of physical objects within the outside perimeter. Use approximate shapes for large objects and symbols for small ones. Place items of evidence in the sketch at the same time you place objects. Use numbers to designate objects and letters to designate evidence. Include such items as point of entry or exit of a bullet, body, hair, gun, fibers, bloodstains and so on. Use exact measurements to show the location of evidence within the room and in relation to all other objects.

Opinions differ on whether to include the location of evidence in this sketch. If evidence is placed within the sketch, some courts have withheld introduction of the sketch until the evidence has been approved. If the evidence is placed only in the finished scale drawing, the sketch can be introduced and used by witnesses to corroborate their testimony.

While sketching, check your measurements frequently. Make corrections if needed, but make no changes after leaving the scene. Measurements may or may not be placed in the sketch itself, depending on how many objects are located in the available space. Measurements can be placed in your notes and later entered in the scale drawing.

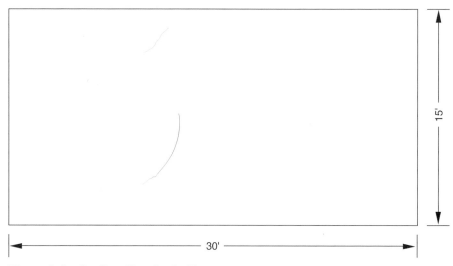

**Figure 2–1    Outline Sketch of a Room**

**59**

**Chapter 2**

**Investigative
Photography
and
Crime-Scene
Sketches**

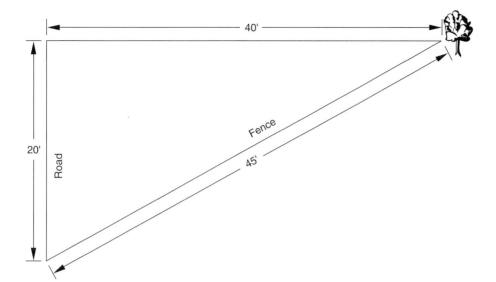

**Figure 2–2    Outline Sketch of an Outdoor Scene**

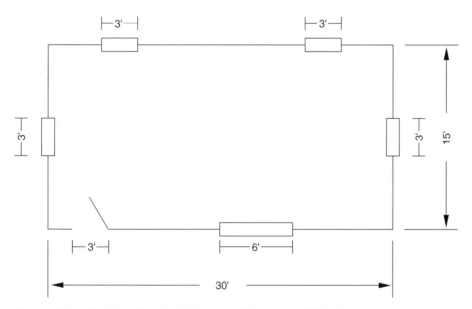

**Figure 2–3    Outline Sketch of Room with Door and Windows**

### Step Three: Plot Objects and Evidence

Accuracy and precision are vital in taking measurements. To plot objects and evidence exactly, determine the fixed points from which to take measurements. There are several methods of plotting and measuring the location of objects.

---

**Plotting methods** are used to locate objects and evidence on the sketch. They include the use of rectangular coordinates, a baseline, triangulation and compass points.

---

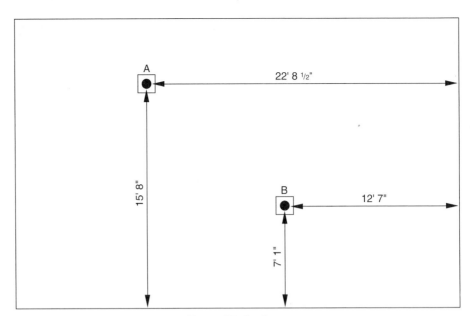

**Figure 2–4    Rectangular-Coordinate Method**

**Rectangular-Coordinate Method.**    The rectangular-coordinate method is a common method for locating objects and evidence in a room. The **rectangular-coordinate method** uses two adjacent walls as fixed points from which distances are measured at right angles. Locate objects by measuring from one wall at right angles and then from the adjacent wall at right angles. Use of this method is restricted to square or rectangular areas (see Figure 2–4).

**Baseline Method.**    Another way to measure by coordinates is to run a baseline from one fixed point to another. The **baseline method** establishes a straight line from one fixed point to another, from which measurements are taken at right angles. Take measurements along either side of the baseline to a

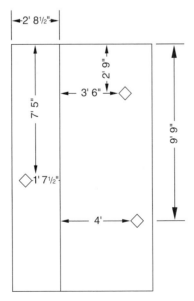

**Figure 2–5    Center Baseline Method**

**61**

**Chapter 2**

**Investigative
Photography
and
Crime-Scene
Sketches**

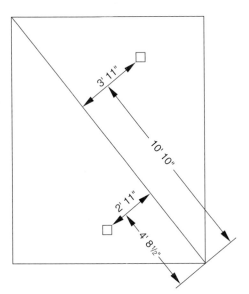

**Figure 2–6   Diagonal Baseline Method**

point at right angles to the object to be located. An indoor baseline method
sketch might look like Figure 2–5 or 2–6. Outdoors, it might look like Figure 2–7.

Sometimes the distance between two locations is important. For example,
the distance from the normal route to a door might be very important if evidence is found in a room. The 34-foot measurement in Figure 2–7 illustrates
this need in an outdoor setting.

**Triangulation Method.**   Triangulation is commonly used in outdoor scenes
but can also be used indoors. **Triangulation** uses straight-line measures from two
fixed objects to the evidence to create a triangle with the evidence in the angle

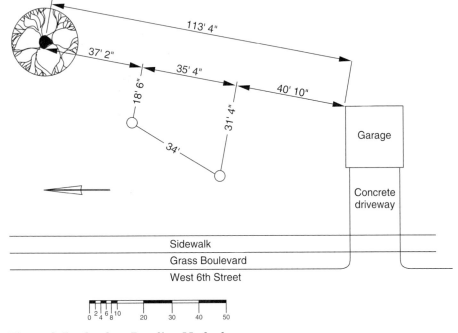

**Figure 2–7   Outdoor Baseline Method**

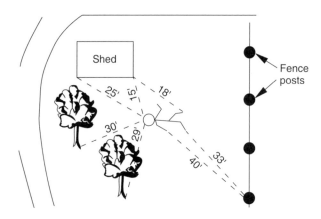

**Figure 2–8   Triangulation Method**

formed by the two straight lines. The degree of the angle formed at the location of the object or evidence can then be measured with a protractor. The angle can be any degree, in contrast to the rectangular coordinate and baseline methods, in which the angle is always a right angle (90°).

Always select the best fixed points possible, with emphasis on their permanency. Fixed points may be closet doors, electrical outlets, door jambs or corners of a structure. It is sometimes impossible to get to the corners of a room for accurate measurements due to obstacles. Triangulation is illustrated in Figure 2–8.

**Compass Point Method.**   The **compass point method** uses a protractor to measure the angle formed by two lines. In Figure 2–9, for example, Object *A* is located 10′7″ from origin *C* and at an angle of 59° from the vertical line through point *C*. Object *B* is 16′7″ from origin *C* at an angle of 47° from the vertical.

**Cross-Projection Method.**   For some interior crime scenes, it is useful to show the relationship between evidence on the floors and the walls. This can be done by sketching the room as though the viewer is straight above it, looking down at a single plane. In effect, the room is flattened out much like a box cut down at the four corners and opened out flat. A **cross-projection sketch** presents the floor and walls as though they were one surface.

Objects of evidence on both the floor and the walls can be measured to show their relationship on a single plane, as shown in Figure 2–10.

### Step Four: Take Notes

After you have completed your sketch, take careful notes regarding factors associated with the scene that are not sketchable, such as lighting conditions, colors, people present at the scene and all other relevant information.

**63**

**Chapter 2**

**Investigative
Photography
and
Crime-Scene
Sketches**

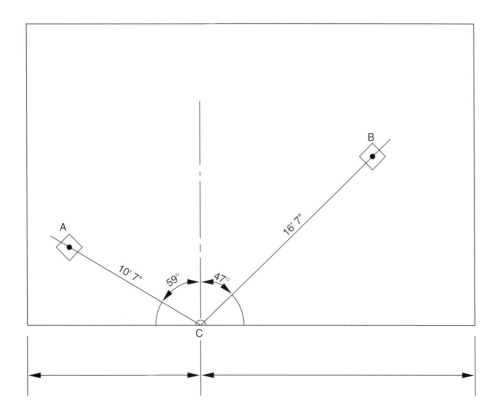

**Figure 2–9   Compass Point Method**

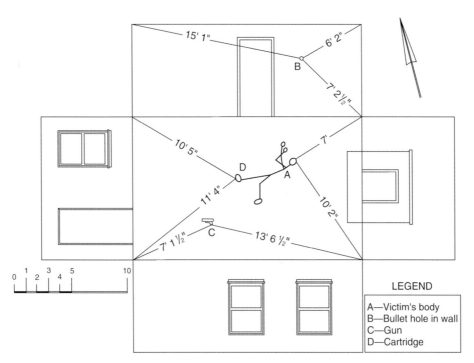

**Figure 2–10   Cross-Projection Sketch**

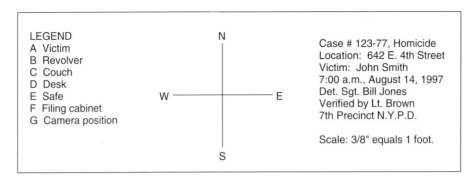

LEGEND
A  Victim
B  Revolver
C  Couch
D  Desk
E  Safe
F  Filing cabinet
G  Camera position

N

W ——————|—————— E

S

Case # 123-77, Homicide
Location:  642 E. 4th Street
Victim:  John Smith
7:00 a.m., August 14, 1997
Det. Sgt. Bill Jones
Verified by Lt. Brown
7th Precinct N.Y.P.D.

Scale: 3/8" equals 1 foot.

**Figure 2–11    Sample Legend**

### Step Five: Identify the Scene

Prepare a **legend** containing the case number, the type of crime, name of the victim or complainant, location, date, time, the investigator, person(s) assisting, scale of the sketch, direction of north and any other identifying information required by your department (see Figure 2–11).

Place a legend in the lower corner of the sketch, outside the room or area outline. Identify the scene completely, the location, type of crime and case number. Give the scale and place an arrow to show north pointing to the top of the sketch. Include the name of the person making the sketch.

### Step Six: Reassess the Sketch

Before leaving the scene, make sure you have recorded everything you need on the sketch. Make sure nothing has been overlooked or incorrectly diagrammed. Once you have left, nothing should be added to the sketch. Compare the scene with the sketch. Are all measurements included? Have all relevant notations been made? Have you missed anything? Figure 2–12 is a completed rough sketch of a crime scene.

## File the Sketch

Place the rough sketch in a secure file. It is the basis for the scale drawing, and it may be used as evidence in court. The rough sketch is a permanent record for all future investigations of the crime. It may be used later to question witnesses or suspects, and it is the foundation for the finished scale drawing. The better the rough sketch is, the better the finished drawing will be.

Keep the rough draft in its original form even after the scale drawing is completed because it may be needed for testifying. Otherwise, the defense may claim that changes were made in preparing the scale drawings.

## The Finished Scale Drawing

Given a well-drawn rough sketch, the finished scale drawing can be completed. The **finished scale drawing** is done in ink on a good grade of paper and is drawn to scale, using exact measurements. The materials used for making scale drawings are listed in Table 2–2.

**65**

**Chapter 2**

**Investigative
Photography
and
Crime-Scene
Sketches**

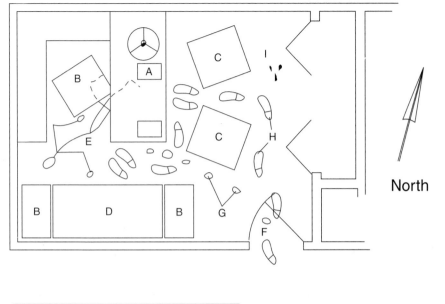

North

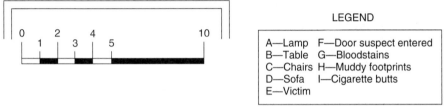

LEGEND

A—Lamp  F—Door suspect entered
B—Table  G—Bloodstains
C—Chairs  H—Muddy footprints
D—Sofa  I—Cigarette butts
E—Victim

**Figure 2–12  Completed Crime Scene Sketch**

The artistic refinements of the scale drawing do not permit it to be made at the crime scene. Instead, it is made at the police station by the investigator or by a drafter. If anyone other than the investigator prepares the finished scale drawing, the investigator must review it carefully and sign it along with the drafter.

The finished drawing can be simple or complex, but it must represent the actual distances, objects and evidence contained in the rough sketch. Color designations and plastic overlays to illustrate other phases of the investigation are often added.

The drawing can be duplicated for other investigators and distributed to the prosecuting attorney. It is usually placed on white mounting board for display in court. A finished scale drawing is illustrated in Figure 2–13.

**Table 2–2  Materials for Making Scale Drawings**

| *Materials* | *Uses* |
|---|---|
| Drawing kit | Contains tools for finer drawing |
| Triangular scale rule | Accurate scaling |
| Templates (assorted shapes, sizes) | Curves, oddly shaped objects |
| Indelible ink | For permanency of finished drawing |
| Drafting table | Ease, perfection in drawing |
| T-square | Accurate, straight lines, right angles |
| Drafting paper | Higher-quality absorption of inks, better display |
| Colors | Show areas of comparison |

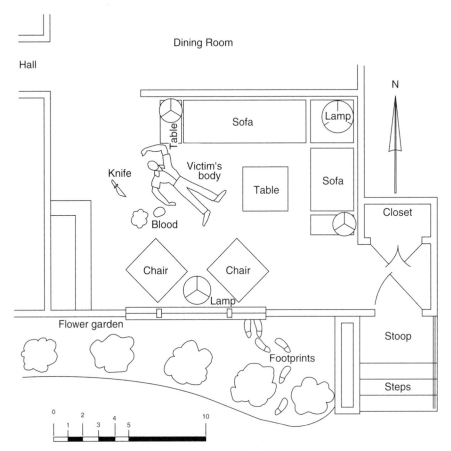

**Figure 2–13   Finished Scale Drawing**

## Legal Admissibility of Sketches and Drawings

An *admissible* sketch is one drawn or personally witnessed by the investigator that accurately portrays the crime scene.

If the sketch is accurate, it is admissible in court. As with all other evidence, the investigator must be prepared to testify as to the information contained in the sketch, the conditions under which it was made and the process used.

A scale drawing also is admissible if the investigating officer drew it or approved it after it was drawn and if it accurately represents the rough sketch. The rough sketch must remain available as evidence.

Well-prepared sketches and drawings help judges, juries, witnesses and other persons to visualize actual crime scenes.

**Chapter 2**

**Investigative
Photography
and
Crime-Scene
Sketches**

Photography, one of the first investigative techniques to be used at a crime scene, helps to establish that a crime was committed and to trace the occurrence of the crime. Photographs and videotapes reproduce the crime scene in detail for presentation to the prosecution, defense, witnesses, judge and jury in court. They are used in investigation, prosecution and police training.

Photography has become increasingly important in criminal investigation because it can immediately preserve evidence, accurately represent the crime scene and evidence, create interest and increase attention to testimony. However, photographs also have disadvantages: they are not selective, do not show actual distances, may be distorted and may be damaged by mechanical errors in shooting or processing.

Take photographs of the entire crime scene before anything is disturbed and avoid inaccuracies and distortions. First photograph the general area, then specific areas and finally specific objects of evidence. Take exterior shots first.

Investigative photography includes crime-scene surveillance, aerial, night, laboratory, mug shot and lineup.

After photographs are taken, they must be properly identified, filed and continuously secured to be admissible as evidence. In addition, rules of evidence dictate that photographs be material, relevant, competent, accurate, free of distortion and noninflammatory.

In addition to photographs, indeed sometimes in place of photographs, crime-scene sketches are often used. A crime-scene sketch assists in (1) interviewing and interrogating people, (2) preparing the investigative report and (3) presenting the case in court. Photographs, sketches and written notes are often needed to provide a clear picture of the scene.

Sketch the scene of a serious crime or accident after photographing it and before moving anything. Include all relevant objects and evidence. Materials needed for making the rough sketch include paper, pencil, long steel measuring tape, carpenter-type ruler, straightedge, clipboard, eraser, compass, protractor and thumbtacks. The steps involved in sketching include (1) observing and planning; (2) measuring and outlining the general area; (3) locating, measuring and recording objects and evidence within the scene; (4) taking notes; (5) identifying the scene; and (6) reassessing the sketch.

Plotting methods useful in locating objects and evidence include rectangular coordinate, baseline, triangulation and compass point. A cross-projection sketch shows the floor and walls in the same plane.

After completing the sketch, record in your notes the lighting conditions, colors, people present at the scene and all other information that cannot be sketched. Then place a legend in the lower corner of the sketch, outside the room or area outline. Identify the scene completely—the location, type of crime and case number. Include the scale and an arrow indicating north pointing to the top of the sketch. Include the name of the person making the sketch. Before leaving the scene, make sure nothing has been overlooked. Keep the sketch secure. It is the basis for the finished scale drawing and may be needed as evidence in court.

The finished scale drawing is done in ink on a good grade of paper and is drawn to scale using exact measurements. Both the rough sketch and the scale drawing are admissible in court if they are made or personally witnessed by the investigator and accurately portray the crime scene. The original rough sketch must remain available as evidence.

Drawing software for investigators has improved significantly over the past decade. "Accurate Crime Scene Diagrams" (1996, p. 13) describes one such program developed by The CAD Zone, "The Crime Zone." Benefits of such programs include that they are:

- Easy to learn.
- Easy to use.
- Flexible.
- Fast.

Figure 2–14 compares a typical hand-drawn diagram with one drawn with a CAD software program.

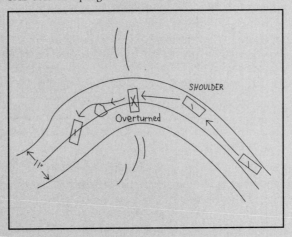

Typical Hand-Drawn Diagram

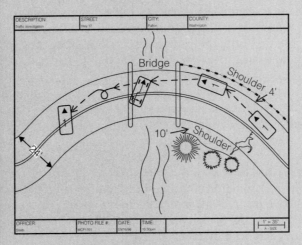

Courtroom Quality Diagrams
Drawn With The Crime Zone

**Figure 2–14   Comparison of a Hand-Drawn and Computer-Generated Crime-Scene "Sketch"**

Source: The CAD Zone, Inc., Beaverton, OR. (1–800–641–9077) Reprinted by permission.

*(continued on p. 69)*

Visatex Corporation has developed software that generates professional crime-scene drawings as well as automated drawings and calculations for automobile accident reconstruction. Visatex's Compuscene™ software allows officers to select images of common household and office items and furniture, various vehicles and weapons and human figures and to show critical distances and dimensions automatically. Final scale drawings can be saved for easy modification or future reference. The drawings can be rescaled automatically and can be enlarged to 4′ × 4′ for courtroom presentation.

Hall and Roberts (1992, p. 50) suggest:

> The advantages of using computer-aided drawings are: ease of use for the investigator or manager, repeatability, accuracy, and the fact that the drawings are useable in other programs, such as Word Perfect, to dress up a report.

In the latter 1990s, the traditional two-dimensional sketches and drawings are being made even more realistic by using three-dimensional computer crime-scene sketches.

A "3-D" crime scene is illustrated in Figure 2–15.

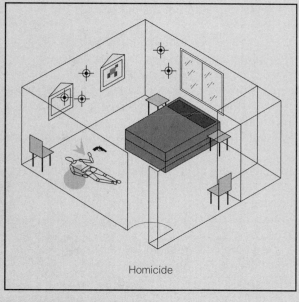

Homicide

**Figure 2–15**   "3-D" Crime Scene
Source: The CAD Zone, Inc., Beaverton, OR. (1–800–641–9077) Reprinted by permission.

# Checklist

## *Police Photography*

- Photograph the entire scene and specific objects before moving anything.
- Include markers where needed to indicate size of evidence.
- Record equipment and techniques used, lighting conditions, etc., in notes.
- Check for other sources of available photographs.

## Questions

- Do the photographs taken at the crime scene depict the scene as you saw it?
- Do they show the exact appearance and condition of the scene as it appeared on your arrival?
- Have exterior pictures been taken to show entrances to the scene and the outside appearance of the crime scene?
- Have close-up shots been taken of the entry and exit points?
- Were aerial photos taken of the crime scene that show routes into and out of the scene area?
- Were interior pictures taken showing the entire layout of the facility in which the crime occurred?
- Do the photographs show the criminal act itself; for example, in a burglary, do the pictures show pry marks on the door, a broken window or shattered glass on the ground or floor?
- Were detailed pictures taken of how the crime was committed? The tools with which it was committed? Any weapon used?
- Do photographs show the victim? Injuries? Were wounds, scratches, bruises or other marks recorded in color as soon as possible after the commission of the crime? A day or two later as well?
- Were pictures taken of the deceased at the scene? Exact position, clothing worn, wounds?
- Were pictures taken at the autopsy?
- Do photographs show the property attacked?
- Were detailed pictures taken of all items of evidence before they were collected, showing exact condition and position at the scene?
- Was anything moved prior to taking the picture? (If so, was it recorded in your notes?)
- Were photographs a true and accurate representation of relevant material?
- Are laboratory photos available for scientific tests conducted?
- Were photographs taken of the suspect to show appearance and condition at the time of the crime? Close-up photos of clothing worn?
- Were all pictures used for identifying suspects placed in special envelopes for later court testimony?
- If a lineup was conducted, were pictures taken of the lineup to show persons selected and their appearance in relation to each other?
- If a motor vehicle was involved, were detailed pictures taken of the vehicle's exterior and interior, color, license plate and any damaged areas?
- What types of photographs are available: moving pictures, black-and-white, color, videotapes?
- Are there crime-in-progress pictures from on-the-scene cameras such as bank surveillance cameras, or were pictures taken by media photographers?
- Have photographs been suitably mounted for presentation in court?
- Have all relevant notes been recorded in the notebook?

### Sketching the Crime Scene

- Is your sketching kit readily available?
- Is the kit completely equipped?
- Have you formed a plan for proceeding to sketch?
- Have you selected the simplest, largest scale?

**71**

**Chapter 2**

**Investigative
Photography
and
Crime-Scene
Sketches**

- Have you sketched the appropriate plotting method to locate objects and evidence?
- Have you sketched the outline of the room or area first?
- Have you then added objects and evidence, including measurements?
- Have you recorded in your notes information that cannot be sketched?
- Have you prepared a legend for the sketch that includes identifying information, the scale and the direction of north?
- Have you reassessed the sketch and compared it with the scene?
- Have you kept the sketch secure?
- Have you prepared or had someone else prepare a finished scale drawing if needed?

## Discussion Questions

  1. In what types of crimes are photographs likely to be important to the investigation?

  2. List the basic equipment you would want to have for a normal crime-scene photographic assignment. Compare it with others' preferences.

  3. What sources outside your police department might contribute photographs of a crime scene?

  4. How are investigative photographs developed and filed in your police department?

  5. In what nationally known cases have photographs played a significant role?

  6. In what well-known cases have rough sketches or scale drawings been important evidence?

  7. What basic sketching materials would you want in an investigative kit?

  8. What method of taking measurements for an outdoor sketch do you prefer? What are the advantages and disadvantages of this method?

  9. By which plotting method could you best locate your precise position in your surroundings at this moment?

10. Who is responsible for making the crime-scene sketch? Should more than one officer sketch the scene?

## References

"Accurate Crime Scene Diagrams." *Law Enforcement Technology,* January 1996, p. 13.

"Documenting Forceful Impact Blood Spatter." *Instant Evidence,* Vol. IX, Spring 1995.

Godin, Norma C. "Photography as an Aid in Burn Injury Evaluation." *Law and Order,* September 1990, pp. 69–70.

Hall, John, and Paul Roberts. "Computer-Aided Drawing." *Law Enforcement Technology,* April 1993, pp. 48–50.

Jensen. "Instant Photography Documents Vandalism." *Law and Order,* October 1995, p. 104.

Lloyd, Robert. "Crime Scene Documentation and Reconstruction." *Law and Order,* November 1994, pp. 35–36.

Mayer, Robert E. "Versatile Compact 35mm Cameras." *Law and Order,* May 1990, pp. 62–66.

Morrison, Richard. "Crime Scene Photography in an Instant." *Law Enforcement Technology,* October 1995, pp. 86–88.

"Mug Shots and Composites." *Law Enforcement Technology,* November 1992, pp. 34–35.

*Polaroid Guide to Instant Imaging: Crime and Accident Scene Documentation.* Cambridge: Polaroid Corporation, 1992.

Schmidt, Jim. "A Changing Picture: The Role of Instant Photography in Policing." *The Police Chief,* December 1991, pp. 45–48.

Stockton, Dale. "In Focus." *Police,* August 1996, pp. 76–77, 116–122.

Unsworth, Stephen H., and Richard M. Forte. "Waltham Police Benefit from Focus on Instant Photography." *Law and Order,* September 1991, pp. 59–61.

"Video Imaging: A Police Tool for the 90s." *Law and Order,* May 1990, pp. 103–105.

# Notes and Reports

## DO YOU KNOW

Why notes are important in an investigation?

When to take notes?

What to record in investigative notes?

How to record the notes?

What the characteristics of effective notes are?

Where to file notes?

How notes are used in court and what problems can arise?

What steps are involved in writing an investigative report?

What types of investigative reports may be required?

Why reports are important to an investigation?

How the narrative should be structured?

What the characteristics of effective investigative reports are?

## CAN YOU DEFINE

active voice     conclusionary language     past tense

best evidence     first person     template

chronological order     narrative

MOST PEOPLE WHO GO INTO LAW ENFORCEMENT ARE AMAZED AT THE amount of paperwork and writing that is required. Dacy (1991, p. 34) notes that although report writing may not be an officer's favorite activity . . .

**Introduction**

> Yet, the reports we write are the fangs of law enforcement, the teeth that "take a bite out of crime." The pen is a vital tool in our profession, as essential as the gun or the baton. By mastering this tool we learn to tame the paper tiger, to harness its power. It's not an easy job, but it's worth the effort.

According to Pilant (1992, p. 34), investigators need:

> Some clerical ability and unending patience for the everpresent piles of paper-work, which comprise about 70 percent of the job. . . . You have special equipment for the crime scene, special equipment for search warrants and other jobs. But in the office, you have to have lots of typewriters, computers, and files. Seventy percent of the job is typing, so you have to have the ability to use a typewriter or a computer.

This chapter begins with a discussion of field notes: when to take them, what to record and where to record. Next is a discussion of various methods of taking notes, the characteritics of effective notes and filing notes. This is followed by an explanation of using notes in court. Then a discussion is presented regarding how to go from field notes to a police report, the types of reports that might be required and the importance of such reports. Next is a thorough, step-by-step method for organizing the information from the field notes and actually writing the reports, followed by a description of the characteristics of effective reports and how to evaluate your reports. The chapter concludes with a look at taping and dictating report writing and the use of a quality control officer for police reports.

## Field Notes

Note taking is not unique to the police profession. News reporters take notes to prepare stories; physicians record information furnished by patients to follow the progress of a case; lawyers and judges take notes to assist in interviewing witnesses and making decisions; students take notes in class and as they read. Quite simply, notes are brief records made of what is seen and/or heard.

---

Investigative notes are a permanent written record of the facts of a case to be used in further investigation, in writing reports and in prosecuting the case.

---

Note taking and report writing are often regarded as unpleasant, boring tasks. Yet no duty is more important, as many officers have found, much to their embarrassment, when they did not take notes, or they took incomplete notes. Accurate notes not only aid later recall but also are used for preparing sketches and reports. Notes are important throughout the entire investigation.

## When to Take Notes

Notes are generally taken as information is received or immediately after.

---

Start to take notes as soon as possible after receiving the call to respond and continue recording information as it is received throughout the investigation.

---

Sometimes it is physically impossible to take notes immediately, for example, while driving a vehicle or in complete darkness. Other times, taking notes immediately will hinder obtaining information if it intimidates a witness or suspect. Whether to take out your notebook immediately in the presence of a person being questioned is a matter of personal insight and experience.

When people are excited, want to get their name in the newspaper or want to get your attention, you can usually record information immediately. Most people are willing to give information if you are friendly and courteous and you explain the importance of the information. In such cases no delay in taking notes is required.

On the other hand, reluctant witnesses and suspects may not talk if you record what they say in your notebook. In such cases, obtain the information first and record it later. You must sense when it is best to delay writing notes. Specific methods of obtaining information from willing and unwilling people are discussed in Chapter 6.

If someone gives you an exact quote or wording of what was said by the person committing the crime, have the witness initial that portion of your notes after reading it to help ensure that it is accurate. If possible, have people who give you information take time to write a statement in their own handwriting. This avoids the possibility they may later claim they did not make the statement or that they were misunderstood or misquoted.

## What to Record

Take notes on everything you do in an official investigative capacity. Record all facts, regardless of where they may lead. Information establishing a suspect's innocence is as important as that establishing guilt. Facts that protect the blameless are as valuable as those that protect society from criminals.

Enter general information first: the time and date of the call, the location, officer(s) assigned and arrival time at the scene. This information is recorded in various ways, depending on department policies and communication systems. Police departments using centrally dispatched message centers may automatically record date, time and case numbers. Even if this is done, make written notes of this initial information because recording tapes may not be kept for extended periods or they may become unusable. The tapes and notes corroborate each other.

---

Record all information that helps to answer the questions: Who? What? Where? When? How? and Why?

---

As you take notes, ask yourself specific questions such as these (Hess and Wrobleski, 1996, pp. 24–25, reprinted by permission.):

When:    did the incident happen? was it discovered? was it reported? did the police arrive on the scene? were suspects arrested? will the case be heard in court?

Where:   did the incident happen? was evidence found? stored? do victims, witnesses and suspects live? do suspects frequent most often? were suspects arrested?

Who:     are suspects? accomplices?
         Complete descriptions would include the following information: sex, race, coloring, age, height, weight, hair (color, style, condition), eyes (color, size, glasses), nose (size, shape), ears (close to head or protruding), distinctive features (birthmarks, scars, beard), clothing, voice (high or low, accent), other distinctive characteristics such as walk.

Who:     were the victims? associates? was talked to? were witnesses? saw or heard something of importance? discovered the crime? reported the incident? made the complaint? investigated the incident? worked on the case? marked and received the evidence? was notified? had a motive?

What:    type of crime was committed? was the amount of damage or value of the property involved? happened (narrative of the actions of suspects, victims and witnesses; combines information included under "How")? evidence was found? preventive measures had been taken (safes, locks, alarms, etc.)? knowledge, skill or strength was needed to commit the crime? was said? did the police officers do? further information is needed? further action is needed?

How:     was the crime discovered? does this crime relate to other crimes? did the crime occur? was evidence found? was information obtained?

Why:     was the crime committed (was there intent? consent? motive?)? was certain property stolen? was a particular time selected?

Make notes that describe the physical scene, including general weather and lighting conditions. Witnesses may testify to observations that would have been impossible, given the existing weather or lighting conditions. Accurate notes on such conditions will refute false or incorrect testimony.

Record everything you observe in the overall scene: all services rendered, including first-aid; description of the injured; location of wounds; who transported the victim and how.

Record complete and accurate information regarding all photographs taken at the scene. As the search is conducted, record the location and description of evidence and its preservation.

Record information to identify the type of crime and what was said and by whom. Include the name, address and phone number of every person present at the scene and all witnesses.

The amount of notes taken depends on the type of offense, the conditions of the case, your attitude and ability and the number of other officers assigned to the case. Make sure you take enough notes to completely describe what you observe and do during an investigation. This will provide a solid foundation for a detailed report and for testifying in court. If in doubt about including a specific detail, record it.

Do *not* jot down information unrelated to the investigation in your notes, for example, the phone number of a friend, an idea for a poem or a doodle. If the defense attorney, judge or jury see your notes, such irrelevant material will reflect poorly on your professionalism.

## Where to Record Notes

Use a notebook to record all facts observed and learned during an investigation. Despite the availability of sophisticated recorders and computers, the notebook remains one of the simplest, most economical and most basic of investigative tools. Notes taken on scraps of paper, on the backs of envelopes or on napkins are apt to be lost, and they also reflect poorly on an officer's professionalism.

Divide the notebook into sections for easy reference. One section might contain frequently used telephone numbers. Another section might contain frequently needed addresses. This information can be a permanent part of the notebook. Identify the notebook with your name, address, telephone number and the address and telephone number of your police department.

Opinions vary as to whether it is better to use a loose-leaf notebook or separate spiral-bound notebooks for each case. If you use a loose-leaf notebook, you can easily add paper for each case you are working on as the need arises, and you can keep it well organized. Most investigators favor the loose-leaf notebook because of its flexibility in arranging notes for reports and for testifying in court. However, use of a loose-leaf notebook opens the opportunity of challenge from the defense attorney that the officer has fabricated the notes, adding pages or deleting relevant pages. This can be countered by numbering each page, followed by the date and case number, or by using a separate spiral notebook for each case.

Disadvantages of the latter approach are that the spiral notebook is often only partially used and therefore expensive and that it may be bulky for storage. Further, if other notes are kept in the same notebook, they also will be subject to the scrutiny of the defense. A final disadvantage is that if you need a blank

*Witnesses are important sources of information regarding crimes committed in their neighborhoods.*

sheet of paper for some reason, you should not take if from a spiral notebook because most such notebooks indicate on the cover how many pages are contained. The defense can only conjecture about loose-leaf pages that might have been removed, but missing pages from a spiral notebook can be construed as evidence that something has, in fact, been removed.

The decision to use a loose-leaf or spiral-bound notebook is sometimes a matter of department policy. The critical point is that all notes should be recorded in some type of notebook, never on a scrap of paper or the back of a napkin. Always have your notebook with you.

In addition to the notebook, always carry pens and pencils. Use pen for most notes because ink is permanent. You may want to use pencil for rough sketches that require minor corrections as you sketch.

## How to Take Notes

Note taking is a skill acquired by practice. Time does not allow for a verbatim transcript. Learn to select key facts and record them in an abbreviated form.

---

Write brief, legible, abbreviated notes that are understandable to others.

---

Do not include words such as *a, and* and *the* in your notes. Omit all other unnecessary words. For example, if a witness were to say, "I arrived here after having lunch at Harry's Cafe, a delightful little place over on the west side, at about 1:30, and I found my boss had been shot," you would record: "Witness arrived at scene at 1:30 (after lunch at Harry's Cafe) to find boss shot." You would not know at the time if the fact that she had lunch at Harry's Cafe was important, but it might be, so you would include it.

**Table 3-1 Abbreviations Commonly Used in Law Enforcement**

| | | | |
|---|---|---|---|
| A&A | Assisted and advised | Memo | Memorandum |
| AKA | Also known as (alias) | M.O. | Modus operandi |
| A/O | Arresting officer | NATB | National Automobile Theft Bureau |
| APB | All points bulletin | N/B | Northbound |
| Arr. | Arrest | NCIC | National Crime Information Center |
| Asst. | Assistant | NFD | No further description |
| Att. | Attempt | NMN | No middle name |
| BAC | Blood alcohol content | OID | Operation Identification |
| Capt. | Captain | P.C. | Penal Code |
| CBA | Cleared by arrest | PIN | Personal identification number |
| CJRS | Criminal justice reporting system | Rec'd | Received |
| Co. | County | R/F | Right front |
| Comp. | Complainant | R/O | Reporting officer |
| Def. | Defendant | ROA | Referred to other agency |
| Dept. | Department | R/R | Right rear |
| Dist. | District | S/B | Southbound |
| DMV | Department of Motor Vehicles | Sgt. | Sergeant |
| DOA | Dead on arrival | Subj. | Subject |
| DOB | Date of birth | Susp. | Suspect |
| DOT | Direction of travel | S/w | Station wagon |
| DUI | Driving under the influence of alcohol | UCR | Uniform Crime Reports |
| DWI | Driving while intoxicated | UTL | Unable to locate |
| E/B | Eastbound | V. | Victim |
| GOA | Gone on arrival | Vict. | Victim |
| Hdqtrs. | Headquarters | VIN | Vehicle identification number |
| HWY | Highway | Viol. | Violation |
| I.D. | Identification | W&R | Warned and released |
| Inf. | Informant | W/B | Westbound |
| Insp. | Inspector | Wit. | Witness |
| Juv. | Juvenile | *WFA | White female adult |
| L/F | Left front | *WFJ | White female juvenile |
| Lic. | License | *WMA | White male adult |
| L/R | Left rear | *WMJ | White male juvenile |
| Lt. | Lieutenant | 2drHT | Two-door hardtop |

*The *W* indicates the race. Use *B* for black, *A* for Asian, *H* for Hispanic, etc.
SOURCE: Kären M. Hess and Henry M. Wrobleski, *For the Record: Report Writing in Law Enforcement*, 4th edition (Blue Lake, CA.: Innovative Systems, Publishers, 1996) p. 187. ©1996 Innovative Systems. Reprinted by permission.

Write or print legibly, especially when recording names, addresses, telephone numbers, license numbers, distances and other specific facts.

Whenever possible, use standard abbreviations such as *mph, DWI, APB* (see Table 3-1). Do *not*, however, devise your own shorthand. For example, if you wrote, "Body removed by A. K.," the initials *A. K.* would be meaningless to others. If you become ill, injured or deceased, others must be able to read and understand your notes. This is necessary to further the investigation even though there may be some question regarding admissibility in court.

If you make an error, cross through it, make the correction and initial it. Do *not* erase. Whether intentional or accidental, erasures raise credibility questions.

### Using a Tape Recorder

Some police departments use tape recorders extensively because of the definite advantage of recording exactly what was stated with no danger of misinterpreting, slanting or misquoting. However, tape recorders do not replace the

*A Boston police officer demonstrates new onboard computers used to provide information to police while on patrol. The computer is tied into the central computer at police headquarters.*

notebook. Despite their advantages, they also have serious disadvantages. The most serious is that they can malfunction and fail to record valuable information. Weak batteries or background noise can also distort the information recorded. In addition, transcribing tapes is time consuming, expensive and subject to error. Finally, the tapes themselves, not the transcription, are the original evidence and thus must be retained and filed.

If information is taped, check the recorder before using it, record the appropriate heading before beginning the questioning, and always play the tape back to ensure that the information is recorded satisfactorily. Supplement the tape with notes of the key points.

## Characteristics of Effective Notes

Effective notes describe the scene and the events well enough to present a view that a prosecutor, judge or jury could visualize.

---

Effective notes are complete, accurate, specific, factual, clear, well organized and legible.

---

The basic purpose of notes is to record the *facts* of a case. Recall the discussion of the importance of objectivity in an investigation. Use this same objectivity in note taking. For example, you might include in your notes the fact that a suspect reached inside his jacket and your *inference* that he was reaching for a gun. Your opinion on the merits of gun-control laws, however, has no place in your notes. If you have a specific reason for including an opinion, clearly label the statement as an opinion. Normally, however, restrict your notes to the facts you observe and learn and the inferences you draw. If, for example, you see a person whom you consider to be nervous and you make a note to that effect, you are recording an inference. If, on the other hand, you record specific observations such as "The man kept looking over his shoulder, checking his watch and wiping perspiration from his forehead," then you are recording facts on which you based your inference. You may not remember six months or a year later what made you infer that the man was "nervous."

Record facts accurately. An inaccurately recorded name can result in the loss of a witness or suspect. Inaccurate measurements can lead to wrong conclusions. Have people spell their names for you. Repeat spellings and numbers for verification. Recheck measurements.

Be as specific as possible. Rather than saying, "tall," "fast" or "far," say "6'8"," "80 mph" or "50 feet." Little agreement may exist on what is tall, fast or far.

Notes are usually taken rapidly, increasing the chance of errors. Take enough time to write legibly and clearly. Legibility and clarity are not synonymous. *Legibility* refers to the distinctness of your letters and numbers. *Clarity* refers to the distinctness of your statements. For example, lack of clarity is seen in a note that states, "When victim saw suspect he pulled gun." *Who* pulled the gun, the victim or the suspect? The same lack of clarity is seen in the statements "When suspect turned quickly I fired" (Did the suspect turn quickly, or did the officer fire quickly?) and "When the suspect came out of the house, I hit him with the spotlight." Make certain your notes are clear and can be interpreted only one way.

Effective notes are also well organized. Make entries from each case on separate pages and number the pages. Keep the pages for each case together and record the case number on each page.

## Filing Notes

Place notes in a location and under a filing system that makes them available months, even years, later. Department policy usually determines where and how notes are to be filed.

---

File notes in a secure location that is readily accessible to investigators.

---

Store notes in an official police department case file or any secure location where they are available on short demand. Some departments file notes with the original file in the official records department. Others permit the officer to keep the original notes and file only the report made from the notes. Wherever notes are filed, they must be secure.

No one filing system is best. Notes may be filed alphabetically by the victim's name, by case number or in chronological order. As long as the system is logical, the notes will be retrievable.

Appeals have been granted as long as twenty years after convictions, with the defendant being granted a new trial. Because of this, many officers retain their notes indefinitely. Other officers destroy all their field notes after they have written their reports. They believe that notes simply duplicate what is in the report and may, in fact, contain information that is no longer pertinent when the report is written. Some police departments also have this as a policy.

## Using Notes in Court

Properly introduced *original* notes made by the officer testifying can be used in a criminal proceeding. Notes may be used by a person other than the officer who wrote them if the other person was present when they were written, witnessed the writing and initialed the notes at the time.

Officers may refer to their notes to refresh their memories, but if they do so, the defense counsel may examine them and read or show them to the judge or jury. The defense may criticize the conditions under which the notes were taken, their readability, spelling errors and other discrepancies. Such attempts to discredit the value of the officer's testimony can be embarrassing, especially if attention is called to material such as doodling that is unrelated to the case contained in the notes.

---

Original notes are legally admissible in court, and officers may use them to refresh their memories. Officers should take to court only those notes that pertain to the particular case.

---

**Best evidence,** in the legal sense, is the original, best and highest evidence; the highest available degree of proof that can be produced (*Cheadle v. Bardwell,* 1933). The best-evidence rule specifies that whenever possible, the original notes are to be used. Legally, original notes are the first or "archetype" notes, from which another instrument is transcribed, copied or imitated (*Arenson v. Jackson,* 1916). However, a copy of the original may be used to testify from if the reason for failing to produce the original is clearly explained. A carbon impression of a letter written on a typewriter, made by the same stroke of keys as the companion impression, qualifies as an original (*United States Fire Ins. Co. of New York v. L. C. Adams Mercantile Co.,* 1926). For example, the original notes may have been destroyed, lost or stolen, or they may have become unreadable. Always state so if you are not using original notes to aid your testimony.

The difficulties that can arise when original notes are not used are illustrated by the case of an investigator who inspected a car believed to be involved in a hit-and-run accident. As the vehicle was raised on a hoist, the investigator made notes regarding a piece of fabric caught on the head of a bolt and a hair located at another spot. Because these notes were smudged and stained from wetness and oil drippings, the investigator typed the notes and later testified from these typed notes. When asked by defense counsel whether the notes were original, the officer said yes. The defense council then asked where and how the notes were made. Hearing the investigator's explanation, he immediately challenged the notes as not original. Fortunately, the investigator could produce the original notes and was allowed to testify from them after they were properly introduced. The officer did not intentionally introduce false evidence, but the notes were *not* original, and the alert defense attorney took the opportunity to attempt to discredit the important testimony.

If your notes are original, factual and accurate, you should have them with you, to refer to them and to testify from them. The use of notes in court is probably their most important legal application. They can help discredit testimony given by a suspect or a defense witness; support evidence already given by a prosecution witness, strengthening that testimony; and defend against false allegations by the suspect or defense witnesses. Notes give you an advantage because others rarely make written notes and, therefore, must testify from memory.

# From Notes to Reports

Notes provide the foundation for the investigative report that is written for each case. Five basic steps are involved in writing a report (Hess and Wrobleski, 1996, p. 42):

---

Steps in report writing:
1. Gather the facts: investigate, interview, interrogate.
2. Record the facts immediately: take notes.
3. Organize the facts.
4. Write the report.
5. Evaluate the report: edit and proofread; revise if necessary.

---

The first two steps have already been completed before you sit down to write the report. If they have not, it is unlikely that your report will be adequate. Before looking at the remaining steps, however, consider the types of police reports you might be required to write, as well as the importance of such reports.

## Types of Reports

Although the types of reports and the forms used vary widely among police departments, most departments use at least three types.

---

Investigators usually complete (1) an initial or preliminary report, (2) supplemental or progress reports and (3) a closing or final report.

---

The initial or preliminary report is completed after the preliminary investigation. This may be followed by a series of supplemental reports to keep the appropriate individuals apprised of progress in the case. The closing or final report is prepared before prosecution of the case.

Some departments have attempted to standardize report writing by using forms. However, most forms still require a narrative account of the investigation.

Law enforcement report forms vary greatly in format. Many report forms contain boxes for placement of descriptive information and addresses and phone numbers of the persons involved (Figure 3–1 provides an example). It is unnecessary to duplicate this information in the narrative unless it is needed for clarity—simply because it tends to interrupt the flow of words and to clutter the narrative. Conversely, narrative reports that are not contained within box-style law enforcement reports should include descriptive information, addresses and phone numbers within the body of the narrative. Note the underlined information in this excerpt from a narrative:

The victim, Harry Brown, <u>1925 West State St., Milwaukee, Wisconsin, phone: 955-4331,</u> told me that taken during the burglary was his diamond ring, <u>one-third karat diamond stone, 14-karat gold setting, with the initials R. S. G. inside the band, valued at $575.00.</u>

If the underlined information was reported on a box-style report form, it could be deleted from the narrative report—unless that information was needed for clarity.

| | | | |
|---|---|---|---|
| **GENERAL** | **3. Specific Offense & NRS/BC Ord.**<br>181.26<br>Theft-Motor Vehicle | | |

**3. Specific Offense & NRS/BC Ord.**
181.26
Theft-Motor Vehicle

| 1. D.R. Number | 2. Reference D.R. Number | 4. Offense Reported: | 5. Teleserve |
|---|---|---|---|
| 90-0906 | 90-0704 | ☒ Dispatch ☐ Citizen<br>☐ On view ☐ Station Rpt. | ☐ Yes<br>☐ No |

**LOC.**

**13. Physical Address and/or Location of Occurrence** (address, city, state)
1423 Shady Beach Rd. Boulder City, Nevada 89005

| 14. Reporting Zone | 8. NCIC Trans. No. |
|---|---|
| 14 | 6034 |

**TIME**

| 9. Date–Time Occurred | on or between | Month<br>Feb | Day<br>15th | Year<br>1994 | Time<br>0213 | 10. Date–Time Reported | Month | Day | Year | Time |
|---|---|---|---|---|---|---|---|---|---|---|

CODE: V - Victim   L - Legal Owner   RO - Registered Owner        LIST FIRM NAME AND CORPORATE NAME IF DIFFERENT

**VICTIMS**

| 11. Code | 12. Name (Last, First, Middle)<br>Timothy Reinke | 13. Sex<br>M | 14. Race<br>W | 15. Age<br>34 | 16. Date of Birth<br>9-12-56 | 17. Occupation<br>Desk Clerk |
|---|---|---|---|---|---|---|

**18. Address**
Residence 4401 Jersey Avenue, Boulder City, Nevada    Zip Code 89005    SS 476-08-1406    Telephone (x=Day) ( ) 239-1082 [ ]
Business

| 11. Code | 12. Name (Last, First, Middle) | 13. Sex | 14. Race | 15. Age | 16. Date of Birth | 17. Occupation |
|---|---|---|---|---|---|---|

**18. Address**
Residence    Zip Code    SS    Telephone (x=Day) ( ) [ ]
Business

| 11. Code | 12. Name (Last, First, Middle) | 13. Sex | 14. Race | 15. Age | 16. Date of Birth | 17. Occupation |
|---|---|---|---|---|---|---|

**18. Address**
Residence    Zip Code    SS    Telephone (x=Day) ( ) [ ]
Business

**20. Additional Persons Listed?**   Yes ☐   No ☐

CODES:   RP-Reporting Party   W-Witness   LP-Last Person in Possession   L-Legal Owner   D-Discovered Crime   PA-Person Accepting Document
P- Person Securing Premise

**WITNESSES**

| 21. Code | 22. Name (Last, First, Middle) | 23. DOB | 24. Address | Zip Code | 25. Telephone (X=Day) Include Area Code |
|---|---|---|---|---|---|
| | None | | Res.<br>Bus. | | |
| | | | Res.<br>Bus. | | |
| | | | Res.<br>Bus. | | |
| | | | Res.<br>Bus. | | |
| | | | Res.<br>Bus. | | |
| | | | Res.<br>Bus. | | |

**VEHICLE**

| 26. Vehicle Year<br>1988 | 27. Vehicle Make<br>Plymouth | 28. Vehicle Model<br>Station Wagon | 29. Vehicle Style<br>4 dr. | 30. Vehicle Colors – Top/Bottom<br>blue |
|---|---|---|---|---|

| 31. Vehicle License No.<br>592-AHU | 32. License Type<br>Passenger | 33. License Year<br>1994 | 34. License State<br>Nevada | 35. Vehicle License Colors – Prime/Numerals<br>Gray-Blue |
|---|---|---|---|---|

| Plates taken off vehicle?<br>☐ Yes ☒ No | 37. Vehicle I. D. No./Motorcycle Frame No.<br>3461426 | 37. Vehicle Engine No.<br>643129 | 38. Vehicle Insured By<br>Farmers Insurance |
|---|---|---|---|

| 39. Additional Vehicle Identifiers (damage, chrome wheels, etc.)<br>Dent right front fender | 40. Evidence Obtained<br>☒ Fingerprints  ☐ Vehicle  ☐ Stains<br>☒ Other Prints  ☒ Photos  ☐ Blood/Semen<br>☐ None  ☐ Weapon/Tools  ☐ Hair  ☐ Other |
|---|---|

**INVEST.**

**41. INVESTIGATION**

| ☒ Dusted for latents | ☒ Photo/Impression Taken | ☐ Diagram of Scene | ☐ Witnesses Contacted |
|---|---|---|---|
| ☐ Tool Marks Noted | ☐ Scene Photographed | ☒ Neighbors Checked | ☒ Victim Contacted |
| ☒ Vehicle Shoe Tracks | ☐ Photos of Victim | ☒ Area Checked | ☐ Scene Processed |

**SUSPECT**

| PRIMARY | Yes | No | SECONDARY | Yes | No | SECONDARY | Yes | No |
|---|---|---|---|---|---|---|---|---|
| 42. Was a suspect arrested? | ☐ | ☒ | 47. Can a suspect be described? | ☐ | ☒ | 50. Is there significant physical evidence? | ☒ | ☐ |
| 43. Can a suspect be named? | ☐ | ☒ | 48. Is there a significant M.O. present? | ☐ | ☒ | 51. Are all elements of crime present? | ☒ | ☐ |
| 44. Can a suspect be located? | ☐ | ☒ | 49. Is stolen property traceable? | ☒ | ☐ | 52. Can suspect vehicle be identified? | ☒ | ☐ |
| 45. Was there a witness to the crime? | ☒ | ☐ | | | | | | |
| 46. Can suspect be identified? | ☐ | ☒ | | | | | | |

53. Is there a significant reason to believe the crime may be solved?        Yes ☒   No ☐

If fingerprint match can be found-several suspect possibilities known

**CERT.**

**54. Reporting Party Signature:** I affirm this information is true and correct.

| ☒ Open | Copy to: | ☐ CSO | ☒ Dept. F.U. | ☐ D.A. | ☐ Other |
|---|---|---|---|---|---|
| ☐ Closed | | ☐ CA | ☐ JO F.U. | ☐ Patrol F.U. | ☐ Records |

| 55. Officer Signature, Number and Division<br>#8 Patrol | 56. Supervisor Initials and Date<br>2-15-97 | 57. Detective Assigned<br>Clifford Sharr | 58. Page ____<br>Of ____ |
|---|---|---|---|

**Figure 3–1   Offense Report Form**

# Importance of Reports

As Cox (1994, p. 8) notes:

There are sergeants and lieutenants who can't spell sergeant or lieutenant. Worse still, they can't organize a report themselves, or help their subordinates craft a report that will stand up in court.

He also suggests (p. 10): "The current level of police report writing often makes the defense attorney's work much easier. As one prosecutor put it: 'Do you want to be a witness for the defense? If not, you need to learn how to write a report.'"

The importance of writing skills in law enforcement is stressed by D'Aulizio and Sheehan (1992, p. 112): "In today's litigious society, it is critical for police officers to articulate their actions in writing. Semiliterate officers are a liability to themselves as well as their department. More than at any other time in the history of law enforcement, the art of report writing must be revived and polished."

Molden (1996, p. 13) also emphasizes: "The more complex our society becomes, the more litigious and demanding the criminal justice system, the greater will be the need for detailed, accurate and complete reporting by officers."

Your reports, like your notes, are a permanent written record that communicates important information to many others. They are *used*, not simply filed away. If investigative reports were not required for efficient law enforcement, you would not have to write them.

---

Reports are a permanent written record of important facts that can be used to examine the past, keep other police officers informed, continue investigations, prepare court cases, provide the court with relevant facts, coordinate law enforcement activities, plan for future law enforcement services and evaluate law enforcement officers' performance.

---

Dacy (1991, p. 76) points out that officers' offense and incident reports "are the memory of the department." Reports are important to others and to you. Your efficiency as an investigator may be partially evaluated by your reports. In fact, report quality is often a criterion used in selecting officers for specialized assignments and promotions.

What you write may be read by many different people: other officers, your supervisor, lawyers, judges, citizens, reporters. It is your responsibility to communicate to these numerous readers what happened, when and how. Well-written reports not only further the cause of justice; they also reflect positively on your education, your competence and your professionalism.

Most law enforcement officers submit their reports for prosecution with concern over the outcome but without much thought about the wheels they've started in motion. This is understandable, for they've done their jobs, and many more cases wait to be investigated. But, what happens when they haven't really done their jobs—when their reports are distorted or incomplete (as many are) because of poor writing? The results not only cost the taxpayers in wasted man-hours, but they also breed disaster in the courtroom.

To cite an all-too-common example, in one recent criminal case the reporting officer, using the passive voice, wrote the following in his report: "The weapon was found in the bushes where the suspect had thrown it." He did not clarify this statement elsewhere in his report. Expectedly, the prosecuting attorney subpoenaed the reporting officer to testify at the preliminary hearing. Unfortunately, the reporting officer's testimony revealed that his partner, not he, had observed the suspect's action and had retrieved the weapon. The partner was unavailable to testify on short notice. Without his testimony the necessary elements of the crime could not be established and the case was dismissed and had to be refiled. The man-hours expended at the time of the dismissal, by witnesses, secretaries, clerks, attorneys and the judge, were virtually wasted because the whole process had to be repeated. The reporting officer could have avoided the problem at the onset through use of the **active voice** which would have provided clarification. Sadly, this basic writing error is not an isolated example; it, and others like it, slip through the system daily, causing delays in the judicial process and depleting dwindling budgets.* [emphasis added]

## Prosecutors' Opinions about Reports

In November 1987 the Alexandria Technical Institute Law Enforcement Program mailed a questionnaire to all eighty-seven Minnesota county attorneys. The purpose of the survey was to learn the prosecutors' opinions about police reports and how these reports could be improved. Fifty-two county attorneys (60 percent) returned the survey. Of those responding, 98 percent felt that police reports were either critically important or very important to the successful prosecution of criminal cases. Among their comments were these:

> The police reports are often the first impression a judge or defense attorney has of an officer's competence, both generally and in regard to the specific elements of the offense charged. If the report is weak, defense attorneys and judges are inclined to require officers to testify and to scrutinize carefully the officer's testimony. A well-written report can often result in a settlement of the case without an Omnibus Hearing or trial.
>
> All prosecution is initiated by the reports submitted by the investigating agency. The decision to charge someone with a crime is based upon the police reports, usually alone.
>
> Good police reports help to speed up the entire system. Delays in prosecution often occur because of incomplete reports.
>
> Poorly phrased reports or reports that are too brief have a tendency to blow up in your face at trial time.
>
> If sloppy or incomplete, they will impeach the officer at trial.
>
> A well-written report alone can settle a case.

In response to the question of what would improve police reports, the Minnesota prosecutors made the following suggestions:

> Use simple, direct language in reports. Reports should be complete and cover all elements of the offense.
>
> There is simply no substitute for well-organized, grammatically correct reports.
>
> Eliminate police jargon.
>
> They need to include in their reports the evidence to establish the crime.
>
> Officers should familiarize themselves with the essential elements of the crimes they are attempting to solve so the reports are focused on the basic

---

*Reprinted with permission from the preface by Floyd T. Stokes in *For the Record: Report Writing in Law Enforcement,* 4th edition by Kären M. Hess and Henry M. Wrobleski, Blue Lake, CA: Innovative Systems Publishers, 1996, p. i.

requirements. . . . Avoid social worker conclusions, write as legibly and concisely as possible, and include as much information as possible.

Do not reach conclusions in the report.

Emphasis should be placed upon writing reports using descriptive phrases rather than legal conclusions. It has been my experience that officers frequently state that the defendant was "intoxicated," "fled," "resisted arrest," rather than describing the conduct of the defendant.

Cover the essential elements of the various crimes and what facts are needed to prove them. Eliminate personal opinion in the report itself. The personal opinions in reports always seem to haunt the prosecution at trial.

### Field Training Officers' Opinions about Reports

Molden (1996, p. 13) reported on a survey of 148 field training officers in Los Angeles County by the National Association of Field Training Officers. In this survey respondents expressed "serious concerns" about law enforcement trainees' ability to write reports. In response to the question, "What concerns do you have with trainees," the greatest number of responses were report writing. Likewise, in response to the question, "In what areas do academies need to improve," the greatest number answered report writing.

With the importance of effective police reports in mind, consider now the third step in creating such reports: organizing the information from your field notes.

## Organizing Information

According to Clark (1996, p. 98), the key to writing good reports is "strict adherence to basic format, *organization* and correct word usage." [emphasis added]

Make an outline before you begin to write. Then jot down what you want to include under each heading in your outline. Reread your notes and number each statement to coincide with a heading in your outline. For example, if section II.B. of your outline is headed "Description of Suspect #1," write *II.B.* in the margin wherever Suspect #1 is described in your notes.

Present the facts of the investigation in **chronological order**; that is, begin with the response to the call and continue in sequence to the end of the investigation. If the report is lengthy, more than four pages, use headings to guide the reader; for example, "Initial Response," "Crime Scene Conditions," "Photographs Taken," "Evidence," "Witnesses," "Suspects" and the like. [emphasis added]

After you complete the outline and determine where each note fits, you are ready to write the report.

## Writing the Report: Structuring the Narrative

The following discussion of structuring the narrative is from *For the Record: Report Writing in Law Enforcement* by Hess and Wrobleski (1996, pp. 51–52, reprinted by permission).

The law enforcement **narrative** is essentially a technical report structured in chronological order describing a sequence of investigative events. Those events are:

**1.** You, the reporting officer, receive information by either viewing something or by being told something, e.g., by examining a crime scene or by interviewing a victim or witness.

**2.** You act on the information you receive, e.g., by collecting evidence, by talking to other witnesses, etc.

**3.** Your actions cause you to receive additional information, e.g., new witnesses to talk to, other areas to search, etc.

**4.** You act on the new information you receive.

This process continues until you have exhausted all leads, completed the investigation or turned the case over to another entity, such as the detective division.

The narrative should first set the stage. Give the date, time, how you came to be involved and the type of incident. For example:

> On 9–7–96 at about 0750 hours, I was dispatched to the Downtown Marina regarding the report of a felony theft. Upon arrival at about 0800 hours, I talked to the victim, Norman Smith.

The next paragraph of the narrative should explain what information you received. For example:

> Smith said he arrived at the Downtown Marina at about 0730 hours to work on his boat. When he went to his walled boat dock, he discovered the dock's door was open and his boat and motor were missing. He did not go inside the dock but immediately phoned the police. He had locked the door the night before at about 1930 hours when he left the dock. The boat and motor were in the dock at that time. He had no idea how the boat and motor were taken. (See Property Loss Section for full description of the missing items.)

The following paragraph should explain what you did about the information you received. For example:

> I checked the open door and saw that the lock appeared to be broken and that the knob had marks on it. The marks appeared similar in pattern to pipewrench jaws. I searched the area and located a 14-inch pipewrench on the dock behind the door. I saw no other items of evidence.

The narrative should then explain what you did about the new information you received. For example:

> I collected the door knob and pipewrench as physical evidence. I photographed the scene. I radioed a description of the boat and motor to dispatch for entry into the NCIC computer system. I checked the area for witnesses but found none. I booked the collected items and negatives into the evidence section (refer to the evidence sheet for details).

The final paragraph of the narrative should explain the disposition of your investigation. For example:

> Case referred to the detective division for follow-up.

---

1. The opening paragraph of a police report states the time, date, type of incident and how you became involved.
2. The next paragraph contains what you were told by the victim(s) or witness(es). For each person talked to, use a separate paragraph.
3. Next record what you did based on the information you received.
4. The final paragraph states the disposition of the case.

---

Steps 2 and 3 may be repeated several times in a report on an incident where you talk to several witnesses/victims.

The completed narrative should look like this:

> On 9–7–96 at about 0750 hours, I was dispatched to the Downtown Marina regarding the report of a felony theft. Upon arrival at about 0800 hours, I talked to the victim, Norman Smith.
>
> Smith said he arrived at the Downtown Marina at about 0730 hours to work on his boat. When he went to his walled boat dock, he discovered the dock's door was open and his boat and motor were missing. He did not go inside the dock but immediately phoned the police. He had locked the door the night before at about 1930 hours when he left the dock. The boat and motor were in the dock at that time. He had no idea how the boat and motor were taken. (See Property Loss Section for full description of the missing items.)
>
> I checked the open door and saw that the lock appeared to be broken and that the knob had marks on it. The marks appeared similar in pattern to pipewrench jaws. I searched the area and located a 14-inch pipewrench on the dock behind the door. I saw no other items of evidence.
>
> I collected the door knob and pipewrench as physical evidence. I photographed the scene. I radioed a description of the boat and motor to dispatch for entry into the NCIC computer system. I checked the area for witnesses but found none. I booked the collected items and negatives into the evidence section (refer to the evidence sheet for details).
>
> Case referred to the detective division for follow-up.

## Characteristics of Effective Reports

In addition to a well-structured narrative that is accurate and complete, an effective report exhibits several other characteristics.

---

An effective report uses paragraphs, the past tense and first person. It is factual, accurate, objective, complete, concise, clear, mechanically correct, written in standard English, legible and reader focused.

---

### Paragraphs

The discussion on structuring the narrative assumed that the writer would *use paragraphs* to guide the reader. Keep the paragraphs short (usually 100 words or less). Discuss only one subject in each paragraph.

Paragraphs are reader-friendly. They will guide the reader through your report. Most paragraphs should be five to six sentences long, although they may be a single sentence or up to ten or fifteen sentences on occasion. Pomerenke (1992, p. 89) suggests using a new paragraph when you:

- Change speakers
  suspect by suspect
  witness by witness
  officer by officer
- Change locations
  room to room
  street to curb
  inside to outside
  scene to post

- Change time
    initial time of call
    return to scene
    move to hospital
    first breath analyzer test to second test
- Change ideas
    observations
    witness descriptions
    suspect statements

### Past Tense

*Write in the past tense throughout the report.* **Past tense** writing uses verbs that denote that events have already occurred. Your report contains what *was* true at the time you took your notes. Use of present tense can cause tremendous problems later. For example, suppose you wrote "John Doe *lives* at 100 South Street and *works* for Ace Trucking Company." One year later you find yourself on the witness stand with a defense attorney asking you: "Now, Officer, your report says that John Doe lives at 100 South Street. Is that correct?" You may not know, and you would have to say so. The next question: "Now, Officer, your report says John Doe works for Ace Trucking Company. Is *that* correct?" Again, you may be uncertain and be forced into an "I don't know" response. Use of the past tense in your report would have avoided this problem.

### First Person

*Use the first person to refer to yourself.* **First person** in English uses the words *I, me, my, we, us* and *our.* The sentence "*I* responded to the call" is written in the first person. This is in contrast to "*This officer* responded to the call," which uses the third person. Whether you remember your English classes and discussions of first, second and third person singular and plural is irrelevant. Simply remember to refer to yourself as *I,* rather than as *this officer.*

### Objective

*Be objective.* Keep to the facts. Include all facts, even those that may appear to be damaging to your case, and use words with no emotional overtones. Word choice is an often overlooked aspect of report writing; yet it is very important. Consider, for example, the difference in effect achieved by these three sentences:

The man cried.

The man wept.

The man blubbered.

Only the first sentence is truly objective. The second sentence makes the reader feel sympathetic toward the man. The third makes the reader unsympathetic. Likewise, a writer who uses the word *nigger* to refer to a black person reveals bias. An alert defense attorney will capitalize on words with emotional overtones and attempt to show bias. Even the use of *claimed* rather than *stated,* for example, can be used to advantage by a defense attorney. The attorney might suggest that the officer's use of *claimed* implies that the officer did not believe the statement.

Also, use the correct word. Do not confuse words that are similar, or you can be made to appear ridiculous. For example, this sentence in an officer's report would probably cast suspicion on the officer's intelligence: "During our training we spent four hours learning to resemble a firearm and the remainder of the time learning defective driving."

Avoid **conclusionary language.** Do not, for example, write "The man *could* not walk a straight line." You do not know what another person can or cannot do. The objective way to report this would be "The man *did* not walk a straight line." Even better would be "The man stepped 18 inches to the right of the line twice and 12 inches to the left of the line three times."

Phrases such as "he saw what happened" or "he heard what happened" are also conclusionary. People can be looking directly at something and not see it either because they are simply not paying attention or because they have terrible vision. The same is true of hearing. Again, you do not know what another person sees or hears. Your report should say "He *said* he saw what happened," or "He looked directly at the man committing the crime."

Another common conclusionary phrase found in police reports is "The check was signed by John Doe." Unless you saw John Doe sign the check, the objective statement would be "The check was signed John Doe." The little two-letter word *by* can create tremendous problems for you on the witness stand!

One area where complete, accurate *objective* reporting is critical is where use of force is involved. Peak (1996, p. 13) suggests that an officer's documentation of his use of force is likely to improve once he realizes that a well-written report is his best defense against excessive force claims. He offers the following advice:

> The report should address why it was necessary for the officer to use force, what force was used, why the force used was reasonable, and the consequences that resulted from its use.
>
> The report should obviously describe any observable injuries sustained by the suspect, any complaints of injury made by the suspect and the officer's response. It is equally important to document the officer's observations and any statements made by the suspect that tend to show that the suspect was not injured. For example:
>
> > I assisted Johnson to his feet and looked him over. I saw no evidence of injuries. I asked if he wanted to see a doctor, and he said, "No." I saw him walk without difficulty, and he had no difficulty entering or exiting my squad. He did not complain of any injuries while he was in my custody.

### Concise

*Be concise.* Avoid wordiness. Length alone does not make for quality. Some reports can be written in half a page; others require twelve or even twenty pages. No specific length can be prescribed, but strive to include all relevant information in as few words as possible. For example, do not say "The car is blue in color"; say "The car is blue." Other wordy phrases to avoid are listed in Table 3–2. Avoiding wordiness does not mean eliminating details; it means eliminating empty words and phrases.

### Clear

Make certain your sentences can be read only one way. Consider, for example, the following unclear sentences:

■ When completely plastered, officers who volunteer will paint the locker room.

Table 3–2  Concise Writing

**91**

Chapter 3

Notes and
Reports

| Wordy | Concise |
|---|---|
| made a note of the fact | noted |
| square in shape | square |
| despite the fact that | although |
| at a high rate of speed | rapidly |
| in the state of California | in California |
| with reference to | about |
| in the amount of | for |
| subsequent to | after |
| is of the opinion | believes |
| in spite of | despite |
| month of February | February |
| red in color | red |
| in the event that | if |
| the perpetrator of the crime | the suspect |
| at that point in time | then |

- Miami police kill a man with a machete.
- Three cars were reported stolen by the Los Angeles police yesterday.
- Police begin campaign to run down jaywalkers.
- Squad helps dog bite victim.

Such sentences should be rewritten so that only one interpretation is possible. For example, the first sentence might read: "Officers who volunteer will paint the locker room after it is completely plastered." The second sentence might read: "Miami police kill a man brandishing a machete." And so on.

Another way to increase clarity is to *use diagrams and sketches.* Diagrams and sketches are especially helpful in investigative reports of accidents, homicides and burglaries. The diagrams do not need to be works of art, but they should be in proportion and help the reader follow the description provided in the report.

## Grammatically and Mechanically Correct

*Use correct grammar and mechanics.* Mistakes in spelling, punctuation, capitalization and grammar give the impression that the writer is careless, uneducated or stupid—maybe all three! Use a dictionary and a grammar book if in doubt about how to write something. The dictionary can tell you not only how to spell a word, but also whether it should be capitalized and how it should be abbreviated. Table 3–3 contains words commonly misspelled in police reports.

A word on spelling: If you are a poor speller, do not let it bother you. As W. C. Fields said, "Anyone who can spell a word only one way is an idiot." In fact, many intelligent people are poor spellers. Why? Because the English language is made up of words from numerous countries, each country with its own spelling rules. This results in a hodgepodge with few rules for spelling. For example, in no other language can the combination of written letters *ough* have seven different sounds: d*ough*, b*ough*t, b*ough*, r*ough*, thr*ough*, thor*ough*, hicc*ough*. Nor can any other language have fourteen different ways to pronounce *sh*, the sound people make when they want someone to be quiet. Check it out: *ch*aperon, cons*c*ious, fuc*h*sia, is*s*ue, man*s*ion, mi*ss*ion, na*ti*on, nau*se*ous, o*ce*an, p*sh*aw, s*ch*ist, *sh*oe, *s*ugar, suspi*c*ion. No wonder people have difficulty mastering English spelling.

### Table 3–3  Words Frequently Misspelled in Police Reports

| | | |
|---|---|---|
| abduction | evidence | robbery |
| accelerated | extortion | sabotage |
| accessories | forcible | scene |
| accident | fraudulent | seize |
| acquitted | homicide | sentence |
| affidavit | indict | sergeant |
| altercation | interrogate | serious |
| apparatus | intimidation | sheriff |
| arson | intoxication | statute |
| assaulted | investigation | strangulation |
| bureau | juvenile | subpoena |
| burglary | larceny | suicide |
| coercion | legal | summons |
| commission | lieutenant | surrender |
| complainant | offense | surveillance |
| conspiracy | official | suspect |
| conviction | pedestrian | suspicion |
| corpse | penalize | testimony |
| counterfeit | possession | thieves |
| criminal | precinct | traffic |
| defendant | premises | trespassing |
| dispatched | prosecute | truancy |
| disposition | prostitution | vagrancy |
| drunkenness | pursuit | victim |
| embezzlement | resistance | warrant |
| emergency | | |

SOURCE: Kären M. Hess and Henry M. Wrobleski, *For the Record: Report Writing in Law Enforcement,* 4th edition (Blue Lake, CA.: Innovative Systems, Publishers, 1996) p. 131. ©1996, Innovative Systems. Reprinted by permission.

To make spelling less difficult, consider using a *speller/divider.* These little reference books contain thousands of the most commonly used words—showing their spelling and how they are divided. The reader is not distracted by definitions, information on the history of the word, synonyms and so on. The most important advantage is that one speller/divider page has as many words on it as fifteen to twenty dictionary pages. Bookstores and office-supply stores carry these handy little books.

Whether you use a dictionary or a speller/divider, when you look up a word, it is a good idea to make a check beside it in the margin. The next time you look that same word up, make another check. As the row of checks gets longer, you can easily see how much time you are wasting looking up the same word. Do something about that word. Either learn it, or write it some place where you can easily locate it, such as the inside cover of your dictionary or speller/divider. This can save you much time and effort in the future.

### Legible

*Write or print legibly.* Ideally, reports should be typed. However, this often is impossible. Many officers prefer to print their reports to increase readability. Whether the reports are typed, written or printed, make certain they can be read easily.

**Reader Friendly**

Always *consider who the reader is.* Among possible readers of police reports, in addition to other police officers, are judges, lawyers, juries, coroners, parole officers, child-welfare-agency personnel and insurance people. Given these varied backgrounds and individuals with limited familiarity with law enforcement terminology, the necessity for reader-focused reports becomes obvious.

One way to be reader friendly is to be certain the narrative portion of your report can stand alone. That calls for eliminating such phrases as *the above.* A reader-friendly report does not begin, "On the above date at the above time, I responded to the above address to investigate a burglary in progress."

Using such phrases presents two problems. First, if readers take time to look "above" to find the information, their train of thought is broken. It is difficult to find where to resume reading, and time is wasted. Second, if readers do *not* take time to look "above," important information is not conveyed, and it is very likely that the reader, perhaps subconsciously, will be wondering what would have been found "above." If information is important enough to refer to in your report, include it in the narrative. Do not take the lazy approach and ask your reader to search for the information "above."

## Evaluating Your Report

Once you have written your report, evaluate it. Do not simply add the final period, staple the pages together and turn it in. Reread it. Make certain that it says what you want it to and that it contains no content or composition errors. You might ask yourself these questions (Hess and Wrobleski, 1996, p. 42):

1. Is the report factual?
2. Is the report accurate?
3. Is the report objective?
4. Is the report complete?
5. Is the report concise?
6. Is the report clear?
7. Is the report mechanically correct?
8. Is the report written in standard English?
9. Is the report legible?

If yes is the answer to all these questions, then your report is probably going to be effective. If you cannot answer yes to the questions, you might want to consider the following ten suggestions Overton and Burns (1994, p. 98) make to improve police reports and increase convictions:

■ Get the details and get them right—no opinions or conclusions.
■ Review your report with the prosecutor before testifying.
■ Find a study buddy and work together toward improvement.
■ Organize in the order things happen.
■ Show; don't tell.
■ Use short sentences.
■ Make sure the subject performs the action (use active voice).
■ Use past tense words to describe what happened.
■ Review to check for mistakes.
■ Practice, practice, practice.

# Taping and Dictating Reports

Taping or dictating reports is common practice in some departments. According to Kelly (1990, p. 49), taping reports during the past fifteen years saved the Fort Collins (Colorado) Police Department in excess of $1 million. The Fort Collins department uses inexpensive cassette recorders for each patrol unit and transcription machines for the records section. Reports needing quick attention are red tagged, and records personnel type all red-tagged cases first. The most frequent problem with this approach, according to Kelly, is malfunctioning tape recorders. Poor dictation skills provide another problem.

In effect, taping or dictating reports shifts the bulk of writing/transcribing time to the records division. Even with taping or dictating, however, officers must still take final responsibility for what is contained in the report.

Davis (1992, p. 3) cautions: "No matter how good the dictating machine, word processor, or hand-held spelling checker, nothing excels the properly trained brain, providing it's functioning effectively. Assuming that [what] you think you spoke into a dictation machine is what will end up on the paper is as risky as strapping on a parachute [packed by] a guy . . . who needed the money to pay his attorney for a prior possession defense." Davis (p. 4) gives an example from a case for which he was called to testify. He was asked to read this sentence from his report on the witness stand:

> I jumped out of the bushes, drew my gun, *pointed it at myself* and yelled, "Police Officer—Freeze!"

Davis learned a lesson from this experience.

> Since I could not recall any training in my ten or so years in law enforcement that called for a "suicide threat to prevent escape," I sheepishly admitted that what was on the paper was not what occurred, nor was it what I had dictated.
>
> I don't know if it was fatigue that caused the error or a typist who watched television while she transcribed, but at that point, it didn't matter. From that day forward, I proofread every (and I do mean *every*) dictated report, and I never hit the witness stand cold.

Following are some humorous illustrations of how some dictated sentences can be misinterpreted:

> He called for a toe truck.
>
> Smith was arrested for a mister meaner.
>
> Jones was a drug attic.
>
> The victim was over rot.
>
> Johnson died of a harder tack.

# Computerized Report Writing

Computers have made significant contributions to efficiency in report writing. In addition to sophisticated spelling- and grammar-checking programs, other programs have been developed to help in the actual preparation of police reports.

Blanchard (1990, p. 53), of the Warwick (Rhode Island) Police Department, reported that after implementing digital dictation: "The gain in productivity over the first six months of the system's operation [was] dramatic—perhaps even sensational. . . . Between January 2 and July 1, 1989, total man-hours spent preparing reports [was] reduced by more than 73 percent."

Using a digital dictation system, officers simply pick up a touch-tone telephone and dictate their report. The digital processor handles the voice much like data, storing it in binary code on a hard disc within the compact microprocessor. Says Blanchard (p. 53):

> Input is simple: just pick up any touch-tone telephone, dial in, punch in your ID, work type, and case number, and begin talking.

Digital systems are superior to conventional tape recorders or dictating systems in their random-access feature; that is, they can locate and play back any item almost instantly.

Another advance is the Computer-Assisted Report Entry (CARE) system developed by the St. Louis County (Missouri) Police Department. This live-entry system centers around a CARE operator who leads officers through preformatted screens and questions, allowing them to complete reports "in a matter of minutes" (George, 1990, p. 46). George states that the CARE system has accomplished five major goals:

1. Freeing officers to spend more time on patrol by reducing report-writing and notification times (the primary goal).
2. Improving the quality, accuracy and timeliness of police reports and management reports by standardizing the collection of information and creating a centralized [legible], on-line database.
3. Providing citizens and county police officers with a convenient, efficient, round-the-clock police reporting service.
4. Improving the availability and timeliness of police report information by electronically processing, aggregating, distributing and filing these documents. (Uniform Crime Reporting information is automatically aggregated.)

*The California Highway Patrol relies heavily on computers to generate reports.*

5. Improving detective follow-up investigation procedures by providing the investigative officer with complete information in a shorter period of time.

Although computerized report writing has greatly increased officers' efficiency, as Cox (1994, p. 8) cautions:

> In many departments, writing skill is diminished due to overconfidence in technological hardware. However data may be disseminated, the facts are selected by humans, and input and retrieved by humans. Machines can't put in what isn't there, or take out what should not be.

## A Quality Control Officer for Police Reports

As pointed out earlier in the chapter, police reports are used by many people, in the department and outside of it. They are, in effect, one of the most important *products* of the department. D'Aulizio (1992, p. 129) suggests that police departments might take a lesson from business:

> In a business, before a finished product is packaged for the general public, it must meet strict standards imposed by the company. These standards are guarded and guided by an individual called the "quality control officer" (QCO). Only when the product meets his approval is it packaged and marketed. Perhaps police departments interested in upgrading their overall image and efficiency should follow the same principle, establishing a QCO for police reports. After all, the police report represents the department's final product—these reports are what we package and market to the courts, the insurance companies, the public, and other agencies.

Just who should serve as the QCO can be determined by the individual department. D'Aulizio suggests: "The right person is one who has the desire and ability to write." This might be a patrol officer, a supervisor, a civilian within the department or an "outsider."

## Summary

Investigative notes and reports are critical parts of a criminal investigation. Notes are a permanent written record of the facts of a case used in further investigation, in writing reports and in prosecuting the case. Start to take notes as soon as possible after receiving the initial call to respond, and continue recording information as it is received throughout the investigation.

Record all relevant information concerning the crime, the crime scene and the investigation, including information that helps answer the questions: Who? What? Where? When? How? and Why? Write brief, abbreviated notes that will be understandable to others. Make them complete, accurate, specific, factual, clear, well organized and legible. After you have used notes to write your report, file them in a secure location that is readily accessible to you.

Original notes are legally admissible in court and may be used to testify from or to refresh your memory. Take to court only those notes that pertain to the case.

Good notes are the foundation for effective reports. The five steps in writing a report are to (1) gather facts, (2) take notes, (3) organize the notes, (4) actually write the report and (5) evaluate it.

*This Austin, Texas, police teletype operator is using a sophisticated communications system.*

The hardware available for word processing has become smaller and faster. It is easier to use and is much more portable. The software too has kept pace. Using computer reporting systems has proven to be efficient and cost effective.

"Pen Computing" (1995, p. 37) describes pen computing as handwriting on a computer screen. The article notes: "Gone are the days of fumbling around for incident forms—not to mention frustrated data processors who have a hard time deciphering an officer's quickly-written notes. Because officers can fill out incident forms right on the screen, it also eliminates the redundancy of data processors keying in the report."

"The greatest advantage of pen-based computers," notes Coumoundouros (1995, p. 50), "is ease of use . . . Code entry is very easy with pen-based computers, which typically display a list from which the user can select the proper code by pressing the pen next to it."

Computerized report writing offers other advantages described by Hawkins and Olon (1995, p. 16):

> Because certain fields *require* an answer, for example, the investigator is forced to enter necessary information. The narratives have also greatly improved with the development of a **template** setting out a logical order of investigative events. Any subsequent investigation is added simply by starting the new paragraph with the date and time the additional investigation was begun. [emphasis added]

Investigators usually complete an initial or preliminary report, supplemental or progress report(s) and a closing or final report. These reports provide a permanent written record of important facts that can be used to examine the past, keep other police officers informed, continue investigations, prepare court cases, provide the court with relevant facts, coordinate law enforcement activities, plan for future law enforcement services and evaluate law enforcement officers' performance.

A police report's narrative might be structured as follows:

- The opening paragraph of a police report states the time, date, type of incident and how you became involved.
- The next paragraph contains what you were told by the victim(s) or witness(es). For each person talked to, use a separate paragraph.
- Next, record what you did based on the information you received.
- The final paragraph states the disposition of the case.

As you write, use paragraphs, past tense and the first person. Be objective and concise, include diagrams and sketches to add clarity, use correct grammar and mechanics, write or print legibly and focus on the reader.

## Checklist

### *Note Taking*
- Is my notebook readily available?
- Does it contain an adequate supply of blank paper?
- Is it logically organized?
- Have I recorded all relevant information legibly?
- Have I identified each page of notes with case number and page number?
- Have I included sketches and diagrams where appropriate?
- Have I filed the notes securely?

### *Report Writing*
- Have I organized my notes and made a rough outline?
- Have I included all relevant information?
- Have I included headings?
- Have I proofread the paper to spot content and composition errors?
- Have I submitted all required reports on time?

## Discussion Questions

1. When else do you take "notes" in your life? How do these notes differ from those taken during an investigation?
2. What do you think is the ideal size for an investigative notebook?
3. What can be done if your writing is illegible?
4. What is *the* most important use of notes? Of reports?
5. Critics of having witnesses read and initial investigative notes contend that witnesses may not be able to read them, that it takes too much time to discuss the notes with witnesses and that the practice inhibits officers from recording all observations. How would you counter such arguments, or do you agree with them?
6. What might be an ideal format for notes? For reports?

**7.** Does your police department use standard forms? If so, for what types of reports?

**8.** Have you ever found yourself in a position where you realized that you did not take sufficient notes? Explain.

**9.** What factors influence the decision of whether to take notes immediately or to wait? When should and should not notes be taken?

**10.** If two investigators take notes and conflicting facts occur in the two sets of notes, how is this resolved? Should more than one person take notes?

## References

Blanchard, Wesley. "Digital Dictation a Boon for Warwick." *The Police Chief,* March 1990, p. 53.

Clark, Lance A. "A Way with Words." *Police,* February 1996, p. 98.

Coumoundouros, John. "Computerized Report Entry Systems." *The Police Chief,* September 1995, pp. 50–52.

Cox, Clarice R. "But Will They Be Able to Write a Report?" *Law Enforcement News,* December 15, 1994, pp. 8, 10.

Dacy, Joe. "Taming the Paper Tiger." *Police,* January 1991, pp. 35–35, 64–67.

D'Aulizio, Michael T. "Instituting Quality Control Measures for Police Reports." *The Police Chief,* October 1992, pp. 129–132.

D'Aulizio, Michael T., and Kathy M. Sheehan. "Writing Reports in an Age of Lawsuits." *Law and Order,* March 1992, pp. 112–114.

Davis, Terry L. "Did I Say That?" *The Journal of Law Enforcement Report Writing,* September 1992, pp. 3–4.

George, Dennis. "Computer-Assisted Report Entry: Toward a Paperless Police Department." *The Police Chief,* March 1990, pp. 46–48.

Hawkins, Michael L., and Nancy L. Olon. "Computerized Reporting and Case Management." *The Police Chief,* July 1995, p. 16.

Hess, Kären M., and Henry M. Wrobleski. *For the Record: Report Writing in Law Enforcement,* 4th edition. Blue Lake, CA: Innovative Systems, Publishers, 1996.

Kelly, Patrick T. "Increasing Productivity by Taping Reports." *The Police Chief,* March 1990, pp. 49–50.

Molden, Jack. "Basic Report Writing." *Law and Order,* February 1996, pp. 13–14.

Overton, W.D., and Dawn A.J. Burns. "Get It All and Get It Right." *Police,* March 1994, p. 98.

Peak, Kevin P. "Reporting the Use of Force." *The Police Chief,* May 1996, pp. 10–13.

"Pen Computing: The Natural 'Next Step' for Field Personnel." *Law and Order,* February 1995, p. 37.

Pilant, Lois. "Spotlight on Outfitting Your Detective Unit." *The Police Chief,* March 1992, pp. 33–41.

Pomerenke, Paula J. "Why Do Report Writers Avoid Using Paragraphs?" *Law and Order,* August 1992, pp. 89–90.

# Chapter 4

# Searches

**Introduction**
SEARCHING IS A VITAL TASK IN MOST CRIMINAL INVESTIGATIONS. IT IS through searching that evidence of crime and against criminals is obtained. Equally vital, however, is the investigator's understanding of the laws relating to searches. Any search must be firmly based on an understanding of the restrictions under which police officers must operate.

To **search** is to go over or look through for the purpose of finding something. A search is not haphazard; it is directed and organized. A search is an examination of a person's house or other buildings or premises or of the person for the purpose of discovering contraband or illicit or stolen property or some evidence of guilt to be used in prosecuting a criminal action with which a person is charged (*Elliott v. State*, 1934).

Investigators make many kinds of searches. They search crime scenes, suspects, dead bodies, vehicles, hotel rooms, apartments, homes and offices. The same basic principles apply to most searches.

This chapter begins with a discussion of investigative searches and the Fourth Amendment, the legal requirements for a search and the consequences imposed by the exclusionary rule if the legal requirements are not met. This is followed by a description of the crime-scene search and specific search patterns that might be used. Next, an explanation is given of specific types of searches, including searches of trash or garbage cans, buildings, vehicles, suspects and dead bodies. The chapter concludes with the use of dogs in searches.

## Investigative Searches and the Fourth Amendment

An understanding of the Fourth Amendment of the U. S. Constitution and its relevance for searches and seizures is critical for any investigator.

The Fourth Amendment to the Constitution forbids unreasonable searches and seizures.

The Fourth Amendment to the U.S. Constitution states:

> The right of the people to be secure in their persons, houses, papers, and effects, against unreasonable searches and seizures, shall not be violated, and no Warrants shall issue, but upon probable cause, supported by Oath or affirmation, and particularly describing the place to be searched, and the persons or things to be seized.

Bruce (1990, p. 100) has noted that "few areas of the law cause more confusion and uncertainty among law enforcement officers than questions about when a warrant is or is not needed to conduct a search."

Several years ago, police officers went to the home of Ted Chimel with an arrest warrant charging him with burglarizing a coin shop. They told Chimel they wanted to "look around." Although Chimel objected, the officers insisted they had the right to search because they had a legal arrest warrant. The officers opened kitchen cabinets and drawers, searched through closets, looked behind furniture in every room and even searched the garage. Their hour-long search turned up several coins that they took with them as evidence. On the basis of this evidence, Chimel was convicted in a California court, but he appealed on the grounds that the coins had been seized illegally. In a historic decision (*Chimel v. California*, 1969), the United States Supreme Court reversed the California decision by ruling that the conviction had been based on illegally obtained evidence.

The case was reversed because the officers conducted their search without a legal search warrant, and any evidence so obtained is inadmissible in court. An arrest warrant is not a search warrant for the premises.

It may seem inappropriate for a judge to refuse to admit incriminating evidence, but the courts are bound by rules and can admit evidence only if it is obtained constitutionally. Thus, the legality of a search must always be kept in mind during the investigation.

To conduct an effective search, know the legal requirements for searching, the items being searched for and the elements of the crime being investigated; be organized, systematic and thorough.

Because evidence obtained in an illegal search will *not* be admissible in court, look first at the legal requirements of a search.

## Legal Requirements for a Search

The courts have adopted guidelines to assure law enforcement personnel that if they adhere to certain rules, their searches or seizures will be reasonable.

A search can be justified if:
- A search warrant has been issued.
- Consent is given.
- The search is incidental to a lawful arrest.
- An emergency exists.

If any one of these *preconditions* exists, a search will be considered "reasonable" and, therefore, legal.

### Search with a Warrant

Technically—that is, according to the Fourth Amendment—all searches are to be conducted under the authority of a warrant. This warrant is to be based "upon probable cause, supported by oath or affirmation, and particularly describing the place to be searched, and the persons or things to be seized."

**Probable cause** is more than reasonable suspicion. Probable cause to search requires that it is thought to be more likely than not that the items sought are where the police believe them to be. *Smith v. United States* (1949) defined *probable cause* as:

> the sum total of layers of information and the synthesis of what the police have heard, what they know, and what they observe as trained officers. We [the Court] weigh not individual layers but the laminated total.

Probable cause is what would lead a person of "reasonable caution" to believe that something connected with a crime is on the premises or person to be searched.

A search warrant must be based on facts and sworn to by the officer requesting the warrant. An address alone is not enough; a description of the location must also be given—for example, *100 S. Main Street, the ABC Liquor Store* or *1234 Forest Drive, a private home.* A warrant for one side of a duplex does not include the other side, even though evidence may be believed to be there also. This is also true of apartments. Only the apartments specified in the warrant may be searched. Figure 4–1 is an example of a search warrant.

The search warrant can be issued to search for and seize any stolen or embezzled property, any property designed or intended for use in committing a

```
                      SEARCH WARRANT                        2-1
STATE OF ANYWHERE, COUNTY OF _____Hennepin_____  ___Justice___ COURT
TO: _Edina Police Department any officer_____

_____ (A) PEACE OFFICER(S) OF THE STATE OF ANYWHERE.
    WHEREAS, _____Patrick Olson_____ has this day on oath, made application to the said Court
applying for issuance of a search warrant to search the following described (premises) (motor vehicle) (person):
   __716 Sunshine Avenue, a private residence,_____

_____

located in the city of ____Edina____,county of ____Hennepin____ STATE OF Minn.
for the following described property and things:  (attach and identify additional sheet if necessary)

    One brown, 21" Panasonic Television,
    Serial Number, 63412X


    WHEREAS, the application and supporting affidavit of _____Patrick Olson_____
(was) (were) duly presented and read by the Court, and being fully advised in the premises.
    NOW, THEREFORE, the Court finds that probable cause exists for the issuance of a search warrant upon
the following grounds:  (Strike inapplicable paragraphs)
    1. The property above-described was stolen or embezzled.
    2. The property above-described was used as a means of committing a crime.
    3. The possession of the property above-described constitutes a crime.
    4. The property above described is in the possession of a person with intent to use such property as a
means of committing a crime.
    5. The property above described constitutes evidence which tends to show a crime has been committed,
or tends to show that a particular person has committed a crime.
    The Court further finds that probable cause exists to believe that the above-described property and things
(are) (will be) (at the above-described premises) (in the above-described motor vehicle) (on the person of _____ ).
    The Court further finds that a nighttime search is necessary to prevent the loss, destruction or removal
of the objects of said search.
    The Court further finds that entry without announcement of authority or purpose is necessary (to prevent
the loss, destruction or removal of the objects of said search) (and) (to protect the safety of the peace officers).
    NOW, THEREFORE, YOU, ____a peace officer of the Edina Police_____
Department_____
THE PEACE OFFICERS(S) AFORESAID, ARE HEREBY COMMANDED (TO ENTER WITHOUT ANNOUNCEMENT OF
AUTHORITY AND PURPOSE) (IN THE DAYTIME ONLY) (IN THE DAYTIME OR NIGHTTIME)     TO SEARCH
(THE DESCRIBED PREMISES) (THE DESCRIBED MOTOR VEHICLE) (THE PERSON OF_____
_____ ) FOR THE ABOVE DESCRIBED PROPERTY AND THINGS.    AND TO SEIZE SAID
PROPERTY AND THINGS AND   (TO RETAIN THEM IN CUSTODY SUBJECT TO COURT ORDER AND ACCORDING
TO LAW) (DELIVER CUSTODY OF SAID PROPERTY AND THINGS TO _____
_____ ).
                          BY THE COURT:

                          ___Oscar Kuntson_____
Dated____4-14___, 19_97_   JUDGE OF              COURT
                          Justice Court
COURT - WHITE COPY • PROS. ATTY. - YELLOW COPY • PEACE OFFICER - PINK COPY • PREMISES/PERSON - GOLD COPY
```

**Figure 4–1   Search Warrant**

crime or any property that tends to show a crime has been committed or that a particular person has committed the crime. The warrant must contain the reasons for requesting it, the names of the persons presenting affidavits, what specifically is being sought and the signature of the judge issuing it.

Once a warrant is obtained, it should be executed promptly. Usually the officer serving the warrant knocks on the particular door, states the purpose of the search and gives a copy of the warrant to the person who has answered the knock. **No-knock warrants** may be issued if evidence might be easily destroyed or if there is advance knowledge of explosives or other specific danger to the officer. Officers may enter by force to execute a search warrant if they are denied entrance or if no one is there to admit them. Even with a search warrant, certain limitations must be observed.

A search conducted with a warrant must be limited to the specific area and specific items named in the warrant.

During a search conducted with a warrant, you can seize items not specified in the warrant if they are similar in nature to the items described, if they are related to the particular crime described, or if they are contraband.

### Search with Consent

Searching without a warrant is allowed if consent is given by a person having authority to do so. This might be a spouse or roommate, a business partner if the search is at a place of business, the owner of a car or the like. As with a search warrant, however, searches conducted with consent have limitations.

Consent to search must be voluntary, and the search must be limited to the area for which consent is given.

The consent must not be in response to an officer's claim of lawful authority, as it was in the *Chimel* case. The request to search must not be phrased as a command or threat but as a genuine request for permission to search. A genuine affirmative reply must also be given; a simple nodding of the head or opening of a door is not sufficient and does not satisfy the consent requirement.

Some officers use a card similar to the Miranda form or a prepared consent form to be signed by the person giving consent. Silence is *not* consent. If consent is given, the person granting it must be legally competent to do so. Further, the person may revoke the consent at any time during the search. If this occurs, officers are obligated to discontinue the search.

*Illinois v. Rodriguez* (1989) held that if the police believe the person giving consent has apparent authority, they may act on this belief, even though it later turns out the person did not have authority to give consent. Any of several individuals occupying a premises may usually give consent for the entire premises.

### Search Following an Arrest

Every lawful arrest is accompanied by a search of the person to protect the arresting officers and others. (This is discussed later in the chapter.) Any weapon or dangerous substance or evidence discovered by the search may be seized. Limitations on a search incidental to arrest are found in the ***Chimel*** **decision**.

The *Chimel* decision established that a search incidental to a lawful arrest must be made simultaneously with the arrest and must be confined to the area within the suspect's immediate control.

In *Chimel*, the U.S. Supreme Court determined that:

> When an arrest is made, it is reasonable for the arresting officer to search the person arrested in order to remove any weapons that the latter might seek to use in order to resist arrest or effect his escape. It is entirely reasonable for the arresting officer to search for and seize any evidence on the arrestee's person in order to prevent its concealment or destruction and the area from within which the arrestee might gain possession of a weapon or destructible evidence.

The Court further specified that the search could extend only to the area within the person's **immediate control**—that is, within the person's reach. The Court noted that using an arrest to justify a thorough search would give police the power to conduct "general searches," which were declared unconstitutional nearly 200 years ago.

Limitations on searches incidental to arrest were further specified in *United States v. Chadwick* (1977), a case in which federal narcotics agents in Boston had probable cause to believe a 200-pound, double-locked footlocker arriving by rail from San Diego contained marijuana. They watched Chadwick and associates remove the footlocker from the depot and put it into the trunk of Chadwick's car. While the trunk was still open, they arrested Chadwick and seized the footlocker and keys. They then took Chadwick and the footlocker to the Boston Federal Building where, more than an hour later, they searched the footlocker and found large amounts of marijuana. Chadwick was charged with possession of marijuana and conspiracy. Before the trial, however, a U.S. district judge suppressed the marijuana evidence on the grounds that a warrant should have been obtained to search the footlocker. Although the government claimed the search was made incidental to a lawful arrest, Chief Justice Warren Burger, writing for the Court, rejected this argument, stating:

> Once law enforcement officers have reduced luggage or other personal property not immediately associated with the person of the arrestee to their exclusive control, and there is no longer any danger that the arrestee might gain access to the property to seize a weapon or destroy evidence, a search of that property is no longer an incident of the arrest.

In other words, a search warrant should have been obtained.

*Buie v. Maryland* (1990) expanded the area of a premises search following a lawful arrest. In this case the Supreme Court added authority for the police to make a protective search of immediately adjoining areas. Before this decision, searches were limited to the arrested person and items within that person's "wingspan" or associated with that person; this did not provide officers sufficient safety. The additional areas of search provided by *Buie v. Maryland* included the automatic right to search any area immediately adjoining the place of arrest and the right to make a protective sweep search of other areas when reasonable suspicion existed that another person might be present who posed a danger to the arresting officers. Protective sweeps are not full searches but include opening closet doors or other areas where someone might be hiding.

The burden of proof is on the government to show that the actions were within the scope of warrantless searches. Factors to be considered include prior information as to the number of individuals on the premises, observance of other people on the premises, the sound of opening doors or windows and unaccounted-for noises.

### Search in an Emergency Situation

Although the letter of the law requires a judge or magistrate to issue a warrant before a search is conducted, this is not always practical. In situations where police officers believe there is probable cause but no time to secure a warrant—for example, if shots are being fired or a person is screaming—they may act on their own discretion.

---

A warrantless search in the absence of a lawful arrest or consent is justified only in emergencies where probable cause exists and the search must be conducted immediately.

---

According to Hawley (1996, p. 25): "Exigent circumstances that create the need for an immediate search arise when there is a danger of violence or injury to officers or others, a risk of the subject's escape or the probability that evidence will be destroyed or concealed."

Such emergencies have established precedents. For example, *Warden v. Hayden* (1967) allowed warrantless entry and search of a house by police in pursuit of a fleeing robber. The Supreme Court has also permitted warrantless searches in cases where a delay would result in loss of evidence. Three such cases are *Kerr v. California* (1963), which allowed police to enter a dwelling unannounced; *Cupp v. Murphy* (1973), which allowed police to take a suspect's fingernail scrapings; and *Schmerber v. California* (1966), which allowed police to take blood samples for an alcohol test.

Searches without a warrant and in the absence of a lawful arrest are often challenged in court. However, officers often must act without benefit of a warrant. The public expects law enforcement officers to *act* when they see suspicious activities. As stated in *United States v. West* (1972): "The local policeman . . . is also in a very real sense a guardian of the public peace and he has a duty in the course of his work to be alert for suspicious circumstances, and, provided that he acts within constitutional limits, to investigate whenever such circumstances indicate to him that he should do so."

The duty of police officers to investigate suspicious circumstances includes stopping and questioning people who are acting suspiciously. The procedures used to stop and question suspects are regulated by the same justifications and limitations associated with lawful searches and seizures.

Two situations require police officers to stop and question individuals: (1) to investigate suspicious circumstances and (2) to make an identification—that is, when they see an individual who looks like a known suspect named in an arrest warrant or an unknown suspect whose description has been broadcast in an all points bulletin (APB). The first circumstance is clearly illustrated in *Terry v. Ohio* (1968), where the U.S. Supreme Court said that a *seizure* exists whenever a police officer restrains an individual's freedom to walk away and that a *search* exists when an officer explores an individual's clothing, even though this is usually referred to as a **patdown** or a **frisk**. The Court warned that such a search is "a serious intrusion upon the sanctity of the person which may inflict great indignity and arouse strong resentment, and it is not to be undertaken lightly."

In the *Terry* case, an officer observed three men who appeared to be casing a store. He approached the men, identified himself and asked their names. Receiving only mumbled replies, he frisked them for weapons, assuming they would be armed if they were planning a robbery in broad daylight. He found weapons on two of the men. The Court upheld the officer's actions:

Where a police officer observes unusual conduct which leads him reasonably to conclude in light of his experience that criminal activity may be afoot and that the persons with whom he is dealing may be armed and presently dangerous, where in the course of investigating this behavior he identifies himself as a policeman and makes reasonable inquiries, and where nothing in the initial stages of the encounter serves to dispel his reasonable fear for his own or others' safety, he is entitled for the protection of himself and others in the area to conduct a carefully limited search of the outer clothing of such persons in an attempt to discover weapons which might be used to assault him.

---

The *Terry* decision established that a patdown or frisk is a "protective search for weapons," and, as such, must be "confined to a scope reasonably designed to discover guns, knives, clubs and other hidden instruments for the assault of a police officer or others."

---

The prime requisite for stopping, questioning and possibly frisking an individual is reasonable suspicion, a concept that is hard to define.

The precedent established by *Terry* was strengthened four years later in *Adams v. Williams* (1972) when the Court said:

The Fourth Amendment does not require a policeman who lacks the precise level of information necessary for probable cause to arrest to simply shrug his shoulders and allow a crime to occur or a criminal to escape. On the contrary, Terry recognizes that it may be the essence of good police work to adopt an intermediate response. . . . A brief stop of a suspicious individual, in order to determine his

*This officer is restricted to a patdown for weapons because no arrest has been made at this point as established by the **Terry** decision. Even with no arrest, however, officers remain on guard.*

identity or to maintain the status quo momentarily while obtaining more information, may be most reasonable in light of the facts known to the officer at the time.

Officers may also stop and question individuals based on information received from informants. In *Adams v. Williams* (1972) the Court held that a known informer's tip is sufficient cause to stop and frisk a suspect. In this case, Williams was asked to open his car door by an officer who had received a tip from a known informant that Williams had a gun and was carrying drugs. When Williams lowered the window, the officer reached into the car and found a loaded handgun in Williams' waistband, exactly where the informant said it would be. A search incident to the arrest revealed heroin as well as other contraband.

*Terry* was further extended in 1988 when a Virginia Court of Appeals ruled that a protective search incident to an investigatory stop may extend to a suspect's dwelling (*Servis v. Virginia*). The court noted that the "frisk" procedure established in *Terry* has been expanded to permit protective searches of automobiles, briefcases and other areas from which a suspect might gain access to a weapon. The primary rationale for this is the protection of police.

In addition, *United States v. Hensley* (1985) established that police officers may stop and question suspects when they believe they recognize them from wanted flyers issued by another police department. In this case the police stopped a man wanted for armed robbery. The police found a weapon in the car and arrested the man. At the trial, the court suppressed the revolver, saying it had been seized improperly.

The U.S. Supreme Court reversed the decision, holding that where police have been able to locate a person suspected of a past crime, the ability to stop that person briefly, ask questions or check identification in the absence of probable cause promotes the strong government interest in solving crimes and bringing offenders to justice. It also held that if a wanted flyer is issued on articulable facts supporting reasonable suspicion that the wanted person has committed an offense, then other police officers may rely on the flyer as a basis for stopping a person answering the description, for checking identification and for posing questions about the offense and may detain the person briefly while attempting to obtain further information from the department issuing the flyer. Police may now sometimes stop, question and even search people when there is less than probable cause to believe they were involved in a past crime.

In California, stop-and-frisk has been validated on the basis of situational criteria, including the following: (1) furtive movements; (2) inappropriate attire; (3) carrying suspicious objects such as a TV or pillowcase; (4) vague, nonspecific answers to routine questions; (5) refusal to identify oneself; and (6) appearing to be out of place.

The majority of court opinions hold that one of the following three conditions must be present for justifiable emergency searches without a warrant:

- A danger to life.
- A danger of escape.
- A danger of destruction or removal of evidence.

In *Mincey v. Arizona* (1978), the Supreme Court stated that the Fourth Amendment does not require police officers to delay a search in the course of an investigation if to do so would gravely endanger their lives or the lives of others. Once the danger has been eliminated, however, any further search should be conducted only after obtaining a search warrant.

**Automobile Searches.** Another type of emergency in which warrantless searches are often justified is the search of mobile vehicles. The precedent for a warrantless search of an automobile was established in *Carroll v. United States* (1925).

---

The **Carroll** decision established that automobiles may be searched without a warrant if (1) there is probable cause for the search and (2) the vehicle would be gone before a search warrant could be obtained.

---

This case occurred during Prohibition. Undercover federal agents arranged to buy a case of whiskey from George Carroll and John Kiro, but the deal did not take place. The agents knew Carroll's car and watched for it during their regular patrol between Detroit and Grand Rapids looking for violations of the Prohibition Act. When the agents spotted the car and recognized Carroll and Kiro inside, they stopped it, believing they would find illegal liquor. They found sixty-eight bottles of Scotch whiskey and gin hidden behind the upholstered seats and arrested the bootleggers.

At the trial the defense argued that introducing the liquor as evidence was improper because the search of the automobile violated the Fourth Amendment. The court did not agree. It ruled that a search without a warrant based on probable cause that an automobile or other vehicle contained items that by law are subject to seizure and destruction is valid, as is the seizure. The Fourth Amendment serves the public interests as well as the interests and rights of individual citizens.

The government has recognized a necessary difference between searching a store or a home for which a proper search warrant could be obtained, and searching a ship, motorboat, wagon or automobile for which it is not practical to secure a warrant because the vehicle could quickly move out of the jurisdiction in which the warrant is sought. However, it would be intolerable and unreasonable if officers were authorized to stop every automobile on the chance of finding contraband and thus subject every person using the highways to the inconvenience and indignity of a search. Those entitled to use the public highways have a right to free passage without interruption or search unless there is known to be a competent official authorized to search and probable cause for believing that their vehicles are carrying contraband or illegal merchandise.

Limitations on warrantless automobile searches were set in *United States v. Henry* (1958). In this case, the Court said: "Once these items [for which a search warrant would be sought] are located, the search must terminate. If, however, while legitimately looking for such articles, the officer unexpectedly discovers evidence of another crime, he can seize that evidence as well."

Unlike a search incidental to an arrest, a vehicle search need not be made immediately, a precedent established by *Chambers v. Maroney* (1970). When the vehicle's contents are inventoried, any evidence found may be seized.

---

*Chambers v. Maroney* established that a vehicle may be taken to headquarters to be searched.

---

The *Chambers v. Maroney* case concerned a service station robbery in Pennsylvania. The robbers took currency from the cash register, and a station attendant was instructed to place coins in a glove, which the robbers also took. Two teenagers had earlier noticed a blue compact station wagon circling the block near the station, and they saw the station wagon speed away from a parking lot near the station. When they learned that the station had been robbed, they reported what they had seen to the police, who had arrived at the scene almost immediately. The teenagers told police that four men were in the station wagon, one wearing a green sweater. The station attendant told police that one of the robbers was wearing a green sweater and another one, a trench coat. This description was broadcast over the police radio.

Within the hour a station wagon with four men was stopped about two miles from the station. The petitioner was wearing a green sweater, and a trench coat was in the car. The occupants were arrested, and the vehicle was driven to the police station. The police searched the vehicle and found two revolvers, a glove containing change and credit cards belonging to an attendant of another station that had been robbed earlier. In subsequent trials the petitioner was convicted of both robberies. The Court held there was probable cause to arrest the occupants of the vehicle based on information the police had: the description of the vehicle, number of occupants, type of clothing of two of them and the proximity of the vehicle to the crime scene.

A question arose in this case that was not present in the *Carroll v. United States* decision. In *Chambers,* the vehicle was stopped at night in a dark parking lot. Officers chose to arrest the petitioner and take the car to the police station for a later search. Was the search then incidental to arrest? Could a search warrant have been obtained because the vehicle was in custody of the police and no longer mobile—lacking the circumstances of mobility described in the *Carroll* decision? Clearly a search warrant would have been a safety net, but it was not obtained in this case. The basic issue was *probable cause* to search, which the officers had. The right to search and the validity of the seizure were not based on the right to arrest but on the officers' reasonable belief that the automobile's contents violated the law, just as in the *Carroll* case.

In addition, when a motor vehicle is taken into custody, property within it is routinely inventoried to prevent claims by the vehicle owner that items were taken. Although, technically, inventory and search are two different processes, in practice they may take place simultaneously. If property found during such an inventory is evidence of a crime, it is admissible in court. It is advisable, however, where a vehicle is no longer mobile or is in the custody of the police, to obtain a search warrant so as not to jeopardize an otherwise perfectly valid case.

In 1981, in *Robbins v. California,* officers stopped a station wagon because of erratic driving. Robbins got out of his car and walked toward the officers. When asked for his driver's license, he fumbled with his wallet. When he opened the car door to get the registration, the officers smelled marijuana smoke. When the officers patted down Robbins, they found a vial of liquid. Searching the passenger portion of the car, the officers found marijuana as well as equipment for using it. They put Robbins, apparently under the influence of marijuana, into the patrol car and then returned to the vehicle. When they searched the rear of the station wagon, they located a recessed luggage compartment, in which they found a tote bag and two packages wrapped in opaque green plastic. Police unwrapped the packages and found that each contained 15 pounds of marijuana. Robbins was charged with various drug offenses and convicted. The case was appealed, and the decision considered another aspect of the "mobility" question.

Two other cases also dealt with the mobility issue: *South Dakota v. Opperman* (1976) and *United States v. Chadwick* (1977). The courts in these cases stated that although an automobile provides a diminished expectation of privacy compared

*An officer may search a vehicle without a warrant if he has probable cause to believe it contains evidence of a crime as established by the* Carroll *decision.*

with a private residence, certain containers within the automobile are not awarded this same degree of protection because of the vehicle's mobility. For example, pieces of luggage and other property may be removed to the custody of the police, and a search warrant may be obtained if there is probable cause. Therefore, searching such items without probable cause at the scene is not justifiable. Closed containers within an automobile are not within the same protection as plain view items and thus do not have the full protection of the Fourth Amendment.

When stopping moving vehicles, if officers have probable cause, they may search the vehicle and any closed containers in the vehicle. If probable cause does not exist, it may be possible to obtain voluntary consent to search, including any closed containers (*Florida v. Jimeno,* 1990). The driver must be competent to give such consent, and silence is not consent. Further, if at any time the driver rescinds consent, the search must cease.

### Inventory Searches

When police take custody of property, the courts have upheld their right to inventory such property for the following reasons:

■   To protect the owner's property. This obligation may be legal or moral, but the courts have supported the police's responsibility to protect property taken into custody from unauthorized interference.

■ To protect the police from disputes and claims that the property was stolen or damaged. Proper inventory at the time of custody provides an accurate record of the condition of the property at the time it was seized.

■ To protect the police and the public from danger. Custody of an automobile or a person subjects the police to conditions that require searching the person or the vehicle for objects such as bombs, chemicals, razor blades, weapons and the like that may harm the officers or the premises where the vehicle or person is taken.

■ To determine the owner's identity. Identifying the owner may be associated with identifying the person under arrest, or it may help the police know to whom the property should be released.

The courts have held that each of these factors outweighs the privacy interests of property and, therefore, justifies an inventory search. The search must be reasonable. To be correct in the inventory procedure, the police must show legal seizure and make an inventory according to approved procedures.

Court cases related to inventory searches include the following:

■ *Florida v. Wells* (1990). State police opened a locked suitcase that contained a closed garbage bag. Inside the bag, police found marijuana. The court ruled that because the police agency did not have any policy regarding opening closed containers, the search was illegal.

■ *California v. Acevedo* (1991). The court ruled that if officers have probable cause to believe that illegal material is in a vehicle, they can use the fleeing target exception.

■ *U.S. v. Williams* (1991). The court ruled that an on-site inventory of property is legally permissible, even though done in advance of impounding, if there is authority and circumstances to justify impound.

■ *U.S. v. Ibarra* (1992). The court ruled that if there is no statutory authority to impound, the vehicle cannot be taken into custody legally; therefore, an inventory search under these circumstances would be inadmissible.

■ *U.S. v. Bowhay* (1993). The court ruled that because a department policy required officers to search everything, the officers had no discretion. Therefore, the presence of an investigative motive did not prohibit the inventory search.

### Student Searches

The Fourth Amendment prohibition of unreasonable searches was determined by the Supreme Court to apply to public school officials. The Court ruled that public school officials are representatives of the state, not merely surrogates of the parents, and therefore do not have immunity from the Fourth Amendment. The Court also held that, although school children have a right to privacy, the school must maintain a climate of learning. In light of these things, the Court eased restrictions on search by school officials. School officials do not need a search warrant if they have probable cause to believe the subject of the search has violated or is violating the law.

The key standard is *reasonableness under all circumstances,* meaning that if there is a reason to believe the search will turn up evidence of a violation of the law or school rules, and if the procedure followed is related to the purpose of the search and not excessively intrusive in view of the student's age and sex and the nature of the infraction, then the search is permissible (*New Jersey v. T.L.O.,* 1985). Cases involving school and student searches have proliferated in recent years with the increased use of drugs. The majority of cases involve searches for drugs, explosives, explosive devices and guns.

## Searches in the Workplace

If a police department employee is under departmental investigation, the right to search the areas of the officer's workplace usually exists. Such areas might include a desk, patrol car, luggage or other items brought to and present in the workplace, including lockers. Several questions might be considered. Is the search connected with an administrative investigation or a criminal investigation? If it is an administrative investigation and is at the workplace where no reasonable expectation of privacy would occur, the search would be legal. If the search is in relation to a criminal investigation or at a workplace location where there is a reasonable expectation of privacy, it may be illegal if conducted without a warrant.

Searches at the workplace should be based on reasonable grounds to believe that evidence will be found as a result of the search. Searches at the private residence of a police employee should be conducted only with a warrant. Criminal investigation searches, even at the workplace, must be based on probable cause. In *United States v. Taketa* (1991), the Court held that a search of an agent's office for administrative purposes was legal, but installing a video camera to gather evidence for criminal charges required a warrant.

## Basic Limitation on Searches

All searches have one limitation.

---

The most important limitation on any search is that the scope must be narrowed. General searches are unconstitutional.

---

## Plain View Evidence

The preceding limitations are intended to protect the rights of all citizens and to ensure due process of law. They are not intended to hamper investigations, nor do they preclude the use of evidence that is not concealed and that is accidentally found.

---

**Plain view evidence,** unconcealed evidence seen by an officer engaged in a lawful activity, is admissible in court.

---

Recall that in *United States v. Henry* (1958) the Court said: "If, however, while legitimately looking for such articles, the officer unexpectedly discovers evidence of another crime, he can seize that evidence as well." In both *Michigan v. Tyler* (1978) and *Mincey v. Arizona* (1978), the Court ruled that while officers are on the premises pursuing their legitimate emergency activities, any evidence in plain view may be seized.

Evidence qualifies as plain view evidence if (1) officers are engaged in a lawful activity when they discover the evidence, (2) the item(s) are not concealed and (3) the discovery is accidental. An officer cannot obtain a warrant and fail to mention a particular object and then use "plain view" to justify its seizure. If the officer is looking for it initially, it must be mentioned in the warrant. Plain view evidence itself is not sufficient to justify a warrantless seizure of evidence; probable cause must also exist.

In one search and seizure case, police officers seized a party balloon during a lawful, routine driver's license check. The officer observed white powder in the glove compartment while the driver was searching it for his license and that the balloon contained a white powdery substance within its tied-off portion. The officer showed the balloon to a fellow officer, and he also "understood the situation." The driver, Brown, was arrested and the items seized. The balloon was found to contain heroin. The Texas court said that the plain view exception required that the officer be in a place he had a right to be and that it be immediately apparent that the items seized were evidence of a crime.

The Supreme Court held (*Texas v. Brown,* 1983) that the plain view doctrine "does not require that the officer know the items to be contraband or evidence. All that is needed is probable cause to associate the property with criminal activity. In this case, the knowledge and experience of the officer as to the practice of putting narcotics in balloons, combined with his observation of the contents of the glove compartment, gave him probable cause to seize the balloon."

In 1990 the Supreme Court ruled again, in *Horton v. California,* that police may seize items not specifically listed in a search warrant but in plain view. In this case police had a warrant to search a residence for the proceeds of a robbery. The warrant listed jewelry that had been stolen. While searching, the officers saw weapons in plain view and seized them. The court ruled that the officers acted properly and that the weapons could be used as evidence in the trial.

Officers may also seize any contraband they discover during a legal search. In *Boyd v. United States* (1886), Justice Bradley stated: "The search for and seizure of stolen or forfeited goods or goods liable to duties and concealed to avoid payment thereof, are totally different things from a search or a seizure of a man's private books and papers. In one case the government is entitled to the property, and in the other it is not."

### Plain Feel/Touch Evidence

"Pat-down Searches" (1993, p. 7) notes: "The 'plain feel' exception is a legitimate extension of the 'plain view' exception." The article explains:

> [I]f a police officer lawfully pats down a suspect's outer clothing and feels an object that he immediately identifies as contraband, a warrantless seizure is justified because there is no invasion of the suspect's privacy beyond that already authorized by the officer's search for weapons (*Minnesota v. Dickerson*).

In *Minnesota v. Dickerson,* the Supreme Court ruled that officers may seize any contraband discovered during a legal patdown IF it is immediately apparent to the officer that the object is an illegal substance.

Laws regulating how and when searches may be legally conducted are numerous and complex. It is critical, however, that officers who are responsible for criminal investigations know these laws and operate within them. The penalty for not doing so is extreme—any evidence obtained during an illegal search will not be allowed at the trial, as established by the exclusionary rule.

## The Exclusionary Rule

In the early 1900s, the federal courts declared that "they would require that evidence be obtained in compliance with constitutional standards" (*Weeks v. United States,* 1914). These standards are contained in the Fourth Amendment. Recall that the Fourth Amendment states: "The right of the people to be secure in their persons, houses, papers, and effects, against unreasonable searches and seizures, shall not be violated, and no Warrants shall issue, but upon probable cause, supported by Oath or affirmation, and particularly describing the place to be searched, and the persons or things to be seized."

---

The **exclusionary rule** established that courts may not accept evidence that was obtained by unreasonable search and seizure, regardless of its relevance to the case (*Weeks v. United States*).

---

Weeks was arrested for using the mail to transport lottery tickets. Officers searched Weeks's home without a warrant and seized several items and documents and turned them over to the U.S. marshal. Later that day the marshal and the officers again searched Weeks's home without a warrant and again seized items and documents. Weeks was convicted of unlawful use of the mail, but the conviction was overturned in *Weeks v. United States* (1914).

The Court ruled that the search had been unreasonable and thus illegal. Consequently, the evidence obtained by the federal officers was inadmissible. This mandate was made applicable to the federal courts in the *Weeks* decision, but that decision was often ignored by state courts. *Mapp v. Ohio* (1961) made it applicable to all courts.

---

*Mapp v. Ohio* made the exclusionary rule applicable to all courts.

---

In 1957 Cleveland police officers forced their way into Ms. Mapp's home, acting on information that a suspect in a bombing was hiding there. The police searched the house thoroughly, including the basement and her child's bedroom. During the search the police found obscene material that Mapp was subsequently convicted of possessing. The Supreme Court overturned the conviction in *Mapp v. Ohio* (1961), saying the methods used to obtain the evidence were an offense to justice.

### The Fruit of the Poisonous Tree Doctrine

The exclusionary rule affects not only any illegally seized evidence, but also any evidence obtained as a result of the illegally seized evidence, referred to as fruit of the poisonous tree. The fruit of the poisonous tree doctrine resulted from the case of *Silverthorne Lumber Co. v. United States* (1920). In this case a U.S. marshal unlawfully entered and searched the Silverthorne Lumber Company's offices and seized several documents. When the company demanded the return of the documents, the government did so, but only after making copies. A district court later impounded these copies, which became the basis for a grand jury indictment. When the company was subpoenaed to produce the original documents, it refused and was then convicted of contempt of court. The Supreme Court, however, reversed the decision, saying:

> [T]he essence of a provision forbidding the acquisition of evidence in a certain way is that not merely evidence so acquired shall not be used before the Court

but that it shall not be used at all. In other words, once the primary source (the "tree") is proven to have been obtained unlawfully, any secondary evidence derived from it (the "fruit") is also inadmissible.

---

The **fruit of the poisonous tree doctrine** established that evidence obtained as a result of an earlier illegality must be excluded from trial.

---

The exclusionary rule may seem to favor criminals at the expense of law enforcement, but this was not the intent of the Court. The Court recognized that important exceptions to this rule might occur. Two of the most important exceptions are the inevitable discovery doctrine and the good faith doctrine.

### The Inevitable Discovery Doctrine

Another Supreme Court decision directly related to the exclusionary rule is *Nix v. Williams* (1984). In this case the defendant's right to counsel under the Sixth Amendment was violated, resulting in his making incriminating statements and leading the police to the body of his murder victim. Searchers who had been conducting an extensive, systematic search of the area then terminated their search. The record supported a finding that if the search had continued, the search party inevitably would have discovered the victim's body. This reasoning is referred to as the inevitable discovery doctrine. Therefore, evidence as to the location and condition of the body was held admissible.

---

The **inevitable discovery doctrine** established that if illegally obtained evidence would in all likelihood eventually have been discovered legally, it may be used.

---

The intent of the exclusionary rule, the Court said, was to deter police from violating citizens' constitutional rights. In the majority opinion, Chief Justice Warren E. Burger wrote: "Exclusion of physical evidence that would inevitably have been discovered adds nothing to either the integrity or fairness of a criminal trial." He stated that the point of the inevitable discovery doctrine was to put the police in the same position they would have been if no police error or misconduct occurred.

### The Good Faith Exception

On July 5, 1984, the United States Supreme Court handed down two cases related to the exclusionary rule: *United States v. Leon* and *Massachusetts v. Sheppard*. In *United States v. Leon*, police in Burbank, California, investigated the involvement of Alberto Leon and others in a drug trafficking operation, following up on a tip from an unreliable informant. Officers acted on the tip, and after considerable surveillance and investigation prepared an application for a search warrant and a supporting affidavit to search automobiles and premises at several locations. The affidavit was based on the initial information, followed by surveillance and investigation. It was reviewed by several deputy district attorneys, and a state superior court judge issued an apparently valid warrant.

The searches revealed large quantities of drugs and other evidence at various locations. The defendants challenged the sufficiency of the warrant and moved to suppress the evidence seized on the basis of the search warrant. The district court held that the affidavit was insufficient to establish probable cause because of the informant's unreliability. The U.S. Court of Appeals affirmed the action of the district court. Then the U.S. Supreme Court reviewed whether the exclusionary rule should be modified so as not to bar admission of evidence seized in *reasonably good faith.*

The Court noted that whereas the Fourth Amendment contains no provision expressly precluding the use of evidence obtained in violation of a person's rights, the exclusionary rule is a *judicially created remedy* intended to serve as a deterrent rather than a guaranteed constitutional right. The Court noted, however, that evidence may be excluded under certain conditions, even where a magistrate approved the search warrant: (1) where police officers were dishonest in preparing the affidavit, (2) where the officers did not have reasonable belief in the probable cause for the search warrant and (3) where the magistrate was not neutral, merely serving as a rubber stamp for the police.

*Massachusetts v. Sheppard* used the principles established in *United States v. Leon* to decide a case where the police relied on the assurances of a state judge and executed a search warrant that had been completed on the wrong form. In this case, a badly burned body was discovered in a vacant lot in Boston. The police were able to determine through investigation that a boyfriend, Osborne Sheppard, might have committed the murder. Based on evidence gathered by the police, a detective drafted an affidavit to support the application for an arrest warrant and a warrant to search Sheppard's residence. The affidavit detailed the items of evidence sought in the search warrant, including a blunt instrument; clothing that might have blood, gasoline or burns on it; jewelry; hair; and wire that might have been used to bind the victim.

The detective first consulted with another police officer and the district attorney to be sure the affidavit sufficiently supported probable cause for the warrants. Because the detective could not find the proper search warrant form, he used a form that pertained to searches for controlled substances. Certain words pertaining to controlled substances were deleted, but others were not. The detective discussed this potential problem with the judge, and the judge advised that he would make the necessary changes so it could be considered a proper search warrant. The judge made some changes and dated and signed the form, but he did not modify the substantive portions of the form to reflect the nature of the search, nor did he alter it to incorporate the affidavit. The judge informed the detective that the warrant was sufficient in form and content to authorize the search.

The search revealed incriminating evidence, and Sheppard was indicted for first-degree murder. The defendant challenged the decision on the basis of the inadequate search warrant. The trial judge, however, denied the motion, holding that the police acted in good faith. On appeal, the Supreme Judicial Court of Massachusetts reversed the defendant's conviction. On review, the Supreme Court stated that it had already ruled on this in *United States v. Leon.* The issue before the Court was whether the officers reasonably believed that the search they were conducting was authorized by a valid warrant and whether there was an objectively reasonable basis for the officers' mistaken belief.

---

The **good faith doctrine** established that illegally obtained evidence may be admissible if the police were truly not aware that they were violating the suspect's Fourth Amendment rights.

---

In rejecting the application of the exclusionary rule to the search, the Court noted that the police conduct in the case was clearly objective, reasonable and largely error-free. An error of constitutional dimensions may have been committed by the judge in issuing the warrant, but that was not the fault of the police who acted on the warrant. In applying the good faith doctrine, the Court refused to rule that a police officer is required to disbelieve a judge who has advised the officer by word and action that the warrant authorizes the search as requested.

These two cases involve search warrants. The Court has not ruled whether the same application would be made in warrantless searches. The officer must still be "objectively reasonable of good faith belief." The Court is still not interested in subjective, personal beliefs or opinions, and ignorance of the laws of search and seizure will still not be excused. Officers are required to have reasonable knowledge of what the law prohibits.

Having looked at the legal restrictions on searching, turn your attention to the search itself, beginning with the search of a crime scene. Although each crime scene is unique, certain general guidelines apply.

## The Crime-Scene Search

A basic function of investigators is to conduct a thorough, legal search at the scene of a crime. Even though not initially visible, evidence in some form is present at most crime scenes. The goal of any search during an investigation, at the crime scene or elsewhere, is to discover evidence that helps to:

- Establish that a crime *was* committed and *what* the specific crime was.
- Establish *when* the crime was committed.
- Identify *who* committed the crime.
- Explain *how* the crime was committed.
- Suggest *why* the crime was committed.

---

A successful crime-scene search locates, identifies and preserves all evidence present.

---

Evidence found at the scene assists in recreating the crime in much the same way that bricks, properly placed, result in the construction of a building. A meticulous, properly conducted search usually results in the discovery of evidence.

The importance of securing the scene was discussed in Chapter 1. The security measures taken by the first officer(s) at the scene determine whether evidence is discovered intact or after it has been altered or destroyed.

Do not search until photographing and sketching are completed. During the search, evidence is often photographed again, this time at closer range to show details. Evidence is also measured and located on the sketch using one of the plotting methods discussed in Chapter 2. The position of objects can often assist in determining the sequence of the crime and the suspect's direction of flight.

During a search, do not change or contaminate physical evidence in any way, or it will be declared inadmissible. Maintain the chain of custody of evidence from the initial discovery to the time of the trial as discussed in the next chapter.

Always be certain the search is justified. In the *Chimel* case, for example, the officers conducted a very thorough search, but the evidence was not admissible because the search itself was illegal. Officers who do not know when they have the right to search not only lose valuable time; they also lose cases.

## Organizing the Crime-Scene Search

After emergencies have been attended to, the scene secured, witnesses located and separated for interviewing and photographing and sketching completed, a search plan must be formulated. Also, a search headquarters needs to be established away from the scene to prevent destruction of evidence.

---

Organizing a search includes dividing the duties, selecting a search pattern, assigning personnel and equipment and giving instructions.

---

Proper organization results in a thorough search with no accidental destruction of evidence. However, even the best-organized search may not yield evidence. Evidence may have been destroyed before the search or removed by the criminal. In a few, rare instances, evidence is simply nonexistent.

In a single-investigator search, one officer conducts the physical search and describes, identifies and preserves the evidence found. If two or more officers conduct the search, the highest-ranking officer on the scene usually assumes command. In accordance with department policy, the officer in charge assigns personnel based on their training. For example, if one officer has specialized training in photography, another in sketching and a third in fingerprinting, they are assigned to their respective specialities. Someone is assigned to each function required in the search. Often two officers are assigned to take measurements to ensure accuracy. These same two officers can collect, identify and preserve evidence as it is found. Evidence should never be removed from the scene without the permission of the search leader.

The search leader also determines the number of personnel needed, the type of search best suited for the area and the items most likely to be found. Personnel are assigned according to the selected search pattern. Members of the search party are given all known details of the crime and are instructed on the type of evidence to seek and their specific responsibilities.

The search leader also determines whether anyone other than the person(s) committing the crime has entered the scene. If so, the person(s) are asked to explain in detail any contacts with the scene that might have contaminated evidence. If no one has entered the scene between the time the crime was committed and when the police arrived, and if the scene was immediately secured, the scene is considered to be a **true, or uncontaminated, scene;** that is, no evidence has been introduced into it or taken from it except by the person(s) committing the crime.

## Physical Evidence

Physical evidence ranges in size from very large objects to minute substances. Understanding what types of evidence can be found at various types of crime scenes is important to the search. Obviously, not everything found at the scene is evidence.

---

Knowing what to search for is indispensable to an effective crime-scene search. Evidence is anything material and relevant to the crime being investigated.

---

*The elements of the crime help to determine what will be useful as evidence.* For example, a burglary requires an illegal entry; therefore, toolmarks and broken glass in a door or window are evidence that assists in proving burglary. A forcible rape requires a sexual act against the victim's will. Therefore, bruises, semen stains or witnesses hearing screams would help to establish evidence of that crime. Specific types of evidence to be sought are discussed in Chapter 5 and throughout Sections Three, Four and Five.

Besides knowing what types of evidence to search for, it is necessary to know where evidence is most likely to be found. For example, evidence is often found on or near the route used to and from the crime. The suspect may drop items used to commit the crime or leave shoe or tire prints. Evidence is also frequently found on or near a dead body.

The **"elephant in a matchbox" doctrine** requires that searchers consider the probable size and shape of evidence they seek, because, for example, large objects cannot be concealed in tiny areas. Ignoring this doctrine can result in a search that wastes resources, destroys potential evidence and leaves the place in a shambles. It may also result in violating the Fourth Amendment requirements on reasonable searches.

## Search Patterns

All **search patterns** have a common denominator: they are designed to locate systematically any evidence at the crime scene or any other area where evidence might be found. Most patterns involve partitioning search areas into workable sizes. The search pattern should be adapted to the area involved, the personnel available, the time limits imposed by weather and light conditions and the circumstances of the individual crime scene. Such patterns ensure thoroughness.

### Exterior Searches

Exterior searches can cover small, large or vast areas. Regardless of the dimensions, the area to be searched can be divided into subareas and diagrammed on paper. As each area is searched, check it off. Be certain sufficient light is available. A search conducted with inadequate light can destroy more evidence than it yields. If weather conditions are favorable, delay nighttime searches until daylight if feasible.

---

Exterior search patterns divide an area into lanes, concentric circles or zones.

---

**Lane Search Pattern.**   One effective search pattern is to partition the area into **lanes,** using stakes and string as illustrated in Figure 4–2. An officer is assigned to each lane. Therefore, the number of lanes to be used depends on the number of officers available to search.

These lanes can be imaginary. Officers' search widths vary from arm's length to shoulder-to-shoulder, either on foot or on their knees. Such searches use no string or cord to mark the lanes.

If only one officer is available for the search, the lane pattern can be adapted to what is commonly called the **strip search pattern.** The officer starts at the beginning of the first lane, goes to the end and then begins at the end of the second lane, as illustrated in Figure 4–3.

For an extensive search, the lane pattern is often modified to form a **grid,** and the area is criss-crossed as illustrated in Figure 4–4.

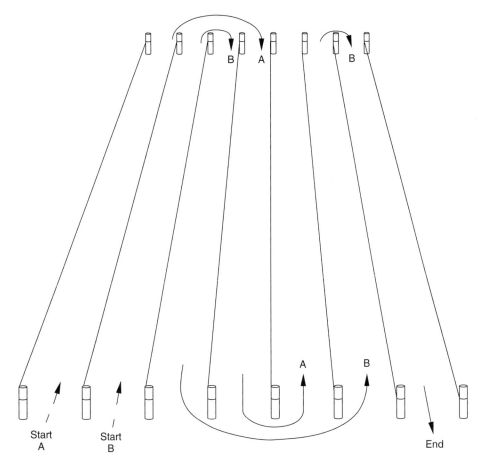

**Figure 4–2   Lane Search Pattern**

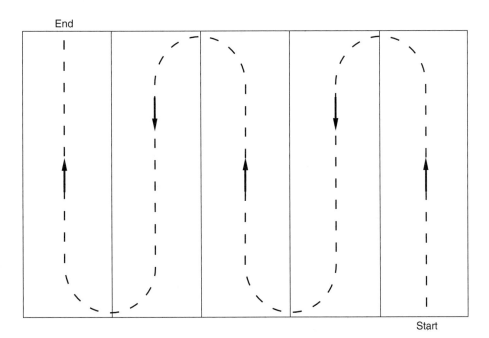

**Figure 4–3   Strip Search Pattern**

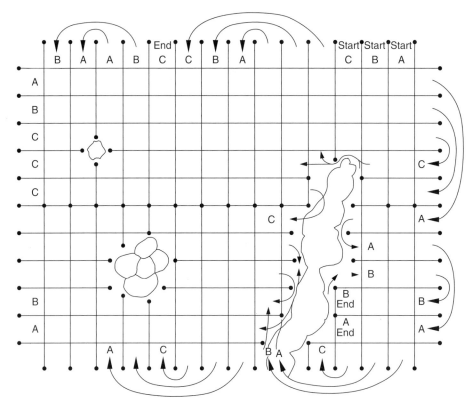

**Figure 4–4  Grid Search Pattern**

**Circle Search Pattern.**   Another commonly used pattern is the **circle search,** which begins at the center of the area to be searched and spreads out in ever-widening concentric circles (see Figure 4–5).

A wooden stake with a long rope is driven into the ground at the center of the area to be searched. Knots are tied in the rope at selected regular intervals. The searcher circles around the stake in the area delineated by the first knot, searching the area within the first circle. When this area is completed, the searcher moves to the second knot and repeats the procedure. The search is continued in ever-widening circles until the entire area is covered.

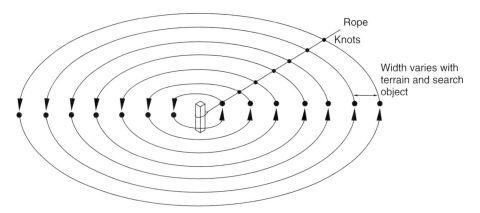

**Figure 4–5  Circle Search Pattern**

**Zone or Sector Search Pattern.** In the **zone** or **sector** search, the area is divided into equal squares on a map of the area, and each square is numbered. Search personnel are assigned to specific squares (see Figure 4–6).

## Interior Searches

The exterior search patterns can be adapted to an interior crime scene. Of prime concern is to search thoroughly without destroying evidence.

---

Interior searches go from the general to the specific, usually in a circular pattern, covering all surfaces of the search area. The floor should be searched first.

---

In making an interior search, look closely at all room surfaces, including the ceiling, walls, floor and all objects on the floor and walls. Evidence can be found on any surface.

The floor usually produces the most evidence, followed by doors and windows. Although the ceiling is often missed in a search, it too can contain evidence such as stains or bullet holes. It can even contain such unlikely evidence as footprints. Footprints were found on the ceiling by an alert officer during the investigation of a bank burglary. Paperhangers had left wallpaper on the bank's floor during the night and had hung it on the ceiling early the next morning before the burglary was discovered. During the night, one of the burglars had stepped on the wallpaper, leaving a footprint that was transferred in a faint outline to the ceiling.

The interior room search usually starts at the point of entry. The floor is searched first so that no evidence is inadvertently destroyed during the remainder of the search. The lane or zone search patterns are adaptable to an interior floor search.

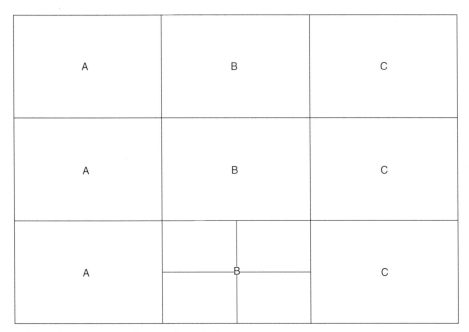

**Figure 4–6   Zone or Sector Search Pattern**

After the floor search, the walls—including doors and windows—and then the ceiling are searched, normally using a clockwise or counterclockwise pattern around the room. Because doors and windows are points of entry and exit, soil, fingerprints, glass fragments and other evidence are often found there. Walls may have marks, bloodstains or trace evidence such as hairs or fibers on them.

After the room is searched in one direction, it is often searched in the opposite direction because lighting is different from different angles. The same general procedures are followed in searching closets, halls or other rooms off the main room. The search is coordinated, and the location of all evidence is communicated to members of the search team.

### General Guidelines

The precise search pattern used is immaterial as long as the search is systematic and covers the entire area. Assigning two officers to search the same area greatly increases the probability of discovering evidence. Finding evidence is no reason to stop the search. Continue searching until the entire area is covered.

## Trash or Garbage Can Searches

In drug and theft cases, evidence is often left in trash or garbage containers left on or near public streets such as at curbside.

Trash and garbage cans in alleys and on public sidewalks are often the depository for evidence of thefts, drugs and even homicides. In *California v. Greenwood* (1988), the Supreme Court ruled that containers left on public property are open to search by police without a warrant. In this Laguna Beach, California, case, police received a tip that drug trafficking was occurring at the residence of Billy Greenwood. After investigation and surveillance, police asked the garbage collector for that location to pick up Greenwood's trash and deliver it to them. In this trash, police found evidence of drug dealing. A search warrant was issued for the residence, and later an arrest warrant was issued for Greenwood on felony drug charges. The California Supreme Court ruled that evidence should be surpressed. On appeal to the United States Supreme Court, this ruling was reversed on the premise that the search of garbage left at the curb for collection does not constitute a violation of the Fourth Amendment or a reasonable expectation of privacy. Justice Byron White stated: "It is common knowledge that plastic garbage bags left on a public street are readily accessible to animals, children, scavengers, snoops, and other members of the public," and therefore, "no reasonable expectation of privacy" is violated by such a search. Trash or garbage containers on private property may not be searched without a warrant.

The most important factor in determining the legality of warrantless trash inspections is the physical location of the retrieved trash. Police cannot trespass to gain access to the trash location, and the trash must not be located within the **curtilage**—that portion of the residence that is not open to the public and is reserved for private owner or family use. This is in contrast to sidewalks and alleys which are used by the public.

According to Griffith (1996, p. 95): "The curtilage is that area where the suspect and his family have the expectation of privacy and are protected from unlawful intrusion."

In *United States v. Dunn* (1987), the Court ruled:

> We believe that curtilage questions should be resolved with particular reference to four factors: the proximity of the area claimed to be curtilage to the home,

whether the area is included within an enclosure surrounding the home, the nature of the uses to which the area is put, and the steps taken by the resident to protect the area from observation by people passing by.

## Building Searches

When executing a warrant to search a building, officers should first familiarize themselves with the location and the past record of the person(s) living there. Check records for any previous police actions at that location. Decide on the least dangerous time of day for the suspect, the police and the neighborhood. For example, when children are coming home from school would not be a good time to execute the warrant.

Do not treat executing a search warrant as routine. Plan for the worst-case scenario. Think *safety* first and last. Arrive safely. Turn off your vehicle's dome light as you approach the building. Stay away from the headlights or turn them off. Use any available cover as you approach the building.

Have a plan before entering the building. Secure the outside perimeter and as many exits as possible—at minimum, the front and rear door. If possible, call for a backup before entering and search with a partner. Once inside, wait for vision adjustments to interior light conditions. Keep light and weapons away from your body. Reduce the level of your radio, and turn off your beeper. Go quickly through doors into dark areas. When moving around objects take quick peeks before proceeding further. Avoid windows. Use light and cover to your advantage. Know where you are at all times and how to get back to where you were. Look for exits.

If the entire building is to be searched, use a systematic approach. Secure each area as it is searched.

## Vehicle Searches

Cars, aircraft, boats, motorcycles, buses, trucks and vans can contain evidence of a crime. Again, the type of crime determines the area to be searched and the evidence to be sought. In a hit-and-run accident, the car's undercarriage can have hairs and fibers, or the interior can reveal a hidden liquor bottle. In narcotics arrests, various types of drugs are often found in cars, planes and boats. An ordinary vehicle has hundreds of places to hide drugs. In some cases, vehicles may have specially constructed compartments.

As with other types of searches, a vehicle search must be systematic and thorough. Evidence is more likely to be found if two officers conduct the search.

---

Remove occupants from the car. First search the area around the vehicle and then the exterior. Finally, search the interior along one side from front to back, and then return along the other side to the front.

---

Before entering a vehicle, search the area around it for evidence related to the crime. Next, examine the vehicle's exterior for fingerprints, dents, scratches or hairs and fibers. Examine the grill, front bumper, fender areas and license plates. Open the hood and check the numerous recesses of the motor, radiator, battery, battery case, engine block, clutch and starter housings, ventilating ducts, air filter, body frame and supports. Open the trunk and examine any clothing, rags, containers, tools, the spare-tire well and the interior of the trunk lid.

Finally, search the vehicle's interior, following the same procedures used in searching a room. Vacuum the car before getting into it. Package collections from different areas of the car separately. Then systematically examine ashtrays, the glove compartment, areas under the seats and the window areas. Remove the seats and vacuum the floor. Hairs and fibers or traces of soil may be discovered that will connect the suspect with soil samples from the crime scene.

Use a flashlight and a mirror to examine the area behind the dashboard. Feeling by hand is not effective because of the numerous wires located there.

Look for fingerprints in the obvious places: window and door handles, underside of the steering wheel, radio buttons, ashtrays, distributor cap, jack, rearview mirror, hood latches and seat adjustment lever.

Figure 4–7 illustrates the areas of vehicles that should be searched. The vehicle is divided into specific search areas to ensure order and thoroughness. As in any other search, take precautions to prevent contaminating evidence.

The searcher must also be alert to what is an original part of the vehicle and what has been added. For example, compartments for concealing illegal drugs or other contraband are sometimes added. The systems and equipment of the vehicle should be validated. Is the exhaust real or phony? Check recesses and cup holders for sneaker flip panels that may contain contraband or weapons. Check the headliner. In convertibles, check the boot.

Blystone and Bodzak (1994, p. 97) cite the following cases related to warrantless searches of vehicles:

- *Belton v. New York* (1981). After a custodial arrest of an occupant of the vehicle, officers may conduct an *immediate* search of the vehicle, following the rule that the search is incident to arrest. The search must be limited to the passenger compartment and may be a general search without a specific object in mind. The search may include closed containers.
- *Florida v. Jimeno* (1991). A warrantless search may be made when consent is obtained from the owner or person in possession of the vehicle. The entire vehicle may be searched, including closed containers, unless the consentor has expressed limitation.
- *United States v. Ross* (1982). A search may be made when probable cause exists to believe that contraband or evidence is within the vehicle. This includes the trunk or closed containers in the vehicle.

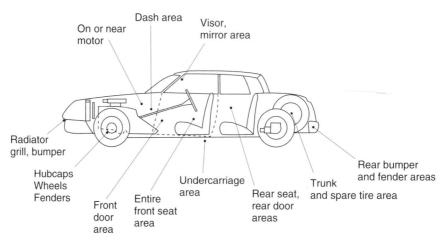

**Figure 4–7   Vehicle Areas That Should Be Searched**

■ *Florida v. Wells* (1990). The contents of a lawfully impounded vehicle may be inventoried for purposes of property accountability, public safety and protection against later claims of damage or loss of property.

■ *Texas v. Brown* (1983). Contraband or evidence in plain view may be confiscated. Two conditions must exist. The officer must be legally present and there must be probable cause to believe that the object in plain view is contraband or the instrumantality of a crime.

In *Alabama v. White* (1990) the Court ruled that if an anonymous tip received by the police had been confirmed before the search and consent to search was voluntarily provided, the search was legal. In this case the police received an anonymous tip about illegal transport of drugs, including a description of the driver and vehicle, when it would be leaving a specific address and where it was going to deliver the drugs which were contained in a brown attaché case. Police followed the car the entire route, thus confirming the credibility of the information. They stopped the vehicle and observed a brown attaché case and requested permission to search, which was voluntarily obtained. They found marijuana in the attaché case and cocaine in the driver's purse. The Alabama court ruled the evidence inadmissible for lack of reasonable suspicion based on the lack of credibility of an anonymous tip. The Supreme Court reversed this decision.

## Suspect Searches

How a suspect should be searched depends on whether you have arrested him or her.

---

If the suspect has not been arrested, confine your search to a patdown or frisk for weapons. If the suspect has been arrested, make a complete body search for weapons and evidence. In either event, always be on your guard.

---

If you have probable cause to stop or arrest a person, be cautious. Many officers are injured or killed because they fail to search a suspect. If you suspect that a person you have stopped for questioning may be armed, conduct a through-the-clothes patdown for weapons. Recall that the *Terry* decision prohibits searching for evidence in this situation. If you feel what may be a weapon, you may seize it.

If a suspect is in a car, have him or her step out of the car, being careful to protect yourself from a suddenly opened door.

On the other hand, if you arrest a suspect, conduct a complete body search for both weapons and evidence. Whether you use an against-the-wall spread-eagle search, a simple stand-up search or a search with all the suspect's clothes removed, follow a methodical, exact procedure. The complete body search often includes taking samples of hair and fingernail scrapings as well as testing for firearm residue when appropriate.

Regardless of whether an arrest has been made, respect the dignity of the suspect while you conduct the patdown or search, but do not let your guard down.

Smith (1993, p. 279) points out a trick that officers conducting searches of suspects should be aware of: the use of a device called a *tip*. The tip is molded to look exactly like a fingertip or a thumb tip and can be used to conceal any number of substances—drugs, written messages or bullets. Smith suggests:

*Balloons full of cocaine
found in a dog's abdomen
and removed.*

To effectively conduct a body search and rule out this form of smuggling, an officer must pinch and pull each finger tip—and especially the thumb.

Strip searches may be conducted only after an arrest and when the prisoner is in a secure facility. Strip searches require the removal of clothing at least down to the underwear. Such searches should be conducted by individuals of the same gender and in privacy, and they should follow written guidelines. All individuals being strip-searched must be treated in the same way regardless of age, gender and race. No comments should be made about the body of the person being searched. Considerations in deciding when a strip search is necessary include the individual's past behavior, the possibility that the person is concealing dangerous drugs or weapons, if the person will be alone or with others in a cell and how long the individual will be in custody. Summers (1991, p. 54) stresses that: "The courts will balance the privacy rights of the arrested individual with the legitimate needs of the agency conducting the search to determine whether it was reasonable."

Cavity searches go beyond the normal strip search and must follow very strict departmental guidelines. As noted by Summers (1991, p. 54): "This procedure is considered to be very intrusive by the courts, and thus receives increased scrutiny and requires greater justification than does a strip search." Normally such searches should be conducted by medical personnel.

The threat of contracting AIDS or hepatitis infections in the line of duty has led police to consider using special equipment when searching suspects—for example, rubber gloves, goggles and face masks. Use of such equipment reduces personal contact with blood and other body fluids, the main carriers of these viruses. Officers must also be alert to suspects who may spit on them or bite them. In reporting on a study of law enforcement officers' knowledge of AIDS, Yearwood (1992, p. 73) notes that: "An alarming 44 percent still thought saliva

**Table 4–1 Possible Transmission of the AIDS Virus**

| Issue Concern | Educational and Action Messages |
|---|---|
| Human bites | A person who bites usually receives the victim's blood; viral transmission through saliva is highly unlikely. If bitten by anyone, milk wound to make it bleed, wash the area thoroughly and seek medical attention. |
| Spitting | Viral transmission through saliva is highly unlikely. |
| Urine/feces | Virus has been isolated in only very low concentrations in urine; not at all in feces; no cases of AIDS or AIDS-virus infection have been associated with either urine or feces. |
| Cuts/puncture wounds | Use caution in handling sharp objects and searching areas hidden from view; needle stick studies show risk of infection is very low. |
| CPR/first aid | To eliminate the already minimal risk associated with CPR, use masks/airways; avoid blood-to-blood contact by keeping open wounds covered and wearing gloves when in contact with bleeding wounds. |
| Body removal | Observe the crime scene rule: Do not touch anything. Those who must come into contact with blood or other body fluids should wear gloves. |
| Casual contact | No cases of AIDS or AIDS-virus infection have been attributed to casual contact. |
| Any contact with blood or body fluids | Wear gloves if contact with blood or body fluids is considered likely. If contact occurs, wash thoroughly with soap and water, clean up spills with one part water to nine parts household bleach. |
| Contact with dried blood | No cases of infection have been traced to exposure to dried blood. The drying process appears to inactivate the virus. Despite low risk, however, caution dictates wearing gloves, a mask and protective shoe coverings if exposure to dried blood particles is likely (e.g., crime scene investigation). |

SOURCE: U.S. Department of Justice, *National Institute of Justice Reports*, December 1987.

and tears were capable of transmitting the virus." As shown in Table 4–1, this is highly unlikely.

According to *AIDS and Lab Procedures for HIV Blood Tests*, by Group Health, Inc. (1992, pp. 2–3), the AIDS virus lives in several fluids contained in the body but is transmitted only through blood, semen and vaginal fluids. People become infected with HIV in one of two main ways:

- Having sexual intercourse—anal, vaginal or oral—with an infected person.
- Sharing drug needles or syringes with an infected person.

When searching, officers should avoid putting their hands into suspects' pockets. They should use patting, rather than grabbing, motions to avoid being stuck by sharp objects such as hypodermic needles. Techniques for collecting evidence that might be contaminated with the AIDS virus are discussed in the next chapter.

## Dead Body Searches

Searching a dead body is unpleasant, even when the person has died recently. It is extremely unpleasant if the person has been dead for a long period. In some such cases, the body can be searched only in the coroner's examination room, where effective exhaust ventilation is available.

Search a dead body systematically and completely. Include the immediate area around and under the body.

The search usually begins with the clothing, which is likely to reveal a wallet or personal identification papers as well as trace evidence. If the body is not fingerprinted at the scene, tie paper bags securely on the hands so that fingerprinting can be done at the coroner's laboratory. If possible, place the body in a body bag to ensure that no physical evidence is lost while it is being transported.

Search the area around and beneath the body immediately after it is removed. A bullet may have passed through part of the body and lodged in the floor or the dirt beneath it. Trace evidence may have fallen from the body or clothing as the body was removed. Inventory and describe all items removed from the deceased.

Department policy determines the extent of the search at the scene. Normally, a complete examination is delayed until the body is received by the coroner's officer. The coroner may take fingernail scrapings, blood and semen samples and possibly some body organs to establish poisoning or the path of a bullet or knife.

Once the body is taken to the funeral home, its organs and fluids will be contaminated by preparation for the burial. Once the body is buried, it is a long, difficult legal process to exhume it for further examination. If the body is cremated, obviously no further examination is possible.

## Use of Dogs in a Search

Because of their acute sense of smell, dogs can be trained to track and locate suspects as well as to detect certain evidence such as explosives and narcotics. Using dogs for such purposes lessens the physical risk to investigating officers.

Dogs can be trained to locate suspects, narcotics and explosives.

Dogs are ideally suited to assist in searching large areas, areas where visibility is poor, areas such as warehouses that may contain thousands of items or any area with numerous hiding places. According to a Michigan study for the city of Lansing reported by Spurlock (1990, p. 91):

> A single K-9 team was able to complete building searches seven times faster than four officers working together to search the same building. And while the dog team found the hidden suspects 93% of the time, the human officers found [them] only 59%. This kind of efficiency and savings in man hours for building searches alone should make any law enforcement administrator take a long, hard look at employing a K-9 program.

Using dogs to sniff out narcotics has been widely publicized. Because narcotics can be concealed in so many different ways, using dogs to locate them has greatly assisted law enforcement officers. Attempts to "mask" drug odors from dogs trained to sniff out drugs are futile because dogs can smell more than one odor simultaneously.

Dogs have also been trained to detect explosives both before and after detonation. Their ability to detect explosives before detonation lessens the risk to officers and can help prevent crimes. A study by the Law Enforcement Assistance

*Specially trained K-9s can be invaluable in searching for drugs. They are often used for inspections conducted at border checkpoints.*

Administration and the Federal Aviation Authority demonstrated that dogs can locate explosives twice as often as a human can. In the case of detonated explosives, dogs have helped locate bomb fragments hidden under piles of debris and at considerable distances from the detonation point.

As agents of the police, dogs are subject to the same legal limitations on searches that officers are. If a police department is not large enough or lacks sufficient need for a search dog and trained handler, learn where the nearest trained search dogs are and how they can be obtained if needed. Many major airports have dogs trained to locate explosives and may make these dogs available to police upon request.

Baratta (1995, p. 23) cites the following results of using K–9s in 1993:

■ Narcotics dogs were involved in more than 17,000 cases, helped confiscate or destroy over 54 million kg of dagga (cannabis) and assisted in more than 6,000 arrests.
■ Explosives dogs attended nearly 2,000 bomb threats and found explosives in 290 cases.
■ Handlers with tracker dogs made nearly 3,000 arrests and recovered lost or stolen property worth $3 million.

## Summary

The Fourth Amendment to the Constitution forbids "unreasonable" searches and seizures. Therefore, investigators must know what constitutes a reasonable, legal search. To search effectively, know the legal requirements for searching, the items being searched for and the elements of the crime. Be organized, systematic and thorough.

A search can be justified if (1) a search warrant has been issued, (2) consent is given, (3) the search is incidental to a lawful arrest or (4) an emergency exists. Each of these four situations has limitations. A search conducted with a warrant must be limited to the area and items specified in the warrant. A search conducted with consent requires that the consent be voluntary and that the search be limited to the area for which the consent was given. A search incidental to a lawful arrest must be made simultaneously with the arrest and be confined to the area within the suspect's immediate control *(Chimel)*. A warrantless search in the absence of a lawful arrest or consent is justified only in emergencies where probable cause exists and the search must be conducted immediately. The *Terry* decision established that a patdown or frisk is a "protective search for weapons" and as such, must be "confined to a scope reasonably designed to discover guns, knives, clubs, and other hidden instruments for the assault of a police officer or others."

Vehicles may be searched without a warrant if there is probable cause and if the vehicle would be gone before a search warrant could be obtained *(Carroll)*. *Chambers v. Maroney* established that a vehicle may be taken to headquarters to be searched in certain circumstances.

The most important limitation on any search is that the scope must be narrowed; general searches are unconstitutional. However, plain view evidence— unconcealed evidence seen by an officer engaged in a lawful activity—may be seized and is admissible in court.

If a search is not conducted legally, the evidence obtained is worthless. According to the exclusionary rule, evidence obtained in unreasonable search and seizure, regardless of how relevant the evidence may be, is inadmissible in court. *Weeks v. United States* established the exclusionary rule at the federal level; *Mapp v. Ohio* made it applicable to all courts.

The fruit of the poisonous tree doctrine established that evidence obtained as a result of an earlier illegality must be excluded from trial. Two important exceptions to the exclusionary rule are the inevitable discovery doctrine and the good faith doctrine. The inevitable discovery doctrine states that if the illegally obtained evidence would in all likelihood eventually have been discovered anyway, it may be used. The good faith doctrine states that illegally obtained evidence may be admitted into trial if the police were truly unaware that they were violating the suspect's Fourth Amendment rights.

A successful crime-scene search locates, identifies and preserves all evidence present. For maximum effectiveness, the search must be well organized. This entails dividing the duties, selecting a search pattern, assigning personnel and equipment and giving instructions. Knowing what to search for is indispensable to an effective search. Anything material and relevant to the crime might be evidence.

Search patterns have been developed that help to ensure a thorough search. Exterior search patterns divide an area into lanes, strips, concentric circles or zones. Interior searches go from the general to the specific, usually in a circular pattern that covers all surfaces of the area being searched. The floor is searched first.

In addition to crime scenes, investigators frequently search vehicles, suspects and dead bodies. When searching a vehicle, remove the occupants from the car. First search the area around the vehicle, then the vehicle's exterior. Finally, search the interior along one side from front to back, and then return along the other side to the front.

Larson (1989, p. 16) reports that police in Orange County, California, are using portable lasers at scenes of major crimes to find and highlight fingerprints. The lasers can even detect fingerprints on the skin of murder victims. Another use of lasers at crime scenes is to trace the path of gunshots.

In addition to lasers, investigators now have available to them gelatin lifters that can lift dusted prints or dust marks (footprints) from a wide variety of surfaces. Used in Europe for decades, the lifters are flexible and easily cut to suit specific needs. They can lift dust prints from any smooth surface, from tile floors to cardboard boxes. The high contrast of the black lifters allows investigators to see dust prints not visible to the naked eye, and the lifted prints photograph extremely well. In addition, the lifters can pick up particle samples such as hair or paint chips. The samples can be removed from the lifter in the laboratory with tweezers or a scalpel without damaging the sampled material.

Another advance reported by Larson is the use of proton magnetometers, devices that sense subtle changes in the earth's magnetic field, in hunting for buried bodies. They are also used by archaeologists to look for ancient burial sites (p. 18).

When searching a suspect who has not been arrested, confine the search to a patdown for weapons *(Terry)*. If the suspect has been arrested, conduct a complete body search for weapons and evidence. In either event, always be on your guard.

Search a dead body systematically and completely; include the immediate area around and under the body.

Specially trained dogs can be very helpful in locating suspects, narcotics or explosives.

## Checklist

### *The Search*

- Is the search legal?
- Was a pattern followed?
- Was all evidence photographed, recorded in the notes, identified and packaged properly?
- Was the search completed even if evidence was found early in the search?
- Were all suspects searched?
- Did more than one investigator search?
- Was plain view evidence seized? If so, were the circumstances recorded?

## Discussion Questions

**1.** What might the officers who arrested Ted Chimel have done differently to ensure that the evidence they obtained would be admissible in court?

**2.** What are the advantages of having several officers search a crime scene? What are the disadvantages?

**3.** What are the steps in obtaining a search warrant?

**4.** What procedure is best for searching a suspect?

**5.** Many court decisions regarding police involve the question of legal searches. What factors are considered in the legal search of a person, a private dwelling, abandoned property, a business building, a car, corporate offices?

**6.** What basic steps constitute a thorough search of a dwelling?

**7.** Should there be legal provisions for an officer to seize evidence without a warrant if the evidence may be destroyed or removed before a warrant can be obtained?

**8.** Under what circumstances are police authorized to conduct no-knock searches?

**9.** Imagine that you are assigned to search a tavern at 2000 hours for illegal gambling devices. Twenty patrons plus the bartender are in the tavern, but the owner is not present. How would you execute the search warrant?

**10.** Police officers frequently stop vehicles for traffic violations. Under the plain view doctrine, what evidence may be taken during such a stop? May the officers search the vehicle? The driver? The occupants?

# References

*AIDS and Lab Procedures for HIV Blood Tests.* Minneapolis, MN: Group Health, Inc., 1992.

Baratta, Rick. "K–9s: Trained to Excel." *Law and Order,* April 1995, pp. 20–25.

Blystone, David A., and Andrew Bodzak. "Warrantless Searches of Vehicles." *Law and Order,* March 1994, pp. 97–98.

Bruce, Theodore A. "The Ten Exceptions to the Search Warrant Requirements." *Law and Order,* October 1990, pp. 100–108.

Griffith, James Andrew. "The 'Open Fields' Doctrine." *Law and Order,* August 1996, pp. 94–96.

Hawley, Donna Lea. "Searching within Fourth Amendment Boundaries." *Police,* August 1996, pp. 24–26.

Larson, Eric. "Getting Away with Murder." *Omni,* September/October 1989, pp. 14–22.

"Pat-down Searches." *NCJA Justice Bulletin,* June 1993, p. 7.

Smith, Lawrence. "The Magic Trick Every Cop Needs to Know." *Law and Order,* January 1993, p. 279.

Spurlock, James C. "K–9." *Law and Order,* March 1990, pp. 91–96.

Summers, William C. "Conducting Strip Searches." *The Police Chief,* May 1991, pp. 54–56.

Yearwood, Douglas L. "Law Enforcement and AIDS: Knowledge, Attitudes, and Fears in the Workplace." *American Journal of Police,* Vol. 11, No. 2 (1992), pp. 65–83.

# Physical Evidence

## DO YOU KNOW

What corpus delicti and associative evidence are?

What is involved in processing physical evidence?

How to determine what is evidence?

What a standard of comparison is and how it is used?

What common errors in collecting evidence are?

How to identify evidence?

What to record in your notes?

How to package evidence?

How to convey evidence to the department or the laboratory?

What types of evidence are most commonly found in criminal investigations and how to collect, identify and package each?

What can and cannot be determined from fingerprints, hairs and bloodstains?

What constitutes "best evidence"?

What DNA profiling is?

How and where evidence is stored?

How to ensure admissibility of physical evidence in court?

How physical evidence is finally disposed of?

## CAN YOU DEFINE

| | | |
|---|---|---|
| associative evidence | DNA | physical evidence |
| automated fingerprint identification system (AFIS) | DNA profiling | plastic fingerprints |
| | elimination prints | prima facie evidence |
| | evidence | probative evidence |
| barcodes | exculpatory evidence | processing evidence |
| biometrics | genetic fingerprint | relevant evidence |
| cast | identifying features | spectrographic analysis |
| chain of evidence | individual | standard of comparison |
| circumstantial evidence | characteristics | toolmark |
| class characteristics | inkless fingerprints | trace evidence |
| competent evidence | integrity of evidence | ultraviolet light |
| corpus delicti | invisible fingerprints | visible fingerprints |
| corpus delicti evidence | latent fingerprints | voiceprint |
| direct evidence | material evidence | X-ray diffraction |

## Introduction

A PRIMARY PURPOSE OF AN INVESTIGATION IS TO LOCATE, IDENTIFY AND preserve **evidence** for determining the facts in a case, for later laboratory examination and for direct presentation in court.

Pilant (1994, p. 48) suggests:

> Forensic science, or more specifically, criminalistics, is one of the few areas of law enforcement where science and crime meet. It is vastly different from the domain inhabited by the detective assigned to the crime scene. Criminalistics

moves from the messy and often emotional crime scene area and into the sterile environs of the crime laboratory.

This chapter begins with a discussion of investigative equipment. Next, the chapter describes how to discover, recognize and examine evidence; how to collect, mark and identify evidence; how to package and preserve evidence and how to transport it. This is followed by a discussion of frequently examined evidence, evidence handling and infectious disease and DNA profiling. The chapter concludes with discussion of protecting and storing evidence, presenting it in court and determining how to dispose of it when no longer needed.

## Definitions

**Physical evidence** is anything real—it has substance—that helps to establish the facts of a case. It can be seen, touched, smelled or tasted; solid, semi-solid or liquid; large or tiny. It may be at the immediate crime scene or miles away; on the suspect or the victim. "Physical evidence, when it is properly collected, marked, and preserved, does not have memory lapses, cannot lie or be corrupted and cannot be impeached" (Pilant, 1992, p. 42).

Some evidence ties one crime to a similar crime or connects one suspect with another. Evidence can also provide new leads when a case appears to be at a dead end. Further, evidence corroborates statements from witnesses to or victims of a crime. Convictions are not achieved from statements, admissions or confessions alone. The crime must be proved by independent investigation and physical evidence.

For example, in a small western town, a six-year-old girl and her parents stated to police that the girl had been sexually molested. The girl told police that a man had taken her to the desert, showed her some "naughty" pictures that he burned and then molested her. Because it was difficult for the police to rely on the girl's statement, they needed physical evidence to corroborate her story. Fortunately, the girl remembered where the man had taken her and led the police there. They found remains of the burned pictures and confiscated them as evidence. The remains of one picture, showing the suspect with a naked young girl on his lap, were sufficient to identify him by the rings on his fingers. This physical evidence supporting the girl's testimony resulted in a charge of lewdness with a minor.

Evidence can be classified in many ways. Extremely small items, such as hair or fibers, are called **trace evidence. Direct evidence** establishes proof of a fact without any other evidence. Evidence established by law is called **prima facie evidence.** For example, 0.1 percent ethanol in the blood is direct or prima facie evidence of intoxication in some states. Evidence that merely tends to incriminate a person, such as a suspect's footprints found near the crime scene, is called **circumstantial evidence.** A popular myth is that circumstantial evidence will not stand alone without other facts to support it, but many convictions have been obtained primarily on circumstantial evidence.

Also of extreme importance to the investigator is **exculpatory evidence,** that is physical evidence that would clear one of blame, for example, having a blood type different from that of blood found at a murder scene.

Two commonly used classifications for evidence are corpus delicti and associative evidence.

**Corpus delicti evidence** establishes that a crime has been committed.
**Associative evidence** links a suspect with the crime.

Contrary to popular belief, the **corpus delicti** in a murder case is not the victim's body but the fact that death occurred as the result of a criminal act. Corpus delicti evidence supports the elements of the crime. Pry marks on an entry door are corpus delicti evidence in a burglary. Associative evidence includes fingerprints, footprints, bloodstains, hairs and fibers.

Finding physical evidence is not enough. To be of value, the evidence must be legally seized and properly and legally processed.

Processing physical evidence includes discovering, recognizing and examining it; collecting, recording and identifying it; packaging, conveying and storing it; exhibiting it in court; and disposing of it when the case is closed.

Before looking at processing a crime scene, consider the basic equipment that may be needed.

## Investigative Equipment

Frontline police personnel who conduct the preliminary investigation need specific equipment to accomplish their assigned tasks. Although not all crime scenes require all items of equipment, you cannot predict the nature of the next committed crime or the equipment that will be needed. Therefore, you should have available at all times a crime-scene investigation kit containing basic equipment. Check the kit's equipment after each use, replacing items as required.

Investigations can be simple or complex and can reveal little or much physical evidence. Consequently, the equipment needs of each investigation are different. The list in Table 5–1, alphabetized for easy reference, contains the investigative equipment most often used. The starred items have been discussed previously in earlier chapters.

Although the list in the table may seem extensive, numerous other items are also often used in investigations: bags, binoculars, blankets, brushes, bullhorns, cable, capsules, chains, checklists, chemicals, chisels, coat hangers (to hang up wet or bloodstained clothing), combs, cotton, cutters, directories, drug kits, eyedroppers, files, fixatives, flares or fuses, floodlamps, forceps, forms, gas masks, generators, gloves, guns, hammers, hatchets, levels, lights, magnets, manuals, maps, matches, metal detectors, moulages (for making impressions or casts), nails, padlocks, pails, plastic sheets, punches, putty, rags, receipts, rubber, saws, scrapers, shovels, sidecutters, solvent, sponges, sprays, stamps, swabs, syringes, tape, tape recorders, thermometers, tin snips, towels, transceivers (to communicate in large buildings, warehouses, apartment complexes or open areas), vacuums, wax, wire and wrenches. The blood test kits, gun-residue kits and other field test kits described in Chapter 1 are also used.

Newer, more specialized equipment for investigation may also include pagers, cellular phones, latex gloves, goggles, electronic tracking systems, camcorders and much more, as will be discussed throughout this section. Many departments are able to use forfeiture assets confiscated during drug busts to purchase specialized investigative equipment.

**Table 5–1  Equipment for Processing Evidence**

| Item | Uses |
|---|---|
| Cameras and film* | (Whatever type is available; perhaps several types) To photograph scene and evidence |
| Chalk and chalk line | To mark off search areas; to outline bodies or objects removed from the scene |
| Compass* | To obtain directions for report orientation and searches |
| Containers | (Boxes, bags of all sizes and shapes; lightweight; plastic or paper; telescoping or collapsible; glass bottles and new paint containers) To contain all types of evidence |
| Crayon or magic marker | To mark evidence |
| Envelopes, all sizes | To collect evidence |
| Fingerprint kit | (Various developing powders, fingerprint camera, fingerprint cards, ink pads, spoons, iodine fumer tube, lifting tape) To develop latent fingerprints |
| First-aid kit | To treat injured persons at the crime scene |
| Flashlight and batteries | To search dark areas, such as tunnels, holes, wells, windowless rooms; to search for latent fingerprints |
| Knife | To cut ropes, string, stakes, etc. |
| Labels, all sizes | (Evidence labels; labels such as "do not touch," "do not open," "handle with care," "fragile") To label evidence and to provide directions |
| Magnifier | To locate fingerprints and minute evidence |
| Measuring tape, steel | To measure long distances |
| Mirror with collapsible handle | To look in out-of-the-way locations for evidence |
| Money | To pay fares in case of vehicle failure, to tip, to purchase small amounts of needed supplies |
| Notebook* | To record information |
| Paper* | (Notebook, graph, scratch pads, wrapping) To take notes, sketch scene, wrap evidence |

Additional heavy-duty, less-portable equipment such as large pry bars or long ladders are frequently contained on fire and rescue vehicles and can be used jointly by the police and fire department.

### Considerations in Selecting Equipment

Survey the types of crimes and evidence most frequently found at crime scenes in your locality. Select equipment to process and preserve the evidence most likely to be encountered. For example, because fingerprints are often found at crime scenes, fingerprint processing equipment should be included in the basic kit. However, you would probably not need to take a shovel along to investigate a rape.

After the basic equipment needs are identified, select specific equipment. Select equipment that is frequently needed, lightweight, compact, high quality, versatile and reasonably priced. For example, boxes should either nest or be collapsible. Containers should be lightweight and plastic. The lighter and smaller the equipment, the more items can be carried in the kit. Consider miniaturized electronic equipment, rather than heavier, battery-operated items. Give preference to equipment that accomplishes more than one function such as a knife with many features or other multiple-purpose tools.

**Table 5-1** (continued)

**139**

Chapter 5

**Physical Evidence**

| Item | Uses |
|------|------|
| Pencils* | (At least two; sharpened) To make sketches |
| Pens* | (At least two; nonsmudge type) To take notes, make sketches |
| Picks | (Door lock picks and ice picks) To use as thumbtacks; to hold one end of a rope or tape |
| Plaster | To make casts of tire treads and footprints |
| Pliers | To pry and twist; to obtain evidence |
| Protractor | To measure angles |
| Rope | (Fluorescent, lightweight, approximately 300 feet) To protect the crime scene |
| Ruler, carpenter-type* | To measure short distances |
| Ruler, straightedge* | To measure small items/distances |
| Scissors | To cut tapes, reproduce size of objects in paper, cut first-aid gauze |
| Screwdrivers, standard and Phillips | To turn and pry |
| Scribe | To mark metal objects for evidence |
| Sketching supplies* | (Ruler, pencil, graph paper, etc.) To make sketches |
| Spatula | To dig; to stir |
| String | To tie objects and boxes containing evidence; to protect the crime scene; to mark off search areas |
| Tags | To attach to items of evidence |
| Templates | To aid in sketching |
| Tongue depressors, wooden | To stir; to add reinforcements to plaster casts; to make side forms for casting; to lift objects without touching them |
| Tubes, glass, with stoppers | To contain evidence |
| Tweezers | To pick up evidence without contamination |
| Wrecking bar | To pry open doors, windows, entryways or exits |

*The use of these items has been discussed earlier in the book.

### Equipment Containers or Kits

The equipment can be put in one container or divided into several containers, based on frequency of use. This is an administrative decision based on each department's needs. Dividing equipment results in a compact, lightweight kit suitable for most crime scenes while ensuring availability of other equipment needed to investigate less common cases. The container or kit must be lightweight, large enough to hold the required equipment and transportable.

Carriers or containers come in all shapes, sizes, colors and designs. Briefcases, attaché cases and transparent plastic bags are often used. Some commercially produced kits include basic equipment. However, many departments prefer to design their own kits, adapting them to their specific needs.

The kit should be small and light enough so that it can be easily transported to and at the scene. The container should look professional, and a list of its contents should be attached to the outside or inside the cover.

### Transporting the Equipment

Crime-scene investigative equipment is transported in a police vehicle, an investigator's vehicle or a crime van. The equipment can be transported in the

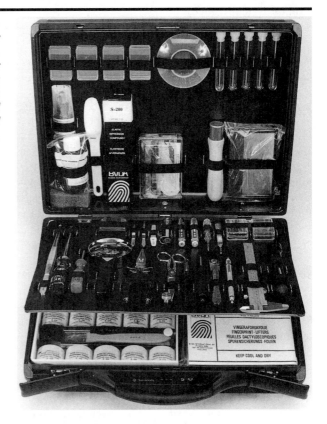

*This all-purpose investigation kit was designed for general crime investigation. It contains materials for lifting and developing fingerprints along with a variety of specialized tools for gathering and storing evidence.*

trunk of a car, or a vehicle can be modified to carry it. For example, special racks can be put in the trunk, or the rear seat can be removed and special racks installed.

A mobile crime lab is usually a commercially customized van that provides compartments to hold equipment and countertops for processing evidence. However, a van cannot go directly to some crime scenes, so the equipment must be transported from the van in other containers. The most frequently used equipment should be in the most accessible locations in the vehicle. Substances that freeze or change consistency in temperature extremes should be protected.

All selected vehicles should be equipped with radio communication and be capable of conveying equipment to disaster scenes as well as to crime scenes—to make them cost-effective. Cost-effectiveness can be further enhanced if the vehicles are made available as command posts, for stakeouts and as personnel carriers.

Regardless of whether you work with a fully equipped mobile crime laboratory or only a small, portable crime-scene investigation kit, your knowledge and skills as an investigator are indispensible to a successful investigation. The most sophisticated, expensive investigative equipment available is only as effective as you are in using it.

### Training in Equipment Use

The largest failure in gathering evidence is not that the equipment is not available but that personnel lack the training to use it effectively. Photographic equipment, for example, need not be highly complex to obtain satisfactory pictures, but basic information is required to take effective pictures. It is important that each officer understand the use and operation of each item of equipment in the kit. Expertise comes with training and experience. Periodic refresher sessions should be held as needed to update personnel on techniques, new equipment, new products, changes in equipment and new administrative decisions regarding investigative equipment.

Review police publications for new equipment and techniques developed by other police departments and laboratories. Make suggestions about other types of equipment that would make investigation more efficient and effective. Those at the crime scene are best qualified to make constructive suggestions for changes in crime-scene investigation equipment.

The first steps in **processing evidence** are discussed next.

## Discovering, Recognizing and Examining Evidence

The importance of legal searches and seizures has been discussed, as has the fact that evidence must be **material**, **relevant** and **competent**. Specific procedures for presenting evidence and testifying in court are discussed in Chapter 20. Of importance at this point is recognizing evidence and then processing it properly.

During the search of a crime scene, it is often difficult to determine immediately what is or might be evidence. Numerous objects are present, and obviously not all are evidence.

---

To determine what is evidence, consider first the type of crime that appears to have been committed. Then look for any objects that are unrelated or foreign to the scene, that are unusual in location or number, that have been damaged or broken or whose relation to other objects suggests a pattern that fits the crime.

---

The relative importance of physical evidence depends on its ability to establish that a crime was committed and to show how, when and by whom it was done. Logic and experience help the investigator to determine the value of physical evidence. Some kinds of evidence are more valuable than others. For example, evidence in its original state is more valuable than evidence that has been altered or damaged.

Probabilities play a large role in determining the value of evidence. Fingerprints, for example, provide positive identification because the probability of two people having the same fingerprints is almost zero. In contrast, blood type does *not* provide positive identification, but it can help eliminate a person as a suspect.

An object's individuality is also extremely important. For example, a heel mark's value is directly proportional to the number of its specific features, such as brand name, number of nails and individual wear patterns that can be identified. Some objects have identification marks on them. Other evidence requires a *comparison* to be of value—a tire impression matching a tire, a bullet matching a specific revolver, a torn piece of clothing matching a shirt.

---

A **standard of comparison** is an object, measure or model with which evidence is compared to determine whether both came from the same source.

---

Fingerprints are the most familiar example of evidence requiring a standard of comparison. A fingerprint found at a crime scene must be matched with a known print to be of value. Likewise, a piece of glass found in a suspect's coat pocket can be compared with glass collected from a window pane broken during a burglary.

Sometimes, how an object fits with the surroundings determines whether it is likely to be evidence. For example, a man's handkerchief found in a women's locker room does not fit. The same handkerchief in a men's locker room is less likely to be evidence.

The value of evidence is affected by what happens to it after it is found. Make sure evidence does not lose its value—its **integrity**—because of improper handling or identification.

### Using Forensic Light Sources

Hoober (1994, p. 103) explains how forensic light sources work:

Many of the things that are invisible to the naked eye are evidence: latent prints, bodily fluids, even altered signatures. That is why UV lights, lasers and other forensic light sources—along with special fluorescent powders for fingerprints and other accessories—have become popular in recent years. . . .

Evidence that fluoresces, or glows, is easier to see—sometimes thousands of times easier. For some kinds of hard-to-see evidence—small amounts of semen, for instance, or fibers—a forensic light source is the only practical way to make the invisible visible.

Pilant (1992) describes the Polilight, which uses several filters and six bands of light to detect latent prints on nearly any surface after other methods have failed. She writes (p. 46): "[T]his portable, tunable device also can be used to decipher erased or altered documents. Using various filters, goggles and light bands, the Polilight can cut through almost any type of alteration to reveal the original writing underneath."

## Collecting, Marking and Identifying Evidence

How evidence is collected directly influences its later value. Remember to photograph and sketch before collecting evidence. Collect and identify all objects that are or may be evidence, leaving the final decision regarding relevance to the prosecuting staff. In deciding what might be useful to collect, it also helps to know the types of analyses crime laboratories can perform.

Collecting evidence requires judgment and care. Put liquids in bottles. Protect cartridges and spent bullets with cotton, and put them in small containers. Put other items in appropriate containers to preserve them for later packaging and transporting.

Use small, versatile tools for collecting evidence. Ideally, each tool can be used in performing several tasks. Extreme care must be taken to avoid cross-contamination. A claim of cross-contamination was one of the key defenses in the O.J. Simpson trial. When using the same tool for several tasks, be certain that it is thoroughly cleaned between each use.

Consider easy replacement and assembly as well as cost in selecting tools. Suggested collection equipment includes tape, knives, labels, containers, a flashlight, wrench, pick, hatchet and screwdriver. (Refer again to Table 5–1.) The scene of a violent crime should be vacuumed with a machine that has a filter attachment. The vacuumed material can then be placed in an evidence bag and submitted to the crime laboratory.

---

Common errors in collecting evidence are (1) not collecting enough of the sample, (2) not obtaining standards of comparison and (3) not maintaining the integrity of the evidence.

---

To simplify testimony in court, one officer usually collects evidence and another officer takes notes on the location, description and condition of each item. The officer collecting evidence enters this information in personal notes or witnesses and initials the notes of the officer assigned to record information. All evidence is identified by the officer who collects it and by any other officer who takes initial custody of it.

---

Mark or identify each item of evidence in a way that can be recognized later. Indicate the date and case number as well as your personal identifying mark or initials.

---

Make your marking easily recognizable and as small as possible—to reduce the possibility of destroying part of the evidence.

Mark all evidence as it is collected or received. Do not alter, change or destroy evidence or reduce its value by the identification marking. Where and how to mark depends on the item. A pen is suitable for some objects. A stylus is used for those that require a more permanent mark that cannot be marked with pen, such as metal boxes, motor parts and furniture. Other objects can be tagged, labeled or placed in containers that are then marked and sealed.

---

Record in your notes the date and time of collection, where the evidence was found and by whom, the case number, a description of the item and who took custody of it.

---

Evidence descriptions can be computer-entered and cross-referenced to current cases in the local jurisdiction and those in the surrounding area.

## Packaging and Preserving Evidence

Careful packaging maintains the evidence in its original state, preventing damage or contamination. Do not mix, or *cross-contaminate,* evidence. Each type of evidence has specific requirements. Some evidence is placed in sterile containers. Other types, such as firing-pin impressions or markings on a fatal bullet, are packed to prevent breakage or wrapped in cotton to prevent damage to individual characteristics. Hairs, fibers and other trace evidence are often placed in paper that is folded so that the evidence cannot fall out. This is called a *druggist fold* (see Figure 5–1).

---

Package each item separately in a durable container to maintain the **integrity of evidence.**

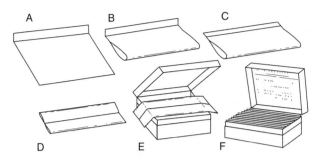

**Figure 5-1    The Druggist Fold**

Packaging is extremely important. Although some authorities recommend the use of plastic bags, few large departments use plastic because it does not "breathe" and hence may cause condensation to form. This can impede the laboratory examination of the evidence. Many departments use new brown-paper grocery bags, especially for clothing. Whereas boxes might be better, they can be impractical to carry and difficult to find. There is usually a supermarket open somewhere if you run out of bags. A means of sealing whatever type of bag is used should be provided to maintain the integrity of the evidence.

Preserve evidence on immovable items at the scene. Often some reproduction of the evidence is made. Fingerprints are developed, photographed, lifted and later compared. Toolmarks are reproduced through photography, modeling clay, moulage, silicone and other impression-making materials. (These methods are acceptable in accordance with the best-evidence rule.) Specific requirements for the most frequently found evidence and best evidence are discussed later.

Submit movable items directly into evidence or send them to a laboratory for analysis. Sometimes an object is both evidence and container of evidence. For example, a stolen radio found in a suspect's car is evidence of theft, and the fingerprints of a second suspect found on the radio are evidence that links that person to the theft.

Before packaging evidence for mailing to a laboratory, make sure it was legally obtained, has been properly identified and is recorded in your notes. Submitting inadmissible evidence is costly and takes time that could be used for valid examinations. Pack any bulky item in a sturdy box, seal the box with tape and mark it "evidence." State if there is any latent evidence such as fingerprints on the surface of the object (see Figure 5-2).

Place a transmittal letter to the laboratory in an envelope attached to the outside of the box. This letter should contain the name of the suspect and of the victim, if any; tell what examinations are desired and which tests, if any, have already been done; and refer to any other correspondence or reports. Include a copy of the letter with the evidence, and mail the original separately. Retain a copy for your files. A sample letter is given in Figure 5-3.

## Transporting Evidence

If the crime laboratory is nearby, evidence can be delivered personally. However, even if the evidence is personally delivered, include with it a letter on department letterhead or a department form.

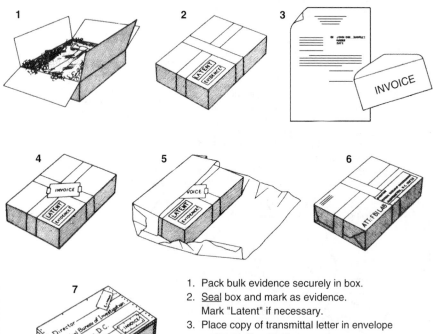

### FEDERAL BUREAU OF INVESTIGATION
### UNITED STATES DEPARTMENT OF JUSTICE

**Proper Sealing of Evidence**

The method shown below permits access to the invoice letter without breaking the inner seal. This allows the person entitled to receive the evidence to receive it in a sealed condition just as it was packed by the sender.

1. Pack bulk evidence securely in box.
2. <u>Seal</u> box and mark as evidence. Mark "Latent" if necessary.
3. Place copy of transmittal letter in envelope and mark "Invoice."
4. Stick envelope to <u>outside</u> of sealed box.
5. Wrap sealed box in outside wrapper and <u>seal</u> with gummed paper.
6. Address to Director / Federal Bureau of Investigation / Washington, D. C. 20535 and mark "Attention FBI Laboratory."
7. If packing box is wooden—tack invoice envelope to top under a clear plastic cover.

**Figure 5–2    Proper Sealing of Evidence**

Source: Courtesy of the FBI.

---

Personal delivery, registered mail, insured parcel post, air express, Federal Express and United Parcel Service are legal ways to transport evidence. Always specify that the person receiving the evidence is to sign for it.

---

How evidence should be transported depends on its size and type and the distance involved. Use the fastest method available. If the package is mailed, a "return receipt" should be requested.

USE OFFICIAL LETTERHEAD

( Police Headquarters
Right City, State zip code
March 17, 19-- )

Director
Federal Bureau of Investigation
U. S. Department of Justice
Washington, D. C. 20535

ATTENTION: FBI LABORATORY

Dear Director:

RE:  GUY PIDGIN, SUSPECT
EMPALL MERCHANDISE MART
BURGLARY

Sometime during the early morning of March 16, 19-- someone entered the Empall Merchandise Mart through an unlocked side window and made an unsuccessful attempt to rip open the safe. The outer layer of metal on the safe door had been pried loose from the upper right corner and bent outward, ripping the metal along the top and down the side of the safe about 12" each way. The burglar may have been scared away because the job was not completed. Investigation led us to Guy Pidgin, who denies complicity. He voluntarily let us take his shoes and trousers and a crowbar that was under his bed in his rooming house.

I am sending by Federal Express a package containing the following evidence in this case:

1. One pair of shoes obtained from Guy Pidgin
2. A pair of grey flannel trousers obtained from Guy Pidgin
3. One 28" crowbar obtained from Guy Pidgin
4. Safe insulation taken from door of safe at Empall Merchandise Mart
5. Piece of bent metal approximately 12" x 12" taken from door of safe at Empall Merchandise Mart. In order to differentiate the two sides cut by us, we have placed adhesive tape on them.
6. Chips of paint taken from the side of safe
7. Fingerprint card for Guy Pidgin
8. Ten transparent lifts

Please examine the shoes and trousers for safe insulation or any paint chips that match the paint taken from the safe. Also, we would be interested to know if you can determine if the crowbar was used to open the safe. Examine items 5 and 8 to determine if latent fingerprints are present. If present, compare with item 7.

This evidence, which should be returned to us, has not been examined by any other expert.

Very truly yours,

James T. Wixling
Chief of Police

**Figure 5–3   Sample Letter to the FBI Lab**

Source: Courtesy of the FBI.

The laboratory analyzes the class and individual characteristics of evidence. **Class characteristics** are the features that place an item into a specific category. For example, the size and shape of a toolmark may indicate that the tool used was a screwdriver rather than a pry bar. **Individual characteristics** are the features that distinguish one item from another of the same type. For example, chips and wear patterns in the blade of a screwdriver may leave marks that are distinguishable from those of any other screwdriver.

---

Frequently examined physical evidence includes fingerprints, voiceprints, shoe and tire impressions, bite marks, tools and toolmarks, weapons and ammunition, glass, soils and minerals, body fluids (including blood), hairs and fibers, safe insulation, rope and tape, drugs, documents and laundry and dry-cleaning marks.

---

## Fingerprints

At the end joint of each finger on the side opposite the fingernail is a rounded area called the *bulb* that has a number of friction ridge outlines. The ridge characteristics on a person's fingers are different from each other and from those of all other persons. These friction ridges and patterns form before birth and do not change during a person's lifetime.

Fingerprints serve two purposes for the investigator. They provide positive personal identification and, if the surface is suitable, they leave evidence of their patterns on objects the person has touched. These prints can be developed and compared with inked prints of the person suspected of leaving them.

Fingerprints are thus a positive way to prove that a suspect was at the crime scene. The implications of finding identifiable prints at the scene vary with each case. For example, prints may not be important if the suspect had a legitimate reason for being at the crime scene. Often, however, this is not the case. For example, in a loan office robbery, the suspect handled a green card-file box in the office safe. At the trial, three witnesses testified that at the time of the robbery the suspect was with them in a tavern 70 miles away. The defendant testified that he had not been in the community where the robbery occurred and had no idea where the loan company was. However, evidence introduced in the trial showed the defendant's fingerprints on the file box. Moreover, a witness testified that she had seen the defendant in the office during the robbery. In view of this evidence, the defendant was found guilty.

Although many laypersons assume that identifiable fingerprints are almost always found at the crime scene, in many cases, none are found. Even when they are, it is often difficult to locate the person who matches the prints. If the person's prints are not on file and there are no suspects, the fingerprints are virtually worthless. Other times, however, fingerprints are the most important physical evidence in a case. Finding fingerprints at a crime scene requires training and experience. Some surfaces retain prints more easily than others. Smooth surfaces, for example, are most apt to retain good latent prints.

Fingerprints are of various types:

■ **Latent fingerprints** are impressions transferred to a surface, either by sweat on the ridges of the fingers or because the fingers carry residue of oil, dirt, blood or some other substance. Latent fingerprints can be visible or invisible.

■ **Visible fingerprints** are made when fingers are dirty or stained. They occur primarily on glossy or light-colored surfaces and can be dusted and lifted.

■ **Plastic fingerprints,** one form of visible print, are impressions left in soft substances such as putty, grease, tar, butter or soft soap. These prints are photographed, not dusted.

■ **Invisible fingerprints** are not readily seen but can be developed through powders or chemicals. They are normally left on nonporous surfaces.

---

Any hard, smooth, nonporous surface can contain latent fingerprints.

---

Nonporous surfaces include light switches; window frames and moldings; enameled surfaces of walls, doors and objects that are painted or varnished; wood; lamps; polished silver surfaces; and glass. Fingerprints often occur on documents, glass, metals, tools and weapons used in the crime as well as on any objects picked up or touched by the suspect. Objects such as firearms, tools, small metal objects, bottles, glassware, documents and other transportable items are submitted to a laboratory where the prints are developed by experts.

Some porous materials also produce latent prints. For example, paper and cloth surfaces have developed excellent prints. Passing a flashlight at an oblique angle over a surface helps to locate possible prints.

Begin the search for fingerprints by determining the entry and exit points and the route through a crime scene. Look in the obvious places as well as less obvious places such as the underside of toilet seats and the back of rearview mirrors in cars. Examine objects that appear to have been moved. Consider the nature of the crime and how it was probably committed.

Prints found on large, immovable objects are processed at the scene by photographing or dusting with powder or chemicals.

**Dusting Latent Fingerprints.**   Fingerprint dusting powders are available in various colors and chemical compositions to provide maximum development and contrasts. When dusting for fingerprints, use a powder contrasting in color to the surface.

---

Do not powder a print unless it is necessary, and do not powder a visible print until after photographing it.

---

To dust for fingerprints, follow these steps (see Figure 5–4):

**1.** Make sure the brush is clean. Roll the handle of the brush between your palms to separate the bristles.
**2.** Shake the powder can to loosen the powder. Apply the powder *lightly* to the print, following the contour lines of the ridges to bring out details.
**3.** Remove all excess powder.
**4.** Photograph.

Use powder lightly. It is better to use too little than to use too much; you can always add a bit more if you need to. Use a camel-hair brush for most surfaces. Use

Apply the powder to the surface to discover the print.

Clean up the print by gently brushing with the flow of the ridges. Do not brush the latent print too vigorously.

**Figure 5–4   Dusting for Fingerprints**

a magnetic brush or aspirator for dusting ceilings and slanted or difficult areas. If in doubt about which powder or brush to use, test them on a similar area first.

Learn to use the various materials by watching an experienced investigator demonstrate the correct powders, brushes and techniques. Then practice placing latent prints on various surfaces and using different colored powders to determine how well each adheres and how much color contrast it provides. Practice until you can recognize surfaces and select the appropriate powder. When photographing developed latent prints, record the color of the powder used, the color of the surface and where the prints were found. Place your identification, date and case number on the back of the photograph and submit it to the crime laboratory. The laboratory will determine whether it is an identifiable print and whether it matches a known suspect or other persons whose prints were submitted for elimination.

**Lifting Prints.**   To lift fingerprints, use a commercially prepared lifter that has both a black-and-white background or a wide transparent lift tape. Use black lifters for light powders and light lifters for black powders. To lift prints on doorknobs or rounded surfaces, use transparent tape so that you can see any spots where the tape is not sticking. Put the tape over the dusted print. Do not use too much pressure. Work out any bubbles that appear under the tape by applying extra pressure. When the print has been lifted, transfer it to a fingerprint card. Figure 5–5 illustrates this procedure.

Common errors in lifting prints include removing too much or too little powder from the ridges, allowing bubbles to develop under the tape and failing to make two lifts where a second lift would be better than the first.

**Chemical Development of Latent Fingerprints.**   Although powders are used to develop latent fingerprints on many surfaces, they are not recommended for unpainted wood, paper, cardboard or other absorbent surfaces. Using powder on such surfaces will smudge any prints, destroying their value as evidence. For such surfaces, use special chemicals such as iodine, silver nitrate or ninhydrin.

The proper method of applying fingerprint tape.

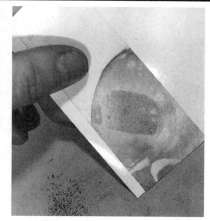

Transfer the lifted print to a fingerprint card.

**Figure 5–5   Lifting Prints**

Use gloves and a holding device to avoid contaminating the evidence by adding your own fingerprints. The chemicals can all be applied to the same specimen because each reacts differently with various types of materials. However, if *all* are used, the order must be iodine first, then ninhydrin and finally silver nitrate.

In the *iodine method,* iodine crystals are placed in a fuming cabinet or a specially prepared fuming gun. The crystals are heated and vaporized, producing a violet fume that is absorbed by the oil in the fingerprints. The fingerprint ridges appear yellow-brown and must be photographed immediately because they fade quickly. Fuming cabinets and guns can be made or purchased from police supply houses.

The *ninhydrin method* develops amino acids. Ninhydrin (highly flammable) is available in spray cans or in a powder form from which a solution of the powder and acetone or ethyl alcohol is made. The evidence is then either sprayed, dipped in or brushed with the ninhydrin. Development of prints can be speeded by applying heat from a fan, pressing iron or oven. At room temperature, prints develop in a minimum of two hours; with a pressing iron, they develop almost immediately. Ninhydrin-developed prints do not fade immediately, but they eventually lose contrast. Therefore, photograph them soon after development.

The *silver nitrate method* develops sodium chloride in the fingerprint ridges into silver chloride that appears as a red-brown print. Because silver nitrate destroys oils and amino acids, it must be used *after* the iodine and ninhydrin methods. Immerse the specimen in a solution of 3 to 10 percent silver nitrate and distilled water. Remove it immediately and hang it to dry. The prints can be developed more rapidly by applying light until they start to develop. They should be photographed immediately because they disappear after several hours.

Fingerprints may also be located and developed by using Magnabrush techniques, laser technology and cyanoacrylate (superglue).

Pilant (1994, p. 48) explains that superglue (cyanoacrylate) fuming has historically been confined to the crime laboratory:

The process involved putting three or four drops of glue in a small plastic dish or on a hot plate and using heat to generate the fumes. Fingerprints developed when the fumes from the glue adhered to the print. Any evidence—from a coffee cup to a car door—had to be carted back to the lab because fuming could not be done at the scene.

Pilant notes that David Weaver has changed that, making the superglue fuming process portable.

A newer process is the *colloidal gold universal fingerprint developer,* developed at Los Alamos National Laboratory. This process, which is used by the FBI and the Secret Service, can effectively develop prints on plastic, bank checks, counterfeit money, metal and skin, even after cyanoacrylate or ninhydrin have failed.

**Inked Prints.** Most police departments have equipment for taking fingerprints. Standard procedure is to fingerprint all adults who have been arrested, either at the time of booking or the time of release. This is done because fingerprint records help ensure that the person arrested is identified correctly. Some departments have portable fingerprint kits in patrol vehicles that allow them to take inked prints and develop latent prints at crime scenes.

To take inked prints, start by rolling the right thumb and fingers in the order stated on the card. Then roll the left thumb and fingers in order. Use a complete roll; that is, go from one side to the other. Next, *press* the fingers and then the thumb of each hand on the spaces provided on the card. The card also has spaces for information about the person and the classification made by the fingerprint examiner. Learn to take inked fingerprints by having someone demonstrate. Figures 5–6a and 5–6b show a fingerprint card.

**Electronic Fingerprinting.** The computer has greatly affected how fingerprints can be taken. An **automated fingerprint identification system (AFIS)** can digitize fingerprint information to produce **inkless fingerprints**. Latent fingerprints are scanned and converted into an electronic image that is stored in a data base for rapid retrieval. According to Burke (1992, p. 75):

> The method of fingerprinting is basically the same as the conventional inked method, with the exception that instead of rolling each finger in ink, each finger is placed in succession onto a glass platen where a laser reads the print and transfers the accepted print into the appropriate finger box on the fingerprint card.
>
> According to Eillen Albrecht, a program analyst with the FBI, this system reduces the possibility of smudging, smearing, over-inking, or under-inking commonly associated with inked prints. Quality fingerprints are generated for later identification.

The live-scan method of fingerprinting records, stores and transmits fingerprints digitally. "Digits Go Digital" (1995, p. 5) says: "The new method allows police to place a suspect's fingers on a glass plate, which is then read by a special device to produce a digital image of the prints. The image can then be transmitted over telephone lines to computerized criminal records centers."

Laser fingerprinting eliminates the mess of inked fingerprints and also many of the problems associated with them. Pilant (1992, p. 39) describes

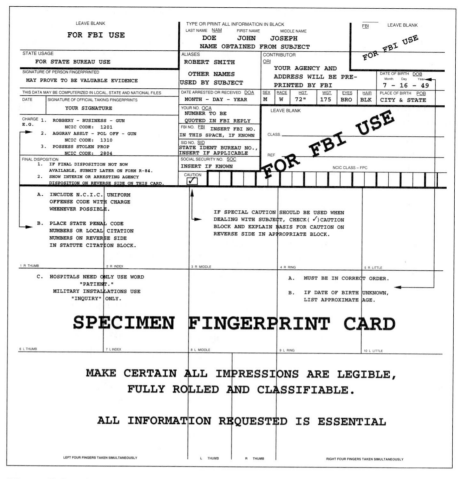

**Figure 5–6a    Sample Fingerprint Card, front**

Source: Courtesy of the FBI.

another form of inkless fingerprinting as well as research underway in fingerprinting:

> In one application [of inkless fingerprinting], a thin chemical pad is attached di-
> rectly to a citation book and is used for suspects or drivers without proper identifi-
> cation. Another application uses a folder the size of a checkbook, a thin inkless
> fingerpad and pretreated sheets of 10-block print cards. It can be used quickly and
> easily for taking prints at the scene.
>
> Still in the research stages are two new applications in the fingerprinting
> field: time-resolved fluorescence imaging, which maximizes the effects of lasers on
> highly fluorescent surfaces, and one-step fluorescent cyanoacrylate, a method that
> incorporates in a single step the superglue tagging process and a dye staining pro-
> cedure that not only will be portable, but will enable investigators to stain large
> areas at a crime scene.

Some systems require pretreated or special card stock; others use standard
cards. Inkless prints are nonsmearable, reduce finger slippage in printing and are
nonerasable. Further, inkless pads do not require the normal preparation inked
prints require. Inkless impressions provide clearer fingerprint patterns, with bet-
ter-defined ridges and spaces.

FEDERAL BUREAU OF INVESTIGATION, UNITED STATES DEPARTMENT OF JUSTICE
WASHINGTON, D. C. 20537

PALM PRINTS TAKEN?  YES ☐  NO ☐

PHOTO AVAILABLE?  YES ☐  NO ☐

IF AVAILABLE, PASTE PHOTO OVER INSTRUCTIONS
IN DOTTED AREA.

(DO NOT USE STAPLES)

SINCE PHOTOGRAPH MAY BECOME DETACHED INDICATE NAME,
DATE TAKEN, FBI NUMBER CONTRIBUTOR AND ARREST NUMBER
ON REVERSE SIDE WHETHER ATTACHED TO FINGERPRINT CARD OR
SUBMITTED LATER   TRIM PHOTO TO FIT IN DOTTED AREA

DATA ON PRIOR ARREST ONLY

IF ARREST FINGERPRINTS SENT FBI PREVIOUSLY AND FBI NO. UNKNOWN,
FURNISH ARREST NO. _____ DATE _____

STATUTE CITATION (SEE INSTRUCTION NO. 9)   CIT

1.    SHOW SEPARATE CITATION OR PENAL
2.    CODE NUMBER FOR EACH CHARGE PLACED
3.    ON FRONT SIDE.

ARREST DISPOSITION (SEE INSTRUCTION NO. 5)   ADN
            HELD FOR GRAND JURY
    IF DISPOSITION IS FINAL, ENTER ON FACE OF CARD.
    ENTER PENDING OR TEMPORARY DISPOSITION HERE.

EMPLOYER: IF U. S. GOVERNMENT, INDICATE SPECIFIC AGENCY.
          IF MILITARY, LIST BRANCH OF SERVICE AND SERIAL NO.

    USEFUL FOR FOLLOW-UP INVESTIGATION

OCCUPATION:
    A GOOD INVESTIGATIVE LEAD

RESIDENCE OF PERSON FINGERPRINTED

    MAY BE VALUABLE IN SUBSEQUENT
        FUGITIVE INVESTIGATION

SCARS, MARKS, TATTOOS, AND AMPUTATIONS   SMT
    FINGER, HAND, AND ARM AMPUTATIONS
    SHOULD ALSO BE NOTED IN APPROPRIATE
    FINGER BLOCKS ON FRONT SIDE.

BASIS FOR CAUTION   ICO      E.G.
    ARMED AND DANGEROUS - SUICIDAL TENDENCIES

DATE OF OFFENSE   DOO   | SKIN TONE   SKN
    IF KNOWN              | E.G.   LIGHT

MISC. NO.   MNU   35-99-49-300   SELECTIVE SERVICE
    IDENTIFY TYPE OF NUMBER            NO.
            ADDITIONAL INFORMATION

---

**INSTRUCTIONS**

1.  UNLESS OTHERWISE PROVIDED BY REGULATION IN YOUR STATE, FINGERPRINTS ARE TO BE SUBMITTED DIRECTLY TO FBI IDENTIFICATION DIVISION. FORWARD IMMEDIATELY FOR MOST EFFECTIVE SERVICE.

2.  FINGERPRINTS SHOULD BE SUBMITTED BY <u>ARRESTING AGENCY ONLY</u> (MULTIPLE PRINTS ON SAME CHARGE SHOULD <u>NOT</u> BE SUBMITTED BY OTHER AGENCIES SUCH AS JAILS, RECEIVING AGENCIES, ETC.). REQUEST COPIES OF FBI IDENTIFICATION RECORD FOR ALL OTHER INTERESTED AGENCIES IN BLOCK BELOW. GIVE COMPLETE MAILING ADDRESS, INCLUDING ZIP CODE.

3.  TYPE OR PRINT ALL INFORMATION.

4.  NOTE AMPUTATIONS IN PROPER FINGER BLOCKS.

5.  LIST FINAL DISPOSITION IN BLOCK ON FRONT SIDE. IF NOT NOW AVAILABLE, SUBMIT LATER ON FBI FORM R-84 FOR COMPLETION OF RECORD. IF FINAL DISPOSITION NOT AVAILABLE SHOW PRE-TRIAL OR ARRESTING AGENCY DISPOSITION, e.g., RELEASED, NO FORMAL CHARGE, BAIL, TURNED OVER TO, IN THE ARREST DISPOSITION BLOCK PROVIDED ON THIS SIDE.

6.  MAKE CERTAIN ALL IMPRESSIONS ARE LEGIBLE, FULLY ROLLED AND CLASSIFIABLE.

7.  CAUTION - CHECK BOX ON FRONT IF CAUTION STATEMENT INDICATED. BASIS FOR CAUTION (ICO) MUST GIVE REASON FOR CAUTION, e. g., ARMED AND DANGEROUS, SUICIDAL, ETC.

8.  MISCELLANEOUS NUMBER (MNU) - SHOULD INCLUDE SUCH NUMBERS AS MILITARY SERVICE, PASSPORT AND/OR VETERANS ADMINISTRATION (IDENTIFY TYPE OF NUMBER).

9.  PROVIDE STATUTE CITATION, IDENTIFYING SPECIFIC STATUTE (example - PL for PENAL LAW) AND CRIMINAL CODE CITATION INCLUDING ANY SUB-SECTIONS.

10. ALL INFORMATION REQUESTED IS ESSENTIAL.

SEND COPY TO:
    INDICATE ANY ADDITIONAL COPIES FOR
    OTHER AGENCIES IN THIS SPACE.  GIVE
    THEIR COMPLETE MAILING ADDRESS,
    INCLUDING ZIP CODE.

REPLY DESIRED?   YES ☐   NO ☐
(REPLY WILL BE SENT IN ALL CASES IF SUBJECT FOUND TO BE WANTED)
IF COLLECT WIRE OR COLLECT TELEPHONE REPLY
DESIRED, INDICATE HERE (WIRE SENT ON ALL UNKNOWN DECEASED)
    DO NOT CHECK UNLESS WILLING TO ACCEPT COLLECT CHARGES.
WIRE REPLY ☐   TELEPHONE REPLY ☐   TELEPHONE NO. AND AREA CODE

LEAVE BLANK
        FOR FBI USE

LEAVE BLANK
        FOR FBI USE

                                    FBI/DOJ

FD-249 (REV. 3-13-72)   :   GPO: 1976 — 218 - 796

---

**Figure 5–6b   Sample Fingerprint Card, back**

Source: Courtesy of the FBI.

**Elimination Prints.**   If fingerprint evidence is found, it is important to know whose prints "belong" at the scene.

---

Prints of persons with good reason to be at the scene are taken and used as **elimination prints.**

---

For example, family members in the home where a crime has occurred or employees of a business that has been robbed should be fingerprinted so that their fingerprints at the scene can be eliminated from suspicion.

**Classifying Fingerprints.**   Experts analyze fingerprint patterns and classify them as *arched, looped* or *whorled*. Variations of these configurations result in the nine basic fingerprint patterns illustrated in Figure 5–7.

An index card is prepared for each person fingerprinted, on which is recorded the person's crime code and number (for example, *BR* for bank robbery, *BB* for bank burglary), name, FBI or arrest number and the type of crime in which the person specializes. The two strips of prints are attached to the card, and the set of prints is assigned to a single fingerprint classification:

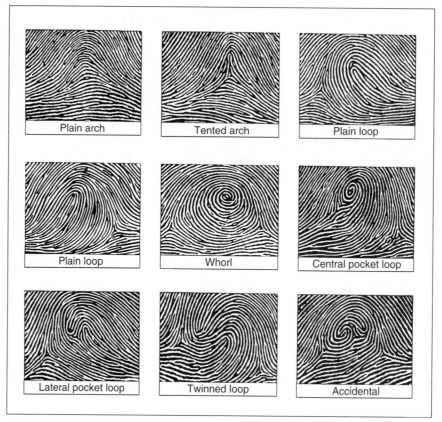

**Figure 5–7   Nine Basic Fingerprint Patterns**
Source: Courtesy of the *FBI Law Enforcement Bulletin.*

0—amputated finger
1—arch pattern
2—tented arch
3—right slope loop
4—left slope loop

5—plain whorl or central pocket loop
6—double (twinned) loop
7—accidental
8—scarred or mutilated patterns

Normally, twelve matchable characteristics are required for positive identification on a single fingerprint (see Figure 5–8).

**Fingerprint Files and Searches.**   Prints are segregated by crime types such as bank robbery, extortion or kidnapping. They are usually filed by name. If files are searched manually, the fingerprints are compared with a name index file. Matching the primary classification with the name file is much faster than searching the fingerprint file classification, and a positive comparison can be made quickly. If the name index does not turn up a possible comparison, the fingerprint is fully classified, and a search is made of the file. If there is still no comparison, the fingerprint card is added to the file for future reference.

Computer searches are often conducted for fingerprints. Fingerprint information stored includes the sex, date of birth, classification formula and each finger's ridge count. When queried, the system selects the cards within the range limitations for the entered classification formula. Fingerprint experts then visually compare the prints.

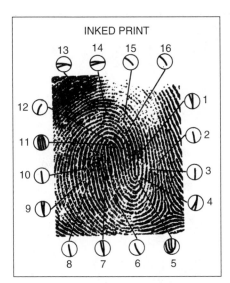
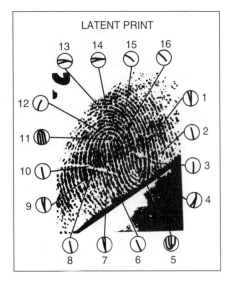

**Figure 5–8 Positive Identification of a Fingerprint**
Three men checked into a motel at 11:00 P.M. Shortly after midnight, when a new desk clerk came on duty, the men went to the office and committed an armed robbery. Police investigating the scene went to the room occupied by the three men and found a latent fingerprint on an ashtray. This print was later matched to one of the suspects whose fingerprints were on file with the police department.

If no match is found in local or state files, prints are submitted to the FBI Identification Division for a further search. This division has on file fingerprints of arrested persons as well as nearly 100 million other persons such as aliens and individuals in government services, including the military.

The automated fingerprint identification system (AFIS) uses computers to review and map fingerprints (see Figure 5–9). It creates a spatial geometry of the minutiae of the print, which is changed into a binary code for the computer's searching algorithm. The capability of registering thousands of details makes it possible for the computer to make a search in minutes that would take days manually.

According to Sparrow (1994, p. 147): "The sale of automated fingerprint identification systems (AFIS) is already a billion dollar per year business worldwide."

Andrae (1993, p. 37) notes: "The combination of a high intensity forensic light, video camera, computer enhancement technology and the Automated Fingerprint Identification System (AFIS) has given police fingerprint staff access to information at a crime scene they have never had before."

For a latent search, the average search time in a fairly substantial size file is 4.5 minutes. The computer makes a comparatively small list of possible comparisons that can then be compared manually. The search success rate has been up to 98 percent in some departments with files under one million.

AFIS has encouraged investigators to obtain better crime-scene prints because they realize it is now possible to make successful comparisons even on "cold makes" in cases with no suspects.

Approximately 35 to 40 percent of crime scenes have latent prints. AFIS has substantially reduced the number of print comparisons the expert has to make. Considering that the FBI fingerprint files contain data on more than 100 million individuals, the AFIS is a tremendous advance in crime fighting.

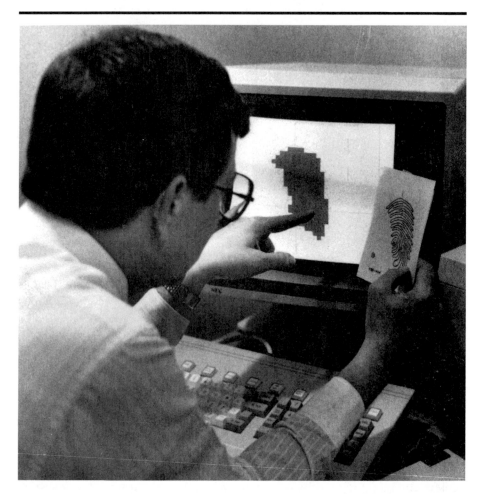

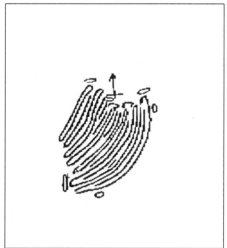

Search-print image                    Candidate-print image

*The Automated Fingerprint Identification System used by the Illinois State Police matches fingerprints recovered at crime scenes with the 1.6 million prints in their files.* Top photo: *Fingerprint examiner edits a print for errors.* Bottom photo: *A search print* (left) *as it appears on the video screen and* (right) *a candidate's print image. The examiner holds a print image match as it would appear on the screen after a match-up* (top).

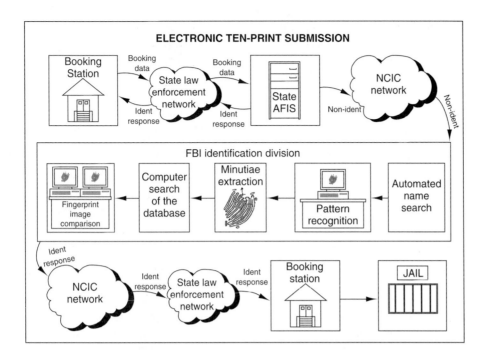

**Figure 5–9   Electronic Ten-Print Submission**
A suspect is booked locally and his fingerprints are sent to the state AFIS. If there is no match, the prints go on to the NCIC Network and from there to the FBI Identification Division for a name search and a fingerprint search. If there is a match with the 10 print card, the FBI electronically sends the state law enforcement network and the requesting (booking) agency the suspect's identity, including the FBI criminal identification number.

Source: J. Van Duyn, 1993. Reprinted by permission.

Departments having similar systems can be interactive. There is also the possibility of unsimilar systems using a basic set of standards, which would make them somewhat compatible.

The FBI is planning for an integrated computer system. Called the 21st Century Integrated ID Automated Systems, or IAFIS, it is an umbrella for seven components, described by Van Duyn (1993, p. 40):

1. A revitalized *NCIC Network,* where all the "hot files" [e.g. wanted persons, stolen vehicles] will be maintained.
2. A completely overhauled *III/FBI [Interstate Identification Index]* where Name Searches, Mug Shots and Arrest Record Responses will be handled.
3. The improved *AFIS/FBI,* which will do the Ten-Print and the Latent-Print searches.
4. The revolutionary *ITN/FBI Network [Image Transmission Network],* which will interface with NCIC 2000 Network, III/FBI, and AFIS/FBI, as a high performance local area network and manage Data Entry, Image Retrieval, Ten-Print and Latent-Print Operations and Document Operations. In short, it will control the processing of all submissions from the time of receipt until the appropriate response is sent back electronically to the requesting party.
5. The reworked *MIDS [Management Information and Decision Support System].*
6. The updated *UCR [Uniform Crime Report].*
7. The finely honed *DTTS [Development Test and Training System].*

**Biometrics,** the statistical study of biological data such as fingerprints, is at the heart of electronic fingerprinting. Zauner (1991, p. 22) states that "biometrics foreshadows the end of ink pads as a means of acquiring and retrieving fingerprint identification." Electronic fingerprints can be invaluable to police officers in the field, as described by Mallory (1992, p. 116):

> With a patrol cruiser equipped with the right equipment, prints of a person . . . can be scanned and transmitted to the National Crime Information Center in a matter of seconds. If there's a hit, the officer can have the suspect's photo and rap sheet displayed in his vehicle. The system can scan local, then state, then NCIC files.

**Usefulness of Fingerprints.** Fingerprints are of extreme evidentiary value in criminal investigations, because they are the strongest possible evidence of a person's identity.

---

Fingerprints are the strongest possible evidence of a person's identity. They cannot, however, indicate the person's age, sex or race.

---

Fingerprints can be sent via communications systems across the country and be visually reproduced. Crime victims are identified by their prints to prove the corpus delicti. Courts, parole and probation officers and prosecutors use fingerprints to positively identify people with multiple criminal records.

Fingerprints also aid in noncriminal investigations. They help to identify victims of mass disasters, missing persons, amnesia victims and unconscious persons. Military agencies use fingerprints recorded at enlistment to identify those killed in combat. Hospitals use fingerprints or footprints to identify newborn babies. Furthermore, fingerprints are becoming widely used as identification for cashing checks and in processing legal documents.

**Other Types of Prints.** Suspects may also leave palm prints, footprints or even prints of body pores. These impressions can be photographed and developed just as fingerprints are.

In one interesting case a burglar shattered a restaurant's plate glass window. The police found no fingerprints around the window but did find footprints and a toe print on a piece of the broken glass. These were developed and lifted. Later a seventeen-year-old was arrested on vagrancy. Learning that he often went barefoot, police also took his footprints and forwarded them to the Latent Fingerprint Section of the FBI's Identification Division. They were identical with those on the plate glass window fragment. It was learned that the youth had taken off his shoes and put his socks on his hands to avoid leaving fingerprints at the crime scene. He was found guilty.

**Admissibility in Court.** Numerous court rulings have upheld the admissibility of fingerprints as evidence when supported by testimony of fingerprint experts.

### Voiceprints

A **voiceprint** is a graphic record of an individual's voice characteristics made by a sound spectograph which records the energy patterns emitted by speech. Like fingerprints, no two voiceprints are alike. Therefore, voiceprints can assist in identifying bomb hoaxers, obscene phone callers and other people who use the telephone illegally. A voiceprint is made during a telephone call and then retained until a suspect is in custody.

The use of voiceprints in criminal trials is controversial. In a number of cases, convictions obtained through the use of voiceprints have been reversed because the voiceprints were not regarded as sufficiently reliable.

### Shoe and Tire Impressions

If shoe or tire prints are found on paper or cardboard, take photographs of them and then submit the originals for laboratory examination. Use latent fingerprint lifters to lift shoe and tire tread impressions from smooth surfaces. Take photographs with and without a marker before lifting the impression. Do not attempt to fit your shoe into the suspect's shoe print to determine size. Too many footprints are destroyed by this attempt. Shoe and tire impressions may have unique wear patterns that should be preserved by casting when possible.

---

Make a plaster cast of shoe or tire tread impressions found in dirt, sand or snow.

---

Some departments prefer dental casting material for such casts.

The steps in making a plaster **cast** of an impression are these (see Figure 5–10):

**1.** Build a retaining frame around the impression about 2 inches from its edges.

Figure 5–10   **Making a Plaster Cast of a Shoe Impression**

**2.** Coat the impression with five or six layers of alcohol and shellac or inexpensive hairspray, allowing each coat to dry before applying the next. Apply talcum powder to the last layer so that the spray can be removed from the cast easily.

**3.** Mix the plaster following directions on the box. Work rapidly.

**4.** Pour the plaster into the impression, using a spatula to cushion its fall and to guide it into all areas of the impression. Fill the impression halfway to the top.

**5.** Add wire or gauze to reinforce the impression.

**6.** Pour in more plaster until it overflows to the retaining frame.

**7.** Before the cast hardens, use a pencil or other pointed instrument to incise your initials, the case number and the date on the back of the impression.

**8.** After the cast is hard, remove it and the retaining frame. Do not wash the cast; the laboratory does this.

**9.** Carefully wrap the cast in protective material to avoid breakage, and place it in a strong box for shipment to the laboratory.

The laboratory compares the cast with shoe and tire-tread files furnished by manufacturers.

**Value of Shoe and Tire Prints.**   In addition to providing unique wear patterns that can be compared to a suspect's shoes, footprints can also indicate if a person was walking or running, was carrying something heavy or was unfamiliar with the area or unsure of the terrain.

Pilant (1992, p. 42) notes that tire marks "can show the direction and approximate speed of travel; whether or not the car leaked oil, transmission fluid or water; and the manufacturer and year the tires were made."

### Bite Marks

When identifiable teeth impressions are found in partially eaten food, they can be cast in the same way shoe and tire-tread impressions are. Dental impression material is preferred because of its fine texture. Saliva samples should be taken using a swab before bite marks are cast.

If the bite mark is not deep enough to cast, you can trace it onto transparent plastic that you have taped over it. A new type of drawing, called a *toneline,* is also available. This is a black photographic outline of the perimeter of a bite mark that can be compared directly with models of an individual's teeth (Pilant, 1992, p. 40).

### Tools and Toolmarks

Common tools such as pliers and screwdrivers are often used in crimes and cause little suspicion if found in someone's possession. Such tools are often found in a suspect's vehicle, on the person or at the residence. If a tool is found at a crime scene, it must be learned if it belongs to the owner of the property. Pieces of broken tools may be found at the crime scene, on the suspect or on the suspect's property (see Figure 5–11).

---

Identify each suspect tool with a string tag. Wrap it separately and pack it in a strong box for sending to the laboratory.

---

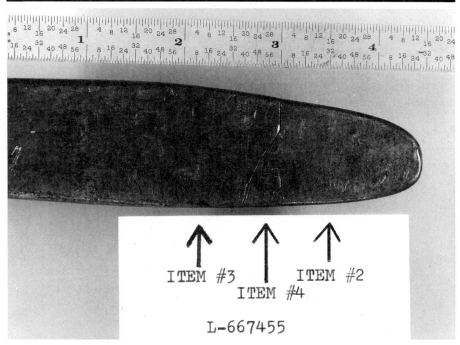

**Figure 5–11   Broken Tool Comparison**
Pry tool used to pry open the rear door of a hardware store. Items 2 and 4 were found at the scene of the burglary. Item 3 was found in a toolbox in the suspect's car. This evidence led to the suspect's conviction for burglary.

A **toolmark** is an impression left by a tool on a surface. For example, a screwdriver forced between a window and sill may leave a mark of the same depth and width as the screwdriver—although the resiliency of the surface may create explainable differences in mark dimensions and tool dimensions. If the screwdriver has a chipped head or other imperfections, it will leave impressions for later comparison. Toolmarks are often found in burglaries, auto thefts and larcenies in which objects are forced open.

A toolmark provides leads as to the size and type of tool that made it. Examining a suspect tool determines, within limits, whether it could have made the mark in question. Even if you find a suspect tool, it is not always possible to match it to the toolmark, especially if the tool was damaged when the mark was made. However, residue from the surface that was forced may adhere to the tool, making a comparison possible on that basis.

Do not attempt to fit a suspected tool into a mark to see if it matches. This disturbs the mark, as well as any paint or other trace evidence on the suspect tool, making the tool inadmissible as evidence.

---

Photograph toolmarks and then either cast them or send the object on which they appear to the laboratory.

---

**Photographing Toolmarks.**   First photograph the location of the tool or toolmark within the general crime scene. Then take close-ups without and then with a marker to show the actual size and detail of the tool or toolmark.

**Casting Toolmarks.**    Casting toolmarks presents special problems because they often are not on a horizontal surface. In such cases, construct a platform or bridge around the mark to hold the casting materials until they harden. The platform can be formed by taping tin or other pliable material to the surface. Plaster of Paris, plasticine and waxes do not provide the detail necessary for tool striation marks. Better results are obtained from moulage, silicone and other thermosetting materials.

**Comparing Toolmarks.**    Toolmarks are easy to compare if a suspect tool has not been altered or damaged since it made the mark. If the tool is found, it is sent to the laboratory where several comparison standards are made.

---

A toolmark is compared with a standard of comparison impression rather than with the tool itself.

---

The material used for the standard is as close as possible to the original material. Ideally, a portion of the original material is used.

The toolmark found at the scene and the standard of comparison are placed under a microscope to make the striation marks appear as light and dark lines. The lines are then adjusted to see whether they match. Variations of approximately 10 degrees in angle are permissible. The fewer the number of striation

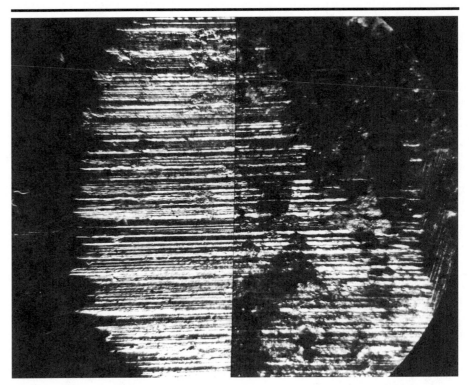

**Figure 5–12    Comparison of Toolmarks**
Striation pattern of a sledgehammer used to open a safe. The white marks are safe insulation. The left half of the photograph is evidence obtained at the scene of the crime; the right half shows the actual hammer seized from the suspect. The marks were matched up under a comparison microscope and magnified.

lines, the more of them that must match. Roughly 60 percent of the lines should match in the comparison (see Figure 5–12).

**Value of Toolmarks.**    Toolmarks are valuable in several ways. A specific mark may be similar to or found in the same relative location as toolmarks found at other crimes. Evidence of the way a tool is applied—the angle, amount of pressure and general use—can tie one crime to another. A toolmark also makes it easier to look for a specific type of tool. Possession of, or fingerprints on, such a tool can implicate a suspect.

## Weapons and Ammunition

The vast majority of violent crimes are committed with a firearm. Use extreme caution when handling firearms found at a crime scene. Tools used to manufacture weapons and defects in weapons acquired through use or neglect are characteristics that often permit positive identification. A bullet or cartridge case can often be linked with the particular weapon from which it was fired.

---

Photograph weapons and then identify them with a string tag. Unload guns. Record the serial number on the string tag and in your notes. Label the packing container "Firearms." Identify bullets on the base, cartridges on the outside of the case near the bullet end and cartridge cases on the inside near the open end. Put ammunition in cotton or soft paper and ship to the laboratory. Never send live ammunition through the mail; use a common carrier.

---

Examine weapons for latent fingerprints. Include in your notes the weapon's make, caliber, model, type, serial number, finish and any unusual characteristics.

Gunpowder tests, shot pattern tests and functional tests of the weapon can be made and compared. The rifling of a gun barrel, the gun's ejection and extraction mechanisms and markings made by these mechanisms can also be compared.

Examination of a cartridge includes the bullet, cartridge case and primer. The bullet is examined for composition and shape. A cartridge case examination includes the head and body of the case and the powder charge, which is either black or smokeless powder. Finding black powder is a significant lead because it is used so little today.

Evidence bullets are compared to determine whether a specific bullet was fired from a specific comparison weapon. Shot patterns determine the distance from which the victim was shot and may disclose the type of choke on the gun and its barrel length. Gun parts found at a crime scene are compared with a weapon, and the trigger pull is tested and measured.

The FBI Laboratory and other laboratories have firearms reference collections, standard ammunition files and national unidentified ammunition files available to all law enforcement officers.

The Bureau of Alcohol, Tobacco and Firearms (BATF) maintains an Integrated Ballistics Identification System (IBIS). This system can identify used cartridges and bullets much like the FBI AFIS identifies fingerprints. Benson (1995, p. 33) cites the example of a wealthy businessman missing in Pennsylvania. A farmer in another community found a gun in the weeds and turned it over to police. ATF ran the weapon through the tracing center and found it belonged to an associate of the missing person. In a third town the victim's body was found in a shallow grave. Bullets removed from the victim's body proved to be fired from the associate's gun. The matching system is also useful in gang murders due to the randomness of the crime and lack of witnesses.

Dees (1994, p. 44) describes an automated forensic ballistics program called Bulletproof: "It is a fully automated system capable of electronically scanning, coding, and storing the signatures of fired bullets, and comparing new specimens with those already in the data base."

Killorin, the ATF's chief spokesperson, says of Bulletproof ("Hey Buddy, Got a Match?" 1994, p. 1): "It's an amazing system. We're literally at a point where the technology is going to allow us to do the same kinds of things using the unique marks left on expended projectiles that's now being done for fingerprints."

The Lawrence Livermore National Laboratory in California has developed a computer-driven system called Lifeguard that tracks bullets in flight and identifies their source, allowing officers facing sniper fire to pinpoint the source in just a fraction of a second ("Ballistics Technology on Track," 1994, p. 1).

Lesce (1995, pp. 47–48) describes several factors that can affect the path of a bullet:

■ Intervening objects can and do deflect bullets.

■ Clothing, and especially the contents of pockets, can affect a bullet's path and velocity.

■ Raising an arm also raises the shirt or jacket, and examination with the arm lowered after the shooting will displace the hole in the clothing. This could produce the illusion that the bullet pierced the clothing and then traveled sideways before penetrating the skin. It could also suggest that the point of impact was lower than it actually was. This is what caused the controversy regarding the first bullet that struck President Kennedy, which hit him in the neck. Because he had his arm raised to wave at the moment of impact, the hole in his jacket suggested that the bullet hit him between his shoulder blades when draped normally.

■ Bullets can also veer within the body after striking a bone.

■ Bullets can also veer on leaving the body.

### Glass

Glass can have great evidentiary value. Tiny pieces of glass can adhere to a suspect's shoes and clothing. Larger glass fragments are processed for fingerprints and can be fit back together to provide information on the direction from which the glass was broken. The source of broken glass fragments also can often be determined.

---

Label glass fragments using adhesive tape on each piece. Wrap each piece separately in cotton to avoid chipping and place in a strong box marked "fragile" for sending to the laboratory.

---

Microscopic, spectrographic and physical comparisons are made of the glass fragments. Microscopic examination of the edges of two pieces of glass can prove that they were one piece. **Spectrographic analysis** can determine the elements of the glass, even of extremely small fragments.

Submit for comparison pieces of glass that are at least the size of a half-dollar. Positive identification is made by matching two or more pieces of glass.

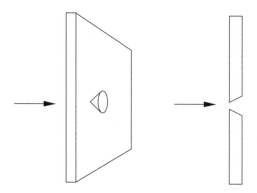

**Figure 5–13    Bullet Entry and Exit Holes**

The direction and angle of a bullet through glass can be determined by re-assembling the pieces of glass. The resulting pattern of cracks indicates the direction of the bullet. A bullet that does not shatter glass will leave a small, round entry hole and a larger, cone-shaped exit hole (see Figure 5–13).

The faster the bullet, the smaller the cracks and/or the tighter the entry point will be. The sequence of bullets fired through a piece of glass also can be determined from the pattern of cracks in the glass.

It is also possible to determine which side of a piece of glass has received a blow, because a blow causes the glass to compress on that side and to stretch on the opposite side. As the blow is struck, circle cracks form around the point of the blow. These circle cracks interconnect with radial cracks to form triangular pieces. The edge of each triangular piece has visible stress lines that tell the direction of the blow. The lines on the side that was struck have almost parallel stress lines that tend to curve downward on the side of the glass opposite the blow (see Figure 5–14). Such an examination can establish whether a burglar broke out of or into a building.

Because larger glass fragments can be matched by fitting the pieces together, a slight mark put on the side of the glass that was facing out helps to reconstruct stress lines. To protect glass needed as evidence, put sharp points in putty, modeling clay or some other soft substance.

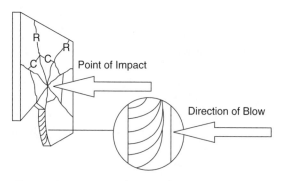

**Figure 5–14    Glass Cracks Caused by a Blow**

## Soils and Minerals

Forensic geologists examine soils and minerals—such substances as mud, cement, plaster, ceramics and insulation—found at the crime scene or on a victim, a suspect, clothing, vehicles or other items. This circumstantial evidence can place a suspect at a crime scene or destroy an alibi.

Although most soil evidence is found outdoors, the suspect can bring soil into structures from the outside. Soils found inside a structure are most valuable if they were brought there on the suspect's shoes or clothing from his or her area of residence. Because soils found in the victim's residence may have been brought there by the victim or by other persons not suspected in the crime, it is necessary to collect elimination samples of soil from the area around the scene.

---

Put one pound of comparison soil into a container, identifying it on the outside of the container. Collect evidence soil the same way. Seal both containers to prevent loss, wrap them and send them to the laboratory.

---

Soils vary greatly in color, particle size, minerals and chemical constituents. Some comparisons are visual; others are made through laboratory analysis. Both differences and similarities have value because soils separated by only a few inches can be very different. Therefore, take sufficient samples directly from and around the suspected area at perhaps 5- to 100-foot intervals, depending on the scene.

If soil evidence is in or on a suspect's clothing, send the entire article with the soil intact to the laboratory. If an object containing soil cannot be moved, use a spatula to gather the soil. Then place the soil in a can or paper bag, properly marked and identified.

Chemical analysis of soil is expensive and not always satisfactory. Soil is generally examined by density, by **X-ray diffraction** (to determine mineral content) and by microscope.

Because varied species of plants grow in different sections of the country, examination of dirt evidence that contains pollen and spores (palynology) is useful. It can refute the alibi of a suspect who is arrested a distance from a crime scene and denies having been there. Electron microscope detection of pollen and spores found at the crime scene and on the suspect's clothing or vehicle will refute the alibi.

## Safe Insulation

Most safes are fire-resistant, sheet-steel boxes with thick insulation. If safes are pried, ripped, punched, drilled or blown open, the insulation breaks apart and falls or sifts out into the room. Burglars often end up with some of this insulation in their clothing. People with safe insulation in or on their clothing must be considered suspects because few people normally come into contact with safe insulation. Tools used to open a safe also can have insulation on them, as may the floor of a vehicle in which the tools were placed after a burglary.

---

Put samples of safe insulation in paper containers, identifying them on the outside.

---

Safe insulation can be compared with particles found on the suspect or on the tools or vehicle used during the crime. Comparison tests can show what make of safe the insulation came from and whether it is the same insulation found at other burglaries.

Insulation is also found with paint chips from safes. Always take standards of comparison if safe insulation is found at a crime scene.

The FBI and other laboratories maintain files on safe insulations used by major safe companies. Home and building insulation materials are also on file. These files are available to all law enforcement agencies.

### Ropes, Strings and Tapes

Ropes, twines, strings and tapes are frequently used in crimes. They also can provide leads in identifying suspects and in linking suspects with crime.

---

Put labeled rope, twine and string in a container. Put tapes on waxed paper or cellophane and then place them in a container.

---

Laboratories have various comparison standards for ropes, twines and tapes. If a suspect sample matches a known sample, the laboratory can determine the manufacturer of the item and its most common uses. Cordage can be compared for composition, construction, color and diameter. Rope ends can be matched if they are frayed. Likewise, pieces of torn tape can be compared to a suspect roll of tape.

Fingerprints can occur on either side of a tape. The smooth side is developed by the normal powder method or by using cyanoacrylate (superglue) if the surface is extremely slick. The sticky-side prints will be visible and are either photographed or retained intact.

### Drugs

Drug-identification kits can be used to make a preliminary analysis of a suspicious substance, but the full analysis must be done at the laboratory.

---

Put liquid drugs in a bottle and attach a label. Put powdered and solid drugs in a pill or powder box and identify the same way.

---

If the drug is a prescription drug, verify the contents with the issuing pharmacist. Determine how much of the original prescription has been consumed.

### Documents

Typing, handwriting and printing can be examined. Typewriters and printers can be compared and paper identification can be attempted. Different types of writing instruments—pens, crayons and pencils—and various types of inks can also be compared. Indented writings, obliterated or altered writings, used carbon paper, burned or charred paper, shoeprint or tire-tread impressions made on paper surfaces—all can be examined in the laboratory. A document's age can also be determined.

---

Do not touch documents with your bare hands. Place them in a cellophane envelope and then in a manila envelope, and identify them on the outside.

---

Standards of comparison are required for many document examinations. To obtain handwriting standards from a suspect, take samples until you believe he or she is writing normally. The suspect should not see the original document or copy. Tell the suspect what to write and remove each sample from sight after it is completed. Provide no instructions on spelling, punctuation or wording. Use the same size and type of paper and writing materials used for the original. Obtain right-handed and left-handed samples as well as samples written at different speeds. Samples of undictated writings, such as school papers or letters, are also helpful as standards. In forgery cases, include the genuine signatures as well as the forged ones.

Chadbourne (1994, p. 57) describes a situation in Walpole, New Hampshire, where a police chief fatally shot his supervisor and then turned the gun on himself. He describes another situation in Clarksville, Tennessee, where a Ft. Campbell soldier went on a shooting rampage one evening, killing four people. He cites Bonnie Lee Nugent who believes these crimes might have been prevented if a handwriting analysis had been done. Nugent has authored a book exploring thinking patterns through writing.

People often type anonymous or threatening letters, believing that typewritten materials are not as traceable as handwritten ones. However, some courts have held that typewriting can be compared more accurately than handwriting and almost as accurately as fingerprints. To collect typewriting standards, remove the ribbon from the suspect typewriter and send the ribbon to the laboratory. Use a different ribbon to take each sample. Take samples using light, medium and heavy pressure. Submit one carbon-copy sample with the typewriter on stencil position. Do not send the typewriter to the laboratory, but hold it as evidence.

Given enough typing samples, it is often possible to determine the make and model of a machine. Typewriter standard files are available for this purpose at the FBI Laboratory in the Department of Justice Building in Washington, D.C.

The information can greatly narrow the search for the actual machine. The most important comparison is between the suspect document and that from a specific typewriter. Several comparisons should be made. Some visual differences can eliminate machines immediately, such as differences in type style, letter size and obvious defects in characters. A typewriter's alignment is often a basis for comparison because few machines are manufactured with perfect alignment. Further, once a typewriter is used, it begins to vary in many ways from all other machines, even those of the same make.

As word processing replaces typewriters across the country, the word processing software program and the printer used become important evidence.

Photographs are also frequently valuable evidence whether taken by an officer at the scene or provided by someone outside the department.

Some researchers in New York are focusing their efforts on techniques to enhance grainy, blurred or poorly contrasted photographs by digitally converting them and subjecting them to a software program called Restoretool (Pilant, p. 39). In Louisiana, a group of researchers are seeking ways to enhance the photographic image of injuries on human skin using reflective and fluorescent ultraviolet imaging. According to Pilant: "Currently in the experimental stage, this research effort will examine images of injuries produced by knives, iron bars, guns, pipes, and baseball bats on victims and offenders."

The best-evidence rule stipulates that the original evidence is to be presented whenever possible.

This precedent, established by *Petit v. Campbell* (1941), forbids substituting evidence for the original if the original evidence is producible. For example, a photograph or photocopy of a forged check is not admissible; the check itself is required.

The FBI also maintains a national fraudulent check file, an anonymous letter file, a bank robbery note file, paper watermarks, safety paper and check-writer standards. When submitting any document evidence to the FBI Lab or another lab, clearly indicate which documents are original and which are comparison standards. Also indicate whether latent fingerprints are requested. Although original documents are needed for laboratory examinations and court exhibits, copies can be used for file searches. A photograph is superior to a photocopy.

### Laundry and Dry-Cleaning Marks

Many launderers and dry cleaners use specific marking systems. The Laundry and Dry Cleaning National Association has files on such marking systems. Many police laboratories also maintain a file of visible and invisible laundry marks used by local establishments. Military clothing is marked with the person's serial number, name and organization.

Use **ultraviolet light** to detect invisible laundry marks. Submit the entire garment to the laboratory, identifying it with a string tag or directly on the garment.

Laundry and dry-cleaning marks are used in identifying the dead and injured in mass disasters such as airplane crashes, fires and floods. The marks can help identify the dead in other circumstances as well. For example, a dead baby was traced by the sheet's laundry marks. Clothing labels can also assist in locating the possible source of the clothing.

### Blood and Other Body Fluids

Blood and other body fluids such as semen and urine can provide valuable information. Blood assists in establishing that a violent crime was committed, in recreating the movements of the suspect or victim and in eliminating suspects. Body fluids can be found on the suspect's or victim's clothing, on the floor or walls, on furniture and on other objects.

Blood is important as evidence in crimes of violence. Heelprints of shoes in blood splashes may be identifiable separate from the blood analysis. It is important to test the stain or sample to determine if it is, in fact, blood.

In addition, because blood is so highly visible and recognizable, many individuals who commit violent crimes attempt to remove blood from items that would incriminate them. A number of reagents—including Luminol, tetramethyl benzedrine and phenolphthalein—can be used to identify the presence of blood at the crime scene. Because crime laboratories are swamped with evidence to examine, such preliminary on-scene testing is important.

Hesskew (1991, p. 33) describes a case in which Luminol played a key role:

A dismembered body was found on the side of the road in a small rural community. The woman had been sexually assaulted and her body mutilated. Police were able to link the victim to a suspect, but lacked evidence to place the victim and suspect together.

The victim was a waitress at a restaurant that the suspect frequented. It was known that the suspect tried to date the victim, but she shunned his advances. On the night she disappeared, the suspect was quite agitated after the victim refused to wait on his table or talk to him. Several days later, her body was found on the side of the road.

The victim's clothing was not located, nor was the murder weapon. According to the autopsy report, the victim's arms and legs had been severed with a saw or large knife with serrated edge.

Information gained several years after the discovery of the body gave investigators the necessary facts to execute a search warrant. A workshop behind the suspect's house contained a large table saw. A close examination of the saw led to the discovery of several hairs that appeared to be human. There was no blood visible on the saw or in the workshop.

The shop interior was sprayed with Luminol, and investigators found the necessary evidence to arrest the subject. A wall in the workshop, the saw, and other items inside the garage contained enough traces of the victim's blood for identification. The suspect was tried for the murder and mutilation, but was found not guilty by reason of insanity. He remains at a state hospital.

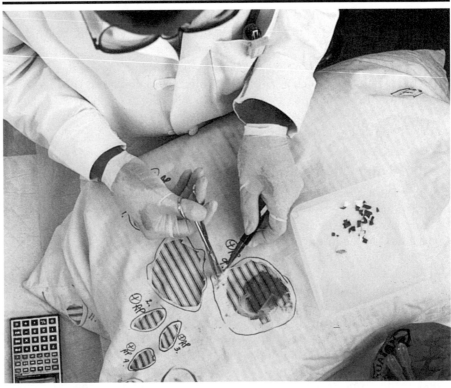

*A laboratory technician recovers samples from a blood-stained pillow found at a crime scene. These samples can be used for DNA testing against blood drawn from a suspect. Good conservation of samples is the only condition required for DNA tests to be reliable, even after a long period of time.*

Advances in how blood patterns can be assessed are also of importance to criminal investigators. Hill (1992, p. 8) reports that a new computer program is making bloodstain analysis "faster, easier, and more accurate." Called BackTrack, the analysis replaces the method of attaching strings to blood droplets, figuring out the rough angle of impact and then projecting the strings back into the room. Using BackTrack, an investigator simply enters the width, length, direction and position of each drop into the computer. The system calculates an angle of attack for each droplet and projects a flight path backwards.

The intersection of two or more back-projection lines indicates the position of the original wound. The more spots used, the more accurate the results (Hill, p. 8).

Another such program, called No More Strings, also calculates bloodstain measurements for point of origin. According to Pilant (1992, p. 45), this program is designed to run on a PC or laptop and "is faster and more accurate than the string method and graphically plots the results for use in court."

As noted by Christman (1994, p. 56):

Blood pattern interpretation has been used in numerous courts around the world as a valid scientific discipline by law enforcement, medicolegal investigators, serologists and crime scene technicians. . . .

Technically speaking, bloodstain pattern analysis is the study of stationary bloodstains that assist in the reconstruction of specific spatial and sequential events that occurred prior to and during the act of bloodshed. . . .

Specifically, blood pattern analysis can help the investigator determine:

- The place where the blood originated from.
- The distance between the origin and where the bloodstain came to rest.
- The types and direction of the impact that created the bloodstains.
- The type of object(s) that produced the bloodstains.
- The minimum number of blows (gunshots, stomps, etc.) that were administered.
- The position of the victim, assailant and items during and after the bloodshed.
- The quality of statements given by the suspects or witnesses about the event.

Blood-spatter patterns can help to determine if a suspect is telling the truth. In many cases suspects have claimed that a death was accidental, but the location and angle of the blood-spatter patterns have refuted their statements. Drops of blood fall in a round shape, and different spatter patterns result depending on the surface and plane of the receiving object. Smooth objects cause a more round pattern. The more perpendicular the surface, the more elongated the pattern.

Collect liquid blood with an eyedropper and put it into a test tube. Write the subject's name and other pertinent information on medical tape applied to the outside of the tube. Send by air express, priority mail or registered mail. Scrape dry blood and put the flakes into a pillbox or envelope, identifying it in the same way. Mark bloodstained clothing with a string tag or directly on the clothing, including the same information as for liquid blood. If the bloodstain is moist, air-dry the clothing before packing.

---

Blood can be identified as animal or human. It is most useful in eliminating suspects. Age, race or sex cannot be determined from blood samples, but DNA analysis can provide positive identification of persons.

---

In some cases, blood characteristics can help to determine race; for example, sickle-shaped red blood cells primarily occur in blacks. DNA analysis as well as precautions that should be taken when handling such evidence are discussed in a later section of this chapter.

### Hairs and Fibers

Hairs and fibers are often difficult to locate without a careful search and strong lighting. They are valuable evidence because they can place a suspect at a crime scene, especially in crimes of violence where an interchange of hairs and fibers is most likely to occur. Hairs and fibers can also be taken from the scene by the suspect.

Place hairs and fibers found at the crime scene in paper, using a druggist fold, or in a small box. Seal all edges and openings, and identify on the outside.

If hairs and fibers are found on an object small enough to send to the laboratory, leave them on the object. Hairs and fiber often adhere to blood, flesh or other materials on the object. If the hairs are visible but are not adhering firmly to the object, record their location in your notes. Then place them in a pillbox or glass vial to send to the laboratory. (Do not use plastic.)

If you suspect that hairs are on an object, carefully wrap the object and send it intact to the laboratory. Attempt to obtain twenty-five to fifty full hairs from the appropriate part of the suspect's body for standards of comparison. A forceps or a comb can be used to obtain the sample.

Hairs and fibers are examined by microscope and compared. Special filter techniques, light sources and photomicrographs can reproduce the specimens in black-and-white or color.

*An LAPD crime lab technician compares two hair strands from a sexual assault case.*

**Examining Hair.** The hair shaft has a *cuticle* on the outside consisting of overlapping scales that always point toward the tip, a *cortex* consisting of elongated cells and the *medulla*—the center of the hair—consisting of variably shaped cells. Variations in these structures make comparisons and identifications possible.

---

Microscopic examination determines whether hair is animal or human. Many characteristics can be determined from human hair: the part of the body it came from; whether it was bleached or dyed, freshly cut, pulled out or burned; and whether there is blood or semen on it. Race, sex and age cannot be determined.

---

As with blood samples, it is extremely difficult to state that a hair came from a certain person, but it can usually be determined that a hair did *not* come from a certain person. DNA analysis can be done on hair for positive identification if the hair root is present.

Hair evidence is important because it does not deteriorate and it is commonly left at the crime scene without the subject's knowledge. Laboratory examination does not destroy hair evidence as it does many other types of evidence. Hair evidence may be subjected to microscopic examination to determine type (e.g., facial, pubic, etc.), biological examination to determine blood-type group and toxicological examination to determine the presence of drugs or poisons.

**Examining Fibers.** Fibers fall into four general groups: mineral, vegetable, animal and synthetic. Mineral fibers most frequently submitted are glass and asbestos. Vegetable fibers include cotton, jute, manila, kapok, hemp and many others. Animal fibers are primarily wool and silk. Synthetics include rayons, polyesters, nylons and others. Each fiber has individual characteristics that can be analyzed chemically.

Fibers are actually more distinguishable than hairs. Fiber examination can determine the fiber's thickness, the number of fibers per strand and other characteristics that help identify clothing. Fibers can be tested for origin, for color and to determine whether the fibers match a comparison garment in type and color.

Although often overlooked, fibers are the most frequently located microscopic evidence. They are often found in assaults, homicides and rapes, where personal contact results in an exchange of clothing fibers. Fibers can be found under the suspect's or victim's fingernails. Burglaries can yield fibers at narrow entrance or exit points where clothing gets snagged. Hit-and-run accidents often yield fibers adhering to vehicles' door handles, grills, fenders or undercarriages.

## Other Types of Evidence

**Paint.** Police laboratories and the FBI maintain files of automobile paints. These standards can help identify the year, make and/or color of a motor vehicle from a chip of paint left at the scene.

Paints are complex and are individual in color, composition, texture and layer composition. In hit-and-run cases, paint samples should be collected from any area of the vehicle that had contact with the victim. Take paint samples down to the original metal to show the layer composition. Use small boxes for submitting paint samples to the crime lab, putting samples from different parts of the vehicle in separate small boxes. If paint chips are on the clothing of the victim or suspect, send the entire article of clothing in a paper bag to the laboratory, properly labeled and identified.

**Skeletal Remains.**    Laboratory examination can determine whether skeletal remains are animal or human. If adequate human remains are available, the sex, race, approximate age at death, approximate height and approximate time since death can be determined. Dental comparisons and X-rays of old fractures are other important **identifying features**.

Busa (1994, p. 36) describes the work of Dr. William Bass, renowned forensic anthropologist and professor, who does identification of dead bodies for the Tennessee Bureau of Investigation and other agencies throughout the county with mysterious deaths. Dr. Bass has become an expert by examining the numerous bodies on his 2-acre research area known as the "body farm." He has identified people by their shoulders, pelvis and vertebrae.

**Wood.**    Wood comparisons are made from items on the suspect, in a vehicle or in or on clothing found at a crime scene. The origin is determined by the size, the fit of the fracture with an original piece of wood or by matching the side or end of pieces of wood. The type of wood is determined from its cellular elements.

**Other.**    Prescription eyeglasses, broken buttons, glove prints and other personal evidence found at a crime scene can also be examined and compared. If there is a problem processing any evidence, the laboratory can provide specific collecting and packaging instructions.

## Evidence Handling and Infectious Disease

Investigators are likely to encounter crimes of violence involving blood and other body fluids of persons with infectious diseases. Patrol officers are likely to encounter these infectious body fluids during routine activities. Edwards and Tewksbury (1996) note:

> Over a decade has passed since the medical and law enforcement communities first became aware of, and concerned about, the implications of HIV/AIDS for police officers. As a result of these concerns, a number of policies and standards have been implemented specifically addressing the training and employment issues relating to what the medical community has labeled the most serious public health threat today.

Pilant (1995, p. 53) suggests: "The statistics [on AIDS] are like a double-edged sword. They do not paint law enforcement officers as impervious to disease, but they do indicate that an officer's chances of contracting one are slim, especially with regard to the AIDS virus." Pilant (p. 54) cautions: "It is the AIDS virus that sparks the deepest fear. . . . Fortunately, the chances are less than 1 percent that an officer will contract the virus on the job. The greater danger lies with tuberculosis (TB), hepatitis and meningitis." She describes these infectious diseases as follows:

■  *Tuberculosis.* This disease is transmitted through the air by suspects who are coughing, hacking and wheezing in the back of the patrol car or in the jail cell.
■  *Hepatitis B.* Known today as HBV, this is a bloodborne pathogen that can live outside the body longer than the HIV virus. . . . A safe and effective vac-

cine to prevent HBV is available and provides at least 90 percent protection
for up to seven years.

■ *Meningitis.* Also spread by airborne transmission, this disease causes in-
flammation of the membranes that surround the brain.

The hepatitis B virus can be found in human blood, urine, semen, cere-
brospinal fluid, vaginal secretions and saliva. Tuberculosis also can be transmitted through saliva, urine, blood and other body fluids.

Precautions for crime-scene processing in the presence of such substances
are suggested by Lopez (1992, p. 22):

> If there are contaminated body fluids at the scene, a minimum of latex gloves,
> goggles, and a face mask should be worn. Evidence should be secured in glass,
> metal, or plastic containers, and any evidence bags should be sealed with tape
> rather than staples (to prevent puncture wounds). Don't eat, smoke, apply
> makeup, or drink at crime scenes. These activities could transfer contaminated
> body fluids to the officer.
>
> The crime scene must be decontaminated after processing. If it is to be left for
> future decontamination, then biohazard warning signs should be placed, and the
> cleaning team must be notified of possible contamination.
>
> Particles of dried blood fly in every direction when a dried blood stain is
> scraped. Because of this, surgical masks and protective eyewear should be considered
> when the possibility exists that dried blood particles or drops of liquid blood may
> strike the face or eyes.
>
> While processing the crime scene, constantly be alert for sharp objects, since
> hypodermic needles and syringes are often secreted in unusual places. . . . Even
> seemingly innocuous items, such as metal staples in paper, present a potential
> hazard. . . .

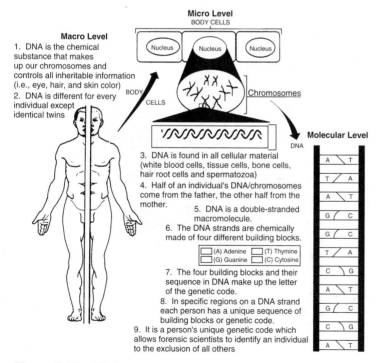

**Figure 5–15　DNA**

Source: Courtesy of the FBI.

If practical, use only disposable items at a crime scene where infectious blood is present. . . . Preferably, the items should be incinerated. . . . All nondisposable items, such as cameras, tools, notebooks, etc., also must be decontaminated. . . . Either a bleach solution or ordinary rubbing alcohol will kill the AIDS virus within 1 minute. . . .

Even after the evidence has been properly dried and packaged, it is still potentially infectious. Therefore, appropriate warnings should be placed on all items.

Further information on procedures for dealing with evidence that has the potential of transmitting an infectious disease can be obtained from the Centers for Disease Control, Office of Biosafety, 1600 Clifton Road N.E., Atlanta, GA 30333.

## DNA Profiling

**DNA** is the abbreviation of *deoxyribonucleic acid,* an organic substance in the nucleus of all living cells that provides the genetic code determining a person's individual characteristics (see Figure 5–15).

According to Zack (1994, p. 1A): "DNA is a basic part of the cell's chromosomes and can be used to create a **genetic fingerprint** to identify a person. It is found in body fluids, hair and tissues."

"DNA Fingerprinting" (1995, p. 3) describes the composition of DNA:

Human cells contain discrete packs of information known as chromosomes. These chromosomes are made of DNA. There are 46 chromosomes within a cell and their arrangement is unique to each individual. Four building blocks, known by their initial letters *A, G, C* and *T,* constitute a DNA chain. The order in which these bases occur provides information necessary to assemble and regulate the construction of a human body.

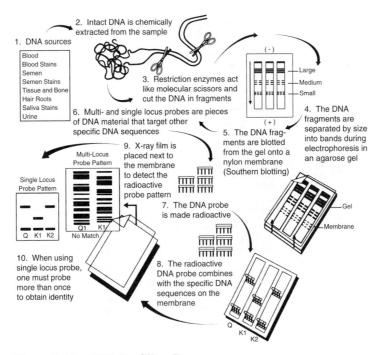

**Figure 5–16   DNA Profiling Process**
Source: Courtesy of the FBI.

**DNA profiling** can be done on blood, hair, saliva, semen, indeed, cells from almost any part of the body (see Figure 5–16).

---

DNA profiling uses material from which chromosomes are made to identify individuals positively. Except for identical twins, no two individuals have the same DNA structure.

---

DNA technology is used in paternity testing, immigration disputes, missing persons cases and unidentified body cases, and, as far as criminal and assailant identification, Geberth (1990, p. 71) says: "It's like the criminal leaving his name, address and social security number at the scene." Geberth notes that DNA "maintains its integrity in dried specimens for prolonged periods" (p. 71) and, consequently, can be helpful in reopening unsolved cases. According to Geberth (p. 73), DNA fingerprinting:

> is the future of forensic medicine, and the experts have only scratched the surface. It is a powerful tool which protects the innocent just as surely as it pinpoints the guilty. . . . It has been established in a number of courts that DNA identification is capable of producing reliable results and that there is general scientific acceptance of the theories underlying DNA identification. The courts have also concluded that DNA forensic tests to determine inclusions are reliable and meet the Frye standard.

Cases are being decided by many courts on a case-by-case basis. In the first appeal from a finding of guilty, the Virginia State Supreme Court upheld the conviction and death sentence of Timothy Spencer in the rapes and murder of two women. The court held that the DNA test results were reliable (*USA Today*, April 5, 1992).

As noted by Brown (1994, p. 51): "The impact of DNA testing in the courts and on the criminal justice system is significant." He suggests:

> The full potential of DNA analysis is only now beginning to be realized. With the advances being made in linking federal, state and local DNA records, otherwise unsolvable crimes will be solved with increasing frequency.

Donohue (1995, p. 1) notes: "DNA testing has proved to be much more than a prosecutorial aid. In rape cases, where DNA testing is used more often than for any other crime, defense attorneys have used the tests not only to clear their clients as suspects, but also to exonerate men previously convicted of rape."

Although DNA profiling has its critics, the Congressional Office of Technological Assessment (1990) gave a strong endorsement to the technology. The FBI Laboratory in Washington, D.C., has been working on processing DNA evidence for a number of years and has been instrumental in training personnel of state and local laboratories.

Advancements have been made in DNA testing. The National Institute of Standards and Technology has developed a quality assurance standards kit for DNA typing that can be used by laboratories to assess the accuracy of their DNA testing procedures within a narrow margin of error. The kit can also be used to test new technicians' knowledge of DNA testing ("DNA Test Kit . . . ," 1992, p. 5).

Because of the expense involved in DNA testing, three criteria must usually be met for the lab to accept DNA samples:

■ Sufficient material must be submitted.

■ Sample (exemplars) must be submitted from both the suspect and the victim.

■ The evidence must be probative.

**Probative evidence** is evidence that is vital for the investigation or prosecution of a case, tending to prove or actually proving guilt or innocence.

DNA evidence not only can prove guilt; it can also prove innocence and thus assists in eliminating suspects. For example, in Baltimore County, Maryland, Robert Scheeler was awaiting trial for rape when DNA test results cleared him. The victim and Scheeler had had a stormy four-year relationship before the assault, and the victim had identified him as her attacker, insisting that it sounded like him, felt like him, was him. While in jail, Scheeler ran into Gregory Ritter, an acquaintance who was strikingly similar to himself in appearance and who was the ex-boyfriend of the rape victim's roommate. Scheeler convinced the authorities to test Ritter's blood, and the DNA test came back positive. In this case DNA cleared an innocent suspect and also convicted the rapist.

In November 1992, the California State Supreme Court changed its course in ruling to admit DNA evidence. However, the findings of guilty by a lower court were upheld against the defendants in the two cases using DNA evidence because the court ruled there was ample non-DNA evidence to incriminate them. This finding supports the advisability of investigating every case thoroughly, even when fingerprint or DNA evidence is seemingly conclusive.

Some states have adopted DNA profiling of violent felons. The Department of Defense has established a military/naval DNA identification system in order to avoid any more "unknown soldiers."

Benefits from DNA analysis include:

■ It requires only a small amount of tissue.

■ It can be applied to old samples.

■ It can be used with mixed stains.

■ The results can be readily checked by another laboratory.

■ A computerized database of DNA patterns can readily be established to aid future investigations.

Disadvantages also exist, however. DNA analysis is time consuming and expensive. In addition, the analysis may be worthless if the defense can attack the methods used to collect and store the evidence on which the DNA analysis was performed.

The trial of O.J. Simpson for the double homicide that occurred in Los Angeles became the "greatest showplace for forensic science ever presented to the public. DNA played a significant role in this showing of scientific investigation" (Laska, 1995, p. 102). Laska suggests: "The 'Dream Team' defense kept its sights centered on the methods used in collection of evidence, and made significant points as to what appeared to be improper collection." He suggests that in the future, defense attorneys are likely to do the same—focus on evidence collection and packaging rather than on the validity of DNA itself.

Suggestions for collecting and preserving DNA evidence are offered by Lifecodes Corporation, the first laboratory in the United States to perform DNA profiling for forensic identification. The suggestions appear in Table 5–2.

## Types of Evidence and Minimal Amounts to Collect

*Blood*

| | |
|---|---|
| Fresh liquid blood | 3 drops |
| Stains | Quarter size |
| Drawn specimens (exemplars) | 1 cc or 1 mL |

*Semen*

| | |
|---|---|
| Fresh liquid semen | 3 drops |
| Stains | Dime size |
| Swabs | 2 swabs |

*Other Types*

Tissues/ Bones/ Teeth: Although small amounts of evidence have provided enough DNA for analysis, the amount that will be needed is unpredictable and depends on many factors including age and concentration of sample.

## How to Collect Biological Evidence

Specimens should be collected and dried as soon as possible to avoid bacterial contamination.

*Wet Specimens*

Quick-dry using a hair dryer on the cool setting.

For large amounts of material, use a large floor fan.

Absorb wet specimen onto sterile gauze, 100% cotton or Q-Tips and then dry.

*Dry Specimens*

Scrape dried specimen from permanent surfaces.

Cut dried specimen out from large areas.

Package whole items if manageable.

## Packaging Specimens

Drying specimens isn't enough. They must be kept as free from moisture as possible. Therefore:

*Small Items*

Place the collected specimen in a zip-lock bag.

Squeeze the air out of the bag.

*Larger Items*

Use paper bags for large items and tape them closed.

## Storing Collected Evidence

Heat can destroy DNA. Therefore, if the evidence is not sent for DNA analysis within a few days, store the packaged evidence as directed.

*Short-Term Storage (less than 30 days)*

Store in freezer.

If freezer is not available, refrigerate evidence.

Store at room temperature for only 1–2 days.

*Extended Storage (more than 30 days)*

Call Lifecodes for recommendations. When it has been collected and stored properly, evidence as old as 10 years has been successfully analyzed.

## Sending Evidence for DNA Analysis

Send evidence and exemplar samples, from the victim and suspect(s), properly labeled, together with a written description of the specimens. Include any other important or relevant facts concerning the case and origin of the sample(s) for the forensic scientist. Send samples via an overnight carrier. The sender is responsible for following the chain-of-custody.

SOURCE: Lifecodes Corporation, Saw Mill River Road, Valhalla, NY 10595 ©1990. By permission.

# Protecting and Storing Evidence

Pilant (1996, p. 38) notes: "Headline after headline points out the lack of control in the property and evidence rooms of small and large agencies." In a survey she conducted, Pilant (pp. 38–39) obtained the following results:

- Only 51 percent of the departments surveyed had written policies and procedures for the property and evidence room.
- 53 percent did not know how much money was stored in the property room.
- 59 percent did not know how many guns were stored in the property room.
- 62 percent had no idea how much evidence came in last year.
- 52 percent did not know the quantity of narcotics stored in the property room.
- 70 percent had no regular inventory process in place.
- 59 percent had no regular auditing system in place.
- 65 percent never changed the locks when personnel changed and did not know how many keys had been issued to department personnel.
- 74 percent did not have an alarm system.

Such results are disturbing given the critical importance of evidence and the chain of custody.

According to Etshman (1995, p. 293):

> It is difficult to properly preserve the chain of custody documentation used in court to determine who has accessed evidence. Too often defendants are able to point out that evidence in the possession of police may have been altered or tampered with because exact chain of custody isn't documented and can't be determined.

Evidence is subject to chemical change, negligence, accident, intentional damage, theft and alteration during handling. Protecting and storing evidence is often the weakest link in the **chain of evidence.** Some evidence requires more care than others.

Improperly sealed containers can allow liquid evidence to evaporate or moisture to enter. Envelopes can split open. Tags can fall off. Writing on labels can become smudged, blurred or faded to the point of illegibility.

Proper storage prevents theft, loss, tampering, contamination and deterioration. The storage area must be secure, well organized and free from pests, insects and excessive heat or moisture.

---

Package evidence properly to keep it in substantially the same condition in which it was found. Document custody of the evidence at every stage.

---

Evidence is stored in vaults, property rooms, evidence rooms, evidence lockers, garages, morgues or under special conditions such as refrigeration. At the crime scene, the officer's vehicle trunk can provide temporary storage. A proper storage area has ample space and is kept at 60 to 80 degrees Fahrenheit. A responsible person is in charge to ensure that established procedures are followed and that the area is secure at all times.

All evidence received is recorded in a register, properly marked and put in the appropriate place. An evidence custodian checks each piece of evidence received to ensure that all forms are properly completed and that the evidence

| BOULDER CITY | EVIDENCE | POLICE DEPT. |
|---|---|---|

| DATE 3-12-97 | DR. NUMBER #97-1640 | | |
|---|---|---|---|
| SUSPECT William Vellum | | JUV ☐ | ADULT ☒ |
| CHARGE Rape | | | |
| LOCATION 1162 Maple Avenue, Boulder City, Nevada | | | |
| BOOKED BY (FINDING OFFICER'S SIGNATURE) Alfred Culp | DATE AND TIME | | |
| INITIALS & P. NUMBER OF BOOKING OFFICER | | | |

**ARTICLES BOOKED**

| ITEM a pair of shorts | ITEM NO. 623 |
|---|---|
| ITEM one womens slacks and panties | ITEM NO. 624 |
| ITEM one bed sheet | ITEM NO. 625 |

| INITIALS USED ON ITEMS BOOKED AC | THIS PACKAGE NO. | TOTAL NO. PACKAGES 3 |
|---|---|---|
| CO-DEFENDANT none | JUV ☐ ADULT ☐ | |
| CO-DEFENDANT | JUV ☐ ADULT ☐ | |

**CHAIN OF CUSTODY**

| SIGNATURE | DATE 3-12-97 | TIME 1940 |
|---|---|---|
| SIGNATURE | DATE | TIME |
| SIGNATURE | DATE | TIME |
| SIGNATURE | DATE | TIME |
| SIGNATURE | DATE | TIME |
| SIGNATURE | DATE | TIME |

**Figure 5–17    Evidence Card**

Source: Courtesy of the Boulder City Police Department.

is the same as described in the forms. A sample evidence card is shown in Figure 5–17.

Strict checkout procedures ensure that the evidence is accounted for at all times. Every person taking any evidence signs for it, giving the date, time, place it is to be taken and the purpose for taking it. When the evidence is returned, it is again signed for, dated and examined to ensure that it is in the same condition as when it was taken. Any change in condition is noted and explained.

Hamilton (1991, p. 146) suggests: "Automation of the evidence function can help prevent many of the problems inherent in managing evidence. With careful preplanning and the right tools for the job, the task is easier, rewards are greater and cost savings are significant."

The amount of property that must be tracked and stored in metro departments is typically 100,000 to 400,000+ pieces of property (Clede, 1991, p. 23). To account for this many items accurately and to maintain the chain of custody, Clede suggests an automated system in which each item is described by its:

- Categorization (NCIC or your own).
- Description (make, model, serial number, etc.).
- Location (within the law enforcement area, warehouse, lab, etc.).
- Ownership (rightful, seized, found, etc., by case).
- Disposition (returned, auctioned, burned, etc.).

Pilant (1992, p. 47) cautions against computerizing "for the sake of computerizing," warning that: "Ultimately, a word-processing system may become a fancier version of an overstuffed file cabinet."

Property control systems that use **barcodes** are used in some departments. According to Barbour and Huestis (1990, p. 53), barcodes "have proven to be efficient and reliable adjuncts to the traditional property/evidence tags." They note (p. 50) that "the things that can go wrong in the property control system often are catastrophic." Yet, an effective property control system is "critically important to the administration of criminal justice, service to the community and the agency's reputation."

The use of barcodes in the Lakewood (Colorado) Police Department has proven to be extremely efficient and effective. At the time property is "booked," it is entered into the computer and given a barcode, which is affixed to the item. During any subsequent signing in/out of the property, the chain of custody is updated by scanning the item's evidence barcode into the log.

Barbour and Huestis (1990, pp. 52–53) report that the system accomplishes the following:

■ Automatically logs in/out evidence and property.
■ Provides an audit trail for money and drugs booked into a property room.
■ Helps locate lost and found property using the computer's search capabilities.
■ Prepares letters to citizens advising them to claim property.
■ Prepares lists from municipal court files when a case disposition has been reached and property is on file.
■ Directs printed "property control notices" to police agents who book-in property or the investigator currently assigned to the case.
■ Prints disposition logs for all items.
■ Prints management and audit reports.
■ Helps with the inventory process.

*Forensic scientist Dr. Henry Lee explains to the O. J. Simpson jury the source of possible shoe prints on murder victim Ron Goldman's blood-soaked jeans shown in photos in the background.*

> Be able to (1) identify the evidence as that found at the crime scene, (2) describe exactly where it was found, (3) establish its custody from discovery to the present and (4) voluntarily explain any changes that have occurred in the evidence.

Typically, the officer who will identify the evidence in court obtains it from the evidence custodian and delivers it to the prosecuting attorney, who takes it to the courtroom and introduces it at the proper time. The identifying officer uses the notes he or she made at the scene to lay the proper foundation for identifying the evidence.

When you are called to the witness stand to identify evidence with your personal mark, take time to examine the item thoroughly. Make sure that all marks are accounted for and that your mark has not been altered. A rapid identification may make a bad impression on the jury and may lead you into an erroneous identification.

## Final Disposition of Evidence

Evidence must be legally disposed of to prevent major storage problems as well as potential problems of pilferage or unauthorized conversion to personal use. State statutes and city ordinances specify how evidence is to be disposed of. The court may order disposition of some evidence such as pornography, narcotics or contraband items.

> Evidence is either returned to the owner, auctioned off or destroyed.

The court or the prosecutor's office usually decides on the manner of disposition. No evidence is destroyed without permission of the prosecutor's office.

Evidence is either disposed of on a continuing basis, during an annual inventory or on a special date set for inventory and disposition. Most evidence is disposed of annually. The status of items is reviewed, and the items are then either returned to storage or disposed of.

Most evidence is held until the case is cleared. In cases where prosecution is not anticipated, contraband items can be released at any time. Other items are returned because the cases have exceeded the statute of limitations.

Witnessed affidavits of disposal list all items sold, destroyed or returned. The affidavits include the date, type of disposition, location and names of all witnesses to the disposition.

## Summary

Criminal investigations rely heavily upon evidence of various types. Corpus delicti evidence establishes that a crime has been committed; associative evidence links a suspect with the crime. To be of value, either type of evidence must be legally and properly seized and processed.

Processing physical evidence includes discovering, recognizing and examining it; collecting, recording and identifying it; packaging, conveying and storing it; exhibiting it in court; and disposing of it when the case is closed. The

Laska (1996, p. 34) describes a computer program distributed by the FBI laboratory called Drugfire. Drugfire is a "PC-based method of storing cartridge case characteristics, comparing the minutiae among various stored cases, sharing this information with other agencies, and even comparing, online, cartridge cases collected by various agencies."

Stowell (1996, p. 18) notes: "Thermal imaging has become a valuable investigation and monitoring tool in at least nine law enforcement applications, ranging from building profiles to search and rescue."

Laska (1995, p. 50) notes: "A new type of inexpensive tool for investigators . . . projects a filtered beam of light onto evidence dusted with fluorescent fingerprint powder. Immediately, a luminescent print appears." He also describes how a portable longwave ultraviolet-light source can be used to illuminate latents on several types of objects. Evidence is usually exposed to superglue and then stained or dusted. After this, it is viewed under the UV light source. Laska (p. 51) contends:

> Forensic light sources have evolved significantly in some 15 years of use. From ponderous expensive units suitable only for laboratory applications, they have slimmed down to units that may attach to a flashlight, or as small, lightweight UV units. The result is that a moderate to large sized agency can equip each crime scene response unit with a forensic light source, and every agency that conducts its own investigations can have a tool that adds significantly to the search for latent fingerprints as well as for trace evidence.

Yet another new area in which investigators should be knowledgeable is in digital forensic imaging. Blitzer (1996, p. 14), program manager of the Law Enforcement Program for Eastman Kodak Company, notes:

> Images are a crucial part of modern crime investigations, and imaging is growing in importance in the practice of law enforcement. Not too long ago, a cover of *Scientific American* magazine showed Marilyn Monroe walking arm-in-arm with Abraham Lincoln. Every day, we see extraordinary special effects in the movies, and even in television advertisements. These new digital technologies make it relatively easy to manipulate images; in turn, this ease makes digital imaging technology suspect in the courtroom.

How can this suspicion be eliminated? Blitzer suggests that any agency using digital imaging establish Standard Operating Procedures and follow them to the letter. He contends that it is the person testifying regarding the digital image who is all-important. He concludes:

> . . . The technology has come a long way since the days of King Kong. However, it is still the integrity of the witness that is in question, not the technology in the lab.

relative importance of physical evidence depends on its ability to establish that a crime was committed as well as how, when and by whom.

Protect the integrity of evidence and the chain of custody by (1) limiting the number of people who handle the evidence and testify in court; (2) following proper procedures for collecting evidence, such as making all relevant notes and properly identifying the evidence; and (3) requiring every person taking evidence to sign for it and explain in writing why it is needed.

To determine what is evidence, consider first the type of crime that appears to have been committed. Then look for any objects that are unrelated or foreign to the scene, that are unusual in their location or number, that have been damaged or broken or whose relation to other objects suggests a pattern that fits the crime. The more individual the evidence, the greater its value.

Often standards of comparison are required. A standard of comparison is an object, measure or model with which evidence is compared to determine whether both came from the same source. Comon errors in collecting evidence are (1) not collecting enough of the sample, (2) not obtaining standards of comparison and (3) not maintaining the integrity of the evidence.

Mark or identify each item of evidence in a way that can be recognized later. Include the date and case number as well as your identifying mark or initials. Record in your notes the date and time of collection, where it was found and by whom, case number, description of the item and who took custody of it. Package each item separately in durable containers to maintain the integrity of evidence. Personal delivery, registered mail, insured parcel post and air express are legal ways to transport evidence. Always obtain the signature of the person receiving the evidence.

Frequently examined physical evidence includes fingerprints, voiceprints, shoe and tire impressions, bite marks, tools and toolmarks, weapons and ammunition, glass, soils and minerals, body fluids (including blood), hairs and fibers, safe insulation, rope and tape, drugs, documents and laundry and dry-cleaning marks.

Know how to locate, develop, photograph, lift and submit fingerprints for classification by experts. Any hard, smooth, nonporous surface can contain latent fingerprints. Do not powder a print unless it is necessary; do not powder a visible print until after photographing it. Inked prints of persons likely to be at the scene are used as elimination prints. Fingerprints and DNA are the strongest possible evidence of a person's identity. Fingerprints cannot, however, indicate the person's age, sex, race or occupation.

Shoe and tire impressions and toolmarks are photographed, and the object on which they appear is submitted to the laboratory if possible. If impressions cannot be submitted intact, cast them.

Blood can be identified as animal or human. It is most useful in eliminating suspects. Age, race or sex cannot be determined from blood samples. DNA analysis, however, can provide positive identification. DNA profiling uses material from which chromosomes are made to identify individuals positively. Except for identical twins, no two individuals have the same DNA structure.

Package evidence properly to keep it in substantially the same condition in which it was found. Document custody of the evidence at every stage. The best-evidence rule stipulates that the original evidence is to be presented in court whenever possible.

When presenting evidence in court, be able to (1) identify the evidence as that found at the crime scene, (2) describe exactly where it was found, (3) establish its custody from discovery to the present and (4) voluntarily explain any changes that have occurred in the evidence.

After a case is closed, evidence is returned to the owner, auctioned off or destroyed.

## Checklist

*Physical Evidence*
- Was all physical evidence photographed before anything was moved?
- Was the physical evidence located in the crime-scene sketch?
- Were relevant facts recorded in your notebook?

■ Was the evidence properly identified, including the date, case number, your initials or mark and a description of the evidence?

■ Was the evidence properly packaged to avoid contamination or destruction?

■ Were standards of comparison obtained if required?

■ Was the evidence sent in a way that kept it secure and provided a signed receipt, such as by registered mail?

■ Was the evidence kept continuously secure until presented in court?

The following types of physical evidence are frequently found at a crime scene and should be searched for, depending on the type of crime committed:

Blood

Cigarettes, cigars, smoking
    materials

Clothing and fragments

Containers and boxes

Documents and papers

Dirt and dust particles

Fibers, ropes and strings

Fingernail scrapings

Fingerprints, visible and latent

Footprints

Glass objects and fragments

Greases, oils, salves, emulsions

Hairs, human and animal

Inorganic materials

Insulation from safes, buildings and
    homes

Metal objects and fragments

Organic materials, plant and
    animal

Paint and paint chips

Palm prints

Personal possessions

Photographs

Plastic impressions

Soils

Tires and tire tracks

Tools and toolmarks

Weapons

Wood chips or fragments

## Discussion Questions

1. What kind of physical evidence would you expect to find at the scene of a burglary?

2. What kind of physical evidence would you expect to find at the scene of an armed robbery? Why does this differ from your response to Question 1?

3. What is meant by evidence that is *material, relevant* and *competent?*

4. What legal rule requires the submission of original evidence and when is this rule followed? When is it permissible to substitute evidence that is not original evidence?

5. What general procedures would you follow in finding and collecting evidence at a crime scene?

6. How would you mark for identification the following items of evidence: A broken window pane? A damaged bullet? Dried blood scraped from a wood floor? A shotgun shell casing? A piece of clothing with semen stains?

7. How would you locate, preserve, lift and identify a latent fingerprint on a wall in a house? How would you have the print examined?

8. What determines whether a government or private laboratory is used to examine evidence? What laboratory facilities are available to your police department?

9. *Continuity of evidence* is a legal term describing the chain of evidence necessary to make evidence legally admissible in court. Describe a chain of evidence from the time of discovery to introduction in court.

**10.** How does your police department dispose of evidence after it is no longer of value or has been released by the court?

## References

Andrae, Dominic. "Fingerprint Technology." *Law and Order*, November 1993, pp. 37–38.

"Ballastics Technology on Track." *Law Enforcement News*, June 15, 1994, pp. 1, 10.

Barbour, Gary R., and Robert P. Huestis. "Barcodes: Technology Enhances Property Control Systems." *The Police Chief*, April 1990, pp. 50–53.

Benson, Kathy. "Matchmakers." *Police*, June 1995, pp. 32–35.

Blitzer, Herbert L. "Forensic Imaging Options: Worth a Thousand Words." *The Police Chief*, October 1996, p. 14.

Brown, John R. "DNA Analysis: A Significant Tool for Law Enforcement." *The Police Chief*, March 1994, pp. 51–52.

Burke, Tod W. "Laser Fingerprinting: Technology of the 1990s." *Law and Order*, August 1992, pp. 75–76.

Busa, Lawrence. "The Bone Experts." *Police*, March 1994, p. 36.

Chadbourne, Robert. "Doing Investigations to the Letter of the Law." *Law and Order*, November 1994, pp. 57–60.

Christman, David. "Handwriting on the Wall: Bloodstain Pattern Analysis Can Be a Signature in Interpreting the Scene of a Crime." *Police*, November 1994, pp. 55–57, 90–91.

Clede, Bill. "Computer Can Save Lost Evidence." *Law and Order*, October 1991, p. 23.

Dees, Timothy. "Automation of Forensic Ballistics." *Law Enforcement Technology*, March 1994, pp. 44–47.

"Digits Go Digital: NYPD Set to Bid Farewell to Ink-Pad Fingerprinting." *Law Enforcement News*, February 28, 1995, p. 5.

"DNA Fingerprinting." *Security Concepts*, December 1995, pp. 3, 21.

"The DNA-Print Guide to Preserving Biological Evidence." Lifecodes Corporation, 1990.

"DNA Test Kit Helps Labs Keep a Handle on Quality." *Law Enforcement News*, October 15, 1992, p. 5.

Donohue, Stephen. "DNA Analysis in High Gear, with Demand for Tests Rising and DOJ Funding New Labs." *Law Enforcement News*, October 15, 1995, pp. 1, 10.

Edwards, Terry D., and Richard Tewksbury. "HIV/AIDS: State Police Training Practices and Personnel Policies." *American Journal of Police*, Vol. XV, No. 1, 1996, pp. 45–62.

Etshman, Todd. "Common-Sense Solutions to Evidentiary Problems." *Law and Order*, January 1995, pp. 293–294.

Geberth, Vernon J. "Application of DNA Technology in Criminal Investigations." *Law and Order*, March 1990, pp. 70–73.

Hamilton, Thomas S. "Developing an Automated Evidence Tracking System." *The Police Chief*, April 1991, pp. 146–149.

Hesskew, Dusty. "Luminol." *Law and Order*, November 1991, pp. 31–33.

"Hey Buddy, Got a Match?" *Law Enforcement News*, April 30, 1994, p. 1.

Hill, Mark. "Bloodstain Analysis Simplified." *Law and Order*, July 1992, p. 8.

Hoober, Scott. "Detecting Fingerprints Easier." *Law and Order*, May 1994, pp. 103–104.

Laska, Paul R. "Computers, Lasers, and Firearms: Investigating Gun Crimes in the '90s." *Law Enforcement Technology*, May 1996, pp. 34–37.

———. "DNA on Trial." *Law Enforcement Technology*, October 1995, pp. 102–104.

———. "Luminescent Fingerprint Techniques." *Law Enforcement Technology*, March 1995, pp. 50–51.

Lesce, Tony. "Bullet Effects." *Law and Order*, June 1995, pp. 47–50.

Lopez, Carl. "The New OSHA Bloodborne Pathogens Regulations." *Law and Order*, November 1992, pp. 21–22.

Mallory, Jim. "Electronic Fingerprint Technology." *Law and Order*, May 1992, pp. 116–118.

Pilant, Lois. "Equipping a Forensics Lab." *The Police Chief*, September 1992, pp. 37–47.

———. "Forensic Science: Forerunners of the Future." *Law Enforcement Technology*, March 1994, pp. 48–51.

———. "Infection Control." *The Police Chief*, November 1995, pp. 53–56.

———. "Property & Evidence Management." *The Police Chief*, July 1996, pp. 37–44.

Sparrow, Malcolm K. "Measuring AFIS Matcher Accuracy." *The Police Chief*, April 1994, pp. 147–151.

Stowell, Charles A. "Heat Made Visible." *Law and Order*, November 1996, pp. 18–21.

Van Duyn, J. "The FBI's 21st Century Integrated Computer System—'IAFIS.'" *Law Enforcement Technology*, April 1993, pp. 40–41.

Zack, Margaret. "Use of DNA Evidence Widened." (Minneapolis/St. Paul) *Star Tribune*, April 30, 1994, pp. A1, A17.

Zauner, Phyllis. "Putting the Finger on Security." *Law and Order*, November 1991, pp. 22–24.

# Obtaining Information

## DO YOU KNOW

What the goal of interviewing and interrogation is?

What sources of information are available to investigators?

What a sources of information file is and what it contains?

How to improve communication?

What the major barriers to communication are?

What the characteristics of an effective interviewer or interrogator are?

When and in what order individuals are interviewed?

What rapport is and how to establish it?

What basic approaches are used in questioning?

What two requirements are needed to obtain information?

What the difference between direct and indirect questions is and when to use each?

What technique is likely to assist recall as well as uncover lies?

What a statement is in a criminal investigation?

What the Miranda warning is and when it is given?

What the two requirements of a place for conducting interrogations are?

What techniques are used in an interrogation?

What third-degree tactics are and their place in interrogation?

What restrictions are placed on obtaining a confession?

What significance a confession has in an investigation?

What to consider when questioning a juvenile?

What a polygraph is and the acceptability of its results in court?

What the polygraph role is in an investigation and if the results are admissable in court?

## CAN YOU DEFINE

| | | |
|---|---|---|
| admission | informant | rapport |
| cognitive interview | information age | sources of information |
| complainant | interrogation | file |
| confession | interview | statement |
| custodial arrest | Miranda warning | suspect |
| custodial interrogation | network | third degree |
| direct question | nonverbal | truth serums |
| hypnosis | communication | victim |
| in custody | polygraph | waiver |
| indirect question | public safety exception | witness |

KNOWLEDGE OBTAINED THROUGH QUESTIONING AND THAT OBTAINED through physical evidence are equally important. Most solved cases rely on both physical evidence and information obtained by interviewing and interrogating. Physical evidence can provide the basis for questioning people about the crime, and questioning can provide leads for finding physical evidence.

**Introduction**

Either or both provide the knowledge required to end the investigation successfully. Although physical evidence is important by itself, supporting oral testimony adds considerable value when presented in court. On the other hand, although a confession may appear to be conclusive, it cannot stand alone legally. It must be supported by physical evidence or other corroboration.

This chapter begins with a discussion of interviews and interrogations. Next, sources of information are described, followed by a discussion of how to enhance communication. Then, an in-depth look at the interview and the interrogation is provided. Evaluating and corroborating information received during an interview or interrogation is the next area to be explored, followed by a discussion of how to question juveniles and young children. The chapter concludes with an explanation of scientific aids available for obtaining information.

## The Interview and the Interrogation

Information is obtained continuously throughout an investigation. Some is volunteered, some the police officer must really work for; some is useful, some worthless or even misleading. Most of a police officer's time is spent meeting people and obtaining information from them, a process commonly referred to by two terms, *interview* and *interrogation*.

An **interview** is the questioning of persons who are not suspects in a crime but who know something about the crime or the individuals involved. An **interrogation** is the questioning of persons suspected of direct or indirect involvement in the crime.

---

The ultimate goals of interviewing and interrogating are to identify those responsible for a crime and to eliminate the innocent from suspicion.

---

All facts supporting the truth must be obtained, whether they indicate a person's guilt or innocence. Much information obtained has no direct bearing on the case. Recognize what information is important and useful. The best information is that which proves the elements of the crime (the corpus delicti) or provides leads for further investigation.

## Sources of Information

In addition to physical evidence, three primary sources of information are available.

---

Important sources of information include (1) reports and records, (2) persons who are not suspects in the crime but who know something about the crime or those involved and (3) suspects in the crime.

---

Often these sources overlap. For example, information in a hotel's records may be supplemented by information supplied by the hotel manager or the doorkeeper.

Because so many informational sources exist in any given community, it is helpful to develop a **sources of information file.** Each time you locate someone who can provide important information on criminal activity in the community, make a card with information on this source. For example, if a hotel manager provides useful information, make a card with the manager's name, name of the hotel, address, telephone number, type of information provided and any other relevant information. File the card under *hotel.*

---

A sources of information file contains cards with the name and location of persons, organizations and records that may assist in a criminal investigation.

---

Intelligence information can be short or long term. It may relate to present cases or future operations. It can be relayed to officers by bulletins, roll call, briefings or through training seminars. Intelligence information is most often associated with organized crime, drug operations, pornography or conspiracy crimes. It is proactive. It anticipates future problems, needs or changes. Such information can be obtained from many sources, for example, from informants, criminals, other police agencies, citizen tips or complaints, school records, other governmental departments, news items, undercover operations and the like.

Futurists note that we have progressed from the stone age to the agricultural age to the industrial age to the **information age.** Knowledge is doubling every two-and-one-half years. In no area have more advances been made than in that of moving information. The challenge is in how to keep abreast of it all.

Among the most important advances for law enforcement is the availability of computerized information. Such information has been in existence for several years but not in individual squad cars, easily accessible by the average "cop on the beat." Officers now receive information on stolen vehicles, individual arrest records and the like within minutes. Parking citations and traffic tickets can also be issued using hand-held computers that not only print out the ticket but also automatically enter the information into the files, greatly reducing officer's paperwork.

## Reports and Records

An important information source is the records and reports of your police department, including all preliminary reports, follow-up investigative reports, offense and arrest records, modus operandi files, fingerprint files, missing persons reports, gun registrations and wanted bulletins.

Read all police reports concerning your case and talk to the officers working in the area where the crime occurred and where the suspect lives. This will help you develop information about the suspect's habits and associates. Closely examine the suspect's prior record and modus operandi. Examine all laboratory and coroner's reports associated with the case.

Other records to check include those maintained by banks, loan and credit companies, delivery services, hospitals and clinics, hotels and motels, newspapers, telephone books, city directories, street cross directories, utility providers, department of motor vehicles, pawnbrokers, storage companies, the Internal Revenue Service and taxi companies. Each time you locate a source whose records are helpful, add a card for that source to your sources of information file.

## Complainants, Witnesses, Victims and Informants

Vast amounts of information come from people with direct or indirect knowledge of a crime. Although legally no one has to provide information to the police except personal identification and accident information, citizens are responsible for cooperating with the police for their own and the community's best interests. Everyone is a potential crime victim and a potential source of information. Interview anyone other than a suspect who has information about a case. This includes complainants, witnesses, victims and informants.

A **complainant** is a person who requests that some action be taken. The complainant is especially important in the initial stages of the case. Listen carefully to all details and determine the extent of the investigative problems involved: the type of crime, who committed it, what witnesses were present, the severity of any injuries and any leads. Thank the complainant for contributing to the investigation.

A **witness** is a person who saw the crime or some part of it being committed. Good eyewitnesses are often the best source of information in a criminal investigation. Record the information a witness gives, including any details that can identify and locate a suspect or place the suspect at the crime scene. Although not always reliable, eyewitnesses' testimony remains a vital asset in investigating and prosecuting a case.

Sometimes a diligent search is needed to find witnesses. They may not want to get involved, or they may withhold or provide information for ulterior motives. Make every effort to locate all witnesses. Check the entire crime-scene area. Conduct a neighborhood canvass to determine whether anyone saw or heard anything when the crime occurred. Check with the victim's friends and associates. Make public appeals for information on radio and television.

Be aware that witness statements are not always reliable. A group of police officers attended a session on reliability of witnesses' memory and were given a memory recall test by Dr. Patrick Robins of the Institute for Police Technology and Management. Every officer failed the test. Robins strongly warned about the susceptibility of human observation to error and suggested paying more attention to expert-witness testimony. Witnesses are often more confident in their knowledge of what happened than they are accurate. Most people observe only a part of the commission of a crime or traffic accident, but they testify as though they witnessed the entire event (Badger, 1995, p. 13).

A **victim** is the person injured by the crime. Frequently the victim is also the complainant and a witness. Victims are emotionally involved and may be experiencing anger, rage and fear. Such personal involvement can cause them to exaggerate or distort what occurred.

An **informant** is any individual who can provide information about the case but who is not a complainant, witness, victim or suspect. Informants may be interested citizens or individuals with criminal records.

Include each source of information *except confidential* sources in your sources-of-information file. Some informants, either because of their position in society or their connection with crime, insist on remaining anonymous. Such contacts are frequently given code names and their true identity is known only to the investigator. Be extremely careful in using such contacts. Never make promises or deals that you cannot legally fulfill.

In some instances, informants may not remain anonymous. Bizzack (1991, p. 125) suggests that investigators who use informants should make them aware of those situations in which their identity might have to be revealed:

- When disclosure is relevant and essential to a fair determination of the case.
- When the informant was an eyewitness to the actual charge being prosecuted.

■  When the informant was a participant in the offense.
■  When the informant could give relevant testimony material to the issues of guilt or innocence.
■  When the accused demonstrates an alibi at the time when the informant incriminated him.

Complainants, victims, witnesses and informants may be greatly aided by cellular phones if in their possession. The majority of the more than 16 million cellular phone owners in the United States own these phones for safety. However, they can also greatly speed reporting of information related to crimes. Police should periodically publicize the importance of calling 911 if cellular phone owners see a crime being committed. Such immediate notification would substantially reduce police response time to calls for police service, increase arrests at the scene and provide for rapid protection of the crime scene to preserve evidence, increasing the chance for convicting a suspect.

### Suspects

A **suspect** is a person considered to be directly or indirectly connected with a crime, either by overt act or by planning or directing it.

Do not overlook the suspect as a chief source of information. An individual can become a suspect either through information provided by citizens or by his or her own actions. Any suspicious individuals should be questioned. Complete a field interview card for any suspicious person you stop. This card places a person or vehicle in a specific place at a specific time and furnishes data for future investigative needs. A sample field interview card is shown in Figure 6–1.

An individual with a known modus operandi fitting the crime may be seen at or near the crime scene. The person may be wanted for another crime or may show an exaggerated concern for the police's presence, or the person may be in an illegal place at an illegal time, often the case with juveniles.

When questioning occurs spontaneously on the street, referred to as a field interview, it is especially advantageous to officers if they can question someone suspected of involvement in a crime right after the crime occurred. Zulawski and Wicklander (1995, p. 114) suggest that several advantages exist in this situation:

■  The suspect has no time to prepare his lies.
■  The suspect must conceal his emotions of having been discovered.
■  The suspect is uncertain as to what is known or not known about the incident.
■  The impact of the suspect's detention causes judgment because he believes his guilt is certain.
■  The field interviewer playing on these advantages can increase the likelihood of the suspect making an admission of involvement in the incident.

✱Zulawski and Wicklander (p. 115) conclude: "Officers on the street, interacting effectively using their interviewing skills, will bring a return on investment found nowhere else in the department. Skilled field interviews increase the department's image, clearance rate, and intelligence gathering while maintaining overhead."

| OP. LIC. NO. | STATE | NAME (Last name first) | | | | | |
|---|---|---|---|---|---|---|---|
| 476-18-4681 | NV | Pirino, John W. | | | | | |

| RESIDENCE ADDRESS | CITY | STATE | SEX | DESCENT | HAIR | EYES |
|---|---|---|---|---|---|---|
| 7801 Dupoint | Las Vegas, Nv. | | M | lt | Bl | Br |

| HEIGHT | WEIGHT | BIRTHDATE | CLOTHING |
|---|---|---|---|
| 5-11 | 187 | 5-14-40 | Blue Jeans, Striped Shirt, Brown Jacket |

| PERSONAL ODDITIES | PHONE NO. |
|---|---|
| Limp-inj. left leg | 421-1170 |

| BUSINESS ADDRESS/SCHOOL/UNION AFFIL. | SOC. SEC. NO. |
|---|---|
| None | 321-14-8645 |

| MONIKER/ALIAS | GANG/CLUB |
|---|---|
| Jack | None |

**SUBJ. INFO.** 1 LOITERER  3 SOLICITOR  5 GANG ACTIVITY  7 ON PAROLE  [X] DRIVER
2 PROWLER  4 HITCHHIKER  6 HAS RECORD  8[X] ON PROBATION  [ ] PASSENGER

| | YEAR | MAKE | MODEL | TYPE | COLOR | VEH. LIC. NO. | STATE |
|---|---|---|---|---|---|---|---|
| **V** | 1986 | Chev St. | Wagon | 4 dr | beige | 491-AMU | Nv |

| **E** | INSIDE COLOR | INT | 1 BUCKET SEATS  2 DAMAGED INSIDE | EXT | 1 CUST. WHEELS  3 LEVEL ALTER.  5 CUST. PAINT  2 PAINTED INSC  4 RUST/PRIMER  6 VINYL TOP |
|---|---|---|---|---|---|
| **H** | Brown | | | | |

**BODY** [X]DAMAGE  [X]STICKER  4 LEFT  6 FRONT    **WIN-DOWS** [X]DAMAGE  3 CURTAINS  4 LEFT  6 FRONT
2 MODIFIED  5 RIGHT  7 REAR    2 CUST. TINT  5 RIGHT  7[X]REAR

**Persons with subject:**

| LAST NAME | 1st init. | SEX | LAST NAME | 1st init. | SEX |
|---|---|---|---|---|---|
| Bixley, W C | | M | Gurley, M S | | F |
| LAST NAME | 1st init. | SEX | LAST NAME | 1st init. | SEX |
| Thoms, G A | | M | Lecher, R L | | F |

ADDITIONAL INFO (ADDITIONAL PERSONS WITH SUBJECT, BKG. NOS., I.D. NOS., NARRATIVE, ETC.)

Vehicle going slow in alley, passengers in rear looking out rear

window.  No other persons or vehicles in alley, late at night.

| DATE | TIME | LOCATION | Rept. Dist. |
|---|---|---|---|
| 5-4-97 | 0130 | Alley behind 602 Pine | |

| OFFICER'S NAME | SERIAL NO. | OFFICER'S NAME | SERIAL NO. |
|---|---|---|---|
| Wesley Jones | 162 | Thomas Begley | 153 |

| **FIELD INTERVIEW** BOULDER CITY POLICE DEPARTMENT | DIVISION | DETAIL | SUPERVISOR'S INITS. |
|---|---|---|---|
| | Patrol | Drug | HVM |

**Figure 6–1   Field Interview Card, front and back**
Source: Courtesy of the Boulder City Police Department.

Sometimes direct questioning of suspects is not the best way to obtain information. In cases where direct contact would tip off the person, it is often better to use undercover or surveillance officers or various types of listening devices. These are discussed in Chapter 8. Important information on suspects is often contained in police files and records or in the records of community agencies and businesses. These are discussed in Chapter 7.

## Enhancing Communication

Successful questioning requires two-way communication between the investigator and the person being questioned. There are several ways to improve communication, whether you are interviewing or interrogating.

> To improve communication: prepare in advance, obtain the information as soon after the incident as possible, be considerate and friendly, use a private setting, eliminate physical barriers, sit rather than stand, encourage conversation, ask simple questions one at a time, listen and observe.

According to Hess and Wrobleski (1996, pp. 43–44), these procedures improve communication with a witness, victim or suspect:

- *Prepare* for each interview in advance if time permits. Know what questions you need to have answered.
- Obtain your information as *soon after* the incident as possible. A delay may result in the subject's not remembering important details.
- *Be considerate* of the subject's feelings. If someone has just been robbed, seen an assault or been attacked, the individual may be upset and emotional. Allow time for the person to calm down before asking many questions. Remember that when emotions increase, memory decreases.
- *Be friendly.* Try to establish rapport with the subject before asking questions. Use the person's name; look at the person as you ask questions; respond to the answers.
- *Use a private setting if possible.* Eliminate as many distractions as you can so that the subject can devote full attention to your questions.
- *Eliminate physical barriers.* Talking across a desk or counter, or through a car window does not encourage conversation.
- *Sit* rather than stand. This will make the subject more comfortable and probably more willing to engage in conversation.
- *Encourage conversation.* Keep the subject talking by:
  Keeping your own talking to a minimum.
  Using open-ended questions, such as "Tell me what you saw."
  Avoiding questions that call for only a "yes" or "no" answer.
  Allowing long pauses. Pauses in the conversation should not be uncomfortable. Remember that the subject needs time to think and organize his or her thoughts. Give the subject all the time needed.
- *Ask simple questions.* Do not use law enforcement terminology when you ask your questions. Keep your language simple and direct.
- *Ask one question at a time.* Allow the subject to answer one question completely before going to the next question.
- *Listen* to what is said and how it is said.
- *Watch* for indications of tension, nervousness, surprise, embarrassment, anger, fear or guilt.

### Barriers to Communication

People often have reasons for not wanting to answer questions asked by the police. Even though these reasons may have no logical basis, be aware of the common barriers to communication.

> Barriers to communication include ingrained attitudes and prejudices, fear, anger and self-preservation.

One important barrier to communication between police and the public is the ingrained attitude that telling the truth to the police is wrong. The criminal element, those closely associated with crime and even the police often use such terms as *fink* and *snitch,* which imply that giving information to the police is wrong, unsavory or illegal.

Prejudices concerning a person's race, beliefs, religion, size, amount of education, economic status or place of upbringing can be barriers to communication. You may encounter prejudice because you are a police officer or because of your race, your physical appearance or religious beliefs. Equally important, prejudices you hold can interfere with your communicating with some individuals and, therefore, with your investigation.

Fear is another barrier to communication. Some witnesses fear that criminals will harm them or their family if they testify, or they fear appearing in court or losing time and wages while testifying.

Persons actually involved in the crime can be reluctant to talk for many reasons, the most important being self-preservation. Although it is natural that suspects do not want to implicate themselves, be aware of other factors that can cause them to not answer questions. Severe guilt feelings can preclude telling anyone about the crime. Fear of the consequences can be so great that no inducement can make them tell the truth. They may fear that if they are sent to prison they will be sexually assaulted or beaten, or they may fear that any accomplices they implicate will seek revenge.

### Characteristics of the Effective Interviewer/Interrogator

Interviewing and interrogating play a critical role in successfully investigating and prosecuting a case. Unfortunately, police are often inadequately trained in questioning techniques and so do not develop the characteristics required of an effective interviewer/interrogator. Many of the emotional and intellectual traits of the investigator discussed in Chapter 1 are especially valuable in communicating with others.

Presenting a favorable appearance and personality and establishing rapport are more important than physical attributes. Sometimes, however, it is an advantage to be of the same race or gender as the person being questioned. Under some circumstances it is better not to wear a uniform when conducting an interview. Sometimes a suit or jeans and a sweater is more appropriate.

---

The effective interviewer/interrogator is adaptable, self-controlled, patient, confident, optimistic, objective, sensitive to individual rights and aware of the elements of crimes.

---

**Adaptability.**   Your cultural and educational background and experience affect your ability to understand people from all walks of life, to meet them on their own level on varied subjects and to adapt to their personalities and lifestyles.

**Self-Control and Patience.**   Use self-control and patience to motivate people to talk. Be sympathetic yet uninvolved, waiting for responses while patiently leading the conversation and probing for facts. Remain professional, recognizing that some persons you interview may be hostile toward you.

**Confidence and Optimism.**   Do not assume that because the person you are questioning is a hardened criminal, has an attorney, is belligerent or is better educated than you that no opportunity exists to obtain information. Show that you are in command, that you already know many answers and want to corroborate what you know. If the conversation shifts away from the subject, steer the discussion back to the topic.

**Objectivity.**    Maintain your perspective on what is sought, avoiding preconceived ideas about the case. Be aware of any personal prejudices that can interfere with your questioning.

**Sensitivity to Individual Rights.**    Maintain a balance between the rights of others and those of society. Naturally, suspects do not want to give information that conflicts with their self-interests or threatens their freedom. Moreover, many citizens want to stay out of other people's business. Use reason and patience to overcome this resistance to becoming involved.

**Knowledge of the Elements of the Crime.**    Know what information you need to prove the elements of the crime you are investigating. Phrase questions to elicit information related to these elements.

## The Interview

Interviewing is talking to people, questioning them, obtaining information and reading between the lines. The main sources of information at the crime scene are the complainant, the victim and any witnesses. (These may be the same person.) Separate witnesses and then obtain a complete account of what happened from each one. Listen, prompt if necessary and explore for new leads.

---

Interview witnesses separately if possible. Interview the victim or complainant first, then eyewitnesses and then individuals who did not actually see the crime but who have relevant information.

---

Finding, detaining and separating witnesses is a high priority. Witnesses who are not immediately detained can drift off into the crowd or decide not to become involved. Obtain the information as rapidly as possible. Identify all witnesses and check their names and addresses against their identification. Ask witnesses not to speak to one another or to compare stories until they have written down in their own words what happened.

If there are many witnesses, discuss the incident briefly with each. Then establish a priority for obtaining statements based on the witnesses' availability and the importance of their information.

In most cases, interview complainants first because they often can provide enough information to determine if a crime has been committed and, if so, what type of crime. If department policy requires it, have complainants read and initial or sign the information you record during the interview.

Anyone who saw what happened, how it happened or who made it happen is interviewed next. Such witnesses can be in a state of panic, frustration or anger. In the presence of such emotions, remain calm and detached; yet show sympathy and understanding—a difficult tightrope act in many cases.

After interviewing witnesses, interview people who can furnish facts about what happened before or immediately after the crime or who have information about the suspect or the victim.

Not all people with information are at the crime scene. Some persons in the general area may have seen or heard something of value. Even people miles away from the scene may have information about the crime or the person committing it. Explain to such individuals why you are questioning them, check their identification and then proceed with your interview.

The main sources of immediate information away from the crime scene are neighbors, business associates, people in the general area such as motel and hotel personnel and longtime residents. Longer-term contacts may include informants, missing witnesses, friends and relatives. Appeals for public cooperation and reports from various agencies and organizations may also produce information.

Record both positive and negative information. The fact that a witness did *not* see anyone enter a building may be as important as if he or she did. Regardless of whether the interview occurs at or away from the crime scene, certain decisions influence the effectiveness of the interview.

Remember that it is counterproductive to appear absolutely "in charge" and to flaunt your badge and authority. This does not elicit information—the goal of interviewing. It is the information of the person being interviewed that is important, not your information.

Interviews should be conducted like a conversation, but with a purpose. Interviewing skills can be learned, and they are honed by applying what is learned to future interviews. After each interview, critique it and identify your mistakes and aspects that you want to improve. Then when you are planning your next interview, review what you have decided you should do differently. Keep doing this with each new interview, and you will become an expert.

Development of rapport with a witness or suspect is not enhanced by a formalized question-and-answer session. Listen intently. Failure to listen is the biggest fault of most police interviewers. If you cannot remember what an interviewee has said, you are not listening; you are thinking more about what you want to say. Curtail this temptation. Let the interviewee help guide the conversation rather than sticking to your prepared questions religiously.

### Advance Planning

Many interviews, at least initial ones, are conducted in the field and allow no time for planning. If time permits, plan carefully for interviews. Review reports about the case before questioning individuals. Learn as much as possible about the person you are going to question before you begin the interview.

### Selecting the Time and Place

Sometimes there is no time to decide when and where to conduct an interview. Arriving at a crime scene, you may be confronted with a victim or witness who immediately begins to supply pertinent information. Recall that these res gestae statements are extremely valuable. Therefore, record them as close to verbatim as possible.

Determine as soon as possible who the complainant is, where and how many witnesses exist and whether the suspect has been apprehended. If more than one officer is present, the officer in charge decides who will be questioned and assigns personnel to do it. People away from the crime scene are normally questioned as they are found.

Immediate contact with persons having information about a crime improves the chances of obtaining information. Although emotions may be running high, witnesses are usually best able to recall details immediately after the incident. They are also less likely to embellish or exaggerate their stories because others present can be asked to verify the information. Moreover, witnesses can be separated so that they will have little opportunity to compare information. Finally, the reluctance to give the police information is usually not so strong immediately after a crime. Given time to reflect, witnesses may fear that they will have to testify in court, that cooperation will take them away from work and cost them financially or that the criminal may retaliate.

Sometimes, however, it is wise to delay interviewing. In such cases, take only preliminary information at the scene; then arrange for an in-depth interview at the witness's convenience. Do not start an interview unless you have the time to fully develop the information. If you appear impatient, the witness may delay giving information, believing the questioning will soon end.

### Beginning the Interview

How an interview is started is extremely important. It is here that the interviewee and the interviewer size each other up and either establish or lose communication. Mistakes in beginning the interview can establish insurmountable barriers. Make your initial contact friendly but professional. Begin by identifying yourself and showing your official credentials. Then ask a general question about the person's knowledge of the crime.

### Establishing Rapport

Rapport is probably the most critical factor in any interview. People who are approached properly and civilly may volunteer a surprising amount of useful information. Most people do not condone criminal behavior and will assist you. However, they often do not know what is important to a specific investigation. Provide every opportunity to establish rapport and to assist citizens in providing information.

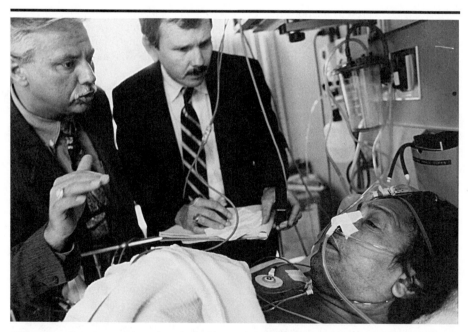

*Some interviews are conducted under extremely difficult circumstances. Here investigators interview a hospitalized convenience store clerk in the intensive care unit of Ben Taub Hospital. The clerk was shot during a robbery of the convenience store.*

---

**Rapport** is the understanding between individuals created by genuine interest and concern.

---

Not everyone with information can provide it easily. People who are emotionally unstable, mentally deficient, have temporary loss of memory or fear police often cannot or will not give information. With them, establishing rapport is critical. If the person is deaf or speaks a foreign language, arrange for an interpreter. If the person appears unwilling to talk, find out why.

Give reluctant witnesses confidence by demonstrating self-assurance. Give indifferent witnesses a sense of importance by showing how the information will help a victim. Remind them that someday they may be victims themselves and will want others to cooperate. Find a way to motivate every witness to talk with you and answer your questions.

Rapport is enhanced by listening carefully to people. Do not indicate verbally or nonverbally that you consider the matter trivial or unimportant; people will sense if you are merely going through the motions. Take a personal interest in people you question. Discuss their family, their work or their hobbies. Offer them a handshake, a soft drink or coffee. Be sympathetic, show personal interest, and assure them that everything possible will be done but that you need their help.

Encourage conversation by letting the person know you represent the victim and the community and that the information you seek is important to the investigation. Praise and thank people for cooperation and helpful information.

### Networking an Interview

Most people are familiar with the concept of a business or professional **network**—a body of personal contacts that can further an individual's career. In reality, networks can extend much further than this. As noted by Noose (1992, p. 101):

> Networks represent relationships, links between people, and between people and their beliefs. Without an understanding of these relationships, these networks, it is often quite difficult, and sometimes even impossible to understand an event or the circumstances that led to it. The answers obtained may have very little in common with the questions asked. . . .
>
> Networks produce the context within which a statement from a complainant, victim, witness or suspect can be most clearly understood. . . .
>
> Besides social networks, there are ethnic, cultural and community networks, business, professional and occupational relationships, religious beliefs, political ideologies and other personal and emotional affiliations that represent links between people and their beliefs. Understanding the networks can help investigators understand the event. . . .
>
> Predictions about American society in the next decade often offer the opinion that the diverse nature of the social groups that will be encountered by police will widen and increase. In order to serve the public, officers will have to be able to uncover the networks . . . within their jurisdiction.

### Interviewing Techniques

Evans (1990, p. 90) contends that most cases are solved through good interviewing techniques and offers these suggestions:

- Select the location of the interview yourself.
- Start with friendly small talk.

- Create a feeling of reciprocity.
- Use deception sparingly.
- Listen carefully and empathize.
- Help subjects to recall events.
- Choose your questions wisely. (Keep them short, confined to one topic.)
- Point out conflicts.
- Be observant for signs of lying.
- Be conscious of body language.

Evans (p. 94) concludes: "The more proficient a police officer becomes in using these interviewing techniques, the higher the dividends will be in successful case resolution."

**Reluctant Interviewees.**    Most people who are reluctant to being questioned respond to one of two approaches: logical or emotional.

---

Appeal to the person's reason or emotions.

---

The *logical approach* is based on reason. Use logic to determine why the person refuses to cooperate and to explain the benefits of cooperating. Explain the problems that result when people who know about a crime do not cooperate.

The *emotional approach* addresses such negative feelings as hate, anger, greed, revenge, pride and jealousy. You can increase these emotions or simply acknowledge them by explaining to the person that "anyone else in the same situation would respond the same way." If such tactics do not work, warn the person of the serious consequences of withholding important information.

Whether to select a rational or an emotional approach depends on the person being interviewed, the type of investigation and your personal preference. No matter which technique or combination of techniques you select, there are two key requirements for obtaining information.

---

Obtain information by listening and observing.

---

How people act during an interview can tell as much as or more than their words. Signs of unusual nervousness, odd expressions, rapid breathing, visible perspiration or a highly agitated state are cause to question the person's truthfulness. Table 6–1 summarizes the guidelines for a successful interview.

Wood (1993, pp. 29–30) makes some suggestions for getting "tough" interviews:

> A person will tell you his secrets only if he feels safe. Your job, from the first handshake, is to put your subject at ease and build his trust in you as a professional.

**Direct vs. Indirect Questions.**    There is a subtle but important difference between direct and indirect questions. A **direct question** is to the point, allowing little possibility of misinterpretation. For example, "What time did you and your husband leave the restaurant?" is direct. In contrast, an **indirect question**

**Table 6–1  Interview Guidelines**

- Ask one question at a time and keep your responses simple and direct.
- Avoid questions that can be answered "yes" or "no"; a narrative account provides more information and may reveal inconsistencies in the person's story.
- Be positive in your approach, but let the person save face if necessary so that you may obtain further information.
- Give the person time to answer. Do not be uncomfortable with pauses in the interview.
- Listen to answers, but at the same time anticipate your next question.
- Watch your body language and tone of voice.
- Start the conversation on neutral territory.
- Tape recorders can be frightening.
- React to what you hear.
- As you move into difficult territory, slow down.
- Don't rush to fill silences.
- Pose the toughest questions simply and directly.
- More room for resistance.
- No meltdowns....You must establish professional distance. Keep your role clear.

is a bit disguised. For example, a question such as "How do you and your husband get along?" could elicit a variety of answers.

> Ask direct questions, that is, questions that come right to the point. Use indirect questions, those that skirt the basic question, sparingly.

The axiom that the shortest distance between two points is a straight line is generally true in obtaining information from a witness. Knowing the elements of the crime you are investigating lets you select questions that will elicit the required information.

**Repetition.**  Anyone who watches detective shows on television has heard victims or suspects complain, "I've already told my story to the police." This is true to life. Individuals *are* asked to tell and retell their version of what happened and for very good reasons. It is difficult for someone who is lying to tell a story exactly the same way several times. A truthful story, however, will contain the same facts but may be phrased differently each time it is retold. After the person has told you what happened, guide the discussion to some other aspect of the case. Later, come back to the topic and ask the person to repeat the story.

> Repetition is the best way to obtain recall and to uncover lies.

Often repeating what someone has told you helps the person provide additional information. Sometimes it also confuses the person being questioned, and if the original version was not true, another repetition will reveal this fact. If inconsistencies appear, go back over the information and attempt to account for them.

**Cognitive Interview Technique.**  Research conducted at the Metro-Dade (Florida) Police Department suggests that interview style has important implications for how much information is received from subjects. According to *Law Enforcement News* ("Interview Style Pays Off...," 1990, p. 1):

> Robbery detectives who conducted interviews with crime victims and eyewitnesses were able to elicit nearly 50 percent more information from their

subjects after being trained to use an experimental technique known as cognitive interviewing. . . .

An interviewer will try to get victims or witnesses to put themselves mentally at the scene of the crime. That is done, the study said, by utilizing several simple mnemonic techniques aimed at encouraging more "focused retrieval." These include allowing the interviewee to do most of the talking; asking fewer short-answer questions and more open-ended ones; allowing more time for the witness to answer; avoiding interruptions as the witness gives details; and encouraging the witness to report all details, no matter how trivial.

This **cognitive interview** method calls for using a secluded, quiet place that is free of distractions for the interview and encouraging subjects to speak slowly. The cognitive interview is especially effective for obtaining information from victims and witnesses who have difficulty remembering the event. Using this technique, the interviewer helps the victim or witness to (Olsen and Wells, 1991, p. 31):

**1.** *Reconstruct the circumstances.* Ask them to think about how they were feeling. Have them focus on the event in their mind's eye. Ask them to describe the weather, the surroundings, objects, people and smells.
**2.** *Report everything.* Ask them to focus on the event and to tell you everything, perhaps telling them not to leave out anything, even if they think it is unimportant. And then try not to interrupt them.
**3.** *Recall the events in a different order.* Ask them to tell the story in reverse chronological order.
**4.** *Change perspectives.* Ask them to assume the role of another person who was present or nearby at the time. What would he or she have been able to see?

Then, depending upon the case, follow the narrative account by asking specific questions:

**1.** *Appearance.* Did the person remind you of anyone? Who? Why?
**2.** *Names.* What was the first letter of the name you heard? (Go through the alphabet.)
**3.** *Numbers.* How many numbers did you see? Were they high? Low? Mixed with letters?
**4.** *Speech.* Who did the voice(s) remind you of? Why?
**5.** *Conversations.* What was your reaction to what was said?

Olsen and Wells (p. 34) point out that this two-pronged approach provides "psychological first aid while facilitating accurate memory recall."

Among the drawbacks of this method are the amount of time it takes and the need for a more controlled environment than may be available. The researchers stress that conducting interviews with witnesses and victims is very different from interrogating suspects—the skills for which are more often taught to police officers.

### Statements

If a person you interview has sufficient information to warrant being a witness in court, obtain a signed statement. Defined by Black's Law Dictionary as "an allegation, a declaration of matters of fact," the **statement** is the foundation of judicial and official proceedings, being a legal narrative description of events related to a crime. It is a more or less formal, exact, detailed presentation. Some officers regard a statement as anything a person says or writes, whose value depends on its content and its admissibility in court.

---

A statement is a legal narrative description of events related to a crime.

---

A statement is not a confession. It begins with an introduction that gives the place, time, date and names of the persons conducting and present at the interview. The name, address and age of the person questioned is stated before the main body of the statement. A sample statement is seen in Figure 6–2.

The body of the statement is the person's account of the incident. A clause at the end states that the information was given voluntarily. The person making

POLICE DEPARTMENT

VOLUNTARY STATEMENT

DR# 943210

DATE OCCURRED 12 Nov. 1997 LOCATION OF

TIME OCCURRED 0315 OCCURRENCE Rear of bar and grill

I, Walter Wilson , am 28 years of age,
home phone: 444-4444

and my address is 100 Main St., this city
bus. phone: 444-4443

1. I left the bar and grill at about 0300 on the 12th of Nov. 1997. I went out the

2. back door, got in my car and drove home. I did not see anyone at the rear of the bar

3. and grill.

4.

5.

6.

7.

8.

9.

10.

11.

12.

13.

14.

15.

16.

I have read this statement consisting of 1 page (s) and I affirm to the truth and accuracy of the facts contained herein.

This statement was completed at (Location) The Police Dept.
on the 14th day of Nov. at 1300 , 19 97 .

WITNESS *Wm Bennett*

WITNESS *Jehut H Scott*

*Walter Wilson*
Signature of person giving
voluntary statement.

**Figure 6–2   Sample Voluntary Statement**

the statement reads each page, makes any needed corrections, initials each correction and then signs the statement.

Obtain statements in private, with no one other than police officers present, and allow no interruptions. However, other persons will need to be called in to witness the signing of the statement.

Statements can be taken in several ways: prepared in longhand by the person interviewed, dictated to a typist in question/answer format or tape-recorded for later typing and signing. A combination of questions and answers, with the answers in narrative form, is often the most effective format. However, a question/answer format is often challenged in court on grounds that questions guide and control the answer provided. Another alternative is for you to write down the words of the person and have the person read and sign your notes. Also record the ending time. Beginning and ending times may be of great value in court testimony.

### Closing the Interview

End each interview by thanking the person for cooperating. If you have established good rapport with the interviewee, you will probably be able to obtain future cooperation from him or her if you need it.

## The Interrogation

Questioning suspects is usually more difficult than questioning witnesses or victims. Once identified and located, a suspect who *is* involved in a crime may make a statement, admission or confession that, corroborated by independent evidence, can produce a guilty plea or obtain a conviction. Jayne and Buckley (1992, p. 65) point out that an interrogation has three primary objectives:

■ To ascertain the probability that the suspect is or is not the offender.
■ To eliminate the innocent by eliciting information, evidence or behavior symptoms that indicate innocence.
■ To obtain a confession from the guilty and/or information from him or her about the involvement of other persons.

Many of the procedures used in interviewing are also used in interrogating, but there are important differences in how you question suspects. One of the most critical is ensuring that you do not violate suspects' constitutional rights so that the information you obtain will be admissible in court.

### The Miranda Warning

Before interrogating any suspect, you must give the **Miranda warning,** as stipulated in *Miranda v. Arizona* (1966). In this decision, the U.S. Supreme Court asserted that a suspect be informed of his or her right to remain silent, to have an attorney present and to have a state-appointed attorney if he or she cannot afford private counsel. Suspects must also be warned that anything they say may be used against them in court.

---

Give the Miranda warning to any suspect you interrogate.

---

> ## Peace Officers
> ## Constitutional Pre-Interrogation Requirements
>
> The following warnings must be given prior to questioning a person who is in custody or is deprived of his freedom of action in any significant way:
>
> THE CONSTITUTION REQUIRES I INFORM YOU THAT:
> 1) YOU HAVE THE RIGHT TO REMAIN SILENT.
> 2) ANYTHING YOU SAY CAN AND WILL BE USED AGAINST YOU IN COURT.
> 3) YOU HAVE THE RIGHT TO TALK TO A LAWYER NOW AND HAVE HIM PRESENT NOW OR AT ANY TIME DURING QUESTIONING.
> 4) IF YOU CANNOT AFFORD A LAWYER, ONE WILL BE APPOINTED FOR YOU WITHOUT COST.
>
> **Waiver of Rights**
> The suspect may waive his rights, but the burden is on the officer to show the waiver is made voluntarily, knowingly and intelligently.
> He must affirmatively respond to the following questions:
> 1) DO YOU UNDERSTAND EACH OF THESE RIGHTS I HAVE EXPLAINED TO YOU?
> 2) DO YOU WISH TO TALK TO US AT THIS TIME?
>
> **Election of Rights**
> A subject can avail himself of his rights at any time and interrogation must then cease. If a subject will not waive his rights or during questioning elects to assert his rights, no testimony of that fact may ever be used against him at trial.

**Figure 6–3   Miranda Warning Card**

Many investigators carry a card, such as the one in Figure 6–3, on which the Miranda warning is printed to guide them on this important consideration.

Ironically, Ernesto Miranda, the defendant in *Miranda v. Arizona,* was stabbed to death in Phoenix, Arizona, on January 31, 1976, ten years after the initial decision. The suspect in his murder was arrested the following day and advised of his rights under the *Miranda* decision.

Thousands of words have been written for and against this decision. The general interpretation and application of the *Miranda* decision is that once you have reasonable grounds to believe a person has committed a crime, that person's constitutional rights are in jeopardy unless the Miranda warning is given *before* any questioning.

Many court cases illustrate the gray area that exists in determining when to give the warning. The terms most often used to describe when it should be given are **in custody** or **custodial arrest.** In custody generally refers to that point when the officer has decided the suspect is not free to leave, there has been considerable deprivation of liberty or the officer has, in fact, arrested the suspect.

In *Oregon v. Mathiason* (1977), the U.S. Supreme Court defined **custodial interrogation** as questioning initiated by law enforcement officers after a person has been taken into custody or otherwise deprived of freedom in a significant way.

The Miranda warning has never applied to voluntary or unsolicited statements, admissions or confessions. Someone can come up to a police officer and say, "I want to confess that I killed Mark Jones. I took a gun from my car and shot him." If this remark was unsolicited and completely voluntary, police officers are under no obligation to interrupt the person giving the confession. In one instance, an individual telephoned the police long distance to voluntarily confess to a felony.

If a suspect chooses to remain silent, ask no further questions. If the suspect requests counsel, ask no more questions until counsel is present.

A suspect can waive the rights granted by *Miranda,* but must do so intelligently and knowingly. A **waiver** is accompanied by a written or witnessed oral statement that the waiver was voluntary (see Figure 6–4).

Silence, in itself, is *not* a waiver. A waiver of rights must be articulated by the suspect. Therefore, many officers read the Miranda warning aloud from a printed card and then have the suspect read and sign the card. The date and time are also recorded. If no card is available, a summary of the Miranda warning can be written, read and signed. Police have the legal burden of proving that the suspect did waive his or her rights. The suspect retains the right to stop answering questions at any point, even when he or she originally waived the right to remain silent.

**ANYWHERE POLICE DEPARTMENT**

DEFENDANT _____ Curtis Remke _____

INTERROGATION:  ADVICE OF YOUR MIRANDA RIGHTS

Before we ask you any questions, you must understand your rights.

You have the right to remain silent . . . . . . . . . . . . . . . . . . . .  *CR*
                                                                                    Initials

If you give up your right to remain silent, anything you say can and will be used against you in a court of law. . . . . . . . . . . . .  *CR*
                                                                                    Initials

You have the right to speak with an attorney for advice before we ask you any questions and to have him with you during questioning . . .  *CR*
                                                                                    Initials

If you cannot afford an attorney, one will be appointed for you without charge before any questioning if you wish . . . . . . . . . . . .  *CR*
                                                                                    Initials

If you decide to answer questions now without an attorney present, you will still have the right to stop answering questions at any time . . . . . . . . . . . . . . . . . . . . . . . . . . . . . . . .  *CR*
                                                                                    Initials

Do you understand each of these rights I have read to you? . . . . . . .  *CR*
                                                                                    Initials

Are you willing to answer questions and make a statement, knowing that you have these rights, and do you waive these rights freely and voluntarily with no threats or promises of any kind having been made to you ? . . . . . . . . . . . . . . . . . . . . . . . . . . . . . .  *CR*
                                                                                    Initials

*Charles Good*
Witness's Signature

*Curtis Remke*
Signature of the defendant

Witness's Signature

Date ___ 3-14-97 ___   TIME ___ 1330 hrs ___  D.R. # ___ 97-860 ___

**Figure 6–4   Miranda Waiver Form**

The Miranda warning does not prevent the suspect from talking. It simply requires that the suspect be advised of and fully understand his or her constitutional rights. The basic intent of the *Miranda* decision is to guarantee the rights of the accused. The practical effect is to ensure that confessions are obtained without duress or coercion, thereby removing any inferences that third-degree tactics were used.

In the 1970s several cases related to the *Miranda* decision were heard. In *Harris v. New York* (1971), the court ruled that a defendant's statements made in violation of *Miranda* may be used to challenge a defendant's trial testimony. *Michigan v. Tucker* (1974) ruled that statements made in violation of *Miranda* may be used to locate prosecution witnesses. In 1975 *Oregon v. Haas* ruled that statements given after the Miranda warning but prior to arrival of an attorney can be used to challenge a defendant's trial testimony, and *Michigan v. Mosley* ruled that a suspect who has invoked the right to remain silent concerning one crime may be asked about another crime.

*Oregon v. Mathiason* (1977) ruled that *Miranda* does not apply to parolees who voluntarily comply with a detective's request to go to the police station for further questioning. *North Carolina v. Butler* (1979) established that police may question suspects who do not specifically relinquish their rights.

Several decisions in the 1980s also relate to the Miranda warning. In 1980 *Rhode Island v. Innis* established that interrogation refers not only to direct questioning, but also to any words or actions the police should know are reasonably expected to elicit an incriminating response. In 1981 *California v. Prysock* ruled that Miranda warnings do *not* have to be given in a specific order or with any specific wording, and *Edwards v. Arizona* (1981) established that once a suspect in custody states that he or she wants an attorney, police must halt all questioning and may not engage in further questioning unless the suspect requests it.

The defendant in *Edwards v. Arizona* interrupted a statement and said to FBI agents, "Maybe I should get a lawyer," but then resumed his story without prompting. The Court ruled that neither the Fourth nor Fifth Amendment prohibits agents from merely listening to a defendant's voluntary statements and using them at the trial. Even if one inferred that the agents' silence amounted to "subtle compulsion," this would not necessarily vitiate the voluntariness of the defendant's statements. This decision was supported in *United States v. Lame* (1983).

*Oregon v. Bradshaw* (1983) also related to the *Edwards* decision. This case established that the *Edwards* decision does not apply when a criminal suspect asks, "What is going to happen to me now?" Police were allowed to resume questioning even though the suspect had asked for a lawyer earlier.

In 1983, in *United States v. Dockery,* the Court ruled that telling a suspect she was "free to leave at any time" and then asking her to wait in a reception area for further questioning was within the Miranda rule. In this case FBI agents first questioned the defendant in the bank where she worked. Although the agents told her she was free to leave, she was, in fact, not. She was summoned back for further questioning. The subsequent interrogation was ruled custodial, and therefore the Miranda warning was required. In addition, the agents lied to the defendant about evidence tying her to the crime under investigation, making the Miranda warning particularly apt.

In 1984 *Minnesota v. Murphy* established that probation officers do not need to give the Miranda warning, and *Berkemer v. McCarty* ruled that the Miranda warning is not required for traffic violations. *Oregon v. Elstad* (1985) established that a suspect's confession given after the Miranda may be used even though a confession before the Miranda was obtained earlier.

The U.S. Supreme Court ruled in *Illinois v. Perkins* (1990) that jailed suspects need not be told of their right to remain silent when they provide information to undercover agents. Justice Anthony Kennedy wrote that the intent of the *Miranda* decision was to assure that police questioning of suspects in custody is not sufficiently coercive to make confessions involuntary. Suspects must be told of their rights not to incriminate themselves. *Miranda* was *not* meant to protect suspects who boast about their criminal activities to individuals they believe to be cellmates, Justice Kennedy wrote in the opinion.

In *Davis v. U.S.* (1994), the Supreme Court ruled that after a knowing and voluntary waiver of *Miranda,* officers may continue to question until the suspect clearly requests an attorney. In *State v. Michael Scales* (1994), the Minnesota Supreme Court ruled that in all custodial interrogations about rights and a waiver of these rights, all questioning should be electronically recorded where feasible and must be recorded when questioning occurs at a place of detention.

One of the most important cases related to the *Miranda* decision is *New York v. Quarles* (1984), which established the public safety exception.

## The Public Safety Exception

On June 12, 1984, in *New York v. Quarles,* the Supreme Court ruled on the **public safety exception** to the *Miranda* warning requirement. In 1980, two police officers were stopped by a young woman who told them she had been raped and gave them a description of her rapist who, she stated, had just entered a nearby supermarket and was armed with a gun. The suspect, Benjamin Quarles, was located, and the officer ordered him to stop. Quarles ran, and the officer momentarily lost sight of him. When he was apprehended and frisked, he was found to be wearing an empty shoulder holster. The officer asked Quarles where the gun was, and he nodded toward some cartons and said, "The gun is over there." The officer retrieved the gun, put Quarles under formal arrest and read him his rights. Quarles waived his rights to an attorney and answered questions.

At the trial, the court ruled pursuant to *Miranda* that the statement "The gun is over there" and the subsequent discovery of the gun as a result of that statement were inadmissible at the defendant's trial.

The U.S. Supreme Court, after reviewing the case, ruled that the procedural safeguards that deter a suspect from responding and increase the possibility of fewer convictions were deemed acceptable in *Miranda* to protect the Fifth Amendment privilege against self-incrimination. However, if Miranda warnings had deterred the response to the officer's question, the cost would have been more than just the loss of evidence that might lead to a conviction. As long as the gun remained concealed in the store, it posed a danger to the public safety.

The Court ruled that in this case the need to have the suspect talk took precedence over the requirement that the defendant be read his rights. The Court ruled that the material factor in applying this "public safety" exception is whether a public threat could possibly be removed by the suspect making a statement. In this case, the officer asked the question only to ensure his and the public safety. He then gave the Miranda warning before continuing questioning.

## Selecting the Time and Place

Like interviews, interrogations are conducted as soon as possible after the crime. Selecting the right place to question a suspect is critical because suspects are usually reluctant to talk to police. Most interrogations are conducted at police headquarters. However, if a suspect refuses to come to the station and evidence is insufficient for an arrest, the interrogation may take place at the crime scene, in a squad car or at the suspect's home or place of work. If possible, suspects should be interrogated in an unfamiliar place, away from their friends and family.

---

Conduct interrogations in a place that is private and free from interruptions.

---

Ideal conditions exist at the police department, where privacy and interruptions can be controlled. Visible movements or unusual noises distract a suspect being questioned. Therefore, if possible, use a private room with little or no opportunity for interruptions.

Only the suspect, his or her attorney and the interrogator(s) should be in the room. Having two officers conduct the interrogation protects against false allegations or other untrue claims by the suspect. Allow no telephone calls and no distracting noises; allow no one to enter the room. Under these conditions, communication is more readily established.

Opinions differ on how interrogation rooms should be furnished. An austere, sparsely furnished room is generally less distracting; pictures can reduce the effectiveness of questioning. Many interrogation rooms have only two chairs, one for the investigator and one for the suspect. Some include a small, bare table. Some officers feel it is better *not* to have a desk or table between the officer and the suspect because the desk serves as some protection to the suspect psychologically. Without it, he or she tends to feel much more uncomfortable and vulnerable. Keep all notebooks, pencils, pens and any objects of evidence to be used in the interrogation out of view, preferably in a drawer, until the appropriate time. An austere setting develops and maintains the suspect's absolute attention and allows total concentration on the conversation.

Other investigators, however, contend that such a setting is not conducive to good rapport. It may remind suspects of jail, and a fear of going to jail may keep them from talking. Instead, some investigators prefer a normally furnished room or office for interrogations. Doctors, lawyers, insurance investigators and others have shown that a relaxed atmosphere encourages conversation. Even background music can reduce anxiety and dispel fear, major steps in getting subjects to talk.

### Starting the Interrogation

Conducting the interrogation at the police station allows many options in timing and approach. A suspect can be brought to the interrogation room and left alone temporarily. Often the suspect has not yet met the investigator and is apprehensive about what the investigator is like, what will be asked and what will happen. Provide time for the anxiety to increase, just as a football team sometimes takes a time-out before the opposing team attempts a critical field goal.

As you enter the room, show that you are in command, but do not display arrogance. The suspect is in an unfamiliar environment, alone, does not know you, has been waiting, is apprehensive and does not know what you will ask. At this point, select your interrogation technique, deciding whether to increase or decrease the suspect's anxiety. Some investigators accomplish their goals by friendliness; others by authoritarianism. Show your identification and introduce yourself to the suspect, state the purpose of the interrogation, and then give the Miranda warning.

Avoid violating the personal zone of the suspect. Try to stay 2 to 6 feet away when questioning.

Do not become so wrapped up in yourself and your quest for information that you overlook body language that may indicate deception, anger or indifference. Most people exhibit body language or **nonverbal communication.** Deception, for example, may be indicated by looking down, rolling the eyes up, placing the hand(s) over the eyes or mouth or rubbing the hands around the mouth. Other possible indicators of deception include continual licking of the lips, twitching of the lips, intermittent coughs, rapid breathing, change in facial color, continued swallowing, pulsating of the carotid artery in the neck, face flushing, tapping the fingers and avoiding eye contact. Excessive protestations of innocence should also be suspect, for example, "I swear on my father's grave."

According to Slahor (1995, p. 95): "Deceptive individuals tend to be less certain in their statements, tend to use fewer factual statements and mention fewer of their personal experiences. They also tend to use fewer past-tense verbs and refer more to the present and future than the past. Their statements tend to be generalities rather than specifics."

### Establishing Rapport

As with interviewing, specific approaches during interrogating may encourage cooperation or may induce silence and noncooperation. The techniques for establishing rapport during an interview are applicable in an interrogation. You might decide to instill the fear that there will be serious consequences if the suspect fails to cooperate. You might choose to appeal to the suspect's conscience, emphasizing the importance of getting out of the present situation and starting over with a clean slate. Try any approach that shows the person that cooperation is more desirable than having you find out about the crime another way.

It also helps to know why the crime was committed. Some crimes are committed out of uncontrollable passion, panic or fear without consideration of the consequences. Other crimes result from the demands of the moment; the presumed necessity of the crime appears to justify it. Some criminals' guilt becomes so overpowering that they turn themselves in to the police. Other criminals turn to drugs, alcohol or leave the area to start over somewhere else.

It takes skill to obtain information from those involved in crime, especially if they know that the consequences can be severe. Suspects who understand that there is no easy way out of the situation may become cooperative. At this point, offering alternatives may be successful. Because most people respond to hard evidence, show suspects the physical evidence against them. Acknowledge to the suspect that there is no totally agreeable solution, but point out that some alternatives may be more agreeable than others.

Make no promises, but remind the suspect that the court decides the sentence and is apt to be easier on those who cooperate. Also point out that family and friends are usually more understanding if people admit they are wrong and try to go straight.

If the suspect will not provide the names of accomplices because they are friends, explain that it is such "friends" who have put him or her in the present predicament.

## Approaches to Interrogation

As with interviews, interrogations can use an emotional or a logical approach. An emotional approach is either sympathetic or authoritarian. After talking with the suspect, select the approach that seems to offer the best chance for obtaining information.

---

Interrogation techniques include inquiring directly or indirectly, forcing responses, deflating or inflating the ego, minimizing or maximizing the crime and combining approaches.

---

**Inquiring Indirectly or Directly.** Indirect inquiry draws out information without mentioning the main subject. For example, an indirect approach would be phrased, "Have you ever been in the vicinity of Elm Street? Grove Street? The intersection of Elm and Grove?" In contrast, a direct question would be, "Did you break into the house on the corner of Elm and Grove Streets on December 16th?"

**Forcing Responses.** A forced response is elicited by asking a question that will implicate the suspect, regardless of what answer is given. For example, the question, "What time did you arrive at the house?" implies that the suspect *did* arrive at the house at some time. Answering the question with a time forces the suspect to admit having been there. Of course, the suspect may simply state, "I never arrived there," or may refuse to answer at all.

**Deflating or Inflating the Ego.** Belittling a suspect is often effective. For example, you might tell a suspect, "We know you couldn't be directly involved in the burglary because you aren't smart enough to pull off a job like that. We thought you might know who did though." Question the suspect's skill in committing the crime known to be his specialty. Suggest that the suspect's reputation is low because his latest burglaries have been bungled. The suspect may attempt, out of pride, to prove that it was a professional job.

The same results can be obtained by inflating suspects' egos, praising the skill shown in pulling off the job. Suspects may want to take the credit and admit their role in the crime.

**Minimizing or Maximizing the Crime.** Concentrate your efforts on the crime itself, ignoring for the moment the person committing it. Instead of using the word *crime,* say "the thing that happened." Refer to stolen property as "the stuff that was taken." Do not use terms such as *robbery, homicide* or *arson.* Use other less threatening terms. For example, asking the suspect "to admit the truth" is much less threatening than asking someone "to confess."

Overstating the severity of the offense can be as effective as understating it. Mentioning that the loot was $5,000 rather than the actual $500 puts the suspect on the spot. Is a partner holding out? Is the victim lying about the losses? Will the suspect be found guilty of a felony because of such lies? Making the offense more serious than it is can induce suspects to provide facts implicating them in lesser offenses.

**Combining Approaches.** Having the suspect tell the story using different methods can reveal discrepancies. If an oral statement has been given, have the suspect put this information in writing and compare the two versions. Then give the story to two different investigators and have them compare the versions.

## Using Persuasion During Interrogation

Sometimes investigators may obtain much better results using persuasive techniques: making sure the suspect is comfortable and has basic needs taken care of, such as being allowed to go to the bathroom and to get a drink of water. Once the suspect has been made comfortable, begin by acknowledging that a problem exists but that before they can talk about it, the suspect needs to be informed of his rights. Then suggest that the suspect probably already knows all about these rights, and ask the suspect to tell what he does know. Usually the suspect can paraphrase the Miranda warning, and you can then compliment him on his knowledge. This will help establish rapport.

Next, encourage the suspect to tell his side of the story in detail, intervening only to give encouragement to continue talking. When the suspect has finished, review it step by step.

Following this, begin "a virtual monolog about robbery" and how some people's desperate circumstances lead them into such a crime. The monolog describes how no one starts out planning a life of crime, but some, like an addict, fall into the criminal pattern that leads either to getting shot and killed or to a lifetime in prison. End the monolog "emphasizing that the inevitable result of this pattern of crime is life in prison or death."

Next, suggest that the suspect can avoid this fate only by breaking this pattern, the first step being to admit that it exists. Add that a person's life should not be judged by one mistake, nor should his or her life be wasted by a refusal to admit that mistake. Following this monolog, begin to talk about the suspect's accomplice(s) and how they are still free, enjoying the "fruits of the crime."

Finally, talk about the suspect's previous encounters with the criminal justice system and how fairly it has treated him (or her). In the past he has probably always claimed to be not guilty. Judges are likely to go easier on suspects they feel are sorry for what they have done. This cannot happen unless the suspect first admits the crime. Point out that "an intelligent person recognizes when it is in his own best interest to admit a mistake."

## Using Deception During Interrogation

Police officers are supposed to be honest, but what happens when they are lied to? Unfortunately, criminal interrogations do not follow a set of rules that mandates everyone to tell the truth. The fact is, criminals lie as a matter of course. Faced with scant evidence, yet a positive belief that a suspect has committed a particular crime, what might the investigator do? According to Dillingham (1996, p. 105):

> We lie to them, using deception as a tool. We lie to make it appear that there is evidence against the criminal, and that we know that this particular criminal committed this particular crime. We lie to suspects because the Supreme Court tells us that not only is it necessary to do so in order to get a confession in most cases, but because it is legal do to so.

Dillingham (pp. 105–106) cites the following cases supporting use of deception:

■ *U.S. ex rel. Caminito v. Murphy* (1955). It is permissible to tell a suspect that he has been identified by witnesses, even though such an event did not occur.
■ *Moore v. Hopper* (1975). It is permissible to tell a suspect that material evidence, such as a weapon used to perpetrate a crime, has been found.

■ *Frazier v. Cupp* (1978). It is permissible to tell a suspect that an accomplice has already confessed, when such has not occurred.

■ *Roe v. State of New York* (1973). It is permissible to tell a suspect that his fingerprints or other physical evidence linking him to the offense was located at the scene of the crime, when such has not occurred.

Dillingham (p. 108) concludes: "While it may not be public knowledge that police can legally lie to suspects, that does not negate the value of deception as a tool. Wisely used, deception can be a great asset in obtaining confessions."

Skolnick and Leo (1992) researched interrogation methods by studying police training manuals from 1942 to the early 1990s, attending local and national interrogation training seminars and courses, listening to recordings of interrogations and interviewing police officers. Based on this research, they reported that the following types of interrogatory deception are being used:

■ Misrepresenting the nature or seriousness of the offense—for example, telling a suspect that the murder victim is still alive.

■ Role-playing manipulative appeals to conscience—for example, projecting sympathy, understanding and compassion; playing the role of father, brother, sister or friend; using the good cop/bad cop routine.

■ Misrepresenting the moral seriousness of the offense—for example, offering the suspect excuses such as that a rape victim "asked for it."

■ Using promises—for example, suggesting that a suspect's conscience will be eased.

■ Misrepresenting identity—for example, pretending to be a reporter or a cellmate.

■ Fabricating evidence—for example, stating that physical evidence such as fingerprints or bloodstains have implicated a suspect or that the suspect's accomplice has confessed.

Recognizing instances of interrogatory deception is relatively straightforward. Determining whether their use is ethical is another matter. Skolnick and Leo (p. 3) found police deception during interrogations to be "more subtle, complex, and morally puzzling than physical coercion." They ask if such deception leads to false confessions or is unfair and should thus be stopped, or if it is a necessary skill that all investigators should attempt to master. If the latter, they point out (p. 9): "Rarely do advocates of greater latitude for police to interrogate consider the effects of systematic lying on law enforcement's reputation for veracity."

A Florida Court of Appeal case, *Florida v. Cayward* (1989), provides a good example of this controversial issue. In this case a nineteen-year-old male was accused of sexually molesting and then killing his five-year-old niece. The defendant maintained his innocence until police showed him fabricated evidence: a report on official-looking stationery stating that semen on the girl's underwear was Cayward's. He confessed. The question became whether it was constitutional to fabricate evidence to obtain a confession from a murdering rapist. The court said no. As reported by Skolnick and Leo (pp. 9–10):

> The Florida police officers who fabricated evidence did so for the best of reasons. The victim was a five-year-old girl, and the crime was abhorrent and hard to prove. Nevertheless, the Florida court excluded the confession on due-process grounds, arguing that police must be discouraged from fabricating false official

documents. . . . Those who affirm the propriety of lying in the interrogatory context tend to undervalue the significance of the long-term harms caused by such authorized deception.

The use of deception in interrogation and what constitutes ethical, professional behavior will remain important issues throughout the 1990s.

### Third-Degree Tactics

Considerable literature deals with the use of the third degree in police interrogations. There is no way to know how widely these methods are used and how much of what is claimed is exaggeration.

**Third degree** is the use of physical force, the threat of force or other physical, mental or psychological abuse to get a suspect to confess to a crime. Third-degree tactics, which are illegal, include striking or hitting a suspect, denying food or water or sleep for abnormal time periods, not allowing the suspect to go to the toilet, having a number of officers ask questions in shifts for prolonged time periods and refusing normal privileges. It is inexcusable to obtain information by these methods.

---

Third-degree tactics—physical force, threats of force or other physical, mental or psychological abuse—are illegal. Any information so obtained, including confessions, is inadmissible in court.

---

The image of police brutality is difficult to offset when third-degree tactics are used. Such tactics cause a loss of respect not only for the officer involved but also for the entire department and the police profession.

Although physical force is not permitted, this does not eliminate physical contact. Placing a hand on the shoulder or touching the suspect's hand can help to establish rapport. Looking directly at the suspect while talking and continuing to do so during the conversation is not using physical force, even though it usually makes the suspect extremely uncomfortable.

If you give the suspect all the privileges you take, there is no substantive cause for a charge of third-degree tactics. Allow the suspect the same breaks for meals, rest and going to the toilet that you take. Law enforcement officers are obligated to protect both the public interest and individual rights. No situation excuses deliberate violation of these rights.

Television and movies often depict the "good cop/bad cop" method of interrogation, portraying one officer as very hostile and another officer as trying to protect the suspect from the hostile officer. Routines such as this could be considered illegal if carried to the extreme. Some interrogation techniques, even if not illegal, may be unethical.

### Admissions and Confessions

When the suspect has become cooperative, you can increase the amount of conversation. Once rapport is established, listen for words indicating that the suspect is in some way connected with the crime, such as "I didn't do it, but I know who did." If the suspect is not implicated in the crime but has relevant information, attempt to obtain a statement. If the suspect is implicated, seek to obtain an admission or confession.

The format for obtaining admissions and confessions from suspects in criminal cases is fairly standard. However, state laws, rules and procedures for taking admissions and confessions vary, so you need to know the rules and requirements of your jurisdiction.

An **admission** contains some information concerning the elements of the crime but falls short of a full confession (see Figure 6–5). A **confession** is information supporting the elements of the crime given by a person involved in committing the crime. It can be oral or written, and it must be voluntary and without threats, promises or rewards. It can be taken in question/answer form or in a narrative handwritten by the suspect or the interrogator (see Figure 6–6).

POLICE DEPARTMENT

ADMISSION

DR# 933210

DATE OCCURRED 12 Nov. 1997 LOCATION OF

TIME OCCURRED 0315 OCCURRENCE Rear of bar and grill

I, Walter Wilson, am 28 years of age,

and my address is 100 Main St.,this city home phone: 444-4444

bus. phone: 444-4443

1. I came out of the bar and grill at approx. 0300 on 12 Nov. 1997 and saw
2. Mr. Victim standing there. He spoke to me and we had an argument. We
3. argued a little while and I left. He was alive when I saw him last.
4.
5.
6.
7.
8.
9.
10.
11.
12.
13.
14.
15.
16.
17.
18.

I have read this statement consisting of 1 page (s) and I affirm to the truth and accuracy of the facts contained herein.

This statement was completed at (Location) The Police Dept.
on the 14th day of Nov. at 1300, 19 97.

WITNESS

WITNESS

Walter Wilson
Signature of person giving voluntary statement.

**Figure 6–5 Sample Admission**

POLICE DEPARTMENT

CONFESSION

DATE ___14 Nov. 1997___ TIME ___1300___ PLACE ___Police Dept.___

I, ___Walter Wilson___ , am ___28___ years of age,

and my address is ___100 Main St., this city___ ,

I have been duly warned by ___police officer name___ , who has identified

himself as ___a police officer___

that I do not have to make any statement at all, and that any statement I make may be used in evidence against me on the trial for the offense concerning which this statement is herein made. Without promise of hope or reward, without fear or threat of physical harm, I freely volunteer the following statement to the aforesaid person:

___I left the bar and grill at about 0300 on 12 Nov. 1997. I went out the back___

___door and I met Mr. Victim coming in. He bumped into me and we got in an argument.___

___He picked up a rock to hit me with, so I took out my knife and stabbed him. I___

___think he was dead when I left.___

I have read the ___1___ pages of this statement and the facts contained therein are true and correct.

WITNESS: _Wm Barnett_

WITNESS: _John H Pratt_

_Walter Wilson_
Signed by the arrested party.
Page __1__ of __1__ pages.

Figure 6–6    Sample Confession

---

A confession, oral or handwritten, must be given of the suspect's free will and without fear, threats, promises or rewards.

---

The voluntary nature of the confession is essential. For example, Ernesto Miranda had an arrest record and was familiar with his rights; yet his confession was ruled inadmissible because these rights had not been clearly stated to him. Although formal education is not required for making a confession, the suspect must be intelligent enough to understand fully everything stated. There must be no opportunity for any misinterpretation that might provide a basis for later denying the confession in court.

In most states, oral confessions are admissible in court, but written confessions usually carry more weight. Put an oral confession into writing as soon as possible, even if the suspect refuses to sign it. Have the suspect repeat the confession before other witnesses to corroborate its content and its voluntariness. In extremely important cases, the prosecutor often obtains the confession to ensure that it meets all legal requirements. Many departments are now videotaping statements and confessions.

After obtaining a confession in such cases, you may also go with the suspect to the crime scene and reenact the crime before witnesses. Take pictures or films of this reenactment. Go over the confession and the pictures with the suspect to verify their accuracy. (Such confessions and reenactments can also be used for police training.)

Even though getting a confession is highly desirable, it may not be true, it may later be denied, or there may be claims that it was involuntary.

---

A confession is only one part of the investigation. Corroborate it by independent evidence.

---

Your investigation will proceed in much the same way with or without a confession. However, a confession often provides additional leads. Although it cannot stand alone, it is an important part of the case.

## Evaluating and Corroborating Information

Do not accept information obtained from interviews and interrogations at face value. Check all information. You cannot know the motives of all those who provide information. Do not assume that all information, even though volunteered, is truthful. Corroborate or disprove statements made during questioning.

To cross-check a story, review the report and the details of the offense. Determine the past record, family status, hobbies and special interests of the persons questioned. If the person has a criminal record, determine his or her prior modus operandi. With such information, you will be able to ask questions in a way that gives the impression that you know what you are talking about and that deceptive answers will be found out.

The person who resorts to half-truths or lies usually ends up on the defensive and becomes entangled in deceit. Knowing the facts of the case allows you to neutralize deliberate lies. If discrepancies in statements occur, question the suspect again or use polygraph or psychological tests. Compare the replies of persons questioned and assess whether they are consistent with the known facts.

### Breaking a Pat Story

A person who is telling the truth can usually repeat the story the same way many times, although he or she may use different words and a different sequence in retelling it. Times and dates may be approximate, and there may be things the person simply cannot remember. In contrast, a person who is telling a fabricated story can usually repeat it word for word innumerable times. Dates and times are usually precise, and all details are remembered. However, it is difficult to repeat lies consistently; each one sounds better than the other, and the story becomes distorted with mistakes and exaggerations.

To break a pat story, ask questions that require slightly different answers and serve to alter memorized responses.

## Questioning Juveniles

Special considerations exist when you question juveniles. Parental permission needs to be obtained before questioning a juvenile, unless the situation warrants immediate questioning at the scene. Parents usually permit their child to be questioned separately if the purpose is explained and there are valid reasons for doing so. Overprotective parents can distract and interfere with an interview or interrogation. Often, however, parents can assist if the juvenile is uncooperative. They can ask questions and bring pressures to bear that you cannot. They know and understand the child and can probably sense when the child is lying. Decide whether to question a juvenile in front of the parents or separately after you determine their attitudes when you explain the reasons for the inquiry to them.

---

Obtain parental permission before questioning a juvenile. Do not use a juvenile as an informant unless the parents know the situation.

---

Your attitude toward juveniles will greatly influence how well you can communicate with them. Ask yourself whether you consider the youth a person who has a problem or a youth who *is* a problem.

Many juveniles act big in front of their friends. For example, in one case a juvenile and some other youths were brought into a room for observation by witnesses. The suspect youth knew he was being watched and challenged his school principal by stating that he had a right to know who was looking at him and why. This ten-year-old boy wanted to impress his friends. A few days later, the boy's parents brought him to the police station at the officer's request. It took two questions to determine that he set the fire that resulted in an $80,000 loss. After a third question, the youth admitted his guilt. Although he was a big shot in front of his friends, his conscience weighed heavily. The presence of the police and the knowledge that his parents were waiting in another room motivated him to cooperate.

Many juveniles also have very active imaginations, tend to exaggerate and may have periods of fantasy. They may describe suspects as bigger than they really are or may view an event as more serious or important than it is.

Finally, juveniles may have definite opinions about the police. Some dislike adults in general and the police in particular. Like adults, however, most of them do not dislike the police and will cooperate with them. Put yourself in their shoes; learn their attitudes and the reasons for them. Time and patience are your greatest allies when questioning juveniles. Explain why they are being questioned and you will probably gain their confidence.

Do not underrate the intelligence or cleverness of young people. They are often excellent observers with good recall. Talk to them as you would an adult. Praise them and impress on them their importance to the investigation.

If a juvenile confesses to a crime, bring in the parents and have the youth repeat the confession to them. The parents will see that the information is voluntary and not the police's account of what happened. Parents often provide additional information once they know the truth. For example, they may be alerted to stolen items at home and report them.

# Questioning Young Children

Geiselman et al. (1992, p. 4) suggest that the cognitive interview technique be adapted for children as follows:

### Phase 1
■ Develop rapport with the child in accordance with recommended guidelines.
■ Prepare child for the interviewer's questions through a set of four instructions.

### Phase 2
■ Ask the child to reconstruct, aloud, the circumstances surrounding the incident. That includes not only such external factors as the appearance of the scene, the people present or nearby and the weather but also the child's thoughts and feelings at the time.
■ Instruct the child to report everything that happened from beginning to end, including what may not seem important.

### Phase 3
■ Ask the child to recall events in backward order, from the end of the incident to the beginning.
■ Use the memory-jogging techniques of asking the child to run through the alphabet as an aid to identifying the first letter of a forgotten name; to reflect on whether the suspect's appearance reminded the child of someone else; to recall unusual speech characteristics; and to remember conversations, unusual words or phrases and reactions to them.

*Police officers should be skilled at communicating with people of all ages and from other cultures. Cultural diversity within the department can be of great benefit.*

- Ask the child to recount the incident from a different perspective, such as through the eyes of someone else who was present, or through the "eyes" of an inanimate object, such as a stuffed animal that was present.

Their research further suggests (p. 5) that: "The impact of a practice cognitive interview about an innocuous event on a child's recall performance during a later, official interview is indeed beneficial." Among the purposes that might be served by staging an event and then conducting a practice cognitive interview are that it:

- Gives the child experience with the usually unfamiliar task of being interviewed by a stranger about details of an event.
- Clarifies the methods used in a subsequent interview.
- Encourages the child to use recall techniques spontaneously so that more of them will be employed.

## Scientific Aids to Obtaining Information

Many attempts have been made to determine the truth through scientific instruments. Even before instruments were developed, however, trials by ordeal and various tests relied on psychological and physiological principles. For example, it was common knowledge for centuries that when a person was lying or nervous, visible or measurable physiological changes in the body occurred. These include dryness of the mouth, shaking or trembling, perspiration, increased heartbeat, faster pulse and rapid breathing. The ancient Chinese capitalized on the symptom of mouth dryness when they made a suspect chew rice. If the rice remained dry after being chewed, the suspect was assumed to be lying.

Science and technology have provided aids to help determine the reliability of information. Among them are the polygraph, hypnosis and truth serums.

### The Polygraph and CVSA

As implied by the name, a **polygraph** (meaning "many writings") records several measurements on a visible graph. One measuring device, the pneumograph, measures respiration and depth of breathing. The galvanograph measures changes in the skin's electrical resistance. The cardiograph measures blood pressure and pulse rate. The person does not actually have to respond verbally for a polygraph to work because the machine measures the mental and emotional responses regardless of whether the person answers questions.

---

The polygraph scientifically measures respiration and depth of breathing, changes in the skin's electrical resistance and blood pressure and pulse.

---

The same factors measured by the polygraph may be visible to a trained observer through such signs as flushing of the face, slight pulsing of the neck arteries, beads of perspiration, rapid breathing and other signs of nervousness such as licking the lips.

Measurements taken by the polygraph can be interpreted when the test is administered or anytime later. The results can be shown to the subject to demonstrate which responses were shown to be truthful and which were not.

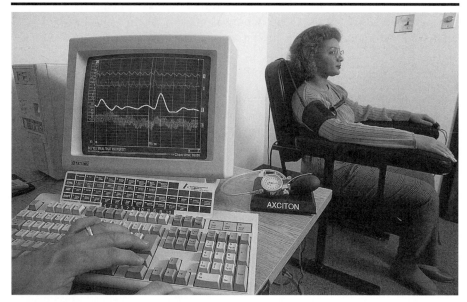

*Computers are now used by many polygraph operators to record and analyze data obtained from individuals who are given polygraphs.*

In a survey of 406 law enforcement agencies in the United States, to which 308 (75.8 percent) responded, McCloud (1991, p. 123) found that 93 percent of the respondents used polygraphs in their investigations. Of these agencies, most (72.5 percent) used sworn personnel as the polygraph examiners.

The effectiveness of the polygraph has been questioned by many, including David Lykken, professor of psychology at the University of Minnesota, who has studied polygraphy since 1959. Lykken suggests (Scalzo, 1991, p. 37):

> Neither a psychologist nor an experienced poker player can possibly believe in the polygraph test. Every poker player knows that the symptoms one person shows when he is bluffing is the exact behavior another person shows when he has a strong hand. To imagine that everyone shares a specific lie response is just loony. We're not constructed like Pinocchio. . . .
>
> Perhaps the major utility of the lie detector is its extraordinary capacity for eliciting confessions.

Among supporters of the polygraph, opinions differ as to its accuracy. Although not infallible, it can detect physiological changes indicating deception anywhere from 75 to 96 percent of the time. Its accuracy depends on the subject, the equipment and the operator's training and experience. In some cases, the machine may fail to detect lies because the subject is on drugs, makes deliberate muscular contractions or is a psychopathic personality.

The subject must be physically, mentally and emotionally fit for the examination. The examination must be voluntary and completed under conditions conducive to cooperation. A clear, concise summary of the test results is furnished only to authorized personnel.

Despite advances in technology and in training polygraph operators, polygraph results are not now accepted by the courts as absolute evidence, except when stipulated by all parties. Some authorities claim that the results violate hearsay rules because it is impossible to cross-examine a machine.

Several court cases have dealt with the admissibility of polygraph results. *Frye v. United States* (1923) upheld a trial court's ruling that refused testimony about lie detector results. Ten years later *State v. Bohner* (1933) recognized the instrument's usefulness, but did not accept the results as evidence. *People v. Kenny* (1938) permitted testimony regarding the psychogalvanometer, but *People v. Forts* (1933) held lie detector evidence to be inadmissible because of doubts about the machine's efficiency.

---

The polygraph is an instrument used to verify the truth, not a substitute for investigating and questioning. Although the results are not presently admissible in court, any confession obtained as a result of a polygraph test is admissible.

---

Many polygraph inaccuracies have been failures to detect lies, not failures to indicate truthful statements. Thus the polygraph is sometimes useful to develop leads, to verify statements and to cross-check information. Moreover, it provides the police with a psychological advantage that may lead to a confession. Such confessions are admissible in court even though the test results are not. Even in jurisdictions where the polygraph is not admissible in court, prosecuting attorneys often give weight to the findings of a polygraph examination in deciding whether to prosecute a case.

Competent questioning is as important as the instrument used. As in an interrogation, the right questions must be asked in the right sequence. Although examiners are trained to give the test and interpret the graphs, they rely heavily on background information provided by the investigator.

All but nine states have licensing or limitation laws that establish minimum requirements for polygraph examiners. The normal procedure for setting up a polygraph test is for the police agency to request, in writing, that a polygraph test be conducted. The examiner should review the complete case in question, including any statements made by the subject before the test is conducted. A pretest interview with the subject should cover the information to be included in the test, a review of the questions to be asked and an advisement of the suspect's constitutional rights.

The polygraph examiner will want the following information before the test:

■ The case facts—the precise criminal offense involved, the complete case file and a summary of the evidence.
■ Information about the subject—complete name, date of birth, physical, mental, emotional and psychological data if known and criminal history.

The proper tests are then decided on and the questions prepared and reviewed with the subject. The test itself may include mixed questions, yes-or-no questions, a card test or a guilt-complex test.

After the test is completed, the subject and the police are advised of the results in person or by letter. If the test indicates deception, it may be followed by an individual interrogation. Any confessions that follow from such tests are almost universally accepted by the courts. The examiner's testimony is not conclusive evidence, but rather, opinion evidence regarding either guilt or innocence.

As noted by Dees (1995, p. 53): "The most recent innovations in polygraph technology occurred in the last few years with the advent of computerized polygraphy." This technology eliminates much of the mechanical equipment such as the streaming graph paper, mechanical pens and wet ink, replacing it with a "virtual" graph on the computer monitor. The graph looks like that produced mechanically and can be printed, if desired.

In the 1970s the Psychological Stress Evaluator (PSE) was introduced. The PSE measured stress in the microtremors of the human voice. A more recent version of this technology is the Computer Voice Stress Analyzer (CVSA). As noted by Whitworth (1993, p. 31):

> In spite of the lack of acceptance by polygraph authorities and a reported lack of scientifically valid objective research, CVSA is a popular device in many law enforcement operations. Several departments have reported unqualified enthusiasm for their CVSA systems, and more departments are investing, budgeting and purchasing new systems. Table 6–2 compares the polygraph and CVSA.

Although the polygraph and CVSA should not be a first or a last-resort investigative technique, it reduces investigative costs, focuses on specific suspects, increases conviction rates (because many tests are followed by confessions) and eliminates suspects. Police agencies should not go on a fishing expedition, however. The suspects should be narrowed to not more than two persons through normal investigative practices before a polygraph examination or CVSA is used.

### Hypnosis and Truth Serums

Like the polygraph, hypnosis and truth serums are supplementary tools to investigation. They are not used as short-cuts but rather in specific cases where the criteria for their use have been determined by thorough review. Criteria cases are normally crimes of violence or cases where loss of memory or ability to recall is involved and where all other standard investigative efforts have been exhausted. Because of the restricted criteria, these techniques are used in a comparatively small number of cases.

**Hypnosis.**   **Hypnosis** is used with crime victims and witnesses to crimes, not with suspects. It should be used only after careful consultation with the person to be hypnotized and after a detailed review of the case as well as of the

**Table 6–2  Comparison of the Polygraph and CVSA**

|  | *Polygraph* | *CVSA* |
|---|---|---|
| Initial Cost: | About $12,000 including machine, room, furniture, training and certification of examiners. | About $7,000 for machine and examiner certification. |
| Accuracy: | 70–95% proven in extensive studies by various sources over many years. | 98% claimed, but shortage of accepted studies based on empirical data. |
| Flexibility: | Normally limited to testing room environment. | Portable, plus flexibility of field recordings. |
| Inputs Measured: | Heartbeat, blood pressure, pulse wave, breathing and skin resistance. | Audible voice microtremors. |
| Admissibility: | By stipulation. | By stipulation. |
| Exam time: | 2 hours. | 2 hours. |

SOURCE: A.W. Whitworth. "Polygraph or CVSA: What's the Truth about Truth Deception Analysis?" *Law and Order*, November 1993, p. 31. Reprinted by permission of the publisher.

subject's mental, physical and emotional condition. Written consent must be obtained from the subject, and permission should be obtained from the prosecutor's office. It is advisable to have an attorney present as well.

A professional should carefully analyze the subject and the case before hypnosis is conducted. The actual act of hypnotism and interrogation should be performed only by a psychiatrist, psychologist or physician specifically trained in the techniques.

Courts have established guidelines for using testimony gained from hypnosis. The guidelines require that a trained professional perform it and that the professional be independent of, rather than responsible to, the prosecution. The number of persons present should be restricted to the hypnotist and the coordinator from the police agency who has knowledge of the case and perhaps an artist who can draw a sketch based on any descriptions of suspects.

The session should be recorded and videotaped, if possible. Questions should relate only to what the witness states under hypnosis. The witness should not be prompted or induced in any way.

**Truth Serums.** **Truth serums** are fast-acting barbiturates of the type used to produce sleep at the approximate level of surgical anesthesia. Alcohol produces somewhat the same effects to a much lesser degree. The theory is that the drug removes the person's inhibitions so the person is more likely to tell the truth. In the past, scopolamine and hyascine were the most used drugs, but sodium amytol and sodium pentathol are more commonly used today.

Truth serums are not used extensively by the police because the accuracy of the information obtained with them is questionable. Truth serum is administered by a physician, preferably a psychiatrist, who remains to monitor the person's condition while the questions are asked. The drugs can cause serious consequences, so the subject must be monitored continually. Some patients also become violently excited. Moreover, individuals vary greatly in their response to truth serums. Some can withhold information even under the influence of a large dose of the serum.

The courts do not officially recognize truth serums or their reliability, nor do they admit the results as evidence.

## Use of Psychics

According to Rachlin (1993, p. 88): "It is usually only in the most desperate and hopeless circumstances that police are willing to consider what for some is the absolute last resort in an investigation: a psychic." Use of psychics in criminal investigations has been popularized by television shows and, to many, the incidents depicted are entirely believable. Although use of psychics in criminal investigations is controversial, Rachlin (1993, p. 88) notes the following similarities between psychics and investigators:

> Both psychics and detectives base their work to some extent on intuition. Psychics claim their instinctual feelings come from special powers within; detectives say their gut feelings and hunches emanate from years of experience, that they have developed a "cop's sense."

The article concludes: "As long as there are psychics, and as long as there are unsolved criminal investigations, the two will probably be linked."

As noted many places in this book, computerization of information is having a significant impact on criminal investigation. Other technological advances important to investigation in the 1990s include optical-disk information-storage systems, computerized polygraphs, cellular telephones and Caller ID.

### Optical-Disk Information-Storage Systems

Optical-disk information-storage systems are allowing law enforcement agencies to store information in a single location on a single disk and to index and recover information very rapidly. Such storage systems are essential in large agencies, which receive numerous requests for services and information from other agencies, insurance companies and the general public each day.

### Computerized Polygraphs

In computerized polygraph systems, the software analyzes physiological changes and reports the probability that the person has answered the question truthfully. According to Cross, a polygrapher since 1979, this "takes the onus off the examiner" (Clede, 1992, p. 43). Cross characterizes the original polygraph as 1940s technology, the electronic polygraph as 1960s technology and computerization as a "quantum leap into the 1990s."

### Cellular Telephones

The use of cellular telephones by police departments is proliferating. Officers in leadership positions have used such phones for several years, but many departments are now issuing them to patrol officers, especially those involved in community policing. The transfer of calls from the police communications center to the officers allows officers to talk directly to victims and complainants.

Some officers buy their own cellular phones and obtain permission from the department to use them on duty. In addition, the possession of cellular telephones by citizens allows direct reporting of their information from the scene. These telephones are enhancing the safety of citizens and officers alike. Although some questions of the security of information have arisen, cellular telephone calls are as secure as radio transmissions. Security safeguards are becoming available.

### Caller ID

Caller ID service records the number of the telephone from which a call is placed, even if the call is not answered. It also provides the date and time of the call and can store numbers in its memory system when more than one call is received.

In some criminal investigations, evidence has been obtained from telephones served by Caller ID. For example, a person who committed a burglary first called the business's office to see if anyone was there. The office telephone recorded the number of the telephone the burglar used, which allowed the police investigating the subsequent burglary to locate the suspect.

Caller ID could be helpful in cases involving telephoned threats, kidnappings and the like.

Most solved cases rely on both physical evidence and information obtained by interviewing and interrogating. The ultimate goals of interviewing and interrogating are to identify those responsible for a crime and to eliminate the innocent from suspicion.

Important sources of information include (1) reports and records, (2) persons who are not suspects in the crime but who know something about the crime or those involved and (3) suspects in the crime. A sources-of-information file contains cards with the name and location of persons, organizations and records that may assist in a criminal investigation. Interview anyone other than a suspect who has information about the case. This includes complainants, witnesses, victims and informants.

Regardless of whether you are interviewing or interrogating, there are several ways to improve communication: prepare in advance and obtain the information as soon after the incident as possible; be considerate and friendly; use a private setting and eliminate physical barriers; sit rather than stand; encourage conversation; ask simple questions one at a time; listen and observe.

Barriers to communication include ingrained attitudes and prejudices, fear, anger or hostility and self-preservation. The effective interviewer/interrogator overcomes such barriers by being adaptable, self-controlled, patient, confident, optimistic, objective, sensitive to individual rights and knowledgeable about the elements of the crime.

Interview witnesses separately if possible. Interview the victim or complainant first, then eyewitnesses and then individuals who did not actually see the crime but who have relevant information. Before beginning the actual questioning, it is important to establish rapport—an understanding between individuals created by genuine interest and concern.

The approach you select can be based on reason or on emotion. Whichever approach you use, obtain information by listening and observing. Ask direct questions that come right to the point. Use indirect questions, those that skirt the basic question, sparingly. Repetition is the best way to obtain recall and to uncover lies. An interview can result in a statement from the person being questioned, that is, a legal narrative description of events related to the crime.

Although many of the same principles apply to interrogating and interviewing, interrogating involves some special considerations. One important consideration is when to give the Miranda warning, which must be given to any suspect who is interrogated. It is also important to conduct interrogations in a place that is private and free from interruptions. Interrogation techniques include inquiring directly or indirectly, forcing responses, deflating or inflating the ego, minimizing or maximizing the crime and combining approaches. Third-degree tactics—physical force, threats of force or other physical, mental or psychological abuse—are illegal. Any information so obtained, including confessions, is inadmissible in court. Any confession, oral or handwritten, must be given of the suspect's free will and without fear, threats, promises or rewards. A confession is only one part of the investigation. It must be corroborated by independent evidence.

Special considerations are also observed when questioning juveniles. Obtain parental permission before questioning a juvenile. Do not use a juvenile as an informant unless the parents know the situation.

In addition to skills in interviewing and interrogating, you can sometimes use scientific aids to obtain information and determine its truthfulness. The polygraph scientifically measures respiration and depth of breathing, changes in the skin's electrical resistance and blood pressure and pulse rate. It is an instrument used to verify the truth, not a substitute for investigating and questioning. Although the results are not presently admissible in court, any confession obtained as a result of a polygraph test is admissible. Other scientific aids include hypnosis and truth serums, but such aids must be monitored closely, and the results are seldom admissible in court.

## Checklist

### *Obtaining Information*

- Were the complainant, witnesses, victim and informants questioned?
- Were all witnesses found?
- Was all information recorded accurately?
- Was the questioning conducted in an appropriate place? At an appropriate time?
- Was the Miranda warning given to all suspects before questioning?
- Were the type of offense and offender considered in selecting the interviewing or interrogating techniques?
- Were answers obtained to the questions of who, what, where, when, why and how?
- Were all available reports and records checked? Sources of information file? Field identification cards? The National Crime Information Center? Other police agencies? Public and private agencies at the local, county, state and national levels?
- Were confidential informants sought?
- Was a request for public assistance or an offer of a reward published?
- Is there a private number to call or a private post office box to write to for persons who have information about a crime?
- Was a polygraph used to check the validity of information given?
- Were all statements, admissions and confessions rechecked against other verbal statements and against existing physical evidence?
- Were those providing information thanked for their help?
- Were all statements, admissions and confessions properly and legally obtained? Recorded? Witnessed? Filed?

## Discussion Questions

**1.** What do you consider to be the essential steps in developing information about a crime?

**2.** What advantages do you see in the concept of *interroview?* What disadvantages?

**3.** Emphasis is often placed on obtaining a confession, or at least an admission, from a suspect in a criminal inquiry. Under what conditions is a confession of greatest value? Of no value?

**4.** The Miranda warning is now accepted by law enforcement agencies as a necessary requirement of interrogation under specific circumstances. What circumstances make it mandatory? What circumstances do not require its use?

**5.** Do you believe use of the Miranda warning has increased or decreased the number of confessions obtained in criminal cases?

**6.** How could polygraph results be used in plea bargaining?

**7.** What categories are included in your police department's sources of information file?

**8.** Should informants be protected by law from having to testify in court about information they have furnished police? What are the effects on investigative procedures and the frequency of cases cleared if informants are not protected?

**9.** Criminals or others who give the police information about a crime that eventually leads to an arrest or a conviction are sometimes paid for the information. Is this a legitimate use of tax funds, or should private donations be used?

**10.** How accurate is the typical television portrayal of an informant?

## References

Badger, Joseph. "Human Error in Memory." *Law and Order,* September 1995, pp. 13–15.

Bizzack, John. *Criminal Investigation: Managing for Results.* Lexington, KY: Autumn House Publishing, 1991.

Clede, Bill. "A Quantum Leap in Polygraphy." *Law and Order,* November 1992, p. 43.

Dees, Timothy M. "Polygraph Technology." *Law Enforcement Technology,* July 1995, pp. 62–54.

Dillingham, Christopher. "Deception in Law Enforcement Interrogations." *Law and Order,* October 1996, pp. 105–108.

Evans, Daniel D. "Ten Ways to Sharpen Your Interviewing Skills." *Law and Order,* August 1990, pp. 90–94.

Geiselman, R. Edward; Gail Bornstein; and Karen J. Saywitz. "New Approach to Interviewing Children: A Test of Its Effectiveness." *National Institute of Justice Research in Brief,* May 1992.

Hess, Kären M., and Henry M. Wrobleski. *For the Record: Report Writing in Law Enforcement,* 4th edition, Blue Lake, CA: Innovative Systems, Publisher, 1996.

"Interview Style Pays Off." *Law Enforcement News,* February 14, 1990, pp. 1, 6.

Jayne, Brian C., and Joseph P. Buckley III. "Criminal Interrogation Techniques on Trial." *Security Management,* October 1992, pp. 64–72.

McCloud, Douglas, G. "A Survey of Polygraph Utilization." *Law and Order,* September 1991, pp. 123–124.

Noose, Gregory A. "Basic Investigative Interviewing Skills: Networking an Interview." *Law and Order,* March 1992, pp. 101–107.

Olsen, Laura, and Robert Wells. "Cognitive Interviewing and the Victim/Witness in Crisis." *The Police Chief,* February 1991, pp. 28–31, 34.

Rachlin, Harvey. "Psychics and Police Work." *Law and Order,* September 1993, pp. 84–88.

Scalzo, Teresa. "To Tell the Truth." *Minnesota Alumni Association,* March–April 1991, pp. 37–38.

Skolnick, Jerome H., and Richard A. Leo. "The Ethics of Deceptive Interrogation." *Criminal Justice Ethics,* Winter/Spring 1992, pp. 3–12.

Slahor, Stephenie. "It's What They Say and How They Say It." *Law and Order,* June 1995, pp. 94–95.

Whitworth, A.W. "Polygraph or CVSA: What's the Truth about Deception Analysis?" *Law and Order,* November 1993, pp. 29–31.

Wood, Toni. "Getting Tough Interviews." *Writer's Digest,* March 1993, pp. 28–31.

Zulawski, David E., and Douglas E. Wicklander. "Field Interviewing." *Law and Order,* September 1995, pp. 111–115.

# Chapter 7

# Identifying and Arresting Suspects

## DO YOU KNOW

When a lawful arrest can be made?

When probable cause for believing that a suspect has committed a crime must exist?

What constitutes an arrest?

When force is justified in making an arrest? How much force is justified?

What field identification is and when is it used?

What rights the suspect has during field identification and what case established these rights?

How a suspect is developed?

How to help witnesses describe a suspect and/or a vehicle?

When mug shots are used?

What the NCIC is and how it assists in criminal investigations?

What the four basic means of identifying a suspect are?

What photographic identification requires and when it is used?

What a lineup requires and when it is used?

What rights suspects have regarding participation in a lineup and which cases established these rights?

When surveillance is used? What objectives are met by surveillance?

What the types of surveillance are?

When wiretapping is legal and the precedent case?

What objectives are met by undercover assignments? What precautions should be taken?

What objectives are met by a raid?

When raids are legal?

What precautions should be taken when conducting a raid?

## CAN YOU DEFINE

arrest
bugging
close tail
cover
electronic
  surveillance
entrapment
field identification
fixed surveillance
lineup identification
loose tail

moving surveillance
National Crime
  Information Center
  (NCIC)
nightcap provision
photographic
  identification
plant
psychological
  profiling
raid

reasonable force
rough tail
stakeout
stationary surveillance
subject
surveillance
surveillant
tail
tight tail
undercover
wiretapping

THE CLASSIC QUESTION IN DETECTIVE STORIES IS "WHODUNIT?" THIS question is also critical in any criminal investigation. In some cases the suspect is very obvious, but in most cases, there is no suspect at first. Although many crimes are witnessed, victims and witnesses may not recognize or be able to describe the suspect. Further, many crimes are not witnessed.

The Rochester (New York) Police Department conducted extensive research on the investigative process and identified solvability factors that are crucial to resolving criminal investigations. Hill (1991, p. 52) reports that five most important solvability factors were found to be:

- Was there a witness to the crime?
- Can the suspect be named?
- Can the suspect be located?
- Can the suspect be described?
- Can the suspect be identified?

The research showed that if one of these five questions could be answered, the crime was potentially solvable. In the majority of their investigations at least one of these factors was present.

Even if the suspect is known or has confessed, you must prove the elements of the crime and establish evidence connecting the suspect with the criminal act. Some cases require that suspects be developed, located, identified and then arrested. Others begin with an arrest and proceed to identification. No pat sequence exists. Regardless of whether an arrest begins or ends an investigation, the arrest must be legal.

This chapter begins with a discussion of what constitutes a legal arrest. This is followed by an explanation of field identification and a discussion of how to develop, locate and identify suspects. The chapter concludes with a description of three specialized areas: surveillances, undercover assignments and raids.

## Legal Arrests

Police powers to arrest (or search) are restricted by the Fourth Amendment, which forbids unreasonable searches or seizures without probable cause. Just as state laws define and establish the elements of crimes, they also define arrest and establish who may make an arrest, for what offenses and when. Most state laws define an **arrest** in general terms as "the taking of a person into custody in the manner authorized by law for the purpose of presenting that person before a magistrate to answer for the commission of a crime." An arrest may be made by a peace officer or by a private person. It may be made with or without a warrant, although a warrant is generally preferred because this places the burden of proving that the arrest was illegal on the defense.

---

Police officers are authorized to make an arrest:
- For any crime committed in their presence.
- For a felony not committed in their presence if they have probable cause to believe the person committed the crime.
- Under the authority of an arrest warrant.

---

Most arrests are for misdemeanors such as disorderly conduct, drunkenness, traffic violations, minor larceny, minor drug offenses, minor assaults, minor sex offenses, nuisances and other offenses of lesser severity. You must see such offenses to make an arrest without a warrant. Exceptions to this requirement exist in some states. In Florida, for example, retail theft and "gas skips" need not be witnessed. In many states an arrest may also be made by a private citizen who witnesses a misdemeanor and then turns the suspect over to law enforcement authorities. A sample citizen's arrest form is seen in Figure 7–1.

If you have probable cause to believe a suspect has committed a felony and there is no time to obtain an arrest warrant, you can make an arrest without the warrant. Facts gathered after the arrest to justify probable cause are *not* legally admissible as evidence of probable cause. They can, however, be used to strengthen the case if probable cause was established before the arrest.

---

CERTIFICATE AND DECLARATION OF ARREST BY PRIVATE PERSON
AND DELIVERY OF PERSON SO ARRESTED TO PEACE OFFICER

DATE _____5-3-97_____

TIME _____1440_____

PLACE _Boulder City -_
_1115 Bolt St._

I, _____Joyce Mayberry_____ , hereby declare and certify that I have arrested

(NAME) _John Mayberry_____

(ADDRESS) _1115 Bolt St. Boulder City, Nevada_____

for the following reasons: _____

John arrived home about fifteen minutes ago and we had

an argument about his drinking and spending all the

money. He struck me twice on the side of my face and

twice in the stomach. He told me that next time he

would kill me.

and I do hereby request and demand that you _____Officer James McGraw_____ ,
a peace officer, take and conduct this person whom I have arrested to the nearest magistrate to be dealt with according to law; and if no magistrate can be contacted before tomorrow morning, then to conduct this person to jail for safekeeping until the required appearance can be arranged before such magistrate, at which time I shall be present, and I will then and there sign, under oath, the appropriate complaint against this person for the offense which this person has committed and for which I made this arrest; and I will then and there, or thereafter as soon as this criminal action or cause can be heard, testify under oath of and concerning the facts and circumstances involved herein. I will save said officer harmless from any and all claim for damage of any kind, nature and description arising out of his acts at my direction.

Signature of private person
making this arrest _____Joyce Mayberry_____

Peace Officer Witnesses to this statement

_____James M. McGraw_____

_____C.J. Stone_____

**Figure 7–1   Certificate of Citizen's Arrest**

Probable cause for believing the suspect committed a crime must be established *before* a lawful arrest can be made.

An arrest for a felony or gross misdemeanor can usually be made any time if there is an arrest warrant or if the arresting officer witnessed the crime. An arrest may be made only in the daytime if it is by warrant, unless a magistrate has endorsed the warrant with a written statement that the arrest may be made at night. This is commonly referred to as a **nightcap provision.**

The officer is allowed to break an inner or outer door to make an arrest after identifying himself or herself, stating the purpose for entry and demanding admittance. This is often necessary when officers are in plain clothes and hence not recognized as police. The courts have approved no-knock entries in cases where the evidence would be immediately destroyed if police announced their intention to enter. You may break a window or door to leave a building if you are illegally detained inside. You may break a door or window to arrest a suspect who has escaped from custody. Finally, you may break an automobile window if a suspect rolls up the windows and locks the doors in attempting to prevent an arrest. Give proper notification of the reason for the arrest and your intention to break the window if the suspect does not voluntarily comply.

The physical act of arrest can be accomplished by taking hold of or controlling the person and stating, "You are under arrest for. . . .

If your intent is to make an arrest and you make this intent known to the suspect and then restrict his or her right to go free, an arrest has been made.

Physical force is not a necessary constituent of an arrest; in fact, most arrests are made without physical force. In most jurisdictions the arresting officer's authority must be stated, and the suspect must be told for what offense the arrest is being made. If you are going to question the suspect, read the Miranda warning first.

When making an arrest, use only as much force as is necessary to overcome any resistance. If no resistance occurs, no force may be used.

McEwen (1996, p. 46) draws an important distinction between use of excessive force and excessive use of force: "*Use of excessive force* means that police applied too much force in a given incident, while *excessive use of force* means that police apply force legally in too many incidents." This distinction is important when discussing police use of force.

**Reasonable force** is the amount of force a prudent person would use in similar circumstances. Use of exceptional force such as striking with a nightstick is justified only when exceptional resistance occurs and there is no other way to make the arrest. Use handcuffs on suspects you believe will harm you, someone else or themselves or who will attempt to escape.

Deciding how much force to use in making an arrest requires logic and good judgment. However, in the heat of the moment, police officers may use more force than intended. Courts and juries have usually excused force that is not blatantly unreasonable, recognizing that many factors are involved in such split-second decisions.

In the aftermath of the Rodney King case in Los Angeles and the alleged use of excessive force in other cities since the King case (such as the Detroit case), much national attention has focused on the question of what constitutes excessive force. Some of these cases are still being processed, but one fact is clear: The public is very aware of and sensitive to police use of force. The instantaneous decisions and actions by police officers at the scene are subject to long-term review by the public and by the courts. Police departments must review their policies on the use of force to ensure that they are clear and in accordance with court decisions as well as effective in assuring officer safety. Officers should know their department's policies regarding use of force. Further, uses of force in making arrests should be critiqued. Any complaints of excessive use of force should be thoroughly reviewed.

*Graham v. Connor* (1989) held that plaintiffs alleging excessive use of force need show only that the officer's actions were unreasonable under the standards of the Fourth Amendment.

Most police departments know of officers who tend to become involved in resistance or violent situations more frequently than others. In some instances, these officers' approach seems to trigger resistance. Voluntary compliance is the "best" arrest. Speak calmly and give the impression that you are in control. In any situation that is not out of control when you arrive, give a friendly greeting and state who you are and your authority if you are not in uniform. Show your badge or identification and give your reason for the questioning. Ask for identification and get their side of the story. Then decide on the appropriate action: warn, release, give a citation or make an arrest.

The amount of resistance to arrest varies, and this determines how much force should be used to make the arrest. With no resistance, no force should be used. There are always situations, however, that are not peaceful. In such cases,

*Police arrest a prolife demonstrator during an abortion clinic sit-in in Cypress, California.*

use only such force as is necessary to overcome the resistance, progressing from control by empty-hand methods (defensive tactics), to the use of control agents such as mace or tear gas, to the use of a police baton or—in the case of life-threatening resistance—to deadly force.

### Nonlethal Weapons

Several nonlethal weapons are available or in development, including the following ("Selecting Nonlethal Weapons, 1994, p. 265):

- *Sticky foam* that is so sticky it renders suspects helpless.
- *Smart guns* that only the owner can activate. This prevents officers from being shot with their own weapon and also prevents accidental shooting of children by their parent's gun.
- Various types of CN, CS and OC (better known as pepper spray), which incapacitate suspects.
- *Rubber bullets* and *stun guns* have also been used.
- *Robots* that can send back images are also in use, some so small they can be sent under closed doorways or hidden in corners.

Fairburn (1996, p. 78) adds to this list the Taser electronic device which fires high-voltage electrical currents to subdue resistant subjects, and the Net Gun which, once it makes contact with a suspect, entangles the person in a net, preventing further resistance. Fairburn (1996, p. 103) notes:

> These less-lethal weapons offer police agencies the means to defend its officers from attack, disperse unruly individuals or crowds, and control dangerous subjects to make apprehension easier. In the future, we may see chemical munitions that will render a subject quickly unconscious.
>
> As much as we might like to have one of Captain Kirk's phasers that could be "set to stun," such weaponry remains in the realm of science fiction. But for now, these very capable less-lethal alternatives will help us control dangerous situations without gunfire.

Use of aerosol weapons, often referred to as aerosol subject restraints or ASRs, is not without problems. According to Ashley (1996, p. 35): "Three issues which consistently raise significant concerns are aerosol training, placement of aerosols on a force continuum, and in-custody death." As far as the third issue is concerned, Ashley (p. 37) contends: "There is far less likelihood of suspect injury with an aerosol weapon than with a baton or firearm, and far less likelihood of officer injury with empty hand control techniques." Figure 7–2 shows a use of force continuum.

### Use of Deadly Force

Whether to use deadly force is a major and difficult decision for police officers. When it should be used is generally defined in state statutes, but three elements should always be present:

**1.** The suspect is threatening the officer or another person with a weapon.
**2.** The officer has probable cause to believe the suspect has committed a crime involving the inflicting or threatened inflicting of serious bodily harm.
**3.** The person is fleeing after committing an inherently violent crime, and the officer has given a warning.

Officers should be aware of and mentally review these elements before making any such decision. Justification for the use of deadly force is based primarily on the facts and circumstances that caused the officer to believe the person to be dangerous.

Everyone understands that force should be used as a last resort. Other non-lethal means should be used when there is opportunity and time. Millions of arrests, many with the potential for use of deadly force, have been made without such force. In making an arrest, the officers' judgment regarding the degree of force is subject to the review and criticism of others who will have ample time to consider all the facts of the situation. Such hindsight is far different from the necessity of making a life-and-death decision within seconds.

Police officers carry guns and are trained in using them. They also have department policy on deadly force as a guide. Unfortunately, the point of last resort may be immediate. Many police situations rapidly deteriorate to the point of "deadly force decision making." When such situations occur, they must be viewed in the light of department policies and the individual situation.

Department policies on deadly force should be reviewed periodically in the light of the most recent Supreme Court decisions. They must be restrictive

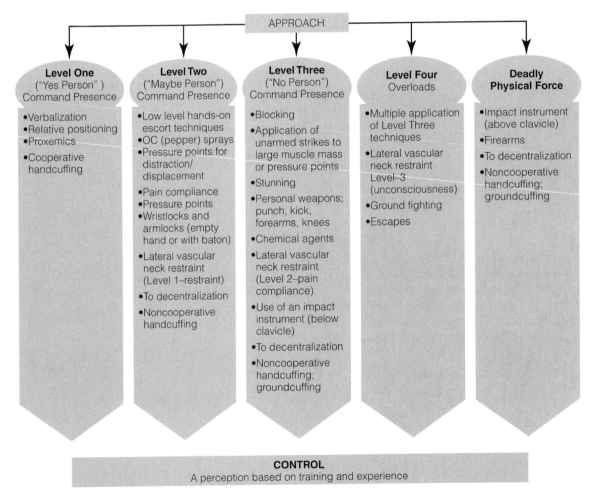

**Figure 7–2   Use of Force Continuum**

Source: *Police*, November 1995, p. 263. Reprinted by permission of Bobit Publishing, Redondo Beach, CA.

*The use of deadly force is sometimes unavoidable. This officer, using his car as a shield, waits
for a bank robber to emerge from the bank.*

enough to limit unreasonable use of deadly force, but they should not be so
restrictive that they fail to protect the lives of officers and members of the
community.

Use of a deadly weapon is carefully defined by state laws and department
policy. Such policies usually permit use of a gun or other weapon only in self-
defense or if others are endangered by the suspect. Some policies also permit use
of a deadly weapon to arrest a felony suspect, to prevent an escape or to recapture a felon when all other means have failed. Warning shots are not usually
recommended because they can ricochet, harming others.

An important Supreme Court ruling, *Tennessee v. Garner* (1985), bans law
enforcement officers from shooting to kill fleeing felons unless an imminent
danger to life exists. This ruling invalidates laws in almost half the states allowing police officers to use deadly force to prevent the escape of a suspected felon.
In this case police shot and killed an unarmed fifteen-year-old boy who had
stolen $10 and some jewelry from an unoccupied house. The Court ruled: "A
police officer may not seize an unarmed, nondangerous suspect by shooting
him dead."

The *Garner* decision did not take away police officers' right to use deadly
force. The Court acknowledged legitimate situations where deadly force is not
only acceptable, but necessary:

> Where the officer has probable cause to believe that the suspect poses a threat of
> serious physical harm, either to the officer or to others, it is not constitutionally
> unreasonable to prevent escape by using deadly force. Thus, if the suspect threat-
> ened the officer with a weapon or there is probable cause to believe that he had
> committed a crime involving the infliction or threatened infliction of serious phys-
> ical harm, deadly force may be used if necessary to prevent escape and if—where
> feasible—some warning has been given.

In situations involving a fleeing felon, officers must assess the situation rapidly, considering the law, department policy and the specific conditions that exist. An officer need not wait to see the flash from the suspect's gun muzzle before taking action. On the other hand, the *Garner* decision brought about policy changes in many departments that had previously approved shooting fleeing felons under all circumstances, including unarmed fleeing felons.

### Off-Duty Arrests

Every department needs to have a policy that allows off-duty officers to make arrests. A suggested policy includes the following guidelines. To make an off-duty arrest, officers should:

- Be within the legal jurisdiction of their agency.
- Not be personally involved.
- Perceive an immediate need for preventing a crime or arresting a suspect.
- Possess the proper identification.

Unless all these conditions exist, officers should not make an arrest but should report the incident to their department for disposition.

### False Arrest

Police officers always face the possibility of false arrest. In fact, as noted by Provost (1992, p. 155): "Any police officer who has been on the job for any length of time has been threatened with a false arrest suit." Some officers carry insurance to protect them against such lawsuits. Most are idle threats, however.

A false-arrest action is a civil tort action that attempts to establish that an officer who claimed to have authority to make the arrest did not have probable cause at the time of arrest. The best protection against false-arrest suits is to be certain that probable cause to arrest does exist, to have an arrest warrant or to obtain a conviction in court.

As Wattendorf (1995, p. 14) notes: "Many false arrest suits stem from drunk and disorderly arrests, a number of which escalate to excessive force claims."

Even when the defendant is found not guilty of the particular offense, a basis for a false-arrest suit is not automatically established. The court will consider the totality of the circumstances at the time of the arrest and whether they would lead an ordinarily prudent person to perceive probable cause and take the same action.

Police officers reduce the probability of valid false-arrest actions by understanding the laws they enforce, the elements of each offense and what probable cause is needed to prove each element. Police officers who honestly believe they have probable cause for an arrest can use the "good faith" defense, as established in *Pierson v. Ray* (1967):

> A policeman's lot is not so unhappy that he must choose between being charged with dereliction of duty if he does not arrest when he has probable cause, and being mulcted [penalized] in damages if he does. Although the matter is not entirely free from doubt, the same consideration would seem to require excusing him from liability for acting under a statute that he reasonably believed to be valid but that was later held unconstitutional on its face or as applied.

# Field Identification

If a suspect is apprehended while committing a crime, you can have witnesses identify the suspect. The same is generally true if the suspect is apprehended at or near the crime scene.

---

**Field identification** is on-the-scene identification of a suspect by the victim of or witnesses to a crime. Field identification must be made within minutes after the crime.

---

The critical element in field identification is *time*. It must be made very soon after the crime was committed (usually fifteen to twenty minutes). If the suspect has fled but is apprehended within minutes, you can either return the suspect to the scene or take the witness(es) to where the suspect was apprehended. It is usually preferable to take the witness to the suspect than to return the suspect to the crime scene.

Whether the identification is made at or away from the scene, the victim or witnesses must identify the suspect as soon after the crime as possible so that details are still clear. However, there must be a reasonable basis for believing that immediate identification is required before using field identification.

---

*United States v. Ash, Jr.* (1973) established that the suspect does not have the right to have counsel present at a field identification.

---

Read suspects the Miranda warning before questioning them. Suspects may refuse to answer questions and may demand a lawyer before any questioning occurs, but they do not have the right to have a lawyer present before field identification is made. Suspects may not even know such identification is occurring. Victims or witnesses may be positioned so that they can see the suspect while the suspect cannot see them.

Field identifications have been attacked on the basis that the victim or witness is too emotionally upset at the time to make an accurate identification, but such objections are seldom upheld. Mistaken identification is less likely if the person committing the crime is apprehended at the scene and is identified immediately. Have the victim or witnesses put their positive identification in writing, sign and date it and then have it witnessed.

# Developing a Suspect

If the suspect is not at the scene and not apprehended nearby, you must develop a suspect.

---

Suspects are developed through:
- Information provided by victims, witnesses and other persons likely to know about the crime or the suspect.
- Physical evidence left at the crime scene.
- Psychological profiling.
- Information in police files.
- Information in the files of other agencies.
- Informants.

---

Many sources are sometimes needed to develop a suspect. Other times, the victim or witnesses provide the required information. Then your task is to corroborate the identification through associative evidence such as fingerprints or DNA analysis, shoe prints, personal belongings left at the scene, tools used, weapons, stolen property in the possession of the suspect, injuries sustained, soil in shoes, safe insulation and other such evidence described in Chapter 5.

Schmitt (1992, p. 33) notes: "Police agencies of today and tomorrow have at their command an impressive array of tools to expedite the process of identifying potential criminals." Several of these technological advances have already been discussed, including automated fingerprint identification systems, computerized imaging systems and the like.

Victim or eyewitness identification of a suspect or the suspect's admission or confession should be corroborated by as much physical and circumstantial evidence as possible.

### Victims and Witnesses

Developing a suspect is much easier if the victim or witnesses can describe and identify the person who committed the crime. Witnesses may not have observed the actual crime but may have seen a vehicle leaving the scene and can describe the vehicle and its occupants. Obtain a complete description of the suspect and any vehicles involved.

---

Ask very specific questions and use an identification diagram to assist witnesses in describing suspects and vehicles.

---

Rather than simply asking a witness to describe a suspect, ask specific questions about each item in Table 7–1. A description sheet with diagram such as Figure 7–3 also helps people to describe suspects.

Also obtain information about how the suspect left the scene—on foot or in a vehicle. If in a vehicle, obtain a complete description of it. Identifying the car may lead to identifying the suspect.

Victims can provide information as to who has a motive for the crime, who has the knowledge required to commit it and who are not likely suspects. For example, in an "inside" burglary, the employer may be able to provide important information about which employees might or might not be suspects.

### Mug Shots

If the victims or witnesses do not know the suspect but saw him or her clearly, mug shots may be used.

---

Have victims and witnesses view mug shots in an attempt to identify a suspect you believe has a record.

---

This procedure, frequently depicted in television detective shows, is very time consuming and is of value only if the suspect has a police record and has been photographed.

### Composite Drawings and Sketches

If witnesses can provide adequate information, a rapid method to produce a composite image of a person who committed a crime is to use a police artist

- Gender
- Height
- Weight
- Build—stout, average, slim, stooped, square-shouldered
- Age
- Nationality
- Face—long, round, square, fat, thin; pimples, acne, or scars
- Complexion—flushed, shallow, pale, fair, dark
- Hair—color; thick, thin, partly bald, completely bald; straight, curly, wavy; long, short
- Forehead—high, low; sloping, straight, bulging
- Eyebrows—bushy, thin, average
- Eyes—color; close together or wide-set; large, small; glasses or sunglasses
- Nose—small, large; broad, narrow; crooked, straight; long, short
- Ears—small, large; close to head or protruding; pierced
- Mustache—color; short, long; thick, thin; pointed ends
- Mouth—large; small; drooping, upturned
- Lips—thick, thin
- Teeth—missing, broken, prominent, gold, conspicuous dental work
- Beard—color; straight, rounded; bushy, thin; long, short
- Chin—square, round, broad; long, narrow; double, sagging
- Neck—long, short; thick, thin
- Distinctive marks—scars, moles, amputations, tattoos
- Peculiarities—peculiar walk or talk, twitch, stutter, foreign accent, distinctive voice or dialect
- Clothing—shabby or well-dressed, monograms, association with an occupation or hobby, general description
- Weapon—(if any) specific type, how carried, how displayed and when
- Jewelry—any obvious rings, bracelets, necklaces, earrings, watches

or an identification kit such as Identi-Kit. Some training is required to use the kit to construct a feature-by-feature composite. The initial composite requires information on the suspect's sex, age, build, height and hairstyle. Then individual facial characteristics are added, including likenesses of the chin, eyes, nose, lips, age lines, hair and beard. Figure 7–4 illustrates the development of a suspect through a composite image using the Identi-Kit.

Composite drawings are most commonly used to draw human faces or full bodies, but they can also be used for any inanimate object described by witnesses—for example, vehicles, unusual marks or symbols, tattoos or clothing.

Computer-generation of composites with such software as CompuSketch or Visatex is becoming more popular. Police officers can also be trained to use professional identification kits such as the Identi-Kit, or they may be trained to sketch freehand while interviewing a victim or witness. Courses in sketching may be available at local colleges or through the FBI Academy at Quantico, Virginia.

Schmitt (1992, p. 43) describes CompuSketch, a computerized system any officer can use to generate a sketch of a suspect:

> The process begins with an on-screen interactive interview—carefully designed with free-form and multiple-choice questions—to solicit all available information from the witness. When the interview is completed, a sketch is automatically created from a library of thousands of facial features. . . .
>
> The witness then views this initial sketch and suggests changes.

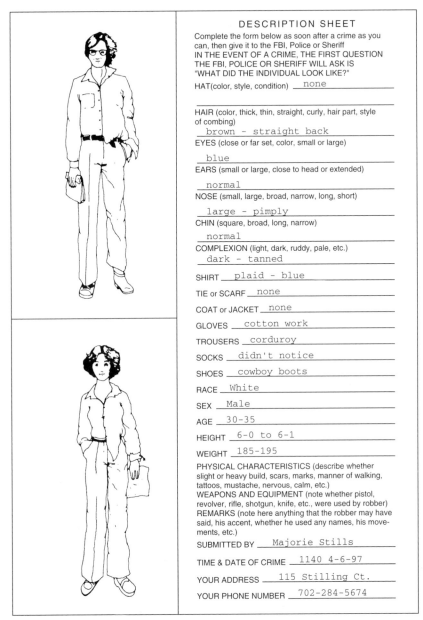

DESCRIPTION SHEET

Complete the form below as soon after a crime as you can, then give it to the FBI, Police or Sheriff
IN THE EVENT OF A CRIME, THE FIRST QUESTION THE FBI, POLICE OR SHERIFF WILL ASK IS "WHAT DID THE INDIVIDUAL LOOK LIKE?"

HAT(color, style, condition) __none__

HAIR (color, thick, thin, straight, curly, hair part, style of combing)
__brown - straight back__

EYES (close or far set, color, small or large)
__blue__

EARS (small or large, close to head or extended)
__normal__

NOSE (small, large, broad, narrow, long, short)
__large - pimply__

CHIN (square, broad, long, narrow)
__normal__

COMPLEXION (light, dark, ruddy, pale, etc.)
__dark - tanned__

SHIRT __plaid - blue__

TIE or SCARF __none__

COAT or JACKET __none__

GLOVES __cotton work__

TROUSERS __corduroy__

SOCKS __didn't notice__

SHOES __cowboy boots__

RACE __White__

SEX __Male__

AGE __30-35__

HEIGHT __6-0 to 6-1__

WEIGHT __185-195__

PHYSICAL CHARACTERISTICS (describe whether slight or heavy build, scars, marks, manner of walking, tattoos, mustache, nervous, calm, etc.)
WEAPONS AND EQUIPMENT (note whether pistol, revolver, rifle, shotgun, knife, etc., were used by robber)
REMARKS (note here anything that the robber may have said, his accent, whether he used any names, his movements, etc.)

SUBMITTED BY __Majorie Stills__

TIME & DATE OF CRIME __1140  4-6-97__

YOUR ADDRESS __115 Stilling Ct.__

YOUR PHONE NUMBER __702-284-5674__

**Figure 7–3    Witness Identification Diagram**

### Psychological Profiling

A method of suspect identification is **psychological profiling,** which attempts to identify the individual's mental, emotional and psychological characteristics. Abnormal, criminal behavior patterns and the characteristics of criminals who have committed specific types of crimes have been studied for many years. This research provides the basis for psychological profiling.

The profile is developed primarily for crimes of violence such as homicides, sadistic crimes, sex crimes, arson without apparent motive and crimes of serial or ritual sequence. The profile provides investigators with corroborative information about a known suspect or with possible leads to an unknown suspect.

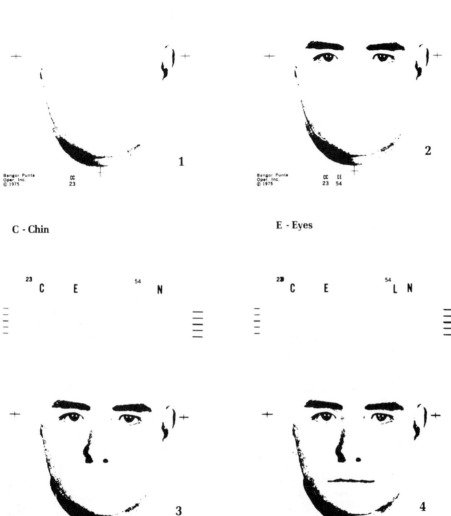

Approximate height and build determines selection of chin...

Approximate age determines selection of eyes, nose, lips and age lines...

1

2

**C - Chin**

**E - Eyes**

3

4

**N - Nose**

**L - Lips**

**Figure 7–4   Use of Identi-Kit to Develop a Composite Image of a Suspect**
M.O.—Subject would get into the rear of a female's car and hide on the floor while she was shopping. When owner returned and drove car away he would attack and rape her. A stakeout was set up in the area he frequented. With composite in hand, the detective apprehended the suspect in the street. He said, "He matched the physical description to a T." A photo lineup was shown to the victim and two other similar cases and all three identified the subject in question.

Reprinted by permission.

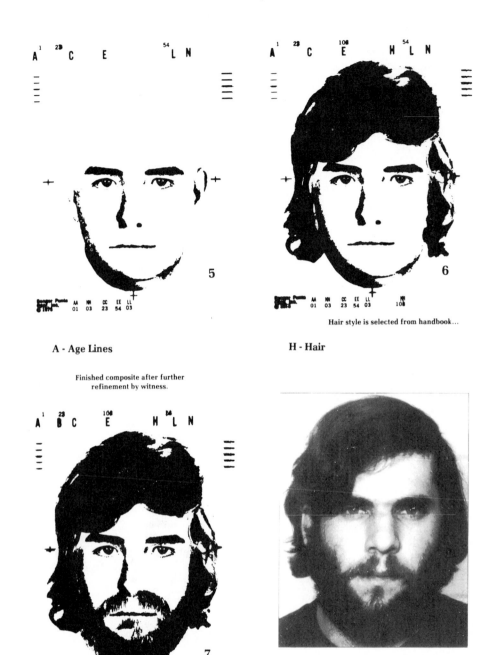

5

A - Age Lines

6

Hair style is selected from handbook...

H - Hair

Finished composite after further
refinement by witness.

7

B - Beard

Figure 7–4   continued

The psychological profile is determined by examining all data and evidence from a specific crime scene, including, but not limited to, crime-scene photographs, detailed photos of bodily injuries to victims, photos of any mutilation evidence, information related to the condition of the victim's clothing or absence thereof, information regarding whether the crime scene was altered or unaltered, photos of the area beyond the immediate crime scene, any available maps of the area, the medical examiner's report and opinion and any other relevant information concerning the crime, particularly any abnormalities such as multiple slashings, disembowelment, drinking of the victim's blood, beheading or dismembering the body.

Specific information is then categorized to produce predictive information regarding the suspect's likely age, sex, race, weight, height; physical, mental and psychological condition; area of residence; whether known to the victim or not; whether the suspect has a prior criminal record; and other details as determined by the information provided by the crime scene.

The psychological profile produced by experts in criminal behavior analysis can provide excellent leads for investigators. Investigators desiring such assistance must provide the complete crime report to the local office of the FBI, Domestic Cooperative Services. If the report is accepted, it is then forwarded to the FBI Behavioral Science Unit in Quantico, Virginia.

In one criminal investigation, the FBI's Behavioral Science Unit advised a police department that the serial rapist they were seeking was probably a 25- to 35-year-old, divorced or separated white male, with a high-school education who worked as a laborer, lived in the area of the rapes and engaged in voyeurism. Based on this information, the agency developed a list of forty suspects having these characteristics. Using other information in the profile, they narrowed their investigation to one suspect and focused on him. Within a week they had enough information to arrest him.

Another case involved the rape/murder of a 25-year-old white married woman. The criminal profiler told a very surprised detective that he had probably already interviewed the killer. The profiler gave the detective a scenario based on color photographs, physical evidence and interviews.

It is of interest to note that William Tafoya of the FBI developed a psychological profile of the Unibomber that many rejected. However, after the arrest of Theodore Kaczynski, it was observed that Tafoya's assessment was much more accurate than many in the FBI had believed.

Psychological profiling is most often used in crimes against persons where the motive is unknown. The profile seeks to disclose a possible motive. Continued use of the technique has shown that the more information the police furnish to the FBI, the greater is the possibility of obtaining accurate leads. Reporting the unusual is extremely important. Psychological profiling can help to eliminate suspects and develop suspects, thereby saving investigative time.

## Tracking

Sometimes a knowledge of tracking is helpful. Tracking skill can be developed and can provide many investigative leads. For example, the direction of vehicle travel from a crime scene can be determined by tire-tread marks. People hiding in outside areas may leave foot, knee, hand, heel or body impressions. Broken tree branches provide some evidence of when the branch was broken; the lighter the color of the break, the more recent it is. Recent overturning of a stone may be indicated by the dirt or by the moist side being on top. The length of stride and depth of impression of footprints can help to determine the size of the person or if the person was carrying a heavy load.

## Other Identification Aids

Visual aids such as newspaper photos or video and news films disseminated to the public may provide rapid identification of suspects. Fingerprints and footprints are other commonly used means of positive identification. Voiceprints and DNA profiling are also becoming more common as means of identification.

If a suspect or victim is deceased and the identity is unknown, dental and orthopedic records may help. Facial reconstruction is also being used in many areas as a means to identify unknown victims or suspects if sufficient skull and facial parts are available. Amazing likenesses can be achieved to assist in identifying unknown deceased persons.

## Developing a Suspect through Modus Operandi Information

A series of crimes often creates a recognizable modus operandi, such as forgers who use the same or a very similar name on each forgery or burglars who take the same type of property. If a series of burglaries occurs at the same time of day, this may be the suspect's time away from a regular job. Such M.O.s furnish important investigative leads.

Check the details of a specific crime against your department's M.O. files. If no similar M.O. is in the file, a new criminal may be starting activity in your area, or it is possible this is the only crime the suspect intends to commit. In such cases, the suspect must be developed through sources other than modus operandi information.

## Information in Police Files and Files of Other Agencies

Police records on solved crimes and on suspects involved in certain types of crimes often develop leads. For example, in the "Son of Sam" case in New York City, one lead to identifying the suspect was provided by a woman who saw an illegally parked car that fit the description of the car reported as being used in the crimes. Police then checked all parking tickets issued on that date for that time and location. This information, combined with other information, eventually led to the suspect.

Police files contain considerable information about people who commit or are suspected of committing crimes. The files contain such information as the person's physical characteristics, date of birth, age, race, general build, kind of clothing usually worn, height, weight, hair color and style, facial features and any unusual marks, tattoos, deformities, abnormalities, alcohol or drug use, M.O. and other information that helps in developing suspects.

Field-interview cards patrol officers file when they stop people under suspicious circumstances can also provide leads. The officer may not know of an actual crime committed at the time of the stop but may later learn that a business or residence in the area of the stop was burglarized at about the same time. Descriptions of vehicles in a high-crime area that do not fit the neighborhood also help to identify suspects.

If the M.O. is discernible or if you have a good description of the suspect, check with other police departments in the area. Review all reports on the case and any cases that seem similar. Many other official sources of information at all levels of government as well as private agencies can also provide leads in developing and locating a suspect.

**Community Level.** Almost every department of community government can provide some type of information during a criminal investigation.

Information sources include the city clerk, city attorney's office, municipal court, finance office, public utilities, building inspectors, public works departments, voter registration records, school files, welfare files and civil service files. Local agencies can often furnish names, birthdates, addresses, changes of address, occupations, places of birth, parents' names, family names, property ownership, legal descriptions of property, proposed businesses and business ownership, prior employment, past criminal offenses and many other details. Banks and credit unions are another excellent source of information.

**County Level.** Sources of information at the county level include the treasury department, the health department, engineering departments, license bureaus, the assessor's office, courts, probate courts, the welfare department, the coroner's office, civil service, the building inspector, the register of deeds, the sheriff's office and the fire marshal. Such sources can furnish information on the payroll of county employees, names, addresses, changes of address, employment and building inspections. County agencies are also a source for birth and death certificates showing parents' names, maps, legal descriptions and values of property, deeds, mortgages, court records, marriage license and divorce records, handwriting specimens, criminal records, business listings, diagrams of buildings and similar information.

**State Level.** State agencies from which information is available include the liquor control board, secretary of state, highway department, highway patrol, bureau of investigation, bureau of narcotics and drug abuse, fish and game agency, insurance department, motor vehicles department, personnel department, state supreme court, state board of probation and parole, state prisons and juvenile detention facilities. These agencies provide access to criminal records within the restrictions of the Privacy and Security Act, vehicle registrations, real estate sales records, licensing information, names, addresses, past addresses, business associates, civil suits, election information, birth and death records and other personal information.

**Federal Level.** The federal government has many agencies, not only in Washington, D.C., but also in regional offices throughout the United States, that provide information valuable in developing and locating suspects. The military departments of the U.S. Navy, Army, Marines, Coast Guard, Merchant Marine and Air Force and their respective investigative agencies can provide much information. Other federal sources include the Civil Service Commission; Department of Health, Education and Welfare; Internal Revenue Service; Department of Commerce; Federal Bureau of Investigation; Central Intelligence Agency; Secret Service; State Department; Immigration and Naturalization Service; Federal Communications Commission; Postal Service; Interstate Commerce Commission; Department of Labor; Federal Aviation Administration; Veterans Administration; Department of the Interior; and task forces on organized crime activities. Such agencies provide information on military service, military criminal records, census data, drug abuse and narcotics involvement, aliens, firearms registration, plane registration and licensing, as well as some information on security investigations.

One of the most important federal-level information sources is the FBI's National Crime Information Center (NCIC) whose data base, according to Nemecek (1990, p. 31), chief of the NCIC, exceeds 20 million records, is queried by 59,362 authorized users who conduct as many as one million transactions per day and whose Wanted Persons File contains 335,000 subjects.

The FBI's **National Crime Information Center (NCIC)** contains criminal fingerprint records and information on wanted criminals and stolen property, including vehicles.

The NCIC data bank is a computerized index of documented criminal justice information about crimes and criminals of national interest. It also includes a locator-type file for missing persons. The Computerized Criminal History (CCH) file provides information on persons currently involved in the criminal justice process. The information is documented by a fingerprint card for each arrest and is restricted to serious violations. Records are placed directly in the NCIC files by an originating agency (a department holding an arrest warrant, significant stolen property, etc.), and the information is then available to every law enforcement agency in the country.

NCIC operates twenty-four hours a day, seven days a week. It provides valuable information for investigators and patrol officers, but the information must be evaluated along with other known facts. If you receive a positive response (a "hit") from NCIC and you have detained an individual or seized stolen property, immediately confirm the information received from NCIC with the agency that filed the report.

The FBI/NCIC staff is developing "image transmission of a black-and-white mug shot and a fingerprint image of wanted subjects over NCIC equipment and telecommunication lines to a two-way radio base station transmitter, and out over a radio frequency into receiving equipment in a patrol car."

As noted by Nemecek: "The ultimate goal of NCIC 2000, relative to image transmission for the Wanted Persons File, is to assist law enforcement in the positive identification of individuals with whom the officer comes in contact. The ability to have a photograph and fingerprint transmitted within seconds to and from the patrol car provides the officer with irrefutable evidence as to whether or not an individual temporarily detained is identical to a wanted person on file at a local, state or national level. This capability will, for all practical purposes, eliminate false or erroneous arrests and could in some instances speed up the overall 'stop' process."

**International Agencies.**   The International Criminal Police Organization, better known as *Interpol,* is a network of national central bureaus in more than 155 member-countries. Interpol compiles and dispenses information on criminals and cases that cross national boundaries. World headquarters is in Lyon, France. The main U.S. office is in Washington, D.C., and Interpol has operations in all the states. It operates twenty-four hours a day. Interpol's telecommunications network links it with nearly all U.S. investigative agencies such as the DEA, FBI, CIA and the Treasury Department.

Interpol is now handling more than 45,000 cases annually. The types of information Interpol can provide include the location of suspects, fugitives and witnesses; criminal history checks; information on terrorists; information on stolen artworks, weapons and motor vehicles; and license plate traces. As noted by Pankau (1993, p. 37): "Technology enables investigators to network with other resources and agencies across the globe and provides an instantaneous transmission of data."

**Private Agencies.**   Many private agencies also assist in developing and locating suspects. These include gas and electric companies, credit bureaus, financial institutions, educational facilities, the National Auto Theft Bureau, telephone companies, moving companies, Better Business Bureaus, taxi companies, real estate sales and rental agencies, laundry and dry-cleaning associations and insurance underwriters. Check your local city directory for possible additional private sources of information.

### Informants

Informants have been a source of police information for centuries. An informant is any person who gives information to the police. Often the information is given voluntarily in the interests of civic duty. Informants may work in a position that places them in frequent contact with criminals, or they may have committed crimes themselves or be associates of active criminals.

Some informants are known to be involved in minor criminal activities and are allowed to remain free in exchange for their continued cooperation with the police, much to the dismay of many citizens. Be careful when working with such informants. Make no promises you cannot keep. Only the prosecutor's office can make concessions to informants in exchange for information.

Most informants closely associated with the criminal world insist on remaining anonymous. This is usually to law enforcement's advantage because much information would no longer be available to informants if their cooperation with the police were known. Assign a code name to such informants and keep records of their information in a confidential file to help preserve their anonymity. Be aware of circumstances under which anonymity cannot be preserved and make informants aware of these circumstances, as discussed in Chapter 6.

One disadvantage of using anonymous informants is that information they provide is not accepted as evidence in court. It must be independently corroborated. However, such information can save much investigative time and lead to the recovery of valuable property or the arrest of suspects.

The information provided by some informants is of such value in solving or preventing crimes that the informants are paid for the information they furnish. Many police agencies, at all levels of government, have informant payment funds. Care must be used in paying informants because the payment motivates some of them to give contrived, false information. Cross-checking for truthfulness is required, and informants' reliability should be documented for future reference. There may be many motives for informing: revenge, a sincere desire to change, a hope of lessening the time to be served in prison, a falling out with cohort criminals, a need for money or a feeling of being threatened.

Departments that use community-oriented policing may develop informants more easily because officers are closer to the people in their patrol area. Because of the negative connotations with the word *informant,* many agencies refer to these individuals as *citizens who assist the police with information.*

## Locating Suspects

Many information sources used to develop a suspect can also help to locate the suspect. If the suspect is local and frequents public places, the victim may see the suspect and call the police. In one instance, a rape victim saw the alleged rapist in a shopping center and remembered that she had seen him there just before her rape occurred. The investigator accompanied the victim to the shopping center for several evenings until the victim saw the suspect and identified him.

Telephone calls to other investigative agencies, neighborhood inquiries at the suspect's last known address, questioning relatives, checking the address on a prison release form, utility checks and numerous other contacts can help locate suspects.

# Identifying Suspects

---

Suspects can be identified through field identification, mug shots, photographic identification or lineups.

---

Field identification and mug shots have been discussed previously.

## Photographic Identification

Often the victim or witnesses get a good look at the suspect and are able to make a positive identification. If you have a good idea of who committed the crime but do not have the suspect in custody or cannot arrange a fair lineup, use **photographic identification.** Photographs for this type of identification can be obtained through surveillance or from files. Select pictures of at least five people of comparable race, height, weight and general appearance.

---

Use photographic identification when the suspect is not in custody or when a fair lineup cannot be conducted. Tell witnesses they need not identify anyone from the photographs.

---

The photographs can be kept separate or mounted on a composite board. Write a number or code on the back of each photograph to identify the individual, but do not include any other information, especially information that the person has a criminal record. Tell witnesses that they need not identify anyone from among the photographs and that it is as important to eliminate innocent persons from suspicion as it is to identify the guilty.

If there are several witnesses, have each one view a separate set of pictures independently—preferably in a different room if other witnesses to the crime are viewing the photographs at the same time. If witnesses recognize a photograph, have them indicate that by placing their initials and the date on the front side. Then have them initial and date the back side of each of the remaining pictures. This procedure establishes the fairness of the identification.

It is unwise to show a single photograph to a victim or witness to obtain identification. Such identification is almost always inadmissible as evidence because it allows little chance of mistaken identity. The Supreme Court decision in *Manson v. Brathwaite* (1977), however, did approve the showing of a single picture in specific circumstances:

### Court Rules on Photo ID*

Washington—An out-of-court photographic identification of a suspect may be admitted as evidence even if it was "unduly suggestive" of guilt, the Supreme Court held by a vote of 7 to 2 Thursday.

---

*Copyright 1977, *Los Angeles Times*. Reprinted by permission.

If the identification is reliable, the court said, it may be admitted for a jury to evaluate. To exclude such evidence flatly might result in the guilty going free, the majority said.

The issue before the court involved the admissibility of a witness's identification based on a single photo of the suspect (a "mug shot"), rather than from an array of photos of the suspect and others similar in appearance—the usual police procedure.

The justices had been urged to rule that a single photo identification could too easily lead to misidentification—and thus always should be inadmissible, as a violation of due process of law.

But the majority declined to go that far, saying instead that the reliability of the identification and the "totality of the circumstances" of the case were the determining factors.

The decision provoked a bitter dissent from the court's two most liberal members, Justices Thurgood Marshall and William J. Brennan, Jr.

"Today's decision can come as no surprise to those who have been watching the court dismantle the protections against mistaken eyewitness testimony," wrote Marshall.

"But it is still distressing to see the court . . . blindly uphold the conviction of a defendant who may well be innocent.

"The use of a single picture (or display of a single live suspect, for that matter) is a grave error, of course, because it dramatically suggests to the witness that the person shown must be the culprit. Why else would the police choose the person? And it is deeply ingrained in human nature to agree with the expressed opinions of others—particularly others who should be more knowledgeable—when making a difficult decision."

In the case before the justices, an undercover Connecticut state police officer purchased heroin from a man in an apartment (*Manson vs. Brathwaite*).

At the time, the officer was about two feet from the seller, conversing with the man during the two-to-three minute period in which the deal was made.

Later, the undercover officer described the suspect to another officer.

The second officer suspected from the description the seller was Nowell A. Brathwaite. He obtained a photo of Brathwaite and two days later the undercover officer identified the man in the photo as the man who sold him the narcotics.

Brathwaite was arrested at the apartment and charged. At trial, the undercover officer described his photographic identification and also identified Brathwaite in court. Brathwaite claimed innocence but was convicted.

On appeal, the U.S. Court of Appeals for the Second Circuit reversed the conviction, holding that the photograph should not have been admitted as evidence because it alone was unduly suggestive of guilt when shown to the undercover officer.

The Supreme Court, in a majority opinion by Justice Harry A. Blackmun, said the appeals court was wrong, even though the photo identification concededly was unduly suggestive.

The majority rejected the argument that the identification should be excluded from evidence whether or not it was reliable. Such a rule, Blackmun wrote, ". . . goes too far, since its application automatically and peremptorily, and without consideration of alleviating factors, keeps evidence from the jury that is reliable and relevant."

". . . Since it denies the (jury) reliable evidence, it may result, on occasion, in the guilty going free," he said, adding, "certainly, inflexible rules of exclusion that may frustrate, rather than promote, justice have not been viewed recently by this court with unlimited enthusiasm."

Blackmun noted that in this case the officer had a good opportunity to see and later identify Brathwaite and that, despite the suspect's claims of innocence, Brathwaite's arrest had taken place where the sale took place earlier—an apartment Brathwaite admitted he visited frequently.

"Surely, we cannot say that under all the circumstances of this case there is a very substantial likelihood of irreparable misidentification," Blackmun said. "Short of that point, such evidence is for the jury to weigh."

After identification is made, review with the witness the conditions under which the suspect was seen, including lighting at the time and distance from the suspect.

---

A suspect does *not* have the right to a lawyer if a photographic lineup is used.

---

At issue in *United States v. Ash, Jr.* (1973) was whether an accused has the right to counsel during a preinvestigation photographic lineup that includes a picture of the accused. The case began on August 26, 1965, when two men in stocking masks robbed a bank in Washington, D.C. An informant gave police the name of Charles Ash, Jr. A photographic lineup of five persons, including Ash, was shown to four witnesses, and all four made nonpositive identifications of Ash. An indictment was returned against Ash and his codefendant in April 1966, but the trial was not set until May 1968, three years after the crime.

In preparing for the trial, the prosecutor arranged for a color photographic lineup with the witnesses to make sure they could identify Ash in court. Three of the four witnesses picked Ash, but did not pick his codefendant. At the trial three of the four witnesses also picked Ash, but were not willing to state so positively. A witness outside the bank who had seen both suspects without their masks identified both Ash and the codefendant, Bailey.

The defense counsel raised doubts because the same witness was accused of not being able to pick out a photograph of the codefendant on a prior occasion. The photographs used in the lineup were introduced into court by the prosecution to avoid a showing by the defense that the witness had picked a third party as the suspect. The informant testified that he had discussed the robbery with both Ash and Bailey, but it was shown that the informer had a long criminal record and a history as an informer.

The jury convicted Ash on all counts, but a motion for acquittal against Bailey was granted. A court of appeals held that Ash's Sixth Amendment rights were violated by not having counsel present at the photographic lineup. The U.S. Supreme Court, however, held that the Sixth Amendment does not grant the right to counsel for photographic displays used to allow a witness to attempt identification of an offender. Because the accused is not present in person and asserts no right to be present, no possibility arises that the witness might be misled by lack of familiarity with the law or overpowered by his or her professional adversary.

Because it is not advisable to have the same witness make an identification from a photograph and then from a lineup, your case will be stronger if you do not show the photographs to all the witnesses. If you have several witnesses and are using photographic identification to build a case strong enough to arrest the suspect, reserve two or three witnesses for lineup identification.

### Lineup Identification

**Lineup identification** is commonly used when the suspect is in custody and there were witnesses to the crime. Police have adopted lineup procedures to ensure accurate and fair identifications and to meet the standards established by Supreme Court decisions. Basically, a lineup has the same requirements as photographic identification.

Use lineup identification when the suspect is in custody. Use at least five individuals of comparable race, height, weight, age and general appearance. Ask all to perform the same actions or speak the same words. Instruct those viewing the lineup that no identification need be made.

Lineups may have from five to ten persons. The suspect must not be of a different race, exceptionally taller or shorter, have longer or shorter hair or be dressed very differently from the other persons in the lineup. The suspect must not be handcuffed unless all persons in the lineup are handcuffed. Nor may the suspect be asked to step forward, turn a certain direction or speak certain words unless every participant in the lineup is asked to do the same.

Suspects may refuse to participate in a lineup, but such refusals can be used against them in court (*Schmerber v. California*). Suspects have a right to have an attorney present during a lineup (*United States v. Wade*).

In *United States v. Wade* (1967) on September 21, 1964, a robber forced a cashier and a bank official to place money in a pillowcase. The robber had a piece of tape on each side of his face. After obtaining the money, he left the bank and drove away with an accomplice who had been waiting outside in a car.

In March 1965, an indictment was returned against Wade and an accomplice for the bank robbery. He was arrested April 2, 1965. Approximately two weeks later, an FBI agent put Wade in a lineup to be observed by bank employees. Wade's counsel was not notified of the lineup. Each person in the lineup had strips of tape similar to those worn by the bank robber, and each was requested to say words allegedly spoken at the robbery. Both bank employees picked Wade out of the lineup as being the robber, and both employees again identified Wade in the courtroom.

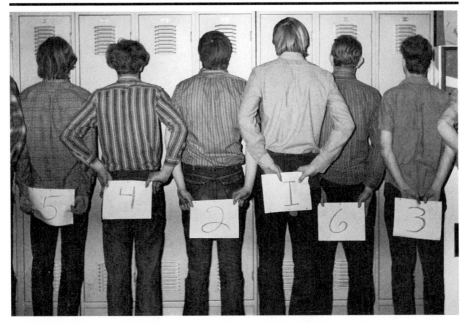

*A back view of a lineup with participants holding numbers behind their backs. Those in a lineup are usually asked to face forward, to the side and to the back.*

The defense objected that the bank officials' courtroom identifications should be stricken because the original lineup had been conducted without the presence of Wade's counsel. The motion was denied, and Wade was found guilty. Counsel held that this violated his Fifth Amendment right against self-incrimination and his Sixth Amendment right to counsel being present at the lineup.

The Court held that a suspect has the right to have counsel present at the lineup because a lineup is held for identification by eyewitnesses and may involve vagaries leading to mistaken identification. The Court pointed to the many cases in which mistaken identification had been made, as well as to the influence of improper suggestion upon identifying witnesses and the improper manner in which the suspect may be presented to the witnesses. The Court commented that neither the lineup nor anything that Wade was required to do in the lineup violated his privilege against self-incrimination.

It stated in *Schmerber v. California* (1966) that protection against self-incrimination involved disclosure of knowledge by the suspect. Both state and federal courts have held that compulsion to submit to photographs, writing, speaking, fingerprints, measurements or giving blood is not self-incrimination within the meaning of the Fifth Amendment.

If the suspect refuses to participate in the lineup or a lineup cannot be conducted for any reason, simply photograph the suspect and each individual in the lineup separately and use photographic identification.

The *Wade* decision ruled that: "Prior to having a suspect participate in a lineup, the officer must advise the suspect of his constitutional right to have his lawyer present during the lineup." Recall that this right to a lawyer does not apply to field identification or photographic identification. If suspects waive their right to counsel, get the waiver in writing. A waiver such as the one in Figure 7–5 can be used.

---

Avoid having the same individual(s) make both photographic and lineup identification. If you do so, do not conduct both within a short time period.

---

If suspects do choose to have a lawyer, they may either select their own or ask you to obtain one. The lawyer may confer with the suspect in private before the lineup and may talk with witnesses observing the lineup, but witnesses are not obligated to talk with him or her. Witnesses may wear face covers to avoid recognition by the suspect. Usually the room used to conduct lineups ensures viewers' anonymity.

Give witnesses clear instructions before the lineup. Tell them that they need not identify anyone in the lineup, that they are not to confer with any other witnesses viewing the lineup and that they are not to indicate in any way if they make an identification. Tape-record or videotape the proceedings and take a color photograph of the lineup to defend against any allegations by the defense counsel of an unfair lineup. The form in Figure 7–6 provides additional evidence of the fairness and reliability of a lineup identification.

## Surveillances, Undercover Assignments and Raids

"Follow that car!" "I think we're being tailed!" "I lost him!" "My cover's blown!" "We've been made!" "It's a raid!" Police officers, criminals and the public are very aware of such investigative practices as observing suspects, their houses or apartments; tailing suspects; staking out locations; and conducting raids. What is usually depicted on television and in movies, however, are the

---

**WAIVER OF RIGHT TO LEGAL COUNSEL AT LINEUP**

Your Rights Are:  The police are requesting you to personally appear in a lineup.  There will be a number of other persons similiar in physical characteristics with you.  The purpose of the lineup is to permit witnesses to observe all persons in the lineup, to make an identification.  You may be asked to perform certain actions such as speaking, walking or moving in a certain manner or to put on articles of clothing.  You must appear in the lineup, but you have a right to have legal cousel of your choice present.  If you do not have an attorney, one can be appointed for you by the court, and the lineup will not be held until your legal counsel is present.  An attorney can help you defend against an identification made by witnesses at the lineup.

You have the right to waive legal counsel being present at the lineup.

**WAIVER**

I have read, or have had read to me, this statement of my rights and I understand these rights.  I am willing to participate in a lineup in the absence of legal counsel.  I fully understand and give my consent to what I am being asked to do.  No promises or threats have been made to me, and no pressure of coercion has been used against me.  I understand that I must appear in the lineup, but this consent is to the waiver of legal counsel being present at the lineup.

Signed                                    Place

Witness                                   Date

Witness                                   Time

---

**Figure 7–5    Sample Waiver**

glamorous, dangerous sides of this facet of investigation. We seldom see the long hours of preparation or the days, even weeks, of tedious watchfulness that are frequently required for obtaining the needed information.

---

Surveillance, undercover assignments and raids are used only when normal methods of continuing the investigation fail to produce results.

---

These techniques are expensive and potentially dangerous. They are not routinely used.

## Surveillance

**Surveillance,** literally meaning "to watch over," is the covert, discreet observation of people or places.

---

The objective of surveillance is to obtain information about people, their associates and their activities that may help to solve a criminal case or to protect witnesses.

---

---

POLICE REPORT OF LINEUP

Boulder City Police
Police Department

Name of suspect ___John Vance___ Birth date ___2-14-1964___

Address ___1424 Colten Street, Boulder City___

Case Number ___6432___ Complainant or victim ___Thelma Crump___

Name of legal counsel ___John Simmons___ Present: Yes _X_ No ___

Was waiver signed:                              Yes _X_ No ___

Place of lineup ___Las Vegas, Nevada, Police Dept.___

Date of lineup ___5-12-97___ Time of lineup ___1640___

Names of persons in lineup (left to right, facing the lineup)

| | Name | Height | Weight | Birth date | Other |
|---|---|---|---|---|---|
| 1. | Charles Upright | 5-11 | 184 | 4-10-1966 | |
| 2. | Gary Starrick | 5-10 | 178 | 2-14-1965 | |
| 3. | Jerry Stilter | 5-11 | 190 | 10-11-1967 | |
| 4. | Ralph Barrett | 5-10 | 185 | 12-24-1968 | |
| 5. | John Vance | 5-10 | 183 | 2-14-1964 | |
| 6. | Christian Dolph | 5-11 | 190 | 6-12-1964 | |
| 7. | | | | | |
| 8. | | | | | |
| 9. | | | | | |
| 10. | | | | | |

Subject identified by witness: Number ___5___ Name ___John Vance___

Recording taken of lineup: Yes _X_ No ___ Photos taken of lineup: Yes _X_ No ___

Persons present at lineup ___Thelma Crump        Alfred Nener___
_____John Simmons        Emmanuel Sorstick___

Person conducting lineup ___Sgt. Lloyd Brenner, LVPD___

---

**Figure 7–6    Police Report of Lineup**

Surveillance can be designed to:

- Gain information required for building a criminal complaint.
- Determine an informant's loyalty.
- Verify the statement of a witness to a crime.
- Gain information required for obtaining a search or arrest warrant.
- Gain information necessary for interrogating a suspect.
- Identify a suspect's associates.
- Observe members of terrorist organizations.
- Find a person wanted for a crime.
- Observe criminal activities in progress.
- Make a legal arrest.

- Apprehend a criminal in the act of committing a crime.
- Prevent a crime from being committed.
- Recover stolen property.
- Protect witnesses.

Because surveillance is a time-consuming, expensive operation that can raise questions of invasion of privacy, exhaust all alternatives before using it. Balance the rights of the individual against the need for public safety.

### The Surveillant

The **surveillant** is the plainclothes investigator assigned to make the observation. Surveillants must be prepared for tedium. No other assignment requires as much patience and perseverance while simultaneously demanding alertness and readiness to respond instantly. Surveillants must display ingenuity in providing a cover for the operation. Lack of resourcefulness in providing adequate answers at a moment's notice can halt the entire case.

The most successful surveillants are those whose appearance and mannerisms do not attract attention and who thus blend into the general populace.

### The Subject

The **subject** is who or what is observed. It can be a person, place, property, vehicle, group of people, organization or object. People placed under surveillance are usually suspects in a crime or their associates. Surveillance of places generally involves a location where a crime is expected to be committed; the residence of a known criminal; a place suspected of harboring criminal activities such as illegal drug transactions, gambling, prostitution, purchase of stolen goods or fencing operations; or the suspected headquarters of a terrorist organization.

### Surveillance Equipment

Surveillance equipment includes binoculars, telescopes, night-vision equipment, body wires and video systems. Pilant (1992, p. 38) notes that surveillance equipment might also include "communications scramblers, pinhole surveillance kits, miniature cameras, drop-ceiling and magnetic surveillance mounts, equipment for surveillance vehicles, miniature and rifle microphones, and various types of telephone recording devices."

Surveillance systems have become extremely sophisticated. One system, for example, conceals a periscope in what looks like a standard air vent in the roof of a van. The periscope rotates 360 degrees and is undetectable. Remote motion detectors activate the system to videotape the area under surveillance.

Many systems have night-vision and/or telephoto lenses as well as time-and-date generators. Many also have hard-copy printers that produce photographic copies on site. The film used can be black-and-white or color.

### Types of Surveillance

The type of surveillance used depends on the subject and the objective of the surveillance. In general, surveillance is either stationary or moving.

---

The types of surveillance include stationary (fixed, plant, stakeout) and moving (tight or close, loose, rough), foot or vehicle.

---

**Stationary Surveillance.**   **Stationary,** or **fixed, surveillance,** also called a **plant** or **stakeout,** is used when you know or suspect that a person is at or will come to a known location, when you suspect that stolen goods are to be dropped or when informants have told you that a crime is going to be committed. Such assignments are comparatively short. An outside surveillance simplifies planning. The observation may be from a car, van or truck or by posting an officer in an inconspicuous place with a view of the location. A "dummy" van or a borrowed business van and a disguise as a painter, carpenter or service technician are often used. Take photographs and notes throughout the surveillance.

In longer surveillances, it is often necessary to photograph people who frequent a specific location such as a store suspected of being a cover for a bookmaking operation or a hotel or motel allowing prostitution or gambling. If the subject of surveillance is a place rather than a person, obtain a copy of the building plan and personally visit the building in advance if possible. Know all entrances and exits, especially rear doors and fire escapes. To properly record what is observed, use closed-circuit camera equipment, movie or video cameras, binoculars with a camera attached, telephoto lenses or infrared equipment for night viewing and photographing.

Lengthy fixed surveillance is often conducted from a room with an unobstructed view of the location, such as an apartment house opposite the location being watched. Naturally, the surveillant(s) must not be noticed entering the observation post.

Ellis (1992, p. 26) notes: "Criminal surveillance brings to mind hot, cold, uncomfortable, long boring hours and, as often as not, very little to show for the misery." He suggests that a well-outfitted surveillance van can be obtained for a reasonable price and can greatly enhance surveillance. It can also be used in other situations, such as when a suspect is barricaded or in a hostage situation. "Being able to put a plain wrapped vehicle near a barricaded subject without causing him any concern would provide a SWAT commander with a wealth of useful information," says Ellis (p. 27).

Such vans can carry a vast array of surveillance equipment. According to Yates (1991, p. 52): "When talking about surveillance vehicles today, however, we tend to think of a van whose interior looks slightly less complex than the bridge of Star Trek's USS Enterprise."

Whether the stationary surveillance is short or long, have adequate communications such as radio, horn signals or hand signals. Use simple hand signals such as pulling up the collar, buttoning the shirt, pulling down the brim on a hat, tying a shoelace, running the hand through the hair or checking a wristwatch. If you use radio communications, find out whether the subject(s) might be monitoring police radio frequencies and, if likely, establish a code.

The surveillance team is selected to fit the case and the area in which it is to be conducted. Have enough surveillants to cover the assignment. Scout the area in person or by studying maps. Make sketches of the immediate area to determine possible ways the subject could avoid observation or apprehension. Be aware of alleys, abnormal street conditions, one-way streets, barricades, parking ramps and all other details. This is especially critical when the objective of the surveillance is to apprehend persons committing a crime. In such cases, all members of the stakeout must know the signal for action and their specific assignments.

**Moving Surveillance.**   The subjects of **moving surveillance** are almost always people. The surveillant may be referred to as a **tail.** The first step in planning for such surveillance is to obtain as much information about the subject(s) as you can. View photographs and, if possible, personally observe the subjects. Memorize their physical descriptions and form a mental image of them. Concentrate on their appearance from behind, as this is the view you normally have while tailing them. Although subjects may alter their physical appearance, this is usually no problem. The major problem is keeping subjects under constant surveillance for the desired time. Know the subjects' habits, where they are likely to go and whether they walk or drive. If they drive, find out what kind of vehicles they use. Also find out who their associates are and whether they are likely to suspect that they are being observed.

Other problems of moving surveillance are losing the subject and having the subject recognize you as a surveillant. Sometimes it is not important if the subject knows of the surveillance. This is often true of material witnesses being protected by the police. It is also true of organized-crime figures, who know they are under constant surveillance and take this into account. In such instances, a **rough tail** is used. No extraordinary means are required to remain undetected. The major problem in using a rough tail is the charge of police harassment or invasion of privacy.

At other times, it is more important to remain undetected than to keep the subject under constant observation. In such cases, a **loose tail** is used. Maintain a safe distance. If the subject is lost during surveillance, you can easily relocate the subject and resume the surveillance. A loose tail is often used when general information is needed about the subject's activities or associates.

Often, however, it is extremely important not to lose the subject, and a very **close (tight) tail** is maintained. On a crowded street this means staying within a few steps of the subject; on a less crowded street, it means keeping the subject in sight. A close tail is most commonly used when it is known that the subject is going to commit a crime, when the subject's exact habits must be known or when knowledge of the subject's activities is important to another critical operation.

*When tailing a subject on foot,* numerous delaying tactics can be used. You can cross to the other side of the street, talk to a person standing nearby, increase your distance from the subject, read a magazine or newspaper, buy a cola, fix the engine in your car, tie your shoe, look in windows or in parked cars or stall in any other way.

If the subject turns a corner, do not follow closely. When you do turn the corner, if you find the subject waiting in a doorway, pass by without paying attention. Then try to pick the tail up again by guessing the subject's next move. This is often possible when you have advance information on the subject's habits.

If the subject enters a restaurant, you can enter and take a seat on the side of the room opposite from the subject, making sure you are near the door so you can see the subject leave, or you can wait outside.

If a subject enters a building that has numerous exits, follow at a safe distance, noticing all potential exits. If the subject takes an elevator, wait at the first floor until the subject returns, noticing the floors at which the elevator stops. If there is a stairway near the elevator, stand near the door so you can hear if the subject has gotten off the elevator and taken the stairs. Such stairs are seldom used, and when someone is going up or down, their footsteps echo and can be easily heard.

When tailing a subject on the street, do not hesitate to pass the subject and enter a store yourself. The less obvious the technique, the more successful it will be.

Use the glass in doors and storefront windows to see behind you.

Subjects who suspect they are being followed use many tricks. They may turn corners suddenly and stand in a nearby doorway, go into a store and duck into the restroom, enter a dressing room, hide behind objects or jump on a bus or into a taxi at the last moment. They may do such things to determine *whether* they are being followed or to lose someone they *know* is following them.

*It is usually better to lose subjects than to alert them to your presence or to allow them to identify you.*

Surveillants often believe that they have been recognized when, in fact, they have not. However, if you are certain the subject knows you are following, stop the surveillance, but do not return to the police department right away because the subject may decide to tail you.

If it is critical not to lose the subject, use more than one surveillant, preferably three. Surveillant A keeps a very close tail immediately behind the subject. Surveillant B follows behind Surveillant A and the subject. Surveillant C observes from across the street parallel with the other two. If the subject turns the corner, Surveillant A continues on in the previous direction for awhile, and Surveillant B or C picks up the tail. Surveillant A then takes the position previously held by the surveillant who picked up the close tail.

*When tailing by vehicle,* have descriptions of all vehicles the subject drives or rides in. The subject's vehicle can be marked in advance by an electronic device or beeper monitored by a receiver in your car, or the beeper can be placed in an object the subject will be carrying. A small amount of fluorescent paint can be applied to the rear bumper of the vehicle to make it easily identifiable day or night.

Your own vehicle should be inconspicuous. Obtain unregistered (dead) plates for it from the motor vehicle authorities and change them frequently, or change your vehicle daily, perhaps using rental cars. Changing the number of occupants tends to confuse a suspicious subject. If surveillance is to be primarily at night, install a multiple contact switch to allow you to turn off one of your headlights at will.

Like subjects being tailed on foot, subjects being tailed by vehicle often use tricks to determine whether they are being tailed or to lose an identified tail. They may turn in the middle of the block, go though a red light, suddenly pull into a parking stall, change traffic lanes rapidly, go down alleys or go the wrong way down a one-way street. In such cases, if temporarily losing the subject causes no problem, stop the surveillance.

If it is critical not to lose the subject, use more than one vehicle for the surveillance. The ideal system uses four vehicles. Vehicle A drives ahead of the subject and observes through the rearview mirror. (This vehicle is not used if only three vehicles are available). Vehicle B follows right behind the subject. Vehicles C and D follow on left and right parallel streets to pick up the tail if the subject turns in either direction.

### Avoiding Detection

Criminals are often suspicious of stakeouts or of being followed and may send someone to scout the area to see if anybody has staked out their residence or their vehicle. This person may stand on the corner near the residence or drive around the block several times to see if everything is clear. Criminals often watch the windows or roofs of buildings across the street for any movements. When they leave their residences, they may have an accomplice trail behind to see if anyone is following. Anticipate and plan for such activities. Sometimes a counter-countersurveillance is used if personnel is available.

Not every surveillance produces the desired results. In some instances, the subject is lost or the surveillant is recognized, despite the best efforts to avoid either. Like any other investigative technique, failure results from unforeseen circumstances such as vehicle failure, illness of the surveillant, unexpected absence of the subject due to illness or emergency, abnormal weather conditions or terrain and other factors beyond control. Usually, however, information and evidence obtained through surveillance is well worth the time and effort invested. In all instances, a form such as the one shown in Figure 7–7 should be completed after a surveillance assignment.

Surveillance Report

Date __4-16-97__ Time started __1130__ Time finished __1330__ Case No. __6432__

Address, location or name of subject __116 7th St-Ralph Burns__

Purpose of surveillance ____Sales of controlled substance____

Weather conditions __Fair__  Equipment used __binoculars__

Conversations with subject __None__

Telephone calls made __None__

Persons contacted by subject __None__

Record of observations during surveillance _____

Time __Female adult entered garage 1142__

Time __Male, adult subject met Burns on step 1154__

Time __2 males in 1974 brown car stopped at above address 1232__

Time __Burns left residence in car 1315 NV; 134-MMN__

Time _____

Signature of surveillant _____

**Figure 7–7  Surveillance Intelligence Form**

# Aerial Surveillance

Aerial surveillance is used to gain information in areas that are inaccessible to foot or vehicle surveillance. Communication between air surveillance and ground vehicles provides guidance for the operational movement in and around the target area. The aerial pilot should be a police officer or be carefully selected by the police. The pilot should know the landmarks of the area because many surveillances of this type involve moving suspect-vehicles.

Clede (1991, p. 54) notes that two STOL—Short Take Off and Landing—aircraft were introduced at the 1991 International Association of Chiefs of Police convention: "These features and safe, slow flight performance are important in a surveillance aircraft."

Photographs taken from navigable air space, usually 1,000 feet, do not violate privacy regulations.

In one aerial surveillance, officers viewed a partially covered greenhouse within the residential curtilage from a helicopter 400 feet above the greenhouse. The greenhouse, which contained marijuana plants, was located 10–20 feet behind the residence, a mobile home. A wire fence surrounded the entire property, and "Do Not Enter" signs were posted. Nonetheless, *Florida v. Riley* (1989) approved the warrantless aerial surveillance, noting there should be no reasonable expectation of privacy from the skies above.

# Audio Surveillance

In special instances electronic devices are used in surveillance. Such **electronic surveillance** devices include wiring a person who is going to be talking with a subject or entering a suspicious business establishment, **bugging** a subject's room or vehicle or **wiretapping** a person's telephone.

The exclusionary rule requires that all evidence against a suspect be acquired according to the standards set forth in the Fourth Amendment. Electronic surveillance and wiretapping are considered by the courts to be forms of search; therefore, they must be based on probable cause and authorized by a judge.

---

Electronic surveillance and wiretapping are permitted only with probable cause and by court order (*Katz v. United States*).

---

In a landmark case, *Katz v. United States* (1967), the U.S. Supreme Court considered an appeal by Charles Katz, who had been convicted in California of violating gambling laws. Investigators had observed Katz for several days as he made telephone calls from a particular phone booth at the same time each day. Suspecting that he was placing horse racing bets, the investigators attached an electronic listening/recording device to the telephone booth and recorded Katz's illegal activities. The evidence was used in obtaining his conviction. The Supreme Court reversed the California decision, saying: ". . . the Fourth Amendment protects people not places. . . . Wherever a man may be, he is entitled to know that he will remain free from unreasonable searches and seizures." The investigators did have probable cause, but they erred in not presenting their information to a judge and obtaining prior approval for their actions.

The importance of electronic surveillance is recognized, however, in the introduction to Title III of the Omnibus Crime Control and Safe Streets Act of

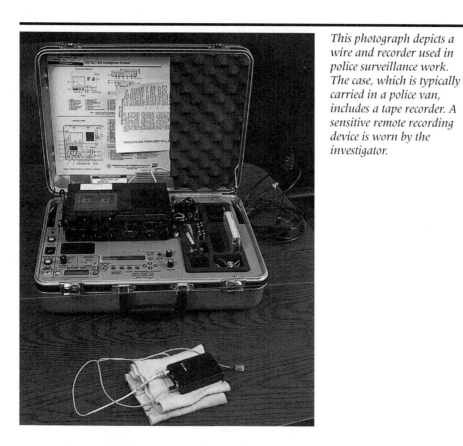

*This photograph depicts a wire and recorder used in police surveillance work. The case, which is typically carried in a police van, includes a tape recorder. A sensitive remote recording device is worn by the investigator.*

1968, which authorized court-ordered electronic surveillance of organized-crime figures. The U.S. Congress stated:

> Organized criminals make extensive use of wire and oral communications in their criminal activities. The interception of such communications to obtain evidence of the commission of crimes or to prevent their commission is an indispensible aid to law enforcement and the administration of justice.

Federal and state laws allow electronic surveillance (eavesdropping), provided it is authorized by a federal or state judge and that specified procedures are followed.

According to Strandberg (1997, p. 40): "Over the past decade the use of court-ordered wiretaps has resulted in the arrest of over thirty thousand felons, and the conviction of over twenty thousand." Strandberg suggests that wiretaps played a significant role in the World Trade Center bombing investigation.

## Undercover Assignments

According to Love et al. (1994, p. 54):

The press and popular media frequently portray undercover police work as glamorous, with unrealistic plots, settings and characters. As most undercover officers and supervisors know, however, the work is very real, entailing a physical and psychological price for all who enter into this type of specialized assignment.

The nonuniformed or plainclothes investigator is in a good position to observe illegal activities and obtain evidence. For example, a male plainclothes officer may appear to accept the solicitations of a prostitute, or any plainclothes police officer may attempt to buy stolen goods or drugs or to place illegal bets. Many such activities require little more than simply "not smelling like the law." Unlike other forms of surveillance in which a prime objective is not to be observed, **undercover** surveillants make personal contact with the subject using an assumed identity or **cover.**

> The objective of an undercover assignment may be to gain a person's confidence or to infiltrate an organization or group by using an assumed identity and to thereby obtain information or evidence connecting the subject(s) with criminal activity.

Undercover assignments can be designed to:

- Obtain evidence for prosecution.
- Obtain leads into criminal activities.
- Check the reliability of witnesses or informants.
- Gain information about premises for use in conducting a later raid or arrest.
- Check the security of a person in a highly sensitive position.
- Obtain information on or evidence against subversive groups.

Undercover assignments are frequently made when criminal activity is greatly suspected or even known, but no legal evidence of it exists. Such as-

*Undercover officers posing as small-time street dealers, sorting out who bought what. While this operation, known as a "reverse sting," has been held legal in the courts, a defense of entrapment is often used.*

signments can be extremely dangerous and require careful planning and preparation. The undercover agent selected must fit the assignment. Age, sex, race, general appearance, language facility, health, energy level, emotional stability and intelligence are all important selection considerations. Undercover agents must be good actors—able to assume their role totally. They must be intelligent and able to deal with any problems that arise, to make quick decisions, to improvise plans and actions and to work with the person or within the group or organization without arousing suspicion.

A good cover is essential to success. Rookies are often used because they are not yet known and because they have not been in law enforcement long enough to acquire expressions or mannerisms that hardened criminals recognize as "the law."

In addition to devising a good cover, the undercover agent learns everything possible about the subject, regardless of whether it is a person or an organization. If you are going to be working undercover, make plans for communicating with headquarters. Make telephone calls from public pay phones, or mail letters to a fictitious friend's post office box. Have a plan for getting emergency messages through, and know what to do if the authorities move in on the subject when you are there. Have a plan for leaving the subject when you have acquired the desired information or evidence.

---

Precautions for undercover agents:
- Write no notes the subject can read.
- Carry no identification other than the cover ID.
- Ensure that any communication with headquarters is covert.
- Do not suggest, plan, initiate or participate in criminal activity.

---

While working undercover, do not suggest, plan, initiate or participate in committing a crime, or the defense can argue that entrapment occurred.

The Supreme Court has defined **entrapment** in *Sorrells v. United States* (1932): "Entrapment is the conception and planning of an offense by an officer, and his procurement of its commission by one who would not have perpetrated it except for the trickery, persuasion or fraud of the officer."

*Sorrells* also explained the need for trickery in obtaining evidence:

> Society is at war with the criminal classes, and the courts have uniformly held that in waging this warfare the forces of prevention and detection may use traps, decoys and deception to obtain evidence of the commission of a crime. Resort to such means does not render an indictment thereafter found a nullity nor call for the exclusion of evidence so procured.

*Sorrells* concludes: "The fact that government agents merely afford opportunities or facilities for the commission of the offense does not constitute entrapment." These Court rulings still stand. In *Sherman v. United States* (1950) the Court explained when entrapment does occur:

> Entrapment occurs only when the criminal conduct was "the product of the creative activity" of law-enforcement officials. To determine whether entrapment has been established, a line must be drawn between the trap for the unwary innocent and the trap for the unwary criminal.

Hawley (1996, p. 8) notes: "Suspects caught red-handed may escape conviction if entrapment is involved." Hawley (p. 9) describes police conduct that might be considered entrapment: "appeals to sympathy, illness, pity or friendship; inducements making the crime unusually attractive to a law-abiding person; guarantees that the act is legal; or an offer of exhorbitant sums of money." Because it is possible that you may be arrested if the subject is arrested, learn ahead of time whether you are to blow your cover or submit to arrest. In some instances, outside sources may interfere with the lawful arrest, posing great danger for an undercover agent whose identity has become known during the arrest.

When the assignment is successfully completed, give the subject a plausible explanation for leaving. It may be necessary to reestablish the undercover contact later.

It is often better to use undercover agents than informants because the testimony of a reliable, trained investigator is not as subject to a defense attorney's attack as that of an informant.

The legality of placing an undercover officer in a high school to investigate student drug use was decided in *Gordon v. Warren Consolidated Board of Education* (1983). High-school officials had put an undercover officer into classes. The claimants alleged deprivation of their civil rights, but the case was dismissed by the federal district court for failure to state a cause of action. On appeal, the Supreme Court affirmed the prior judgment, stating that the presence of the undercover police officer did not constitute any more than a "chilling" effect on the First Amendment right because it did not disrupt classroom activities or education and it did not have any tangible effect on inhibiting expression of particular views in the classroom.

## Raids

A police **raid** is a planned, organized operation based on the element of surprise. Consider all other alternatives before executing a raid.

---

The objectives of a raid are to recover stolen property, seize evidence or arrest a suspect.

---

Sometimes all three objectives are accomplished in a single raid.

The first consideration is whether there are alternatives to a raid such as waiting and arresting the suspect at a location not requiring a raid. A second consideration is the legality of the raid.

---

A raid must be the result of a hot pursuit or be under the authority of a no-knock arrest or search warrant.

---

If you are in hot pursuit of a known felon and there is no time to plan a raid, make sure enough personnel and weapons are available to reduce danger. Call for a backup before starting the raid.

If the raid is conducted to obtain evidence or property, obtain a legal search warrant. Most raids are planned and result from an arrest warrant being issued. In such cases, the subject is usually living under circumstances that make it evident that the only way an arrest can be made is to raid the premises. The individual may also be extremely dangerous. Therefore, adequate fire power and personnel are essential for minimizing danger.

Planning, organizing and executing a raid is somewhat similar to undertaking a small military attack on a specific target. Begin by gathering information on the premises to be raided. This includes such things as exact address and points of entry and exit for both the raiding party and the suspect. Obtain a picture or sketch of the building and study the room arrangement. Study the suspect's background. What crimes has the suspect committed in the past? What difficulties were encountered in making past arrests? Is the suspect a narcotics addict? An alcoholic? Likely to be armed? If so, what type of weapon?

If the raid is to recover evidence or stolen property, obtain an exact description of the property sought and its likely location on the premises.

If possible, evacuate all other persons from the area of the raid without making the suspect suspicious. It is not always possible to do this without losing the element of surprise that is vital to the success of the raid. Therefore, it is important to include in your planning the fact that other people are in the vicinity of the raid.

Plan for enough personnel to minimize violence, to overcome opposition through superiority of forces and to prevent the escape of the suspect or destruction of evidence. One person should be assigned to be in command.

Obtain the appropriate warrants. Specify that you require a no-knock warrant to conduct the raid. You may want to specify a nighttime warrant to enhance the element of surprise.

Decide how to transport the raiding party to the scene and how to take the suspect(s) or evidence and property away. Also determine which weapons and equipment are required. Keep the raid plan as simple as possible. Make sure all entrances and exits will be covered and that a communication system is established.

The raid should occur only after a careful briefing of all members of the raiding party. Each participant must know the objective, who the suspect is or what evidence or property is sought and the exact plan and organization of the raid itself. Give each participant proper equipment such as body armor, weapons, radios, whistles, megaphones and signal lights. Give each participant a specific assignment, and answer all questions about the raid before leaving the briefing. The raid commander directs the raid, giving the signal to begin and coordinating all assignments. Surprise and swiftness are essential elements of a successful raid.

Decisions about the initial entry and control phase of a raid must be made rapidly since control is usually established within the first fifteen to thirty seconds of a successful raid. No two raids are executed in precisely the same way. The immediate circumstances and events dictate what decisions and actions must be made at the raid scene.

Handguns are still the most versatile weapon during a raid, but shotguns and other assault-type weapons are useful in the perimeter operations and to control arrested individuals. If guard animals are known to be inside the raid area, provisions must be made for their control. Special equipment such as sledgehammers or rams may be needed for breaking down fortified entrances. An ambulance should be on standby, or, at the least, raid personnel should know the fastest route to the nearest hospital.

Because raids are highly visible, the public and the news media are often aware of them. Therefore, raids are likely to be the object of community praise or criticism. They are also often vital to prosecuting a case successfully.

Precautions in conducting raids:
- Ensure that the raid is legal.
- Plan carefully.
- Assign adequate personnel and equipment.
- Thoroughly brief every member of the raiding party.

Many metropolitan areas have developed tactical squads, sometimes called *Special Weapons and Tactics (SWAT) teams,* to execute raids. These units are thoroughly trained to search areas for criminals, handle sniper incidents and hostage situations, execute arrest and search warrants and apprehend militants who have barricaded themselves inside a building or other location.

Drugs busts and raids on crackhouses have become increasingly common. In some instances police have used front-end loaders and other tanklike vehicles to break through the walls of suspected crackhouses. They have, unfortunately, sometimes had the wrong address.

Sometimes a raid is unsuccessful and results in a standoff or a hostage situation as in the ATF raid on the Branch Davidian cult in Waco, Texas, in February of 1993. In such situations, according to Sanow (1993, p. 35): "Tactical teams should depend on stealth, and the three T's—Time, Talk, and Tear Gas—are still the best special response policy." The results of this raid are discussed in Chapter 19.

*Minneapolis police officers raiding a suspected crackhouse. Surprise, swiftness and sufficient personnel are required for a successful raid.*

Recent advances have increased the capability of audio, video and remote equipment in surveillance and undercover operations. Advances in surveillance are described by Clede (1991, p. 53), who notes: "Surveillance is a matter of extending the five senses, and technology is enabling agencies to do that better and more inexpensively. It will soon enable us to do what we've never been able to do before." Among the advancements Clede reports are the following:

- Smaller body wires and better audio quality.
- Body transmitters are now available with scrambling capabilities.
- Aircraft are being fitted with digital communications, forward-looking infrared imaging (FLIR), GPS positioning display and complete video systems.
- Laser technology can direct a beam at the glass in a window with a beam modulated by the sonic vibrations inside the room, bouncing the sound back to a receiver so officers can hear what is being said.

Clede (p. 55) writes that: "Eavesdropping with easier-to-plant bugs is a quantum leap away from where the technology was a decade ago." He also notes, however, that sophisticated criminals are using high-tech electronic countermeasures to "cleanse" a room before they hold a meeting or conversation there.

Surveillance is also being used as a crime deterrent in cities such as Newark. Newark police use "Video Patrol" to monitor the city's two main downtown streets by closed-circuit television. According to the city's mayor ("Monitoring Crime," 1992, p. 48): "This system takes one officer and allows him to do more, see more, and be in a position to coordinate. . . . Persons who are considering a criminal act know that 'Big Brother' is watching, and that 'Big Brother' can tape them."

Advertisements in police magazines describe state-of-the-art surveillance systems designed to make undercover work more efficient and effective.

Siuru (1997, p. 38) describes a new technology—laser radar—to the "increasing menu of techniques to see the bad guys in the dark." The Advanced Ranging Imaging Sensor (ARIS) is "a scannerless laser radar imaging system that simultaneously generates both two-dimensional reflectance images and three-dimensional radar images." Siuru explains: "ARIS uses diffused, infrared energy from a scannerless laser transmitter to floodlight the entire surveillance scene to produce instantaneous three-dimentional images."

Another innovation to aid in surveillance are the laser range-finding binoculars described by Morrison (1997, p. 35):

> The Leica binoculars offer high-quality optics giving bright, sharp images in a wide range of conditions, and are ideal for surveillance and sniper work. . . .

Such binoculars can eliminate judging distance errors. Among the most sophisticated is the Vector 1500 that, according to Morrison, "is a binocular, laser range finder, digital magnetic compass and an inclinometer."

## Summary

Developing, locating, identifying and arresting suspects are primary responsibilities of investigators.

An arrest may occur at any point during an investigation. You may make an arrest (1) for any crime committed in your presence, (2) for a felony not committed in your presence if you have probable cause to believe the person committed the crime or (3) under the authority of an arrest warrant. A lawful arrest requires that probable cause for believing the suspect committed a crime be established *before* the arrest.

If you make it known that you intend to arrest a suspect and then restrict his or her right to go free, you have made an arrest. When making an arrest, use only as much force as is necessary to overcome any resistance. If no resistance occurs, force must not be used.

If you arrest a suspect at or near the scene of a crime, use field, or on-the-scene, identification. This must be conducted within fifteen to twenty minutes after the crime to be admissible. Suspects do not have the right to counsel at a field identification (*United States v. Ash, Jr.*).

If the suspect is not immediately identified, you must develop a suspect through information provided by victims, witnesses and other persons likely to know about the crime or the suspect; through physical evidence at the crime scene; through psychological profiling; through information in police files; through information in the files of other agencies; or through informants. Help witnesses describe suspects by asking very specific questions and using an identification diagram.

Use the FBI's National Crime Information Center (NCIC) to assist in developing or identifying suspects. The NCIC contains criminal fingerprint records and information on wanted criminals as well as on stolen property and vehicles.

Suspects can be identified through field identification, mug shots, photographic identification or lineups. Use field identification when the suspect is arrested at or near the scene. Use mug-shot identification if you believe the suspect has a police record. Use photographic identification when the suspect is not in custody or a fair lineup cannot be conducted. The pictures should portray at least five people of comparable race, height, weight and general appearance. Tell witnesses they need not identify anyone from the photographs. A suspect does *not* have the right to a lawyer if a photographic lineup is used.

Use lineup identification when the suspect is in custody. Have at least five individuals of comparable race, height, weight, age and general appearance. Ask all to perform the same actions or speak the same words. Instruct those viewing the lineup that no identification need be made. Suspects may refuse to participate in a lineup, but such refusal may be used against them in court (*Schmerber v. California*). Suspects have a right to have an attorney present during a lineup (*United States v. Wade*). Avoid having the same individual(s) make both photographic and lineup identification. If you do so, do not conduct both within a short time period.

Some investigations reach a point where no further progress can be made without using surveillance, undercover agents or a raid. Before taking any of these measures, make sure all alternatives have been exhausted.

The objective of surveillance is to obtain information about people or their associates and activities that may help solve a criminal case or protect witnesses. Surveillance can be stationary (fixed, plant, stakeout) or moving (tail or shadow). Moving surveillance can be rough, loose or close (tight). Electronic surveillance and wiretapping are permitted only with probable cause and by direct court order (*Katz v. United States*).

The objective of an undercover assignment is to gain a person's confidence or to infiltrate an organization or group by using an assumed identity and to thereby obtain information or evidence connecting the subject with criminal activity. If you are working undercover, write no notes the subject can read, carry no identification other than the cover ID, make sure any communication with headquarters is covert and do not suggest, plan, initiate or participate in any criminal activity.

The objective of a raid is to recover stolen property, to seize evidence or to arrest a suspect. To be legal, a raid must be the result of a hot pursuit or under authority of a no-knock arrest warrant or a search warrant. Precautions in conducting raids include ensuring that the raid is legal, planning carefully, assigning adequate personnel and equipment and thoroughly briefing every member of the raiding party.

## Checklist

### *Identifying and Arresting Suspects*

- Was a suspect observed by police on arrival at the scene?
- Was a suspect arrested at the scene?
- Was any person observed at the scene by any other person?
- Was a neighborhood check made to determine suspicious persons, vehicles or noises?
- Was the complainant interviewed?
- Were statements taken from witnesses or persons having information about the crime?
- Was a description of the suspect(s) obtained?
- Was the description disseminated to other members of the local police force? To neighboring police departments?
- Was any associative evidence found at the scene or in the suspect's possession?
- Were informants checked?
- Were similar crimes committed in the area? The community? Neighboring communities?
- Were field identification cards checked to determine who was in the area?
- Were modus operandi files reviewed to determine who commits the type of crime? Are the suspects in or out of prison?
- Were traffic tickets checked to see if any person or vehicle was in the area at the time of the crime? Does the vehicle or crime compare with the suspect vehicle or person?
- Have other agencies been checked? Municipal? County? State? Federal?
- How was the person identified? Field identification? Mug shots? Photographic identification? Lineup identification? Was it legal?
- Was the arrest legal?

### *Surveillance*

- Is there any alternative to surveillance?
- What information is needed from the surveillance?
- What type of surveillance is needed?
- Have equipment and personnel needs for the area of surveillance been determined?
- Are the required equipment and personnel available?
- Are proper forms available for recording necessary information during the surveillance?
- Are all signals preestablished?

*Undercover Assignments*

- Is there any alternative to undercover work?
- What information is needed from the assignment?
- Is adequate information about the subject available?
- Have you established a good cover?
- How will you communicate with headquarters?
- What are you to do if you are arrested?
- Do you have an alternative plan if the initial plan fails?
- Do you have a plausible explanation for leaving once the assignment is completed?

### *Raids*

- Is there any alternative to a raid?
- Have appropriate warrants been obtained?
- Have the objectives of the raid been clearly specified?
- Has a presurveillance of the raid location been conducted?
- Are adequate personnel and equipment available?
- Has a briefing been held?

## Discussion Questions

**1.** Imagine that a burglary has occurred each of the last four nights in a ten-block residential area in a city of 200,000 people. How might an investigator start to determine who is committing these crimes? What sources of information and techniques are used in developing a suspect?

**2.** Suppose you have obtained information concerning a suspect in a rape case. Two witnesses saw an individual near the rape scene at about the time of the offense, and the victim was able to describe her assailant. How should identification be made?

**3.** How do cooperation of the public and of other police agencies each help in identifying and arresting suspects? Which is more important, public cooperation or the cooperation of other police agencies?

**4.** How are persons selected to be in a lineup? How should a lineup be conducted—what are the legal requirements? What is done if the suspect refuses to participate?

**5.** What balance must be maintained between the individual's right to privacy and the public interest when using surveillance in an investigation?

**6.** Under what conditions should a police raid be considered?

**7.** In what types of crimes would the use of an undercover agent be justified?

**8.** What type of tail would you use for each of the following: Checking the loyalty of an informant? A suspected bank robber planning to case a bank? A burglar known to meet with another burglar frequently? An individual suspected of being an organized-crime leader?

**9.** How much risk is involved in undercover assignments and raids? How can this risk be minimized?

**10.** When do outside agencies participate in carrying out surveillances, undercover assignments and raids?

# References

**273**

**Chapter 7**

**Identifying
and Arresting
Suspects**

Ashley, Steven D. "Managing Aerosol Issues." *Law and Order,* March 1996, pp. 35–37.

Clede, Bill. "Surveillance Equipment." *Law and Order,* December 1991, pp. 53–55.

Ellis, Tom. "Cutting the Cost of Surveillance." *Law Enforcement Technology,* September 1992, pp. 26–28.

Fairburn, Dick. "To Kill . . . Or Not To Kill." *Police,* August 1996, pp. 78–103.

Hawley, Donna Lea. "Undercover Officers Walk a Fine Legal Line." *Police,* November 1996, pp. 8–9.

Hill, Scott C. "Technology Making IDs Quicker, Easier, More Accurate." *The Police Chief,* April 1991, pp. 52–64.

Love, Kevin G.; James L. Tolsma; and Gary Kaufmann. "Effective Management of Undercover Officers." *The Police Chief,* September 1994, pp. 54–55.

McEwen, Tom. *National Data Collection on Police Use of Force.* Washington, DC: Bureau of Justice Statistics and the National Institute of Justice. April 1996.

"Monitoring Crime on CCTV: Newark's Video Patrol." *Law Enforcement Technology,* June 1992, pp. 48–49.

Morrison, Richard. "Target Control: Laser Range-Finding Binoculars." *Law Enforcement Technology,* January 1997, pp. 35–36.

Nemecek, David F. "NCIC 2000: Technology Adds a New Weapon to Law Enforcement's Arsenal." *The Police Chief,* April 1990, pp. 31–33.

Pankau, Edmund J. "The Consummate Investigator." *Security Management,* February 1993, pp. 37–41.

Pilant, Lois. "Outfitting Your Detective Unit." *The Police Chief,* March 1992, pp. 33–41.

Provost, John R. "The Facts on False Arrest." *Law and Order,* October 1992, pp. 115–116.

Sanow, Ed. "SWAT Update." *Law Enforcement Technology,* March 1993, pp. 34–38.

Schmitt, Judith Blair. "Computerized ID Systems." *The Police Chief,* February 1992, pp. 33–45.

"Selecting Nonlethal Weapons." *Police,* March 1994, p. 265.

Siuru, William D., Jr. "Seeing in the Dark." *Law Enforcement Technology,* January 1997, p. 38.

Strandberg, Keith W. "Wiretapping." *Law Enforcement Technology,* January 1997, pp. 40–44.

Wattendorf, George. "High-Risk Cases May Lead to False-Arrest Liability." *The Police Chief,* June 1995, p. 14.

Yates, Tom. "Surveillance Vans." *Law and Order,* December 1991, pp. 52, 56–58.

# Investigating Crimes against Persons

**P**art One of the FBI's *Uniform Crime Reports* contains statistics on eight types of serious crimes: murder, aggravated assault, forcible rape, robbery, burglary, larceny/theft, motor vehicle theft and arson.

The FBI *Uniform Crime Report* for 1995 reported a combined total of 13.9 million offenses against persons and property, a decrease of 1 percent, 1995 versus 1994, and was the fourth consecutive annual decline. Of this total, 1,798,785 were violent crimes, down 3.2 percent from the 1994 figure of 1,857,670 violent crimes. Caution must be used in looking at such figures. A National Crime Survey conducted by the United States Census Bureau found that 2.92 million crimes were reported for the same period, suggesting that about half of all crimes are *not* reported to police.

The largest number of crimes were reported in the southern states, which accounted for 38 percent of the total, with western states accounting for 25 percent, midwestern states for 21 percent and northeastern states for 16 percent. All regions, except the western states, showed decreases in 1995. As in previous years, most crime index offenses occurred in August and least in February. (See the table below.)

A 21 percent clearance rate was reported nationwide on all crimes, for an estimated 2.9 million arrests. The number of persons arrested for Index Crimes in 1995 decreased 1 percent from 1994. Juvenile arrests for Index Crimes decreased 2 percent, while those of adults showed virtually no change.

**Violent Crime Total by Month, 1991–1995** (Percent distribution)

| *Months* | *1991* | *1992* | *1993* | *1994* | *1995* |
|---|---|---|---|---|---|
| January | 7.6 | 8.0 | 8.0 | 7.7 | 7.9 |
| February | 7.0 | 7.6 | 6.7 | 7.3 | 7.1 |
| March | 7.8 | 8.1 | 8.2 | 8.4 | 8.1 |
| April | 7.8 | 8.3 | 8.0 | 8.3 | 8.0 |
| May | 8.6 | 8.7 | 8.4 | 8.5 | 8.5 |
| June | 8.7 | 8.5 | 8.7 | 8.6 | 8.5 |
| July | 9.2 | 9.0 | 9.3 | 9.1 | 9.1 |
| August | 9.5 | 8.9 | 9.1 | 9.2 | 9.2 |
| September | 8.8 | 8.5 | 8.4 | 8.6 | 8.8 |
| October | 8.8 | 8.6 | 8.6 | 8.7 | 8.9 |
| November | 8.0 | 7.8 | 7.8 | 7.8 | 8.0 |
| December | 8.2 | 8.0 | 8.9 | 7.6 | 7.9 |

SOURCE: *Uniform Crime Report* 1995. Published 1996, p. 11. Courtesy of the FBI.

Violent crimes decreased 4.1 percent in 1995 from 1994. Despite this decrease, the United States had 8.9 homicides per 100,000 population compared with 1.0 per 100,000, in Great Britain.

According to the *Uniform Crime Reports* for 1995, a violent crime occurred nationally every 18 seconds:

1 robbery every 54 seconds

1 aggravated assault every 29 seconds

1 forcible rape every 5 minutes

1 murder every 24 minutes

Investigating crimes against persons is made more difficult by the emotionalism usually encountered, not only from the victim but from the public. Generally, however, investigating crimes against persons results in more and better information and evidence than investigating crimes against property, discussed in Section Four. In crimes against persons, the victim is often an eyewitness, an important source of information and a key to identifying the suspect. The victim and other witnesses are often able to provide important information on the type of crime, the person attacked, how and by what means the attack was made, what the attacker's intent or motive was and what words may have been spoken. Weapons may provide physical evidence, as may any injuries suffered by the victim. Typically, crimes against persons yield much physical evidence, with the type of evidence to anticipate directly related to the type of crime committed. Normally, you can expect to find such evidence as a weapon, blood, hair, fibers, fingerprints, footprints and the like, depending on the specific crime. Subsequently the arrest rate is high.

In recent years, violent-crime investigations have been enhanced by the establishment of the Violent Crime Apprehension Program (VICAP) at the FBI National Police Academy in Quantico, Virginia. The goal of this program is to coordinate major violent-crime cases, regardless of their location, in the United States. Information considered viable is published in the FBI's *Law Enforcement Bulletin*. If the case merits interagency cooperation, a major case investigation team of investigators from all involved agencies may be formed.

Viability is determined by specialists at VICAP who review the materials submitted and compare this information with information received from other departments about similar cases and modus operandi. This is especially important in serial killings and other major violent crimes where the suspects have moved to other areas and committed similar crimes.

The chapters in this section of the book discuss specific considerations in investigating robbery (Chapter 8), assault (9), rape and other sex offenses (10), child abuse (11) and homicide (12). In actuality, more than one offense can occur in a given case. For example, what begins as a robbery can progress to an assault, then a forcible rape and finally a homicide. Each offense must be proven separately. Section Four discusses the remaining Index Crimes. The frequency of occurrence of the eight Index Crimes is shown in the FBI's Crime Clock below.

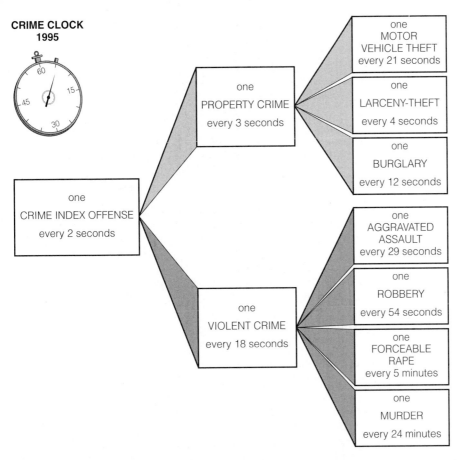

**CRIME CLOCK
1995**

one
CRIME INDEX OFFENSE
every 2 seconds

one
PROPERTY CRIME
every 3 seconds

one
VIOLENT CRIME
every 18 seconds

one
MOTOR VEHICLE THEFT
every 21 seconds

one
LARCENY-THEFT
every 4 seconds

one
BURGLARY
every 12 seconds

one
AGGRAVATED ASSAULT
every 29 seconds

one
ROBBERY
every 54 seconds

one
FORCEABLE RAPE
every 5 minutes

one
MURDER
every 24 minutes

The crime clock should be viewed with care. Being the most aggregate representation of UCR data, it is designed to convey the annual reported crime experience by showing the relative frequency of occurrence of the Index Offenses. This mode of display should not be taken to imply a regularity in the commission of Part 1 Offenses; rather, it represents the annual ratio of crime to fixed time intervals.

# Chapter 8

# Robbery

## DO YOU KNOW

How robbery is defined?

How robberies are classified?

What home invaders are?

In what types of robbery the FBI and state officials become involved?

What new category of robbery has become a national concern?

What the elements of the crime of robbery are?

What special problems are posed in a robbery investigation?

What factors must be considered in responding to a robbery-in-progress call?

How to prove each element of robbery?

What descriptive information is needed to identify suspects and vehicles?

What modus operandi information needs to be obtained in a robbery case?

What physical evidence can link the suspect with the robbery?

## CAN YOU DEFINE

bait money
carjacking
robbery

**Introduction**

DURING THE 1930s, JOHN DILLINGER, AMERICA'S NUMBER-ONE desperado, captured the attention of citizens and law enforcement officers alike. This notorious bank robber's tools of the trade were a Thompson submachine gun and a revolver. Although admired by many for his daring and cast as a folk hero, Dillinger gunned down ten men. "Pretty Boy" Floyd began his criminal career by robbing a local post office of $350 in pennies. Like Dillinger, he killed ten people. Who can forget the murder and robbery spree of Bonnie Parker and Clyde Barrow through Missouri, Texas and Oklahoma?

The preceding are vivid examples of the violent nature of many robberies. Robbery is one of the three most violent crimes against the person. Only homicide and rape are considered to be more traumatic to the victim.

This chapter begins with an overview of robbery and a description of how robberies might be classified. This is followed by an explanation of the elements of the crime of robbery. Next is a discussion of special problems in investigating robberies, the preliminary investigation, proving the elements of the offense and conducting the complete investigation. The chapter concludes with a look at the problem of false robbery reports.

## Robbery: An Overview

**Robbery** is the felonious taking of another's property, either directly from the person or in his or her presence, through force or intimidation.

Robbery takes many forms, from the daring exploits of criminals such as Dillinger to purse-snatching and muggings. Whatever the form, the potential for violence exists.

Most robbers carry a weapon or other threatening item or indicate to the victim that they are armed. Therefore, little direct personal contact occurs between the robber and the victim, which reduces the probability of physical evidence remaining at the crime scene. Despite the inherent danger to the victim during a robbery, most robberies do not result in personal injury. Sometimes, however, a violent physical act is performed against the victim early in the robbery, either by original intent or because of unexpected circumstances or resistance. Such cases involve additional charges of aggravated assault or, in the case of death, murder.

According to the FBI's *Uniform Crime Reports,* the use of violence during robberies has increased during the past ten years, but such violence is not nearly as frequent as the general public might expect. One theory explaining the low rates of injury and death during robberies is that threats of force, use of force or the presence of a weapon reduce the likelihood of the victim resisting. Confronted with threatening statements, a threatening note or a visible weapon, most robbery victims obey the robber's demands.

However, the behavior of an armed robber is unpredictable. In some cases when the victim resists, the robber may flee without completing the robbery. In one case, a man armed with a shotgun demanded and obtained $10,000 from a bank teller. Instead of leaving, he talked to the teller for fifteen minutes, telling her that he was drunk and was considering suicide. Then he handed the money back to the teller and walked out of the bank. In another case, a robber handed a bank teller a note that said, "Please put the money in this bag and no one will get hurt. Thank you very much." The teller called a bank guard and handed him the note. The guard read the note and told the robber, "Get out, you bum, or I'll blow your brains out." The robber quickly left the bank. In other instances, however, resisting victims have been injured or killed.

Violence against the victim also occurs in muggings and purse-snatchings where the victim is struck with a weapon, club or the fists or is knocked down. Older people are often injured by the fall resulting from such violent acts. Any

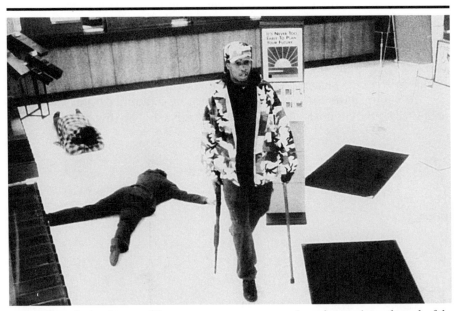

*As seen from the bank's surveillance camera, a gunman carries a shotgun into a branch of the Commercial Bank branch in northeast Detroit as two customers lay on the floor during the robbery attempt. The gunman killed two bank employees and wounded another before taking the life of a hostage outside the bank. He was later killed by police.*

such violent contact increases the probability of hair, fibers, scratches or other evidence being found on the victim or the suspect.

Most robbers are visibly armed with a weapon or dangerous device and make an *oral demand* for the desired money or property. For example, a robber uses a gun to obtain money from an attendant inside a service station. The gun is either visible, or the robber's hands are in a coat or jacket pocket and he or she indicates possession of a weapon.

Some robbers present a *note* rather than speaking. Figure 8–1 shows the actual wording of a note used in a robbery in Los Angeles on July 2, 1980. The robber may or may not ask for the note to be returned. It is important evidence if it is left behind.

*Hostages* are held in some robberies. In one case a bank's head cashier, his wife and their child were held captive by a robber for five hours on a Saturday. The cashier was ordered to go to the bank and get money. The wife and child were tied up but left unharmed. In another case, a woman was taken from her home and forced to drive two men to a bank in her car. They forced her to accompany them into the bank, robbed it, left her there and used her car for their getaway. Bank robberies and hostage situations are discussed later in this chapter.

Robbers use various ruses to get themselves into position for the crime. They may loiter, pose as salespersons or feign business, watching for the opportune moment to make their demands known. Once the opportunity presents itself, robbers act quickly and decisively. Sometimes, however, their actions before the robbery give them away. One such case involved a robber who was captured by two FBI agents just as the teller was handing over the money. The robber was unaware that the FBI agents had been watching him since he entered the bank. His nervous actions had attracted their attention, even though they were in the bank on other business at the time.

Stolen jewelry or cash usually cannot be recovered unless an arrest is made immediately after the crime. Stolen purses and wallets are usually discarded within minutes of the robbery. According to the FBI *Uniform Crime Report* for 1995, there were 580,545 robberies, the lowest since 1989. Robberies decreased 6.2 percent from 1994, when there were 618,949 robberies reported. Firearms were the most frequently used weapons, 41 percent in 1995. The majority of robberies occurred on streets, parking lots and alleys. About 2 percent were banks. In 1995, 25 percent of robberies were cleared by arrest.

The vast majority (91 percent) of robberies are committed by males. Robbers are usually serial criminals and may commit fifteen to twenty-five robberies before

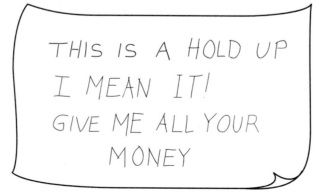

**Figure 8–1   Bank Robbery Note**

being apprehended. People who commit robberies are often egotistical braggarts, prone to boasting of their crimes. Because of this, informants can provide excellent leads in robbery cases.

The most frequent victims of robberies are banks, dope houses, liquor stores, fast-food places, jewelry stores, convenience stores, motels, gambling houses and private residences. The elderly are frequently victims of robbery. Most such robberies are snatches of purses or packages committed by amateurs or juveniles.

Other characteristics of robberies include the following:

- They are committed with the use of stolen cars, stolen motor-vehicle license plates or both.
- They are committed by two or more people working together.
- The offender lives within 100 miles of the robbery.
- Robberies committed by a lone robber tend to involve lone victims and are apt to be crimes of opportunity (on the spur of the moment).
- Youths committing robberies tend to operate in groups and to use strongarm tactics more frequently than adults.
- Less physical evidence is normally found than in other violent crimes.
- They take much less time than other crimes.
- Middle-aged and older people tend to be the victims.

Rand (1995, p. v) reports on a study conducted by the Bureau of Justice Statistics that found that:

> In confrontational robberies, regardless of the weapon possessed by the offender, victims who defended themselves in some way were less likely to lose property than victims who took no actions. Victims who did nothing to defend themselves lost property in about nine-tenths of robberies committed with guns or knives and in three-fourths of robberies committed with or without other weapons. Victims who took action lost property in 60 percent of all confrontational robberies committed with handguns, 50 percent of robberies committed without a weapon and less than 50 percent of those committed with knives or other weapons.
>
> Victims who defended themselves against offenders armed with guns were more likely than those who took no actions to be injured during the crime.

The report on the study concludes (p. 22): "Data on confrontational robberies support the conventional wisdom that victims who do nothing to defend themselves or their property are the most likely to avoid injury, but are also the most likely to lose property."

## Classification

Robberies are classified into four categories, each committed by different types of people using different techniques.

---

Robberies are classified as residential, commercial, street and vehicle driver.

---

### Residential Robberies

Residential robberies include those that occur in hotel and motel rooms, garages, elevators and private homes. These robberies are less frequent than the other types but are dangerous and traumatic because they tend to involve entire families.

Entrance is frequently gained by knocking on the door and then forcing entrance when the occupant appears. Most residential robberies occur in the early evening when people are apt to be home. Victims are frequently bound and gagged or even tortured as the robber attempts to learn the location of valuables.

Hotel, motel, garage or elevator robberies are carried out rapidly, and they frequently involve injury. Information from employees that a person has a large amount of jewelry or money determines the victim for some robberies.

In some cases, people are robbed because they arrive home to discover a burglary in progress. The burglar is thus "forced" to become a robber.

A relatively new type of residential robber that is challenging police departments across the country has been dubbed the *home invaders*. Hurley (1995, p. 122) suggests: "Home invasion robbery (HIR) represents an especially troubling crime trend and a formidable challenge to law enforcement." He (p. 144) also notes: "Home invaders usually target the resident, not the residence. They often choose women, senior citizens or drug dealers."

---

Home invaders are usually young Asian gang members who travel across the country robbing Asian families, especially Asian business owners.

---

Burke (1990, p. 23) writes:

Home invaders are young men who travel around the country terrorizing selected community members until the victims surrender their valuables. . . . Aware that many Asian families have a great distrust of the banking industry and therefore keep large amounts of cash and jewelry in their homes, these organized gang members travel across the country, selecting Asian business owners as their primary victims.

The article "Growing in Power . . ." (1991) characterized them as "highly organized and extremely vicious Vietnamese youth gangs . . . preying on their fellow Southeast Asian refugees." The article notes that many of the gang members were hardened by the cruelties and violence they witnessed as children: "mutilations, mayhem and robberies." Although not an excuse, such experiences may help to explain their willingness to resort to violence on a whim.

### Commercial Robberies

Convenience stores, loan companies, jewelry stores, liquor stores, gasoline or service stations and taverns are especially susceptible to robbery. Drugstores are apt to be targets of robberies to obtain narcotics as well as cash.

Commercial robberies occur most frequently toward the end of the week between 6 P.M. and 4 A.M. Stores with poor visibility from the street and few employees on duty are the most likely targets. Many stores now keep only a limited amount of cash on hand during high-risk times. Stores also attempt to deter robbers by using surveillance cameras, alarm systems, guards and guard dogs.

Many commercial robberies are committed by persons with criminal records; therefore, their M.O.s should be compared with those of past robberies. Because of the offenders' experience, commercial robberies are usually better planned than street or vehicle-driver robberies.

Many robbers of convenience stores are on drugs or rob to pay for drugs. Convenience stores that are robbed once are the most likely targets to be robbed again. In fact, about 8 percent of the stores account for more than 50 percent of the robberies.

The National Association of Convenience Store *Robbery Deterrence Manual* lists these deterrents:

- Keep the cash-register cash balance low.
- Provide good lighting outside and inside the store.
- Elevate the cash-register area so the clerk has better viewing ability and is in sight of passersby.
- Remove outdoor pay phones from the premises.

Yarbrough and Meyer (1996, p. 33) describe the robbery of a major computer chip manufacturer having normal physical security. A heavily armed Asian gang took hostage an employee having a cigarette break outside the plant. The robbers used this employee's proximity access card to gain entrance and then tied and blindfolded the few employees working the night shift. They then unloaded a pallet of packaged computer chips valued at a half-million dollars— loaded them into their car and drove off.

This type of robbery should be anticipated, and preventive measures should be taken. Computer chips are an easy target: small, impossible to identify and extremely valuable. They are often seen as worth the risk of a strong-arm robbery.

**Bank Robbery.** "'Bank robbery!' The call could mean a possible shootout or a hostage situation. It is not a nice thought, but you are on your way to whatever fate awaits you" (Morrison, 1996, p. 159).

Pearson (1996, p. 48) stresses: "The actions of the first officer on the scene of a hostage situation can mean the difference between life and death."

As Morrison (1996, p. 160) notes: "It is paramount that the first officer on the scene, the investigator and all members of the department know and understand the bank's policies and procedures for a robbery call. Knowing how the employees are trained to respond will make the job easier and safer."

Bank robbery is both a federal and a state offense. U.S. Code Title 18, Section 2113, defines the elements of the federal crime of bank robbery. This statute applies to robbery, burglary or larceny from any member bank of the Federal Reserve system, any bank insured by the Federal Deposit Insurance Corporation (FDIC), any bank organized and operated under the laws of the United States, any federal savings and loan association or any federal credit union.

---

Bank robberies are within the jurisdictions of the FBI, the state and the community where the crime occurred and are jointly investigated.

---

Because of the large sums of money involved, bank robberies are committed by rank amateurs as well as by habitual criminals. Amateurs are usually more dangerous because they are not as familiar with weapons and often are nervous and fearful.

Bank robbers often act alone inside the bank, but most have a getaway car with lookouts posted nearby. These individuals pose additional problems for the approaching police. The robbery car often has stolen plates or is itself stolen. This hot car is used to leave the robbery scene and to transport the robber(s) and loot to a "cold" car left a distance from the robbery.

Morrison (1996, p. 160) suggests: "A cardinal rule is that even if only one robber has been reported at the scene, an armed accomplice may be nearby."

The number of bank robberies has increased with the number of branch banks, many of which are housed in storefront offices and outlying shopping centers and thus provide quick entrance to and exit from the robbery scene.

Adding clerks is not necessarily a deterrent because a person with a gun has the advantage regardless of the number of clerks. The association also reports that adding bulletproof glass around the cashier increased the incidence of hostage taking.

## Street Robberies

Robberies are most frequently committed on public streets and sidewalks and in alleys and parking lots. Most are committed with a weapon, but some are strong-arm robberies where physical force is the weapon. Both victim and robber are usually on foot.

Speed and surprise typify street robberies. They are often crimes of opportunity with little or no advance planning. Because such robberies happen so fast, the victim is often unable to identify the robber. Sometimes the victim is approached from behind and never sees the attacker.

Nearly half of street-robbery victims are injured by being struck or shoved to the ground. Women and older men are the most frequent victims. Because most street robberies yield little money, the robber often commits several robberies in one night.

In areas where there are large influxes of diverse groups of immigrants, especially of undocumented ones, special problems occur. Sullivan (1992) describes the problem in Yonkers, New York, where great numbers of illegal immigrants from Mexico, Central America and South America were being preyed upon by robbers. In fact, officers found that a new derogatory term was being used to describe these robberies: *taco hunting.* According to Sullivan (p. 2):

> This term referred to the attackers' beliefs that members of the target group were easy victims. Analysis showed that because of the illegal status of the victims, few had social security numbers. Without a social security number, they were unable to open a bank account or get paid by check. Therefore, they tended to carry large amounts of cash on their persons, sometimes their entire savings.

Compounding the problem are the language barrier, fear and mistrust of police, fear of deportation and lack of understanding of the justice system.

## Vehicle-Driver Robberies

Drivers of taxis, buses, trucks, milk trucks, various types of delivery and messenger vehicles, armored trucks and personal cars are frequent targets of robbers. Taxi drivers are vulnerable because they are often alone while cruising for fares or are dispatched to addresses in vulnerable locations. Some taxi companies have taken such preventive steps as placing protective shields between the passenger and driver and reducing the amount of cash drivers carry. Buses in many cities require passengers to have the exact change to reduce the amount of cash in the driver's possession.

Delivery vehicle drivers may be robbed of their merchandise as they arrive for a delivery, or the robbers may wait until after the delivery and take the cash.

Armored-car robberies are of special concern because they are usually well planned by professional, well-armed robbers and involve large amounts of money. Gates and Roberge (1991, p. 41) suggest that one approach to this problem is to develop an intelligence-type network between the police department and the armored car industry. Their criminal/intelligence files might include the following:

*Somerville, Massachusetts, police and federal authorities gather at the scene of a fatal armored car robbery outside a Star Market at the Twin City Mall, where three masked men attempted to rob the vehicle, fatally shot a guard at the scene and escaped in a van.*

- Known robbery suspects.
- Potential robbery suspects and associates.
- Photo file of suspects.
- Automated Vehicle Intelligence File (AVIF) of known vehicles of suspects and potential suspects.

Drivers of personal cars are often approached in parking lots or while stopped at red lights in less-traveled areas. These robberies are generally committed by teenagers. Drivers who pick up hitchhikers leave themselves open not only to robbery but also to assault and auto theft. Some robbers force people off roads or set up fake accidents or injuries to lure motorists into stopping. A combination of street and vehicle-driver robberies that has increased drastically over the past few years is carjacking.

## Carjacking

A new category of robbery appeared late in 1990 and increased substantially in 1991 and 1992—carjacking.

---

**Carjacking,** a category of robbery, is the taking of a motor vehicle by force or threat of force. It may be investigated by the FBI.

---

The force may consist of use of a handgun, simulated handgun, club, machete, axe, knife or fists. The violence associated with this crime is described by Burke and O'Rear (1993, p. 18):

On Tuesday, September 8, 1992, armed carjacking received national attention when Pamela Basu, a senior research chemist from Maryland, was dragged for almost two miles after her vehicle was commandeered at a stop sign near her home. Her 22-month-old daughter, who was strapped in a car seat, was tossed into the roadway a few blocks after the vehicle was stolen. Mrs. Basu was killed, while her daughter survived the tragedy.

According to USAA ("Carjacking," 1993, p. 16): "Carjacking, the violent and sometimes deadly offspring of auto theft, has become the latest road hazard for motorists."

Burke and O'Rear (1993, p. 24) agree: "Armed carjackers are terrorizing the nation in epidemic proportions. . . . Armed carjacking represents such an assault on the fabric of our lives that it requires the focused attention of the law enforcement community." This threat was recognized by former FBI Director William S. Sessions when he said the crime "has become so extensive that it would no longer be considered simple auto theft, but rather would be treated as a violent crime" ("Carjacking Takes Hold...," 1992, p. 1).

Nearly every major city has experienced armed carjacking offenses in sufficiently substantial numbers that *Uniform Crime Reports* may soon be required to use this as a designation rather than being reported without uniformity as armed robbery, auto theft or some other offense.

Carjackings have resulted in car thefts, injuries and deaths. Initially, the more expensive vehicles were involved, but this trend has changed to any type of motor vehicle. The stolen vehicle is then used as in the conventional crime of vehicle theft: for resale, resale of parts, joyriding or use in committing another crime. Burke and O'Rear (1992, p. 165) note: "Many stolen luxury vehicles are showing up for sale in Third World countries."

Rand (1994, pp. 1–2) reports the following statistics related to carjacking:

- Men were more likely than women, and blacks were more likely than whites, to be victimized by carjacking.
- Most carjacking victims escaped without injury.
- Offenders used a weapon in 77 percent of all attempted and completed carjackings.
- Carjackings were more likely to occur in the evening or at night.
- Most carjackings occurred away from the victim's home.
- Offenders between ages 21 and 29 committed about half of all completed carjackings.
- Victims identified the offenders' race as white in 32 percent of all carjackings, black in 49 percent and Asian or American Indian in 6 percent.
- Men committed 87 percent of all carjackings.
- The median value of automobiles stolen in carjackings was $4,000.
- About half (54 percent) of all completed or attempted carjackings were committed by groups of two or more offenders.

A 1993 FBI study of 169 carjacking cases revealed the following: Most carjackings occur in urban areas between 8 to 11 P.M. on Friday, Saturday or Sunday. Most are committed by amateurs, but some are by serial offenders. Carjacking is a crime of opportunity in which force, including murder, is often used. The offenders know it is a high-risk offense but seem unconcerned about the consequences.

Parking lots are the favorite location for carjacking, followed by city streets, private residence driveways, sporting events, car dealerships, gas stations and bank teller machines. Handguns are the most frequently used weapon. The average age of carjacking victims is between 18 and 36. Three-fourths of the victims were men.

The motivation for carjacking is not clear because the vehicles are taken under so many different circumstances and for so many different reasons. One theory for the sudden increase is that the increased use of alarms and protective devices on vehicles, especially on more expensive ones, makes it more difficult to steal a vehicle by traditional means. The downturn in the economy may also be a factor. The "discount-priced" vehicles are easily sold here and overseas, as are their parts. Car operators are easy prey compared to convenience stores or other commercial establishments that may have surveillance cameras and other security measures in effect. Another theory suggests that status is involved; that a criminal who carjacks a vehicle is accorded higher status in the criminal subculture than one who steals it in the conventional manner. In addition, some police officers believe the crime is becoming a fad among certain groups of young people as a way to prove their "bravado."

Many ruses have been used to engage a victim. Some carjackers stage accidents. Others wait for their victims at workplace parking lots or private residential driveways. Other likely locations include commercial parking lots, stoplights, service stations, automatic teller machines, drive-up bank windows and pay telephones. According to Burke and O'Rear (1992, p. 165): "Armed carjackers usually do not work alone. An accomplice is often nearby in another vehicle as a back-up to the armed robber. The accomplice also provides the initial transportation to the crime scene."

Carjackings have become a serious problem for police, and police investigate them in the same way as other armed robberies. Publication of prevention techniques has become standard policy for police agencies in an effort to prevent losses of property, injuries and deaths. Some agencies are using decoys in an effort to apprehend carjackers. In addition, Burke and O'Rear (1993, p. 24) list these recommendations for law enforcement agencies:

- Maintain a special carjacking modus operandi file.
- Assign a specialized task force to focus upon carjackings.
- Be aware of the possibility of false reports for fraudulent insurance claims.

In October 1992, Congress passed, and President Bush signed, the Anti-Car Theft Act of 1992, making armed carjacking a federal offense. Under this law, automakers must engrave a seventeen-digit vehicle identification number on twenty-four parts of every new car. In addition, the act ("Anti-Car Theft Act," 1992, p. 6): "provides start-up funding to link state motor vehicle departments by computer so that each state will have access to other states' lists of valid titles . . . and requires insurance companies selling junk or salvage vehicles to verify that the vehicles are not stolen."

Burke and O'Rear (1992, p. 23) noted that federal agencies are becoming active in investigating carjacking, with former FBI Director William Sessions stating: "Carjackings will be included with gang activity and drug-related violence as crimes investigated by a 300-member arm of the agency . . . with former foreign counterintelligence agents. . . . The FBI will use undercover officers, decoys, and informants to pursue carjackers."

In a further effort to curtail carjacking, Congress passed the Carjacking Correction Act of 1996. This act establishes strict penalties for the crime of carjacking, with longer sentences, up to twenty-five years in prison, for cases involving "serious bodily injury" to a victim. When President Clinton signed the legislation, he commented: "Sexual assault causes serious bodily injury. Carjackers who rape their victims will meet with nothing less than the full force of the law" ("Carjacking Correction Act," 1996, p. 3).

In addition to knowing how robberies are generally classified, investigators must be familiar with the elements of the crime of robbery in their particular jurisdictions.

## Elements of the Crime: Robbery

State laws define *robbery* precisely. Although the general public tends to use the term *robbery* interchangeably with *burglary, larceny* and *theft,* the specific elements of robbery clearly distinguish it from these offenses. A businessman might say that his store was robbed when, in fact, it was burglarized. A woman may have money taken from her purse at work while she is busy waiting on customers and say that she was robbed when, legally, it was larceny. Such thefts are not robbery because the necessary elements are not present.

Some states have only one degree of robbery. Others have simple and aggravated robbery. Still others have robbery in the first, second and third degree. However, in most state laws common elements exist.

---

The elements of the crime of robbery are:
- The wrongful taking of personal property.
- From the person or in the person's presence.
- Against the person's will by force or threat of force.

---

**Wrongful Taking of Personal Property.**   Various statutes use phrases such as *unlawful taking, felonious taking* or *knowing he is not entitled thereto.* Intent is an element of the crime in some, but not all, states. To take "wrongfully," the robber must have no legal right to the property. Moreover, property must be *personal property,* as distinguished from real property.

**From the Person or in the Presence of the Person.**   In most cases, *in the presence of the person* means that the victim sees the robber take the property. This is not always the case, however, because the victim may be locked in a room with no opportunity to see the property taken. For example, robbers often take victims to a separate room such as a restroom or a bank vault while they search for the desired items or cash. Such actions do not remove the crime "from the presence of the person" as long as the separation from the property is the direct result of force or threats of force used by the robber.

**Against the Person's Will by Use of Force or Threat of Force.**   This essential element clearly separates robbery from burglary and larceny. As noted, most robberies are committed with a weapon or dangerous device or by indicating that such is present. The force is generally sufficient to deter resistance. The force or threat of force can be immediate or threatened in the future. It can be directed at the victim, the victim's family or another person with the victim.

## Special Problems in Investigation

As a violent crime, robbery introduces problems that require special attention from the dispatcher, patrol officers, investigators and police administrators. Three major problems occur in dealing with robberies: (1) they are usually not reported until the offenders have left the scene; (2) it is difficult to obtain good descriptions or positive identification from victims; (3) the items taken, usually currency, are difficult to identify.

The speed of a robbery, its potential for violence and the taking of hostages and the usual lack of evidence at the scene pose special problems for investigators.

Police response time can be reduced if the robbed business or residence has an alarm system that is connected to the police department or a private alarm agency. Silent alarms can provide an early response, and audible alarms sometimes prevent a robbery. The lag time—that is, the elapsed time between the commission of a robbery and the time the police are notified—is usually much longer than the actual police response time. Police can develop plans and response procedures for locations likely to be robbed.

A robbery-in-progress call involves an all-units response, with units close to the scene going there directly while other units cover the area near the scene, looking for a possible getaway vehicle. Other cars go to checkpoints such as bridges, converging highways, freeway entry and exit ramps, dead-end streets and alleys. Observe all vehicles as you approach a robbery scene. Whether to use red lights and sirens depends on the information received from the dispatcher. It is often best to arrive quietly to prevent the taking of hostages. If shooting is occurring, using lights and siren may cause the robber(s) to leave before you arrive.

When responding to a robbery-in-progress call:
- Proceed as rapidly as possible, but use extreme caution.
- Assume the robber is at the scene unless otherwise advised.
- Be prepared for gunfire.
- Look for and immobilize any getaway vehicle discovered.
- Avoid a hostage situation if possible.
- Make an immediate arrest if the suspect is at the scene.

With no information to the contrary, assume the suspect is still at the scene and probably armed. Use extreme caution. The biggest problem is often initially getting too close to the scene and not knowing where the suspects or lookouts are.

Upon arrival, attempt to locate any vehicle that might be used by the suspects, even if you have no description of it. It will probably be within a block of the crime scene, and its engine may be running. It generally has a person in it (the wheelman or lookout) waiting for the robber(s) to return. If the vehicle is identified through prior information and is empty, immobilize it by removing the distributor cap or letting the air out of a tire. If a cohort is waiting in the car, arrest the person and then immobilize the vehicle.

Decide whether to enter the robbery location immediately or to wait until sufficient personnel are in position. Department policy determines if it is an immediate or a timed response. Too early an entry increases the chances of a hostage situation or of having to use weapons. The general rule is to avoid a confrontation if it will create a worse situation than the robbery itself.

If you arrive at the robbery scene and find a suspect there with the victim, surround the building and order the suspect to come out. Get other people in the area to leave because of possible gunfire. Know the operational limitations imposed by the number of officers and the amount of equipment available at the scene. Take advantage of vehicles and buildings in the area for cover.

Because the robber is committing a violent crime and is usually armed, expect that a weapon may be used against the police and that a hostage may be taken.

**Hostage Situations.**    The priorities in a hostage situation are to (1) preserve life, (2) apprehend the hostage taker and (3) recover or protect property. To accomplish these priorities requires specialized training in hostage situations.

In general, consider a direct assault only if there has already been a killing or if further negotiations would be useless. The negotiator in a hostage situation must be prepared for a long ordeal and, therefore, must be mentally alert and emotionally and physically fit, as well as well trained. Hostage situations may last from less than an hour to more than forty hours; the average length is approximately twelve hours. This is a long time to be involved in a tense situation that involves lives in each decision reached during the negotiation.

The need for negotiation is based on the principle that preserving life—that of the hostages or the hostage takers, as well as police or innocent bystanders—is the main priority. SWAT teams or expert sharpshooters are often at or near the scene, but they do not participate in the negotiations and in some cases are not visible except as a last resort.

DiVasto and Newman (1993, pp. 82–87) suggest four key phases of hostage situations: contain, communicate, convince and conclude.

*Contain.* Determine exactly what is happening and who is involved. Establish control by setting up an inner and outer perimeter. Use the existing chain of command. Keep the hostage taker in a confined space and appoint one person to record all that occurs.

*Communicate.* Appoint one person to establish voice contact with the hostage taker but not face-to-face contact. Keep communication between the negotiator

*After a bank robbery in Germany, the robbers took the cashier and a female advisor as hostages. They later captured a town bus with thirty-two passengers aboard. The bus continued to the Netherlands and then back to Germany. During an attack by a special unit of German police officers, one robber and one hostage were killed. The other robber and hostage sustained serious injuries.*

and the hostage taker only; do not use third-party negotiators unless absolutely necessary. Let the hostage taker vent his or her grievances.

*Convince.* Persuade the perpetrator to cooperate by finding subjects of discussion to create a bond between the negotiator and hostage taker. Understand that the passage of time usually works to the negotiator's advantage. Be truthful in your statements, and provide for the basic needs of the hostage taker if requested. Assure that the safety of the hostage taker relies on talking to and reaching an agreement with the negotiator. However, in some incidents there is no possibility of a successful conclusion other than use of force.

*Conclude.* Accept surrender. Keep any promises made leading to the surrender. Protect everyone until the actual surrender is made and the subject is in custody. Then hold a debriefing to learn what went right and what went wrong.

Time is normally a valuable ally for the police in negotiations. Strentz (1995, p. 71) describes the typical emotions hostage taker's experience during negotiations, illustrated in Figure 8–2.

There is usually no need to rush into the scene immediately and proceed with direct contact. In a few cases it may be better not to do anything, to let the hostage taker resolve the situation. The passage of time can accomplish the following:

- Provide the opportunity for face-to-face contact with the hostage taker.
- Allow the negotiator to attempt to establish a trustful rapport.
- Permit mental, emotional and physical fatigue to operate against the hostage taker.
- Increase the hostage taker's needs for food, water, sleep and elimination.
- Increase the possibility of reducing demands to reasonable compliance levels.
- Possibly foster the "Stockholm syndrome," by which hostages begin to identify with their captors and sympathize with them.
- Allow hostage-escape possibilities to present themselves.
- Provide for more rational and logical thinking, in contrast to the emotionalism usually present during the initial stage of the crime.

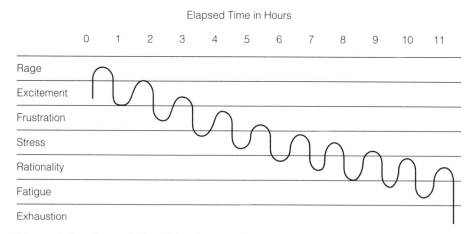

**Figure 8–2    General Time Line Pattern for Successful Negotiation**

Source: Thomas Strentz. "The Cyclic Crisis Negotiations Time Line." *Law and Order,* March 1995, p. 73. Reprinted by permission of the publisher.

■ Lessen the hostage taker's anxiety and reduce his or her adrenalin flow, allowing more rational negotiations.

■ Allow for important intelligence gathering concerning the hostage taker, hostages, layout, protection barriers and needed police reinforcement.

The negotiator chosen should have street knowledge and experience with hostage incidents. Sometimes the first officers at the scene have established rapport with the hostage taker, and the negotiator only advises. In some cases a trained clinical psychologist may be called to the scene, not as a negotiator but as a consultant regarding possible behavioral deviations of the hostage taker.

Strentz (1996, p. 72) reports on a survey of 100 sworn West Coast officers. There was a high level of agreement (90 percent or better) on the following characteristics of effective negotiators: adaptable, alert, calm, capable, clear thinking, mature, patient, sociable and tactful. There was also a high level of agreement (95 percent) on one characteristic of the ineffective negotiation: argumentative.

The most ideal contact is face-to-face negotiations because this provides the best opportunity for gathering knowledge about and personally observing the reactions of the hostage taker. Such contact should be undertaken only if circumstances indicate the negotiator will not be in danger. An alternative is telephone contact. Telephone contact allows for personal conversation and establishing rapport without the dangers of face-to-face contact. The use of bullhorns is not the personal type of communication desired. Nonetheless, it may be the only available method of communication.

Negotiable items may include food and drink (but not liquor unless it is known that liquor would lessen the hostage taker's anxieties rather than increase them); money; media access and reduced penalties for the hostage taker. Mobile transportation is generally not negotiable because of the difficulty in monitoring such transportation and controlling the situation. Some negotiators feel any item is negotiable as long as the police have control of the situation and it is within reasonable limitations. Police departments should set forth policies regarding hostage negotiations in advance of such incidents. In general, nothing should be granted to a hostage taker without something being received in return.

Table 8–1, prepared from a number of sources, presents information related to hostage takers, their characteristics and possible motives and guidelines for possible actions. FBI reports concerning hostage taking indicate that 52 percent of these incidents involve mentally disturbed persons; therefore, the first four categories in the table are especially important.

In the several instances in which the author has been a negotiator, each incident lent itself to the general guidelines, but each incident was also unique. Decisions had to be made based on the immediate factors involved. In the vast majority of cases, effectively handled negotiations can resolve the situation without injury or death.

If the robber emerges on request or is already outside the building, arrest him or her immediately. Have the victim and any witnesses make a field identification, and then remove the suspect from the scene immediately.

A wounded suspect presents an especially dangerous situation. Be alert to a suspect feigning more serious injury than exists to draw you off guard and get close enough to shoot you. Keep the suspect covered at all times. Immobilize him or her with handcuffs as soon as possible. If the suspect is seriously injured, arrange for an armed escort in the ambulance and for taking a dying declaration if necessary. If the suspect is killed, notify the coroner or medical examiner immediately.

**Table 8–1 Hostage Takers**

| Type | Characteristics | Motives | Guidelines for Action |
|---|---|---|---|
| Paranoid schizophrenic | Out of touch with reality<br>Hallucinations, delusions<br>Above-average intelligence | Needs to carry out plans<br>Imagines perceived wrongs<br>Feels he or she is right | Do not lie or attempt to trick<br>Do not argue about beliefs<br>Accept statements<br>May negotiate |
| Manic depressive | Out of touch with reality<br>Feels unworthy<br>Suicidal<br>Slow speech | To remove hostages from "this horrible life" | Needs understanding and support<br>Try to induce subject to talk about something positive |
| Inadequate personality | Homicidal<br>Loser complex<br>In touch with reality<br>Fired from many jobs | To get attention<br>To prove him- or herself<br>High point of life | Needs understanding and acceptance<br>Can be negotiated with<br>Make only promises that can be kept<br>Do not bring parents to scene |
| Antisocial personality—sociopath or psychopath | Absence of conscience or guilt; no moral values<br>Con man; snow jobs<br>Impulsive<br>Self-centered<br>Street- and police wise | Manipulates people for own gain | Do not use tricks<br>Do not make unrealistic promises<br>Stimulate ego |
| Prisoners | Usually not mentally disturbed<br>Guards likely to be hostages and likely to be killed | Improve prison conditions<br>Bargaining power | Requires rapid police action<br>Do not allow a leader to develop |
| Criminals | Know what to expect from police<br>Usually a spontaneous reaction to being cornered | Media attention<br>To escape safely from a crime<br>Demand additional money | Accept physical safety of criminal in return for release of hostage<br>Obtain all facts |
| Terrorists | Much planning<br>Hostages are in serious jeopardy<br>Local police may not be able to meet demands<br>May need state or federal assistance | Media attention<br>Fast, intense media attention<br>Further a cause<br>Martyr complex<br>Demand money<br>Hope government will overreact, so blame is on government, not terrorists | Admit points are well made<br>Let it be known demands are understood and action is being considered<br>Impress that killing hostages will only discredit cause<br>Activate SWAT teams |

## The Preliminary Investigation

Frequently, officers arriving at the scene of a robbery find that the robber has just fled. After taking care of emergencies, broadcast initial information about the suspect(s), the getaway vehicle and the direction of travel. Follow-up vehicles dispatched to the general area of the robbery can then attempt to apprehend the escaping robbers. Early information helps determine how far the suspect may have traveled and the most likely escape routes.

Robbery usually leaves the victim and any witnesses feeling vulnerable and fearful. Fear and stress make it difficult for them to give accurate descriptions and details of what occurred. Be patient.

Witnesses to a robbery suffer varying degrees of trauma even though they have not lost any property. They may have had to lie on the floor or been placed in a locked room or a bank vault, possibly fearing that the robber would return and kill them. Their ability to recall precise details is further impaired by the suddenness of the crime. Victims and witnesses may be asked to complete a form such as the one in Figures 8–3a and b.

## Proving the Elements of the Offense

Know the elements of robbery in your jurisdiction so you can determine if a robbery has, in fact, been committed. Each element must be proven separately. Proving some of the elements is not sufficient.

**Was Personal Property Wrongfully Taken?** *Taking of property* necessitates proving that it was carried away from the lawful owner or possessor to deprive the owner permanently of the property. Prove that the robber had no legal right to the property taken.

---

Determine the legal owner of the property taken. Describe completely the property and its value.

---

*Who is the legal owner?* Take statements from the victim to show legal possession and control of the property before and during the robbery.

*Was property taken or intended to be taken?* Obtain a complete description of the property and its value, including marks, serial numbers, operation identification number (if available), color, size and any other characteristics that might identify the property.

Obtain proof of what was lost and its value. In a bank robbery, the bank manager or auditor can give an accurate accounting of the money taken. In a store robbery, any responsible employee can help determine the loss. Cash register receipts, sales receipts, retail and wholesale prices, reasonable estimates by persons in the same business or the estimate of an independent appraiser can be used to determine the amount of the loss. In robberies of the person, the victim determines the loss. Some robbery victims claim to have lost more or less than was actually taken; this complicates the case.

**Was It Taken from the Person or in the Person's Presence?** *From the person or in the presence of the person* necessitates proving that the property was under the victim's control before the robbery and was removed from the victim's control by the robber's direct actions.

---

Record the exact words, gestures, motions or actions the robber used to gain control of the property.

---

Answer such questions as:

- Where was the property before it was taken?
- Where was the victim?
- How was the property taken?
- Was the removal against the victim's will by force or the threat of force?

## ROBBER IDENTIFICATION FORM

DO NOT DISCUSS DETAILS OF THE CRIME OR ROBBER DESCRIPTIONS WITH ANYONE EXCEPT OFFICER IN CHARGE OR LAW ENFORCEMENT OFFICIALS.

RECORD YOUR OWN OBSERVATIONS, NOT WHAT SOMEONE TELLS YOU.

Use separate form for each robber.

Time of Robbery _____ A.M. _____ P.M.    No. of robbers involved _____   This form describes Robber No. _____

**Race**   White ☐      Black ☐      Am. Indian ☐
Mexican Am. ☐  Puerto Rican ☐  Cuban ☐
Asian ☐      Other _____

**Sex:**   Male ☐  Female ☐

**Age** _____  **Height** _____  **Weight** _____

**Build:**  Small ☐  Medium ☐  Large ☐

**Stature:**  Thin ☐  Medium ☐  Heavy ☐

**Complexion:**  Light ☐  Medium ☐  Dark ☐
Ruddy ☐  Fair ☐  Wrinkled ☐

**Hair:**  Bald ☐  Partially Bald ☐
Color _____ Very Short (close cropped) ☐
Short ☐  Medium ☐
Long ☐  Very Long ☐

**Beard:**  No ☐  Yes ☐   **Mustache:**  No ☐  Yes ☐

**Sideburns:**  No ☐  Yes ☐
If Yes — Short ☐  Medium ☐  Long ☐

**Glasses:**  No ☐  Yes ☐
If Yes — Regular ☐  Sunglasses ☐

**Size of Frame:**  Small ☐  Medium ☐  Large ☐

**Type of Frame:**  Wire ☐  Plastic ☐  Color _____

**Shape of Frame:**  Regular ☐  Round ☐
Square ☐  Rectangular ☐

**Hat:**  No ☐  Yes ☐  If Yes — Color _____
**Type** _____

**Tie:**  No ☐  Yes ☐  If Yes — Color _____

**Shirt or Blouse:**  Color _____

**Type:**  Work ☐  Sport ☐  Dress ☐  T-Shirt ☐
Sweatshirt ☐  Other Data _____

**Sweater:**  No ☐  Yes ☐  If Yes — Color _____

**Type:**  Button ☐  Pullover ☐
Other Data _____

**Pants:**  Color _____

**Type:**  Work ☐  Jeans ☐  Dress ☐

**Shoes:**  Color _____

**Style:**  Work ☐  Sport ☐  Dress ☐
Type of Heel _____

**Coat:**  No ☐  Yes ☐  If Yes — Color _____

**Type:**  Business Suit ☐  Sport Suit ☐
Jacket ☐  Overcoat ☐  Raincoat ☐

**Style:**  Button ☐  Zipper ☐  Other _____

**Length:**  Hip Level ☐  Knee Level ☐
Thigh Level ☐  Other _____

**Gloves:**  No ☐  Yes ☐  If Yes — Color _____

**Type** _____

**Mask or Disguise:**  No ☐  Yes ☐
If Yes — Describe _____
_____
_____
_____

Continued other side

**Figure 8–3a   Robber Identification Form, front**

Obtain a complete description of the robber's words, actions and any weapon used or threatened to be used.

If nothing was said, find out what gestures, motions or other actions compelled the victim to give up the property.

The force need not be directly against the robbery victim. For example, a woman may receive a call at work, telling her that her husband is being held hostage and will be killed unless she brings money to a certain location, or the robber may grab a friend of the victim or a customer in a store and direct the victim to hand over money to protect the person being held from harm.

**Weapon:** None Seen ☐   Gun ☐   Knife ☐

Other (describe) _____

If gun,   Rifle ☐   Shotgun ☐

Pistol ☐   Revolver ☐   Automatic ☐

**Color of Gun:**   Black ☐   Chrome ☐   Blue ☐

**Speech:**   Coarse ☐   Refined ☐   High ☐   Low ☐

Accent ☐   Drawl ☐   Stutter ☐

Lisp ☐   Normal ☐

**Manner:**   Polite ☐   Gruff ☐   Nervous ☐

Calm ☐   Alcoholic ☐

Direction of Escape: _____

_____

**Motor Vehicle:**   Colors:

Top _____

Bottom _____

Make: _____

Model: _____

2 Dr. ☐   4 Dr. ☐   Sedan ☐   Wagon ☐

Van ☐   Other _____

License Plate No.: _____

State _____

Color of Plate: _____

Color of numbers _____

Number of people in vehicle _____

Scars, marks or moles _____

Does subject resemble any acquaintance? _____

Subject first observed: Remarks _____

_____

Actions of subject: Remarks _____

_____

Words spoken by subject: _____

_____

Was the money placed in a container?   No ☐   Yes ☐   If Yes — Describe _____

_____

Other remarks; peculiarities; jewelry, etc. _____

_____

Other Details _____

_____

_____

_____

Location of Employee/Customer in relation to subject(s) _____

_____

Name of Witness (Print) _____ Tele. Home _____ Business _____

Address _____ City _____ State _____ Zip _____

Signature _____ Date _____

**Figure 8–3b   Robber Identification Form, back**

Describe any injuries to the victim or witnesses. Photograph them, if possible, and have them examined by a doctor, emergency room personnel or ambulance paramedics.

## The Complete Investigation

Most robberies are solved through prompt actions by the victim, witnesses and the police patrolling the immediate area or by police at checkpoints. In many cases, however, a robbery investigation takes weeks or even months. Begin your investigation with an immediate canvass of the neighborhood because the suspect may be hiding in a parked car, in a gas station restroom or on the roof of a building. Check motels and hotels in the area. If there is another city nearby, check the motels there. Look for discarded property such as the weapon, a wallet, money bag or other item taken from victims. Check car rental agencies if no vehicle was reported stolen. Check airports, bus and train stations and taxi companies for possible links.

Recheck all information and physical descriptions. Have a sketch of the suspect prepared and circulate it. Alert your informants to listen for word of the robbery. Check known fences. Check field interview and modus operandi files.

Prepare your report carefully and thoroughly and circulate it to any officers who might assist. Even if you do not apprehend your suspect, the suspect may be apprehended during a future robbery, and his or her M.O. and other evidence may implicate him or her in the robbery you investigated.

### Identifying the Suspect

The various techniques used in suspect identification (discussed in Chapter 7) are relevant at this point.

---

Obtain information about the suspect's general appearance, clothing, any disguises, weapon(s) and vehicle(s).

---

If the suspect is apprehended within a short time (twenty minutes or so), he or she may be taken back to the scene for identification by the victim. Alternatively, the victim may be taken to where the suspect is being held. Several people should be in the area of the suspect to witness that the victim makes any identification without assistance from the police. This should be done within three to five hours after the incident if possible. Photo lineups may be used if no suspect is arrested at or near the scene of the crime. Photo lineups should include five other people in addition to the suspect. A person who has been arrested does not have the right to refuse to have a photo taken.

Eyewitness identification is affected by many factors: the distance between the witness and the suspect at the time of the robbery, the time of day and lighting conditions, the amount of violence involved, whether the witness had ever seen or knew the suspect and the time it took for the crime to be committed.

**Disguises.** Many robbers use face masks such as ski masks, nylon stockings pulled over the head and paper sacks with eye holes. Other disguises include wigs, dyed hair, sideburns, scarves, various types of false noses or ears and makeup to alter appearance. Gauze is sometimes used to distort the shape of the cheeks or mouth and tape to simulate cuts or to cover scars.

Clothing also can serve as a disguise. Collars can be pulled up and hats pulled down. False heels and soles can increase height. Various types of uniforms that fit in with the area of the robbery scene, such as delivery uniforms or work clothes, have been used.

Clothing and disguises may be discarded by the robber as he or she leaves the scene. They are valuable evidence if discovered.

**Weapons.** Pistols, revolvers and automatic weapons are frequently used weapons in robberies. Sawed-off shotguns, rifles, airguns, various types of imitation guns, knives, razors and other cutting and stabbing instruments, explosives, tear gas and various acids have also been used. Such weapons and devices are often found on or near the suspect when arrested, but many are hidden in the vehicle used or are thrown away during the escape.

**Vehicles.** Most vehicles used in robberies are inconspicuous, popular makes that attract no attention and are stolen just before the robbery. Some robbers leave the scene on foot and then take buses or taxis or commandeer vehicles, sometimes at gunpoint.

### Establishing the Modus Operandi

Even if the suspect is apprehended at the scene, the M.O. can help link the suspect with other robberies.

Important modus operandi information includes:
- Type of robbery.
- Time (day and hour).
- Method of attack (real or threatened).
- Weapon.
- Number of robbers.
- Voice and words.
- Vehicle used.
- Peculiarities.
- Object sought.

Finding that an M.O. matches a previous robbery does not necessarily mean that the same robber committed the crime. For example, in one instance three masked gunmen robbed a midwestern bank of more than $45,000 and escaped in a stolen car. The M.O. matched a similar robbery in the same town a few weeks earlier in which $30,000 was obtained. The three gunmen were identified and arrested the next day and more than $41,000 of the loot recovered. One gunman told the FBI agent that he planned the robbery after reading about the successful bank robbery three other masked gunmen had pulled off. The FBI agent smiled and informed the robber that the perpetrators had been arrested shortly after the robbery. Aghast, the copycat robber bemoaned the fact that he had seen no publicity on the arrest.

### Physical Evidence

Physical evidence at a robbery scene is usually minimal. Sometimes, however, the robbery occurs where a surveillance camera is operating. The film can be processed immediately and used as evidence.

Physical evidence that can connect a suspect with a robbery includes fingerprints, shoe prints, tire prints, restraining devices used, discarded garments, fibers and hairs, a note or the stolen property.

Fingerprints may be found at the scene if the suspect handled any objects, on the holdup note if one was left behind, on the getaway car or on recovered property. They might also be found on pieces of tape used as restraints, which, in themselves, are valuable as evidence.

In one residential robbery, the criminal forced entrance into the home, bound and gagged the residents, stole several items of value and then left. As he backed up to turn his car around, he inadvertently left the impression of the vehicle's license plate clearly imprinted on a snowbank. He was apprehended within hours of the robbery.

Recovering stolen property is a major problem. Jewelry and cash are particularly difficult to identify and are easily disposed of or hidden. Some banks

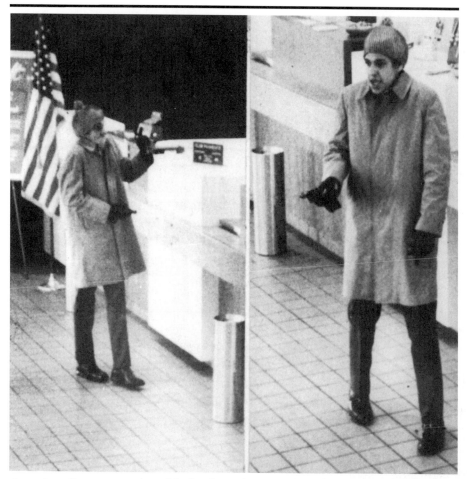

*An automatic camera activated by bank employees in the Bala Cynwyd, Pennsylvania, Continental Bank records the activities of bank robbers holding bank staff at gunpoint.*

and establishments with a high risk of robbery keep **bait money** on hand. This is currency whose serial numbers are recorded and that is kept accessible so that it can be added to any robbery loot. In one bank robbed, bait money had been placed in each teller's case so that it would trip the alarm system when it was moved. Unfortunately, the teller forgot about the bait money, and the robber made off with $5,000.

## False Robbery Reports

Investigators need to rule out the probability that the robbery report is false. Among the indicators of a false robbery report are these (*Learning Objectives*, 1991, p. 134):

- Unusual delay in reporting the offense.
- Amount of the loss not fitting the victim's apparent financial status.
- Lack of correspondence with the physical evidence.
- Improbable events.
- Exceptionally detailed or exceptionally vague description of offender.
- Lack of cooperation.

*News stories reflect actual crime committed in the United States. Similar crimes occur daily. You are a police detective assigned to some of these cases. Each has different elements of the offense. What evidence would you need to identify and convict the person who committed each type of crime? How would you coordinate your investigation with other local, state or federal police agencies? There are unlimited details in investigating a crime. Just use your imagination and Get Real.*

## Police nab robbery suspects

**By Glenn Puit**
*Review-Journal*

A suspect wanted in a convenience store robbery escaped injury early Saturday after he was shot at by a Las Vegas police officer who was pursuing the man off East Tropicana Avenue, police said.

Las Vegas police Lt. Larry Spinosa said the officer was chasing the man on foot through the Liberace Plaza, 1775 E. Tropicana, at 2:09 a.m. when the shooting occurred. Spinosa said the officer ordered the fleeing suspect to stop when the man apparently turned and reached into his waistband.

"The officer, fearing for his personal safety, fired one round from his service weapon," Spinosa said. "The round missed the suspect."

The suspect and two other men were eventually taken into custody on charges of robbery with the use of a deadly weapon, Spinosa said. Police were not able to confirm the identities of the three men early Saturday.

The three suspects were wanted in connection with a 2 a.m. robbery of a convenience store in the 4200 block of Las Vegas Boulevard South, Spinosa said. The men entered the store, produced knives and ordered a clerk to give them money from a cash register.

After receiving the money, the men fled the store parking lot in a car, Spinosa said. The name of the store was not released.

A witness who called police on his cellular phone gave officers a description of the suspects' vehicle, which was later stopped by the officer at the intersection of Tropicana Avenue and Spencer Street. One of the suspects exited the vehicle and was running through the parking lot when the officer shot at him.

Source: *Las Vegas Review Journal,* 22 September 1996. Reprinted by permission of the *Las Vegas Review Journal.*

## Robber has targeted 5 banks in suburban grocery stores

One robber apparently has hit five banks in Twin Cities grocery stores a total of eight times.

On Monday, the man robbed the TCF Bank in Cub Foods on Meadowland Dr. in White Bear Township. Investigators believe he is responsible for seven other recent robberies at TCF banks in Cub stores in Blaine, Crystal and Eden Prairie and the Marquette Bank in the Rainbow Foods in Blaine.

Grocery-store banks are not a typical target for robbers, said Kevin Rickett of the Minneapolis FBI office. He said agents don't know why the robber prefers in-store banks. "When we get him, then we'll know," he said.

In the most recent robbery, the man gave the teller a note, took the money and left the bank. He was last seen on Hwy. 96 in a gray and black Subaru.

He is described as white, in his late 20s, approximately 145 pounds, with blue eyes and sandy blond hair worn in a ponytail. He was wearing a red, white and black flannel shirt and a black baseball cap with a green brim.

Anyone with information about that robbery is asked to call the FBI at 376-3200, the Ramsey County Sheriff's Department or CrimeStoppers. A reward of up to $5,000 is being offered for information leading to a conviction.

**—James Walsh**

Source: *Star Tribune,* 2 April 1997. Reprinted by permission of the *Star Tribune,* Minneapolis-St. Paul.

Robbery is the felonious taking of another's property from his or her person or in his or her presence through force or intimidation. Robberies are classified as either residential, commercial, street or vehicle-driver robberies. One category of robbery is carjacking, the taking of a motor vehicle by force or threat of force. It may be investigated by the FBI.

A relatively new type of residential robber is the home invader. Home invaders are usually young Asian gang members who travel across the country robbing Asian families, especially Asian business owners. Bank robberies are jointly investigated by the FBI, state and local law enforcement personnel.

The elements of the crime of robbery are (1) the wrongful taking of personal property, (2) from the person or in the person's presence, (3) against the person's will by force or threat of force.

The rapidity of a robbery, its potential for violence and the taking of hostages and the usual lack of evidence at the scene pose special problems in robbery investigations. When responding to a robbery-in-progress call, proceed as rapidly as possible, but use extreme caution. Assume the robber is at the scene unless otherwise advised, and be prepared for gunfire. Look for and immobilize any getaway vehicle discovered. Avoid a hostage situation if possible, and make an immediate arrest if the situation warrants.

Prove each element of robbery separately. To prove that personal property was wrongfully taken, determine the legal owner of the property and describe the property and its value completely. To prove that it was taken from the person or in the person's presence, record the exact words, gestures, motions or actions the robber used to gain control of the property. To prove the removal was against the victim's will by force or threat of force, obtain a complete description of the robber's words, actions and any weapon used or threatened to be used.

Obtain information about the suspect's general appearance, clothing, any disguises, weapon(s) and vehicle(s) used. Important modus operandi information includes type of robbery, time (day and hour), method of attack (threatened or real), weapon, object sought, number of robbers, voice and words, vehicle used and any peculiarities. Physical evidence that can connect the suspect with the robbery includes fingerprints, shoe prints, tire prints, restraining devices used, discarded garments, fibers and hairs, a note and the stolen property.

# Checklist

### Robbery

■ Are maps and pictures on file of banks and other places in the community that handle large amounts of cash?

■ Are there plans for police response in the event these facilities are robbed?

■ Was the place that was robbed protected by an alarm? Was the alarm working?

■ Was the place that was robbed protected by a surveillance camera? Was the camera working? Was the film immediately removed and processed?

■ What procedure was used in responding to the call? Did the police enter directly? Did they wait until the robber had left the premises to avoid a hostage situation?

■ Were all persons in the place that was robbed interviewed separately, and were written statements obtained from each?

■ Are all elements of the crime of robbery present?

■ How was the robber dressed? Was a disguise used?

■ What were the exact words and actions of the robber?

■ What type of weapon or threat was used?

■ Was anybody injured or killed?

■ Was there a getaway car? Description? Direction of travel? A second person in the car?

■ Was a general description of persons and vehicles involved broadcast to other police agencies as soon as possible?

■ Was the scene secured and photographed?

■ What property was taken in the robbery? What was its value?

■ Who is the legal owner?

■ If a bank, were the FBI and state officials notified?

■ If the suspect was arrested, how was identification made?

■ If money or property was recovered, was it properly processed?

## Application*

Read the following account of an actual robbery investigation. As you read, list the steps taken by the investigators. Review the list and determine whether all necessary steps were taken.

On December 16, close to midnight, a woman looked in the window of the grocery store owned by Efimy Romanow at 187 Ashmun Street, New Haven, Connecticut, and saw Romanow lying behind the counter with the telephone receiver clutched in his right hand. Thinking Romanow was sick, the woman notified a neighbor, Thomas Kelly, who went to the store and then called an ambulance. Romanow was pronounced dead on arrival at the hospital.

Autopsy revealed he had been shot near the heart. The bullet was removed and turned over to detectives, who immediately began an investigation. Officers protected the crime scene and made a thorough search for possible prints and other evidence. They found a small amount of money in the cash register. At the hospital, $15.50 was found in Romanow's pockets, and $313 in bills was found in his right shoe. A thorough check of neighborhood homes was made without result. One report received was that two white men were seen leaving the store before Romanow's body was discovered.

About 1 A.M., December 17, Mrs. Marion Lang, who lived directly opposite the store but was not home when the officers first went there, was contacted. She stated that at about 11:10 P.M. she had heard loud talking in the street, including the remark, "Damn it, he is shot, let's get out of here." She did not look out the window, so she was unable to describe the persons she heard talking.

The investigation continued without any tangible clues until 9:25 P.M., December 17, when a phone call was received from George M. Proctor, owner of a drugstore on a street parallel to Ashmun Street and one block away. He had just overheard a woman talking in the telephone booth in his store say, "I will not stand for her taking my fellow away. I know who shot the storekeeper on Ashmun. It was Scotty and Almeda at 17 Dixwell." Mr. Proctor did not know the woman whom he had overheard.

Two detectives were assigned to this lead, and they began a search. A few hours later they learned that Scotty and Almeda were in a room at 55 Dixwell Avenue. Arriving with several uniformed officers, they entered and found Francis Scott and

---

*Adapted from a report by Captain Raymond J. Eagan, New Haven, Connecticut.

Henry Almeda in bed with their clothes on. Both had previous records and were well known to the local police. The detectives took the two men to headquarters for questioning and then returned to the room. Their search revealed five .32 caliber bullets at the top of a window casing where plaster had been broken up.

They also received information that Almeda and Scott had earlier visited Julia Redmond, who had a room in the same house. They asked Ms. Redmond if Almeda and Scott had left anything there. She responded, "They put something under the mattress." Turning over the mattress, the detectives found a .32 caliber Harrington and Richardson revolver, serial number 430-087. Ms. Redmond said, "That belongs to Almeda and Scott."

The detectives returned to headquarters and searched the stolen gun files. They discovered that this gun had been reported stolen in a burglary at the home of Geoffrey Harrell, 46 Webster Street, in November. Both suspects were questioned during the night and denied any part in the shooting.

The questioning resumed on the morning of December 18 at 9:00 A.M. At 3:45 P.M. that day, Almeda broke and made a confession in which he involved Scott. Almeda's statement was read to Scott with Almeda present. When Almeda identified the confession and stated it was true, Scott also admitted his part in the shooting.

When Almeda was shown the .32 caliber H & R revolver, he identified it as the gun used in shooting Romanow. He explained that they had to shoot Romanow because he refused to give up his money and placed himself between them and the door. In order to get out, he shot Romanow. Both stated that they had no car and that no one else was involved.

A preliminary examination of the bullet taken from Romanow's body did not satisfy the detectives that the bullet had been fired from the gun in their possession, even though it had been identified by both Almeda and Scott as the one used.

A detective took the gun and bullet to the FBI Technical Laboratory in Washington, D.C., where a ballistics comparison established that the gun furnished for examination was not the gun that fired the death bullet. A search of the Technical Laboratory files revealed that the gun matched a bullet furnished by the same department as evidence in a holdup of Levine's Liquor Store on December 1 of that year. One shot had been fired, striking a chair and deflecting into a pile of rubbish in the rear of the store. The bullet had been recovered by detectives after sifting through the rubbish.

When confronted with this information, Scott and Almeda admitted that they had committed this holdup and shooting while masked. They also admitted they had stolen an automobile to use that night and that they had burglarized Harrell's home in November when they took the gun.

The detectives conducted an extensive search for the gun used in killing Romanow. They cut a hole in the bottom of the flue leading from the room occupied by Almeda and Scott and even had the sewer department clean out fifteen sewer-catch basins in the area of the crime, but no weapon was discovered.

Both Almeda and Scott were indicted by the grand jury for first-degree murder. They were scheduled for trial February 13. The night before the trial was to begin, they told their lawyers that a third man had furnished the gun and driven the getaway car. In a conference with the state's attorney and detectives, the lawyers identified the third man as William Sutton. Within half an hour, Sutton was apprehended and brought to the state attorney's office where, in the presence of Scott and Almeda, their statements were read to Sutton. He admitted participating in the crime.

This new turn in the case also revealed that the gun used in the killing was loaned to Sutton by John Foy, who knew the gun was to be used in a holdup.

The morning after the shooting, Sutton brought the gun back to Foy and left it with him. A short time later Sutton returned and asked for the gun. He had decided he should get rid of it because it was hot. Sutton then took the cylinder from the gun while Foy broke the rest of it into small parts, which he threw in various places. Foy, who admitted that he knew the gun was to be used in a holdup, was charged with conspiracy.

Sutton, Almeda and Scott pled guilty to second-degree murder and received life sentences in the Connecticut State Prison. Foy received a one-year jail sentence.

1. List the steps the investigators followed in the investigation.
2. Were any necessary steps omitted?
3. What comparison evidence was helpful in the case?
4. How did law enforcement agencies cooperate?
5. What interrogation techniques were used?
6. How important was citizen information?

## Discussion Questions

1. In a robbery of a neighborhood grocery store, how important is citizen information? Should a neighborhood check be made if the incident occurred at 3 A.M.? How would you attempt to locate two witnesses who saw the robber enter the store if the owner does not know their names? How else could you develop information on the robber's description, vehicle and the like?

2. Imagine that you are a police officer responding to the scene of a bank robbery. Should you enter the bank immediately? Should you close the bank to business during the investigation? Can the drive-up window be used for business if it was not involved in the robbery? What should be done with the bank employees after the robbery? With customers in the bank at the time of the robbery? What agencies should work jointly on this type of crime?

3. How important is an immediate response in responding to a robbery call? What vehicles should respond to the scene? To the area surrounding the scene? What types of locations near the scene are most advantageous to apprehending the suspect?

4. If a robber takes a hostage inside a building being robbed, what are immediate considerations? If the hostage situation is not resolved in the first fifteen minutes, what must be considered? Should a police officer offer to take the place of the hostage? What might you say to the robber to induce him or her to release the hostage? To surrender after release of the hostage?

5. Why is a robbery in progress dangerous for the police? For the victim? What can the police do to reduce the potential danger while responding to the scene? To reduce the danger of the victim being taken hostage?

6. Which takes priority: taking the robber at all risks to remove him or her from the street and prevent future robberies, or ensuring the safety of the victim and any witnesses?

7. What other crimes often occur along with a robbery?

8. What types of establishments are most susceptible to robbery? What types of establishments are most often robbed in your community?

9. What measures can a police department take to prevent robbery? What preventive measures are taken by your department?

10. What measures can citizens take to help prevent robberies? How can the police assist citizens in these preventive measures?

"Anti-Car Theft Act of 1992." *Subject to Debate,* September/October 1992, p. 6.

Burke, Tod W. "Home Invaders: Gangs of the Future." *The Police Chief,* November 1990, pp. 23–24.

Burke, Tod W., and Charles E. O'Rear. "Armed Carjacking: A Violent Problem in Need of a Solution." *The Police Chief,* January 1993, pp. 18–24.

———. "Armed Carjacking: The Latest Nightmare." *Law and Order,* October 1992, pp. 165–168.

"Carjacking." *The Car Guide.* San Antonio, TX: USAA Foundation, 1993.

"Carjacking Correction Act." *Criminal Justice Newsletter,* Vol. 27, No. 21, November 1, 1996, p. 3.

"Carjacking Takes Hold in Washington, and the Feds Sit Up and Take Notice." *Law Enforcement News,* October 15, 1992, pp. 1, 7.

DiVasto, Peter V., and Stephanie L. Newman. "The Four Cs of Hostage Negotiation." *Law and Order,* May 1993, pp. 82–87.

Gates, Daryl F., and Norman N. Roberge. "Updated Solutions for Armored Car Robberies." *The Police Chief,* October 1991, pp. 141–143.

"Growing in Power and Viciousness, Vietnamese Gangs Flex Their Muscles." *Law Enforcement News,* May 15/31, 1991, pp. 3, 10.

Hurley, James T. "Violent Crime Hits Home: Home Invasion Robbery." *Law Enforcement Technology,* October 1995, pp. 112–114.

*Learning Objectives.* St. Paul, MN: Minnesota P.O.S.T. Board, 1991.

Morrison, Richard D. "Bank Roberry." *Law and Order,* October 1996, pp. 159–160.

Pearson, Cecil. "No Nonsense Negotiations." *Police,* April 1996, pp. 48–51.

Rand, Michael R. *Carjacking: Crime Data Brief.* Washington, DC: Bureau of Justice Statistics, March 1994.

———. *The Effects of Offender Weapon Use and Victim Self-Defense on Robbery Outcomes.* Washington, DC: Bureau of Justice Statistics, August 1995.

Strentz, Thomas. "The Cyclic Crisis Negotiations Time Line." *Law and Order,* March 1995, pp. 73–76.

———. "Hostage/Crisis Negotiation." *Law and Order,* June 1996, pp. 70–73.

Sullivan, Thomas. "Solving Crimes against Immigrants in Yonkers." *Problem Solving Quarterly,* Summer 1992, pp. 1–2, 9.

Yarbrough, Kenneth R., and Ted Meyer. "Investigating High-Tech Robbery and Theft." *The Police Chief,* July 1996, pp. 33–35.

# Chapter 9

# Assault

## DO YOU KNOW

How to define assault?

How assaults are classified?

How simple assault differs from aggravated assault?

When force is legal?

What the elements of the crime of simple assault are? Of aggravated (felonious) assault? Of attempted assault?

What special problems are posed in an assault investigation?

How to prove the elements of simple and aggravated assault?

What evidence is likely to be at the scene of an assault?

What offenses might be categorized as separate crimes rather than simply as assault?

## CAN YOU DEFINE

| | | |
|---|---|---|
| aggravated assault | felonious assault | simple assault |
| assault | in loco parentis | stalker |
| elder abuse | | |

**Introduction**

TWO PEOPLE HAVE A VIOLENT ARGUMENT AND HURL INSULTS AT EACH other. A bouncer physically ejects a belligerent drunk from a bar; an enforcer breaks all the fingers of a man who is past due on a gambling debt. An angry wife hurls a frying pan, striking her husband in the back. A teacher slaps a disrespectful student. A group of teenagers mug an old man. A jealous lover stabs a rival with a knife. Each of these preceding has one thing in common—each is an assault.

This chapter begins with a discussion of the classification of assault. This is followed by an explanation of the elements of the crime and special problems involved in investigating assaults. Next the chapter provides a discussion on the investigation and proving the elements of the crime. The chapter concludes with a close-up look at considerations in investigating domestic violence, stalking and elder abuse.

## Assault: An Overview

**Assault** is "an intentional, unlawful act of injury to another by force, or force directed toward another person, under circumstances that create fear of imminent peril, coupled with apparent state of ability to execute attempt, if not prevented. The intention to harm is of the essence. Mere words, although provoking or insulting, are not sufficient" (*Naler v. State*, 1933).

*Assault* is unlawfully threatening to harm another person, actually harming another person or attempting unsuccessfully to do so.

Assaults range from violent threats to brutal gangland beatings, from a shove to a stabbing. Many assaults arise from domestic conflicts, often during periods of heavy drinking by one or both parties. Some result from long-developing ill feelings that suddenly erupt into open violence. Some result from an argument such as a barroom dispute that ends in a brawl. They often are connected with robberies. In fact, 50 percent of all robberies include an assault of some form.

Formerly, in many states the term *assault* referred to threats of or attempts to cause bodily harm, whereas *battery* referred to the actual carrying out of such threats. Actual physical contact is not required for assault. The threat or fear of an assault along with ability to commit the act is sufficient.

In most revised state statutes, the term *assault* is synonymous with *battery*, or the two terms have been joined in a single crime termed *assault*. Some states, however, still have separate statutory offenses of assault and battery. Where one statute remains, battery includes the lesser crime of assault.

The 1995 *Uniform Crime Report* indicates 1,099,179 aggravated assaults, a 1.3 percent decline from 1994 figures of 1,113,179 offenses. Southern states were highest with 40 percent. Most aggravated assaults were committed in July and least in February; 22.9 percent were committed with firearms, 18.3 percent with cutting instruments, 32.9 percent with blunt objects and 25.9 percent with personal weapons such as fists or feet; 56 percent were cleared by arrest. Of the more than 437,000 arrested, whites comprised 60 percent and blacks 38 percent; 82 percent were males and 85 percent adults.

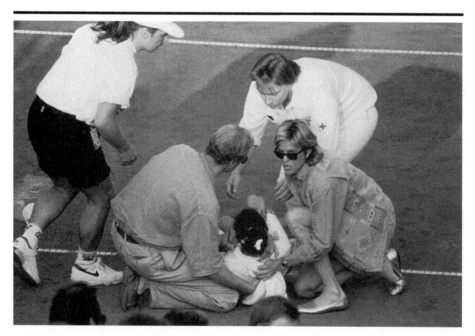

*Tennis star Monica Seles was stabbed during a tournament's qualification and was carried away on a stretcher. The assault interrupted her promising career.*

# Classification

Assaults are classified as either simple or aggravated (felonious).

---

**Simple assault** is intentionally causing another person to fear immediate bodily harm or death or intentionally inflicting or attempting to inflict bodily harm on the person. **Aggravated (felonious) assault** is an unlawful attack by one person on another to inflict severe bodily injury.

---

Simple assault is usually a misdemeanor. It does not involve a deadly weapon, and the injuries sustained, if any, are not severe or permanent. Aggravated assault, on the other hand, is a felony. Nationally, it is the most frequent of the crimes against the person. Aggravated or felonious assault is sometimes further classified as assault with a deadly weapon or as assault with intent to commit murder.

## Legal Force

Physical force may be used legally in certain instances.

---

In specified instances, teachers, persons operating public conveyances and law enforcement officers can legally use reasonable physical force.

---

Teachers have the authority of **in loco parentis** ("to take the place of the parent") in many states and are allowed to use minimum force to maintain discipline, to stop fights on school property or to prevent destruction of school property. Bus drivers, train conductors, airplane pilots and ship captains have authority to use force to stop misconduct by passengers. Law enforcement officers may use as much force as needed to overcome resistance to a lawful arrest. Force used in self-defense is also justifiable.

## Elements of the Crime

### Simple Assault

Most state statutes have common elements.

---

The elements of the crime of simple assault are:
- Intent to do bodily harm to another.
- Present ability to commit the act.
- Commission of an overt act toward carrying out the intention.

---

**Intent to Do Bodily Harm to Another.**   Evidence of specific *intent* to commit bodily injury must be present. Injury caused accidentally is not assault. The suspect's words and actions or any injuries inflicted on the victim imply this intent. The injury must be to another person; injury to property or self-inflicted injury, no matter how serious, is not assault.

The bodily harm or injury in simple assault need not cause severe physical pain or disability. The degree of force necessary in simple assault ranges from a shove or a slap to slightly less than that required for the great bodily harm that distinguishes aggravated assault.

**Present Ability to Commit the Act.** The suspect must have been physically able to commit the act at the time. A suspect who hurled a knife at a victim who was obviously out of range would not have had the ability to hit his or her target.

**Commission of an Overt Act.** An overt act, more than a threat or gesture, must have been completed. If the suspect was in range to strike the victim, even if someone intervened, an assault can be proven. Intentionally pushing, shoving or physically preventing someone from entering or leaving property is often determined to be simple assault.

## Aggravated Assault

Aggravated assault includes the three elements of simple assault plus an element relating to the severity of the attack. Aggravated assault is usually committed with a weapon or by some means likely to produce great bodily harm or death.

---

An additional element in the crime of aggravated assault is that the intentionally inflicted bodily injury must have resulted in:
- A high probability of death.
- Serious, permanent disfigurement.
- Or permanent or protracted loss or impairment of the function of any body member or organ or other severe bodily harm.

---

As with simple assault, the act must be intentional, not accidental.

**High Probability of Death.** An assault is considered aggravated if it is committed by any means so severe that a reasonable person feels it would result in a high probability of death. Examples include a blow sufficient to cause unconsciousness or coma, a gunshot or knife wound causing heavy bleeding or burns inflicted over most of a person's body.

**Serious, Permanent Disfigurement.** Permanent disfigurement includes such things as losing an ear, eye or part of the nose or permanent scarring of the face or other parts of the body that are normally visible. It cannot be a temporary injury that will subsequently heal and not be evident.

**Loss or Impairment of Body Members or Organs.** Regardless of the part of the body affected, a charge of aggravated assault is supported by the loss or permanent impairment of body members or organs, or maiming. "Maiming signifies to cripple or mutilate in any way which deprives of the use of any limb or member of the body, to seriously wound or disfigure or disable" (*Schackelford v. Commonwealth,* 1945).

Only one of these additional elements is needed to show aggravated assault, although two or all three are sometimes present. Some states do not require permanent or protracted injury or loss if the weapon used in the assault is a dangerous weapon that causes fear of immediate harm or death.

### Attempted Assault

Attempted aggravated assault is also a crime in many states. If the suspect intended to assault someone but was prevented from doing so for some reason, it is still a punishable offense categorized as "unlawful attempt to commit assault."

---

Attempted assault requires proof of intent along with some overt act toward committing the crime.

---

Intent or preparation is not enough to prove attempted assault. For example, a suspect must have done more than obtain a weapon or make a plan or even arrange to go to the scene. Rather, the suspect must actually have gone there and have had the weapon in possession when the effort was aborted.

A person who intends to rob a grocery store and whose gun accidentally discharges while she is in the store has indeed committed an overt act. However, if the gun discharges while she is driving to the store, there is no overt act to support an attempted assault charge. Likewise, if a potential rapist approaches a woman and has raised his arm to strike her when he is apprehended, an overt act toward an assault has been committed. But if the man is apprehended while still lurking behind a bush, there is reasonable doubt.

## Special Problems in Investigation

---

Special problems in assault investigations include distinguishing the victim from the suspect, determining if the matter is civil or criminal and determining if the act was intentional or accidental. Obtaining a complaint against a simple assault also is sometimes difficult. Moreover, such calls may be dangerous for responding officers.

---

Sometimes it is difficult to know who started a fight. Both parties may claim the other person struck the first blow. In such cases, both may be charged with disturbing the peace until more information is obtained.

Also it is necessary to determine whether the altercation is a civil or a criminal matter. A person who accidently injures someone is not guilty of a criminal offense but may be sued in a civil court by the victim.

It is sometimes difficult, especially in cases of wife and child beating, to obtain a complaint from the victim. If it is simple assault, a misdemeanor, you must see the offense committed or obtain a complaint and arrest warrant or have the victim make a citizen's arrest.

Patrol officers usually make the first contact with the complainant or assault victim. Police on regular patrol sometimes observe an assault occurring. Usually, however, they are sent to the assault scene by the dispatcher. Assault calls are potentially dangerous for the police. In fact, according to the FBI's *Uniform Crime Reports*, more police officers are injured and killed in response to domestic and assault calls than in response to robbery and burglary complaints.

You may arrive at the point of most heated emotions and end up in the middle of a situation that stems from a deep-rooted problem entirely unknown to you. Your first act is to stop any assaultive action by separating or arresting the people involved. This reduces the possibility of further conflict.

Be on your guard, and do not take sides in any dispute. If people are injured, administer first aid or summon emergency personnel to the scene. Determine whether more help is needed and if a description of the suspect must be broadcast.

In most assault cases, arriving police officers find the assault has been completed. However, verbal abuse and considerable confusion may exist. The victim is normally conscious and, even if severely injured, can provide information about the assailant. Interview the victim as soon as possible to obtain details about the injury, the degree of pain, medical assistance rendered and other facts related to the severity of the attack. The extent and nature of the injury determines the degree of assault to be charged. Further facts supporting the severity of the attack are obtained by noting what treatment the victim requires and by talking to medical personnel.

The victim frequently knows who committed the assault, either by name or by an association that can be checked. Determine the reason for the assault. Find out what actions the victim and assailant took before, during and after the assault. If the victim of an aggravated assault is severely injured and indicates by words, gestures or appearance that death is possible soon, obtain a dying declaration.

If the suspect is at the scene, make an arrest if the situation warrants, or have the victim make a citizen's arrest. If the suspect is known but is not at the scene, broadcast the suspect's description and begin your investigation.

## The Preliminary Investigation

At minimum, an officer arriving on the scene of an assault should:

- Control and disarm those involved in the altercation.
- Provide medical aid to either suspects or victims.
- Separate suspects.
- Protect the crime scene.
- Give the Miranda warning if applicable.
- Obtain preliminary statements.
- Photograph evidence.
- Collect and preserve evidence.
- Reconstruct the crime.

## Proving the Elements of Assault

An assault that involves no dangerous weapon and results in no serious injury is a relatively minor crime. In contrast, aggravated assault is an extremely serious crime.

---

To prove the elements of assault, establish the intent to cause injury, the severity of the injury inflicted and if a dangerous weapon was used.

---

Intent can be established by determining what events led up to the assault. Record the suspect's exact words and actions and take statements from the victim and any witnesses.

Establish the severity of the assault by taking photographs and describing all injuries in your notes. Describe the size, location, number, color, depth and amount of bleeding of any injuries. Some bruises do not become visible for several hours or even a day or two. Assault victims should be advised of this and told that additional photographs should be taken. Obtain an oral or written statement from a qualified medical person as to the severity and permanence of the injuries and any impairment of bodily functioning.

Determine the means of attack and the exact weapon used. Was it hands, fists, feet, a gun or a knife?

### Evidence in Assault Investigations

Corroborate the victim's information with physical evidence.

---

Physical evidence in an assault includes photographs of injuries, clothing of the victim or suspect, weapons, broken objects, bloodstains, hairs, fibers and other signs of an altercation.

---

Two important pieces of evidence are photographs of injuries and the weapon used in the assault. If the hands, fists or feet were used, examine them for cuts and bruises, and photograph any injuries. Obtain fingernail scrapings from both the victim and the suspect.

Take as evidence any weapons found at the scene. The victim's clothing may contain evidence such as bullet holes or tears made by a knife or other cutting instrument. If you suspect alcohol or drug use may have contributed to the assault, arrange for the appropriate urine, blood and saliva tests. Photograph and make notes regarding evidence that indicates the intensity of the assault; for example, overturned furniture, broken objects, torn up sod and bent shrubs.

*In 1996, the LAPD released a new tool that they hope will finally break the cycle of domestic abuse: a top-of-the-line Polaroid camera for immediate documentation of spousal attacks. Four hundred patrol units will be equipped with the new cameras. Officers will be trained to take high quality photographs that will stand up in court.*

Reflective ultraviolet photography can reveal injuries not visible to the naked eye. Aaron (1991, p. 34) contends: "A little-known photographic technique exists which in many cases allows investigators to document injuries on flesh up to nine months after they have visibly healed." Reflective ultraviolet photography can reveal pattern injuries—that is, injuries that have a recognizable shape—including cigarette burns, whip or belt marks, bruising, contusions, abrasions, injury margins from immersion burns, bite marks, scratches and almost any skin injury imaginable (Aaron, p. 34).

## Considerations in Investigating Domestic Violence

Domestic violence is one of the most frequent crimes in the United States and one of the most underreported. Many women do not report domestic assaults because of a threat such as "I'll take the kids and you'll never see them again," or "I'll kill you if you call the police." In many instances the wife fails to report the abuse (and to leave the relationship) because she has no work skills and no independent income, because of the stigma and embarrassment associated with the offense or because she has one or more children to support.

It is estimated that six million women and men are battered by their spouses each year. One out of six murders are domestic crimes, most of them being the murder of a spouse or lover. Four out of five murders by females are reported to be responses to present or continuing domestic violence.

Sanow (1995, p. 64) states: "More than four million women are battered by their partners each year, and approximately one million of these seek medical assistance for their injuries."

Also, Hinds (1993, p. 86) states: "Statistics show that in the United States, a woman is battered by a husband or partner every 15 seconds. . . . Police estimate that 40 to 60 percent of their calls are in some way related to domestic violence."

On a more conservative note, Holmes (1993, p. 101) says: "Some reports have stated that as much as 20 percent of all calls are related to domestic violence."

According to Jarret (1996, p. 16), abuse generally occurs in a three-stage cycle:

- Tension building.
- The acute battering episode.
- The honeymoon.

Jarret believes that this cycle typically increases both in frequency and severity.

The importance of dealing with domestic violence effectively cannot be underestimated. Domestic violence is a vicious cycle (Paisner, 1991, p. 35):

> Violence is learned behavior. Children who have witnessed abuse or have been abused themselves are 1,000 times more likely to abuse a spouse or child when they become adults than are children raised in a home without violence.

Litaker (1996, p. 87) explains the historic acceptance of wife beating:

> Historically, English common law gave husbands the right to chastise their wives. There once existed a "rule of thumb" which held that a husband had the right to beat his wife with a stick, but the stick must not be any thicker than his thumb.

Although wife beating is not accepted in the twentieth century, the law-enforcement approach to it has varied with time. Breci and Murphy (1992, p. 53) describe these differences:

> Prior to the middle 1970s, police response was characterized by officers' non-involvement in family affairs. . . . During the 1980s, many police departments implemented mandatory or presumptive arrest procedures in response to the criticism [of noninvolvement]. Recent research, however, questions the claims made by mandatory arrest advocates.

Domestic violence is found at all income levels and in all races, and it may or may not involve alcohol or drugs. The crime occurs with heterosexual and homosexual partners and with married, divorced, separated and living-together couples. It can be male or female aggression, although most instances of heterosexual domestic violence involve male suspects. The offense may be a misdemeanor, a gross misdemeanor or a felony, depending on the severity of the assault.

Characteristics of women violently victimized by intimates include the following (*Violence Between Intimates*, 1994, p. 2):

- White and black women had equivalent rates.
- Hispanic and non-Hispanic females had about the same rates.
- Women age 20 to 34 had the highest rates.
- Women who graduated from college had the lowest rates.
- Women with family incomes under $9,999 had the highest rates.
- Divorced or separated women had higher rates.
- Women living in central cities, suburban areas and rural locations experienced similar rates.

Bachman and Saltzman (1995, p. 1) report similar findings:

- Women of all races and Hispanic and non-Hispanic women were about equally vulnerable to violence by an intimate.
- Women age 19–29 and women in families with incomes below $10,000 were more likely than other women to be victims of violence by an intimate.

They also report that women were about six times more likely than men to experience violence committed by an intimate.

Responding to domestic violence calls is one of the most disagreeable duties of police officers. In some instances, officers who are not trained for this type of duty may have preconceptions or prejudices that it is a "family matter." Additionally, domestic assault calls are dangerous for the police. Connor (1990, p. 66) notes: "In reference to frequency and intensity of actual as well as perceived danger to the police, no other call qualifies to the degree as that of a domestic complaint."

Russo (1995, p. 47) agrees: "Domestic violence incidents are among the most difficult calls an officer can respond to."

According to Jackson (1996, p. 33): "The highly emotional atmosphere accompanying domestic abuse situations, the raw violence often displayed, the family lives destroyed and the victim's frequent hesitancy to prosecute or seek shelter all place a heavy burden on the officers sent to these disturbances."

Garner (1994, p. 32) provides some insight into the danger presented by disturbance calls, noting that domestic disturbances have long been a major cause of on-duty police deaths, accounting for approximately 17 percent. Forty percent were killed making arrests or answering crimes in progress calls. Fourteen percent were killed answering suspicious persons calls. Indeed, the statistics support what has long been known: disturbance calls are potentially high-risk police responses.

Garner also explains that examining domestic calls reveals that most officers were killed when they failed to wait until a second officer arrived, failed to watch the suspect's hands, acted under false or dangerous assumptions, failed to practice good weapons retention, had a poor approach or were generally apathetic and careless.

Russo (1995, p. 46) contends:

> One of the reasons officers get a lot of flack about ignoring domestic violence incidents is they often receive several calls a week which do not directly come from the parties involved. Anyone can call the police about a disturbance for example, and what often happens is a neighbor has called regarding the couple across the hall who might be shouting at each other, or one party can create a false situation or even lie about a domestic violence incident just to see the other party punished or the threat of punishment inflicted. Sometimes neither party wanted the police there and when the officer arrives, the couple is either embarrassed or angry because this is their way of arguing.

### Domestic Violence as a Crime

According to Bourn (1996, p. 36): "Domestic violence is a silent epidemic, often leaving its victims fearful, voiceless and uncooperative. To increase the likelihood of a conviction, police should treat the call and investigation as they would a homicide." Indeed, as noted by Holder (1996, p. 54): "Domestic violence is a serious social problem that is said to be at the root of all other social ills. It is also a criminal problem—a crime that can be prevented."

Domestic violence should be investigated as the crime that it is. O'Dell (1996, p. 21) stresses:

> The research in this area is conclusive. In every community across the country where domestic violence is viewed as the crime that it is and steps are taken to change the criminal justice system, lives are saved.

She gives as an example San Diego, California, where in two years the domestic violence homicide rate was reduced by 59 percent.

Martin (1994, p. 38) concurs: "If the police treat domestic violence as a serious criminal offense, then the community will also perceive it as serious."

---

Domestic assault may be categorized as a specific crime.

---

As has been documented time and time again, many batterers eventually kill their intimate. Quinn (1996, p. 59) cites the following indicators, provided by the San Diego Police Department's Domestic Violence Unit, for assessing a batterer's potential to kill:

- Threats of homicide or suicide.
- Fantasies of homicide or suicide.
- Depression.
- Weapons.
- Obsessiveness about partner or family.
- Centrality of battered woman.
- Rage.
- Drug or alcohol consumption.
- Pet abuse.

In some instances, the batterer becomes the victim of homicide. In such cases the defense often relies on attributing the murder to the "battered-woman syndrome." This syndrome is based on the concept of duress and results from a cycle of violence. Wallace (1994, p. 82) says of duress: "Duress is composed of three basic components: lack of fault, proportionality and necessity. Each must be present to perfect a valid defense of duress." Wallace suggests that battered women's claims of duress affect both prosecution and sentencing.

Several departments throughout the country have adopted a "zero tolerance" approach to domestic violence, including the Tampa Police Department (Holder, 1996, p. 35) and the Hillsborough County Sheriff's Office, Tampa, Florida (Henderson and Reder, 1996, p. 54). This approach appears to be highly successful.

**Legislation.**    Jarret (1996, p. 16) notes: "In response to public pressure, state legislatures across the United States have enacted legislation that makes domestic violence investigations and prosecutions a law enforcement priority." He concludes (1996, p. 19): "The current state of affairs in domestic violence policy is emotionally charged, politically sensitive and highly visible."

Many departments across the country have a mandatory arrest policy. In fact, some states have legislated that police have and implement such a policy. This was due in large part to the "Minneapolis Experiment" conducted by Sherman and Berk in early 1981 to mid-1982 that concluded that arrest was a more effective deterrent to repeat offenses than advising or sending the suspect away. See Figure 9–1. This report, sometimes summarized as "arrest works best," had a "significant impact in helping to turn the tide toward a nationwide pro-arrest sentiment regarding domestic violence." (Gartin, 1995, p. 93). However, since that time Sherman and others have stated that alternatives to arrest might be better in specific circumstances.

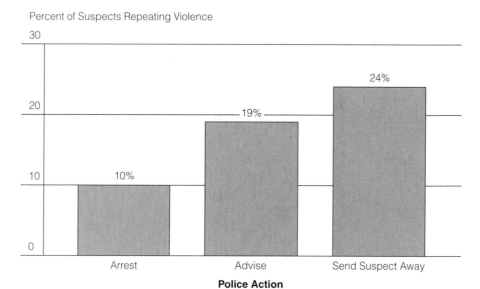

**Figure 9–1    Percentage of Repeat Violence Over Six Months For Each Police Action**

Source: Lawrence W. Sherman and Richard A. Berk. *The Minneapolis Domestic Violence Experiment.* Washington, DC: Police Foundation, April 1984. Reprinted by permission of the Police Foundation.

## A Model Pro-Arrest Policy

The following model pro-arrest policy, developed by Greg Connor (1990, p. 67, reprinted by permission), provides guidelines for investigating domestic violence and assaults:

### Communication Networking

In most cases the police dispatcher is the first line of action in reference to a domestic violence situation. This person must recognize the priority nature of this contact and remain a positive focus for facilitating the safe and effective police response.

Communication personnel must be trained in trauma assessment and interpretation skills to process calls for service involving domestic violence as efficiently as possible. Police unit(s) will be immediately dispatched as appropriate with a two-officer response as a minimum. Communication personnel will gather necessary response information including:

1. Exact location of the incident (street, house number, apartment number, etc.).
2. The nature of the contact and its emergency status.
3. Complainant's identity and involvement.
4. Victim's(s) injury and involvement and need for emergency equipment.
5. Perpetrator identity and immediate location.
6. Weapon description and presence.
7. Perpetrator probable location or route of escape if not present at the scene.
8. Other participants at the scene subject to risk (children, witnesses, etc.).
9. Nature of the perpetrator (mentally unstable, intoxicated, etc.).
10. Is a current Order of Protection in effect?
11. Previous contact with police and resolution.

### Responding Officer Strategies

1. Develop a plan en route to the scene. Past action at the location may not be the predictor of present problem.
2. Respond to the location in a safe and expeditious manner.
3. Approach and deploy in a tactical manner maximizing officer and victim safety.
4. Assess risks on arrival, requesting support units if needed:
   A. Assess risks to officer and others. If the officer believes occupant(s) is in imminent danger, is suffering from bodily harm or is in need of medical assistance, forced entry is permitted if consistent with officer safety;
   B. If entry is refused but no immediacy is felt to force entry, a supervisor should be summoned to the scene to initiate possible negotiation procedures;
   C. If entry is permitted, officers must reassess risks of entry and do so only if tactically feasible. Survey the scene; sense the environment.

### Initial Contact

1. Attempt to control involved subjects, using crisis intervention techniques.
2. Separate perpetrator and victim if tactically feasible.
3. Facilitate necessary medical assistance to injured parties.
4. Attempt to gain control of the situation. Center on facts rather than assumptions.
5. Display empathic energy to reinforce the calming effect of the intervention as well as the serious nature of the situation.
6. Conduct selective and separate preliminary interviews with involved parties and witnesses.
7. Survey the scene for supportive information to develop probable cause for arrest.

8. When probable cause for an arrest exists and tactical advantage is maximized, arrest subject and facilitate transport.
9. If perpetrator has left the scene and probable cause exists to make an arrest, check likely locations where the subject may be.

### Supplemental Contact

1. Once scene has been secured and perpetrator removed, conduct intensive interviews with victim and other witnesses. Focus upon supportive information of evidentiary value including the frequency of violence, intensity of the assaultive action, previous police contacts, etc.
2. Develop a crime scene sketch of the incident to support spatial features relevant to the crime.
3. Photograph the crime scene including broken objects, damage to fixed objects, displaced items, etc.
4. If appropriate, photograph injuries to victim if visible on the body. Personal injuries to areas of the body requiring disrobing should be done in a clinical setting.
5. Collect and record items of evidence present at the scene: possible weapons, ripped clothing, damaged property, etc.
6. Provide victim with appropriate information and assistance prior to contact closure:
   A. Transport to medical facility or shelter if present residence is unsafe;
   B. Present a verbal overview of the judicial procedures to be expected relative to the incident. This overview should be done to aid in preparing the person for judicial events rather than to create fear or paranoia about the future;
   C. Provide the victim with a written summary of procedures involved with assistance alternatives recognized as rights under domestic violence statutes;
   D. Actively and supportively refer the victim to appropriate social service agencies for follow-up counseling and assistance.

### Investigative Contact

1. Investigators shall conduct a follow-up or supportive investigation relative to the seriousness and frequency of the offense.
2. If follow-up contact is necessary, it should be made as soon as possible after the incident within a maximum of 24 hours.
3. Maintain contact with victim during interim period of court appearances.
4. Advise officers involved of concluding disposition of case.

## The Initial Response

Salafia and Irons (1995, p. 61) note: "The time from when the call comes in to the time officers arrive is the dispatcher's responsibility. They can make or break an investigation, save hours of leg work, explore the scene with the victim, the frame of mind of the caller and the potential attacker." From that point on, however, it is the officer's response which is critical.

Pentelei-Molnar (1996, p. 32) reported:

The most important ingredient to an effective domestic violence policy is properly addressing the initial response and procedure of the responding officer. What you do as the primary officer will often determine what happens in court—whether an effective arrest will be conducted and whether or not proper evidence will be collected. . . .

When responding to a domestic violence call, remember that the situation can involve many other crimes as well. It could involve simple battery, assault, kidnapping, trespassing, murder, stalking, terrorist threats, spousal rape and many others. The key is to never assume that the people you're going to encounter are merely involved in the types of squabbles that mom and dad used to get in over the television remote. . . .

Upon arrival, don't park your patrol car within view of the location you are responding to. This may allow the suspect to see you, become even more enraged at the thought of going to jail, inflict more injury on the victim or have time to gather weapons to assault you with.

Pentelei-Molnar (1996, p. 34) also suggests how to proceed when you arrive on the scene:

> The first rule, of course, is to interview the suspect and victim separately. When initially contacting a suspect, do not immediately Mirandize him or her. At this point, until you have determined both the nature of the crime and relationship between the suspect and victim, the suspect is not under arrest for domestic violence. They are simply under detention for investigation, since you have reasonable suspicion to detain them.
>    This is critical because many domestic violence suspects, based on their agitated emotional state, will make admissible, spontaneous statements that can be used against them later in court. Let them make all the spontaneous statements they want.

Police officers must listen to the facts and determine who is the offender if the assault is not continuing when they arrive. Officers need to reduce the level of tension at the scene by separating and talking to the participants. Officers must consider the safety of the participants and any children present.

Basically, any evidence that would lead an officer to make an arrest in any other situation also applies to spousal situations. Most states permit an arrest on probable cause. A number of states make it mandatory for the officer to make an arrest, even without a signed complaint by the victim, if there is probable cause. According to Connor (1990, p. 66):

> Research indicates that an arrest tends to prevent further criminal behavior, reduces risks to officers as a result of incident reduction, reduces risks to the victim, encourages and supports the victim's perception of rights, initiates an increased opportunity for long-term therapeutic treatment for those involved, and positions the officer in less likelihood of future civil litigation.

In Nevada, for example, if the police have sufficient reason to believe that a person, within the preceding four hours, committed an act of domestic violence or spousal battery, the officer is required to arrest that person, absent mitigating circumstances. Officers must *not* base their decisions regarding arrest on their perception of the willingness of the victim or witnesses to testify. The victim need not sign a complaint. If the battery was a mutual battery committed by both people involved, officers must try to determine who was the primary physical aggressor and then arrest that person. Factors to consider in making this determination include:

- Prior domestic violence involving either person.
- The relative seriousness of the injuries inflicted upon each person involved.
- The potential for future injury.
- Whether one of the alleged batteries was committed in self-defense.
- Any other factor that helps the officer decide which person was the primary physical aggressor.

Obtain all evidence, which may include photographs of injuries, victim's statements, prior police reports, doctor or hospital reports, weapons used, damaged clothing or other property and statements from neighbors or other witnesses. Explain to the victim that an order of protection may be obtained from a court to help prevent future assaults.

Bourn (1996, pp. 37–38) suggests that department policies and protocols address the following:

- Medical attention. Have victim sign a release for medical records.
- Victim's statements. Also include the victim's demeanor.
- Degree of pain.
- Victim's written statement.
- Defendant's statements.
- Photographs.
- Follow-up investigation. Check back a few days later because bruises do not typically appear until a day or two after an assault.

Pentelei-Molnar (1996, p. 35) stresses the importance of the report regarding the incident:

> As with any crime report, the better your report, the better chance you have of obtaining a conviction in court. When writing your report, remain objective in the documentation of the crime. . . .
>
> Be sure to include all elements of the crime, the relationship and background of the suspect and victim—and whether or not the victim was advised of a private person's arrest during evaluation. Of course, describe in detail the origin of the call, the investigation and any evidence and drawing you may want to provide of the scene. . . .
>
> Also, be sure to accurately label and describe each photograph that you've taken of injuries and the victim's physical condition. Some departments have a supplement report form to document evidence in domestic violence cases [see Figure 9–2].

*Police responded to a woman's call for help as she cried that her husband had gone berserk because dinner was not ready when he got home from work. They held the husband in another room so she could talk freely. He denied everything and said she would be afraid to press charges. Police left without making an arrest, and as they did so, the woman whispered to them "Remember you were here. The next time, I will be dead."*

PAGE ___ OF ___

SAN DIEGO POLICE DEPARTMENT DOMESTIC VIOLENCE SUPPLEMENTAL 137000 P.C.

VICTIM'S NAME (L, M, F) DATE OF BIRTH SDPD CASE NUMBER

ORIGIN/CRIME DESCRIPTION

I responded to a call of at (SDPD Dispatch Center # )

I found the victim The victim displayed the following emotional and physical conditions:

VICTIM — DESCRIBE ALL CONDITIONS OBSERVED; PHYSICAL, EMOTIONAL AND CRIME SCENE

☐ ANGRY ☐ APOLOGETIC ☐ CRYING ☐ FEARFUL ☐ HYSTERICAL ☐ CALM ☐ AFRAID ☐ IRRATIONAL ☐ NERVOUS ☐ THREATENING ☐ OTHER: EXPLAIN

☐ COMP. OF PAIN ☐ BRUISE (S) ☐ ABRASION (S) ☐ MINOR CUT (S) ☐ LACERATION (S) ☐ FRACTURE (S) ☐ CONCUSSION (S) ☐ OTHER: EXPLAIN

ALWAYS explain OPPOSITES in narrative.

SUSPECT

☐ ANGRY ☐ APOLOGETIC ☐ CRYING ☐ FEARFUL ☐ HYSTERICAL ☐ CALM ☐ AFRAID ☐ IRRATIONAL ☐ NERVOUS ☐ THREATENING ☐ OTHER: EXPLAIN

☐ COMP. OF PAIN ☐ BRUISE (S) ☐ ABRASION (S) ☐ MINOR CUT (S) ☐ LACERATION (S) ☐ FRACTURE (S) ☐ CONCUSSION (S) ☐ OTHER: EXPLAIN

ALWAYS explain OPPOSITES in narrative.

RELATIONSHIP BETWEEN VICTIM AND SUSPECT
MARK ALL THAT APPLY

☐ SPOUSE ☐ FORMER SPOUSE ☐ COHABITANTS ☐ FORMER COHABITANTS ☐ DATING/ENGAGED ☐ FORMER DATING ☐ SAME SEX ☐ EMANCIPATED MINOR ☐ PARENT OF CHILD FROM RELATIONSHIP

LENGTH OF RELATIONSHIP

___ YEAR(s) ___ MONTH(s)

IF APPLICABLE, DATE RELATIONSHIP ENDED: ________

PRIOR HISTORY OF DOMESTIC VIOLENCE? ☐ YES ☐ NO
PRIOR HISTORY OF VIOLENCE DOCUMENTED? ☐ YES ☐ NO
NUMBER OF PRIOR INCIDENTS ☐ ☐ MINOR ☐ SERIOUS
CASE NUMBER(S) ________
INVESTIGATING AGENCY ________

MEDICAL TREATMENT

☐ NONE ☐ WILL SEEK OWN DOCTOR ☐ FIRST AID ☐ PARAMEDICS ☐ HOSPITAL ☐ REFUSED MEDICAL AID

PARAMEDICS AT SCENE ☐ YES ☐ NO
UNIT NUMBER: ________
NAME(S) ID#:

HOSPITAL: ________
ATTENDING PHYSICIAN(S):

EVIDENCE

EVIDENCE COLLECTED — DESCRIBE ALL EVIDENCE AND DISPOSITION

FROM: ☐ Crime Scene ☐ Hospital ☐ Other; Explain
PHOTOS: ☐ Yes ☐ No Number ________
TYPE: ☐ 35mm ☐ Polaroid

TAKEN BY: ________

*DESCRIBE ALL PHOTOGRAPHS*

Photos of victim's injuries: ☐ Yes ☐ No
Photos of suspect's injuries: ☐ Yes ☐ No
Weapon used during incident: ☐ Yes ☐ No

Type of weapon used: ________
Weapon impounded: ☐ Yes ☐ No
Firearm(s) impounded for safety: ☐ Yes ☐ No

PROPERTY TAG NUMBER: ________ ☐ CONTINUED

REPORTING OFFICER | ID NUMBER | DIV. WATCH | DATE & TIME | APPROVED BY: NAME & ID

PD-965-FDS (Rev. 10/94) *This information is available in alternate formats upon request.*

**Figure 9–2a Sample Report Form to Document Evidence in Domestic Violence Cases, front**

Source: Kathryn Bourn. "Battles on the Homefront." *Police Magazine,* March 1996, p. 62. Reprinted by permission of Bobit Publishing, Redondo Beach, CA.

## When the Abuser Is a Police Officer

When the abuser is a police officer, special challenges may exist. According to Clark (1995, p. 1): "Domestic violence victims believe that no one will help them. When the abuser is a person with authority and the people from whom the victims are seeking help are the abuser's colleagues, that makes it much more difficult."

In addition, as Bonderman (1995, p. 1) notes: "Police officers under restraining orders for domestic violence are exempted from a federal ban on such abusers owning guns. . . . In a number of cases, abusive police officers have used their service weapons to injure or kill their spouses."

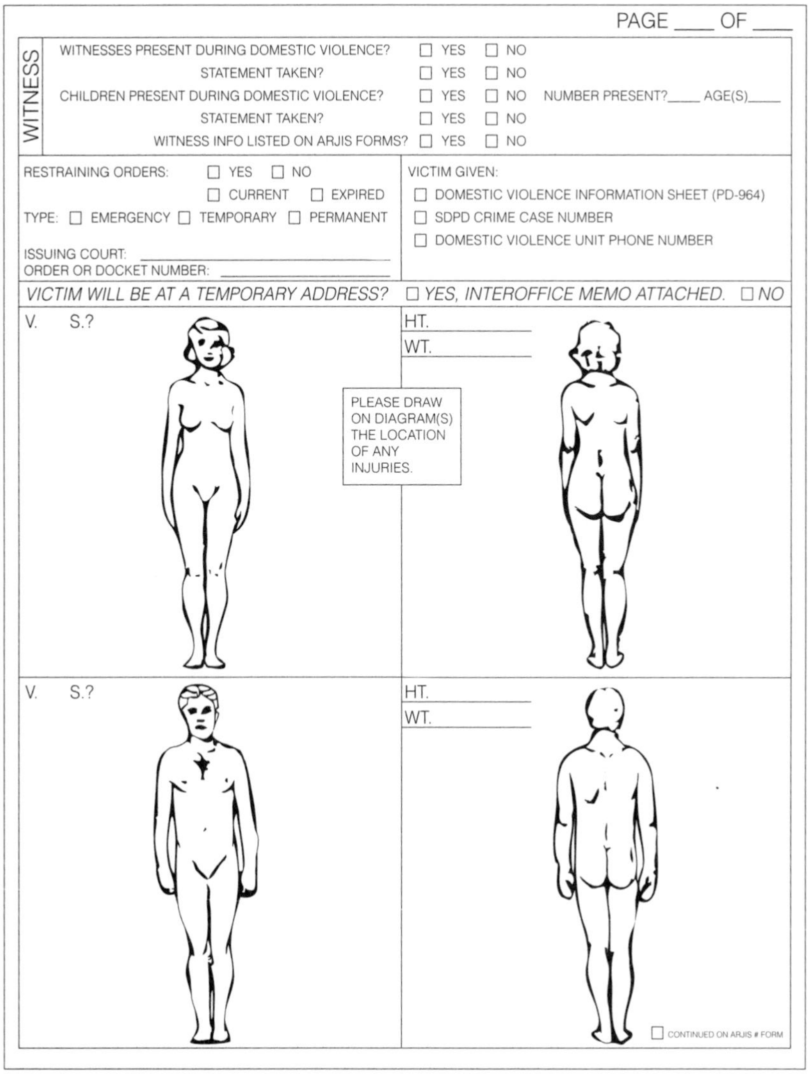

PAGE ____ OF ____

WITNESS

WITNESSES PRESENT DURING DOMESTIC VIOLENCE? ☐ YES ☐ NO
STATEMENT TAKEN? ☐ YES ☐ NO
CHILDREN PRESENT DURING DOMESTIC VIOLENCE? ☐ YES ☐ NO NUMBER PRESENT?____ AGE(S)____
STATEMENT TAKEN? ☐ YES ☐ NO
WITNESS INFO LISTED ON ARJIS FORMS? ☐ YES ☐ NO

RESTRAINING ORDERS: ☐ YES ☐ NO
☐ CURRENT ☐ EXPIRED
TYPE: ☐ EMERGENCY ☐ TEMPORARY ☐ PERMANENT
ISSUING COURT: ____________
ORDER OR DOCKET NUMBER: ____________

VICTIM GIVEN:
☐ DOMESTIC VIOLENCE INFORMATION SHEET (PD-964)
☐ SDPD CRIME CASE NUMBER
☐ DOMESTIC VIOLENCE UNIT PHONE NUMBER

*VICTIM WILL BE AT A TEMPORARY ADDRESS?* ☐ *YES, INTEROFFICE MEMO ATTACHED.* ☐ *NO*

V. S.?

HT. ________
WT. ________

PLEASE DRAW ON DIAGRAM(S) THE LOCATION OF ANY INJURIES.

V. S.?

HT. ________
WT. ________

☐ CONTINUED ON ARJIS # FORM

**Figure 9–2b Sample Report Form to Document Evidence in Domestic Violence Cases, back**

Source: Kathryn Bourn "Battles of the Homefront." *Police Magazine*, March 1996, p.62. Reprinted by permission of Bobit Publishing, Redondo Beach, CA.

Feltgen (1996, p. 42) describes this problem as follows:

> When officers were dispatched to suspected calls of domestic violence involving one of their co-workers, any policy or law regarding the enforcement of domestic violence procedures was quickly abandoned. Responding officers would often speak only briefly with the "off-duty officer" and, predictably, dismiss the call without any further investigation, written report or—most importantly—a check on the spouse's welfare and safety.
>
> In case after case, victims of domestic violence at the hands of a police officer had made emergency requests for law enforcement intervention, only to have their calls fall on deaf ears. . . .
>
> Abused spouses of police officers become even more traumatized by a system assumed to protect "all" victims of domestic violence as they become tragically lost in a system that fails even to record them as statistics.

## Cooperative Efforts to Deal with Domestic Violence

As noted by Martin (1994, p. 39): "Law enforcement alone cannot shoulder the burden of fighting domestic violence. To this end, many police departments now work in tandem with social service agencies to serve both victims and abusers." Hamilton (1996, p. 32), likewise, says that police departments need "to establish networks in the community to address the needs of domestic violence victims and their families."

According to Lyons (1996, p. 34): "The key to working together is to eliminate turf boundaries, rethink past practices and work as a community team to tackle the problem." For example, as Mullen (1996, p. 35) says:

> If an abuser violates his probation, we enlist the the aid of the entire community in an effort to secure his quick arrest and incarceration. Photographs are displayed in local newspapers with a description of his criminal history. Thanks to public tips, our apprehension rate is over 85 percent, with most violators arrested before they commit any new crime or abuse.

Another example of cooperative efforts is described by Kramer and Black (1996, p. 5), Colorado Springs Police Department. This department collaborates with multiple rural law-enforcement agencies to provide them assistance through equipment, training and support of community volunteer advocates. They also collaborate with Pikes Peak Legal Services to provide legal aid, advocacy and advice to domestic violence victims who do not have financial resources.

### Avoiding Lawsuits

As noted by Snow (1993, p. 94), domestic violence can be a serious financial liability to local governments:

> Increasingly, victims of family violence [are] suing local governments for not protecting them. The most famous case was that of Tracy Thurman in Torrington, CT, where the local police department had to pay almost a million dollars because of their failure to protect Tracy from her husband, Charles, who had a history of battering her (*Thurman v. City of Torrington*, 1984).

Wattendorf (1995, p. 11) suggests the following ways to reduce exposure to lawsuits:

■  Having a policy encouraging or mandating arrest when the officer has probable cause to believe a domestic assault has occurred.
■  Sponsoring training sessions that reinforce a pro-arrest policy and ensure consistent response by department members.
■  Requiring officers to document when no arrest is made—for example, noting lack of probable cause because there was no sign of struggle or injury to the victim.

Wattendorf concludes: "A police department that develops and implements a pro-arrest policy in domestic assaults can substantially reduce the risk of being sued. . . . "

Payne (1996, p. 58) emphasizes the second suggestion, saying: "Training is a key component of the department's domestic violence procedures—truly essential if effective and professional results are to be accomplished."

# Considerations in Investigating Stalking

A **stalker** is someone who "intentionally and repeatedly follows, attempts to contact, harasses, and/or intimidates another person" (Geberth, 1992, p. 138). The seriousness of this problem can be seen in the fact that almost one-third of the women killed in the United States are murdered by their husbands or boyfriends and that as many as 90 percent of them are stalked before the murder (*Newsweek,* July 13, 1992).

Holmes (1994, p. 89) notes:

> Many husbands and wives seek out their former mates to terrorize. Troubled and disturbed people send letters and make telephone calls to popular personalities and target strangers for the purpose of terrorizing. Some follow up these acts with sexual assaults and even murder. Few people are truly safe from a predatory stalker.

The Los Angeles Police Department has established an antistalking squad called the Threat Management Unit. Research conducted by the squad's officer-in-charge has placed stalkers into three categories (Geberth, 1992, p. 143):

- *Erotomania* (9.5 percent of the cases studied). Stalker falsely believes that the target, usually someone famous or rich, is in love with the stalker.
- *Love obsession* (43 percent). Stalker is a stranger to the target but is obsessed and mounts a campaign of harassment to make the target aware of the stalker's existence.
- *Simple obsession* (47 percent). Stalker, usually a male, knows the target as an ex-spouse, ex-lover or former boss and begins a campaign of harassment.

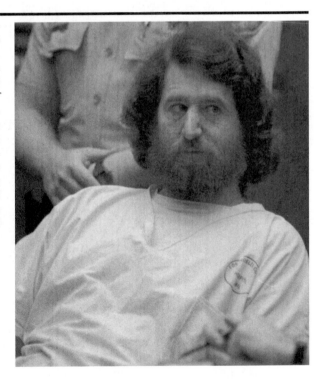

*Robert Dewey Hoskins sits quietly as he is sentenced to ten years in prison for stalking and terrorizing pop star Madonna. Prosecutors said Hoskins scaled the walls of Madonna's 25,000-square-foot Hollywood Hills estate in April 1995 and again in May 1995 and told her assistants he would either marry her or slash her throat from ear to ear. A bodyguard shot and wounded Hoskins the second time he scaled the wall.*

An example of love-obsessional stalking would be John Hinckley, Jr.'s shooting of Ronald Reagan in an attempt to impress actress Jodie Foster.

The traditional law enforcement response to stalkers has been to issue restraining orders. Unfortunately, such orders are often ineffective, as Geberth noted (1992, p. 138):

> One offender quite graphically indicated his contempt for both the order of protection and the criminal justice system. He stabbed his wife to death and knifed the court order to her chest.

Recently, many states have issued antistalking legislation, giving law enforcement the tools they need to combat the stalking problem. Antistalking laws describe specific conduct considered threatening and hold the suspect responsible for proving that his or her actions were not intended to frighten or intimidate the victim.

---

Stalking is a specific crime in several states.

---

Jarrett (1996, p. 18), after reviewing various stalking laws, found two types of stalking—misdemeanor and felony:

> Misdemeanor stalking, in which the offender willfully, maliciously and repeatedly follows or harasses another, is most frequently punishable by up to one year in jail. Felony, or aggravated, stalking—most commonly punishable by up to five years in jail—is defined as willfully, maliciously and repeatedly following or harassing another person and making a credible threat with the intent to place that person in reasonable fear of death or bodily injury.

When dealing with stalkers, investigators should encourage victims to make police reports of the incidents and document the harassment. Such records can serve as the basis for action against the stalker.

## Considerations in Investigating Elder Abuse

In 1996 there were 3 million Americans older than 95. About 30 percent have Alzheimer's disease and 24 percent live in nursing homes. By 2020 there will be 7 million of the "oldest old," many living in nursing homes or requiring care from children who themselves are elderly ("Baby Boomers Creating Elderly Boom," 1996, p. A4). Martin (1994, p. 52) notes: "Demographic shifts indicate that older Americans will double their ranks within the next 25 years."

A national crime-victimization survey (*Elderly Crime Victims*, 1994, p. 1) found that persons age 65 or older are the least likely of all age groups in the nation to experience crime. (See Table 9–1.)

As the U.S. population ages, a growing concern in law enforcement is elder abuse. Like carjacking, elder abuse is not a specific crime category in many states, which makes its frequency data difficult to obtain. It is typically included in the assault, battery or murder category.

**Table 9–1  Victimization by Age**

| Age | Number of victimizations per 1,000 persons or households | | |
|---|---|---|---|
| | *Violent crime* | *Personal theft* | *Household crime* |
| 12–24 | 64.6 | 112.7 | 309.3 |
| 25–49 | 27.2 | 71.2 | 200.2 |
| 50–64 | 8.5 | 38.3 | 133.0 |
| 65 or older | 4.0 | 19.5 | 78.5 |

SOURCE: *Elderly Crime Victims*, Washington, DC: Bureau of Justice Statistics, March 1994, p. 1.

**Elder abuse** may be categorized as a separate crime to aid data collection and enforcement.

The American Medical Association (AMA) estimates that 2 million older Americans are mistreated every year ("Doctors Advised on Finding Elderly Abuse," 1992, p. A1).

In addition to the difficulty in determining the extensiveness of the problem due to the lack of data, investigators are also faced with reluctance to report the crime—similar to the situation with domestic assault.

According to Fox (1995, p. 95): "The abuse of seniors has been described as a 'hidden' or 'silent' crime because cases often go unreported or undetected."

The American Medical Association says that by one estimate only one in fourteen cases is reported to authorities ("Doctors Advised on Finding Elderly Abuse," 1992, p. A1).

Victims may fear further abuse or fear losing the care of the only provider they have, or they may be embarrassed that a child of theirs could treat them this way. In other cases, elderly individuals are physically incapable of providing information or may be suffering from conditions such as senility or Alzheimer's disease that might cause people not to believe their statements.

## Signs of Physical Abuse of the Elderly

Signs of physical abuse of the elderly that investigators should be aware of include:

■ Injury incompatible with explanation.
■ Burns (possibly caused by cigarettes, acids, friction from ropes).
■ Cuts, pinch marks, scratches, lacerations or puncture wounds.
■ Bruises, welts or discolorations.
■ Dehydration and/or other malnourishment without illness-related causes; unexplained loss of weight.
■ Pallor; sunken eyes, cheeks.
■ Eye injury.
■ Soiled clothing or bedding.
■ Lack of bandages on injuries or stitches where needed, or evidence of unset bone fractures.
■ Injuries hidden under the breasts or on other areas of the body normally covered by clothing.
■ Frequent use of the emergency room and/or clinic.

The American Medical Association provided doctors with the following guidelines, which are equally applicable to law enforcement officers. They recommend the following questions:

- Has anyone at home ever hurt you?
- Has anyone ever scolded or threatened you?
- Have you ever signed any documents that you didn't understand?
- Are you alone often?
- Are you afraid of anyone at home?
- Has anyone ever touched you without their consent?
- Has anyone ever made you do things you didn't want to?

Controversy exists as to the role of law enforcement in dealing with elder abuse, especially in identifying "hard to detect" cases. Some departments believe this is the responsibility of social services, not law enforcement. Other departments feel they are in an ideal position to learn from and to assist social services in dealing with cases of elder abuse.

One coordinated approach to reducing elderly victimization is TRIAD. As Miller (1991, p. 96) explains:

> A joint resolution was recently adopted by the International Association of Chiefs of Police (IACP), in cooperation with the American Association of Retired Persons (AARP) and the National Sheriffs' Association (NSA). These three organizations expressed concerns about criminal victimization of older people and agreed to work effectively together to bring about interjurisdictional approaches and programs designed to reduce the victimization of older persons, assist those who have been victimized, and generally enhance law enforcement services to older adults and communities at large.

## Summary

Assault is unlawfully threatening to harm another person, actually harming another person or attempting unsuccessfully to do so. Simple assault is intentionally causing another to fear immediate bodily harm or death or intentionally inflicting or attempting to inflict bodily harm on another. It is usually a misdemeanor. Aggravated assault is an unlawful attack by one person on another to inflict *severe* bodily injury. It often involves use of a dangerous weapon and is a felony. In specified instances, teachers, persons operating public conveyances and law enforcement officers use physical force legally.

The elements of the crime of simple assault are (1) intent to do bodily harm to another, (2) present ability to commit the act and (3) commission of an overt act toward carrying out the intent. An additional element in the crime of aggravated assault is that the intentionally inflicted bodily injury results in (1) a high probability of death, (2) serious, permanent disfigurement or (3) permanent or protracted loss or impairment of the function of any body member or organ or other severe bodily harm. Attempted assault requires proof of intent and an overt act toward committing the crime.

Special problems in investigating assaults include distinguishing the victim from the suspect, determining if the matter is civil or criminal and determining if the act was intentional or accidental. Obtaining a complaint against simple assault also is sometimes difficult.

## Woman charged with assault attempt on police

COLD SPRING, MINN.—A Willmar woman who authorities say pulled a gun on two police officers during a traffic stop has been charged with attempted second-degree assault.

According to the criminal complaint, Sandra Lynn Waterman, 35, was pulled over Monday night when two Cold Spring officers spotted a headlight burned out on her car. As officer Todd Weeres walked up to the driver's side of the car and asked Waterman to get out, he saw her raise a semiautomatic handgun toward the steering wheel. Weeres and officer Chris Boucher drew their weapons.

Waterman dropped the gun and concealed it under the armrest, the complaint says, and then got out of the car.

Authorities say a bullet was in the gun chamber and its safety device was off.

Crispin Silvas Rodriguez, 39, a passenger in Waterman's car, faces felony weapons charges in connection with the incident. He said he owned the gun.

—**Associated Press**

Source: *Star Tribune*, 21 June 1996. Reprinted by permission of Associated Press.

## La Crosse cellar abuse case reveals more odd stories about couple

LA CROSSE, WIS.—Muriel Smith denies she took advantage of her husband, who'd sat and slept in a chair in a small cellar room for the past few years. "Everything you read in that newspaper about what I did and about what the neighbors said about me is lies," Smith, 53, said after her appearance in La Crosse County Circuit Court on charges of felony abuse of a vulnerable adult and unlawful use of a telephone. "I can't make Leroy do anything he don't want to do."

*(continued on p. 329)*

To prove the elements of the offense of assault, establish the intent to cause injury, the severity of the injury inflicted and if a dangerous weapon was used. Physical evidence in an assault includes photographs of injuries, clothing of the victim or suspect, weapons, broken objects, bloodstains, hairs, fibers and other signs of an altercation.

Domestic assault, stalking and elder abuse all are candidates for categorization as separate crimes, rather than being lumped in the general category of assault for reporting and research purposes.

## Checklist

*Assault*

- Is the assault legal or justifiable?
- Are the elements of the crime of assault present?
- Who committed the assault?
- Is the suspect still at the scene?

*(continued)*

The couple's adult daughter, Patricia Smith, told police that she saw her mother routinely beat her father with a broom and that the bruises on his legs were so bad that he could not wear shorts. She described her mother as a "control freak" who locked the refrigerator and allowed her and her 26-year-old brother, who is developmentally disabled, to wash only once a week, according to the criminal complaint.

The La Crosse woman was released on a $25,000 signature bond after appearing Monday before Judge Dennis Montabon. She was barred from contacting her husband or her children and was ordered to return to court Thursday. She faces a $10,000 fine and two years in prison on the felony abuse charge and a $10,000 fine and 90 days for the phone charge, which stems from a call that allegedly included threats against the water-meter reader who called police to report seeing her husband in the 6-by-8-foot room.

Leroy Smith, 63, a janitor at the local Stroh brewery, also appeared before Montabon on Monday. After hearing a physician's testimony, the judge found probable cause to place him in temporary protective custody.

Police said he was banished to the cellar three years ago after he urinated in his pants because of a leg infection that made it difficult for him to walk to the bathroom.

Muriel Smith said he went to the cellar after they argued about his urination episodes: "A couple hours after the fight, I went down to the cellar and begged him to come up, but he said 'No, I like it down here,'" she said. ". . . He told me he peed deliberately. He's mean and abusive, mentally, emotionally and physically."

Co-workers said he sometimes came to work with bruises and cuts and was often seen going through garbage and smoking cigarette butts from ashtrays. Union stewards once took him to the county Human Services Department because of his bruises and sores, but he refused to talk to department workers.

**—Associated Press**

Source: *Star Tribune,* 2 April 1997. Reprinted by permission of Associated Press

- Who signed the complaint? Who made the arrest?
- Has the victim made a written statement? Have witnesses?
- Are injuries visible?
- Have photographs been taken of injuries? In color?
- If injuries are not visible, has the victim received medical attention?
- If medical attention was received, has a report on the nature of the injuries been received? Was permission obtained from the victim?
- What words were used by the assailant to show intent to do bodily harm?
- Was a dangerous weapon involved?
- Has a complete report been made on regular department forms?
- If the assault is severe enough to be aggravated assault, what injuries or weapons support such a charge?
- If the victim died as a result of the attack, was a dying declaration taken?
- Was it necessary and legal to make an arrest at the scene? Away from the scene?
- How was the suspect identified?

# Application

Read the following and then answer the questions.

Mike S. was drinking beer in a local park about 9:00 P.M. It was dark. He knew Tom C. was at the other end of the park and that Tom had been seeing Mike's girlfriend, Susy H. Susy was with Mike, trying to talk him out of doing anything to Tom. Mike said he was going to find Tom and "pound him into the ground. When I get through with him, they'll have to take him to the hospital."

Mike left the group and Susy then, telling them to wait for him. Tom C. was found later that night two blocks from the park, lying unconscious on a boulevard next to the curb. His clothes were torn and his left arm was cut. When he regained consciousness, he told police he was walking home from the park when someone jumped out from some bushes, grabbed him from behind, beat him with fists and then hit him over the head with something. He did not see his assailant.

Mike S. was arrested because a person at the park overheard his threats.

### Questions

1. What is the probability that Mike committed the assault?
2. Did he have the intent? The present ability to commit the act?
3. Did he commit the act? Should he have been arrested?

## Discussion Questions

1. If a police officer wearing a concealed armored vest confronts a man burglarizing a store and the burglar fires a gun at the officer, striking him in the chest, is this assault? If so, what type? Which elements of the offense are and are not present?

2. What if the same situation existed except that, as the burglar fired, he slipped and the bullet struck a tree some distance from the officer?

3. Under what circumstances is a person justified in using force against another person? When is a police officer justified in using force?

4. Imagine that Mrs. Jones has reported to the police department that she and her husband were arguing over his drinking and that Mr. Jones had just beaten her. She wants the police to come to their home and arrest her husband. How would you proceed with this complaint? What precautions would you take?

5. Do your state's laws differentiate between the crimes of assault and battery?

6. Suppose a teacher is having a serious discipline problem with a five-year-old student and sends the student to the principal's office. The principal spanks the student. Under the *in loco parentis* doctrine, is this action legal? Do you agree with the *in loco parentis* doctrine? Does your state have such a law?

7. Does a sniper firing on a crowd commit assault?

8. In what crimes is assault often an additional crime?

9. If two people become involved in a violent struggle that seriously injures one or both of them, and if both claim the other started the fight, what do you do?

10. Can police officers be sued for making verbal threats to a suspect?

Aaron, J. Michael. "Reflective Ultraviolet Photography Sheds New Light on Pattern Injury." *Law and Order,* November 1991, pp. 34–36.

"Baby Boomers Creating Elderly Boom." (Minneapolis/St. Paul) *Star Tribune,* May 21, 1996, p. A4.

Bachman, Ronet, and Linda E. Saltzman. *Violence against Women: Estimates from the Redesigned Survey, Special Report.* Washington, DC: Bureau of Justice Statistics, August 1995.

Bonderman, Judith. "Why Are the Rules Different for the Police?" *Subject to Debate.* Washington, DC: Police Executive Research Forum, Vol. 9, No. 8, August 1995.

Bourn, Kathryn. "Battles on the Homefront." *Police,* March 1996, pp. 36–38, 62–63.

Breci, Michael G., and John E. Murphy. "What Do Citizens Want Police To Do at Domestics: Enforce the Law or Provide Services?" *American Journal of Police,* Vol. XI, No. 3, 1992, pp. 53–68.

Clark, Jacob R. "When Brutality Hits Close to Home." *Law Enforcement News,* January 31, 1995, pp. 1, 6.

Connor, Greg. "Domestic Disputes: A Model Pro-Arrest Policy." *Law and Order,* February 1990, pp. 66–67.

"Doctors Advised on Finding Elderly Abuse." (Minneapolis/St. Paul) *Star Tribune,* November 24, 1992, pp. A1, A11.

*Elderly Crime Victims.* Washington, DC: Bureau of Justice Statistics, March 1994.

Feltgen, John. "Domestic Violence: When the Abuser Is a Police Officer." *The Police Chief,* October 1996, pp. 42–49.

Fox, Christopher. "Shattering the Silence of Senior Abuse." *Law and Order,* March 1995, pp. 95–99.

Garner, Gerald. "Surviving Disturbance Calls." *Police,* June 1994, p. 32.

Gartin, Patrick R. "Examining Differential Officer Effects in the Domestic Violence Experiment." *American Journal of Police,* Vol. XIV, No. 3/4, 1995, pp. 93–110.

Geberth, Vernon J. "Stalkers." *Law and Order,* October 1992, pp. 138–143.

Hamilton, Douglas. "Domestic Violence: Challenges for Law Enforcement." *The Police Chief,* February 1996, p. 32.

Henderson, Cal, and R.D. Reder. "'Zero-Tolerance' Policy in Hillsborough County." *The Police Chief,* February 1996, pp. 54–55.

Hinds, David L. "Domestic Violence Documentation." *Law and Order,* July 1993, pp. 86–89.

Holder, Bennie R. "A Three-Pronged Strategy." *The Police Chief,* February 1996, pp. 35–36.

Holmes, Ronald. "Stalking." *Law and Order,* May 1994, pp. 89–92.

Holmes, William H. "Police Arrests for Domestic Violence." *American Journal of Police,* Vol. 12, No. 4, 1993, pp. 101–125.

Jackson, James G. "Ending the Cycle." *The Police Chief,* February 1996, pp. 33–34.

Jarret, Joseph G. "Domestic Violence: Developing Policies and Procedures Poses Challenge for Law Enforcement." *The Police Chief,* February 1996, pp. 16–19.

Kramer, Lorne, and Howard Black. "Taking Domestic Violence Investigation to the Next Level." *Subject to Debate,* Vol. 10, No. 11/12, November/December 1996, pp. 5–6.

Litaker, G. Ed. "Dealing with Domestic Violence." *Law and Order,* June 1996, pp. 87–89.

Lyons, Scott. "Cooperative Efforts." *The Police Chief,* February 1996, p. 34.

Martin, Deirdre. "Domestic Violence." *Law Enforcement Technology,* October 1994, pp. 38–40.

———. "Triads Help the Elderly to Handle Crime." *Law Enforcement Technology,* March 1994, pp. 52–53.

Miller, William D. "The Graying of America: Implications Towards Policing." *Law and Order,* October 1991, pp. 86–87.

Mullen, Francis E. "Long-Term Effectiveness." *The Police Chief,* February 1996, pp. 34–35.

O'Dell, Anne. "Domestic Violence Homicides." *The Police Chief,* February 1996, pp. 21–23.

Paisner, Susan R. "Domestic Violence: Breaking the Cycle." *The Police Chief,* February 1991, pp. 35–38.

Payne, Lee. "Training Is Key." *The Police Chief,* February 1996, pp. 55–58.

Pentelei-Molnar, John. "Putting Out the Fire." *Police,* March 1996, pp. 32–35.

Quinn, Steve. "Too Close for Comfort." *Police,* March 1996, pp. 58–66.

Russo, Lorraine. "Tightening the Cinch on Domestic Violence." *Law Enforcement Technology,* July 1995, pp. 46–51.

Salafia, Phil, and Nick Irons. "Changing Times: The Dispatcher's Role in Domestic Violence." *Law and Order,* February 1995, pp. 61–63.

Sanow, Ed. "Preventing Domestic Violence." *Law and Order,* December 1995, pp. 64–66.

Snow, Robert L. "Battling Family Violence." *Law and Order,* March 1993, pp. 94–98.

*Violence Between Intimates.* Washington, DC: Bureau of Justice Statistics, November 1994.

Wallace, Harvey. "Battered Woman Syndrome." *Law and Order,* July 1994, pp. 82–85.

Wattendorf, George. "Pro-Arrest Policy for Domestic Violence Minimizes Liability Exposure." *The Police Chief,* November 1995, p. 11.

# Sex Offenses

## DO YOU KNOW

How sex offenses are classified?

How rape is defined and classified?

What the elements of sexual assault are?

What special problems exist in investigating sex offenses?

What modus operandi factors are important in investigating a
sexual assault?

What evidence is often obtained in sex offense investigations?

What agencies can assist in a sexual assault investigation?

## CAN YOU DEFINE

bigamy

child molestation

cunnilingus

exhibitionist

fellatio

forcible rape

incest

indecent exposure

intimate parts

oral copulation

pedophile

penetration

prostitution

rape

sadist

sadomasochistic abuse

sexual contact

sexual penetration

sexually explicit
   conduct

sodomy

statutory rape

voyeurism

**Introduction**

ACCORDING TO THE AMA ("SEXUAL ASSAULT . . .," 1995, p. 5): "MORE
than 700,000 women are sexually assaulted in the United States each year—
with the vast majority of victims under the age of 18." The AMA calls sexual
assault "a silent, violent epidemic" that is "the fastest-growing category of
violent crime in the country."

Physically attractive or unattractive people of any age—from very young
children to senior citizens—may be victims of sexual assault. Sex offenses
range from **voyeurism** (the Peeping Tom) to rape and murder. Sex offenses
can be difficult to investigate because the victim is often emotionally distraught.
Moreover, investigating officers may be uncomfortable because they lack
special training in interviewing sex offense victims or offenders.

Some sex offenders are emotionally disturbed and feel no remorse for
their actions. For example, a thirty-eight-year-old man with a twenty-year
history of sex offenses admitted to a prison psychiatrist that even he could not
remember how many rapes and sexual assaults he had committed. The suspect also talked freely about his sexual exploits with children and showed no
emotion at all. A **pedophile,** a person who is sexually attracted to young
children, can be extremely dangerous, as can a **sadist,** a person who derives
sexual gratification from causing pain to others, often through mutilation.

Although some sex offenders are emotionally disturbed, the fact remains
that most victims know their attacker and that most attacks occur not in
dark alleys but in living rooms and bedrooms.

This chapter begins with a discussion of the classification of sex offenses,
a definition of rape/sexual assault and the elements of the crime. This is
followed by an explanation of sex offense terminology and special problems
in investigating sex crimes, including the problem of investigating obscene

phone calls. Next a description of sexual offenders and psychological profiling in rape cases is provided. Then the chapter explains how to interrogate sex offenders, what physical evidence might be important and how to conduct the follow-up investigation and clearance. The chapter concludes with a discussion of prosecuting rape and statutory changes which have taken place in this area.

## Classification

---

Sex offenses include bigamy, child molestation, incest, indecent exposure, prostitution, rape and sodomy.

---

Sex crimes are sometimes classified according to whether they involve physical aggression and a victim—for example, rape—or are victimless acts between consenting adults, such as sodomy. The former are most frequently reported to police and investigated. The latter are often simply offensive to others and are seldom reported or investigated.

**Bigamy** is marrying another person, knowing that one or both are already married.

**Child molestation** is usually a felony and includes lewd and lascivious acts, indecent exposure, incest or statutory rape involving any child, male or female, under age fourteen. This is a difficult charge to prove because children frequently are not believed. Moreover, parents are often reluctant to bring charges in such cases. (This offense is discussed in depth in the next chapter.)

**Incest** is sexual intercourse with another person nearer of kin than first cousin when the relationship is known.

**Indecent exposure** is revealing one's genitals to another person to such an extent as to shock the other's sense of decency. It is not necessary to prove intent. The offense is a misdemeanor, although repeated offenses can be charged as a felony in many states. Ordinarily, exhibitionists are not dangerous, but they may become so if they are humiliated or abused.

**Prostitution,** soliciting sexual intercourse for pay, not only contributes to the spread of venereal disease, but profits from it often go to organized crime. Of special concern to law enforcement officers is the practice of enticing very young girls into prostitution. Attempts to prevent such actions have been made through legislation such as the Mann Act. Section 2423 of the act prohibits "coercion or enticement of minor females and the taking of male or female persons across the state line for immoral purposes." Of more recent concern is the role of male and female prostitution in spreading the acquired immune deficiency syndrome (AIDS).

**Rape** is having sexual intercourse with a person against his or her will. Rape is usually considered the most serious crime except murder and carries a heavy penalty in most states. It has come to be viewed as a violent assault rather than a type of deviance.

**Sodomy** is any form of anal or oral copulation. Although commonly thought of as being performed by homosexual males, sodomy can occur between a male and female, between two females or between a human and an animal (bestiality). Oral or anal penetration must be proven. Both parties are guilty if it is voluntary. Because sodomy is usually a private act between consenting adults, it is difficult to obtain sufficient evidence for prosecution. In some states sodomy between consenting adults is no longer a crime. Such acts between adults and juveniles remain crimes, however.

Sex offenses may include a wide range of forbidden sexual activity, including the following:

**Cunnilingus,** sexual activity involving oral contact with the female genitals.

**Fellatio,** sexual activity involving oral contact with the male genitals.

**Oral copulation,** the same as cunnilingus and fellatio; it is the act of joining the mouth of one person with the sexual organ of another person.

**Penetration,** any intrusion, however slight, of any part of a person's body or any object manipulated or inserted by a person into the genital or anal openings of another's body, including sexual intercourse in its ordinary meaning.

**Sadomasochistic abuse,** fettering, binding or otherwise physically restraining, whipping or torturing for sexual gratification.

**Sexually explicit conduct,** any type of sexual intercourse between persons of the same or opposite sex, bestiality, sadomasochistic abuse, lewd exhibition or mutual masturbation.

## Rape/Sexual Assault

Rape is often classified as either forcible or statutory.

**Forcible rape** is sexual intercourse against a person's will by the use or threat of force. **Statutory rape** is sexual intercourse with a minor, with or without consent.

Forcible rape is the only sex offense that is an Index Crime, and it is to this offense that most of the remainder of the chapter is addressed. According to the *Uniform Crime Reports,* forcible rape, like robbery and assault, doubled in frequency in the past ten years, even though it is known to be the least reported of the Index Crimes. Rape is underreported for a variety of reasons. Many victims feel worthless or guilty afterward. Some fear the social stigma associated with rape. Others have a close relationship with their rapist and fear that a charge of rape would damage the relationship. Many victims appear to be intimidated by the criminal justice system in general or by how the system appears to have dealt with rape cases in the past.

In 1995, 97,460 forcible rape offenses were reported to police, a decline of 4.6 percent from 1994. Slightly more than half were cleared by arrest; 56 percent were white; 43 percent were black.

When investigating cases of sexual assault, officers should be aware of several assumptions that are not based on fact, as shown in Table 10–1.

By 1993, at least twenty-two states had substituted the term *sexual assault* for *rape,* and the number of states adopting this definition has been growing steadily. In this chapter the words *rape* and *sexual assault* are used synonymously and interchangeably. In some states statutory rape is classified as "illegal intercourse." In other states it is classified as "assault with intent to commit rape" or as "attempted rape" when the suspect is prevented from completing the act. Some states, including Minnesota and Illinois, have broadened their definition to provide that the victim *and* the perpetrator may be of either sex. In addition, several states provide greater penalties for attacks on the very young and the very old.

**Table 10–1   Assumptions v. Facts about Sexual Assault**

| Assumption | Fact |
| --- | --- |
| Most rapes are impulsive acts. | Most rapes are planned. |
| Victims are attacked suddenly, without conversation. | The attack is usually preceded by conversation. |
| Men rape because they lack sexual outlets. | Many rapists have access to sex; they want to express power, dominance and control. |
| Rape is a sex crime. | Rape is a crime of violence. Sex is often not the goal. |

SOURCE: Minnesota P.O.S.T., *Learning Objectives,* 1989, p. 135.

## Elements of the Crime

Rape is defined in various ways by state laws, but certain elements of the offense are fairly universal.

The elements of the crime of rape commonly include:
- An act of sexual intercourse.
- With a female other than the wife.
- Committed without the victim's consent.
- Against the victim's will and by force.

**An Act of Sexual Intercourse.**   The element of sexual intercourse does not require establishing that a complete sex act accompanied by ejaculation occurred. Any degree of penetration of the vagina by the penis is sufficient to constitute sexual intercourse. An emission of semen is not required.

**With a Female Other than the Wife.**   This element precludes the possibility of a man being raped, either by a male or female. Some states, as noted, are revising their laws to include as rape forcible sex acts committed by an adult male against another male.

Although most states require that the victim not be the man's wife, a husband can be charged with assault. Moreover, some states include forced sexual intercourse with the wife during a legal separation as rape if the act fulfills the other requirements of rape. Other states are considering laws that would include as rape a husband's forced sexual intercourse accompanied by serious assault threats against the wife's life. Oregon has such a law and has tried (and acquitted) a husband.

**Committed without the Consent of the Victim.**   Consent that is given because of fear, panic, emotional disturbance, mental illness, retardation; while on drugs or unconscious; or given by a child is *not* considered true consent.

**Against the Victim's Will and by Force.**   This element has traditionally been the most difficult to prove and the most subject to attack by the defense. Although laws require the woman to use the utmost resistance possible, such resistance can result in additional violence and even death. A man who is willing to rape is often willing to injure. Therefore, legislation in many states emphasizes the words, actions and intent of the rapist rather than the degree of resistance by the victim.

Police officers are often asked if it is better for a woman to resist or to submit to a sexual attack. Does resistance increase the attacker's violence? It is a difficult question to answer because researchers have arrived at different conclusions. Some results indicate that resisting reduces the likelihood of continued assault; others, that it makes the attacker more violent. Some people who have been sexually assaulted report that they fought back only after they had already been harmed, which would appear to preclude that resisting caused increased violence. It has been found that people who have been attacked previously are more apt to resist.

One study pointed out that in no other crime are victims expected to resist or not to resist their assailants. Certainly, everyone has a right to defend themselves, but whether it is more harmful to the victim to choose to defend is not possible to state. This must be an individual decision. Some police departments do not give advice on this question because of the possibility of lawsuits.

What works in one instance may not in another. It is an individual decision that must be based on individual circumstances. More emphasis should be placed on the behavior of the attacker than on that of the victim. Increasing the penalty where extreme violence is used by the attacker may help reduce the severity of the attacks, although this is problematic because of the emotional status and possible mental instability of this type of criminal.

## Sex Offense Terminology

**Intimate parts** usually refers to the primary genital areas, groin, inner thighs, buttocks and breasts.

**Sexual contact** usually includes any act committed without the complainant's consent for the suspect's sexual or aggressive satisfaction. This includes touching the complainant's intimate parts, forcing another person to touch one's intimate parts or forcing another person to touch the complainant's intimate parts. In any of these cases, the body area may be clothed or unclothed.

**Sexual penetration** includes sexual intercourse, cunnilingus, fellatio, anal intercourse or any other intrusion, no matter how slight, into the victim's genital, oral or anal openings by the suspect's body or by an object. An emission of semen is not required. Any act of sexual penetration by the suspect without the affirmative, freely given permission of the victim to the specific act of penetration constitutes the crime of sexual assault.

## Special Problems in Investigation

The initial call concerning a rape (or other sexual offense) is normally taken by the dispatcher, communications officer or complaint clerk. The person taking the call immediately dispatches a patrol unit, not only because rape is a felony but also because it is a crime in which the offender may be known or be close to the scene. The person taking the call then tells the victim to wait for the police to arrive if she (assuming the victim is a female) is at a safe location and not to alter her physical appearance or to touch anything at the scene. The victim is asked if she can identify or describe the suspect, if there are serious injuries and if medical assistance is needed immediately. The victim also should be advised not to wash, shower or douche before having a medical exam. As with any crime against the person, early response is critical not only in apprehending the suspect but also in reducing the victim's anxiety.

Special problems in investigating rape include the sensitive nature of the offense, social attitudes and the victim's horror and/or embarrassment. A rape investigation requires great sensitivity.

The first officers to arrive can make or break a rape case depending on how they approach the victim. All police officers should have special training in handling sexual assault victims. Whenever possible, an officer without such training should not be assigned to this kind of case.

As soon as you arrive at the scene, announce yourself clearly to allay fears the victim may have that the suspect is returning. Explain to the victim what is being done for her safety. If the rape has just occurred, if there are serious injuries or if it appears the victim is in shock, call for an ambulance.

Protect the crime scene and broadcast a description of the assailant, means and direction of flight and the time and exact location of the assault. The victim may be unable to describe the suspect because of stress or darkness or because the perpetrator wore a mask or other identity-concealing clothing.

A time lapse before reporting the offense can occur because of the victim's embarrassment, confusion or shock, or because the victim was taken to a remote area, giving the suspect time to escape.

Establish a command post away from the scene to divert attention from the address of the victim and to preserve the scene. Conduct the preliminary

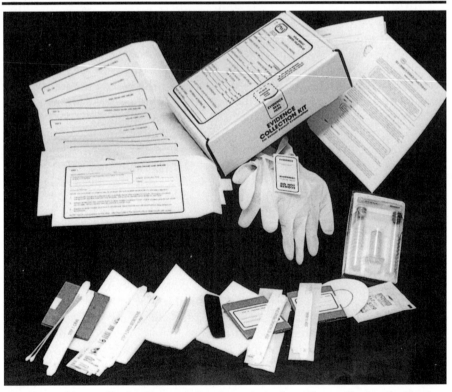

*Sex crimes evidence collection kits are designed to assist in the uniform collection of evidentiary specimens in sexual assaults. Most kits include instructions for trace evidence, clothing and underwear, debris, dried secretions, fingernail scrapings, head and pubic hairs, saliva, blood, vaginal/penile smears and anal smears.*

investigation as described in Chapter 1. Ascertain the background of both the accuser and, if possible, the accused. At minimum, officers on the scene should do the following:

- Record their arrival time.
- Determine the victim's location and condition. Request an ambulance if needed. Obtain identification of the suspect if possible.
- Determine if the suspect is at the scene.
- Protect the crime scene.
- Identify and separate witnesses. Obtain valid identification from them and then obtain preliminary statements.
- Initiate crime broadcast if applicable.

Sometimes it is difficult to determine if an assault or homicide is a sex-related crime. Gerberth (1996, p. 77) lists the following evidence of sexual activity observable at the crime scene or upon the victim's body:

- The type of, or lack of, attire on the victim.
- Evidence of seminal fluid on, near or in the body.
- Evidence of sexual injury and/or sexual mutilation.
- Sexualized positioning of the body.
- Evidence of substitute sexual activity, that is, fantasy, ritualism, symbolism and/or masturbation.
- Multiple stabbing or cutting to the body, including slicing wounds across the abdomen of the victim, throat slashing and overkill-type injuries that are considered suggestive of a sexual motivation.

### Taking a Suspect into Custody

If a suspect is apprehended at the scene, record any spontaneous statements made by the suspect and photograph him. (Again, it is assumed the victim is female and the offender, male, in this discussion.) If more than one suspect is present, separate the suspects. Do not allow communication between suspect(s), the victim and witnesses. Remove the suspect(s) from the scene as soon as possible.

After emergency matters have been taken care of, interview the victim separately from any witness and in private.

### Interviewing the Victim

Rape is typically a horrifying, violent experience of violation to the victim. Reporting it to the police is frequently a courageous act because the victim knows she will be forced to relive the experience through numerous retellings and that her word may be doubted. In addition, rape is humiliating, and it can involve numerous undesirable repercussions such as ostracism by friends and family, hospitalization, pregnancy, venereal disease and even AIDS. At the time of the interview the rape victim may be hysterical or unusually calm. Remember: rape is a crime of aggression and hostility and is usually conducted violently. Attempt to establish rapport by using sympathetic body language and explaining the necessity for asking sensitive questions.

Attempt to reinforce the victim's emotional well-being, but obtain the facts. The pressure and stress caused by rape can make victims uncooperative.

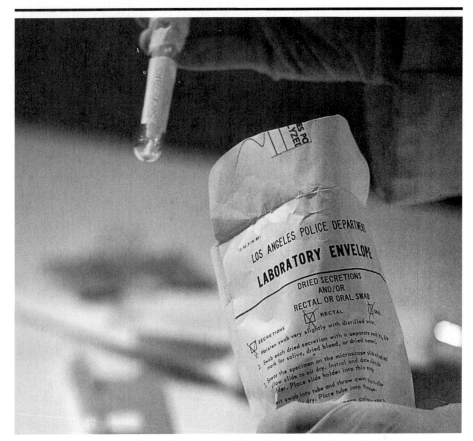

*LAPD scientific investigation staff examine evidence from a sexual assault case.*

Insensitive actions by a male investigator may reinforce the female victim's image of male aggressiveness and result in refusal to answer any questions.

Rape victims sometimes complain that investigative personnel question the validity of the complaint even before hearing the facts, are rude and overly aggressive, fail to explain the procedures used in the investigation, ask highly personal questions too early in the interview, have unsympathetic attitudes or express negative attitudes about the victim's personal appearance, clothing or actions, implying that the victim may be partly responsible for the crime.

Both uniformed and investigative personnel, male and female, can help the victim cooperate if they are sympathetic, understanding and supportive. Such an approach not only contributes to the victim's psychological well-being but also helps obtain information and evidence required to apprehend and prosecute the offender.

Although some police feel professional medical personnel should obtain the personal details of a sex attack, this is shirking responsibility. Deal with the emotional and psychological needs of the sex offense victim while making a complete investigation of the case and preserving evidence.

Whether the gender of the investigator affects the cooperation of the victim is debatable. Some believe a female investigator should interview the female victim. Others feel a male can better show the victim that men can be understanding and nonaggressive. How much the victim cooperates usually depends less on the gender of the interviewer than on the interviewer's attitude, patience, understanding, competence and ability to establish rapport. Treat the victim with care, concern and understanding. Assume that the sexual assault is real unless facts should prove it otherwise.

The location of the interview is also important. The police station may be unsatisfactory. The victim's home may be ideal, if the rape did not occur there. Tell the victim you must ask questions about the incident and ask where she would be most comfortable talking about it. If the victim is hospitalized, consult with the medical staff as to when you can question her.

No matter where the interview is conducted, do it privately. Although the victim should be allowed to have a relative or friend near to talk to, it is better to be alone when specific questions are asked. If the victim insists on having someone with her, discuss the procedure to be followed with this person. Explain that the person's presence is important to the victim for reassurance and security but that the person must allow the victim to talk freely and not interrupt.

The victim's family and friends can considerably influence whether the victim relates the entire story. A wide range of emotional feelings can occur from mothers, fathers, husbands or other family members. They may be silent, hysterical or angry to the point that they are "going to kill him if I find him." Sometimes such anger is turned against the victim.

Make a complete report of the victim's appearance and behavior: presence of liquor or drugs; bruises, scratches or marks; manner of speech; emotional condition; appearance of clothes or hair; color of face; smeared makeup; torn clothes; and stains. Take photographs to supplement your notes.

The needed initial information includes the victim's name, age, address, work address, telephone numbers and any prior relationship with the offender, if the offender is known. Additional information investigators should obtain about the victim at a *later* interview includes the following:

- Children, ages.
- Educational level.
- Family and parents, nature of relationship with them.
- Fears.
- Financial status, past and present.
- Friends and enemies.
- Hobbies.
- Marital status.
- Medical history, physical and mental.
- Occupation, past and present.
- Personal habits.
- Physical description, including attire at the time of the incident.
- Recent court actions.
- Recent changes in lifestyle.
- Reputation on the job and in the neighborhood.
- Residence, past and present.
- Social habits.
- Use of alcohol and drugs.

Obtain a detailed account of the crime, including the suspect's actions and statements, special characteristics or oddities and any unusual sexual behaviors. Determine exactly where and how the attack occurred, what happened before and after the attack and if the victim can give any motive for the attack. Explain what you need to know and why, the procedures that will be followed and how important the victim's cooperation is. Use open-ended questions such as, "Take your time and tell me exactly what happened."

Determine the exact details of resistance, even if not required by law. Was there any unconsciousness, paralysis or fainting? Was there penetration? Who did the victim first talk to after the assault? How soon was the report made, and if there was a delay, what was the reason?

Establish lack of consent. Obtain the names of any witnesses. Determine where the victim was before the attack and whether someone might have seen her and followed her. The suspect's description can then be used at that location to see if anyone there can identify him. Obtain as much information as possible about the suspect: voice, mannerisms, clothing, actions and, of course, general appearance.

It is important to obtain as many details as possible, even though they may appear insignificant at the time. How the initial contact was made; attempts at concealment; the suspect's voice, appearance and exact words; any unusual behavior, including any unusual sexual acts performed—all these things can be helpful. Because rapists are generally recidivists (about 70 percent of them commit more than one rape), it is possible that the details and M.O.'s of offenses in another area of the same city or another community may be identical to the present case.

End the interview with an explanation of available victim assistance programs, such as Sexual Offense Services (S.O.S.). Arrange for relatives, friends or personnel from a rape crisis center to help the victim. If the victim refuses to be questioned, is incapable of answering questions because of shock or injuries or begins the interview but then breaks down emotionally, terminate the interview for the time being, but return later.

Following the interview of the victim, officers should determine whether the crime scene or evidence has been altered or contaminated. Dealing with physical evidence in sexual assaults is discussed in detail later in the chapter. Investigators should also interview all possible witnesses to the offense.

### Interviewing Witnesses

Locate witnesses as soon as possible, and obtain their names, addresses and phone numbers. Canvass the neighborhood for possible witnesses. Even though witnesses may not have seen the incident, they may be able to describe the suspect or his vehicle. They may have heard screams or statements made by the victim or the offender.

Establish if a relationship exists between the witness and the victim or offender. Determine exactly what they saw and heard. Did they see the victim before, during or after the assault? Was the victim seen with the suspect? How did they happen to be in the vicinity where the offense occurred? Check out acquaintances and individuals known to the victim because many victims know their rapists. In fact, the incidence of date rape has been increasing. In such cases it is a matter of proving lack of consent.

A particularly difficult type of sexual assault is *date rape,* where the victim knows the suspect. According to Morrison (1997, pp. 48–49):

> Whether or not the sex was consensual is the pivotal question. Often the suspect will admit the act, but give a statement denying the victim was forced, drugged or intimidated. . . . The testimony of the victim is often viewed with skepticism by the defense attorney, the jury and sometimes even the judge because of the blame-the-victim mentality many have acquired.

### Investigating Obscene Telephone Calls

Making obscene telephone calls is a crime. Police departments receive complaints of many types of harassment calls that are not of a sexual nature and have established procedures for investigating such calls. The same procedures apply to telephone calls with sexual implications.

In most obscene phone calls, the callers want to remain anonymous, using the telephone as a barrier between themselves and their victims. The callers receive sexual or psychological gratification from making contact with victims, even from a distance. Calls involving sexual connotations are threatening to the victims because they have no way of knowing the caller's true intent. Although such calls may be made randomly, in many cases the caller knows the victim.

If the victim wants to prosecute, the first contact may be the telephone company. The information section at the front of most telephone directories provides information about what constitutes a violation of telephone company regulations and the law and provides instructions on what to do if you receive obscene or harassing calls (stay calm, do not respond, quietly hang up the phone; if the calls persist, call the telephone company). The company will assist the victim in contacting the police for further investigation. The advent of Caller ID may discourage obscene calls because the caller's phone number will be provided to the victim and the victim can give it to the police. Traps and traces may also be used by police if they are given a signed affidavit from the victim stating the facts related to the obscene calls.

## Sexual Offenders

Some sexual assault offenders are sadistic and commit physical abuses in such hostile, vicious manners that they result in injury or even death to the victim. Others seek to control their victims through threats and physical strength but do not cause permanent physical injuries. Still others act out aggression and hatred in short attacks on women selected as random targets. Bradway (1990, p. 119) categorizes rapists as being motivated by either power or anger. Each category is further divided into two subcategories; see Table 10–2.

No personality or physical type can be automatically eliminated as a sex offender. Sex offenders include those who are married, have families and good jobs, are college educated and are active churchgoers.

Suspects fall into two general classifications: those who know the victim and those who are known sex offenders. In the first category are friends of the victim, persons who have daily contact with the victim's relatives, those who make

**Table 10-2   Profiles of Rapists**

| | Power Rapists | | Anger Rapists | |
|---|---|---|---|---|
| | *Manhood Reassurance* | *Manhood Assertive* | *Retaliatory/ Punishing* | *Excitation/ Sadistic* |
| *Purpose* | Confirm manhood to self | Express manhood to victim | Punish women for real or imagined wrongs | Obtain pleasure from inflicting pain |
| *Preassault behavior* | Fantasizes about successful sexual relationships<br>Plans attack | Seldom pre-planned<br>Crime of opportunity | Spontaneous act in response to a significant stressor | Violent fantasies<br>Careful planning |
| *Victim selection* | Observes (prowler, window peeker) | By chance | Spontaneous | Cruises |
| *Victim characteristics* | Same race<br>Meek, nonassertive | Same age and race | Resembles female in his life | Same age and race |
| *Location of approach* | Inside victim's residence | Singles bars | Near his residence or job | Any location |
| *Type of approach* | Stealth<br>Hand over mouth | Smooth talker<br>Con | Blitz<br>Immediate excessive use of force | Brandish a weapon |
| *Weapon* | Of opportunity if used | Of opportunity if used | Of opportunity if used | Of choice or planned |
| *Time of day* | Nighttime | Nighttime | Anytime | Anytime |
| *Sexual acts* | Normal | Self-satisfying<br>Vaginal/penile intercourse<br>Vaginal/anal intercourse<br>Fellatio<br>Spends long time | Violent, painful sex acts<br>Degrading, humiliating acts<br>Spends short time | Experimental sex<br>Inserts objects into body cavities<br>Spends long time |
| *Sexual dysfunction* | Erection problems<br>Premature ejaculation | Retarded ejaculation | — | — |
| *Other behaviors* | Relatively nonviolent | Tears clothing off | Profanity<br>Injury-provoking, assaultive | Excessive, brutal force; bondage; torture; cuts clothing off<br>Protects identity (mask, gloves)<br>Most likely to kill |
| *Postassault behavior* | Likely to apologize<br>Takes personal items<br>Keeps a diary | Likely to threaten<br>Takes items as trophies<br>Boasts of conquests | Leaves abruptly<br>May or may not threaten | Straightens scene<br>Shows no remorse |

SOURCE: William C. Bradway. "Stages of a Sexual Assault." *Law and Order,* September 1990, pp. 119–124. Reprinted by permission of the publisher.

deliveries to the victim's residence or business and neighbors. In the second category are those on file in the police records as having committed prior sex offenses. Known offenders with prior arrests are prime suspects because rehabilitation is often unsuccessful.

If a suspect is arrested at or near the scene, conduct a field identification. If much time has elapsed between the offense and the report, use other means of identification. If the victim knows the assailant, obtain his name, address, complete description and the nature of their relationship. Then obtain arrest and search warrants. If the suspect is unknown to the victim, check modus operandi files and have the victim look at photo files on sex offenders.

---

Modus operandi factors important in investigating sex offenses include type of offense, words spoken, use of a weapon, actual method of attack, time of day, type of location and age of the victim.

---

Morrison (1995, p. 100) believes: "Many rapists, lust murderers or sexually motivated serial killers have histories of sexual behavior that include . . . abnormal acts." Among these acts, he suggests the following:

- Voyerism or scoptophilia. A voyeur or scoptophiliac achieves sexual arousal by looking at intimate sexual scenes.
- Triolism. A form of scoptophilia where the person achieves erotic stimulations by watching himself or herself in sexual scenes.
- Exhibitionism. The **exhibitionist** exposes himself to others in a public place.
- Frottage. A step beyond exhibitionism, a frotteur achieves sexual gratification by rubbing against another person.

D'Arcy (1995, p. 112) describes sexual predators as "a very mobile, sophisticated group of culprits." According to D'Arcy (1995, p. 90):

Sexual predators are not like dopers and drug dealers. The paranoia about cops being everywhere, always checking for a tail, is not usually exhibited by sex deviates. Surprisingly, most sex offenders have never considered someone might be stalking them, especially the police.

Geberth (1995, p. 82) says: "Examination of the case studies published on male serial killers revealed that the majority of those known to us violated their victims sexually." Sometimes the assault is sadistic.

The American Psychiatric Association (*Diagnostic and Statistics Manual . . . ,* 1994) describes sexual sadism as follows:

Over a period of at least six months, recurrent intense sexual urges and sexually arousing fantasies involving acts (real, not simulated) in which the psychological or physical suffering (including humiliation) of the victim is sexually exciting to the person. These behaviors are sadistic fantasies or acts that involve activities that indicate the dominance of the person over his victim, e.g., forcing the victim to crawl or keeping the victim in a cage, or restraint, blindfolding, paddling, spanking, whipping, pinching, beating, burning, electrical shocks, rape, cutting or stabbing, strangulation, torture, mutilation, or killing.

## The Psychological Profile in Rape Cases

Considering the numerous descriptors frequently applied to sex offenders, the usefulness of psychological profiling becomes apparent. Interviews with victims of sex offenders should focus on the offender's behavior.

Several specific areas should be covered in the behavior-oriented interview of rape victims, including three essential basic steps: (1) carefully interview the victim about the rapist's behavior, (2) analyze that behavior to ascertain the motivation underlying the assault, and (3) compile a profile of the individual likely to have committed the crime.

The three types of rapist behavior of concern to investigators are physical (use of force), verbal and sexual behavior. First, the method of approach should be ascertained. Three common approaches are the "con" approach, where the offender is initially friendly, even charming, and dupes the victim; the "blitz" approach, where the offender directly physically assaults the victim, frequently gagging, binding or blindfolding the victim; and the "surprise" approach, where the offender hides in the back seat of a car, in shrubbery or behind a wall or waits until the victim is sleeping.

After determining how the approach was made, it should be determined how control was maintained. Four common methods of control are (1) mere presence, (2) verbal threats, (3) display of a weapon and (4) use of physical force.

If physical force was used, it is important to determine the amount of force, as this gives insight into the offender's motivations. Four levels of physical force may be used: (1) *minimal,* perhaps slapping; (2) *moderate,* repeated hitting; (3) *excessive,* beating resulting in bruises and cuts and (4) *brutal,* sadistic torture. This offender is typically extremely profane, abusive and aggressive, and the victim may require hospitalization or may die.

Hazelwood et al. (1992, p. 17) suggest that a sexual sadist becomes sexually excited in reponse to the victim's degree of suffering. As one sadist wrote: "The most important radical aim is to make her suffer, since there is no greater power over another person than that of inflicting pain on her to force her to undergo suffering without being able to defend herself." The pleasure of complete domination over another person is the essence of the sadistic drive.

Hazelwood et al. also suggest that the sadist is cunning, deceitful and feels no remorse, guilt or compassion. He considers himself superior to society, particularly the police. He often uses devices such as pliers, hammers, electric cattle prods, whips, fire, bondage, amputation and objects inserted into the vagina. He also often keeps diaries, tape recorders, sexual devices, photographs of his victims, devices to torture victims and other incriminating evidence—all items to be included in a search warrant.

In addition to the offender's sexual behavior, investigators should inquire about the offender's verbal behavior. Themes in rapists' conversation include threats, orders, personal inquiries of the victim, personal revelations, obscene names, racial epithets and inquiries about the victim's sexual "enjoyment."

The verbal behavior of the victim should also be asked about. Did the offender demand that the victim say certain words or demand that she beg or plead or scream? Such demands shed insight into the offender's motivation.

Victims should be specifically asked about any change in the offender's behavior, either verbal, physical or sexual. Such changes can indicate weakness or fear if the offender lessens his efforts, or anger and hostility if he suddenly increases his efforts.

A further area of inquiry relates to the offender's experience level. Did he take actions to protect his identity, to destroy or remove evidence or to make certain he had an escape route? The novice rapist may take minimal or obvious actions to protect his identity, for example, wearing a ski mask and gloves, changing his voice tone, affecting an accent, ordering the victim not to look at him or blindfolding and binding the victim. These are common precautions a person not knowledgeable of phosphotate tests of hair and fiber evidence would be expected to take. In contrast, the experienced rapist may walk through the residence or prepare an escape route, disable the telephone, order the victim to shower or douche, bring bindings or gags, wear surgical gloves or take or force the victim to wash items the rapist touched or ejaculated on, such as bedding and the victim's clothing.

Investigators should also determine if any items other than those of evidentiary value were taken by the offender. Of interest are not only items of value but also items of a personal nature. It is important to determine not only if items were taken but also why. Again, such information may provide insight into the offender's motivation.

**Serial Rapists.** Interviews were conducted with 41 serial rapists who had raped at least 10 times and were responsible for 837 sexual assaults and more than 400 attempted rapes. The information has value for officers responsible for questioning suspects, interviewing suspects' former wives or girlfriends and preparing search warrants.

The sample was made up of thirty-five white males, five black males and one Hispanic male, and the mean age was 35.2 years. Fifty-four percent had stable employment histories, with a mean annual income of $16,446. Seventy-one percent had been married, and all but one had participated in consensual sexual activities previously. They showed an "unusually high level of general intelligence" and had a mean educational level of 11.3 years. The majority (58 percent) had been institutionalized in a correctional center or mental facility at least once. The majority surrendered without resistance, and almost half admitted fully to the offense.

The majority were living with their parents, spouses and/or children or with a roommate. The vast majority were well-groomed, expressive though guarded, distrustful, articulate and conversational. More than half (54 percent) were raised in average or above-average socioeconomic environments, and more than three-fourths (76 percent) had been sexually abused as children. Tables 10–3, 10–4, 10–5 and 10–6 summarize the family structure, sexual history and current sexual behaviors of the serial rapists and the victims' characteristics and demographic characteristics.

## Interrogating Sex Offenders

When interrogating sex offenders, obtain as much information as possible and yet remain nonjudgmental. According to Hertica (1991, p. 39), an effective approach to the questioning is to invite the suspect to come to the police department to clarify a situation in which he appears to be involved. When this initial contact is sufficiently vague, most rapists are anxious to come to the police station and tell their side of the story.

The suspect should be the last person interviewed. This allows the interviewer to have all information possible by the time of the suspect interview: facts about the victim, the type of offense and the location of the crime; statements from witnesses, neighbors and informants; and information about the suspect's background.

As in most interrogation situations, building rapport is the first step. Suggest to the suspect that you understand what he is going through. Ask about his family,

**Table 10-3   Serial Rapists' Family Structure**

|  | N | Percent |
|---|---|---|
| *Assessment of Socioeconomic Level of Subject's Preadult Home (N = 41)* | | |
| Advantaged | 7 | 17% |
| Comfortable, average | 15 | 37% |
| Marginal, self-sufficient | 11 | 27% |
| Submarginal | 8 | 20% |
| Variable | — | — |
| *Dominant Parental Figures (N = 40)* | | |
| Mother | 20 | 50% |
| Father | 16 | 40% |
| Other | 4 | 10% |
| *Quality of Relationship to Mother or Dominant Female Caretaker (N = 39)* | | |
| Warm, close | 14 | 36% |
| Variable | 12 | 31% |
| Cold, distant | 2 | 5% |
| Uncaring, indifferent | 4 | 10% |
| Hostile, aggressive | 7 | 18% |
| *Quality of Relationship to Father or Dominant Male Caretaker (N = 39)* | | |
| Warm, close | 7 | 18% |
| Variable | 10 | 26% |
| Cold, distant | 12 | 31% |
| Uncaring, indifferent | 3 | 8% |
| Hostile, aggressive | 7 | 18% |
| *Evidence that Subject Was Physically Abused by Parents/Caretakers (N = 40)* | | |
| Yes | 15 | 38% |
| No | 25 | 62% |
| *Evidence that Subject Was Psychologically Abused by Parents/Caretakers (N = 41)* | | |
| Yes | 30 | 73% |
| No | 11 | 27% |
| *Evidence that Subject Was Sexually Abused (N = 41)* | | |
| Yes | 31 | 76% |
| No | 10 | 24% |

SOURCE: Robert Hazelwood and Janet Warren. "Serial Rapists." *FBI Law Enforcement Bulletin,* January 1989, p. 10. Reprinted by permission.

his job, his interests. Assess the suspect's character. After rapport is established, ask the suspect to tell his side of the story from beginning to end, and do not interrupt him. Show interest in what he is saying and keep him talking. The interrogator's approach should be one of "you tell me what happened and I will understand," even though that may not be the investigator's feelings.

The objective of the interview is to obtain the truth and the information necessary for proving guilt or innocence. To help accomplish this goal, attempt to gain the suspect's confidence. Many suspects feel they can justify their actions by putting some blame on the victim; for example, "She came on to me."

During the interrogation, remember that the seriousness of the charge to be brought will be based on the information that is obtained. All elements of the charged offense must be proven, so keep the possible charges in mind and prepare questions that will elicit supporting information.

**Table 10-4   Serial Rapists' Sexual History and Current Sexual Behaviors**

|  | N | Percent | Total/N |
|---|---|---|---|
| *Childhood or Adolescent Sexual Trauma* | | | |
| Witnessing sexual violence of others......................... | 8 | 25% | 32 |
| Witnessing disturbing sexual activity of parents ....... | 17 | 44% | 39 |
| Witnessing disturbing sexual activity of other family members or friends.................................... | 9 | 25% | 36 |
| Physical injury to sexual organs; venereal disease .... | 5 | 14% | 36 |
| Multiple sexual assault ......................................... | 11 | 31% | 35 |
| Sex stress situations (e.g., punitive parental reaction to masturbation, etc.) .............................. | 17 | 46% | 37 |
| *Adult Sexual Behavior* | | | |
| Marked inhibition or aversion to sexual activity....... | 4 | 10% | 40 |
| Compulsive masturbation......................................... | 21 | 54% | 39 |
| Exhibitionism ...................................................... | 12 | 29% | 41 |
| Voyeurism (peeping) .............................................. | 27 | 68% | 40 |
| Fetishism.............................................................. | 16 | 41% | 39 |
| Cross-dressing...................................................... | 9 | 23% | 39 |
| Obscene phone calls ............................................... | 15 | 38% | 40 |
| Prostitution (as prostitute or pimp) ........................ | 6 | 15% | 41 |
| Sexual bondage ..................................................... | 10 | 26% | 39 |
| Collects detective magazines ................................... | 11 | 28% | 39 |
| Collects pornography............................................... | 13 | 33% | 39 |

SOURCE: Robert Hazelwood and Janet Warren. "Serial Rapists." *FBI Law Enforcement Bulliten*, January 1989, p. 10. Reprinted by permission.

Hertica (1991, pp. 42–43) suggests the following tactics when interrogating sexual assault suspects:

> One tactic that is frequently successful is to ask the subject to explain why the victim would have lied about what happened. He will have difficulty answering this, particularly . . . where there is no motivation for a false accusation.
>
> Another effective tactic that can be used here, if there is a relationship between the suspect and the victim, is to play on the suspect's sympathies. The investigator can explain that the last thing the victim said was how much she loved him and how, although she wanted the abuse to stop, she didn't want anything bad to happen to him. The investigator might also remind the suspect of how much he loves the victim and how he can spare her the trauma of the court proceedings. . . .
>
> All evidence assembled in the case should be at the investigator's fingertips for the interview, and he or she should be aware of—and prepared to use—all available sanctions.

Mann (1996, p. 117) describes "fantasy-based interviewing" as an investigations approach for predatory sex offenders. He suggests that although everyone has fantasies, "the fantasies of sex offenders are mental rehearsals for actual, hands-on acts." Therefore, investigators should "assertively go after this type of information." The fantasy-based interview consists of six steps (Mann, pp. 118–119):

**1.** Create a comfortable, relaxed environment.
**2.** Establish a common ground for discussion (human fantasy). Emphasize that all humans fantasize.
**3.** Speak in the language and tone a therapist would use, for example, *disclosure, deviant thoughts, urges.*
**4.** Make the suspect feel safe enough to disclose his fantasies.

**Table 10–5    Victim Characteristics**

| Why Subject Selected Victim | Percentage | |
|---|---|---|
| | *Yes* | *No* |
| Availability | 98% | 2% |
| Gender | 95% | 5% |
| Age | 66% | 34% |
| Location | 66% | 34% |
| Race | 63% | 37% |
| Physical characteristics | 39% | 61% |
| Other specific reasons | 31% | 69% |
| No special reasons | 25% | 75% |
| Clothing | 15% | 85% |
| Vocation | 7% | 93% |

| | First Rape | | Middle Rape | | Last Rape | |
|---|---|---|---|---|---|---|
| | *N* | *%* | *N* | *%* | *N* | *%* |
| *Relationship to Victim* | | | | | | |
| Stranger | 33 | 80% | 35 | 85% | 36 | 88% |
| Acquaintance | 3 | 7% | 5 | 12% | 2 | 5% |
| Other | 2 | 5% | 0 | 0% | 1 | 2% |
| Date | 1 | 2% | 0 | 0% | 0 | 0% |
| Friend | 1 | 2% | 0 | 0% | 0 | 0% |
| Neighbor | 1 | 2% | 1 | 2% | 2 | 5% |
| Subordinate on job | 0 | 0% | 0 | 0% | 0 | 0% |
| *Scene of Sexual Assault* | | | | | | |
| Victim's residence | 21 | 52% | 20 | 53% | 18 | 45% |
| Street/alleyway | 4 | 10% | 1 | 3% | 2 | 5% |
| Other | 11 | 28% | 10 | 26% | 15 | 38% |
| Parking lot | 1 | 2% | 1 | 3% | 1 | 2% |
| Subject's residence | 2 | 5% | 3 | 8% | 1 | 2% |
| Public facilities | 1 | 2% | 0 | 0% | 1 | 2% |
| Victim's place of work | 0 | 0% | 0 | 0% | 0 | 0% |
| Subject's place of work | 0 | 0% | 1 | 3% | 0 | 0% |
| Highway | 0 | 0% | 2 | 5% | 2 | 5% |

SOURCE: Robert Hazelwood and Janet Warren. "Serial Rapists." *FBI Law Enforcement Bulliten*, January 1989, p. 10. Reprinted by permission.

**5.** Get the suspect to discuss his fantasies openly. The details can provide a blueprint for past criminal acts or future planned acts.
**6.** Match the fantasies to criminal behavior.

Mann (p. 119) concludes:

> Do not ignore fantasy behavior! Look for it in all forms (verbal and nonverbal). . . . As distasteful as the fantasy-based interview might be, it works. The benefits are worth the discomfort. You just might be instrumental in preventing a crime from occurring.

## Physical Evidence

Evidence in a rape case shows the amount of force that occurred, establishes that a sexual act was performed and links the act with the suspect.

---

Evidence in a rape case consists of stained or torn clothing; scratches, bruises or cuts; evidence of a struggle and semen and bloodstains.

---

**Table 10–6    Victims' Demographic Characteristics**

|  | First Rape | | Middle Rape | | Last Rape | |
| --- | --- | --- | --- | --- | --- | --- |
|  | N | % | N | % | N | % |
| *Age* | | | | | | |
| 0–9 | 0 | 0% | 0 | 0% | 5 | 12% |
| 10–17 | 7 | 17% | 6 | 15% | 4 | 10% |
| 18–25 | 15 | 37% | 15 | 38% | 13 | 32% |
| 26–33 | 14 | 34% | 14 | 35% | 11 | 27% |
| 34–41 | 4 | 10% | 4 | 10% | 7 | 17% |
| 42+ | 1 | 2% | 1 | 2% | 1 | 2% |
| *Race* | | | | | | |
| Caucasian | 36 | 88% | 39 | 95% | 38 | 93% |
| Black | 3 | 7% | 2 | 5% | 1 | 2% |
| Hispanic | — | — | — | | 1 | 2% |
| Asian | 1 | 2% | — | | 1 | 2% |
| Native American | 1 | 2% | — | | | |
| Sex | | | | | | |
| Female | 40 | 98% | 41 | 100% | 40 | 98% |
| Male | 1 | 2% | — | | 1 | 2% |

SOURCE: Robert Hazelwood and Janet Warren. "Serial Rapists." *FBI Law Enforcement Bulliten,* January 1989, p. 10. Reprinted by permission.

Because such evidence deteriorates rapidly, obtain it as soon as possible. Some police departments have a rape kit that contains the equipment needed to collect, label and preserve evidence.

Photograph all injuries to the victim, and take as evidence any torn or stained clothing. Examine the scene for other physical evidence such as fingerprints, footprints, a weapon, stains or personal objects the suspect may have left behind. Examine washcloths or towels the suspect may have used. Photograph any signs of a struggle such as broken objects, overturned furniture or, if outdoors, disturbed vegetation.

If the assault occurred outdoors, take soil and vegetation samples for comparison. If the assault occurred in a vehicle, vacuum the car seats and interior to obtain soil, hairs and other fibers. Examine the seats for blood and semen stains. DNA analysis has become increasingly important in sexual assault cases.

If a suspect is apprehended, photograph any injuries, marks or scratches on the suspect's body. Obtain blood and hair samples, and give the appropriate tests to determine whether he is intoxicated or on drugs. Obtain any clothing or possessions of the suspect that might connect him with the rape. If necessary, obtain a warrant to search his vehicle, home or office. Such searches may reveal items associated with perversion or weapons of the type used in the assault.

## The Victim's Medical Examination

The rape victim should have a medical examination as soon as possible to establish injuries and if intercourse occurred and to protect against venereal disease and pregnancy. Some hospitals provide drugs at the initial examination to lessen the possibility of pregnancy. Further examination for venereal disease is also conducted.

Although each hospital has its own procedures, emergency room doctors and nurses are trained to observe and treat trauma; therefore, they can provide counseling and support services to the victim during this initial critical phase. Good examination-stage care promotes later cooperation from the victim.

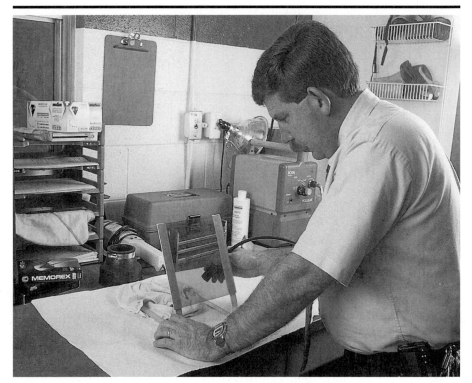

*A lab technician conducts a forensic test using ultra-violet light that shows semen samples on underwear. The underwear was collected as evidence in a rape case.*

Medical-legal evidence to be obtained by the hospital includes a detailed report of an examination of the victim for trauma, injuries and intercourse. Precise descriptions of all bruises, scratches, cuts or other injuries are entered in the medical report. The physician's report contains descriptions of the physician's findings and treatment, the victim's statements, a report of a social worker's interview with the victim or the history of the sexual assault taken by the doctor, documentation of the presence or absence of semen, the specific diagnosis of trauma and any other specific medical facts concerning the victim's conditions. No conclusions as to whether or not the woman was raped should be included. This is a legal matter for the court to decide. However, in some states, hospitals are required by law to report suspected rape cases to the police.

Most hospitals have a sexual assault and vaginal kit in the examination room with the proper forms and tests for sperm and semen. Tests can be made of the vagina, anus or mouth, depending on the type of assault. After the examination, these kits are given to the police at the victim's request and sent to a crime laboratory for analysis.

The victim should be asked to sign a release form that authorizes a copy of the medical examination record to be provided to the police. Hospital reports may be introduced as evidence even if a police officer was not present during the examination. Also ask the hospital and the victim for the clothing the victim was wearing at the time of the assault if it was not obtained earlier.

The victim is reimbursed for medical examination costs in jurisdictions that have victim compensation laws. In other states, local or state health agencies may cover the costs. Rape crisis center personnel can assist in these arrangements. Such information is important to many victims.

## Follow-Up Investigation and Clearance

After the preliminary investigation and medical examination are completed, conduct a follow-up investigation. Interview the victim again in two to five days to obtain further information and to compare the statements made after time has elapsed.

Some victims decide not to prosecute because of pressure from family or friends, fear of reprisal, shame, fear of going to court or emotional or mental disturbance. Sometimes the prosecuting attorney refuses to take the case to court because the case is weak and thus has little chance of conviction. For example, there may not be enough physical evidence to corroborate the victim's complaint or the victim may be a known prostitute, a girlfriend of the rapist or pregnant because of prior sexual relations with the assailant.

Other times the report is unfounded, unsubstantiated by the evidence.

### False Reports

Women make false reports of sexual assault for a number of reasons including to get revenge on a lover who has jilted her, to cover up a pregnancy or to get attention. Such circumstances need to be ruled out when investigating a reported sexual assault. The credibility of rape reports is probably questioned more frequently than that of any other felony reports. A polygraph can help to determine the truth of the complainant's statements. If the evidence of a false report is overwhelming, include all facts in your close-out report.

If the victim admits orally or in writing that her story was false, close the case. Where the credibility of the victim is in serious doubt because of contradictory evidence, the investigating officer's superior or the prosecutor can close the case.

### Coordination with Other Agencies

A number of other agencies and individuals assist in handling a rape case.

A rape case often involves cooperation with medical personnel, social workers, rape crisis-center personnel and the media.

The public and the news media can greatly influence the prosecution of a rape case. Medical and hospital personnel influence the victim's attitude and her cooperation in obtaining facts for medical reports and the right evidence for use in court. Rape crisis centers can provide various kinds of support to the victim and encourage her to sign a complaint.

## Prosecution of Rape and Statutory Changes

Few criminal cases are as difficult to prosecute as rape is, at least under older laws. Despite changes in the law, it is virtually impossible to obtain a conviction on the victim's testimony alone. Conviction requires medical evidence, physical evidence such as torn clothing, evidence of injuries and that a complaint be reported reasonably close to the time of the assault.

Defendants usually want a jury trial because of present laws and attitudes regarding rape. The defendant is not required to testify, but the victim not only must relate a very difficult ordeal but also is subjected to cross-examination that can make her appear to be on trial.

Juries tend to be unsympathetic with a victim who was drinking heavily, hitchhiking or using drugs or who left a bar with a stranger or engaged in other socially "unacceptable" actions. Many newer laws make it very explicit that such conditions are not to be considered during the trial. Newer laws also state that the victim's testimony need not be corroborated and that testimony about the degree of resistance, although it may be admitted, is not required. Moreover, testimony about the victim's previous sexual conduct is not admissible unless (1) the woman has had prior sexual relations with the defendant, (2) there is evidence of venereal disease or pregnancy resulting from the assault, (3) circumstances suggest that consent occurred within the calendar year or (4) the victim has not told the truth or has filed a false report.

Juries must not be instructed that a victim who consented to sexual intercourse with other persons would be likely to have consented with the defendant, that the victim's prior sexual conduct may be used to determine her credibility or that the victim's testimony should be subjected to any greater test of credibility than in any other crime.

Some states have made it illegal to publish the names or addresses of sex crime victims and have required that the county where the crime occurred pay the medical examination expenses. Many recent laws have reduced the penalties for sexual assault, which should lead to more convictions. Former penalties were so severe that many juries hesitated to convict. More recent laws usually include both oral and anal sexual conduct, and many classify sexual offenses by degrees.

## Summary

Sex offenses include bigamy, child molestation, incest, indecent exposure, prostitution, rape (sexual assault) and sodomy. The most serious of the sex offenses is rape, sexual intercourse with a person against the person's will. Rape is classified as forcible (by use or threats of force) or statutory (with a minor, with or without consent).

Most states include the following elements in defining the crime of rape or sexual assault: (1) an act of sexual intercourse, (2) with a female other than the wife, (3) committed without the victim's consent, (4) against the victim's will and by force.

Special problems in investigating rape include the sensitive nature of the offense, social attitudes and the victim's embarrassment. A rape investigation requires great tact. Modus operandi factors important in investigating sex offenses include type of offense, words spoken, use of a weapon, method of attack, time of day, type of location and age of the victim. Physical evidence commonly found in rape cases includes stained or torn clothing; scratches, bruises and cuts; evidence of a struggle and semen and bloodstains.

A rape case often involves cooperation with the news media, medical personnel, social workers and personnel from rape crisis centers.

*Read the following articles and imagine yourself as the officer/detective assigned to each case. What elements of the crime are present? What evidence would you need to prosecute the case? Who else might you need to coordinate your efforts with? What is the likelihood of solving each crime?*

## Convicted sex offender is suspect in crime spree

**Associated Press**

SALT LAKE CITY—Convicted sex offender Keith LaMar Shepherd, who escaped from Gunnison prison last year, continues to elude authorities who believe he has committed new crimes in four states including Utah.

Shepherd, 37, escaped by hiding in the storage compartment of a delivery truck on Nov. 4, nearly three years to the day after he broke out of the Utah State Penitentiary in 1992.

After his earlier escape, Shepherd committed a string of robberies in Utah and six other states during his four months of freedom. A high-speed chase with police in Sparks ended his crime spree and resulted in his capture.

In a little more than two months as a free man this time, Shepherd is believed to have committed at least four robberies and one sexual assault, according to investigators.

He was sentenced to prison in 1985 for an aggravated sexual assault.

Just hours after his escape from the Gunnison prison in Sanpete County, police believe Shepherd robbed a bank in Provo. Shepherd has been indicted by a federal grand jury in that robbery, which netted $2,000.

Leo Lucey, supervising investigator for the Department of Corrections, said Shepherd is a suspect in the robbery of a bank in Colorado 11/2 months ago; the robbery of a Baskin Robbins ice cream store in Flagstaff, Ariz., two weeks ago, and the robbery of a Baskin Robbins in Cheyenne, Wyo.

In the Cheyenne robbery last week, Lucey said, the robber raped the cashier working in the store. He used a semi-automatic handgun that authorities believe he stole from a sporting goods store in Laramie, Wyo.

Source: *Las Vegas Review Journal,* 16 January 1997. Reprinted by permission of the Associated Press.

## Former Scout leader charged in sex assault

A former St. Paul Boy Scout leader has been charged with having sexual contact with a 9-year-old boy. Robert N. Heinze, 22, charged with second-degree criminal sexual conduct, is accused of having sexual contact with the boy on three occasions since July 1996. According to a criminal complaint, he told police that he sexually touched the boy on two occasions.

The complaint said the boy's mother found a note in her son's desk last month allegedly written by Heinze in which he said he would "never do those things" to the boy again. When she asked her son about the note, he told her about the sexual contact.

Heinze is being held in the Ramsey County jail in lieu of $20,000 bail. He became an assistant scout leader in September 1994 with Troop 115 at the Apostolic Bible Church in St.Paul, but has not been a registered Boy Scout volunteer in 1997, said Kent York, communications director of the Boy Scout Indian-head Council.

York said, "This is certainly something about which we are going to find out everything we can."

**Paul Gustafson**

Source: *Star Tribune,* 8 March 1997. Reprinted by permission of the *Star Tribune,* Minneapolis-St. Paul.

*(continued on p. 356)*

*(continued)*

## Serial-rape suspect faces charges in Washington County

**By Herón Márquez Estrada**
*Star Tribune Staff Writer*

A 23-year-old St. Paul man was charged Friday in Washington County with two counts of rape, and authorities say he is a suspect in sexual assaults in St. Paul and Inver Grove Heights in the past three weeks.

"We have very strong evidence to link the sexual assaults in all four communities," said Greg Orth, Woodbury's director of public safety, after the arrest.

The series of rapes began in Cottage Grove on May 4 and spread to St. Paul on May 8, Inver Grove Heights on May 17 and Woodbury on Thursday, where the man was arrested about 9 p.m. after allegedly raping a woman in her home about 1 a.m.

He was identified Friday as Tony Dejuan Jackson, the manager of Sunsets Restaurant in Woodbury. He faces seven charges, ranging from rape to assault, in connection with the attacks in Cottage Grove and Woodbury.

He is being held in the Washington County jail in Stillwater on two counts of first degree criminal sexual conduct, two counts of false imprisonment, two counts of burglary, one count of first degree assault and one count of second degree assault.

Authorities initially said that attacks were on strangers, but then found links between the suspect and some of the victims. One woman was a co-worker and another victim had a roommate who reportedly dated the suspect.

"We feel pretty confident he's tied to the other incidents," said Sylvia Burgos, spokeswoman for the St. Paul Police Department, one of five agencies working on the case.

All four victims provided similar descriptions of their attacker, and all of the women were bound before being raped.

In the May 4 attack, an 18-year-old Cottage Grove woman was handcuffed and raped after letting a man in to use the phone. She said he was wearing a blue fanny pack with "The St. Paul" written on it.

The 22-year-old victim in Thursday's attack in Woodbury was bound with duct tape, and the assailant wore a mask and a wig. She told police she thought he had a pack because she could hear him searching through it.

Police had stopped Jackson earlier in the week, cited him on a weapons violation and released him. Among the items police have connected to him, according to the criminal complaint, is a fanny pack with "The St. Paul Company" written on it. The pack was found when St. Paul police arrested Jackson Monday and cited him for having a pistol without a permit.

The weapon was found inside a fanny pack, along with a set of handcuff keys. Police also found a knife, ammunition, a roll of duct tape, rope and a blue nylon skull cap with eye holes cut out.

The car he was driving at the time of the Monday arrest in St. Paul is the one linked to the sexual assaults, according to the Washington County attorney's office.

The car belongs to Jackson's fiancée. Police said he moved to the Twin Cities after she was hired by the St. Paul Companies. Police did not say when the couple moved into the area or where they came from.

St. Paul police said investigators also are looking "into the possibility that this suspect may have been involved in other criminal sexual assaults," said Lt. Lisa McGinn.

Source: *Star Tribune*, 24 May 1997.
Reprinted by permission of the *Star Tribune*, Minneapolis-St. Paul.

### Sexual Assault

- What specific sex offense was committed?
- Are all the elements of the crime present?
- Who is the victim? Were there any injuries? Were they described and photographed?
- Were there any witnesses?
- Was the surrounding area canvassed to locate possible leads?
- Is there a suspect? A description of a suspect?
- Has there been a relationship between the suspect and the victim?
- What evidence was obtained at the scene?
- Was evidence submitted to the crime laboratory? Reports received?
- Was the victim taken to the hospital for a medical examination?
- What evidence was obtained at the hospital? Is a medical report available?
- Was the victim interviewed? Will she sign a complaint?
- Was the victim reinterviewed four to five days after the assault?
- Was a background check made of the victim?
- Were other police agencies in the area notified and queried?
- Were field interrogation cards, M.O. files and other intelligence files checked?
- Have patrol divisions been checked for leads on cars or persons in the area?
- Has a sexual assault or rape crisis center been contacted for help?

## Application

Several young people in a car wave down a police car and tell the officers that screams are coming from the south end of a nearby park. At about the same time, the police dispatcher receives a call from a resident who says she hears screams and cries for help but cannot tell exactly what part of the park they are coming from. The officers talk to the juveniles, get their names and a description of the area and then head for the park without red lights and siren to avoid warning the attacker. Arriving at the south end of the park, the officers see a man running from some bushes. He is wearing a dark jacket and is bareheaded. One officer goes to find the victim; the other attempts to follow the fleeing man. At the scene, the officer observes a woman with torn clothing and a cut on the side of her head. She is unable to speak coherently, but it is obvious that she has been assaulted. The juveniles have followed the squad car to the scene and crowd around the victim to offer help. The officer chasing the suspect has lost him and has returned to the scene. Both officers help the victim into the squad car and leave the scene with red lights and sirens, heading for the hospital. After leaving the victim at the hospital, they return to the scene. They find that branches are broken from some of the bushes. They also find an article of clothing from the victim and a switchblade knife on the ground. They secure the scene by posting several of the juveniles around the area until further help arrives.

### Questions

1. Should red lights and siren have been used in going to the scene?
2. Was it correct for the officers to split up as they did?
3. Evaluate the effectiveness of the officers' actions after arriving at the scene.

# Discussion Questions

**1.** What myths and prejudices have you heard about prosecuting rape cases? Are rape cases more difficult to prosecute than other crimes?

**2.** What are the penalties for rape in your state? Are these penalties adequate, or should they be more or less severe?

**3.** Past rape laws have required the utmost resistance on the part of the victim. Present laws have reduced this requirement. Do you support this change?

**4.** What persons or agencies can assist the police in rape investigations? What functions or services can they provide? What resources are available in your community? Your state?

**5.** Should the rape victim be interviewed by male or female investigators?

**6.** Rape victims often complain about the attitudes of police and medical personnel during a rape investigation. Do you believe this is justified, or is it due to the victim's emotional stress?

**7.** In the late 1970s, a case in Oregon received wide publicity because a husband was charged with raping his wife during a temporary separation and was acquitted. Do you agree with this verdict? Are there circumstances where such a charge should be supported?

**8.** What environment is best for interviewing the victim of a rape or sexual assault? How would you start the interview? How supportive of the victim would you be? What questions would you ask? Who would you allow to be present? How would you close the interview?

**9.** How vigorously should sex offenses such as sodomy, indecent exposure and prostitution be investigated? Should unnatural sexual acts between consenting adults be considered criminal acts?

**10.** Why is semen, rather than sperm, the evidence sought in a rape case?

# References

Bradway, William C. "Stages of a Sexual Assault." *Law and Order,* September 1990, pp. 119–124.

D'Arcy, Stephen. "An Old Problem, A New Approach." *The Police Chief,* October 1995, pp. 90–94.

———."Tracking Habitual Offenders." *Law and Order,* March 1995, pp. 111–112.

*Diagnostic and Statistical Manual of Mental Disorders,* 4th ed. rev. Washington, DC: American Psychiatric Association, 1994.

Geberth, Vernon J. "Psychopathic Sexual Sadists." *Law and Order,* April 1995, pp. 82–86.

———. "Sex-Related Crimes." *Law and Order,* August 1996, pp. 78–81.

Hazelwood, Robert; Park Eliot Dietz and Janet Warren. "The Sexual Sadist." *FBI Law Enforcement Bulletin,* February 1992, pp. 12–20.

Hertica, Michael A. "Interviewing Sex Offenders." *The Police Chief,* February 1991, pp. 39–43.

Mann, Mark. "Fantasy-Based Interviewing." *Law and Order,* May 1996, pp. 117–119.

Morrison, Richard D. "Profiling Aberrant Sexual Behavior." *Law and Order,* March 1995, pp. 100–102.

———. "The Victim's Viewpoint."*Police,* January 1997, pp. 48–51.

"Sexual Assault Is a 'Violent Epidemic'—and Getting Worse." *Law Enforcement News,* November 30, 1995, p. 5.

# Crimes against Children

## DO YOU KNOW

What crimes against children are frequently committed?

What effects child abuse can have?

What the Child Protection Act involves?

What special problems are involved in investigating crimes against children?

Who usually reports crimes against children?

When a child should be taken into protective custody?

If children are generally truthful when talking about abuse?

What factors to consider in interviewing child victims?

What things can indicate child neglect or abuse?

What types of evidence are important in child neglect or abuse cases?

What a pedophile is?

What types of sex rings exist in the United States?

How a pedophile might typically react to being discovered?

How crimes against children can be prevented?

## CAN YOU DEFINE

| | | |
|---|---|---|
| abandonment | lewdness | physical abuse |
| chicken hawk | misoped | sexual exploitation |
| child sexual abuse | molestation | sexual seduction |
| commercial exploitation | Munchhausen | sexually explicit |
| emotional abuse | Syndrome | conduct |
| exploitation | Munchhausen | temporary custody |
| hebephile | Syndrome by Proxy | without hearing |
| incest | (MSBP) | visual medium |
| indecent exposure | neglect | visual print |
| kidnapping | pedophile | |

**Introduction**

A MAN ADMITTED TO A LAW ENFORCEMENT INVESTIGATOR THAT HE had molested 5,000 boys in his lifetime; a forty-two-year-old man admitted more than 1,000; and a 62-year-old oil executive stated he had molested a boy a day for 30 years. Child molestation is but one type of crime against children. Other crimes against children may occur repeatedly with the same victim, as in most instances of child abuse, whether physical, emotional or sexual abuse.

It is estimated that a child is abused physically or sexually every forty-five seconds in the United States. Ten percent of the children who are raped are under five years old, and 20 percent are under the age of twelve. Further, it is estimated that for every report of abuse the police and child protective services receive, there are ten unreported cases (Duvall, 1991, p. 109). Duvall writes:

The sad ugly truth in today's society is: with 85 to 90% of all the sexually abused children, the offender is someone the child knows, loves or trusts. The place most people remember as a safe haven is most likely the very place children are being raped; anally, orally, and vaginally; by someone they know, love or trust. . . .

Children are our biggest asset for the future. If society doesn't wake up and hear the screams and see the tears, the next time they see these abused victims may be on the front page of newspapers or worse yet, holding a pistol in your face.

One report ("Report . . .," 1995, p. A2) states:

There is no disease or natural disaster or trauma that is killing more children under 4 than abuse and neglect. . . . The level of violence aimed at young children in this country has reached public health crisis proportions, annually claiming the lives of at least 2,000 children and seriously injuring nearly 140,000.

This chapter begins with a classification of crimes against children, the effects of child abuse and important terminology. This is followed by an examination of the police response and special problems in investigation. Next the chapter describes the initial report, the importance of protecting the child, the preliminary investigation and indicators of child neglect and abuse. The chapter next provides guidelines for interviewing sexually abused children and a sample protocol. This is followed by a discussion of the evidence to collect and who might be possible suspects. Then child sexual rings are described. The chapter concludes with an examination of children as witnesses in court and a discussion of preventing child abuse.

## Classification

Law enforcement agencies are charged with investigating all crimes, but their responsibility is especially great where crimes against children are involved. Children need the protection of the law to a greater degree than other members of society because they are so vulnerable, especially if the offense is committed by one or both parents. Even after the offense is committed, the child may still be in danger of further victimization.

Crimes against children include kidnapping, abandonment, neglect, exploitation, physical abuse, emotional abuse, incest and sexual assault.

**Kidnapping** is taking someone away by force, often for ransom. In the case of child kidnapping, it is especially traumatic for the parents and for those called upon to investigate. A highly publicized child kidnapping case in 1988 involved the abduction of eleven-year-old Jacob Wetterling, who was taken at gunpoint from near his home by a masked man. No ransom was demanded, and despite national publicity and a nationwide search, Jacob remains missing.

Some child kidnappings are committed by a parent who has lost custody of the child in divorce proceedings. In such cases, ransom is not demanded. Rather, the parent committing the kidnapping may take on a new identity and move to another part of the country. Childless couples have also been known to kidnap babies or young children to raise as their own.

**Abandonment** refers to a parent's desertion of a child. This may occur not because the parents no longer love the child but because they feel the child would have a better life without them. It sometimes occurs when a young girl has a child and does not want anyone to know about it.

**Neglect** refers to failure to care for a child properly. This can include not providing humane living quarters, adequate food or adequate love and attention.

Briscoe (1994, p. 26) states: "In 1994, an American child [was] abused or neglected every 13 seconds." She further notes (p. 28): "On a national basis, reports of neglect are three times as high as those for abuse. What's worse, unless there is neurological damage from the abuse, neglect has a longer term, more damaging impact to the development of a child."

An example of physical abuse or neglect is a couple who raped, drugged and fed fried rats and boiled cockroaches to their four children over a period of at least four years ("Chicago Couple. . .," 1996, p. A8). These children were fed "as a regular diet, skinned and boiled rats rolled in flour and deep-fried and boiled cockroaches served with hot sauce."

**Exploitation** refers to taking unfair advantage of children or using them illegally. This includes using children in pornography and prostitution. It can also involve forcing children to perform physical labor beyond what could be reasonably expected of a child.

**Physical abuse** refers to beating, whipping, burning or otherwise inflicting physical harm upon a child. Child abuse has been identified as the biggest single cause of death of young children. One study, in fact, found that between three and four million children have at some time been kicked, beaten or hit with a fist by their parents; between 1.4 and 2.3 million have been "beaten up" by their parents; and between 900,000 and 1.8 million have been assaulted with a knife or gun.

**Emotional abuse** refers to causing fear or feelings of unworthiness in children by such means as locking them in closets, ignoring them or constantly belittling them.

**Incest** includes parents having sexual relations with their children.

**Child sexual abuse** includes sexually molesting a child, performing sexual acts with a child and statutory rape and seduction. Holmes et al. (1993, p. 77) stress: "Other than homicide, there is no greater crime committed against children than that of sexual abuse." They estimate that sexual assault victims range in the millions and that perhaps more than 90 percent of child molestations are not reported to the criminal justice system.

## The Effects of Child Abuse

The effects of child abuse can be devastating.

---

Child abuse can result in permanent and serious physical, mental and emotional damage.

---

Physical damage may involve the brain, vital organs, eyes, ears, arms or legs. Severe abuse may also cause mental retardation, restricted language ability, restricted perceptual and motor-skill development, arrested physical development, blindness, deafness, loss of limbs or even death.

Emotional damage may include impaired self-concept as well as increased levels of aggression, anxiety and tendency toward self-destructiveness. These self-destructive tendencies can cause children to act out antisocial behavior in the family, the school and the community at large.

Another likely effect of child abuse is that, as an adult, the former victim very frequently becomes a perpetrator of child abuse, thereby creating a vicious circle.

According to Widom (1992, p. 1): "Being abused or neglected as a child increased the likelihood of arrest as a juvenile by 53 percent, as an adult by 38 percent, and for a violent crime by 38 percent." This is substantiated by a study of 14,000 inmates imprisoned for violent crimes. Of these, two-thirds victimized a child, and one-third raped or sexually assaulted their own child or stepchild ("Direct from the Source . . .," 1996, p.7).

Likewise, Widom (1995, p. 1) refers to the "cycle of violence" or the "intergenerational transmission of violence." She states:

> The research clearly reveal[s] that a childhood history of physical abuse predisposes the survivor to violence in later years, and that victims of neglect are more likely to engage in later violent criminal behavior as well.

## Terminology

Any discussion of crimes against children must take into account that state statutes differ in their definitions of *minor*, with the most common being under the age of sixteen and under the age of eighteen.

When classifying crimes against children, several state statutes are applicable, including offenses of physical assault, sexual assault, incest, sexual seduction, indecent exposure, lewdness and molestation. Physical and sexual assault and incest have been previously defined. **Sexual seduction** means ordinary sexual intercourse, anal intercourse, cunnilingus or fellatio committed by a non-minor with a consenting minor. **Indecent exposure** means publicly showing the genitals. **Lewdness** means touching a minor to arouse, appeal to or gratify their sexual desires. The touching may be done by the perpetrator or by the minor under the direction of the perpetrator. **Molestation** is a broader term, referring to any act motivated by unnatural or abnormal sexual interest in minors that would reasonably be expected to disturb, irritate or offend the victim. Molestation may or may not involve touching of the victim.

*Melissa Drexler, an 18-year-old New Jersey high school graduate, allegedly went to her prom in June 1997, gave birth, disposed of the baby in a trash bin and then returned to the dance. Drexler faces murder charges and, if convicted, from 30 years to life in prison.*

Legislatures in a number of states are attempting to broaden penalties to make them match the severity of the offense, especially if the victim is very young. There is also a concerted effort to expand the offenses to make genders equal, recognizing that victims and offenders may be male or female. The age of the offender as well as the type of the crime are all taken into account. Illinois, for example, has consolidated nine sex offenses into four, but provides for twenty-four combinations of how a person may be charged.

On the federal level, statutes related to child abuse pertain mainly to exploitation, but they also set forth some important definitions that apply to any type of child abuse. Public Law 95-225 (1978) defines **sexual exploitation:**

> Any person who employs, uses, persuades, induces, entices, or coerces any minor to engage or assist in engaging in any sexually explicit conduct for the purpose of producing any visual or print medium, knowing that such visual or print medium will be transported interstate or in foreign commerce or mailed, is guilty of sexual exploitation. Further, any parent or legal guardian who knowingly permits such conduct, having control and custody of the child, is also subject to prosecution.

**Sexually explicit conduct** is defined as any type of sexual intercourse between persons of the same or opposite sex, bestiality, sadomasochistic abuse, lewd exhibition or masturbation. **Visual print** or **medium** means any film, photograph, negative, slide, book, magazine or other visual print or medium. **Commercial exploitation** means having as a direct or indirect goal monetary or other material gain.

On May 21, 1984, Congress passed the Child Protection Act.

---

The Child Protection Act prohibits child pornography and greatly increases the penalties for adults who engage in it.

---

The law describes child pornography as being highly developed into an organized, multimillion-dollar industry operating on a national level, exploiting thousands of children including runaways and homeless youth, producing and distributing pornographic materials. It states that such exploitation is harmful to the physiological, emotional and mental health of the individual and to society.

Many states have passed similarly worded statutes and have also increased penalties for sexual abuse and the production and distribution of child-pornographic materials. Although adult pornography has always been objectionable to many people, it has not resulted in the aggressive public and legislative action that child pornography has received. In 1977 Congress passed the Protection of Children Against Sexual Exploitation Act. This and other federal and state laws have prohibited commercial and noncommercial distribution of pornographic materials and more recently have made it a violation of law to *possess* such materials. The basis for these laws has been the acceptance of a relationship between child-pornographic materials and child sexual abuse offenders and offenses.

Indeed, in many cases, arrested pedophiles have had in their possession child-pornographic literature used to lower their selected victims' inhibitions. It is often necessary to obtain search warrants for the suspect's premises to obtain these materials. It is necessary in the investigation to gain as much evidence as possible because the problems of child testimony in court are well established.

# The Police Response

Overton et al. (1994, p. 97) provide insight into the traditional approach to child sexual abuse and the current approach:

Ten years ago, law enforcement viewed child sexual abuse as a family problem—a social issue. It was not considered a crime. As such, it was relegated to the domain of child protection agencies. . . .

Today police are more inclined to recognize that child sexual abuse is a crime and as such falls under the jurisdiction of the criminal justice system. Dealing with the problem, however, is still woefully behind. As a crime, child sexual abuse needs to be investigated by trained criminal investigators. Yes, this is an emotionally charged issue, but so is murder and other violent crimes.

No police agency would send a welfare worker to investigate a murder, and yet for years we have asked welfare workers to investigate child sexual abuse and then blame them when the case does not hold up in court. This is why the multi-disciplinary team involved in the crime of child abuse must come together to identify roles and then, as a team, put together the strongest criminal case possible, with emphasis on the welfare of the child victim.

A survey of 59 urban police and sheriff's departments suggests that they are informed of and investigate more than 200,000 cases of child abuse and neglect annually (Martin and Besharov, 1991, p. 5). In 56 percent of the agencies surveyed, responsibility for investigating sexual abuse cases rests with specialized individuals or squads in the criminal investigation unit (p. 21). The survey also found that the following areas were covered in written child abuse policies (p. 27):

■ Notification of child protective agency, 75 percent of the agencies
■ Conducting initial investigation, 64 percent
■ Evidence collection, 63 percent
■ Follow-up investigations, 49 percent
■ When a child is to be taken into protective custody, 49 percent
■ Obtaining medical diagnosis or treatment for victim, 46 percent
■ Handling protective custody (for example, notifying parents, transporting child), 40 percent
■ Statement of law enforcement responsibilities in joint investigation, 37 percent
■ Identifying cases of physical abuse, 36 percent
■ Specifying which cases are to be investigated jointly with child protective agency, 34 percent
■ Identifying cases of sexual abuse, 30 percent
■ Identifying neglect, 30 percent
■ Interviewing abuse victims, 29 percent
■ Resolving protective custody disagreements between law enforcement and child protection investigators, 27 percent
■ When to arrest, 16 percent
■ Interviewing alleged abuser, 14 percent
■ Looking for child abuse in spouse-abuse cases, 13 percent

## Special Problems in Investigation

Crimes against children are perceived by many prosecutors at all levels of the judiciary as being among the most difficult to prosecute and obtain convictions for.

Therefore, officers interviewing child witnesses and victims should have specialized training, not only to convict the guilty but also to protect those who are innocent. Regardless of whether crimes against children are handled by generalists or specialists within the department, certain problems are unique to these investigations.

---

Problems in investigating crimes against children include the need to protect the child from further harm, the possibility of parental involvement, the difficulty in interviewing children and the potential need to involve other agencies.

---

Because taking written statements from children is difficult, it is sometimes better to videotape the interview. Videotapes may be used by other officers, prosecutors and the courts, which eliminates having to requestion the victim. Make the child feel comfortable, and keep in mind that questioning children is apt to be more of a sharing experience than a formal interview. Questions should be relative to what happened, who did it, when it happened, where it happened and whether force, threats or enticements were involved.

The decision must be made whether to conduct the interview and investigation as a police matter or to invite the participation of a social services agency. If the child must be removed from the parents, it will be necessary, at least at that point, to involve a social services agency. Social service personnel may have more formal training and experience in interviewing children at their level and, therefore, be able to establish better rapport.

The importance of a coordinated response to crimes against children is supported by numerous studies. The U.S. Department of Justice and the U.S. Department of Health and Human Services conducted a symposium on *Joint Investigations of Child Abuse* (1993, p. 3) and reported the following benefits from a coordinated response; coordinated responses can:

- Reduce the number of interviews a child undergoes.
- Minimize the number of people involved in a case.
- Enhance the quality of evidence discovered for civil litigation or criminal prosecution.
- Provide information essential to family service agencies.
- Minimize the likelihood of conflicts among agencies with different philosophies and mandates.

The report on this symposium (p. 6) suggested that a coordinated investigative system includes at least four components:

- Educating all participating disciplines in the dynamics of victimization, child development and the criminal justice process as it relates to children.
- Establishing and maintaining consistent reporting practices.
- Providing better quality investigations and eliminating duplication of effort.
- Ensuring sensitive treatment of the child victim and her/his family throughout the investigative and trial process.

Corporal punishment such as rapping knuckles with a ruler or paddling a student used to be commonplace as a means to maintain discipline. Now, however, as reported by Benshoff (1993, p. 4B), paddling in the schools has decreased greatly, and twenty-six states have banned its use entirely.

Tjaden (1995, p. 8) describes a study funded by a grant from the National Center on Child Abuse and Neglect which examined more than 1,800 cases of serious physical and sexual abuse reported to the child protective service agencies in five sites across the country: Las Vegas, Denver, Colorado Springs, Honolulu and DuPage County, Illinois. The study found that "joint investigations resulted in significantly more victim corroborations and perpetrator confessions than did independent investigations." Tjaden concludes:

> Because joint investigations resulted in more corroborations and confessions, they also resulted in more substantiated allegations, protective custody removals of children, criminal prosecutions and court-enforced treatment plans. These extremely important legal interventions send the message that our society is ready to view child abuse as a crime rather than as a mere family problem.

Referral agencies are available to provide support and assistance to families and victims experiencing child abuse or neglect. Steidel (1992, p. 66) notes: "Recent years have witnessed a move away from a singular agency approach toward a comprehensive, community-based, collaborative approach to address problems associated with children and youth. This has resulted in the identification, development, and implementation of more effective, multiagency solutions and responses to many of these problems."

A Child Protection Center (CPC) such as the one developed in Cedar Rapids, Iowa, can be of great assistance in child abuse cases. The Cedar Rapids Center is connected to a regional hospital, and, according to Hinzman and Blome (1991, p. 24): "Specially trained in examination of abused children, the center's medical personnel know how to conduct the exam and what evidence to collect for prosecution purposes. They are also briefed by the detective concerning legal requirements for collecting specimens and maintaining chain of custody."

Burden (1992, p. 5) describes a project of the National Center for Missing and Exploited Children (NCMEC) to enlist the aid of retired law enforcement officers as volunteers to assist in such ways as the following:

- Investigate old cases that have been dormant.
- Provide fast response to a police department that requests help for recent abduction cases.
- Provide security assessments for day-care centers, schools, infant wards in hospitals and other children's facilities.

The Center hopes to have 100 volunteers ready to assist around the country.

In addition, Burden (1995, p. 325) notes that the National Fingerprint for Children Identification project can provide information to law enforcement agencies about the identification of children who have been fingerprinted and are listed in their files. These files contain some 40,000 children and are confidential. The prints are submitted by parents, police and sometimes civic organizations as a community project.

Most reports of child neglect or abuse are made by third parties such as teachers, neighbors, siblings or parents. Seldom does the victim report the offense.

In most states, certain individuals who work with or treat children are required by law to report cases of suspected neglect or abuse. This includes teachers, school authorities, child-care personnel, camp personnel, clergy, physicians, dentists, chiropractors, nurses, psychologists, medical assistants, attorneys and social workers. Such a report may be made to the welfare department, the juvenile court or the local police or sheriff's department. It may be made verbally, but it should also be put into writing as soon as possible after the initial verbal report is made. Some states have special forms for child abuse cases. These forms are sent to a central location in the state, thereby helping to prevent child abusers from taking the child to different doctors or hospitals for treatment and thus avoiding the suspicion that would accompany multiple incidents involving the same child.

Child neglect/abuse reports should contain the name, age and address of the child victim; the name and address of the child's parents or other persons responsible for the child's care; the name and address of the person suspected of the abuse; the nature and extent of the neglect or abuse and any evidence of this or previous neglect or abuse. These reports are confidential.

In most states, action must be taken on a report within a specified time, frequently three days. If in the judgment of the person receiving the report it is necessary to remove the child from present custody, this is discussed with the responsible agency, such as the welfare department or the juvenile court. If the situation is deemed life threatening, the police may temporarily remove the child. No matter who receives the report or whether the child must be removed from the situation, it is the responsibility of the law enforcement agency to investigate the charge.

## Protecting the Child

When a report of child abuse is received, investigators may initiate the investigation on their own, or they may investigate jointly with the welfare department. Regardless of the source of the report, and regardless of whether the investigation is a single or joint effort, the primary responsibility of the investigator(s) assigned to the case is the immediate protection of the child.

If the possibility of present or continued danger to the child exists, the child must be removed into protective custody.

Under welfare regulations and codes, an officer may take a child into temporary custody without a warrant if there is an emergency or if the officer has reason to believe that leaving the child in the present situation would subject him or her to further abuse or harm. **Temporary custody without hearing** usually means for forty-eight hours. Conditions that would justify placing a child in protective custody include the following:

- The child's age or physical or mental condition makes him or her incapable of self-protection.
- The home's physical environment poses an immediate threat to the child.
- The child needs immediate medical or psychiatric care, and the parents refuse to get it.
- The parents cannot or will not provide for the child's basic needs.
- Maltreatment in the home could permanently damage the child physically or emotionally.
- The parents may abandon the child.

Consultation with local welfare authorities is sometimes needed before asking the court for a hearing to remove a child from the custody of the parents or for protective custody in an authorized facility because police rarely have such facilities. As soon as possible the child should be taken to the nearest welfare facility or to a foster home, as stipulated by the juvenile court. The parents or legal guardians of the child must be notified as soon as possible.

## The Preliminary Investigation

The investigator must talk with people who know the child and obtain background information on the child. For example, does the child have behavior problems? Is the child generally truthful?

If interviews are conducted with the parents, every attempt should be made to conduct the interviews in private. Explain why the interview is necessary. Be direct, honest, sympathetic, understanding and professional in your approach. Do not accuse, demand, give personal opinions about the situation, request information from the parents unrelated to the matter under discussion, make judgments, place blame or reveal the source of your information. If the parents are suspects, provide them the due process rights granted by the Fourth and Fifth Amendments, including the Miranda warning.

### Interviewing a Child Abuse Victim

Interviewing a child abuse victim takes special understanding, skill and practice. Children often have difficulty in talking about sexual abuse, and often they have been instructed not to tell anyone about it. They may have been threatened by the abuser, or they may have a close relationship with the abuser and not want anything bad to happen to that person.

---

When interviewing children, officers should consider the child's age, ability to describe what happened and the potential for retaliation by the suspect against a child who "tells."

---

The initial interview should be brief, merely to establish the facts supporting probable cause, with a second interview later. It should be explained to the child that it is important to tell the truth.

---

In the vast majority of child abuse cases, children tell the truth to the best of their ability.

---

People who work with child abuse cases point out that children will frequently lie to get out of trouble, but they seldom lie to get into trouble. Although most child abuse reports are valid, caution must be used to weed out those cases reported by a habitual liar or by a child who is telling a story to offset some other misdeeds he or she has committed. A child's motivation for lying may be revenge, efforts to avoid school or parental disapproval, efforts to cover up for other disapproved behavior or, in the case of sexual abuse, an attempt to explain a pregnancy or to obtain an abortion at state expense.

As repulsive as society finds child abuse, particularly sexual abuse, investigators must exercise great care to protect the innocent. No other crime is so fraught with stigma. Consequently, accusations of this type are extremely difficult to dispel, even if they are false.

When conducting an interview with a child, investigators must establish rapport. Generally it is best to conduct the interview in private in the home or in a small room at the police station, hospital or a friend's home. If the interview is to take place at the child's home, it might be best not to wear a uniform, especially if the child thinks he or she is to blame. The uniform could be too authoritative and frighten the child into thinking he or she is going to be arrested. Plainclothes, casual and comfortable, are usually best.

Slahor (1992, p. 281) describes how an interview room in a police station can be converted into a "friendly, nonthreatening environment suited for any age youngster" using painting, decorating and accessories donated by the officers, staff and the community. Regardless of whether the interview is conducted at the child's home or at the police station, it is usually not advisable to have a family member present—but if the child so desires, the wish should be respected. The family member should be seated out of the child's view so as not to influence the interview. However, if a parent is suspected of being the offender, neither parent should be present. It is recommended that the investigator record the time the interview begins and ends.

The interviewer should sit next to the child and speak in a friendly voice, without talking down to the child. It may help to play a game with the child or to get down on the floor at the child's level to get attention and to encourage the child to talk naturally. Allow the child freedom to do other things during the interview, but do not allow distractions from the outside. Learn about the child's abilities by asking questions about everyday activities.

A young child's attention span is very short, so questions should be short and understandable. This is difficult and requires training and practice. Interviewers who are excellent with adults may not be successful with children. The gender of the interviewer generally does not matter. The ability to elicit accurate information is the key quality.

Lynch and Bussiculo (1991, p. 91) caution that because young children have a short attention span, fact-finding interviews should last no more than fifteen or twenty minutes. They suggest the following questions:

- Who abused the child? Can you tell me about it?
- How did it begin?
- What happened next?
- Where did it happen? What room? On furniture? The floor?
- Was anyone else home?
- When did it happen (time and day)?
- How long has this been going on?
- Did anyone else know?
- Why didn't they tell someone?
- Was pornography used?
- Did drugs play a part in the abuse?
- Were games played?

■ What did the suspect say to the victim?
■ Why is the child telling now?

It is extremely important not to put words into the child's mouth. When the child answers your questions, be certain you understand the meaning of his or her words. A child may think "sex" is kissing or hugging or touching. If the child uses a word, learn what the word really means to the child in order to get to the truth and avoid later embarrassment in court.

In the case of sexual abuse of young children, it may be helpful to use anatomical dolls to assist the child in describing exactly what happened and the positions of the child and the abuser when the offense took place.

## Guidelines for Interviewing Sexually Abused Children

The following guidelines were developed by the Sexual Assault Center, Seattle, Washington. (Reprinted by permission.)

### Background

Several factors affect the child's ability to give a history of sexual assault and influence the cooperativeness of victim and family.

Characteristics of the assault affect the child's emotional perception of the event and to a great extent determine the response. The closeness of the child's relationship to the offender, the duration of the offense, the amount of secrecy surrounding the assault and the degree of violence are the factors that have the greatest impact on the child's reaction. The child may very well have ambivalent feelings toward the offender or be dependent on him or her for other needs.

The child may be fearful of the consequences of reporting a sexual assault. The response of the family support system and official agencies will directly affect the resolution of the psychological trauma and his or her cooperativeness as a witness. The child may fear he or she will be disbelieved or blamed for the assault and almost always is hesitant about reporting.

*Anatomical dolls are sometimes used to diagnose and treat sexual abuse victims. The dolls enable victims (generally children) to better express thoughts and actions by "acting out" their trauma. Each doll features a male or female sex organ, breasts, jointed legs, ears, navel and individual fingers.*

## Preparing for the Interview

Before interviewing the child, obtain relevant information from the parents or guardian, and if applicable, from the Child Protective Services caseworker, physician and Sexual Assault Center or Rape Relief counselor. Explain to them your role and procedures and enlist their cooperation.

Determine the child's general developmental status (age, grade in school, siblings, family composition, capabilities, ability to write, read, count, ride a bike), any problems (physical, intellectual, behavioral), knowledge of anatomy and sexual behavior and family terminology for genital areas.

Review the circumstances of the assault (as reported already by the child to another person): what, where, by whom and to whom reported; exact words of child; other persons told by child; how many persons have already interviewed the child; child's reaction to assault; how the child feels about it and what, if any, behavioral signs of distress (nightmares, withdrawal, regression, acting out) have occurred.

Determine what reactions and changes the child has been exposed to following revelation of the assault(s): believing, supportive, blaming, angry, ambivalent, parents getting a divorce, move to a new home.

## Beginning the Interview

**Setting.**    The more comfortable for the child, the more information he or she is likely to share.

■  Flexibility—A child likes to move around the room, explore and touch, sit on the floor or in an adult's lap.
■  Activity—Playing or coloring can occupy a child's physical needs and allows him or her to talk with less guardedness.
■  Privacy—Interruptions distract an already-short attention span, divert the focus of the interview and make a self-conscious or apprehensive child withdraw.
■  Support—If the child wishes a parent or other person present, it should be allowed. A frightened or insecure child will not give a complete statement. If a parent must be present, it is important for the officer to discuss some do's and don'ts on the parent's part. It is usually best for a parent not to be present unless the child really wants one or both there.

**Establishing a Relationship.**    It is important to establish rapport with the child before asking specific questions.

■  Introduction—Name, brief and simple explanation of your role and purpose: "I'm Officer Jones and I'm going to help you."
■  General exchange—Ask for the child's name (including last name), age, grade, school and teacher's names, siblings, family composition, pets, friends, activities, favorite games or TV shows. It often helps to share personal information when appropriate, such as children or pets.
■  Assess the child's level of sophistication and ability to understand concepts—Does the child read, write, count, tell time; know colors or shapes; know the day or date; know birthdate; remember past events (breakfast, yesterday, last year); understand before and after; know about money; assume

responsibilities (goes around neighborhood alone, stays at home alone, makes dinner, etc.).

## Obtaining a History of the Sexual Assault

**Preliminaries.** Several factors are important to consider when obtaining a history of a sexual assault.

■ Use language appropriate to the child's level; be sure the child understands the words you use. Watch for signs of confusion, blankness or embarrassment; be careful with such words as *incident, occur, penetration, prior* or *ejaculation.*

■ Do not ask "why" questions: "Why did you go to the house?" "Why didn't you tell?" They tend to sound accusatory.

■ Never threaten or try to force a reluctant child to talk. Pressure causes a child to clam up and may further traumatize him or her.

■ Be aware that the child who has been instructed or threatened not to tell by the offender (*especially* if a parent) will be very reluctant and full of anxiety. (You will usually notice a change in the child's inflection while talking about the assault.) The fears often need to be allayed.

"It's not bad to tell what happened."

"You won't get in trouble."

"You can help your dad by telling what happened."

"It wasn't your fault."

"You're not to blame."

■ The interviewer's affective response should be consonant with the child's perception of the assault. For example, do not hint that the offender may be sent to jail if the child has expressed positive feelings toward him or her.

■ Ask direct, simple questions that are as open-ended as allowed by the child's level of comprehension and ability to talk about the assault.

## The Statement

■ What . . .

"Can you tell me what happened?"

"I need to know what the person did."

"Did he or she ever touch you? Where?"

"Where did he (she) put his (her) finger?"

"Have you ever seen him (her) with his (her) clothes off?"

"Did you ever see his penis get big?"

"Did he ever put it into your mouth?"

"Did he ever make you touch him on his penis?"

■ Who . . .

The child's response will probably not be elaborate here. Most children know the offender and can name him or her, although in some cases the child may not understand the relationship to self or family. Ascertain from other sources what is the exact nature and extent of the relationship.

■ When . . .

The response to this question will depend on the child's ability, how recently the assault happened, the lapse between the last incident and the report and the number of assaults. Children tend to confuse or mix separate incidents. If the child is under six, information regarding time is unlikely to be reliable. An older child can often narrow down dates and times using recognizable events or associating an assault with other incidents.

"Was it before your birthday, the weekend, Valentine's Day?"

"Was it nighttime or daytime?"

"Did it happen after dinner, your brother's bedtime?"

■ Where . . .

The assault usually occurs in the child's or offender's home. Information about which room, where other family members were and where the child was before the assault may be learned.

■ Coercion . . .

What kind of force, threat, enticement or pressure was used to ensure cooperation and secrecy?

"Did he (she) tell you not to tell?" "What did he (she) say?"

"Did he (she) say something bad would happen or that you would get in trouble if you told?"

"Did he (she) say it was a secret?"

## Assessing Credibility and Competency

■ Does the child describe acts or experiences to which a child of his or her age would not have normally been exposed? The average child is not familiar with erection or ejaculation until adolescence at the earliest.

■ Does the child describe circumstances and characteristics typical of a sexual assault situation? "He told me that it was our secret"; "He said I couldn't go out if I didn't do it"; "She told me it was sex education."

■ How and under what circumstances did the child tell? What were the child's exact words?

■ How many times has the child given the history, and how consistent is it regarding the basic facts of the assault (times, dates, circumstances, sequence of events, etc.)?

■ How much spontaneous information does the child provide? How much prompting is required?

■ Can the child define the difference between truth and a lie? (This question is not actually very useful with young children because they learn this by rote and may not understand the concepts.)

## Closing the Interview

After the interview is completed, praise and thank the child for the information and cooperation.

Do not extract promises from the child regarding testifying. Most children cannot project themselves into an unknown situation and predict how they will behave. Questions about testifying in court or undue emphasis on a trial will have little meaning and may frighten the child, causing nightmares and apprehension.

Provide the parents with simple, straightforward information about what will happen next in the criminal justice system and approximately when, the likelihood of trial and so on. Enlist their cooperation. Let them know who to contact for status reports or in an emergency; express appreciation and understanding for the efforts they are making by reporting and following through on the process. Answer any questions the parents or child have.

## Importance of the Interview

Exact notes are critical in interviews of child sexual abuse victims because such cases are an exception to the hearsay rule. An officer *may* testify in court as to statements made by the victim; therefore, officers should be meticulous in recording all verbatim statements. The child may not be able to repeat the statements due to fear or anxiety. Whenever possible, the interviews should be videotaped.

## A Sample Protocol

The following portion of the Boulder City (Nevada) Police Department's protocol for investigating reports of sexual and physical abuse of children is typical. (Reprinted by permission.)

It is the policy to *team* investigate all abuse allegations.

When a report comes in, a juvenile officer is immediately assigned all abuse cases. This officer is responsible for maintaining a 72-hour time frame. Contact is made as soon as possible.

The investigative process includes the following:

A. The investigator contacts Nevada Welfare, and together they contact the victim at a location where the victim can be interviewed briefly, and not in the presence of the alleged perpetrator of the crime.

B. During the initial interview the juvenile officer tries to determine if the report is:
   1. a substantiated abuse
   2. unsubstantiated
   3. unfounded

C. If the report is substantiated, the juvenile officer or Nevada State Welfare remove the child from the home and book the child into protective custody. If the juvenile officer and Nevada State Welfare investigator determine the child is not in danger of *any* abuse, the child can be allowed to remain in his/her home environment. (This is indeed rare, but does occur.)

D. If the report is unsubstantiated, the child is left in the home.

E. If the report is unfounded, the reason for the false report is also investigated to identify other problems. . . .

F. If the case is substantiated abuse, the victim is housed at Child Haven, and there is a detention hearing at 9:00 A.M. on the following working day.

An in-depth interview is conducted with the victim by the juvenile officer and the Nevada State Welfare investigator. Several aids are used, depending on the child's age and mental abilities: structured and unstructured play therapy, picture drawings and use of anatomical dolls.

The juvenile officer also contacts the accused person(s) and interviews him/her about the specific allegations, makes a report or statement relevant to the interview and makes these reports available to Nevada State Welfare and/or Clark County Juvenile Court. Nevada State Welfare is encouraged to attend these interviews, and a team approach is used during this phase of the investigation also.

The juvenile officer also interviews other people, including witnesses or victims, anyone who might have information in the case. The officer prepares an affidavit and presents the case to the District Attorney's Office to determine if the case is suitable for prosecution. If so, a complaint is issued and a warrant or summons is issued for the accused. Once a warrant is obtained, the investigating officer locates and arrests or causes the person accused to be arrested.

As noted by Martin and Besharov (1991, p. 29): "To meet the special needs of child victims, most experts have recommended 'child-friendly' interview rooms to put young victims at ease, anatomical dolls and drawings for diagnostic purposes, and videotaping of statements to reduce the trauma of repeated interviews." Martin and Besharov have developed a self-assessment guide to help law enforcement agencies evaluate their responsiveness to the problems of child abuse and neglect. The guide includes assessments of departmental commitment, the specialized investigative unit, investigative capabilities, the role of patrol, relations with prosecutors, training, written policies and interagency agreements. The self-assessment is reprinted in Appendix A.

## Indicators of Child Neglect and Abuse

---

Indicators of neglect or abuse may be physical or behavioral or both.

---

*A caution:* The lists of indicators in this section are not exhaustive; many other indicators exist. In addition, the presence of one or more of these indicators does not prove that neglect or abuse exists. All factors and conditions of each specific case must be considered before making a decision.

### Neglect Indicators

The *physical* indicators of child neglect may include frequent hunger, poor hygiene, inappropriate dress, consistent lack of supervision (especially in dangerous activities or for long time periods), unattended physical problems or medical needs and abandonment.

The *behavioral* indicators may include begging, stealing food, extending school days by arriving early and/or leaving late, constant fatigue, listlessness or falling asleep in school, alcohol or drug abuse, delinquency, stealing and stating that no one is at home to care for them.

### Emotional Abuse Indicators

*Physical* indicators of emotional abuse may include speech disorders, lags in physical development and general failure to thrive.

*Behavioral* indicators may include habit disorders such as sucking, biting and rocking back and forth and conduct disorders such as antisocial, destructive behavior. Other possible symptoms are sleep disorders, inhibitions in play, obsessions, compulsions, phobias, hypochondria, behavioral extremes and attempted suicide.

### Physical Abuse Indicators

*Physical* indicators of physical abuse include unexplained bruises or welts, burns, fractures, lacerations and abrasions. These may be in various stages of healing.

*Behavioral* indicators include being wary of adults, being apprehensive when other children cry, showing extreme aggressiveness or extreme withdrawal, being frightened of parents and being afraid to go home.

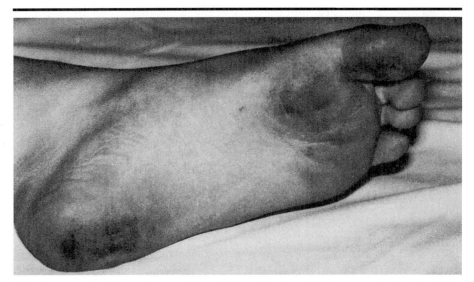

*This is an actual evidence photo used in a high-profile domestic abuse case in New York City. The victim, Lisa Steinberg, was beaten by her father, Joel Steinberg. Evidence of physical abuse may be concealed under clothing or in areas not normally viewed, such as the bottom of the feet.*

*Parental* indicators may include contradictory explanations for a child's injury; attempts to conceal a child's injury or to protect the identity of the person responsible; routine use of harsh, unreasonable discipline inappropriate to the child's age or transgressions and poor impulse control.

### Sexual Abuse Indicators

*Physical* indicators of sexual abuse are rarely observed. Venereal disease or pregnancy, especially in preteens, are two indicators.

*Behavioral* indicators of sexual abuse may include being unwilling to change clothes for or participate in physical education classes; withdrawal, fantasy or infantile behavior; bizarre sexual behavior, sexual sophistication beyond age or unusual behavior or knowledge of sex; poor peer relationships; delinquent or runaway; reports of being sexually assaulted.

*Parental* indicators may include jealousy and overprotectiveness of a child. Incest incidents are insidious, commonly beginning with the parent fondling and caressing the child between the ages of three and six months and then progressing over a long time period, increasing in intensity of contact until the child is capable of full participation, usually between the ages of eight and ten. A parent may hesitate to report a spouse who is sexually abusing their child for fear of destroying the marriage or for fear of retaliation. Interfamily sex may be viewed as preferable to extramarital sex.

Holmes et al. (1993, p. 78) cite the following behavioral indicators of the sexually abused child:

> These behaviors include: seductive behavior with classmates, teachers or other adults; excessive masturbatory behavior; sudden school problems; abrupt changes in personality or behavior; suicide threats; use of alcohol or drugs; depression, low self-esteem; excessive crying; indirect hints about the incident(s); and drastic changes in appetites.

# Evidence

All the investigator's observations pertaining to the physical and emotional condition of the victim must be recorded in detail.

---

Evidence includes the surroundings, the home conditions, clothing, bruises or other body injuries, the medical examination report and other observations.

---

Photographs may be the best way to document child abuse and neglect where it is necessary to show injury to the child or the conditions of the home environment. Pictures should be taken immediately because children's injuries heal quickly and home conditions can be changed rapidly. Pictures in both color and black-and-white should be taken, showing bruises, burns, cuts or any injury requiring medical treatment. These photographs should be witnessed by people who can later testify as to the location and extent of the injuries, including medical personnel who examined the child.

Explain the need for the pictures to the child to avoid further fear or excitement. All procedures for photography at a crime scene, discussed in Chapter 2, should be followed.

Stephenson ("When Adults Hurt Kids," 1996, p. 9) stresses:

> Photos are a powerful reinforcement to the information contained in the police report. Broken glass, exposed electrical wiring, matches, explosives, knives, squalid and foul living quarters—when photos of these conditions are taken and attached to the report, I don't have to rely on the narrative for documentation. I can see it. It's one thing to read about a roach infested house; it's another to see photos of the roaches crawling all over the kitchen counter.

Additional types of evidence that may be obtained in sexual assault cases include photographs, torn clothing, ropes or tapes and trace evidence such as the hair of the offender and the victim and, in some instances, semen.

## The Suspect

In most instances of child neglect and physical or emotional abuse, the suspect is one of the parents. In instances of sexual abuse, however, the suspect may be a close family member or a complete stranger.

Persons having normal behavior patterns in all other areas of living may have very abnormal sexual behavior patterns. Child sexual abusers may commit only one offense in their lifetime, or they may commit hundreds. Surveys indicate that 35 to 50 percent of the offenders know their victims. Some studies indicate an even higher percentage. Therefore, the investigator of a child sexual crime may not be looking for an unknown suspect or stranger.

### The Parent as Suspect

Sexual abuse of one or more children in a family is one of the most common child sexual-abuse problems, but it is not often reported. It is the least known to the public because of the difficulties in detecting it. The harm to the child from continued, close sexual relationships with a family member may be accompanied by shame, fear or even guilt. Additional conflict may be caused by admonitions of secrecy.

Although girls are more frequently victims, investigators should keep in mind that if a girl is sexually abused by a family member, a boy in the same family also may be a victim.

Incest usually involves children under eleven and becomes a repeated activity, both in severity and frequency. Courts have ruled that the spousal immunity rules do not apply to child sexual abuse cases. One spouse may be forced to testify against the other in court.

A less-commonly encountered form of child abuse involving the parent is Munchhausen Syndrome. Another consideration with this syndrome is that the child is self-inflicting the harm.

## Munchhausen Syndrome and Munchhausen Syndrome by Proxy (MSBP)

**Munchhausen Syndrome** involves self-induced or self-inflicted injuries. Boros and Brubaker (1992, p. 18) note that if a child's injuries appear to be self-induced or self-inflicted, the child may be causing its own condition for attention, sympathy or to avoid something they do not want to do. They also note that parents, most often the mother, may cause the same condition for basically the same reasons.

"**Munchhausen Syndrome by Proxy** (MSBP) is a form of child abuse whereby the parent or adult caregiver deliberately stimulates or causes medical distress in a child," says Geberth (1994, p. 95). He states that usually MSBP is done to gain attention or sympathy of family, friends and others. Geberth (p. 97) stresses:

> The potential for death as well as life-impairing physical damage makes this disorder a genuine cause for concern for both the medical profession and law enforcement. From an investigative perspective, MSBP should be considered as a possible motive in any questionable or unexplained death of a child.

The following checklist might be used by investigators who suspect MSBP (*FBI Law Enforcement Bulletin*, June 1992, reprinted by permission).

### Investigators' Checklist

*Investigators assigned to work child abuse cases should investigate cases of MSBP as they do similar cases of abuse. In general, however, when confronted with possible cases of MSBP, investigators should:*

- Review the victim's medical records to determine condition and illness
- Determine from contact with medical personnel the reporting parent's concerns and reactions to the child's medical treatment
- Compile a complete history of the family to determine previous involvement with law enforcement agencies, medical facilities, and social and child protection services
- Compile a detailed social history of the family, including deaths, injuries, and illnesses
- Interview family members, neighbors, and babysitters
- Use video surveillance in the hospital in accordance with state law
- Use a search warrant for the family's residence when collecting evidence of the assaults.

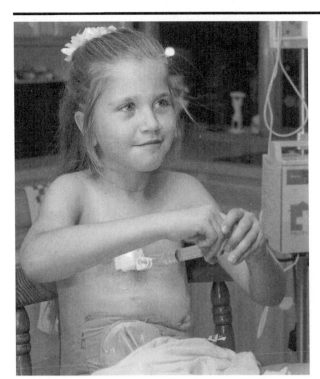

*At her Coral Springs, Florida, home, Jennifer Bush applies medicine from a syringe as treatment for a rare disease. She has been hospitalized more than 200 times, undergone 40 operations and accumulated $3 million in medical expenses. Jennifer has been placed under state care and her mother jailed for allegedly causing her illnesses, known as Munchhausen Syndrome by Proxy, a rare form of child abuse in which an adult intentionally makes a child ill to get attention.*

## The Nonparent Suspect

Habitual child sex abusers, whether they operate as loners or as part of a sex ring, have been classified into three types. First is the **misoped,** the person who hates children, who has sex with them and then brutally destroys them. The second type is the **hebephile,** a person who selects high-school-age youth as his or her sex victims. Third, and most common, is the pedophile.

---

The **pedophile** is an adult who has either heterosexual or homosexual preferences for young boys or girls of a specific, limited age range.

---

Holmes et al. (1993, p. 77) caution: "A pedophile is typically male. But this is not always the case. Women are involved in the sexual abuse of children more than is commonly thought."

Rarely deviating from the preferred age range, the pedophile is an expert in selecting and enticing young people. The pedophile frequently selects children who stand apart from other children, who are runaways or who crave attention and love. Although some pedophiles are child rapists, the majority rarely use force, relying instead on befriending the victims and gaining their confidence and friendship. They may become involved in activities or programs that interest the type of victims they want to attract and that provide them with easy access to these children. They may also use drugs or alcohol as a means of seduction, reducing the child's inhibitions.

Pedophiles may obtain, collect and maintain photographs of the children with whom they are or have been involved with. Many pedophiles maintain diaries of their sexual encounters with children. They may also collect books, magazines, newspapers and other writings on the subject of sexual activities with children. They may also collect addresses, phone numbers or lists of persons who have similar sexual interests.

D'Arcy (1995, p. 112) suggests: "Pedophiles are often plugged into the high-tech information super-highway, frequently communicate and socialize with one another and suddenly relocate in unsuspecting communities with ease."

Dees (1994, p. 53) explains the term *chickenhawk,* coined by Ingram of the Alameda County California District Attorney's office. A **chickenhawk** is simply an online pedophile who is "cyberhip." He reports that chickenhawks use chat lines and member profiles to locate potential victims, sometimes posing as another youth to establish a bond.

According to McCauley (1996, p. 33):

One of the more repulsive crimes of the computer age is the proliferation of child pornography on the Internet. Low-cost technology has proved a boon to those who sexually victimize children. Readily available scanning equipment converts photos into computer graphics, while electronic mail transmits digital images anywhere in the world. Data encryption and anonymous e-mail services make enforcement more difficult. . . . Fortunately for law enforcement, however, many of the areas that are accessible to online perverts can be monitored by police as well. These include public chat rooms where pedophiles have been known to recruit young victims (p. 34).

Many pedophiles are members of sex rings.

## Child Sexual Abuse Rings

This section condenses an article by Lanning and Burgess (1984) that describes the results of a study of sex rings developed for the purpose of child sexual abuse.

### Adult Leaders of the Rings

In all cases (forty) studied, adults (at least ten to fifteen years older than the victims) were the dominant leaders, organizers and operators of the sex rings. In no case did children or youths seek out an adult for sex, pornography or prostitution; young people were selectively gathered together for a sexual purpose, which was usually implicit in the initial stages. The involvement varied from the first contact to months, with the longest time periods occurring in those cases where prepubescent children were involved. All cases involved male ringleaders, but a few cases involved female codefendants, usually husband/wife pairs. The youngest adults were in their twenties and the oldest in their seventies.

To organize a ring, whether for child molesting, pornography, prostitution or any combination of these, the offender needs access to a group of children. The access routes for group victimization include occupation, a child and the neighborhood.

Almost half (twenty) the offenders used their *occupation* as the major access route to the child victims. The adult had a legitimate role as an authority figure in the lives of the children selected for the ring or was able to survey vulnerable children through access to family records or history.

On occasion, a ring is formed by the adult targeting a *child*, who then uses his or her connections via peer pressure to bring other children into the group. The initial child may be a relative of the offender, or the adult may solicit the help of a previously unknown child. One technique used was posting a notice on a store bulletin board requesting girls to help with housework.

The adult's status in the *neighborhood* sometimes helped to legitimize his presence with the children and their parents and permitted the unquestioned movement of young people into his home. Such an offender often is well liked by his neighbors.

### Types of Sex Rings

Investigators should be aware of three types of sex rings: solo, transition and syndicated sex rings. Certain cults also are involved in sexual abuse of children.

**Solo Sex Rings.**   The organization of solo sex rings is primarily by the age of the child—for example, toddlers (ages two to five), prepubescent (six to twelve), or pubescent (thirteen to seventeen). Sex rings are interactional situations involving an adult as organizer or ringleader and a child or adolescent as victim. This type of offender prefers to have multiple children as sex objects, in contrast to the offender who seeks out one child at a time.

**Transition Sex Rings.**   Although pedophilia is a sex offense in all states, there is a strong need among pedophiles to communicate with others regarding their interest in children. In transition rings, experiences are exchanged, whereas in solo rings, the pedophile keeps his or her activities and photographs totally secret. Photographs of children as well as sexual services may be traded and sold.

The trading of pornography appears to be the first move of the victim into the possession of other pedophiles. The photographs are traded, and victims may be tested by other offenders and eventually traded for their sexual services.

**Syndicated Sex Rings.**   The third type of ring noted in the sample was the syndicated ring. This ring involves a well-structured organization that recruits children, produces pornography, delivers direct sexual services and establishes an extensive network of customers. The number of adults operating these rings ranged from two to nine. Syndicated rings have involved a Boy Scout troop, a boys' farm operated by a minister and a national boy prostitution ring.

**Cults.**   According to Wrobleski and Hess (1997, p. 278): "Of great concern to law enforcement is growing evidence of rather widespread ritualistic abuse of children." Crimes associated with cults are discussed in Chapter 19.

### Sex Crimes by Other Children

Although seldom discussed, an increasing number of child sex crimes are being committed by other children. Many people think that such crimes would not occur because children are often viewed as not being sexually capable. However, arrests of twelve- to fourteen-year-olds for sexual offenses increased 70 percent during the 1980s. Some child sexual abusers were molested themselves.

When investigators receive reports of children committing sex crimes against other children, they must not automatically dismiss them as fantasy. All such reports must be thoroughly investigated.

### Victimology

Persons involved in the intervention, investigation or prosecution of child pornography and sex ring cases must recognize that a bond often develops between the offender and the victims. Many victims find themselves willing to trade sex for attention, affection and other benefits. Pedophile ring operators are, by definition, skilled at gaining the continued cooperation and control of their victims through well-planned seduction. They are skilled at recognizing and then *temporarily* filling the emotional and physical needs of children. They know how to listen to children—an ability many parents lack. They are willing to spend all the time it takes to seduce the child.

This positive offender/victim bond must not be misinterpreted as consent, complicity or guilt. In one case, a prosecutor announced to the television media that the victims were as guilty, if not more guilty, than the offenders. Police investigators, in particular, must be sensitive to this problem.

### Offender Reactions

When a child pornography and sex ring is discovered, certain reactions by the pedophile offenders are fairly predictable. The intensity of these reactions may depend on how much the offenders have to lose by their identification and conviction.

Usually the first reaction of pedophiles to discovery is complete denial. The offenders may act shocked, surprised or even indignant about such an allegation of sexual activity with children. This denial frequently is aided by their friends, neighbors, relatives and co-workers, who insist that they are such wonderful people there is no way they could have done what is alleged.

If the evidence rules out total denial, offenders may switch to a slightly different tactic, attempting to minimize what has been done in both quantity and quality. Pedophiles are often knowledgeable about the law and might admit to acts known to be lesser offenses or misdemeanors.

Either as part of the effort to minimize or as a separate reaction, pedophiles typically attempt to justify their behavior. They might claim that they care for these children more than their parents do and that what they do is beneficial to the children. They may claim to have been under tremendous stress, have a drinking problem or not to have known how young a certain victim was. The efforts to justify the behavior often center around blaming the victim. Offenders may claim they were seduced by the victims, that the victims initiated the sexual activity or that the victims were promiscuous or even prostitutes.

When various reactions do not result in termination of the investigation or prosecution, pedophiles may claim to be sick, unable to control themselves. Pedophile manuals advocate this tactic when all else fails.

---

Pedophiles' reactions to being discovered usually begin with complete denial then progress through minimizing the acts, justifying the acts and blaming the victims. If all else fails, they may claim to be sick.

---

With the increase in criminal cases involving physical and sexual abuse of children, the problems associated with children providing testimony in court have increased proportionately. Court procedures and legal practices that benefit the child witness may not be balanced with the rights of the accused, and vice versa. To resolve some of these problems, the courts have changed a number of rules and procedures. The following are some of the changes:

- Some courts give preference to these cases by placing them ahead of other cases on the docket.
- Some courts permit videotaping child interviews and then providing access to the tapes to numerous individuals to spare the child the added trauma of multiple interviews.
- Privileges for repeated medical and psychological examinations of children are being limited.
- To reduce the number of times the child must face the accused, the courts are allowing testimony concerning observations of the child by another person who is not a witness, allowing the child to remain in another room during the trial and/or using a videotape of the child's testimony as evidence.
- Some courts remove the accused from the courtroom during the child's testimony.

Many of these changes in rules and procedures are being challenged, however. Future court decisions will establish precedents to be followed in child abuse and neglect cases.

## Preventing Child Abuse

---

Child abuse may be prevented by educating children and by keeping the channels of communication with them open.

---

The following specific suggestions should assist in preventing child abuse. Although the suggestions refer to parents, they apply equally to guardians or any other individuals who care for children.

**1.** Parents should teach their children about sexual abuse, what forms it might take and what to do about it. Children should learn to discuss sex questions with their parents. They should know what sexual abuse is, including anyone touching their anus, penis, vagina or breasts. They should learn to tell their parents if they encounter any abnormal sexual behavior from adults.

**2.** Parents should listen to their children. Children may drop subtle hints such as "Uncle Charlie was not very nice to me today." An appropriate response might be "Oh? How was he not nice?" Such a response might elicit a statement such as "He asked me to take down my pants when I was in the car."

**3.** Children should be instructed to tell their parents when someone tells them, "Don't tell anyone." Usually if someone says not to tell, it is about something that is wrong.

**4.** Parents should understand that children do not usually tell tales about sexual abuse. Experience has taught parents and police that the vast majority of sexual abuse incidents as told by children are true. Therefore, if a child tells a parent about being sexually abused, the parents should report it to the police immediately.

**5.** Older children should be taught to tell their parents where they are going, with whom and approximately when they expect to return. They should learn to call home if plans change.

**6.** Children should be taught to stay with the group when they are on picnics or at events away from home and that if they become lost, they are to go to an area where people are present and seek help.

**7.** Children should be taught that when they are home alone they should lock the doors and windows and should never let strangers into the home. Parents should see that doors and windows are locked before they leave the child alone. They should also give proper instructions for leaving the home in case of fire.

**8.** Children should be taught that sometimes it is all right to tell a lie. For example, if a child is home alone and receives a phone call for one of the parents, it is all right to say the parents are home but cannot come to the phone because they are resting or in the shower or some other excuse.

**9.** Parents should help children plan safe routes to and from school and their friends' homes. Children should then travel these routes. "Block parent" programs can provide places where children can stop if in danger, or the parents should tell their children what houses they can stop at where friends of the family live. Children should be taught to play in groups; to avoid vacant buildings, alleys and restrooms; and to walk with friends when possible.

**10.** Baby sitters should be selected carefully. References should always be requested and checked.

Child abusers can be of any race, age or occupation; someone close or a complete stranger. When they are given adequate information, children can avoid sexual molestation situations and they can protect themselves against them.

## Summary

Crimes against children include kidnapping, abandonment, neglect, exploitation, physical abuse, emotional abuse, incest and sexual assault. Such crimes can result in permanent and serious damage physically, mentally and emotionally. The Child Protection Act prohibits child pornography and greatly increases the penalties for adults who engage in it.

Problems in investigating crimes against children include the need to protect the child from further harm, the possibility of parental involvement, the difficulty in interviewing children and the potential need to involve other agencies.

Generally, reports of child neglect or abuse are made by third parties such as teachers, neighbors, siblings and parents. Seldom does the victim report the offense. When such reports are received, if the possibility of present or

*Read the following articles and imagine yourself as the officer/detective assigned to each case. What elements of the crime are present? What evidence would you need to prosecute the case? Who else might you need to coordinate your efforts with? What is the likelihood of solving each crime?*

### Killing of children 'fits with trend'

*Child abuse, slaying on rise*

**By Misti Snow**

***Star Tribune* Staff Writer**

Their names read like a classroom roster—Hannah, Jordyn, Tuyet, Alex, Brandon, Byron, Jacob, Eric, Jeremiah and Jody. But these are not the names of friends in an schoolroom. These are the 10 children under age 14 who were slain in Minnesota in just the past two months.

Their ages ranged from 7 months to 13 years. They died violently, most at the hands of adults: their parents, a mother's boyfriend, an elderly neighbor, a drive-by shooter. And they're not the only Minnesota children to be slain this year. Four other children in this age group have been killed since January.

Roy Garza, director of the Minnesota Committee for the Prevention of Child Abuse, said he was saddened but not surprised by the deaths.

The killings "fit with the trend of increasing child abuse," he said. "We are a society that accepts, condones and glamorizes violence."

Source: *Star Tribune,* 16 July 1996. Reprinted by permission of the *Star Tribune*, Minneapolis/St. Paul.

### Girl, 17, charged with trying to abduct boy

A 17-year-old girl with a history of sexually abusing children was charged Monday with trying to kidnap an 8-year-old boy at a Kmart store in St. Paul.

The boy's father was shopping Sunday evening in the store at 245 Maryland Ave. when "somebody runs up to him and tells him a girl is trying to take his kid out of the store," said police Inspector Doug Holtz. The father ran to the parking lot, where the girl was surrounded by a group of shoppers and store security people, he said.

"The kid turned on his father and runs right toward him," he said.

*(continued on p. 386)*

continued danger to the child exists, the child must be placed in protective custody. In the vast majority of child abuse cases, children tell the truth to the best of their ability. Investigators should listen carefully to children and should look for indicators of neglect or abuse. These indicators may be physical or behavioral or both. Evidence includes the surroundings, the home conditions, clothing, bruises or other body injuries, the medical examination report and other observations.

Investigators should also be aware of pedophiles, adults who have either heterosexual or homosexual preferences for young boys or girls of a specific, limited age range. Many pedophiles are members of sex rings. Three types of sex rings have been identified: solo, transition and syndicated. Certain cults also practice sexual abuse of children. Pedophiles' reactions to being discovered usually begin with complete denial and progress through minimizing the acts, justifying the acts and blaming the victims. If all else fails, they may claim to be sick.

Child abuse can be prevented by educating children about it and by keeping the channels of communication with them open.

Holtz said witnesses said the girl dragged the boy by his hair out of the store while covering his mouth with one hand. He said she has a history of sexually abusing children, but didn't know specific details.

He said that the girl ran away from a group home, but that he didn't know if it is in the Twin Cities. She was held Monday evening at the Anoka County Juvenile Detention Center. Holtz said she may be charged as an adult.

Source: *Star Tribune*, 11 June, 1996. Reprinted by permission of the *Star Tribune*, Minneapolis/St. Paul.

## Release of 6-year-old in beating considered

**Associated Press**

MARTINEZ, Calif.—A Contra Costa County juvenile court referee on Wednesday agreed to consider releasing a 6-year-old boy charged with attempted murder from Juvenile Hall as long as he lives in a suitable environment.

Juvenile referee Stephen Easton denied a request by the boy's lawyers to release him to his mother. Easton said he was considering a suggestion to move the boy to a foster home away from his old neighborhood, although it was not immediately clear when that decision would be made.

The kindergartner is charged with breaking into a Richmond apartment and beating and kicking then-4-week-old Ignacio Bermudez Jr. and stealing a Big Wheel tricycle. Charged with robbery were 8-year-old twins, who were with the boy during the attack.

Also Wednesday, Easton appointed two psychiatrists from Children's Hospital in Oakland to evaluate the 6-year-old. The evaluation is due June 5.

That evaluation could show whether the boy knows the difference between right and wrong and help determine whether the case is handled by the courts or social services, said the boy's lawyer, John Burris.

Source: *Las Vegas Review Journal*, 9 May, 1996. Reprinted by permission of the Associated Press.

# Checklist

## *Crimes Against Children*

- What statute has been violated, if any?
- What are the elements of the offense charged?
- Who initiated the crime?
- Are there witnesses to the offense?
- What evidence is needed for proving the elements of the offense charged?
- Is there physical evidence?
- Has physical evidence been submitted for laboratory examination?
- Who has been interviewed?
- Are written statements available?
- Would a polygraph be of any assistance in examining the victim? The suspect?
- Is there probable cause to obtain a search warrant?
- What items should be included in the search?
- Is the victim able to provide specific dates and times?

- Is the victim able to provide details of what happened?
- What physical and behaviorial indicators are present in this case?
- Were photographs taken of injuries to the victim?
- Is the victim in danger of continued abuse?
- Is it necessary to remove the victim into protective custody?
- Has the local welfare jurisdiction been notified? Was there a joint investigation to avoid duplication of effort?
- Is there a file on known sexual offenders in the community?
- Is a child sexual abuse ring involved in the offense?
- Could the offense have been prevented? How?

## Application

**A.** A police officer receives an anonymous call reporting sexual abuse of a ten-year-old white female. The caller states that the abusers are the father and brother of the girl and provides all three names and their address. When the officer requests more details, the caller hangs up. You are assigned the case and initiate the investigation by contacting the alleged victim at school. She is reluctant to talk to you at first but eventually admits that both her father and brother have been having sex with her for almost a year. You then question the suspects and obtain written statements in which they admit the sexual abuse.

### Questions
**1.** Should the investigation have been initiated on the basis of the anonymous caller?
**2.** What type of crime has been committed?
**3.** Was it appropriate to make the initial contact with the victim at her school?
**4.** Who should be present at the initial interview of the victim?
**5.** What should be done with the victim after obtaining the facts?
**6.** What would be the basis for an affidavit for an arrest warrant?

**B.** A police officer receives an anonymous phone call stating that a child is being sexually assaulted at a specific address. The officer goes to the address, an apartment and through an open door sees a child lying on the floor, apparently unconscious. The officer enters the apartment and, while checking the child for injuries, notices blood on the child's face and clothing. The child regains consciousness, and the officer asks, "Did your dad do this?" The child answers, "Yes." The officer then goes into another room and finds the father in bed, intoxicated. He rouses him and places him under arrest.

### Questions
**1.** Was the officer authorized to enter the apartment on the basis of the initial information?
**2.** Was the officer authorized to enter without a warrant?
**3.** Should the officer have asked if the father had done it? If not, how should the question have been phrased?
**4.** Was an arrest of the father justified without a warrant?
**5.** What should be done with the victim?

**C.** A woman living in another state telephones the police department and identifies herself as the ex-wife of a man she believes is performing illegal sexual acts with the daughter of his present lover. The man resides in the police department's jurisdiction. The woman says the acts have been witnessed by her sons who have been in the area visiting their father. The sons told her that the father goes into the bathroom and bedroom with his lover's eight-year-old daughter and closes the door. They also have seen the father making suggestive advances to the girl and taking her into the shower with him. The girl has told her sons that the father does "naughty" things to her. Her sons are currently at home with her, but she is worried about the little girl.

### Questions

1. Should an investigation be initiated based on this third-hand information?
2. If the report is founded, what type of crime is being committed?
3. Who has jurisdiction to investigate?
4. What actions would be necessary in the noninitiating state?
5. Where should the initial contact with the alleged victim be made?

**D.** A reliable informant has told the police that a man has been molesting children in his garage. Police establish a surveillance of the suspect and see him invite a juvenile into his car. They follow the car and see it pull into the driveway of the man's residence. The man and the boy then go into the house. The officers follow and knock on the front door, but they receive no answer. They knock again and loudly state their purpose. When they continue to receive no answer, they enter the house through the unlocked front door, talk to the boy and based on what he says, they arrest the suspect.

### Questions

1. Did the officers violate the suspect's right to privacy and domestic security?
2. Does the emergency doctrine apply?
3. What should be done with the victim?
4. Was the arrest legal?

*Note:* In each of the preceding cases, the information is initially received not from the victim but from third parties. This is usually the case in child abuse offenses.

## Discussion Questions

1. At what age does a child cease to be a minor in your state?
2. What is the child sexual-abuse problem in your community? How many offenses were charged during the past year? Is there any method of estimating how many unreported offenses occurred?
3. What are some common physical and behavioral abuse indicators?
4. What evidence is commonly found in child sexual-abuse cases?
5. What types of evidence are needed for establishing probable cause for a search warrant?
6. Who are suspects in child sexual-abuse cases?

7. What statutes in your state or community are applicable to prosecuting child sexual-abuse cases?

8. What are some special difficulties in interviewing children? In having children testify in court?

9. What is being done in your community to prevent crimes against children?

10. Have any sex rings been exposed in your community? Your state?

## References

Benshoff, Anastasia. "Schools to Shelve Paddles." *The Rockford Register Star,* Saturday, October 16, 1993, p. 4B.

Boros, Stephen, and Larry Brubaker. "Munchhausen Syndrome by Proxy." *FBI Law Enforcement Bulletin,* June 1992, pp. 16–20.

Briscoe, Judy. "The Cost of Child Abuse and Neglect." *Corrections Today,* December 1994, pp. 26–28.

Burden, Ordway. "National Fingerprint Program for Child Identification." *Law and Order,* January 1995, p. 325.

———. "Retirees Aid Search for Missing Kids." *Law Enforcement News,* October 15, 1992, p. 5.

"Chicago Couple Face Multiple Charges of Long-Term Abuse of Four Children." (Minneapolis/St. Paul) *Star Tribune,* February 7, 1996, p. A8.

D'Arcy, Stephen. "Tracking Habitual Offenders." *Law and Order,* March 1995, pp. 111–112.

Dees, Timothy M. "Cyberhip Chickenhawks: A Mix of Kids, Computers and Pedophiles." *Law Enforcement Technology,* October 1994, pp. 52–56.

"Direct from the Source: Sex Offenders Prey on Young Family Members." *Law Enforcement News,* March 15, 1996, p. 7.

Duvall, Ed, Jr. "What Is Happening to Our Children?" *Law and Order,* November 1991, p. 109.

Geberth, Vernon J. "Munchausen Syndrome by Proxy (MSBP)." *Law and Order,* August 1994, pp. 95–97.

Hinzman, Gary, and Dennis Blome. "Cooperation Key to Success of Child Protection Center." *The Police Chief,* February 1991, pp. 24, 27.

Holmes, Ronald M., Stephen T. Holmes and Jerrie Unholz. "Female Pedophilia." *Law and Order,* 1993, pp. 77–79.

*Joint Investigation of Child Abuse: Report of a Symposium.* Washington, DC: U.S. Department of Justice and U.S. Department of Health and Human Services, July 1993.

Lanning, K., and A. W. Burgess. "Child Pornography and Sex Rings." *FBI Law Enforcement Bulletin,* January 1984.

Lynch, Raymond, and Michael Bussiculo. "A Law Enforcement Officer's Guide to Interviewing Child Sex Abuse Victims." *Law and Order,* May 1991, pp. 90–94.

Martin, Susan E., and Douglas J. Besharov. *Police and Child Abuse: New Policies for Expanded Responsibilities.* Washington, DC: U.S. Department of Justice, National Institute of Justice, 1991.

McCauley, Dennis. "Hi-Tech Crooks." *Police,* December 1996, pp. 32–49.

Overton, W.C., D. Burns and J. Atkins. "Child Sexual Abuse Investigation." *Law and Order,* July 1994, pp. 97–100.

"Report: Violence Kills 2,000 Kids a Year." (Minneapolis/St. Paul) *Star Tribune,* April 26, 1995, p. A2.

Slahor, Stephenie. "Just for Kids." *Law and Order,* January 1992, p. 281.

Steidel, Stephen E. "M/Cap: Addressing the Issue of Missing and Exploited Children." *The Police Chief,* June 1992, pp. 65–66.

Tjaden, Patricia G. "Joining Forces for the Good of the Victim." *Law Enforcement News,* October 15, 1995, p. 8.

U.S. Public Law 95–225 (1978). *An Act Relating to Sexual Exploitation of Children.*

"When Adults Hurt Kids." *Instant Evidence,* Summer 1996, pp. 8–9.

Widom, Cathy Spatz. *The Cycle of Violence: Research in Brief.* Washington, DC: National Institute of Justice, October 1992.

———. *Victims of Childhood Sexual Abuse—Later Criminal Consequences: Research in Brief.* Washington, DC: National Institute of Justice, March 1995.

Wrobleski, Henry M., and Kären M. Hess. *Introduction to Law Enforcement and Criminal Justice,* 5th ed. St. Paul: West Publishing, 1997.

# Homicide

## DO YOU KNOW

What a basic requirement in a homicide investigation is?

What the four categories of death are?

How to define and classify homicide, murder and manslaughter?

What degrees of murder are frequently specified?

How criminal and noncriminal homicide differ?

How excusable and justifiable homicide differ?

What the elements of each category of murder and manslaughter are?

What special problems are encountered in a homicide investigation?

What first priority in a homicide investigation is?

How to establish that death has occurred?

How to identify an unknown homicide victim?

What factors help in estimating the time of death?

What cadaveric spasm is and why it is important?

What effect water has on a dead body?

What the most frequent causes of unnatural death are and what
indicates whether a death is a suicide or a homicide?

What information and evidence is obtained from the victim?

Why determining a motive is important in homicide investigations?

What physical evidence is usually found in homicides?

What information is provided by the medical examiner or coroner?

## CAN YOU DEFINE

adipocere
asphyxiation
autoerotic asphyxiation
cadaveric spasm
criminal homicide
criminal negligence
defense wounds
excusable homicide
first-degree murder

heat of passion
hesitation wounds
homicide
involuntary
     manslaughter
justifiable homicide
malicious intent
manslaughter
mummification
murder

noncriminal homicide
postmortem lividity
premeditation
rigor mortis
second-degree murder
serial murder
suicide
third-degree murder
toxicology
voluntary manslaughter

## Introduction

YOU ARRIVE AT THE SCENE OF A DEATH IN RESPONSE TO AN EMERGENCY
call and find the body of a fifty-five-year-old white male crumpled at the bottom of a steep staircase—obviously dead. Did the victim trip and fall (accidental death)? Did he suffer a fatal heart attack at the top of the stairs and then fall (natural death)? Did he throw himself down the stairs to end some intense physical or mental suffering (suicide)? Or was he pushed (homicide)?

Only the fourth explanation involves a criminal action meriting an official police investigation. However, because the police must determine whether it actually was homicide, the other three possible explanations must be investigated.

A basic requirement in a homicide investigation is to establish that death was caused by a criminal action.

Statistically, murder is the least significant of the Index Crimes. However, deaths reported as accidents or suicides can actually have been murder, and vice versa.

"Murder in America" (1995, p. 18) states: "Murder remains a problem that undermines the security and quality of life of all Americans." In addition, according to "Murder in the U.S." (1995, p. 20), the nature of murder has changed, making investigations more difficult. This article suggests that there are more murders between strangers, more juvenile gang killings and more guns involved than in past years.

The FBI *Uniform Crime Report* (1995) indicated that there were 21,597 murder offenses, 7.4 percent less than in 1994 when there were 23,326. Firearms were the most frequently used weapon (68 percent), accounting for seven out of ten victim deaths. Cutting instruments were used in 13 percent; personal weapons, such as hands and feet, 6 percent; blunt weapons, 5 percent; 15 percent were killed by strangling. Less than half were related to their assailants: 26 percent of females were killed by husbands or boyfriends; 18 percent occurred while committing felony crimes; 28 percent resulted from arguments; 8 percent were related to gang activities.

In 1995, 65 percent of murders were cleared by arrest. This is a higher percentage than any other index crime. Persons under 18 accounted for only 9 percent of murders; 91 percent were males, 9 percent females. Blacks comprised 54 percent and whites 43 percent. There were 21,230 arrests for murder: 56 percent were under 25 years of age, with the 18–24 age group accounting for 41 percent.

In some instances, suicides and homicides *appear to* encourage other suicides and homicides. This raises the question, might suicide or murder be contagious in the short term? David Phillips, a sociologist at the University of California, San Diego, conducted a six-year study of media-linked violence and found a connection between certain news stories and suicides or murders ("A Plague Called Violence," by Sherry Baker, *Omni*). Phillips's study was based on actual acts of violence. In a number of instances, increases in violence occurred after acts of violence were reported by the media.

There is also evidence that violence increases when temperatures rise, and this includes indoor and outdoor violence. It has been reported that violence increases on holidays and weekends and that suicide rates increase in April and May. Violence rates are higher in southern states than in northern states.

Homicides draw media attention, and police may be plagued by the press when homicides occur in their jurisdiction. Homicides also receive the most attention by police. This is not only because they are considered the most serious crime but also because they are complex cases to investigate. It must first be determined if death was due to accident, suicide or homicide. It may be necessary to determine whether the crime was a murder made to appear as a suicide to eliminate further investigation or a murder made to appear as an accident to collect life insurance.

This chapter begins with a classification of homicide and descriptions of criminal homicide, noncriminal homicide and suicide. This is followed by a discussion of the elements of the crime, special problems in investigating homicides and the preliminary investigation. Next the chapter focuses on identifying the victim and estimating the time of death. Then a discussion of unnatural causes of death and the method used, as well as drug-related homicides, is presented. This is followed by an examination of victims, witnesses and suspects and a look at the physical evidence often found in homicide investigations. The chapter concludes with a description of the role of the medical examination, the importance of collaborative efforts in investigating homicides and the unpleasant task of death notification.

## Classification

The four types of death:

| | |
|---|---|
| Natural <br> Accidental <br> Suicide | } Noncriminal |
| Homicide — | Noncriminal or criminal |

### Natural Causes

Natural causes of death include heart attacks, strokes, fatal diseases, pneumonia, sudden crib deaths and old age. Frequently, a person who dies of natural causes has been under a physician's care, and it is easily established that death was from natural causes.

Sometimes, however, a death is made to look as though it resulted from natural causes. For example, drugs that simulate the effects of a heart attack might be used in a suicide or homicide.

### Accidental Deaths

Among the causes of accidental death are falling, drowning, unintentionally taking too many pills or ingesting a poisonous substance, being caught in industrial or farm machinery or being involved in an automobile, boat, train, bus or plane crash.

As with natural deaths, an apparent accidental death can actually be a suicide or a homicide. For example, a person can jump or be pushed from a roof or in front of a vehicle or can voluntarily or involuntarily take an overdose of pills.

### Suicide

**Suicide,** the intentional taking of one's own life, can be committed by shooting, stabbing, poison, burns, asphyxiation or ingesting drugs or poisons. However, homicides are often made to look like suicides, and many suicides are made to look like accidents, usually for insurance purposes or to ease the family's suffering. In most states it is not a crime to commit suicide, but aiding and abetting, or assisting, suicides is controversial. Is it a crime or not?

### Homicide

If another individual is the direct or indirect cause of the death, it is classified as **homicide.**

---

Homicide is the killing of one person by another.

---

Homicide includes the taking of life by another human or by an agency, such as a government. It is either **criminal** or **noncriminal,** that is, felonious or nonfelonious.

Criminal homicide is subdivided into murder and manslaughter, both of which are further subdivided. Noncriminal homicide is subdivided into excusable and justifiable homicide.

---

Classification of homicides:
    Criminal (felonious).
      Murder (first, second and third degree).
      Manslaughter (voluntary and involuntary).
    Noncriminal (nonfelonious).
      Excusable homicide.
      Justifiable homicide.

---

Thus, *murder* and *homicide* are not synonymous. All murders are homicides (and criminal), but not all homicides are murders (or criminal).

## Criminal Homicide

The two classes of criminal homicide—murder and manslaughter—have several similarities but also important differences.

### Murder

**Murder** is the most severe statutory crime, one of the few for which the penalty can be life imprisonment or death. (In some states treason and ransom kidnapping carry a similarly severe penalty.) Some laws classify murder as first, second or third degree. **First-degree murder** requires premeditation (advanced planning) and the intent to cause death. Some statutes include in this classification any death that results while committing or attempting to commit a felony such as rape or robbery. **Second-degree murder** includes the intent to cause death but not premeditation. An example is a violent argument that ends in one person spontaneously killing the other. **Third-degree murder** involves neither premeditation nor intent. It results from an act that is imminently dangerous to others and shows a disregard for human life, such as shooting into a room where people are likely to be present or playing a practical joke that could result in someone's death.

### Manslaughter

**Manslaughter** is the unlawful killing of another person with no prior malice. It may be voluntary or involuntary.

**Voluntary manslaughter** is intentionally causing the death of another person in the heat of passion, caused by words or acts that provide adequate provocation. For example, the law generally recognizes such acts as adultery, seduction of a child or rape of a close female relative as outrageous enough to constitute adequate provocation. This provocation must result in intense passion that replaces reason and leads to the immediate act. The provocation, passion and fatal act must occur in rapid succession and be directly, sequentially related; that is, the provocation must cause the passion that causes the fatal act.

**Involuntary manslaughter** is accidental homicide that results from extreme (culpable) negligence. Examples of involuntary manslaughter include handling a firearm negligently, leaving poison where children might take it or operating an automobile, boat or aircraft in a criminally negligent manner. Some states, such as California, have a third category of manslaughter: manslaughter with a motor vehicle.

Other acts that can be classified as involuntary manslaughter include shooting another person with a firearm or other dangerous weapon while mistakenly believing that person to be an animal; setting a spring gun, pitfall, deadfall, snare or other dangerous device designed to trap animals but capable of harming humans; and negligently and intentionally allowing an animal known to be vicious to roam free.

---

Murder:
| | |
|---|---|
| First degree | Premeditated and intentional, or while committing or attempting to commit a felony. |
| Second degree | Intentional but not premeditated. |
| Third degree | Neither intentional nor premeditated, but the result of an imminently dangerous act. |

Manslaughter:
| | |
|---|---|
| Voluntary | Intentional homicide caused by intense passion resulting from adequate provocation. |
| Involuntary | Unintentional homicide caused by criminal (culpable) negligence. |

---

## Noncriminal Homicide

Although the term *homicide* is usually associated with crime, not all homicides are crimes.

---

Excusable homicide is the unintentional, truly accidental killing of another person. Justifiable homicide is killing another person under authorization of the law.

---

**Excusable homicide** results from an act that normally would not cause death or from an act committed with ordinary caution that, because of the *victim's* negligence, results in death, as when a person runs in front of a car.

**Justifiable homicide** includes killing in self-defense or in the defense of another person if the victim's actions and capability present imminent danger of serious injury or death. This classification includes capital punishment, death caused by a public officer while carrying out a court order and deaths caused by police officers while attempting to prevent a dangerous felon's escape or to recapture a dangerous felon who has escaped or is resisting arrest. Killing an enemy during wartime is also classified as justifiable homicide.

## Suicide

Although suicide is not a criminal offense, in most states it is a crime to attempt to commit suicide. This allows the state to take custody of such individuals legally for hospitalization or treatment. It may be a crime to help someone commit or attempt to commit suicide either by intentionally advising, encouraging or actually assisting the victim in the act, as previously noted.

At the center of the controversy are the actions of Jack Kevorkian, "Dr. Death," an assisted-suicide crusader who has assisted in more than thirty suicides since 1990 and who has never been convicted ("Jury Hands Kevorkian His Third Acquittal," 1996, p. A4).

## Elements of the Crime

Laws on criminal homicide vary significantly from state to state, but certain common elements are usually found in each, as summarized in Table 12–1. The degree eventually charged is decided by the prosecuting attorney based on the available evidence. For example, the only difference between first- and second-degree murder is the element of premeditation. If thorough investigation does not yield proof of premeditation, a charge of second-degree murder is made.

**Causing the Death of Another Human.** Usually, the death of a human is not difficult to prove; a death certificate completed by a physician, coroner or medical examiner suffices. If a death certificate is not available, the investigator must locate witnesses to testify that they saw the body of the person allegedly killed by the suspect. When insufficient remains exist to identify the body positively, death is proven by circumstantial evidence such as examination by a qualified pathologist or by other experts and their expert testimony regarding dental work, bone structure and the like.

A more difficult portion of the element to prove is the causation of death. To show that the suspect's act caused the death: (1) prove the cause of death and (2) prove that the suspect, through direct action, inflicted injury sufficient to cause the death with some weapon or device. For example, if the cause of death was a fatal wound from a .22-caliber weapon, it is necessary to show that the

**Table 12–1 Degrees of Homicide**

| | Murder | | | Manslaughter | |
|---|---|---|---|---|---|
| Element | First Degree | Second Degree | Third Degree | Voluntary | Involuntary |
| Causing the death of another human | ** | ** | ** | ** | ** |
| Premeditation | * | | | | |
| Malicious intent | * | * | | | |
| Adequately provoked intent resulting in the heat of passion | | | | * | |
| †While committing or attempting to commit a felony | * | | | | |
| †While committing or attempting to commit a crime not a felony | | | * | * | |
| When forced or threatened | | | | * | |
| Culpable negligence or depravity | | | * | | |
| Negligence | | | | | * |

†indicates that the other single-starred elements need not be proven.

suspect produced the cause of death. Did the suspect own such a weapon? Can witnesses testify that the suspect had such a weapon immediately before the fatal injury? Was the suspect seen actually committing the offense? Did the suspect admit the act by statement or confession?

**Premeditation.**   **Premeditation** is considering, planning or preparing for an act, no matter how briefly, before committing it. Laws use such terms as *premeditated design to kill* or *malice of forethought.* Whatever the law's wording, it is necessary to prove some intention and plan to commit the crime before it was actually committed.

---

Premeditation is the element of first-degree murder that sets it apart from all other classifications.

---

Were oral statements made during a heated argument? Threats? Did the suspect buy or have a gun just before the crime was committed or travel a long distance to wait for the victim? Premeditation can be proved in many ways. Sometimes the time interval between thought and action is only a minute; other times it may be hours, days, weeks, months or even years.

Determine at what time before the killing the suspect considered, planned, threatened or made some overt act to prepare to commit the murder. This might be established by statements from witnesses or from the victim before death, from evidence at the crime scene or through a review of the suspect's past criminal history and statements.

**Intent to Effect the Death of Another Person.**   Intent is a required element of most categories of criminal homicide. Evidence must show that the crime was intentional, not accidental. **Malicious intent,** an element of first- and second-degree murder, implies ill will, wickedness or cruelty. How the act was committed shows the degree of intent. The type of weapon used, how and when it was acquired and how the suspect and victim came together helps prove the intent as well as the act that caused the death.

Intent and premeditation are not the same. Premeditation is not a requirement of intent. Most crimes of passion involve intent but not premeditation or malicious intent.

This element also applies to a death caused to someone other than the intended victim. For example, in one case a woman intended to kill her husband by placing poison in a bottle of whiskey he kept under the seat of the family car. Unknowingly, the husband offered a drink from the bottle to a friend, who died as a result. The wife was charged with first-degree murder and convicted even though the person who died was not her intended victim. It was a reasonable consequence of her act. An explosive set for one person may detonate prematurely and kill someone else. A person shooting at an intended victim may miss and kill an innocent bystander. Both of these would constitute first-degree murder.

**Adequately Provoked Intent Resulting in Heat of Passion.**   This element is the alternative to premeditation. It assumes that the act was committed when the suspect suddenly became extremely emotional, thus precluding premeditation. **Heat of passion** results from extremely volatile arguments between two people, from seeing a wife or family member raped, from a sudden discovery of adultery or from seeing a brutal assault being committed against a close friend or family member.

**While Committing or Attempting to Commit a Felony.**   In some states, a charge of first-degree murder does not require that the murder was committed with premeditation if the victim died as a result of acts committed while the suspect was engaged in a felony such as rape, robbery or arson. Proof of the elements of the felony must, of course, be established.

**While Committing or Attempting to Commit a Crime Not a Felony.** If a death results from an act committed by a suspect engaged in a nonfelonious crime such as purse-snatching or petty theft, it can be charged as either third-degree murder or voluntary manslaughter, depending on the state where the offense occurs.

**Culpable Negligence or Depravity.**   The act and the way it is committed establish this element. The act must be so dangerous that any prudent person would see death of a person as a possible consequence. A person causing a death while depraved and committing acts evident of such depravity is guilty of third-degree murder.

**Negligence.**   A fine line separates this element from the preceding element. Some laws make no distinction, classifying both in a separate category of **criminal negligence.** Where separate categories exist, this lesser degree of negligence involves creating a situation that results in an unreasonable risk of death or great bodily harm.

## Special Problems in Investigation

Police have an obligation to act on behalf of the deceased and their families. They are expected to conduct a professional investigation to identify, arrest and prosecute suspects. One apparent injustice in the criminal justice system is that, to an outsider, it appears that the police are constantly trying to protect the rights of the perpetrator and pay slight attention to the rights of the deceased or the family.

Special problems in homicide investigations include pressure by the media and the public, the difficulty of establishing that a crime has been committed, identifying the victim and establishing the cause and time of death.

Homicides create high interest in the community, as evidenced by increased sales of newspapers and higher ratings for the broadcast media. Indeed, the news media have a special interest in police investigations of deaths—accidental or otherwise. Police officers who have dealt with the news media understand the important relationship between law enforcement and the media, as noted in Chapter 1. Although the media need the police and the police need the media, their needs do not necessarily coincide in time or place. Whenever possible, it is desirable to establish guidelines and understandings with the press. In larger departments, a public relations officer may be assigned to deal with the media. In smaller departments, it is generally the supervisor in charge or a higher-ranking officer who handles this responsibility. Officers at the scene or investigating the crime should refer inquiries to their immediate supervisor. This centralizes responsibility for what is released and permits officers to perform their functions at the scene without interruption.

Police policies and guidelines should specify what information is to be released: the deceased's name, accused's name and general identifying information, any details regarding formal charges and general facts about the investigation that are not harmful to the continuing investigation of the case.

Information that could be prejudicial should be omitted—for example, personal opinions, conjectures as to future pleas or charges, any prior record of the accused, any details of admissions or confessions, results of laboratory tests—as should the names of juveniles and the identity of victims of certain crimes.

Do not pose the accused for photographs, and do not permit the accused to talk to the press. If investigators have details that are known only to them and the accused, that information must not be released. Exercising good sense, getting to know the reporters personally and refraining from giving "off the record" comments will prevent many problems. Reporters have a right to be at the scene, and cooperation is the best policy—within the policies and guidelines of the department.

From time to time, public outrage over particular crimes places increased pressure on the police to solve murders. A more serious problem is the difficulty of establishing that a crime has, in fact, been committed. Search warrants can be issued if proof of a crime exists; however, such proof may not be legally available without a warrant. It can also be difficult to determine whether the death was homicide or suicide.

Geberth (1996, p. 89) cautions investigators to be conscious of staged crime scenes, where an offender consciously attempts to thwart an investigation:

> The facts are vague or misleading. . . . A common type of staging occurs when the perpetrator changes elements of the scene to make the death appear to be a suicide or accident in order to cover up a murder. Also common is when the perpetrator attempts to redirect the investigation by making the crime appear to be a sex-related homicide.

In addition, many perpetrators attempt to make the crime scene look as if a robbery or burglary has taken place.

## Suicide

According to Geberth (1996, p. 163): "More suicides are occurring in the 1990s and the rate among pre-teens and the elderly has increased."

The reason(s) for an apparent suicide needs to be determined. An act that appears to be too violent for suicide and is therefore a suspected homicide might actually be a natural death. Never exclude the possibility of death from natural causes in the initial phase of an investigation because of the presence of obvious marks of violence. The appearance of a struggle can be created by the abnormal activity of a person suffering from an acutely painful attack. The onset of more than seventy diseases can produce sudden death. A person experiencing such an attack may disarrange his clothing and injure himself severely by falling. In one case, a man shot himself to relieve excruciating pain, and the autopsy showed that a ruptured aorta caused his death, not the gunshot. What appeared to be suicide was declared to be death by natural causes.

When investigating suspected suicides, attempt to find a note or letter. However, lack of a note does not eliminate the possibility of suicide. If there is a note, have it compared with the deceased's handwriting. Preserve all evidence until the medical examiner or coroner's office rules the death a suicide.

Check for weapons on or near the body. Were there any prior attempts, a history of mental illness or recent traumatic incidents? What was the cause of death: overdosing, gassing, hanging, drowning, poisoning or stabbing? Was the hanging intentional or accidental? In addition to written notes, look for videos or cassettes describing the actions taken. Examine any pads of paper near the body for the presence of indented writing remaining from sheets of paper torn from the pad and destroyed. Look for manuals on how to commit suicide. Check on prior arrangements with an undertaker or other evidence of "putting things in order."

Learn if the victim was left- or right-handed and see if this fits with the method of committing suicide. Note lividity conditions and the body's location to determine how long the person has been dead and if the body has been moved. Note the condition of rigor mortis. Are there "hesitation marks" indicating indecision before the final act? Do not assume that any blood on the victim is the victim's; it may be from a murderer. (These things are discussed later in the chapter.)

A suicide note is left in only a fourth of the cases investigated. When smaller calibre weapons are fired, there may not be blood on the hands of the person firing the gun. In fact, in most suicide cases there is no blood on the hands. In more than 75 percent of suicide cases in which a gun is used, the gun is not found in the victim's hand but is near the body. In a number of suicides the victims have had multiple wounds. If evidence surfaces after the initial investigation that proves a suicide was actually a homicide, do not hesitate to reopen the case.

What appears to be a double suicide can also present problems. It may be a murder-suicide. Determine who died first or who inflicted the fatal wounds. Attempt to determine the motive. Search for a note. Look for signs of a violent struggle before death. Sometimes suicide is very obvious, as when suspects kill themselves to avoid being captured by the police.

Geberth (1996, p. 165) suggests that investigators be aware of three basic considerations to establish if a death might be a suicide:

- The presence of the weapon or means of death at the scene.
- Injuries or wounds that are obvious or self-inflicted or could have been inflicted by the deceased.
- The existence of a motive or intent on the part of the victim to take his or her own life.

### "Suicide by Police"

Clinton Van Zandt, supervisory special agent with the FBI's National Center for the Analysis of Violent Crimes in Quantico, Virginia, has coined the phrase "suicide by police," which he defines as "someone deciding he or she wants to die but doesn't want to pull the trigger. So the person sets up a situation where police are forced to shoot" (Graves, 1992, p. B1). Many such cases involve a "man-with-a-gun" call, and police are confronted with a person who is acting bizarre and threatening to shoot him/herself, a hostage or the responding officers. In many instances, the gun is not loaded or is a fake or inoperative, but if it is pointed at the police, the police are forced to shoot.

Van Zandt explains the psychology behind "suicide by police" like this:

> A person who chooses "suicide by police" is too frightened to kill himself or views death by his own hand as socially or religiously unacceptable. When someone commits suicide, he is seen as a loser. But if police kill him, society may view him both as victim and hero because he died in a blaze of glory.

Such victim-precipitated homicide is also known as "Suicide by Cop" or SbC. Van Zandt (1993, p. 24) notes: "Too often, a person armed with a weapon that is later discovered to be broken or unloaded—if not a toy—has confronted police in such a manner as to elicit a violent, self-defense action by the officer." He also notes: "Others have fired shots at officers or innocent bystanders in an attempt to have the authorities make the choice between life and death for them."

According to Geberth (1993, p. 105): "Seemingly, these events [suicide-by-cop] are on the increase." He (p. 109) suggests: "Practically speaking, a suicide-by-cop incident should be investigated as both a homicide and a suicide."

Van Zandt* (1993, p. 29) lists the following indicators of a potential SbC:

- As the subject of a self-initiated hostage or a barricade situation, he refuses to negotiate with the authorities.
- He has just killed a significant other in his life, especially if the victim was a child or the subject's mother.
- He demands that he be killed by the police.
- He sets a deadline for the authorities to kill him.
- He has recently learned he has a life-threatening illness or disease.
- He indicates an elaborate plan for his own death, one that has taken both prior thought and preparation.
- He says he will only "surrender" (in person) to the officer in charge, e.g., the chief or the sheriff.
- He indicates he wants to "go out in a big way."
- He presents no demands that include his escape or freedom.
- He comes from a low socioeconomic background.
- He provides the authorities with a "verbal will."
- He appears to be looking for a manly or macho way to die.
- He has recently given away money or personal possessions.
- He has a criminal record indicating past assaultive behavior.
- He has recently experienced one or more traumatic events in his life that affect him, his family or his career.
- He expresses feelings of hopelessness and helplessness.

He concludes (p. 29): "If an individual is identified as a potential SbC, the police response should be low key and non-dramatic."

Police departments should train their officers to recognize the "suicide by police" phenomenon and develop alternative strategies for dealing with it.

## Suicide of Police Officers

"A 'silent epidemic' is eating away at America's police departments. . . . Experts believe the number of police officers who have committed suicide has increased sharply in recent years" ("By Their Own Hands," 1994, p. 9). This article suggests:

Typically, the cop who commits suicide is a male, white, 35, working patrol, abusing alcohol, separated or seeking a divorce, experiencing a recent loss or disappointment. Typically, a domestic dispute is involved.

A study by the FOP's Center for Criminal Justice Studies ("National FOP Looks at Police Suicide . . . ," 1995, p. 1) which analyzed the life insurance

---

*Excerpt used by permission. Copyright held by the International Association of Chiefs of Police, 515 N. Washington Street, Alexandria, VA 22314. Further reproduction without express written permission from IACP is strictly prohibited.

policies of 38,800 FOP members found that 37 percent of accidental police deaths—or 17 out of 46—were the result of suicide.

Stack and Kelley (1994, p. 75) give the following "suicidogenic" conditions that place police officers at high risk:

■ The prevalence of alternating shiftwork in policing can contribute to suicide by creating difficulties in marital relationships, maintaining and developing friendships and participating in community organizations.

■ Officers often experience considerable apathy from the public and occasional antipolice sentiments, which can create negative definitions of the police role and foster alienation from work.

■ Working with the other units of the "fragmented" criminal justice system is often demoralizing, given perceived injustices, contradictions and unfair decisions of the courts and corrections establishment.

■ The constant danger of death both to oneself and others can lead to generalized psychological consequences contributing to suicide potential.

■ Because police officers carry firearms, the *opportunity* or means for suicide is unusually high.

■ Police officers are overwhelmingly male, and males in this culture have a suicide rate that is three to four times that of females.

■ Suicide has also been linked to alcohol abuse.

## The Preliminary Investigation

The initial investigation of a homicide is basically the same as for any other crime, although it may require more flexibility, logic and perseverance. The primary goals of the investigation are (1) to establish that there is a human death caused by the criminal act or omission of another and (2) to determine who caused the death.

The homicide case normally begins with a report of a missing person or the discovery of a body. The officer in the field seldom makes the initial discovery. The first notification is received by the police communications center or a dispatcher who records the date, time and exact wording used. Because the original call is sometimes made anonymously by a suspect, a voice recording is made for comparison with later suspects.

---

The first priority is to give emergency aid to the victim if he or she is still alive or to determine that death has occurred.

---

As noted before, if the suspect is still at the scene, priorities may differ drastically. Normally, however, the suspect is not at the scene, and the victim is the first priority. If the victim is obviously dying, take a dying declaration. The live victim is taken to a hospital as rapidly as possible.

The Federal Rules of Evidence established that, to be admissible, a dying declaration must pass a three-part test (Bourn, 1996, p. 8):

■ The declarant (the person who made the statement) believed his death was "imminent" when he spoke.

■ The statement concerned "the cause or circumstances" of what the declarant believed to be his impending death.

■ The declarant is "unavailable."

To be admissible, the victim making the statement need not die to be "unavailable." Bourn (p. 9) explains:

> A person who is unavailable under the federal rule includes someone who is privileged from testifying, someone who persistently refuses to testify, someone who has lost his memory or someone who cannot be made to attend the legal proceeding.

The first-arriving officer determines the path to the victim that will least disturb evidence. If the victim is obviously dead, the body remains at the scene until the preliminary investigation is complete. It is then taken to the morgue by the medical examiner or coroner for postmortem examination or autopsy.

A death scene checklist developed by the FBI can help assure a thorough preliminary investigation. This checklist is reprinted in Appendix B.

## Determining That Death Has Occurred

Medically, death is determined by cessation of three vital functions: heartbeat, respiration and brain activity. The first two signs are observable.

---

Signs of death include lack of breathing, lack of heartbeat, lack of flushing of the fingernail bed when pressure is applied to the nail and then released and failure of the eyelids to close after being gently lifted.

---

Cessation of respiration is generally the first visible sign of death. However, in cases such as barbiturate overdoses, breathing can be so shallow that it is undetectable. Therefore, always check for a heartbeat and pulse. Except in some drug overdoses and with certain types of blindness, failure of the pupils to dilate in reaction to light is also a sign of death.

If it appears that the victim has just died, attempt resuscitation with the standard cardiopulmonary resuscitation methods.

## The Focus of the Homicide Investigation

As with any other criminal investigation, the homicide scene must be secured, photographed and sketched, and all evidence must be obtained, identified and properly preserved.

Geberth (1996, p. 97) suggests that videotaping the crime scene is "being employed with excellent results in the investigation of homicides." He also notes that a dying declaration can be videotaped.

---

After priority matters are completed, the focus of the homicide investigation is to:
- Identify the victim.
- Establish the time of death.
- Establish the cause and method used to produce death.
- Develop a suspect.

---

The preliminary investigation either accomplishes these things, or it provides leads that are followed up.

# Identifying the Victim

In some cases there is no body. It may have been burned or cut up beyond recognition, weighted and sunk in a body of water or dissolved in a vat of acid. Some states allow the use of circumstantial evidence to prove the corpus delicti. In most homicides, however, a body does exist. The problem sometimes is to identify the victim.

---

Homicide victims are identified by family, relatives or acquaintances; personal effects, fingerprints, DNA analysis, dental and skeletal studies; clothing and laundry marks; or through missing-persons files.

---

In many cases identifying the deceased is no problem. The parents, a close friend or a relative makes the identification. If possible, have several people identify the body because people make mistakes under stress. In a number of cases, a homicide victim has been identified only to turn up later alive. Although personal identification by viewing the deceased is ideal, corroborate it by other evidence.

Personal effects found on the victim assist in identification. However, such personal effects may not, in fact, belong to the deceased. Therefore, check them carefully.

If identification cannot be made by relatives or acquaintances or by personal effects, the most positive identification is by fingerprint or DNA analysis. Comparative fingerprints are not always available, however, and blood type does not provide a positive identification, although it can prove that a body is *not* a specific person.

For an unknown victim, record a complete description and take photographs if possible. Check these against missing-persons files. Circulate the description and photograph in the surrounding area. Check the victim's clothing for possible laundry marks or for labels that might provide a lead as to where the clothes were purchased.

If the body is badly decomposed, the bones provide a basis for estimating height, sex and approximate age as well as proof that the deceased was a human. If there are leads as to whom the victim might be, identification can be attempted by comparing dental charts and X-rays of prior fractures and by examining prior surgical procedures, scars or other abnormalities.

## Estimating the Time of Death

The time of death relates directly to whether the suspect could have been at the scene and to the sequence of multiple deaths. It is also important to the victim's family in settling insurance claims and social security and pension payments.

Both the investigator and the medical examiner or coroner are responsible for estimating the time of death. Knowing how the professional examiner estimates time of death helps the investigator to understand better what circumstances are important at the crime scene and alerts you to observe and record specific factors that aid in estimating the time of death. Some of these factors are available only to the first officers at the scene.

The time of death is seldom completely accurate without eyewitnesses. Normally, however, the time of the death—if it has occurred within the past four days—can be determined to within four hours, depending on the examiner's

*Bones often assist in identification of victims through comparison with health and dental records.*

expertise and the factors available for examination. Figure 12–1 shows the timing of various body changes after death.

Factors that are helpful in estimating the time of death are body temperature, rigor mortis, postmortem lividity, appearance of eyes, stomach contents, stage of decomposition and evidence suggesting a change in the victim's normal routine.

### Recent Death

A time of death that is less than a half-hour before examination is normally the easiest determination to make. The body is still warm; mucous membranes are still moist but drying; blood is still moist but drying; the pupils have begun to dilate; and the skin is becoming pale white in Caucasians.

### Death That Occurred One-Half Hour to Four Days Prior

Generally, if the death occurred within the past four days but more than one-half hour ago, the mucous membranes and any blood from the wounds are dry, there are skin blisters and skin slippage, the body is slightly pink, body temperature has dropped, rigor mortis and postmortem lividity are present and the pupils are restricted and cloudy.

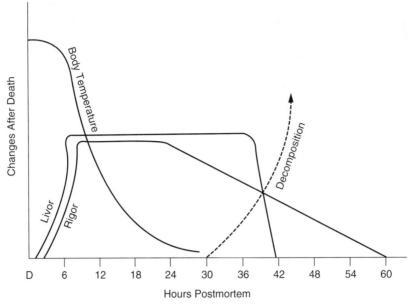

**Figure 12–1    Timing of Postmortem Body Cooling, Livor and Rigor Mortis and Putrefactive Changes**

Source: Irwin M. Sopher. "The Law Enforcement Officer and the Determination of the Time of Death." *FBI Law Enforcement Bulletin*, October 1973. Reprinted with permission.

**Body Temperature.**    Although not an accurate measure of time of death, body temperature is helpful in conjunction with other factors. After death, the body tends to assume the temperature of its environment. Record the temperature of the surroundings and the amount of clothing worn. Reach under the clothing to determine the warmth or coldness of the body. Compare this with exposed parts of the body to determine if body heat is being retained by the clothing.

---

Body temperature drops 2 to 3 degrees in the first hour after death and 1 to 11/2 degrees for each subsequent hour up to eighteen hours.

---

These amounts vary in abnormally hot or cold environments. Also, body temperature drops more slowly in large or obese people, if a high fever was present before death, if humidity prevents evaporation and if strenuous physical activity occurred immediately before death.

**Rigor Mortis.**    The body is limp after death until rigor mortis sets in. **Rigor mortis** is a stiffening of parts of the body after death, presumably because of enzyme breakdown. It begins in the jaw and head five to six hours after death and then moves downward through the entire body. The body remains rigid from eighteen to twenty-six hours. However, within about thirty-six hours, rigor mortis normally disappears in the same sequence as it appeared.

---

| Rigor mortis: | |
| --- | --- |
| Appears in head | 5 to 6 hours |
| Appears in upper body | 12 hours |
| Appears in entire body | 18 hours |
| Disappears in same order | 36 hours |

---

The degree of rigor mortis as an indicator of time of death is usually accurate to within four hours when used along with other factors. Excitement, vigorous activity, heavy clothing and abnormally high temperatures increase the rapidity of rigor; cold slows it. Babies and the aged have little rigor.

Closely associated with rigor mortis is **cadaveric spasm,** a condition that occurs in specific muscle groups rather than the entire body. It occurs most often when the victim is holding something in the hand at the time of death. The hand closes tightly around the object because of the stress and tension of death occurring. The condition does not disappear as rigor mortis does, and it cannot be induced by another person. Cadaveric spasm does not always occur, but when it does, it helps to establish whether death was homicide or a suicide. If a dead person is found with a gun or knife tightly clutched in the hand and this is the only area of the body showing this condition, the victim was holding the weapon at the moment of death.

---

A weapon tightly clutched in the victim's hand as the result of cadaveric spasm indicates suicide.

---

Ensure that the weapon clutched *was* the murder weapon. It might be that both the victim and an assailant were armed and that the death was not suicide. Likewise, absence of cadaveric spasm does not preclude suicide because it does not always occur.

**Postmortem Lividity.**   When the heart stops beating at death, the blood no longer circulates, and gravity drains the blood to the body's lowest levels. This causes a dark blue or purple discoloration of the body called **postmortem lividity.** Lividity is cherry red or a strong pink if death is caused by carbon monoxide poisoning, and various other poisons give lividity other colors.

If a body is on its back, lividity appears in the lower portion of the back and legs. If on the front, it appears on the face, chest, stomach and legs. If on the side, lividity appears on the side on which the body is resting, and if the body is upright, it appears in the buttocks and lower legs.

---

Postmortem lividity starts one-half to three hours after death and is congealed in the capillaries in four to five hours. Maximum lividity occurs within ten to twelve hours.

---

Any part of the body that is pressing directly on a hard surface does not show lividity because the pressure of the body's weight prevents blood from entering the blood vessels in that area. If there are large gaping wounds from which blood has been released, very little if any lividity occurs.

Postmortem lividity and bruises appear similar, but they are easy to distinguish. When bruises are pressed with the thumb or fingers, they remain the same, whereas lividity turns white, or blanches, when pressure is applied. If the blood has already congealed, an incision reveals whether the blood is still in the vessels (lividity) or outside them (bruise). In addition, the color of a bruise varies, whereas the color of lividity is uniform.

---

The location of lividity can indicate whether a body was moved after death.

---

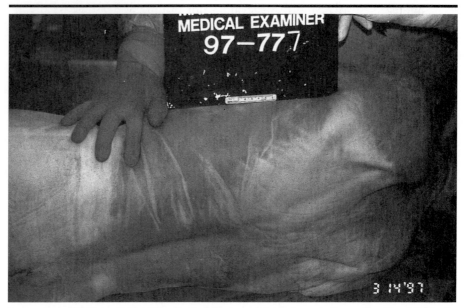

*Postmortem lividity pattern. After death, blood coagulates down to the underside of the body. Such patterns can indicate if a body has been moved after death.*

Besides helping to establish time of death and sometimes the cause, lividity helps determine if the body was moved after death occurred. Postmortem lividity in a body moved immediately after death would provide no clues. However, if the body was moved to a different position after lividity had set in, lividity will occur in unlikely areas, indicating that the body was moved.

**Examination of the Eyes.** The appearance of the eyes also assists in estimating the time of death. After death, eye muscle tone lessens and tends to disappear. The pupils tend to dilate.

A partial restriction of the pupil occurs in about seven hours. In twelve hours the cornea appears cloudy.

The cornea clouds more rapidly if the eyes are open after death.

During the medical examination, fluid can be withdrawn from the eyeball (or the spine) to determine the level of potassium, which tends to rise at a predictable rate after death.

**Examination of Stomach Contents.** Although the stomach contents must be examined during the medical examination, the investigator can provide important information for the examiner.

Determine when and what the victim last ate. If any vomit is present, preserve it as evidence and submit it for examination.

Attempt to find out when the victim last ate. The medical examiner can often determine how long the victim lived after eating because digestion is a fairly constant process, measurable in hours. Food remains in the stomach one to two hours after eating and then empties into the small intestine, where it takes two to four hours to pass into the large intestine. If the stomach is full, death occurred within one to two hours after eating. If the small intestine is full, death occurred four to six hours after eating. If the large intestine is empty, twelve or more hours passed after the victim ate and before death occurred.

Digestive time is affected by many factors, however. Mental and emotional upsets, poor health, fatigue and constipation decrease digestive time; diarrhea increases it.

If the victim has vomited, the stomach is empty and will distort the estimate of time of death; therefore, report the presence of any vomit near the body. Preserve such vomit as evidence as it may provide information on drugs or poisons related to the cause of death.

### Many Days after Death

It is more difficult to estimate the time of death if death occurred several days before discovery of the body. The cadaver is bloated, lividity is darkened, the abdomen is greenish, blisters are filled with gas and a distinct odor is present.

**Decomposition.**    The medical examiner makes a rough estimate of time of death based on the body's state of decomposition. Decomposition is first observed as an extended stomach and abdomen, the result of internal gases developing. In general, decomposition is increased by higher temperatures and decreased by lower temperatures.

If the body is in a hot, moist location, a soapy appearance called **adipocere** develops. This takes up to three months to develop fully. Attacks by insects, bacteria, animals and birds also increase the decomposition rate.

The presence on the body of insect eggs, their stage of development and the life cycle of the species, as well as various stages of vegetation on or near the body, also provide information on the time of death.

A forensic entomologist (F. E.) can examine various types of insects to assist in estimating the time of death. Examination of insects is especially helpful when death occurred more than a week before. Insects can detect newly dead body odors 2 miles away. Because particular insects work or rest during the day or the night, the types of insects at the scene provide clues as to the timing of the body's deterioration. Expert entomologists examine this type of evidence at the Forensic Science Research and Training Center at Quantico, Virginia. According to Ullman (1992, p. 28):

> Through the forensic entomologist, it is often possible to pinpoint a specific geographic area where the remains originated. . . .
>
> It is possible to tie a suspect to the area based upon the insects that are found smashed into the grill or on other areas of vehicle.

Ullman cites the example of a body found in a coastal area, 100 miles from where the suspected assailant lived. The suspect denied ever being in the area, but a technician obtained samples of dead insects from the suspect's car's radiator and windshield and submitted them to a forensic entomologist for examination:

> They discovered a species of mayfly that was only found in the area where the body was dumped. In addition, the insects were active in that stage during a short period of time. When the time of death was found to be consistent with when the mayflies were active, the case was clinched.

Complete dehydration of all body tissues results in **mummification.** A cadaver left in an extremely dry, hot area will mummify in about a year and will remain in this condition for several years if undisturbed by animals or insects.

## Effects of Water

Bodies immersed in water for a period of time undergo changes that help to determine time of death. A body immersed in water may decompose rapidly, depending on the water temperature and the effects of fish and other marine life.

A dead body usually sinks in water and remains immersed for eight to ten days in warm water or two to three weeks in cold water. It then rises to the surface unless restricted. The outer skin loosens in five to six days, and the nails separate in two to three weeks.

The medical examination also determines if the person was alive or dead at the time the body was immersed in water. This provides evidence to support homicide, suicide or accidental death.

## Factors Suggesting a Change in the Victim's Routine

Check telephone calls made to and by the victim. Check dates on mail, newspapers, food in the refrigerator. Determine who normally provides services to the victim, such as dentists, doctors, barbers, hairdressers and clerks. Find out if any appointments were not kept. Were any routines discontinued, such as playing cards or tennis, going to work on schedule, riding a particular bus? Was there food on the stove or the table? Was the stove on? Were the lights, television, radio or stereo on or off? Were pets fed? Were dirty dishes on the counters or in the sink? Was this normal for the victim? Was a fire burning in the fireplace? Was the damper left open? All such facts help to estimate the time of death and can corroborate the estimate based on physical findings.

# Unnatural Causes of Death and Method Used

In all cases of violent death, industrial/accidental death or suicide, the medical examiner determines the cause of death. A number of deaths involve circumstances that are investigated by police and the medical examiner, even though many are not criminal homicides.

Among the most common causes of unnatural death are gunshot wounds; stabbing and cutting wounds; blows from blunt instruments; asphyxia induced by choking, drowning, hanging, smothering, strangulation, gases or poisons; poisoning and drug overdose; burning; explosions, electric shock, and lightning.

Table 12–2 indicates the probability of a specific cause of death being the result of an accident, suicide or homicide.

## Gunshot Wounds

Most deaths due to gunshot wounds result from handguns, rifles or shotguns. Knowing the type of weapon is important for making comparison tests and locating unknown weapons. The major cause of death from gunshot

**Table 12–2 Causes of Death**

**411**

**Chapter 12**

**Homicide**

| Cause of Death | Accident | Suicide | Homicide |
|---|---|---|---|
| Gunshot wound | * | * | * |
| Stabbing and cutting wounds | rare | * | * |
| Blow from blunt instruments | | | |
| Fall | * | * | * |
| Hit-and-run vehicle | | | * |
| Asphyxia | | | |
| Choking | * | | |
| Drowning | * | * | * |
| Hanging | autoerotic | * | rare |
| Smothering | * | | rare |
| Strangulation | autoerotic | rare | * |
| Poisoning and overdose | * | * | * |
| Burning | * | | |
| Explosion | * | | |
| Electric shock | * | rare | |
| Lightning | * | | |

*means reasonable to suspect as the cause of death.

wounds is internal hemorrhaging and shock. The size, number and velocity of the ammunition used and the type of weapon determine the effect on the body.

A number of things occur, almost simultaneously, when a gun is fired: exit of the bullet or projectile, expansion of gases due to the explosion of the powder, cartridge-case metal fragments, carbons, soot and various elements from the primer firing. Shots fired from a distance produce little or no powder tattooing or carbons on the skin around where the bullet entered the body, and it is difficult to determine the exact distance—even though the angle of trajectory can be determined from the bullet's path through the body. In the middle-distance range, tattooing appears on the clothing or the body when handguns are fired from up to approximately 2 feet away. Powder tattooing results from both burned and unburned powder. By using test-firing pattern comparisons with the same weapon and ammunition, the actual firing distance can be determined.

If the muzzle of the weapon was in direct contact with the body, contact wounds will be evident. There may be a muzzle impression on the skin and soot or powder fragments in the entrance area or around the wound. At the entry point, the hole is smaller than the bullet because the skin's elasticity closes the entry point slightly. Entrance wounds are normally round or oval in appearance. Little bleeding occurs at the entry wound. As the bullet passes through the skin, it leaves a gray to black abrasion collar around the edges of the entry wound.

The exit wound is larger, bleeds more profusely and has no abrasion collar. It is larger because gases build up in the body, especially from shots at close range, and tissues bunch up ahead of the bullet until reaching the outer skin. Elasticity then forces the skin outward until it breaks, permitting the bullet and the gases to pass through. The exit wound is generally jagged and torn. The difference between entry and exit wounds is observable.

Shotgun wounds are distinctly different because numerous pellets penetrate the body. At close range these leave a much larger hole than does a bullet, and at farther range they produce a discernible pellet pattern. Both the entry and exit wounds are larger than those produced by single bullets.

Shotgun-wound patterns and the appearance of entrance and exit wounds from handguns and rifles help determine the distance from which the gun was

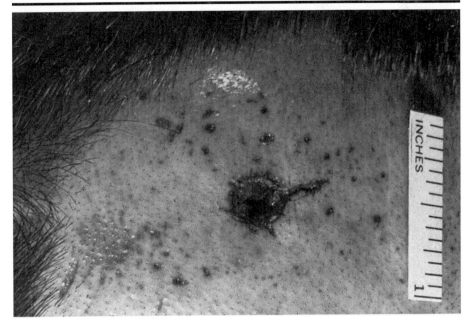

*This photo shows a cleaned, close-range (1–6 inches) gunshot wound with stippling. The wound resulted from an accidental shooting.*

fired. Contact wounds (fired at point-blank range) cause a large entry wound with smudging around the edges. The principal damage is due to the blasting and flame of the powder. Smudging around a wound can be wiped off, but the tattooing pattern cannot be eliminated. If the gun is more than 18 inches from the body when fired, no tattooing or smudging occurs.

In addition, a bullet or pellets from any weapon produce a path or track through the body that follows the angle between the weapon and the victim at the time of firing. The bullet's path or angle helps to determine the angle at which the weapon was fired and, therefore, the suspect's possible location at the time of firing. This angle also helps differentiate between suicide and murder.

When investigating gunshot deaths, determine whether the death was due to the wound or to some other injury. Was the wound impossible for the victim to have produced? What is the approximate distance from which the weapon was fired? Were there one or more wounds? Examine the victim's hands to determine if he or she fired the gun. What was the position of the body when found?

Suicide Indicators:
  Gun held against skin.
  Wound in mouth or in right temple if victim is right-handed, left temple if
    left-handed.
  Not shot through clothing, unless shot in the chest.
  Weapon present, especially if tightly held in hand.
Murder Indicators:
  Gun fired from more than a few inches away.
  Angle or location that rules out self-infliction.
  Shot through clothing.
  No weapon present.

## Stabbing and Cutting Wounds

Stabbing and cutting wounds differ in shape, size and extent of external and internal bleeding. A knife is the most frequent weapon used. The weapon and wound can be different sizes, depending on the depth and severity of the wound and whether it is into or across the tissues and fibers.

**Stab Wounds.**    Stab wounds are caused by thrusting actions. They vary in size in different areas of the body but are usually smaller than cutting wounds. A stab wound in a soft part of the body produces a larger hole than one in the head or a bony area. Ice-pick wounds in a skull covered by a substantial amount of hair can easily be missed on initial examination.

The major damage in stab wounds is to internal tissues, followed by bleeding, primarily internal. The extent and rapidity of internal bleeding depends on the size of the blood vessels affected. In most cases, the cause of death is bleeding, rather than damage to a vital organ. A stab wound can be deeper than the length of the weapon used because the force of the thrust on the softer tissues can compress the body's surface inward.

Even if a weapon is found, it can rarely be designated as the murder weapon unless part of it separates and remains in the body or it contains blood, tissue and fibers from the deceased.

Most stabbing deaths are murders. In murders, stab wounds can be single or multiple and can be in several areas of the body if the victim tried to defend him- or herself. **Defense wounds**—cuts on the hands, arms and legs—result from the victim attempting to ward off the attacker.

**Cutting Wounds.**    With cutting wounds, external bleeding is generally the cause of death. Cutting wounds are frequently the result of suicide. It is common in such cases to observe **hesitation wounds** in areas where the main wound occurs. These less severe cutting marks are caused by attempts to build up courage to make the fatal wound.

Suicidal cutting wounds are made at an angle related to the hand that held the weapon, generally in a downward direction because of the natural pull of the arm as it is brought across the body.

---

Suicide Indicators:
> Hesitation wounds.
> Wounds under clothing.
> Weapon present, especially if tightly clutched.
> Usually throat, wrists, ankles.
> Seldom disfigurement.
> Body not moved.

Murder Indicators:
> Defense wounds.
> Wounds through clothing.
> No weapon present.
> Usually vital organs.
> Disfigurement.
> Body moved.

---

## Blows from Blunt Objects

Fatal injuries can result from hands and feet and blows with various blunt objects, including hammers, clubs, heavy objects and rocks. It is often impossible to determine the specific type of weapon involved. The injuries can occur to any part of the body and can result in visible external bruises. The size of the bruise may not correspond to the size of the weapon because blood escapes into a larger area. Severe bruises are not often found in suicides.

In a battered-child investigation, death rarely results from a single blow or a single series of blows but rather from physical abuse over an extended period. An autopsy reveals prior broken bones or injuries. Death may also have been caused by starvation or other forms of neglect.

Falls can cause death or can be used to conceal the real cause of death. In some cases, the victim is taken to a staircase and pushed down after being severely beaten. Intoxication is often given as the reason for the fall, but this can easily be checked through blood tests.

### Asphyxia

**Asphyxiation** results when the body tissues and the brain receive insufficient oxygen to support the red blood cells. An examination of blood cells shows this lack of oxygen.

Discoloration occurs in all dead bodies, but in asphyxia deaths, it is usually more pronounced and varied due to the lack of oxygen—especially in the blood vessels closest to the skin surface. It is most noticeable as a blue or purple color around the lips, fingernails and toenails. Although you need not know the varied coloration produced by different causes and chemicals, be certain to record precise descriptions of coloration that can be interpreted by the medical examiner and related to probable cause of death.

Asphyxia deaths result from many causes, including choking, drowning, smothering, strangulation, hanging, swallowing of certain chemicals, poisoning and overdosing on sleeping-pills.

**Choking.**    Foreign bodies in the throat cause choking, as do burial in grain or sand slides or rapid pneumonia of infants in cribs. Such deaths are almost always accidental.

**Drowning.**    The majority of drownings are accidental. Murder is rarely proven unless witnesses are present. If a dead body is placed in water to make it appear as though death was caused by drowning, the medical examination can establish that the person was dead when immersed.

**Smothering.**    Smothering is an uncommon means of murder, despite many fictional adaptions of this method. Intoxicated persons, the elderly and infants are most likely to be victims of smothering, usually by the hands or a pillow. Often, however, such deaths are accidental. For example, an infant weak from disease may turn over, face downward or become tangled in bedclothes and accidentally suffocate.

**Hanging.**    Hangings are normally suicides, but murders have been made to appear as hanging suicides. Some hangings result from experimentation to achieve sexual satisfaction, as discussed later. In suicides, the pressure on the neck is usually generated by standing on a chair or stool and kicking the support away, jumping off or simply letting the body hang against the noose. (A body need not be completely suspended to result in death by hanging.) Although it is commonly thought that death results from a broken

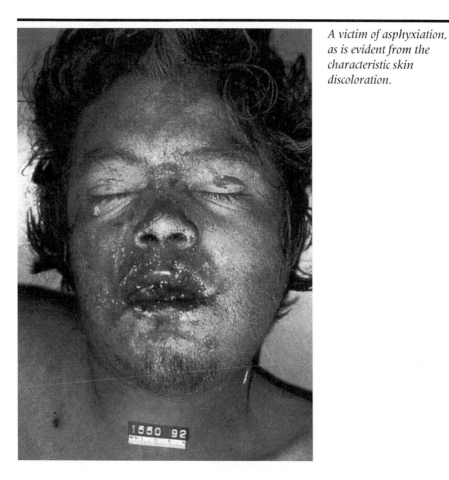

*A victim of asphyxiation, as is evident from the characteristic skin discoloration.*

neck, it is usually the result of a broken trachea or a complete constriction of the air supply.

In hangings the ligature marks start from the area of the neck below the chin and travel upward to the point just below the ears. Observe the condition and angle of these marks, and save the entire rope, including the knot, as evidence.

**Strangulation.**   Strangulation by rope, hands, wire or scarves produces the same effect as hanging. In both, the cause of death is total restriction of air. In contrast to hangings, however, the ligature marks caused by strangulation are normally evenly grooved and are horizontal around the neck. In cases of manual strangulation, marks often remain from the hand pressure.

**Poisons, Chemicals and Overdoses of Sleeping Pills.**   Asphyxiating chemicals, including ammonia and chloroform, can cause irritation severe enough to totally constrict the breathing passages. Examination of the air passages indicates paralysis.

---

Asphyxiation deaths: most cases of choking, drowning and smothering are accidental; most cases of hanging are suicides; most cases of strangulation are murder.

---

**Autoerotic Asphyxiation.** In autoerotic asphyxia, sexual gratification has been sought by placing a rope around the neck and causing just enough restriction to result in semiconsciousness. Such experimentation may be successful a number of times but then result in total unconsciousness rather than semiconsciousness. In such a case, the body goes limp in the noose, and the weight of the body causes the noose to tighten, causing death. Two conditions often exist with this type of death: a nude body and mirrors placed to observe the ritual. Evidence of masturbation is often found.

Although not common, **autoerotic asphyxiation** should be recognized by police officers. According to Geberth (1990, p. 274):

> Approximately 500–1,000 people die from autoerotic asphyxiation each year in the U.S. Many times this type of case has either been misclassified or has gone unrecognized due to lack of knowledge, misinformation, or misguided efforts on the part of the surviving family to cover up an embarrassing situation.

In these instances, suicides are, in fact, tragic accidents that occurred during dangerous autoerotic acts. As noted by Geberth (p. 275): "A combination of ritualistic behavior, oxygen deprivation, danger, and fantasy appears to bring about sexual gratification for these people."

Such deaths are classified into three categories: suffocation, strangulation and chemical asphyxia, with strangulation resulting from suspension of the body being most common. In such cases, the body is usually touching the ground and often the victim is bound. Analysis will show, however, that the binding could have been done by the victim.

Common indicators of accidental death during autoerotic practices include the following (Geberth, p. 279):

- Evidence of physiological mechanism for obtaining or enhancing sexual arousal and dependence on either a self-rescue mechanism or the victim's judgment to discontinue its effect.
- Evidence of solo sexual activity.
- Evidence of sexual fantasy aids.
- Evidence of prior dangerous autoerotic practice.
- No apparent suicidal intent.

Geberth provides a checklist to help determine autoerotic asphyxia (pp. 291–292):

- Is the victim nude, sexually exposed or, if a male, dressed in feminine attire? Transvestism, make-up, wigs?
- Is there evidence of masturbatory activity? Tissues, towels or hanky in hand or in shorts to catch semen?
- Is there evidence of infibulation? Piercing or causing pain to the genitalia, self-torture masochism?
- Are sexually stimulating paraphernalia present; vibrators, dildos, sex aids, pornographic magazines?
- Is bondage present; ropes, chains, blindfolds, gags, etc.? Are any constrictive devices present; corset, plastic wrap, belts, ropes or vacuum cleaner hoses around the body or chest constraints?
- Is there protective padding between the ligature and the neck to prevent rope burns or discomfort?

- Are the restraints interconnected? Do ropes and ties come together or are they connected, are the chains interconnected through one another? Is the victim tied so that by putting pressure on one of his limbs the restraints are tightened?
- Are mirrors or other reflective devices present and positioned so that victim can view his activities?
- Is there evidence of fantasy (diaries, erotic literature, etc.) or fetishism? Woman's panties, bras, girdles, leather, high heel shoes, etc.?
- Is the suspension point within reach of the victim? Or is there an escape mechanism (keys, lock, slip knot, etc.)?
- Is there evidence of prior such activities (abrasions or rope burns)? Unexplained secretive behavior or long stays in isolated areas?
- Does the victim possess literature dealing with bondage, escapology or knots?
- Is there a positioned camera? (View any film or video tapes present.)

### Poisoning

Poisoning, one of the oldest methods of murder, can occur from an overwhelming dose that causes immediate death or from small doses that accumulate over time and cause death. Poisons can be injected into the blood or muscles, inhaled as gases, absorbed through the skin surface, taken in foods or liquids or inserted into the rectum or vagina.

**Toxicology** (the study of poisons) experts can determine the type of poison, the amount ingested, the approximate time ingested and the effect on the body.

An overdose death is not necessarily a suicide. It might have been accidental—a result of the person not knowing when medication was last taken or of being in a semistupor and taking more pills than intended. If a prescription bottle is found, determine from family members how many pills were in the bottle before the death. Check with the issuing pharmacist to determine whether it was a legal prescription, how many pills were prescribed and the date the prescription was last filled. Preserve all evidence until the coroner's office rules the death accidental or a suicide. Other important evidence in poisoning cases includes the contents of the medicine cabinet, any excretions or vomit present at the scene and any food the victim recently ate.

If a child is poisoned by accidentally ingesting cleaning fluid, detergents, pills or other such substances, the parents are sometimes charged with manslaughter or negligent homicide.

### Burning

Most deaths by burning are accidental. However, a death resulting from burns received in a fire caused by arson is classified as murder. Moreover, people sometimes try to disguise murder by burning the victim's body. Even in the most destructive fires, however, considerable information is available from an autopsy because bones are not easily burned. Even in extreme heat, enough blood usually remains to enable a carbon monoxide analysis to determine if the victim was alive at the time of the fire. However, in extremely hot fires the heat may cause the skin to break open on the surface, and the resulting wounds may appear to be knife or other wounds inflicted by an assailant prior to the fire.

## Explosions, Electrocution and Lightning

Death due to explosives can result from the direct tearing force of the blast, from a shock wave or from the victim being blown off the top of a structure or against an object with enough force to cause death. Such deaths are usually accidental.

Electrocution paralyzes the heart muscle, causing rapid death. Nearly all electrocution deaths are accidental (except, of course, in capital punishment cases). High-voltage lines and lightning are the main causes. Lightning leaves linear stripes on the body, turns the skin blue and burns the skin, especially at the lightning bolt's entry and exit points.

---

Poisoning deaths can be accidental, suicide or murder. Most deaths caused by burning, explosions, electrocution and lightning are accidental, although burning is sometimes used in attempting to disguise murder.

---

## Drug-Related Homicides

According to Hougland (1994, p. 57): "The basic techniques used in routine death investigations apply also to drug-related death investigations, with some minor modifications."

Geberth (1990, p. 76) identifies four types of drug-related homicides:

- Drug hits, premeditated murders intended to eliminate competition or enforce control or killing undercover police officers or informants.
- Interpersonal drug disputes, occurring between individuals under the influence of drugs and/or involved in illicit drug activity.
- Murder of innocent bystanders, caught in crossfire or hit by random shots fired between rival gangs or participants in drug-related disputes.
- Drug assassinations, premeditated murders directed toward government officials, law enforcement personnel and civilians.

Geberth suggests that each category presents specific investigative options. These are summarized in Table 12–3. Most of these investigative options are discussed in detail in Chapter 18.

## The Victim

In most crimes the victim provides verbal details of what occurred. In homicides, the victim may be able to provide such information if witnesses or the police are present before death occurs. However, the information usually comes from the crime scene, witnesses, physical and circumstantial evidence and the suspect.

Victims often know the person who killed them, so information about the deceased can furnish leads to the suspect. Obtain the victim's name, address, age, sex, nationality and type and place of work. Also find out the names of family members, close friends and known enemies and learn about the victim's

**Table 12–3  Drug-Related Homicides and Investigative Options**

| Category | Investigative Options |
|---|---|
| Drug hit | Intelligence information<br>Narcotics buy operation<br>Buy and bust operation<br>Informant information |
| Interpersonal drug disputes | Buy and bust operation<br>Informant information<br>Narcotics buy operation |
| Murder of innocent bystanders | Reward money<br>Crime Stoppers program<br>Use of news media<br>Community activists<br>Buy and bust operation<br>Informant information |
| Drug assassinations | Intelligence operations<br>Electronic eavesdropping<br>Narcotics buy operations<br>Reward money<br>Crime Stoppers program<br>Use of news media |

SOURCE: Vernon J. Geberth. "Investigation of Drug-Related Homicides." *Law and Order,* November 1990, p. 76. Reprinted by permission.

habits. Ask about any religious, political or business actions or remarks that might have enraged someone. Take the victim's fingerprints and determine if any criminal history might lead to a suspect.

Interview personal contacts such as doctors, pastors or counselors to find out about the victim's physical and emotional condition, especially if it has not yet been determined whether the death was an accident, suicide or homicide. The person's medical background may provide information about an extremely painful or terminal disease that could motivate suicide. Inquire about the victim's mental stability. Most suicide victims attempt to avoid inflicting severe pain on themselves when they take their lives, but this is not always true. One woman cut off both her feet before fatally stabbing herself in the chest. Some people set themselves on fire to commit suicide.

---

The victim's background provides information as to whether the death was an accident, suicide or homicide. If homicide, the background often provides leads to a suspect. Evidence on the victim's body also can provide important leads.

---

In violent murders, the victim may grab the suspect's hair, buttons or clothing or scratch or claw the suspect. A victim may leave injuries on the suspect, and traces of the suspect's flesh may be found under the victim's fingernails. Identify and preserve all belongings and evidence on or near the deceased. Carefully examine the location where the body was found if it is not where death occurred.

After the entire scene and the evidence have been photographed and sketched, the body is taken to the morgue. Use care in moving the body. Lift it a few inches off the surface and slide a sheet under it to catch any evidence that might fall while transporting the body to the vehicle. Itemize other possessions and send them to the morgue for later release to the family if they are not evidence.

Although a body bag may be used, the body should first be wrapped in a clean, white sheet. Evidence on the body that falls off is much easier to see on a sheet. Also, the sheet absorbs moisture.

## Partner Homicide

Holmes (1992, p. 85) notes the following facts about partner homicide:

■   Nearly 70 percent of incidents of domestic violence are committed by a husband, boyfriend or ex-boyfriend.
■   In more than 75 percent of partner homicides, the police had been called to the home at least once during the two years preceding the fatal incident. In more than half of these cases, they had been called five times or more.
■   Most acts of spouse homicide occur in the home.
■   The methods and weapons used in partner homicide vary: knives, guns, pushes, shoves, poisons, rifles, blunt instruments, asphyxiation, explosives are all evident.

## Law Enforcement Officers Killed

The risk of being killed in the line of duty "comes with the job." According to Whetsel (1995, p. 6): "One police officer is killed somewhere in America every 52 hours." In 1995, according to Walchak (1996, p. 7): "162 federal, state and local officers were killed—the highest total since 1989. On average, the officers who died were 37 years old and had served for nine years. Four of the officers were women." These statistics include the twelve federal officers killed in the Oklahoma City bombing.

As Simms (1996, pp. 26–27) explains:

These deaths include automobile crashes, accidental deaths and deaths at
the hands of others. They are all traumatic events and will have a lasting and
profound emotional impact.

Rachlin (1994, p. 145) further explains: "The gloom if there's a line-of-duty death is indescribable."

Pinizzotto and Davis (1993, p. 36) give the following demographic description of "cop killers:"

| | |
|---|---|
| Gender: | 96% male; 4% female |
| Average Age: | 26 years |
| Race: | 60% white; 40% nonwhite |
| Average Height: | 5′ 9″ |
| Average Weight: | 176 pounds |
| Marital Status: | 12% married; 54% single; 2% separated; 32% divorced |
| Education: | 34% no diploma; 60% high school diploma; 4% some college; 2% college degree. |

Rachlin (1994, p. 130) stresses: "Any agency might experience such a tragedy [a line-of-duty death] and each should be prepared to properly handle the situation." Gist and Taylor (1996, p. 37) suggest: "The well-developed responses of a well-integrated agency—including its families as well as its employees—provide the best framework for recovery from tragic loss." In addition to having prepared-in-advance procedures for coping with line-of-duty deaths, Rachlin (1994, p. 94) notes: "Peer support can validate, normalize and legitimize reactions. It can encourage survivors to cope positively and constructively." One such organization is C.O.P.S. (Concerns of Police Survivors), a national organization described by Nyberg (1993, p. 45): "If death in the line of duty is the prevailing cloud in the police profession, then C.O.P.S. is the silver lining." Investigators dealing with line-of-duty deaths should be familiar with organizations such as this so that they can refer the survivors to them.

## Witnesses

In violent criminal deaths, struggles often create noise and attract the attention of neighbors or passersby. Witnesses may know and name the suspect, or they may have seen the suspect or vehicle. Often, however, there are no witnesses, and information must be sought from family members, neighbors and associates.

St. Louis police have set up a homicide hotline with an untraceable number that murder witnesses can call to offer anonymous tips. According to *Law Enforcement News* ("'Untraceable' Hotline Debuts . . .," 1992, p. 1):

> When you have a group of about thirty onlookers, nobody wants to be pin-pointed as a snitch. . . . So what we came up with was the homicide hotline and the hotline card. We pass them out to everyone at a scene—not just people who we think are witnesses.

The hotline is answered by a message machine and requires no staffing to implement. Figure 12–2 shows the card distributed to bystanders at homicide scenes.

---

"STOP THE KILLING"

If you have information regarding this or
any homicide investigation,
contact the

## HOMICIDE HOTLINE
## 444-5830

*THE HOTLINE IS CONFIDENTIAL AND NONTRACEABLE
St. Louis Metropolitan Police Department

---

**Figure 12–2    The Card Handed Out to Bystanders at St. Louis Murder Scenes**
Source: Courtesy of the St. Louis Police Department

# Suspects

If the suspect is arrested at the crime scene, follow the procedures described in Chapter 1. If the suspect is known but is not at the scene, immediately disseminate the description to other investigators, field officers and police agencies.

If the suspect is not known, identification becomes a priority of the investigation. Often, several suspects are identified and eventually eliminated as information and evidence is obtained and the list is reduced to one or two prime suspects. In major cases, any number of suspects may be developed from information at the scene, from informants and from intelligence files.

Discovering a motive is not a specific requirement in the investigation, but motive is so closely tied to intent and to developing a suspect that it should be determined. Murders are committed for many reasons. Common types of criminal homicide include the anger killing, the love-triangle killing, the revenge or jealousy killing, killing for profit, random killing, murder-suicide, the sex and sadism killing and felony murder. Anger killings often begin as assaults. The possibility of killing for profit almost always exists. Thus, it is always critical to determine who would stand to profit from the victim's death.

> Determine the motive for a killing; it provides leads to developing suspects and strong circumstantial evidence against a suspect.

Some murders are contracted or hired. This is frequently the case in murders of organized-crime figures.

## Serial Killers

**Serial murder** is defined by Geberth (1990, p. 72) as "the killing of three or more separate victims with emotional time breaks between the killings." Some serial killers belong to gangs and cults, as discussed in Chapter 19. A number of serial killers in the United States have received national attention. These include Henry Lucas, who confessed to 188 murders in 24 states; the Green River murderer, 46 murders; Theodore Bundy, 40 murders; John Gacey, 33 murders; Elmer Henley, 27 murders; Bobbie Joe Long, 10 murders; and others. "Jack the Ripper," who killed at least seven prostitutes in one London district in the autumn of 1888, is probably the best-known serial killer internationally.

Initially, investigating a murder committed by a serial killer may seem the same as investigating any other murder. As a case is investigated, however, and no suspect can be developed, the investigator should consider reporting the crime to the FBI's National Center for the Analysis of Violent Crime (NCAVC) at Quantico, Virginia. NCAVC provides a profiling program, as well as research and development, training and the Violent Criminal Apprehension Program (VICAP). Police departments investigating cases that they believe involve serial murder can submit the cases to VICAP. Other cases with similar modus operandi submitted by other agencies are then compared, and information is furnished to the submitting agencies. It is obvious that in the Henry Lucas cases, for example, where murders were committed in twenty-four states, that VICAP is an important resource in investigating and prosecuting this type of killer. If VICAP determines that a serial murderer is probably involved, a multijurisdictional

Major Crime Investigation Team may be assembled from the jurisdictions to be in charge of the case.

Geberth (1992, p. 107) points out that police officers who understand the psychology underlying serial killings will be more effective in investigating the murders and in interviewing the murderers:

> If we apply free will and freedom of choice to a serial killer's murderous and sadistic activities, we are confronted by the reality of an evil human predator; an evil entity, who has made a conscious decision to kill. . . .
>
> Serial murderers are extremely selfish and narcissistic. Their goal is power and sexual gratification. . . .
>
> Most serial murderers are psychopathic sexual sadists. If you could crawl into their minds and examine the elements of their psyche, you would find their superego or conscience missing. This is perhaps the most significant characteristic of the psychopath, because it allows full and violent expression without significant hesitation, guilt, shame, or remorse. He knows right from wrong—he simply does not care. . . .
>
> They obviously have a profound personality disorder, but they are keenly aware of their own criminality and certainly not out of touch with reality. If serial killers were psychotic, they wouldn't be as successful in eluding the police.

Given this personality, it is logical that when interviewing serial killers, any attempts to evoke sympathy for the victims or surviving relatives will probably be futile. Appeals to their ego, on the other hand, may meet with success. It is also important not to display shock at the atrocities that may have been committed, as this is often what the serial murderer wants. Geberth suggests (p. 110) that serial murderers "possess a sadistic nature and are fascinated by violence, injury and torture. They often enjoy disclosing certain particularly outrageous and cruel aspects of the crime. They do this not only to shock the investigator but also to psychically relive the event in a selfish and perverse manner of continuing their own sadistic fantasies."

The acts of serial murderers seem incomprehensible to "normal" people. For example, the killing and mutilation of sixteen young men and boys by Jeffrey Dahmer in 1991 made national headlines. When police entered Dahmer's stench-filled apartment they found body parts of eleven males—painted human skulls, severed heads and body parts in cold storage and torsos disintegrating in an acid-filled vat. Dahmer's murders can also be classified as lust murders.

## Lust Murderers

Geberth (1991, p. 70) defines a lust murder as "a sex-related homicide involving psychopathology manifested in sadistic and deviant assault." In lust murder, the killer depersonalizes the victim, sexually mutilates the body and may displace body parts.

Geberth describes two types of lust murderers, the organized offender and the disorganized offender. The organized offender is usually of above-average intelligence, methodical and cunning. He plans his crime carefully. He has a car but usually commits the offense close to where he lives or works. He is socially skilled and cons his victims into a position where he can torture and then murder them. He brings his own weapon, may take a "trophy" of the crime, often moves the body from the crime scene and avoids leaving evidence behind.

In contrast, the disorganized offender is usually of below-average intelligence, has no car and is a loner who acts on impulse. Geberth (p. 71) writes:

The disorganized offender usually depersonalizes his victim by facial destruction or overkill type of wounds. Any sexually sadistic acts are performed post mortem. Mutilation to the genitalia, rectum, breasts of females, neck, throat and buttocks are performed because these parts of the body contain a strong sexual significance to him.

Like the organized offender, the disorganized offender usually murders a victim from his own geographic area. Regardless of whether the offender is organized or disorganized, most lust murders involve elements of fantasy, ritual, fetishes and symbolism.

### Homosexual Serial Murder Investigations

Geberth (1995, p. 83) also discusses homosexual homicides where victims are killed by lovers of the same sex. He notes: "Homosexual serial murders involve sadomasochistic torture, lust murders, thrill killings, and child killings as well as robbery homicides which are homosexually-oriented." He divides homosexual serial killers into three groups:

- Those who exclusively target other homosexuals of the same gender.
- Those who attack heterosexual and homosexual victims.
- Male pedophiles who attack young males and boys.

## Physical Evidence

Physical evidence can be found on the body, at the scene or on the suspect.

---

Physical evidence in a homicide includes a weapon, a body, blood, hairs and fibers.

---

Any of the various types of evidence discussed can be present at a homicide scene. Especially important are the body and the weapon. In automobile homicides, physical evidence often consists of paint chips, glass fragments or tire impressions that can serve to identify the vehicle involved. If the vehicle is located, it may contain evidence of the impact and it usually has traces of the victim's blood, flesh, hair or clothing.

## The Medical Examination

After the preliminary investigation, the body is taken to the morgue for an autopsy by the coroner or medical examiner. Most large departments have medical examiners and forensic pathologists on staff or available as consultants for autopsies. The medical or forensic pathologist assists investigations by relating the evidence to the findings of the autopsy.

The major purpose of the coroner's or medical examiner's office is to determine the cause of death. If no unnatural cause is determined, no crime exists. Much of the evidence that leads the examiner to determine that the death was murder also provides corroborating evidence for investigating and prosecuting the case; therefore, pathologists and investigators work together closely.

As noted by Morrison (1994, p. 56): "The medical examiner is charged with conducting a medicolegal investigation of death. Forensic pathology, the science of recognizing and interpreting diseases and injuries in the human body, is the basis of any medicolegal investigation." Morrison (p. 62) suggests that an autopsy helps homicide investigators answer such questions as the following:

- What type of weapon was used?
- Are injuries consistent with the circumstances?
- Was the deceased under the influence of drugs or alcohol?
- Was there a sexual assault before or after the death?
- Which was the fatal wound?

Certain types of death must be investigated. These include all violent deaths, whether homicide, suicide or an accident; sudden deaths not caused by a recognizable disease; deaths under suspicious circumstances; suspicious deaths of persons whose bodies will be cremated, dissected, buried at sea or otherwise made unavailable for further examination; deaths of inmates in prisons or public institutions other than from disease; deaths due to disease that may constitute a public threat; and deaths due to hazardous employment.

Before an autopsy, the body condition is not changed in any way. An investigator present at the autopsy records the location, date, time, names of the persons in attendance and the name of the person who performs the autopsy. The body is weighed, measured and photographed before the autopsy begins. It is then periodically photographed as each stage is completed. Facial features and any marks, cuts, wounds, bruises or unusual conditions are photographed close up. The deceased, including clothing, is completely described. The clothing is tagged, marked for identification and sent to the police laboratory for examination. Fingerprints are usually taken, even if the body has been personally identified.

---

The medical examination provides evidence related to the cause and time of death.

---

Morrison (1994, p. 63) notes: "Attending an autopsy is difficult, even for many police investigators. . . . Competent homicide investigators accept the ritual as part of the job." Morrison (1996, p. 29) suggests that homicide investigators prepare in advance for attending their first autopsy by knowing what to expect:

Usually the morgue is a morbid place hidden away in a basement or some other out-of-the-way place, but there are a few modern facilities around the country. . . .

The cold storage lockers, stainless steel tables, weight baskets, sinks and drains all depict the stark reality of the business.

Morrison (p. 30) offers the following tips for the first encounter:

- Don't eat a big breakfast.
- Review forensic protocol prior to exam.
- Use the glass window, if possible.
- Be prepared to converse with the M.E. on the physical aspects of the case.
- Don't think of the body with emotional attachments.
- Be prepared for the dry humor of M.E. personnel.
- Expect odors, brilliant colors and noisy saws.
- The brain removal will be the most unsettling step; be ready for it.
- Know your capabilities and weaknesses before entering the morgue.
- Don't go to an infant autopsy as your first one.

After the autopsy is completed, the cause of death, if determined, is recorded. Deaths not recorded as natural, suicide or accidental are recorded as either undetermined or homicide. Before making the final determination, the medical examiner reads a copy of the police investigation reports to date. These reports indicate prior symptoms such as vomiting, a comatose state, partial paralysis, slow or rapid respiration, convulsions and various colorations. A close relationship between the pathologist and the investigator helps ensure effective exchange of information. During the investigation, report everything relating to cause of death to the pathologist. Likewise, information discovered by the pathologist is immediately conveyed to the investigative team.

Pennsylvania has passed a new law mandating that before any body is cremated, the cremation must be approved by the coroner. Although an autopsy is not done, the body is examined and X-rays are usually taken. This law is intended to decrease the likelihood of a murder going unnoticed.

### Exhuming a Body for Medical Examination

It is not common procedure to exhume a body. Usually this is done to determine if the cause of death stated on the death certificate is valid. It may also be done if the body is suspected of having been buried to conceal the cause of death or if the identity of the body is in question.

Exhuming a body requires adherence to strict legal procedures to prevent later civil action by relatives. First obtain permission from the principal relatives. If this is not granted, it is necessary to obtain a court order to proceed. Arrange to have the coroner or medical examiner, a police representative, grave digger, cemetery official and family member present at the exhumation. Have the cemetery official or the person who placed the marker identify the grave. Photograph the general area, the specific grave with the marker and the coffin before exhumation.

At the morgue, the coroner, police, family, undertaker and pathologist are present at the lid opening. The body is then identified by the persons present if they know the deceased, and the examination is conducted.

## Collaborative Efforts

In addition to working with the medical examiner, investigators involved in homicide cases have other resources available to them. As noted by Geberth (1994, p. 65):

> For many years investigators from different jurisdictions have worked on similar cases independently of one another. They did not have access to the information available elsewhere that could speed and enhance investigations in their own jurisdiction. . . .
>
> In addition to lack of information, some violent crimes are so unusual, bizarre, and vicious that they are only rarely encountered by detectives working in smaller agencies. Serial violent criminals often transcend boundaries as they travel from city to city and state to state.

The crimes of these highly transient criminals are sometimes never linked together. One solution to this problem is the Homicide Investigation and Tracking Systems (HITS), which provides for information sharing on a statewide and regional basis via computer.

Keppel and Weis (1993, p. 1) describe HITS as follows:

> The Homicide Investigation and Tracking System (HITS), a program that began in Washington State, is helping investigators work better by allowing them access via computer to a wide range of information about serious crimes and to resources that can help solve them.

HITS is a computerized murder and sexual-assault investigation program that collects and analyzes information pertaining to specific serious criminal offenses.

Another type of collaboration is available through the FBI's Violent Criminal Apprehension Program (VICAP), introduced earlier in the chapter. As described by Green and Whitmore (1993, p. 38):

> Founded within the FBI in 1985, VICAP attempts to track this type of criminal [highly mobile serial murderers who commit their crimes across jurisdictional boundaries] nationally by matching cases that could be linked to the same individual. The program provides a nationwide clearinghouse to collect, review and analyze reports submitted by law enforcement agencies with regard to the following:

- Solved or unsolved homicides or attempts, especially those that involve an abduction; are apparently random, motiveless or sexually oriented; or are known or suspected to be part of a series.
- Missing persons, where the circumstances indicate a strong possibility of foul play and the victim is still missing.
- Unidentified dead bodies, where the manner of death is known or suspected to be homicide.

## Death Notification

"Of all the tasks in police work," writes Sly (1992, p. 26), "death notification ranks as one of the most difficult." It is best to make death notifications in person whenever possible because there are so many variations of circumstances. If the relative is in another community or state or is out of the country, it is best to ask police of that jurisdiction to make the notification. Notification may be made by a police dispatcher, police officer, police chaplain or a pastor of the religious faith of the deceased.

When you arrive at the location of the person to be notified, identify yourself, determine or confirm the exact relationship of the person to the deceased and then tell the person of the death, providing whatever details are known and are proper to release. Offer care, concern and compassion. Offer assistance in notifying others. Leave a name or agency to contact for further information and offer future assistance if needed. Generally, if the police chaplain or another pastor accompanies the officer, the chaplain or pastor performs the initial notification, and the officer fills in the details.

Sly suggests the following ten guidelines for making death notifications effective and efficient (pp. 26–28):

1. Assign a chaplain or clergy person with the officer.
2. Verify that correct information has been received.
3. Take separate vehicles (so the officer can return to duty and the chaplain can remain).

4. Plan the notification procedure. (Who will say what.)

5. The team's presence already indicates something has happened. Don't hedge with small talk.

6. Try to get people into a comfortable setting.

7. Be sensitive to surroundings.

8. Provide a police department contact.

9. Initiate a follow-up.

10. Ask if there is a relative, friend or clergy person they would like to have contacted.

It is best to have some training seminars on this subject because police officers are seldom trained to perform this function. Seek the advice of an older officer, the coroner or the medical examiner before making your first death notification if there is no formal policy or procedure established in your department.

## Summary

Homicide investigations are challenging and frequently require all investigative techniques and skills. A basic requirement is to establish that death was caused by a criminal action. The four basic types of death are death by natural causes, accidental death, suicide and homicide. Although technically you are concerned only with homicide, frequently you do not know at the start of an investigation what type of death has occurred; therefore, any of the four types of death may require investigation.

Homicide, the killing of one person by another, is classified as criminal (felonious) or noncriminal. Criminal homicide includes murder and manslaughter. Noncriminal homicide includes excusable homicide—the unintentional, truly accidental killing of another person—and justifiable homicide—killing another person under authorization of law. Premeditation is the essential element of first-degree murder, distinguishing it from all other murder classifications.

Special problems in homicide investigations include pressure by the public and the media, difficulty in establishing that it is homicide rather than suicide or an accidental or natural death, identifying the victim and establishing the cause and time of death.

First priority in a preliminary homicide investigation is to give emergency aid to the victim if he or she is still alive or to determine that death has occurred—provided the suspect is not at the scene. Signs of death include lack of breathing, lack of heartbeat, lack of flushing of the fingernail bed when pressure is applied and then released and failure of the eyelids to close after being gently lifted. After priority matters are completed, the focus of the homicide investigation is to identify the victim, establish the time of death, establish the cause of death and the method used to produce it and to develop a suspect.

Homicide victims are identified by their relatives, friends or acquaintances; by personal effects, fingerprints, DNA analysis, skeletal studies including teeth, clothing and laundry marks; or through missing-persons files.

General factors used to estimate time of death are body temperature, rigor mortis, postmortem lividity, appearance of the eyes, stomach contents, stage of decomposition and evidence suggesting a change in the victim's normal routine. Body temperature drops 2 to 3 degrees in the first hour after death and 1 to 1½ degrees

*Read the following articles and imagine yourself as the officer/detective assigned to each case. What elements of the crime are present? What evidence would you need to prosecute the case? Who else might you need to coordinate your efforts with? What is the likelihood of solving each crime?*

## Ex-convict, woman found dead in Wisconsin

**Associated Press**

James R. Wentala and a woman, found dead in a van near where officials say he buried a slain teenage girl 20 years ago, apparently died in a murder-suicide, authorities said Monday. Greg Guenard, Douglas County chief deputy sheriff, said the bodies were identified as those of Wentala, 42, and Susan Irene Stingley, 48, whose most recent address was in Superior. Stingley, whose body was nude, was reported missing by her son about three weeks ago.

The bodies were found Friday near Brule, in a minivan near where Wentala buried the body of Charmaine Louis, 14, of Iron River, whom he was convicted of killing, Guenard said.

Preliminary pathology reports indicate that the two people died more than a month ago, Guenard said. Tests indicate that Wentala strangled the woman with a piece of fabric and then rigged the vehicle's exhaust system to asphyxiate himself, Guenard said.

Wentala's crime record includes convictions for attempted rape, murder and mayhem, court records said.

Source: *Star Tribune*, 16 July 1996. Reprinted by permission of the Associated Press.

## Suspect held in slaying of home alone student

**Associated Press**

MIDDLEBORO, Mass.—An 18-year-old man is charged with killing an Indiana University student during a botched robbery attempt at her father's home.

Tara Gillon's father and stepmother found her body when they returned home from a New Year's Eve supper Tuesday night, apparently surprising the killer while he ransacked the house. They told police they heard him run outside.

Nothing seemed to be missing, but "drawers were taken out and tipped over," District Attorney Michael Sullivan said.

The 20-year-old victim's stab wounds indicated she tried to fend off the intruder with her hands, Sullivan said.

Neighbors reported hearing nothing suspicious. Police used dogs to track footprints from the door of the house, but the trail broke off.

Source: *Las Vegas Review Journal*, 3 January 1997. Reprinted by permission of the Associated Press.

## Selection for du Pont jury starts

**Associated Press**

MEDIA, Pa.—After six hours of painstaking questions, four jurors were seated Tuesday for the trial of John du Pont, the millionaire who has said he was insane when he fatally shot an Olympic wrestler.

Three men and one woman were chosen, including one bank employee who said he occasionally heard about the case but had not formed an opinion on du Pont's role in the death of Olympic gold-medalist Dave Schultz.

Du Pont's lawyers do not deny that du Pont, one of the richest murder defendants in U.S. history, pulled the trigger on Jan. 26, 1996. But they claim he did not know the difference between right and wrong at the time.

Source: *Las Vegas Review Journal*, 22 January 1997. Reprinted by permission of the Associated Press.

*(continued on p. 430)*

*(continued)*

## FBI may soon add Cunanan to its 10-most-wanted list*

Almost four weeks after the start of an alleged nationwide killing spree, Andrew Cunanan is on the verge of making the FBI's 10-most-wanted list.

One of the fugitives currently on the list was arrested in the past couple of days.

"We do have a slot available," Minneapolis FBI spokeswoman Colleen Rowley said Friday. Cunanan, who is wanted in connection with the deaths of two Twin Cities friends, a wealthy developer in Chicago and a cemetery caretaker in New Jersey, "could be a candidate."

Local police across the country, 56 FBI offices and even the 176 member nations of Interpol, the international police organization, are now alerted to Cunanan, Rowley said. Adding him to the list would be a way to further intensify that attention.

Meanwhile, the Boston area has been added to the investigation. In efforts similar to those of gay activists in New York City and police in San Francisco, police in Boston are showing photos of Cunanan in neighborhoods known to have a substantial gay population.

There have been no confirmed sightings of the accused killer in the Boston area, said FBI spokesman Peter Ginieres, but agents and police in the area are on alert as a precaution.

Cunanan, who is openly gay and known to travel extensively and enjoy a free-spending lifestyle, has been charged with murder in Chisago County and is also wanted for killings in Minneapolis, Chicago and New Jersey.

Reports of Cunanan sightings continue to flow in, Rowley said, but investigators are wary of giving specifics because he may be monitoring news reports. They also urged people to call if they think they see him, even if they believe he's in another part of the country.

**—James Walsh**

Source: *Star Tribune*, 24 May 1997.
Reprinted by permission of the *Star Tribune*, Minneapolis-St. Paul.

*The manhunt ended in July in Miami Beach, where Cunanan committed suicide aboard a houseboat.

for each subsequent hour up to eighteen hours. Rigor mortis appears in the head 5 to 6 hours after death; in the upper body after about 12 hours; and in the entire body after about 18 hours. After about 36 hours, rigor mortis usually disappears in the same sequence as it appeared. Any weapon tightly clutched in the victim's hand as the result of cadaveric spasm indicates suicide rather than murder. Postmortem lividity starts one-half to three hours after death and is congealed in the capillaries in four to five hours. Maximum lividity occurs within ten to twelve hours. The location of lividity can indicate whether a body was moved after death. A partial restriction of the pupil occurs in about seven hours. In twelve hours the cornea appears cloudy. The investigator should determine when and what the victim last ate. If any vomit is present, it should be preserved as evidence and submitted for examination. A dead body usually sinks in water and remains immersed for eight to ten days in warm water or two to three weeks in cold water. It then rises to the surface unless restricted. The outer skin loosens in five to six days, and the nails separate in two to three weeks.

Among the most common causes of unnatural death are gunshot wounds; stabbing and cutting wounds; blows from blunt instruments; asphyxia induced by choking, drowning, hanging, smothering, strangulation, gases or poisons;

poisoning and drug overdoses; burning; explosions; electric shock; and lightning. In the case of a gunshot wound, suicide may be indicated if the gun was held against the skin, the wound is in the mouth or temple, the shot did not go through clothing or the weapon is present. Murder may be indicated if the gun was fired from more than a few inches away or from an angle or location that rules out self-infliction, if the victim was shot through clothing or if there is no weapon present. Stabbing and cutting wounds may be the result of suicide if the body shows hesitation wounds; if the wounds appear under clothing or on the throat, wrists or ankles; if the weapon is present; or if the body has not been moved. Defense wounds, cuts through clothing or to vital organs, disfigurement, the absence of a weapon and signs that the body has been moved indicate murder. Most cases of choking, drowning and smothering are accidental; most cases of hanging are suicides; most cases of strangulation are murder. Poisoning deaths can be accidental, suicide or murder. Most deaths caused by burning, explosions, electrocution and lightning are accidental, although burning is sometimes used in attempting to disguise murder.

The victim's background can also provide information as to whether the death was accidental, suicide or homicide. This background and evidence on the victim's body often provide leads to a suspect.

Determine a motive for the killing to develop a suspect and to provide strong circumstantial evidence against the suspect. Physical evidence in a homicide includes a weapon, a body, blood, hairs and fibers.

A medical examination or autopsy provides legal evidence related to the cause and time of death and corroborates information obtained during the investigation.

## Checklist

### Homicide

- How were the police notified? By whom? Date? Time?
- Was the victim alive or dead at the time of arrival?
- Was medical help provided?
- If hospitalized, who attended the victim at the hospital? Are reports available?
- Was there a dying declaration?
- What was the condition of the body? Rigor mortis? Postmortem lividity?
- How was the victim identified?
- Has cause of death been determined?
- Was the medical examiner notified? Are the reports available?
- Was the evidence technician team notified?
- Was the crime scene protected?
- Were arrangements made to handle the news media?
- Are all the elements of the offense present?
- What types of evidence were found at the scene?
- How was the time of death estimated?
- Was the complainant interviewed? Witnesses? Suspects? Victim if alive at time of arrival?
- What leads exist?
- Was a description of the suspect(s) obtained? Disseminated?
- Was a search or arrest warrant necessary?
- Was all evidence properly collected, identified and preserved?
- Were photographs taken of the scene? Victim? Evidence?
- Were sketches or maps of the scene made?

# Application

**A.** Mary Jones, an eighteen-year-old high-school girl, quarreled with her boyfriend, Thomas Smith. At 3 A.M. following the evening of their quarrel, Mary went to Smith's home to return his picture. Smith stated that after receiving the picture, he went to his room, took a nap and awoke about 8 A.M. When he looked out his window, he saw Mary's car parked out front. Looking into the car, he discovered Mary sitting erect behind the steering wheel, shot through the chest, a .22 revolver lying beside her on the front seat. She was dead—apparently a suicide. The revolver had been a gift to Mary from her father. Smith called the police to report the shooting.

Mary had been shot once. The bullet entered just below the right breast, traveled across the front of her body and lodged near her heart. The medical examiner theorized that she did not die immediately. When found, she was sitting upright in the car, her head tilted slightly backward, her right hand high on the steering wheel, her left hand hanging limp at her left side.

When questioned, Smith steadfastly denied any knowledge of the shooting. Mary's clothing, the bullet from her body and the gun were sent to the FBI Laboratory for examination. An examination of her blouse where the bullet entered failed to reveal any powder residues. The bullet removed from her body was identified as having been fired from the gun found beside her body.

### Questions

1. Is the shooting likely to be a suicide or a homicide? What facts support this?
2. How should the investigation proceed?

**B.** Ten-year-old Denise was playing in a school parking lot with her nine-year-old stepbrother, Jerry. A car pulled up to the curb next to the lot, and the man driving the car motioned for Denise and Jerry to come over. When the man asked where they lived, Denise described their house. The man then asked Denise to take him to the house, saying he would bring her right back to the lot afterward. Denise got into the car with the man, and they drove away. When they did not return after an hour, Jerry went into the school and told a teacher what had happened. Denise did not return home that evening. The next day the police received a report that a body had been found near a lover's lane. It was Denise, who had been stabbed to death with a pocketknife.

### Questions

1. What steps should be taken immediately?
2. Where would you expect to find leads?
3. What evidence would you expect to find?
4. Specifically, how would you investigate this murder?

# Discussion Questions

1. Questions still remain regarding the assassination of President John F. Kennedy. Why is this murder so controversial? What special problems were involved in the investigation?

2. What special problems were encountered in investigating the shooting of Lee Harvey Oswald?

**3.** How many murders were committed in your community last year? In your state?

**4.** How do your state laws classify criminal homicide? What are the penalties for each classification? Are they appropriate? Are they more or less severe than in other states?

**5.** Are you for or against capital punishment for persons convicted of first-degree murder? Is execution of murderers a deterrent to crime? Is media publicity concerning such cases a deterrent to murder? Do TV shows and movies showing criminal violence contribute to such crimes? Would gun-control laws deter murder?

**6.** If patrol officers are dispatched to a murder scene, what are their duties and responsibilities there?

**7.** An investigator is called to a murder scene by the patrol officer at the scene. What are the duties and responsibilities of the investigator? What activities can be performed jointly by the patrol officer and the investigator? Who is in charge?

**8.** The investigation of murder is considered the classic crime investigation. Are there factors that make this crime more difficult to investigate, or is it basically the same as any other criminal investigation?

**9.** What investigative procedures are required in homicides resulting from drowning? Gunshot? Electrocution? Stabbing? Hanging? Poisoning?

**10.** Mass deaths during World War II in concentration camps, in Guyana involving a religious cult and the more recent mass deaths in Waco, Texas, introduce entirely new problems into homicide investigation. Who should be charged and with what degree of murder? What special problems are associated with such investigations?

## References

Bourn, Kathryn. "Preserving a Victim's Deathbed Declaration." *Police,* September 1996, pp. 8–9.

"By Their Own Hands." *Law Enforcement News,* March 31, 1994, p. 9.

Geberth, Vernon J. "Homosexual Serial Murder Investigation." *Law and Order,* June 1995, pp. 83–86.

———. "Investigation of Drug-Related Homicides." *Law and Order,* November 1990, pp. 76–81.

———. "Lust Murder: The Psychodynamics of the Killer and the Psychosexual Aspects of the Crime." *Law and Order,* June 1991, pp. 70–74.

———. *Practical Homicide Investigation Tactics, Procedures, and Forensic Techniques,* 2nd edition. New York: Elsevier Science Publishing Company, Inc., 1990.

———. "The Psychology of Suicide." *Law and Order,* October 1996, pp. 163–166.

———. "A Return to the Scene of the Crime." *Law and Order,* March 1996, pp. 97–100.

———. "The Serial Killer and the Revelations of Ted Bundy." *Law and Order,* May 1990, pp. 72–77.

———. "Serial Murder: A Psychology of Evil." *Law and Order,* May 1992, pp. 107–110.

———. "The Staged Crime Scene." *Law and Order,* February 1996, pp. 89–91.

———. "State-Wide and Regional Information Systems." *Law and Order,* April 1994, pp. 64–67.

———. "Suicide-By-Cop." *Law and Order,* July 1993, pp. 105–109.

Gist, Richard M, and Vickie Harris Taylor. "Line-of-Duty Deaths and Their Effect on Co-Workers and Their Families." *The Police Chief,* May 1996, pp. 34–37.

Graves, Chris. "Suicide by Police." (Minneapolis/St. Paul) *Star Tribune,* December 15, 1992, pp. B1–B2.

Green, Terence J., and Jane E. Whitmore. "VICAP's Role in Multiagency Serial Murder Investigations." *The Police Chief,* June 1993, pp. 38–45.

Holmes, Ronald M. "Partner Homicide: America's Shame." *Law and Order,* August 1992, pp. 85–88.

Hougland, Steven M. "Conducting Drug-Related Death Investigations." *Law and Order,* April 1994, pp. 57–60.

"Jury Hands Kevorkian His Third Acquittal." (Minneapolis/St. Paul) *Star Tribune,* May 15, 1996, p. A4.

Keppel, Robert D., and  Joseph G. Weis. *Improving the Investigation of Violent Crime: The Homicide Investigation and Tracking System.* A Research in Brief. Washington, DC: National Institute of Justice, August 1993.

Morrison, Richard D. "Attending an Autopsy." *Law and Order,* November 1996, pp. 29–30.

———. "Solving Homicide Cases: The Medical Examiner Can Provide Some Answers." *Law and Order,* April 1994, pp. 56–63.

"Murder in America." *The Police Chief,* August 1995, pp. 18–28.

"Murder in the U.S." *Law Enforcement Technology,* November 1995, p. 20.

"National FOP Looks at Police Suicide and How to Prevent It." *Law Enforcement News,* April 30, 1995, pp. 1, 8.

Nyberg, Ramesh. "C.O.P.S. at Work." *Law and Order,* September 1993, pp. 45–48.

Pinizzotto, Anthony J., and Edward F. Davis. "Cop Killers and Their Victims." *Law Enforcement Technology,* July 1993, pp. 34–39.

Rachlin, Harvey. "Police Officer Deaths: Killed in the Line of Duty." *Law and Order,* September 1994, pp. 129–150.

———. "When Tragedy Strikes." *Law and Order,* November 1994, pp. 94–98.

Simms, Thomas H. "Your Worst Nightmare Has Just Come True." *The Police Chief,* May 1996, pp. 26–33.

Sly, Randy. "I'm Sorry to Inform You." *Law and Order,* May 1992, pp. 26–29.

Stack, Steven, and Thomas Kelley. "Police Suicide: An Analysis." *American Journal of Police,* Vol. XIII, No. 4, 1994, pp. 73–90.

Ullman, Kurt. "Forensic Entomology: Aiding Investigations." *Law and Order,* November 1992, pp. 26–29.

"'Untraceable' Hotline Debuts in St. Louis for Homicide Tips." *Law Enforcement News,* December 31, 1992, p. 1.

Van Zandt, Clinton R. "Suicide by Cop." *The Police Chief,* July 1993, pp. 24–30.

Walchak, David G. "In the Line of Duty." *The Police Chief,* May 1996, p. 7.

Whetsel, John T. "Honoring Our Fallen Officers." *The Police Chief,* April 1995, p. 6.

# Investigating Crimes against Property

**M**ost of the crimes discussed in this section do not involve force or violence against persons and, therefore, are often not considered to be as serious as assault, robbery, rape or murder. However, according to the *Uniform Crime Reports,* crimes against property occur much more frequently than crimes against persons. For example, larceny/theft accounted for 57.7 percent of the crimes reported in 1995. The figure below presents the percentage breakdown for 1995 Crime Index offenses.

In 1995, a crime against property occurred every 3 seconds in the United States:

1 larceny/theft every 4 seconds

1 burglary every 12 seconds

1 motor vehicle theft every 21 seconds

Many property crimes are difficult to investigate because there is little evidence and usually no eyewitnesses.

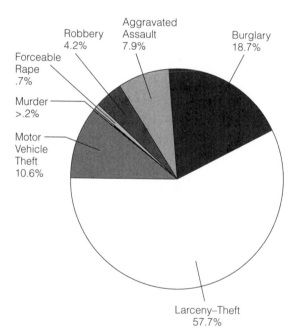

**Crime Index Offenses in 1995, percent distribution**

Source: FBI *Uniform Crime Report,* October, 1996, p. 8.

Physical evidence in property crimes is often similar to that found in crimes against persons: fingerprints, footprints, tire impressions, hair, fibers, broken glass and personal objects left at the crime scene. Other important evidence in crimes against property includes tools, tool fragments, toolmarks, safe insulation, disturbance of paint and evidence of forcible entry. The modus operandi of a property crime often take on added importance because there are no other significant leads. Further, crimes against property tend to occur in series, so solving one crime may lead to solving an entire series of similar crimes.

The chapters in this section discuss specific considerations in investigating burglary (Chapter 13), larceny/theft (Chapter 14), computer-related crime (Chapter 15), motor vehicle theft (Chapter 16) and arson (Chapter 17).

# Burglary

## DO YOU KNOW

How to define *burglary?*

What the basic difference between burglary and robbery is?

What the two basic classifications of burglary are?

What three elements are present in laws defining burglary?

What additional elements can be included in burglary?

What determines the severity of a burglary?

What the elements of the crime of possession of burglary tools are?

How to proceed to a burglary scene and what to do on arrival?

What special considerations are involved in burglary investigations?

What is the most frequent means of entry to commit burglary?

How safes are broken into and what evidence to look for?

What physical evidence is often found at a burglary scene?

What modus operandi factors are important in burglary?

Where to search for stolen property?

## CAN YOU DEFINE

| | | |
|---|---|---|
| blowing a safe | dragging a safe | punching a safe |
| burglary | peeling a safe | safe |
| burning a safe | pulling a safe | vault |
| chopping a safe | | |

**Introduction**

IN A WESTERN CITY, POLICE OFFICERS NOTICED WHAT THEY BELIEVED was safe insulation on the steps of a cabin occupied by a known burglar. They obtained a warrant and searched the premises for evidence of a burglary. The substance found on the steps and some burglary tools found inside the home were mailed to the laboratory, where the substance was confirmed as safe insulation. The suspect was arrested and convicted of burglary. On appeal, the courts held that such knowledge on the officers' part was, in effect, an extension of the laboratory and was, therefore, probable cause even without the laboratory examination. The verification by the laboratory only strengthened the probable cause. The charge of burglary was sustained.

The FBI's *Uniform Crime Reports* define **burglary** as "the unlawful entry of a structure to commit a felony or theft, even though no force was used to gain entry." All such attempts also count as burglaries. The common-law definition of *burglary* (originating in sixteenth-century England) required that the breaking and entering be committed during the nighttime or "between sunset and sunrise." Many changes have been made in burglary statutes since that time, including eliminating the requirement that it occur between sunset and sunrise.

---

Burglary is the unlawful entry of a structure to commit a crime.

---

The word *burglar* comes from the German words *burg* meaning "house" and *laron* meaning "thief"; thus the meaning "house thief."

Burglary is reported by frequency and by the value of the property stolen and recovered. This is because many burglaries yield low losses, although a single burglary can yield a high loss. The public regards burglary as a major crime problem. Many people fear arriving home or at work and confronting a burglar, a situation that can develop into an assault. Moreover, it is traumatic for people to realize that they have been doubly victimized when someone has invaded the privacy of their home or business and stolen their possessions. Although the items taken may be covered by insurance, they may be irreplaceable because of their great sentimental value.

The FBI *Uniform Crime Report* for 1995 indicated that 2,594,995, burglaries were reported that year, a decrease of 4.3 percent from 1994 figures of 2,712,774. Two out of three burglaries in 1995 were committed in private residences; 67 percent included forcible entry. The value of property stolen in burglaries was estimated at $3.3 billion. All four regions in the United States reported decreases. In 1995, burglaries were down 18 percent from 1991 rates and 20 percent from 1986 rates.

Harman (1994, p. 43) stresses: "Burglary is a serious crime because it devastates the lives, hopes, ambitions and memories of a vast number of people."

This chapter first explains the basic differences between burglary and robbery and presents a classification of various types of burglary. This is followed by a discussion of the elements of the crime of burglary and how to determine its severity, as well as a discussion of the elements of the crime of burglary tools in possession. Next is an explanation of the "typical" burglar and how to conduct the preliminary investigation. Then the chapter explores precautions to take if explosives are discovered at the scene of a burglary. This is followed by a description of the Scene Team experiment, modus operandi factors to consider and the possibility of fake burglaries. The chapter concludes with a discussion of effective case management and recovering stolen property.

---

## Burglary versus Robbery

A burglar seeks to avoid contact with persons near the scene or on the premises.

Burglary differs from robbery in that burglars are covert, seeking to remain unseen, whereas robbers confront their victims directly. Burglary is a crime against property; robbery is a crime against a person.

Most burglaries occur in unoccupied homes and businesses; therefore, few witnesses exist, and few alarms are given to provide advance notice to the police. The best chances of apprehending a burglar in the act are when a silent alarm is tripped, a surveillance camera records the crime, a witness hears or sees suspicious activities and reports them immediately to the police or when alert patrol officers observe a burglary in progress. However, most burglaries are not solved at the crime scene but through subsequent investigation.

*This burglar, operating under the cover of darkness, pries open the window of a home.*

## Classification

Burglaries are classified as residential or commercial.

### Residential Burglaries

*Residential burglaries* are defined as those that occur in buildings, structures or attachments that are used as or are suitable for dwellings, even though they may be unoccupied at the time of the burglary. Residential units include private homes, tenements, mobile homes, cabins, apartments, rooms within a house that are leased by a renter, houseboats used as dwellings and any other structure suitable for and used as a dwelling. About 67 percent of all burglaries are residential burglaries.

Residential burglaries are often committed by one or more juveniles or young adults who live in the same community. The targets are cash, items to convert to personal use or items to fence or sell such as televisions, radios, computers, guns, jewelry, tools and other small household goods.

### Commercial Burglaries

*Commercial burglaries* are defined as those that involve churches, schools, barns, public buildings, shops, offices, stores, factories, warehouses, stables, ships and railroad cars.

Most commercial burglaries are committed in service stations, stores, schools, manufacturing plants, warehouses and office buildings. Burglars often specialize in one type of facility. Businesses located in out-of-the-way places are most susceptible to burglary because of lack of police coverage and street lighting and because there are usually few witnesses to observe wrongdoing and notify the police.

Commercial burglaries are often committed by two or more people, depending on the type of premises, size and location of the building and the burglary attack planned. Some use a lookout who acts like a drunk, works on a stalled car or walks an animal near the location.

The building is cased in advance to learn about protection devices, opening and closing times, employee habits, people in the neighborhood and presence of a private security guard. Casing is also done by obtaining information from an employee or by posing as a worker, repairperson or salesperson to gain legitimate entrance.

## Elements of the Crime: Burglary

Although burglary laws vary from state to state, statutes of all states include three key elements.

Elements of the crime of burglary include:
- Entering a structure.
- Without the consent of the person in possession.
- With the intent to commit a crime therein.

*Burglars often ransack rooms looking for valuables, making it difficult for the victim to know what is missing. Often there are no leads and, therefore, little hope of apprehending the burglar or recovering the stolen property.*

**Entering a Structure.**　Entry may be by walking through an open door, crawling through an open window or transom, reaching through an open door or window with a long stick or pole or climbing through a hole in the wall, through a tunnel or through a ventilation shaft. Entry can be made by jimmying a door or window, using a celluloid strip to open a door lock, climbing a ladder or stairs outside a building, descending through a skylight, hiding in an entryway or breaking a window and taking items from the window display. Entry also includes remaining in a store until after closing time and then committing a burglary.

Some state laws include vehicles, trailers and railroad cars as structures.

**Without the Consent of the Person in Possession.**　To constitute burglary, the entry must be illegal and must be committed without permission of a person with lawful authority, that is, the owner of the property, the legal agent of such person or the person in physical control of the property such as a renter or part owner.

Entering a public place is done with consent unless consent has been expressly withdrawn. The hours for legal entry usually are posted on public buildings; for example, "Open Weekdays 9 A.M. to 5 P.M." Entrance at any other time is without consent. If a specific individual is restricted from entering a public place during its open hours, that individual must be notified orally or in writing that consent has been withdrawn.

**With Intent to Commit a Crime.**　Regardless of whether the burglary is planned well in advance or committed on the spur of the moment, intent must be shown. When the first two elements are present, the third is often presumed present; that is, if a person enters a structure without the owner's consent, the presumption is that it is to commit a crime, usually larceny or a sex offense.

## Additional Elements

Three additional elements are found in the laws of some states.

---

Elements of burglary can also include breaking into the dwelling of another during the nighttime.

---

**Breaking Into.**　Actual "breaking" is a matter of interpretation. Any force used during the burglary to enter or leave the structure, even if a door or window is partly opened or closed, constitutes breaking. Entrance through trick or ruse or through threats to or collusion with any person residing in the building is also considered breaking.

Breaking and entering is strong presumptive evidence that a crime is intended. Some laws include such wording as:

> Every person who shall unlawfully break and enter a building or dwelling or other structure, shall be deemed to have broken and entered or entered the same with intent to commit grand or petit larceny or a felony therein, unless such unlawful breaking and entering entry shall be explained by testimony satisfactory to the jury to have been made without criminal intent.

This, in effect, places the burden of proof on the defendant.

**The Dwelling of Another.** Some states still require that the structure broken into be a dwelling, that is, a structure suitable for sheltering humans. This remnant from common law restricts burglary to residential burglaries.

**During the Nighttime.** Common law also specified that burglary occur under the cover of darkness, an element still retained in some state laws. Nighttime is defined as the period from sunset to sunrise that is specified by official weather charts.

## Establishing the Severity of the Burglary

Most burglary laws increase the crime's severity if the burglar possesses a weapon or an explosive. Obtain the weapon and connect it with the burglar if possible. Check with the National Crime Information Center. If the weapon is stolen, a separate felony charge of theft or illegal possession of a weapon can be made.

---

A burglary's severity is determined by the presence of dangerous devices in the burglar's possession or the value of the property stolen.

---

If other crimes are committed along with the burglary or if the burglary is for the purpose of committing another crime such as rape, the additional crime is separate and must be proven separately.

## Elements of the Crime: Possession of Burglary Tools

A companion crime to burglary is possession of burglary tools, an offense separate from burglary. The charge of possession of burglary tools can be made even if a burglary has not been committed if circumstances indicate that the tools were intended for use in a burglary.

---

Elements of the crime of possessing burglary tools include:
- Possessing any device, explosive or other instrumentality.
- With intent to use or permit their use to commit burglary.

---

Burglary tools include nitroglycerin, explosives and any engine, machine, tool, implement, chemical or substance designed for cutting or burning open buildings or protective containers.

A person with a large number of automobile keys probably intends to use them to open varied makes and models of vehicle doors. Portable key cutters, codes and key blanks such as those used in hardware stores and key-making shops are also classified as burglary tools, as are slam pullers, devices that look like an oversized screwdriver and are inserted in car locks to force them open.

Many other tools used in burglaries are commonly obtained in hardware stores. These include pry bars, screwdrivers, bolt cutters, extension cords, pipe wrenches, channel locks and tire irons. Lock picks and tension wrenches, lever-type wrenches, warded pass keys, pick guns, cylinder drill jigs and various types of metal blades to open car doors can also be used as burglary tools.

Because many people, especially mechanics and carpenters, have tools that might be used in a burglary in their car or on their person, circumstances must clearly show an intent to use or allow their use in committing a crime.

## The Burglar

The burglar is often portrayed as a person with a mask over the eyes and a bag over the shoulder loaded with silverware and candlesticks. In reality, burglars fit no set image; they are of all sizes, ages, races and occupations. They are either amateurs or long-time professionals whose sole income is derived from burglaries.

Most amateur burglars are between the ages of fifteen and twenty-five; most professionals are twenty-five to fifty-five. The amateur is usually an unskilled, "infancy level" burglar who steals radios, televisions, cash and other portable property and who learns through trial and error. In contrast, the professional burglar usually steals furs, jewelry and more valuable items and has been carefully trained by other professional burglars.

Even though amateurs gain experience in committing burglaries, they are apt to make a mistake sooner or later and be observed by the police while committing a burglary. If caught and sentenced to prison, amateur burglars gain the opportunity to learn more about the "trade" from the professionals.

Professional burglars may have lookouts in communication through two-way radios. The getaway vehicle is usually close to the burglary site and the lookout monitors police radio frequencies.

Although most burglars' motives are monetary or drug related, sometimes the excitement of committing burglary and evading detection is equally or more important. One burglar said it was a "thrill" not to know what was waiting for him and if he would get away with the crime.

## The Preliminary Investigation

---

Proceed to a burglary scene quietly. Be observant and cautious at the scene.

---

On the way to the burglary scene, watch for persons fleeing the area, suspicious-looking persons still at the scene and suspicious automobiles. Do not use a siren on the way to the scene. Cut your flashing lights some distance from the scene, and do not use a spotlight or flashlight to determine the address. Park several doors away from the address of the call, turn the radio down and close car doors quietly. Approach the immediate area with low-tone conversation and avoid jangling keys or coins or flashing lights.

The first two officers arriving place themselves at diagonally opposed corners of the building. This places them out of the other's line of fire but in position to protect each other.

---

Search the premises inside and outside for the burglar.

---

Use maximum cover and caution in going around corners. In a dark room, use a flashlight rather than room lights to prevent silhouettes. Hold the flashlight in front of you at a 45-degree angle. Have your gun drawn but not cocked.

If no suspect is found, conduct the preliminary investigation as described in Chapter 1. Obtain detailed information about the type of structure burglarized, the means of entry, the time and date, the whereabouts of the owner, other persons recently on the premises, the property taken and the M.O.

Determine who the occupants are and where they were at the time of the burglary. Were they on the premises? If not, when did they leave? Were the doors and windows locked? Who had keys? What visitors had recently been there? Obtain descriptions of peddlers, agents, service installers or maintenance people on the premises recently.

Was the burglar familiar with the premises? Could the location of the stolen items be known only to a person who worked on the premises; that is, was it an inside job?

Obtain a complete list of the property taken. Estimate the value and find out where the property was obtained and where it was stored. Where and when did the owner last see it? What type of property was *not* stolen?

### Residential Burglaries

The preliminary investigation of a residential burglary should include the following as a minimum:

■ Contact the resident(s).
■ Establish points and methods of entry and exit.
■ Determine the type and amount of loss.
■ Describe the M.O.
■ Check for recent callers such as friends of children, salespeople and maintenance people.
■ Canvass the neighborhood for witnesses, evidence, discarded stolen articles, etc.

Interviews of burglars have revealed that they prefer middle- to upper-class homes and corner homes that allow them to see people approaching from more directions. They may knock on doors before entering to determine if a dog is inside, and they may call in advance to see if anyone is home. The advent of Caller ID may bring about some change in this technique.

When processing the crime scene in a residential burglary, process the exit as well as the entry area. When looking for fingerprints, check the inside of drawers that have been ransacked, smooth glass objects, papers strewn on the floor, countertops and clocks. The same procedures are followed if the burglary has occurred in a multiple-dwelling or a commercial lodging establishment such as an apartment building or a hotel.

### Commercial Burglaries

Preliminary investigation of a commercial burglary (for example, markets, shops, offices, liquor stores) should minimally include the following:

■ Contact the owner.
■ Protect the scene from intrusion by owners, the public and others.
■ Establish the point and method of entry.
■ Establish the point and method of exit.
■ Locate, collect and preserve possible evidence.
■ Narrow the time frame of the crime.
■ Determine the type and amount of loss.

- Determine who closed the establishment, who was present at the time of the crime and who had keys to the establishment.
- Describe the M.O.
- Identify friends of employees, maintenance people and any possible disgruntled employees or customers.
- Rule out a faked or staged burglary for insurance purposes.

## Special Problems in Investigation

---

Special considerations in investigating burglary include the problem of false alarms, determining the means of entry into a structure as well as into objects such as safes or vaults and recovering the stolen property.

---

**False Burglar Alarms.** "False alarms from personal security systems are a huge problem for law enforcement across the country," contends Strandberg (1992, p. 28). Daughtry (1993, p. 14) notes that "police studies consistently show that 95 to 99 percent of alarm calls are false—that is, non-police emergencies . . . a staggering 14 million calls."

Daughtry (1993, p. 14) also notes: "A National Institute of Justice report indicates that alarm responses account for 10 to 30 percent of all calls for police service and, since almost all of them are false alarms, the result is millions of hours in wasted police time." This is not only a frustrating waste of time for responding officers; more important, it may cause officers to be caught off guard when the alarm is "for real." Officers responding to alarms should not be "psychologically disarmed."

**Determining Entry into Structures.** Burglary is a crime of opportunity and concealment. Entry is made in areas of a structure not normally observed, under the cover of darkness, in covered entryways, through windows screened by shrubbery or trees or through ruse and trickery. Sometimes, however, the burglar breaks a shop window, removes some items on display and rapidly escapes by jumping into a nearby vehicle driven by an accomplice.

---

Jimmying is the most common method of entry to commit burglary.

---

Almost every means imaginable has been used, including tunneling; chopping holes in walls, floors and ceilings; and using fire escapes. Some burglars have keys made. For example, some people leave their car at a repair shop along with their full set of keys—an open invitation to make a duplicate house or office key. Other times, burglars hide out inside a building until after closing. In such cases, they often leave behind evidence such as matches, cigarettes or candy wrappers because their wait is often lengthy.

The hit-and-run burglary, in which a window is smashed to steal merchandise, is most frequently committed by younger, inexperienced burglars. Jewelry and furs are the most common targets.

Toolmarks, disturbed paint, footprints and fingerprints, broken glass or forced locks help determine how entry was made.

**Determining Entry into Safes and Vaults.** Safes are usually considered a good way to protect valuables, but most older safes provide little more than fire protection. Unless they are carried away or demolished by a burglar or lost in a fire, safes last many years; therefore, many old safes are still in use.

A **safe** is a semiportable strongbox with a combination lock. The size of the safe or lock does not necessarily correlate with its security. A **vault** is a stationary room of reinforced concrete, often steel lined, with a combination lock. Both safes and vaults are common targets of burglars.

---

Safes and vaults are entered illegally by punching, peeling, pulling, blowing, burning and chopping. Sometimes safes are simply hauled away by burglars.

---

In **punching,** the burglar shears the dial from the safe door by holding a chisel to the dial and using a sledge to knock the dial off, exposing the safe mechanism spindle to view. Next, a drift pin is held against the spindle. The sledge is then used to knock the spindle backward, which releases the tumblers. Many safes are now constructed to defeat punching.

In **peeling,** the burglar drills a hole in the upper left corner of the safe and then makes this hole successively larger by other drills until the narrow end of a jimmy can be inserted in the hole to pry the safe door partially open. The burglar then uses the larger end of the jimmy to complete the job. Although slow, this method is less noisy than other methods and so attracts less attention.

In **pulling,** also called **dragging,** the burglar inserts a *V* plate over the dial with the *V* in place behind the dial. Screw bolts are then tightened one at a time

*Some burglars use a rock or brick to smash a display window and to then steal valuable merchandise. Such smash-and-grab burglaries often set off an alarm.*

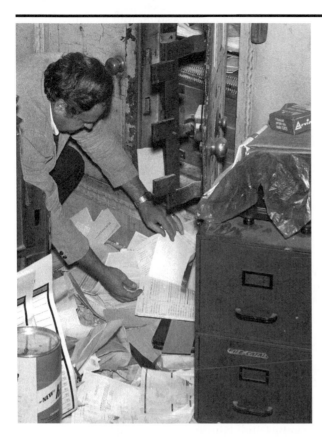

*Safes are a frequent target of burglars.*

until the dial and the spindle are pulled out. This method, the opposite of punching, works on many older safes but not on newer ones.

In **blowing,** the burglar drills a hole in the safe near the locking bar area or pushes cotton into an area of the safe door crack and puts nitroglycerin on the cotton. The burglar then places a primer cap against the cotton, tapes it in place and runs a wire away from the safe to a protected area. Mattresses and blankets are often used to soften the blast. Finally, the burglar ignites the nitroglycerin, and the safe is literally blown open. This dangerous, noisy method requires experience and is rarely used today.

The **burning** process often uses a "burning bar," a recently developed safe-cracking tool that is portable and easily brought to the scene. Whatever equipment is used, a hole is burned into the safe to gain entry to the contents. This hole may be burned near the safe's locking mechanism, or the safe may be tipped over and the hole burned through the bottom.

According to Lloyd (1994, p. 31), one of the newest tools of the safe and vault burglar is the oxy-arc burning cutting torch. A refinement of this tool is described by Dunckel (1994, p. 93). The device is an arc-air burning tool that can punch a hole completely through a 1-inch steel plate in about 10 seconds.

In **chopping,** the burglar uses chisels to chop out a hole in the bottom of the safe large enough to remove the property. This difficult, noisy process is seldom used.

Some burglars decide to use one or more of the entry methods just explained at a site of their own choosing. They steal the entire safe, hauling it away in a truck to another location, where they open it.

The preceding methods are used on older safes still found in many smaller stores. Often, the safe can be entered in less than fifteen minutes. More modern safes, however, do not have spindles and cannot be punched or peeled. Pulling the dial is unsuccessful because it removes only the dial and does not provide access to the safe's interior. Safes of newer steel alloys are highly resistant to burning and drilling.

### Obtaining Physical Evidence

Most burglars are convicted on circumstantial evidence. Any physical evidence at the burglary scene is of utmost importance.

---

Physical evidence at a burglary scene includes fingerprints, footprints, tire prints, tools, toolmarks, broken glass, safe insulation, paint chips and personal possessions.

---

Tools and toolmarks are especially important items of evidence that can connect one burglary with another. Be alert to the variety of containers used to carry burglary tools—handbags, suitcases, musical-instrument cases and packages appearing to contain merchandise. Tools can also be concealed under coats, inside pant legs or under car seats. Tools on the premises also are sometimes used to avoid being caught with burglary tools in possession.

Evidence at the scene of a safe burglary also may include safe insulation. The burglar often has some of this insulation in his or her clothing, either in pants, coat or jacket pockets or in the nailholes of shoes. Take comparison standards of safe insulation to be matched with particles found on the suspect, on tools used by the suspect or in the vehicle used during the crime. In some cases, safe insulation can also be matched with a series of burglaries.

*A door frame at a burglary scene may contain evidence such as fingerprints and toolmarks.*

DNA is also becoming of importance in burglary investigations. If a burglar cuts himself or herself breaking into a structure, he or she may leave blood behind that can be analyzed for DNA, perhaps linking this burglary to others. In fact, Harman (p. 44) suggests: "In the future, it may be possible to give a basic picture of an offender from DNA material left at the crime scene."

## Precautions for Explosives at the Scene

Sometimes explosives are encountered at a burglary scene. Use extreme caution in handling and preserving such evidence.

If a bomb threat is connected with a burglary, notify the FBI. If explosives are actually detonated, notify the Alcohol, Tobacco and Firearms Division of the U.S. Treasury Department. To dispose of explosives at the scene or in the suspect's possession, call the bomb squad of the nearest large metropolitan area or the explosives ordnance unit of the closest military installation. If an explosion has already occurred at the burglary scene, intentionally or accidentally, identify and preserve fragments from the explosive device and send them to the crime laboratory.

## The Scene Team Experiment

To increase discovery of fingerprints at burglary crime scenes, the Philadelphia Police Department began a "scene team" experiment in January 1987. In this experiment one detective processed burglary locations for latent fingerprints and other physical evidence while another detective interviewed neighbors in the immediate area.

According to Seamon (1990, p. 87): "An examination of the statistical information indicates that for the period surveyed, the team's efforts were resulting in approximately one arrest per month. . . . Also significant is the fact that of the 10 suspects identified by latents, one was charged with 100 burglaries and another was charged with 30 burglaries."

Identifiable lifts were produced from 17.2 percent of the scenes. The problem for this police department was that they had no capability to make cold searches of their tenprint files. If they had had an Automated Fingerprint Identification System, this 17.2 percent rate would be much higher.

The scene team's efforts at finding latent prints were considered to be successful, but this was not true of the neighborhood interviews. As noted by Seamon (p. 88):

> In general, if neighbors observe anything that may be useful to the police, they will call police to report the burglary or they will notify their neighbor—the complainant—who will direct the investigator to the source of information. Residents who do not want to get involved will not give any information to detectives who are canvassing the area. . . .
>
> In the future, scene team detectives will be sent to process scenes solo rather than as a two-officer team.

## Modus Operandi Factors

Effective M.O. files are essential in investigating burglaries because most burglars commit a series of burglaries. Look for patterns in the location, day of week, time of day, type of property stolen and method of entry or exit. The burglar may commit vandalism, ransack, write with lipstick on mirrors, take only cash or jewelry, drink liquor from the scene or eat from the refrigerator. Such peculiarities can tie several burglaries to one suspect.

---

Important modus operandi factors include the time, type of victim, type of premises, point and means of entry, type of property taken and any peculiarities of the offense.

---

Suspects often commit burglaries only on a certain day of the week, perhaps related to their day off from a regular job. The time of the burglary should be as accurate as possible, but when victims are gone on vacation, this is not easy to determine. Knowing the time also helps in checking alibis, interviewing witnesses and, in some states, determining the degree of the burglary or whether it is legally a burglary.

Determine any peculiarities of the offense, including oddities of the suspect. What method of search was used? Was anything else done besides committing the burglary? Did the burglar eat food, drink liquor, take a bath, use the shelter, leave matches? Did the burglar telephone first to ensure that no one was home or pose as a deliveryperson? Did neighbors see such activities? Determine any trademarks of the burglar. Some burglars take such pride in their professionalism that they leave a calling card of some type to let the police know whose work it is.

Check the M.O. with local files. Talk to other officers, inquire at other agencies within a 100-mile radius and discuss the case at area investigation meetings. Other officers may have encountered a similar M.O.

## Fake Burglaries

Do not overlook the possibility of faked burglaries, especially in commercial burglaries where the owner appears to be in financial difficulty. Check the owner's financial status.

So-called combination safe jobs, in which the safe is opened by the combination without the use of external force, are usually due to the combination being found on the premises, the safe being carelessly left open or improperly locked, a dishonest present or former employee using the combination or selling it to the burglar or the employer faking a burglary to cover a shortage of funds.

## Effective Case Management

Because burglary is predominantly a serial crime, the serial burglar should be the primary target of the burglary unit. This requires effective case management, including an effective system for prioritizing cases.

Effective case management also recognizes the mobility of burglars and makes assignments on the M.O. rather than geographic area; for example, burglaries involving forcible entry, daytime burglaries involving no force and nighttime residential burglaries.

All information should be shared with the drug enforcement unit because many burglaries are drug related.

### Using Computers to Investigate Burglaries

Kruse (1996, p. 66) describes the impact of use of computers on criminal investigations: "The computers have helped clear cases by discovering that some piece of evidence is duplicated in several different cases, sometimes a witness's name comes up several times and that information has been very helpful."

Using the computer's search capabilities, information retrieval is fast and simple, and investigations can proceed on information that in the past would have taken hundreds of hours to retrieve if, indeed, it could have been retrieved at all.

### Showing Concern for Burglary Victims

Surveys have indicated that victims' impressions of the police are related to how professionally investigators conduct the crime scene investigation. If officers are thorough, courteous, considerate, concerned and conscientious about keeping victims informed of the progress of the investigation, victims generally express favorable opinions of the investigators. Solving the crime is first priority for the police, but the victims' feelings must be considered as well. They may feel devastated, violated, angry or completely dejected. These feelings must be considered by investigators as they conduct interviews with victims.

## Recovering Stolen Property

Most burglars take money, jewelry, precious stones, negotiable bonds and other property that can be easily disposed of through a fence, pawnshop or secondhand store.

---

Check with fences, pawnshops, secondhand stores, flea markets and informants for leads in recovering stolen property.

---

Informants can often locate stolen property because they usually know who is active in the area. Surveillance of pawnshops and fences also often pays off. Circulate a list of the stolen property to all establishments that might deal in such merchandise in your own community and surrounding communities. If the property is of extreme value, enter it into the FBI's NCIC files.

If property is recovered, determine how it got to where it was found. Have the owner identify the property. Although the burglar is not normally identified by a fence, a pawnshop or secondhand store owner can often make such an identification.

There is often a higher ratio of property recovered than cases cleared by arrest because some property is discovered abandoned and some victims make deals with the burglars to recover their property when little hope of obtaining a conviction exists. The property recovery rate is between 25 and 40 percent in most communities.

Recovering stolen property and returning it to the rightful owner is aided by Operation Identification programs. In such programs, homeowners mark all easily stolen property with a Personal Identification Number (PIN). The numbers are recorded and placed in a secure location.

*Read the following articles and imagine yourself as the officer/detective assigned to each case. What elements of the crime are present? What evidence would you need to prosecute the case? Who else might you need to coordinate your efforts with? What is the likelihood of solving each crime?*

## Burglars use high-tech gadgets

**By Amanda Covarrubias**

*Associated Press*

SAN DIEGO—Jim Boyle came home from work one Tuesday and noticed his garage door was open. Strange, because he had closed it when he left that morning.

Inside his single-story house, someone had rifled through every closet, drawer and cupboard, making off with $8,000 in leather jackets, fur coats, power tools and camera gear.

Boyle had received a rude awakening to the high-tech world of garage door opener burglaries. Like cellular fraud and computer hacking, this type of crime is another example of criminals using electronic gadgetry to ply their illicit trade.

Police and security systems experts say burglars using electronic "code grabbers" can record and play back the signal from an automatic garage door opener from hundreds of feet away.

When Boyle left his house and activated his garage door opener, a thief with a "code grabber" was able to retransmit the signal and open the door. He walked in—and walked off with no telltale signs of breaking and entering.

"It's like having a key to your house," said Mark O'Keefe, a salesman at Street Smart Security in La Mesa, a San Diego suburb.

His colleague, Michael Lamb, 27, markets a device called a "code rotator" to combat the thievery trend. Each time the remote control is pressed, the code rotates to a new one, rendering a "code grabber" useless.

Although some garage door opener manufacturers offer a similar device with their units, Lamb's has 70 billion codes, making it virtually impossible to repeat the same code twice, he says.

If someone were to close his garage door 100 times a day, it would take 1.2 million years to repeat a code, Lamb claims.

He sells automobile and home alarm systems at his store, Street Smart Security. The rotator retails for $159.

A state law passed last year makes it a misdemeanor in California to use a code-grabber for illegal activity.

And Rep. Ron Packard, R-Oceanside, has introduced similar legislation at the federal level.

"They don't want another cell phone theft industry," Lamb said, referring to the estimated $2.5 billion the industry loses each year to electronic rip-offs.

Lamb's familiarity with the code grabber, which has surfaced in the past year, has made him an expert among law enforcement officials. He

*(continued on p. 453)*

## Summary

Burglary is the unlawful entry of a structure to commit a crime. It differs from robbery in that burglars are covert, seeking to remain unseen, whereas robbers confront their victims directly. Burglary is a crime against property; robbery is a crime against a person.

Burglaries are classified as residential or commercial. The elements of the crime of burglary include (1) entering a structure (2) without the consent of the person in possession (3) with the intent to commit a crime therein. Additional elements of burglary that may be required include (1) breaking into (2) the dwelling of another (3) during the nighttime. A burglary's severity is

*(continued)*

has spoken to numerous police departments and FBI officials about the code grabber and given them demonstrations on how it works.

"There's a device being manufactured that can compromise your home if you use your garage door opener," said Det. Chuck Nowotny of the Huntington Beach Police Department and president of the Western Association of Police Investigators.

Source: *Las Vegas Review Journal*, 5 April 1994. Reprinted by permission of the Associated Press.

## Man charged in Red Wing church burglary after mom called police

A rural Goodhue County man was charged Monday with theft in connection with the July 3 burglary of a Red Wing, Minn., church.

Glen Michael Dougherty, 25, is being held in the Goodhue County jail in lieu of $15,000 bail.

Investigators said Dougherty admitted that he took nearly $1,500 worth of electronic equipment from Christ Episcopal Church, including several VCRs, a color TV, computer system, tape recorder and microphone. Police later recovered most of the stolen goods at a Twin Cities pawn shop.

Dougherty also has admitted stealing electronic equipment from 10 other churches in Goodhue County since June 19, according to a criminal complaint filed in court Monday. Police said he had sold most of the stolen items to pawn shops.

Additional charges are expected to be filed today, an assistant county attorney said.

Source: *Star Tribune*, 16 July 1996. Reprinted by permission of the *Star Tribune*, Minneapolis-St. Paul.

## Man is arrested in burglaries of Goodhue County churches

A man from rural Goodhue, Minn., has been arrested in connection with a rash of church burglaries in southeastern Minnesota the past three weeks.

Glen Michael Dougherty, 25, was arrested by Goodhue County authorities Friday after investigators questioned him. They say he admitted being involved in the burglaries.

Since June 19, a dozen churches have been burglarized in Red Wing, Bellechester, Goodhue, Cannon Falls, Hay Creek, Holden Township and Pine Island.

Some were burglarized during the day, some at night. In each case, hundreds to thousands of dollars worth of electrical equipment was stolen, including televisions, VCRs, microphones and recording equipment.

Source: *Star Tribune*, 13 July 1996. Reprinted by permission of the *Star Tribune*, Minneapolis-St. Paul.

---

determined by the presence of dangerous devices in the burglar's possession or by the value of the property stolen. Attempted burglary and possession of burglary tools are also felonies. The elements of the crime of possessing burglary tools include (1) possessing any device, explosive or other instrumentality (2) with intent to use or permit their use to commit burglary.

When responding to a burglary call, proceed to the burglary scene quietly. Be observant and cautious. Search the premises inside and outside for the burglar.

Special considerations in investigating burglary include the problem of false alarms, determining the means of entry into a structure, as well as into objects such as safes or vaults and recovering the stolen property. Jimmying is the most common method to enter a structure to commit burglary. Attacks on safes and vaults include punching, peeling, pulling or dragging, blowing, burning, chopping and, for safes, hauling them away.

Physical evidence at a burglary scene often includes fingerprints, footprints, tire prints, tools, toolmarks, broken glass, safe insulation, paint chips and personal possessions.

Important modus operandi factors include the time, the types of premises, the type of victim, point and means of entry, type of property taken and any peculiarities of the offense.

Check with fences, pawnshops, secondhand stores, flea markets and informants for leads in recovering stolen property.

## Checklist

### Burglary

- Was a thorough preliminary investigation conducted?
- What is the address and description of the structure burglarized?
- What time and date did the burglary occur?
- What means was used to enter? Was it forcible?
- Who is the rightful owner? Was consent given for the entry?
- What visitors had recently been on the premises?
- Was the burglar familiar with the premises?
- What was taken (complete description and value of each item)?
- Where was the property located, and when was it last seen by the owner?
- What was *not* taken?
- What pattern of search did the burglar use?
- What was the burglar's M.O.?
- What physical evidence was found at the scene?
- Did any witnesses see or hear anything suspicious at the time of the burglary?
- Does the owner have any idea who might have committed the burglary?
- Have the M.O. files been checked?
- Have neighboring communities been informed of the burglary?
- Have you checked with fences, pawnshop owners and secondhand stores for the stolen property? Circulated a list to owners of such businesses?
- Might this be a fake burglary?

## Application

Read this account of a criminal investigation and evaluate its effectiveness:

In a California city, two janitors were met at the door of the restaurant they were cleaning by two armed men. One janitor was taken inside; the other escaped and notified the police. When the police arrived, both suspects were outside the building in different areas and claimed they knew nothing of a crime being committed. Inside, the one janitor was tied up in the kitchen, unharmed. The safe had been ripped open. A substance believed to be safe insulation, along with paint chips, was found in the trouser cuffs and shoes of both suspects. Both janitors made a positive field identification of the two suspects. Laboratory analysis of the substance found in the suspects' clothing and shoes matched a comparison sample of the safe insulation, and the paint chips matched the top two layers of paint on the safe. The men were charged with burglary.

*Questions*

1. Was it legal to take the men into custody?
2. Was field identification appropriate?
3. Was it legal to submit the safe insulation and paint chips for laboratory analysis?
4. Was the charge correct?
5. What additional evidence should have been located and seized?

## Discussion Questions

1. Many people think of *burglary* and *robbery* as interchangeable terms. What is the principal difference between these two offenses from an investigative viewpoint?

2. Describe the following methods of entering a safe: a pull job; a peel job; a chopping; blowing a safe; burning.

3. What types of evidence would you expect to find at the scene of a safe burglary? How would you collect and preserve it?

4. What are the elements of burglary in your state? What is the penalty for burglary?

5. How frequent is burglary in your community? Your state? Has burglary been increasing or decreasing in the past five years?

6. If you are investigating a burglary, which persons would you be most interested in talking to at the scene? Away from the scene?

7. What other crimes are often committed along with burglary?

8. Is it legal to "steal back" your own property if someone has stolen it from you?

9. If the object stolen in a burglary is valued below $100, is the crime a misdemeanor?

10. What can the police do to increase the reporting of burglaries? What can they do to help the public prevent burglaries?

## References

Daughtry, Sylvester, Jr. "False Alarm Reduction: A Priority for Law Enforcement." *The Police Chief,* January 1993, pp. 14, 16.

Dunckel, Kenneth. "Safe and Vault Burglary Trends." *Law and Order,* September 1994, pp. 91–95.

Harman, Alan. "Operation Bumblebee." *Law and Order,* November 1994, pp. 43–44.

Kruse, Warren. "2001—A Computer Odyssey." *Law Enforcement Technology,* April 1996, pp. 63–66.

Lloyd, Robert. "Crime Scene Documentation and Reconstruction." *Law and Order,* November 1994, pp. 31–32.

Seamon, Thomas. "Burglary Scene Investigation Experiment." *The Police Chief,* January 1990, pp. 87–89.

Strandberg, Keith W. "False Alarms Ignite Controversy." *Law Enforcement Technology,* November 1992, pp. 28–29.

# Chapter 14

# Larceny/Theft, Fraud, White-Collar and Environmental Crime

## DO YOU KNOW

How to define *larceny/theft?*

How larceny differs from burglary and robbery?

What the elements of larceny/theft are?

What the two major categories of larceny are and how to determine them?

What legally must be done with found property?

What the common types of larceny are and how to investigate each?

When the FBI becomes involved in a larceny/theft investigation?

What the elements of the offense of receiving stolen goods are?

What fraud is and how it differs from larceny/theft?

What the common means of committing fraud are and how to investigate each?

What the common types of check fraud are?

What the elements of the crime of larceny by credit card are?

What white-collar crime is and what specific offenses are included in this crime category?

## CAN YOU DEFINE

| | | |
|---|---|---|
| credit card | grand larceny | property |
| embezzlement | holder | shoplifting |
| floor-release limit | kleptomaniacs | short-con games |
| forgery | larceny/theft | white-collar crime |
| fraud | long-con games | zero floor release |
| goods | petty larceny | |

## Introduction

LARCENY/THEFT IS ONE OF THE EIGHT PART-ONE INDEX CRIMES. Although fraud, white-collar crime and environmental crime are not Index Crimes, they are so closely related to larceny/theft that they are included in this chapter. All three have elements in common and are investigated in similar ways.

Some states eliminate the distinctions between larceny, fraud and white-collar crimes, combining them into the single crime of *theft.* However, because many states do have separate offenses, they are discussed separately in this chapter. The distinction may be unimportant in your jurisdiction.

This chapter begins with an overview of larceny/theft, a discussion of the elements of the crime of larceny/theft, classification of such crimes and how "found property" fits. This is followed by a description of the preliminary investigation, the various types of larceny/theft that might be investigated and proving the elements of the crime. Next is presented an explanation of recovering stolen property and receiving stolen goods. Then the chapter focuses on the various types of fraud investigators might encounter. The chapter concludes with a discussion of white-collar crime and environmental crime.

## Larceny/Theft: An Overview

Reported larcenies exceed the combined total of all other Part One Index Crimes (58 percent), and have increased more rapidly than any other Index Crime, rising 500 percent over the past twelve years. In 1995 there were 8,000,631 reported larcenies, a 1.5 percent rise over 1994, when 7,879,812 larcenies were reported. Larceny was the only crime category in 1995 that showed an increase over 1994. Only 20 percent of larcenies were cleared by arrest in 1995.

**Larceny/theft** is the unlawful taking, carrying, leading or riding away of property from the possession of another.

Larceny is committed through the cunning, skill and criminal design of the professional thief or as a crime of opportunity committed by the rank amateur. The adage that "there is a little larceny in everyone" has considerable truth. Although some thefts result from revenge or spite, the motive for most larceny is the same for the professional and amateur thief—monetary gain, either actual cash or articles that can be converted to cash or to personal use. Compulsive thieves, called **kleptomaniacs,** are responsible for only a small number of offenses.

Both larceny and burglary are crimes against property, but larceny, unlike burglary, does not involve illegally entering a structure. Larceny differs from robbery in that no force or threat of force is involved.

## Elements of the Crime: Larceny/Theft

The crime of larceny/theft takes many forms, but the basic elements of the offense are similar in the statutes of every state.

The elements of the crime of larceny/theft are:
- The felonious stealing, taking, carrying, leading or driving away.
- Of another's personal goods or property.
- Valued above (grand) or below (petty) a specified amount.
- With the intent to permanently deprive the owner of the property or goods.

**Felonious Stealing, Taking, Carrying, Leading or Driving Away.** This element requires an unlawful, wrongful or felonious removal of the property; that is, the property is removed by any manner of stealing. Taking items such as fuel and electricity is also included in this element. Withholding property is a form of larceny by a failure to return, or to properly account for, the property or to deliver the property to the rightful owner when it is due. Failure to pay a debt is *not* larceny, even though there is a failure to pay. Civil remedies are sought for this type of theft.

**The Personal Goods or Property of Another.** **Goods** or **property** refers to all forms of tangible property, real or personal. It includes valuable documents; electricity, gas, water and heat supplied by municipalities or public utility companies; and domestic animals such as cats, dogs and farm animals. It also includes property in which the accused has co-ownership, a lien, pledge, bailment, lease or other subordinate interest. Larceny laws also cover cases in which the property of a partnership is converted to personal use adverse to the partner's rights, except when the accused and the victim are husband and wife.

In the definition of larceny/theft *another* refers to an individual, government, corporation or organization. This element refers to the true owner or the one authorized to control the property. Care assignment, personal custody or some degree of legal control is evidence of possession. In numerous cases, ownership of property has been questioned. Ownership usually means the true owner or the person having superior rights at the time of the theft. The owner must support the charge of larceny or there is no prosecution.

**Of a Value Above or Below a Specified Amount.** Value determines whether the offense is grand or petty larceny. Value means the market value at the time of the theft. Determine value by learning the replacement cost, legitimate market value, value listed in government property catalogues, fair market value or reasonable estimates.

If the property is restored to the owner, value means the value of the property's use or the damage it sustained, whichever is greater, while the owner was deprived of its possession. However, this cannot exceed the original value declared.

If several items are stolen in a single crime, the value of *all* items combined determines the value of the loss, even if the property belonged to more than one owner. Identical items stolen from different larceny locations are not combined but are treated as separate offenses.

**With the Intent to Permanently Deprive the Owner of the Property or Goods.** Intent either exists at the time the property was taken or is formed afterwards. The person may have intended only to borrow the property but then decided to keep it permanently. This element is usually the most difficult to prove. Establish ownership through documents of purchase, statements describing how the property was possessed, for how long and details of the delegation of care and control to another by the true owner.

Because of its frequency, much police time is devoted to larceny, and individual merchants and private security forces are also involved. Millions of dollars in losses go unreported each month. Those that are reported are usually reported to collect insurance rather than in the hope of recovering the property or clearing the case.

## Classification of Larceny/Theft

Most statutes have two major categories of larceny/theft based on the total value of the property stolen.

---

The categories of larceny/theft are **grand larceny,** a felony, and **petty larceny,** a misdemeanor—based on the value of the property stolen.

---

In many states the amount for grand larceny is $100 or more; any lesser amount is petty (petit) larceny. Check the laws in your jurisdiction for the dollar value that distinguishes petty and grand larceny. It is important to know whether the crime is a misdemeanor or a felony before proceeding with the investigation.

## Found Property

Keeping or selling property lost by the owner is a form of theft.

In most states, taking found property with the intent to keep or sell it is a crime.

Although the finder has possession of the property, it is not legal possession. Thieves apprehended with stolen property often claim to have found it, an invalid excuse. Some reasonable effort must be made to find the owner of the property, such as by making inquiries or advertising in a newspaper. The owner, if located, must pay the cost of such inquiries before the property is returned.

If the owner is not located after reasonable attempts are made to do so and after a time specified by law, the finder of the property can legally retain possession of it.

## The Preliminary Investigation

Investigating larceny/theft is similar to investigating a burglary, except that in a larceny/theft even less physical evidence is available because no illegal or forcible entry occurred. Physical evidence might include empty cartons or containers, empty hangers, objects left at the scene, footprints and fingerprints.

Do not give the complainant or victim the impression that the investigation of the reported theft is unimportant. If there is little hope of recovering the property or finding the thief, inform the complainant of this but only after all facts are obtained.

## Types of Larceny/Theft

Common types of larceny are purse-snatching, picking pockets, theft from coin machines, shoplifting, bicycle theft, theft from motor vehicles, theft from buildings, theft of motor vehicle accessories and jewelry theft.

The *Uniform Crime Report* for 1995 indicates the relative frequency of these types of larceny (see Figure 14–1).

### Pickpockets and Purse-Snatchers

Pickpockets are difficult to apprehend because the victim must identify the thief. This is rare unless the thief is observed by someone else or is caught in the act. The purse-opener and purse-snatcher are modern versions of the pickpocket. These thieves use force if necessary but count on their skills to avoid

**Figure 14–1   Larceny
Analysis**

Source: FBI *Uniform Crime Report,*
October 1996, p. 47.

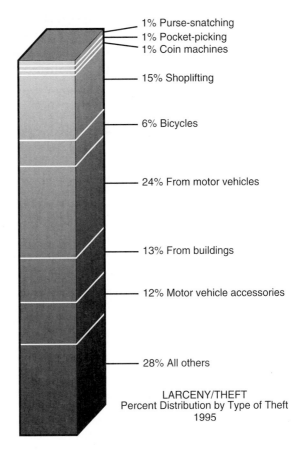

1% Purse-snatching
1% Pocket-picking
1% Coin machines

15% Shoplifting

6% Bicycles

24% From motor vehicles

13% From buildings

12% Motor vehicle accessories

28% All others

LARCENY/THEFT
Percent Distribution by Type of Theft
1995

force and identification. Lost wallets and purses, often the work of the pick-pocket, are not reported as thefts because the victims do not realize that theft has occurred.

Obtain from the victim a description of what was stolen and its value. Ask if the victim recalls being jostled or distracted momentarily, and if so, obtain complete details. Keep careful records of pickpockets and purse-snatchers, as often they are caught.

## Employee Theft

Most thefts from stores are internal, committed by employees of the establishment. The National Retail Foundation recently reported that 38 percent of the losses in the retail industry were due to employee thefts. Shoplifting accounted for 25.2 percent, bookkeeping errors for 22.5 percent and other types of problems for 14.4 percent. Employee theft is a serious problem that is increasing in the difficult economy of the 1990s. Employee embezzlement has bankrupted some smaller corporations. In some surveys conducted by loss specialists, 30 percent of the employees interviewed admitted to stealing from their employers.

One recommendation for reducing employee theft is to keep more expensive items under security lock and to have frank discussions with employees regarding the problem. Employees who are aware of management's policy regarding employee theft are less likely to steal.

Another action taken by some companies is to eliminate some potential employee thieves by informing job applicants that a drug test is required, even if it is not. This announcement alone may weed out applicants who have a drug habit and, therefore, are more prone to steal to support the habit.

## Shoplifting

**Shoplifting,** also known as *boosting,* involves taking items from retail stores without paying for them. It is normally committed by potential customers in the store during normal business hours. It does *not* include thefts from warehouses, factories or other retail outlets or thefts by employees.

Shoplifting has increased with the modern merchandising techniques that display the goods for sale, remove barriers between customer and merchandise and permit the potential buyer to pick up and handle the goods. Such efforts to increase sales also tend to increase shoplifting. Most items shoplifted are on the main floor, where it is easy to leave the store.

Shoplifting losses are astronomical. According to "Survey of U.S. Retailers (1994)," stores lose $9 billion + annually to shoplifting. Unfortunately, the customer ultimately pays because prices are usually increased 1 or 2 percent to make up for losses due to theft. The amount not recovered is part of the business operating expense, resulting in lower profits. It may be enough to put a small business out of business.

Like burglars, shoplifters are amateur (95 percent) or professional (5 percent). Most amateur shoplifters are law-abiding people who act on impulse and feel the big store can afford their small theft. Unfortunately, juries often uphold this belief, especially when shoplifters are charged during holidays. Most amateur shoplifters steal primarily for their own use, although some steal goods to sell for money to buy drugs.

Juveniles frequently shoplift on a dare, to be initiated into a shoplifters' gang, for status among their peers or because of a real or imagined need for the item itself. Juveniles may be given money and sent to the store to buy an item and then steal the item and keep the money. They may have their own money but steal needed items and use their money for something they cannot steal, such as drugs, or they may not have any money and steal the item simply because they want it. Other juveniles are semiprofessional and steal for monetary gain.

The transient or vagrant steals food or items for resale to obtain such items as liquor or drugs. The alcoholic and drug addict shoplift items they can sell to support a habit, not to make financial profit.

The professional shoplifter makes a living at stealing and thus develops many techniques to avoid detection. For example, a cohort may pretend to faint, drawing attention while the other steals the desired item. Sometimes stolen articles are kept on the person. Other times they are left in another area of the store and reclaimed at an opportune moment. Professionals operate alone, in pairs or in groups. They usually steal expensive objects. Cases on record show professionals who have stolen more than a million dollars worth of merchandise over a ten-year period. The items were rapidly converted to a lesser amount of cash (usually 25 percent of the value) by a fence. Some professionals have their own fences and steal on order. The professional rarely steals for personal use. Almost all thefts are for profit received through resale of the stolen property.

**Shoplifting Techniques.**   Many shoplifting techniques are used by the amateur and the professional. Most frequently, the amateur simply puts an item into a pocket or purse. Hiding items under garments or coats or putting them on under other clothing is the next most frequently used method. Some shoplifters place the items between their legs and walk out in the "shoplifter's shuffle." More sophisticated techniques involve using false-bottom boxes, baby buggies, hollowed-out books, empty lunch containers and shopping bags to steal items. Women sometimes use "booster bloomers," underpants with a false pocket sewn on the backside. The shoplifter may palm the item and carry it out or later put it into the pocket, use large coats or baggy pants, or hide an expensive stolen item between two cheaper, legitimately purchased items.

The apprehension rate for shoplifters is extremely low compared with the total number of shoplifting offenses committed. Police officers usually catch shoplifters only by luck or after being tipped off to a professional group operating in the community. Most apprehensions are by private security forces working for department stores and shopping centers or by floorwalkers or supervisory personnel. Clerks, in general, are not trained to make apprehensions and thus avoid making arrests, preferring to watch suspicious persons in an attempt to deter them from stealing. Although they have the most contact with potential shoplifters, clerks are often busy waiting on customers, are usually restricted to one department and are often told to simply inform their supervisor of any suspicious person.

Stores that detect and apprehend shoplifters often do not prosecute for fear of losing a good customer, of being humiliated and embarrassed in court or of

*One of the shoplifter's tools is the "booster box," a box made up to look like an ordinary giftwrapped package, but with a hinged lid that allows the shoplifter to put merchandise into it. The spring-loaded lid snaps shut, presenting an innocent appearance.*

facing a false arrest suit. Other reasons for not prosecuting are concern for the cost of attorney's fees, the hope that a reprimand will cure the problem or the belief that notifying a juvenile shoplifter's parents will control the situation.

Managers sometimes call the police for the effect it will have on the shoplifter, but if the property is recovered, they often decline to sign a complaint. Normally, even though the police can initiate a complaint on information and belief, their actions are based primarily on the store policy unless they personally witness the offense. In some states, store personnel are encouraged to interview the suspect because they are not police officers and thus do not have to warn suspects of their rights.

**Elements of Larceny by Shoplifting.** The elements of shoplifting are very similar to those required for general larceny:

- Intentionally taking or carrying away, transferring, stealing, concealing or retaining possession of merchandise or altering the price of the merchandise.
- Without the consent of the merchant.
- With intent to permanently deprive the merchant of possession or the full purchase price.

---

Altering the price of an item is considered larceny. It is usually not required that the person leave the premises with the stolen item before apprehension.

---

Early laws required that the shoplifter leave the store before an apprehension could be made. However, many laws have been changed to permit apprehension after the suspect has passed the last cashier's counter in the store for the particular level or department. The farther the suspect is from the normal place of payment, the greater the degree of intent that is shown to permanently deprive the merchant of the item. The suspect may be detained, after being told why, for a reasonable length of time and then delivered to a police officer, parent or guardian.

It is not a crime for a person to walk out of a store after simply forgetting to pay for an item because intent is absent. This is a common problem for individuals who suffer from Alzheimer's disease. Such people may forget they have picked up an item, may forget to pay for it or may honestly believe they have paid for it when, in fact, they have not. Such incidents require officers to exhibit patience, understanding and excellent communication skills in resolving the situation.

Because shoplifting can be either petty or grand larceny, a misdemeanor or a felony, establish the value of the property. If the shoplifter is placed under arrest, recover and retain the stolen item(s) as evidence. Whether the individual is prosecuted depends on the individual's attitude, the policy of the store and the police department, the value of the property taken and how many of the legal requirements for prosecution are fulfilled. Evidence to support shoplifting or altering a price requires an eyewitness or proof that the item could not have been removed except by the person charged. The property must be carried away or removed, but not necessarily to outside the store.

Have the manager or clerk identify the property and show proof of the store's ownership.

Proving the intent to permanently deprive is the most difficult problem in investigating shoplifting. Show this intent by the shoplifter's actions from the time the item was stolen until the arrest was made.

*A security guard monitors the facilities of a California computer company using multi-image closed-circuit televisions sets.*

Specific information to obtain in a shoplifting investigation includes the following:

■ Were store personnel deliberately avoided?
■ Was there flight to avoid arrest?
■ What did the shoplifter do to avoid detection?
■ Were any price tags or other identifying marks or tags removed?
■ Was the property concealed? How? Where was the property found?
■ Was the property taken to other locations in the store before stealing it?
■ Was any attempt made to locate the checkout register, or was it deliberately avoided?
■ Did the suspect have any money on his or her person? If so, how much?
■ Were there any incriminating actions such as attempts to hide the item when the store detective approached?
■ Was the suspect carrying order lists for merchandise that would indicate intent to steal for others?
■ Were any special shoplifting devices used such as booster bloomers, false boxes, empty bags?
■ Were there any other witnesses? How reliable are they?
■ What acts made the apprehending person suspicious?

Stores are legally within their rights to recover items taken from the store if there is no proof of purchase. This does not mean the person is guilty of shoplifting. It may be impossible to prove an intent to steal.

If a store manager wants to prosecute, review the store's reports to determine if a crime has been committed. If it has, take the shoplifter to the police station and book and search him or her for any other property. The person making the arrest must sign a complaint. Most shoplifters never reach the stage of arrest and release to the police. When it does occur, encourage store cooperation

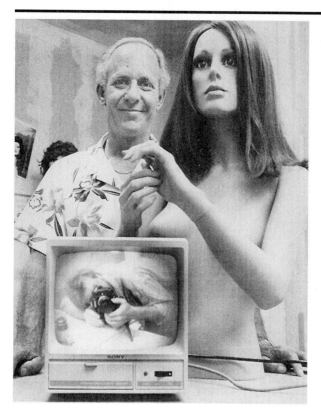

*Inventor F. Jerry Gutierrez demonstrates one of his surveillance mannequins designed to watch for shoplifters. They are being photographed by the photographer shown on the TV monitor.*

because good arrests by store personnel aid convictions and can deter shoplifting in the particular store.

Overcrowded courts have become a problem to retailers who want to prosecute for shoplifting. Prosecutors have difficulty obtaining convictions. Forty-three states have passed statutes providing for civil fines instead of, or in combination with, criminal penalties. Retailers are not satisfied with the criminal prosecution approach because of the delays, low rate of convictions and lack of restitution for the lost property. The new approach permits the retailer to sue civilly in small claims court, even in cases where the offender is not convicted of a crime. Penalties under civil action range from $50 to $500 or in some cases actual damages plus five times the value. Using a combination of civil and criminal approaches results in more satisfactory resolution of shoplifting cases.

### Bicycle Theft

As bicycles have increased in popularity, so has bicycle theft, which accounts for 6 percent of reported larcenies. Identification of bicycles is difficult due to the failure to have a registration system or to use one that exists, the complex method of providing serial numbers and the fact that stolen bikes are often altered, dismantled, repainted and resold.

Bicycles are most frequently stolen from schoolyards, college campuses, sidewalk parking racks, driveways and residential yards. Juveniles are responsible for the majority of thefts, although some professional bike theft rings operate interstate. In many bicycle thefts, the crime is grand larceny due to the high value of many bicycles.

A single bike theft is best investigated by the patrol force. Determine the bicycle's value and have the owner sign a complaint. A juvenile apprehended for a single theft can be prosecuted, especially with a prior record of similar or other offenses. Restitution for damage and an informal probation is usually initiated. If multiple thefts have occurred, the offender usually goes to juvenile court. Adults are prosecuted by the same procedures used for other larcenies.

The investigative division compiles a list of bike complaints organized by make of bike, serial number and color. Bike thefts are also entered into the police computer system. All patrol officers are given a bike hot sheet similar to that for stolen vehicles and periodically check bike racks at parks, schools and business areas against this sheet.

Bikes are sometimes reported stolen to defraud insurance companies. Even if the bike is recovered, the owner has already collected its value, and there will seldom be a prosecution.

Large numbers of thefts in a short time period may indicate that an interstate ring has moved into the community. Roaming interstate groups of bicycle thieves may hit neighborhoods resulting in a large number of thefts in a short time. They use covered trucks to transport the bicycles from the area, making recovery almost impossible without information from informants.

Stolen bicycles are used for transportation or are sold to bike stores, repair shops or bargain hunters. The professional thief, often using a van or covered truck, steals several expensive bikes at one time, takes them to a garage and repaints or dismantles them for parts.

Bicycles are easy to disguise by painting over or removing ID tags. Many are immediately disassembled and sold for parts, easily taken from one location to another by riding them or placing into a vehicle trunk, van or truck. One problem in identifying stolen bikes is the lack of a uniform state or national registration system such as that used for motor vehicles.

## Jewelry Theft

Jewelry, most often stolen by professional thieves, is also the target of armed robbers and burglars. Jewel thieves know the value of jewels, that they are extremely difficult to identify once removed from their settings and that the rewards are higher for the amount of risk involved than in other types of larceny. They also have ready outlets for disposition.

Most jewelry thefts are from vehicles owned by jewelry salespeople and from private individuals known to be careless about the security of their jewelry.

Frank and Serpico (1995, p. 51) state that a traveling jewelry salesperson (TJS) typically carries from $50,000 to $1 million worth of jewelry during daily visits to jewelry retailers: "Dressed to impress customers in an industry that deals in some of the most beautiful baubles in the world, the TJS is easily targeted by cunning predators."

Jewel thieves also operate in stores, distracting the salesperson and then substituting a cheap facsimile for expensive jewelry. Jewel thieves are ordinarily not local; they tend to operate interstate and to use locally known fences. They have many ingenious methods to steal and hide jewelry.

Because jewel thieves operate interstate, the FBI becomes involved. The local FBI office maintains files of known jewel thieves and their last known operations; their pictures, descriptions and modus operandi; and information about whether they are in or out of prison.

**467**

Chapter 14

**Larceny/Theft,
Fraud, White-
Collar and
Environmental
Crime**

Always inform the FBI of jewel thefts, even without immediate evidence of interstate operation.

---

FBI jurisdiction is attained under Title 18, Sections 2314 and 2315. Section 2314 gives jurisdiction when the value exceeds $5,000 and the items are transported interstate or in foreign commerce and when the criminal knows the goods to be stolen, converted to personal use or obtained fraudulently. Section 2315 gives jurisdiction when buyers of the goods know they are stolen, that they have been transported interstate or by foreign commerce and that they are worth more than $5,000. Mailing packages that contain illegally obtained jewels to another state also constitutes interstate operation.

Investigating jewelry theft is the same as for any other larceny. Search the crime scene as you would in a burglary to obtain physical evidence. Obtain the names of people in neighboring rooms at motels and hotels. Interview employees and other possible witnesses. Review the victim's account of the theft. Obtain a complete description of the jewelry, the value of each item and the amount of insurance carried. Contact informants and alert them to watch for information about the location of the stolen items and those responsible.

## Art Thefts

Art thefts are increasing, and to cope with the problems resulting from the interstate and international nature of these thefts, the FBI created the National Stolen Art File in 1979. Objects must have a value of at least $2,000 to be entered into this file. Local FBI offices have the reporting forms that must be submitted by a police agency, not the owner.

The FBI reports that $50 million worth of art is stolen annually in the United States and more than $1 billion worth internationally. This offense usually comes to the attention of law enforcement through an art gallery's report of a burglary or theft. In other instances, art objects are recovered during the investigation of another crime, or the theft is reported by another police agency. Two unique factors in art thefts are that the objects are frequently held for long time periods and are then sold or moved coast to coast or internationally for disposition.

Baker (1996, p. 19) suggests: "Art theft and related crime are almost always international. Art stolen in one country typically ends up in another—after passing through numerous hands."

Theft of art objects is the second most important international criminal activity. Because of this, thefts of valuable art should be reported to the FBI and to Interpol, which also has an international stolen art file. Few police officers have any training in identifying art, so they should conduct only the normal burglary, theft or fraud investigation. Then an authenticity check of the art object should be conducted by the FBI and national art dealers. People who own art objects rarely have adequate descriptions or photos of each piece, and the pieces rarely have identification numbers. Investigators should submit to the FBI all known information concerning the theft and a photograph of the art if one is available.

## Numismatic Thefts: Coins, Metals and Paper Money

Thefts of coins, metals of various types and paper money also have been increasing. These types of thefts have existed for many years.

Coin collections are typically stolen during commercial and residential burglaries. Obtain the exact description of the coins, the condition, any defects, scratches, dye breaks, how they were jacketed and any other identifying information. To a high degree, the condition of coins determines their value; a coin in mint condition may be worth double the value of a coin in poor condition. Stolen coins may be taken from one coast to the other for disposition. Large coin shows are held throughout the year in larger cities, usually at convention centers or hotels. If interstate transportation is suspected, notify the FBI.

Metals of various types, such as gold, copper, silver and aluminum, are valuable. Copper is obtained from electrical and telephone lines or from storage yards of these companies. Thieves have been known to cut down telephone lines and to strip electrical lines in remote areas. A weekly check of scrap yards may be advisable in some jurisdictions.

### Trash Theft

Lehman and Dion (1996, p. 39) call stealing trash a "gray-collar crime." They note: "The national average cost to haul and dispose of a ton of trash is estimated at $125. This means that the trash disposal industry is a $67 million per day—$24.5 billion per year—operation in the United States. This is big business and a big opportunity for theft." They cite as an example a trash hauler who claims the garbage being dumped is residential rather than commercial, meaning the city pays for it. A typical 25-yard compactor truck hauling 10–13 tons of trash a day would cost $500 to $650—an "instant theft of the same amount from the town." They note that if this happens once a day, five days a week, in a year the hauler has stolen $130,000 to $160,000, and that's just *one* truck. Lehman and Dion (p. 44) conclude:

> Policing trash crime hardly has the glamourous aura of traditional police work. Yet this form of theft is just as real as taking cash from the till of the corner store. The difference is that there is a lot more money in the trash industry, and the crime is a lot more insidious.

## Proving the Elements of the Crime

To prove the felonious stealing, taking, carrying, leading or driving away of property, gather evidence to prove the property is missing, not simply misplaced. Take statements from the owner regarding the circumstances of the purchase, where the property was located and what security was provided. Also obtain evidence that the owner no longer has possession of the property.

Obtain proof of ownership through bills of sale or receipts, or through evidence that the owner had custody, possession or responsibility for the item.

Determine the item's value by ascertaining its replacement cost, legitimate market value or reasonable estimates. The owner can testify to the actual value if he or she is familiar with the specific item and its quality and condition at the time of the theft. Persons with business knowledge of the value of similar items can help determine value. If certain items obviously exceed the petty larceny limitation, it is not necessary to know their exact value.

Intent to permanently deprive the owner of the property is shown by the suspect's selling, concealing, hiding or pawning the property or converting it to personal use. It is proven by a motive of revenge, possession under circumstances of concealment, denial of possession where possession is proven or flight from normal residence.

## Recovering Stolen Property

Stolen property is disposed of in many ways. Often it is sold on the streets to obtain a higher profit than would be paid by a fence and to avoid a record of the sale. Because many people are looking for a bargain, thieves usually can dispose of the property on the streets, but this involves a risk of being reported to the police by someone who sees the transaction.

If property is sold to pawnshops or secondhand stores or is left at a store on consignment for sale, most states and communities have statutes or ordinances requiring a permanent record of the transaction. The seller must be given a receipt describing the property purchased, the seller's name and address and the amount paid. A copy of the transaction is often sent to the police department of the community listed as the seller's home address. If the property is identified as being stolen, the police contact the shop owner and, upon proof that the property is stolen, can recover it. Shop records are open to police inspection at all times. Information in these records can lead to the arrest of the seller as the person who committed the theft.

When you recover stolen property, record when the property was recovered, where, who turned it in and the circumstances surrounding the recovery. List the names and addresses of any persons present at the time of recovery. Mark the property as evidence and take it into custody. In some ways, it is legal to return the property as long as its identification is recorded and a photograph is taken. There is no reason the original property must be produced in court unless it was an instrument that caused death or serious injury.

## Receiving Stolen Goods

A go-between who receives stolen goods for resale is referred to as a *fence*.

---

The elements of the offense of receiving stolen goods are:
- Receiving, buying or concealing stolen or illegally obtained goods.
- Knowing them to be stolen or illegally obtained.

---

Receiving stolen property for resale is a crime, as is concealing stolen property, even though not purchased. The thief does not have to personally sell goods to the fence. An "innocent" third party can sell the property for the thief, but it is still an offense if the buyer knows the property was stolen.

Knowing is difficult to prove. The property must be found in the receiver's possession and identified as the stolen property by the owner's testimony, marks, serial numbers or other positive identifying marks. Knowing can then be proved by the very low price paid for the goods in comparison with the true value.

Usually, evidence of the sale is provided through an informant who made the sale or knows who did. The property may have been resold, and the person buying the item may be the informant who identifies the receiver of stolen goods. This person assists the police in making another sale or identifying property in the receiver's possession.

The receiver of stolen goods is often discovered when the person who stole the property is arrested and identifies the receiver. It is necessary to show that the receiver could not legitimately own the item unless he or she had bought it from a thief. Show that it was not purchased through a normal business transaction. The character of the person selling the property or any indication that the property was being concealed is evidence. Evidence that markings or serial numbers have been altered or removed indicates concealment and intent to deprive the rightful owner of the property. The seller can testify to conversations with the receiver about the property and the fact that it was stolen. The receiver's records may not show the transaction, which would be evidence of intent to conceal. The charge of receiving stolen goods can be used when possession of stolen items can be shown but there is not sufficient evidence to prove theft.

**Sting Operations.**    Many cities have established sting operations, in which the police legally establish a fencing operation. A suitable shop is set up as a front for the operation. Normally, secondhand stores, repair shops, salvage dealers, appliance dealers or pawnshops make good front operations. The store is stocked with items to support the type of business selected.

Word is spread through informants and the underworld that the business will "buy anything." Attractive prices are paid to get the business started. Closed-circuit television records all transactions between the fence and the seller of stolen goods. The camera is usually focused on an area in which a calendar and clock are clearly visible, to establish the date and time of each transaction. Video equipment records the transaction, the actual sale and the person selling the stolen goods. A parking lot surveillance camera shows the vehicle used to transport the property and its license number.

When an item is presented at the counter, the seller, the amount paid for the property and the buyer are recorded. The property is then dusted for fingerprints to further prove the seller's possession. The stolen goods are checked through normal police channels to determine where they were stolen.

The shop is run for two to three months and then discontinued. Arrest warrants are then issued for the persons implicated during the store's operation.

# Fraud

**Fraud** is a general term used for deceit, trickery and cheating as well as to describe individuals who pretend to be what they are not. Legally, however, fraud has a narrower meaning.

---

Fraud is an intentional deception to cause a person to give up property or some lawful right. It differs from theft in that fraud uses deceit rather than stealth to obtain goods illegally.

---

Fraud victims are in a good position to provide information regarding suspects because they have had firsthand dealings with the suspects.

---

Fraud is committed in many ways, including the use of checks, credit cards, confidence games and embezzlement.

---

## Check Fraud

Losses from bad-check operations cannot be determined exactly because no single clearinghouse gathers statistics on this offense. Checks used to defraud include personal, business, counter, draft and universal checks, as well as money orders. Fraudulent checks are made to appear genuine in many ways. The check blank can be similar to the one normally used and difficult to detect. In fact, many fraudulent and forged checks are written on stolen check blanks. Handwriting is practiced to look authentic. Various stamps, checkwriters, date stamps and cancellation stamps are placed on the front and back of the check to give it a genuine appearance.

Scott (1996, p. 46) cautions: "One myth commonly associated with check cases is that these violators are all rather petty offenders, and police should concentrate on 'real criminals.' Unfortunately, 'real criminals' also frequently write bad checks to finance their activities."

---

Common types of check fraud are insufficient-fund checks, issuing worthless checks and forgeries.

---

The *insufficient-* or *nonsufficient-fund check* falls into one of two categories: (1) accidental, in which people carelessly overdraw the checking account and are generally not prosecuted unless they do so habitually or (2) intentional, in which professionals open a checking account with a small deposit, planning to write checks well in excess of the amount deposited. This is intent to defraud, a prosecutable offense.

Most bad checks are not written with intent to defraud. They may have been mistakenly drawn against the wrong bank, the account balance may have been less than the person thought, two or more people may have used the same account without knowing the actual balance or the bank may have made an error. These nuisance-type checks are usually paid in full on request of the payee.

*Issuing a worthless check* occurs when the issuer does not intend the check to be paid. Proof of intent is shown if the issuer has no account or has insufficient funds or credit or both. A worthless check is normally prosecuted the same as one for insufficient funds. Obtain the check as well as statements from the person who accepted it, any other witnesses and bank representatives. Also obtain a signed complaint.

**Forgery** is signing someone else's name to a document with the intent to defraud. This includes actually signing the name and using a rubber stamp or a check-writing machine. To prosecute, obtain the forged check or document, statements from the person whose name is forged, any witnesses to the transaction and the testimony of a handwriting expert if necessary. Blank checks are often obtained through burglaries or office thefts committed by professionals. The check is authentic and, therefore, easier to cash once the endorsement is forged.

It is also forgery to alter the amount on the check or to change the name of the payee. The person who initially draws the check must testify as to the authorized amount and payee. It is also forgery to change a name on a charge account slip.

**The National Fraudulent Check File.** Professional check passers who write several checks in a city in a short time and then move to another city or state often use the same technique. The FBI's National Fraudulent Check File helps identify such persons and often shows a pattern of travel. The FBI maintains other files that assist in tracing bad-check writers. These include files on check-writer standards, watermarks, confidence operators, safety paper standards, rubber stamps, anonymous letters and typewriter standards.

Investigating bad or fraudulent checks requires precise details about the check and the entire transaction. The check itself is the main evidence. Carefully examine the front and back of the check and note peculiarities. Describe the check: type, firm name and whether it is personal, payroll, federal or state. Was it written in pencil or ink or typed? Were any special stamps used? If the check was altered, was it by change of payee, change of date, change of amount or a forged signature? Were there erasures and misspellings? Were local names and addresses used? Put the check in a protective polyethylene envelope or plastic container. It can also be processed for fingerprints at the laboratory.

Where was the check passed? Who took it? Were there other witnesses? If so, obtain their names and addresses. If currency was given, what were the denominations?

Obtain an exact description of the check passer. Was the suspect known to the person taking the check? Had he or she ever done business with the store before? What identification was used: driver's license, social security card, bank identification card, credit card? Was the suspect left- or right-handed? Was the suspect alone? If with others, what did they look like? What approach was used? What words were spoken? If the check passer used a car, did anyone notice what it looked like or the license number?

If the check passer is apprehended, look for devices used to make checks such as check writers, ink pads, typewritten date stamps or other rubber stamps on the person or in the vehicle.

Scott (1996, p. 44) suggests: "Police investigations tend to concentrate on individual checks, treating each one passed as a separate offense. While this inflates the number of cases handled, it also promotes duplication of effort and fails to reflect the actual extent of the problem."

### Counterfeiting

Counterfeiting of money generally comes to the attention of the police through a retailer or a bank. The Secret Service publishes pamphlets on identifying counterfeit money. The most common denominations of counterfeit money are $10, $20 and $50. The paper of authentic bills has red and blue fibers imbedded in it, and the bills have intaglio printing. The portrait is detailed and lifelike; the Treasury seal is clear and distinct on sawtooth points; the borders are clear and unbroken; and serial numbers are distinct, evenly spaced and the same color as the Treasury seal.

If a bill is suspect, a receipt should be given to the retailer or bank, and the bill should be turned over to the nearest Secret Service Office to determine its authenticity. Obtain details of how the bill came into the complainant's possession as well as an accurate description of the bill passer.

A newly developed felt-tip marker can instantly detect even the finest-quality counterfeit money with a single stroke. With the felt-tip marker, a dot or short line is made on the suspect bill. If the "ink" remains gold, the bill is authentic. If the "ink" turns black, the bill needs scrutiny.

### Credit-Card Fraud

**Credit card** refers to any credit plate, charge plate, courtesy card or other identification card or device used to obtain a cash advance, a loan or credit or to purchase or lease property or services on the issuer's credit or that of the holder. The **holder** is the person to whom such a card is issued and who agrees to pay obligations arising from its use.

Use of credit cards has become a way of life in the United States. The credit card opened a new avenue for criminals to obtain goods and services by theft and fraud. On the other hand, the credit card, like the check, reduces cash thefts from individuals and reduces the amount of cash-on-hand in places such

**473**

**Chapter 14**

**Larceny/Theft,
Fraud, White-
Collar and
Environmental
Crime**

*A secret service agent compares a counterfeit $100 bill, top, and a genuine one, bottom, in his Richmond, Virginia, office in May 1996. At least fourteen fake $100 bills were passed at fast-food restaurants, grocery stores, convenience shops and discount outlets in Chesterfield County, Petersburg and Hopewell, Virginia. Local counterfeiters are apparently using computers, image scanners and full-color copiers or printers.*

as filling stations, as well as the amount of cash transferred to banks from businesses. Use of credit cards also aids in identifying criminals who have the cards in their possession, more so than does cash, which is not as easily identifiable.

Masuda (1992, p. 72) writes:

> The economic rewards of credit fraud far outweigh the risks of apprehension since no system is in place to identify, apprehend, and manage the prosecution of offenders. . . .
>
> Cards are discounted on the street from $50 to $300. An initial investment of $250 for five cards with credit limits of $2,000 per card, enables a criminal entrepreneur to obtain a 30-day maximum yield of $9,750 or a profit of 3,900 percent. This scheme represents an extraordinary return on a low-risk investment that virtually outperforms all of the major stock exchanges and futures markets.

Because credit-card fraud is often spread throughout many jurisdictions, many police departments place low priority on this type of offense. Further complicating this crime, many businesses accept credit-card telephone purchases. Fraudulent orders are placed, and if the victims do not review their bills, the fraud can go completely undetected.

As noted by Dees (1994, p. 51) many of the best counterfeit credit cards are made in Asia where they have overcome problems with technical aspects of the card such as the hologram and the magnetic strip for signature, personal identification number and account number.

Most people involved in credit-card fraud are also involved in other types of crimes. The credit cards are obtained principally by muggers, robbers, burglars, pickpockets, purse-snatchers, thieves and prostitutes. They can also be obtained through fraudulent application or by counterfeiting the card.

Credit cards can be stolen by mailbox thieves who may have been tipped off by a postal employee, at apartment boxes or by dishonest employees of the card manufacturer. Cards from the manufacturer are desirable because they are unsigned. The criminal can sign the holder's name in his or her own handwriting. These cards also provide more time for use before the theft is discovered. For the same reasons, these cards are more valuable for resale to other fraudulent users.

To take maximum advantage without being detected, the criminal obtains the card by fraud, theft or reproduction, uses it for a short time and then disposes of it.

---

The elements of the crime of larceny by credit card include:
- Possessing a credit card obtained by theft or fraud.
- By which services or goods are obtained.
- Through unauthorized signing of the cardholder's name.

---

To use another person's credit card illegally, the criminal must either forge the cardholder's signature on sales slips or alter the signature on the card. The latter is made difficult by colored or symbol undertones that indicate when erasures and alterations are attempted.

The criminal must also operate under the floor-release limit to avoid having the clerk check the card's validity. The **floor-release limit** is the maximum dollar amount that may be paid with a charge card without getting authorization from the central office, unless the business assumes liability for any loss. The limit is set by each company and is subject to change. It can be $50 or $100; in some gas stations, it is only $10. **Zero floor release** means that all transactions by credit card must be checked. A suspicious merchant usually runs a check regardless of the amount of credit requested. Often the criminal is asked for additional identification, which is difficult to produce unless other identification was also obtained in the theft.

Credit cards are attractive to criminals who operate interstate. Such criminals know that few companies will pay the witness fees for out-of-state prosecutions and that extradition is difficult to obtain unless the losses are great.

Many laws cover larceny or fraudulent use of credit cards. Possessing a forged credit card or one signed by a person other than the cardholder is the basis for a charge of possession of a forged instrument. Possessing two such cards is the basis for presuming intent to defraud. Illegally making or embossing a credit card or changing the expiration date or account number also subjects the person to a charge of intent to defraud. In most jurisdictions, it is not necessary to prove that the person possessing the card signed it. Persons having machinery or devices to counterfeit or forge credit cards can be charged with possession of forgery devices.

It is larceny to fail to return a lost credit card or to keep one that is sent by mistake if the finder or recipient uses the card. Airline tickets bought with a stolen or forged credit card also are stolen property. The degree of larceny, petty or grand, is determined by the ticket's value. It is also larceny to misrepresent credit information or identity to obtain a credit card. If a person sells his or her credit card to someone who uses it and the original cardholder then refuses to pay, the cardholder can be charged with larceny.

Not all merchants and businesspeople are the victims of credit-card fraud. Some of them commit such fraud. For example, a merchant may direct an employee to make more than one authorized record of charge per sale and then forward the charges for payment or raise the amount on the credit-card charge slip. This is larceny, with the degree determined by the difference between the actual charge and that forwarded for payment. It is also forgery because a document was altered. It is an attempt to commit larceny if such actions are not completed because of intervening circumstances such as the cardholder becoming suspicious.

Most large credit-card issuers assign personnel to work with local police in cases of credit-card larceny. These people can be contacted for help or to obtain information on the system used to manufacture and issue the cards.

When investigating credit-card fraud, obtain samples of handwriting from sales slips signed by the suspect. If a card is obtained by false credit application, handwriting is available on the credit application form. If the card is used for a car rental, other information about the vehicle rented is available. Gas stations often record the state and license number of vehicles serviced. Drivers' licenses are used for identification. If a suspect is arrested, obtain a warrant to search the suspect's vehicle and room for copies of sales slips or tickets obtained with the card, even though it has been discarded or sold.

Examine credit cards for alteration of the signature panel; the numbers or name can be shortened by using a razor blade to shave off numbers or letters. New numbers can be entered to defeat the hot card list. Merchandise on sales slips found in the criminal's possession can provide further proof of illegal use. If the service obtained is a motel room, telephone calls can be traced to determine accomplices. The clerks who handle the transactions often initial the sales slip, which enables the company or store to furnish the name of a witness.

## Phone and Mail Fraud

Telemarketing fraud and other types of fraud using the telephone have also proliferated. In one such scam, a "representative" informs potential victims that they have won a sweepstakes prize and that the company needs their name, address and social security number to process the award. "The company" then uses the social security number for fraudulent purposes.

Sharp (1994, p. 91) notes: "U.S. consumers are bilked out of approximately $100 billion a year, almost half of which is attributed to telemarketing scams.

Clede (1993, p. 87) notes that cellular-phone fraud is a growing problem that police must be prepared to deal with:

> While there are no official statistics, fraud is thought to be now costing the industry between $100 million and $300 million per year. This "cost of doing business" is passed on to the consumer.

One type of cellular fraud is access fraud, the unauthorized use of a cellular phone service by tampering with the phone's programming. A specific form of this type of fraud involves cloning—monitoring calls and capturing the electronic serial number (ESN) or MIN (mobile identification number), decoding it and cloning a new chip to make another phone appear to be a duplicate of that phone.

Caller ID can enhance *and hinder* fraud investigations. It can be used to identify perpetrators of fraud, but it can also pose a danger to officers who work undercover. Morrison (1992, p. 48) suggests that Caller ID is a "serious threat to officer safety when conducting investigations. . . . Special investigation units, narcotics bureaus and other covert police agencies are concerned that they will be exposed by having their telephone numbers exposed to the criminals they telephone."

If mail fraud is suspected, police officers should contact the Postal Inspector through their local post office.

### Confidence Games

Confidence games have separated people from their money for centuries; in fact, con games were known as early as 100 B.C. Changing times require changing techniques, but four basic elements are always present: locating a mark from whom the money is to be obtained, selecting the game, conducting it and then leaving the area as rapidly as possible.

A confidence game obtains money or property by a trick, device or swindle that takes advantage of a victim's trust in the swindler. The confidence game offers a get-rich-quick scheme. The victim is sworn to secrecy and told that telling anyone could cause the deal to fall through or the profits to be divided among more people. The game may require the victim to do something dishonest or unethical, thus making the victim less apt to report it to the police. It is often conducted away from the victim's hometown so that the victim cannot obtain advice from friends.

A particular type of person is needed to make the con game work. Con artists develop cunning, guile and skills through their own systems of learning and education. They are taught by older persons in the "trade," usually starting as the "number two" or "straight man." As they gain experience, they work their way up until they are the "number one" in a swindle of their own. Con artists understand human nature, are extremely convincing with words, lack conscience, have an uncanny ability to select the right victim and have no mercy for their victims, often extracting the life savings of elderly people.

Two basic approaches are used in con games: the short con and the long con. **Short-con games** are schemes that take the victims for whatever money they have with them at the time of the action. For example, "Three-Card Monte," similar to the old shell game, entices victims to bet on whether they can select one card from among three. "Huge Duke" involves betting on a stacked poker hand, with the victim dealing the final hand. "The Wipe" involves tying money into a handkerchief for safekeeping and then switching it with one containing newspaper bits.

**Long-con games** are usually for higher stakes. For example, in "The Wire," the original long-con game, the victim is enticed to bet on horse races, convinced through an elaborate telegraph office setup that the manager can beat the bookmaker by delaying the results of the race long enough to let the victim and other cohorts in the scheme make bets. After allowing the victim to win a few games at low stakes, the "big bet" is made in which the victim may lose anywhere from $10,000 to $25,000.

When investigating con-game fraud, obtain a complete description of the confidence artists and the type of fraud, trick or false pretense they used, as well as the exact amount of money involved.

Because the victim usually sees and talks with the con artists, it is often easy to identify them, but unless the police are notified quickly, the suspects will be gone from the area. Obtain descriptions of the perpetrators and their M.O. Keep this information on file for future reference. The FBI maintains a confidence artist file to assist in locating such suspects, as well as a general appearance file of con artists (even though photographs are not available). The FBI assists in investigating violations that occur on interstate conveyances such as planes, boats and trains. It also assists if there is evidence that radio, television or telegraph was used in committing the crime or if a money order was sent to a person in another state. If the swindle exceeds $5,000, the FBI has jurisdiction under the Interstate Transportation of Stolen Property Act. (Many con games exceed this amount.)

Postal authorities can assist in investigating if the confidence artists use the mails to obtain victims or to transport profits from their crime.

Most states include con games in laws relating to larceny by trick and to obtaining money under false pretenses. Check the laws in your jurisdiction for the specific elements that must be proven.

One type of fraud that may be unfamiliar to law enforcement is called "gypsy crime." According to Harman (1996, p. 97):

> A crime family specializing in fraud has operated successfully throughout the world for almost 2,000 years. Millions of dollars are lost each year to these perpetrators, but fewer than 5% of the victims ever complain—and those that do are most often met with laughter.

Harman explains that the gypsy population is a close-knit family, superb at keeping secrets and speaking their own language. In addition to fortune-telling fraud, gypsies also operate major welfare frauds and are often involved in extortion schemes.

## Embezzlement

**Embezzlement** is the fraudulent appropriation of property by a person to whom it has been entrusted. The property is then used by the embezzler or another person contrary to the terms of the trust. The owner retains title to the property during the trust period. The property so entrusted may be real or personal property. Even though the title remains with the owner, the embezzler usually has control through appointment as agent, servant, bailee or trustee. Because of the relationship between owner and embezzler, the embezzler has custody of the property. Most embezzlements involve employees.

Most bank losses are from embezzlement, often involving large sums of money.

---

Bank embezzlement is jointly investigated by the local police and the FBI.

---

Bank embezzlements often start small and gradually increase. Surprisingly, many embezzlements are not committed for the benefit of the embezzler. Many start by providing unauthorized credit extensions to customers. As the amount increases, the employee is afraid to make the error known to the employer and attempts to cover the losses. In other cases, the employee uses funds to start other businesses, fully intending to replace the borrowed funds, but the businesses often fail. Other motives for embezzlement are to cover gambling debts, to support a drug habit, to make home improvements, to meet heavy medical expenses or to get even with the employer for real or imagined grievances. The FBI must be involved in the investigation of bank fraud.

Businesses, industries and other financial institutions are also victims of embezzlement. Embezzlement includes committing petty theft over a period of time, kiting accounts receivable, overextending credit and cash returns, falsifying accounts payable records and falsifying information put into computers, a highly sophisticated crime. (Computer-related crimes are discussed in the next chapter.)

Embezzlement is increasing at 15 percent per year and has an estimated annual cost of $4 billion. The prosecution rate is low because of adverse publicity for the individual and the company. Often the employee has been trusted for many years, and sympathy overrules justice.

Embezzlement losses may be discovered by accident, by careful audit, by inspection of records or property, by the embezzler's abnormal behavior, by a sudden increase in the embezzler's standard of living or by the embezzler's disappearance from employment. Because police training rarely includes accounting courses, investigating embezzlement cases often requires help from professional accountants. In embezzlement cases, prove fraudulent intent to convert property contrary to the terms of a trust by establishing how and when the property was converted, what the exact amount was and who did the converting. Establish that a financial loss did, in fact, occur. Determine the amount of the loss. Describe the property accurately if it is not money. Describe and prove the method of obtaining the property. Establish the nature of the trust. Seize all relevant books and financial records as evidence. It is necessary to determine the motive to prove fraudulent intent.

## White-Collar Crime

**White-collar crime** refers to business-related or occupational crime. White-collar crime is big business. According to Burkhart and Lantz (1996, p. 3): "Estimates start at $40 billion a year and growing." And, as Turner and Stephenson (1993, p. 57) caution: "Statistics are unreliable, however, because many of the crimes are never reported. White-collar crime is also responsible for a significant loss in productivity that is not reflected in the statistics."

Murray (1995, p. 52) suggests: "For years, statistics have pointed to an upward trend in white-collar crime. As this trend continues, every law enforcement agency must be properly equipped to react to fraud-related complaints."

"National White Collar Crime Center" (1996, p. 11) notes: "While its impact on the economy may be measured in the hundreds of billions of dollars, the crime known as white-collar, economic or financial, is often misperceived as victimless." The article explains:

> Typically, there is no body and no blood. The individual involved in economic criminal activity is generally smarter and more sophisticated than his or her street crime counterpart, and the victim, for a number of reasons, doesn't report the crime. Fighting economic crime is a complicated undertaking involving tedious financial research and analysis.

Many instances of larceny/theft and fraud can also be classified as white-collar crime. Perpetrators of white-collar crime seldom "look like" criminals. They are often highly educated, socially accepted people who hold high-level positions of trust within a company. Because of such positions, they are able to commit crimes involving millions of dollars.

*Michael Milken, former junk bond chief at Drexel Burnham Lambert, leaves the U.S. District Court in New York with his wife, Lori, after pleading guilty to six felony counts of securities fraud. He agreed to pay the court a record $600 million, but remained a very rich man.*

According to Turner and Stephenson (1993, p. 57): "White-collar crime probably costs U.S. businesses more than $40 billion each year. . . . It is highly profitable, relatively risk free, and almost socially acceptable."

Much white-collar crime is never reported because it involves top-level executives whose reputations their organizations do not want to damage. White-collar crimes may be committed by individuals against other individuals such as family members, lawyers, real estate agents, insurance agents and physicians. They may be committed against organizations by insiders such as business partners, office managers, computer programmers and senior executives. White-collar crimes may also be committed by individuals with no relationship to the victim, such as corporate spies, forgers, counterfeiters, computer hackers and information pirates.

Turner and Stephenson (p. 57) note some of the tactics used by white-collar criminals:

> White-collar criminals' tactics include trickery, deceit, or misrepresentation. Some familiar schemes are customer impersonations, medical and insurance frauds, real estate and banking swindles, and embezzlements. The crimes may involve forged or counterfeit checks, receipts, business records, or other legal documents, or the criminals may be aided by technologies, such as on-line computer terminals, fax machines, and color copiers.

Regan (1995, p. 51), a special agent with the financial crimes division of the U.S. Secret Service, notes:

Today's financial criminal runs the gamut from the embezzling bank employee to the armed robber at an ATM to the heroin-trafficking West Africans to the Asian Triad committing bank fraud on global scale. Clearly, the misconception that all financial crimes are victimless, white-collar crimes that are very rarely connected with violent, recidivistic defendants must be changed.

The United States Chamber of Commerce has identified nine categories of white-collar crime:

---

White-collar or business-related crime includes (1) securities theft and fraud, (2) insurance fraud, (3) credit-card and check fraud, (4) consumer fraud, illegal competition and deceptive practices, (5) bankruptcy fraud, (6) computer-related fraud, (7) embezzlement and pilferage, (8) bribes, kick-backs and payoffs and (9) receiving stolen property.

---

Investigate these crimes as you would any larceny case. Whether they are felonies or misdemeanors depends on the value involved.

White-collar crimes can be committed by any employee within a business or organization. However, low-level employees usually do not have the opportunity to steal a large amount from their employer. Most often their crimes consist of pilferage from the employer. Many employees do not see taking office supplies or placing personal long-distance phone calls from a work phone as dishonest. However, they would not think of doing the same thing in a place where they did not work. Over time, the losses from pilferage are often much more than what a high-level employee might embezzle.

Morrison (1995, p. 34) states: "The investigation of economic or white collar crimes frequently presents a challenge to the police investigator because of the complexity involved in such cases. Conceivably, part of the reason for these intricacies is that there are usually some special accounting problems associated with auditing transactions and analyzing records of activity involving perpetrators and criminal acts."

### Public/Private Cooperation

Few law enforcement agencies are equipped to investigate white-collar crime, encouraging such investigations to be conducted internally by in-house or contracted private investigators. Turner and Stephenson (p. 57) suggest: "Security managers should plan their investigations as if they are to receive no assistance from local law enforcement." This advice is echoed by Biancardi (1992, p. 77): "In most countries, it would be unrealistic to expect much cooperation from law enforcement in preventing corporate fraud." Biancardi suggests:

The first investigative steps should be taken within the company being victimized. The company should use its own or contracted resources before approaching the police.

Biancardi urges that such investigation should be conducted by a competent professional because: "Unintentional damage done by a nonprofessional during the first steps of a criminal investigation is almost always irreparable—and detrimental to morale."

The National White Collar Crime Center (NWCCC) links criminal justice agencies across international borders and also bridges the gap between local and state criminal justice agencies. This center provides assistance in preventing, investigating and prosecuting economic crime.

## Environmental Crime

Hammett and Epstein (1993, p. 2) state: "Environmental crime is a serious problem for the United States, even though the immediate consequences of an offense may not be obvious or severe. Environmental crimes do have victims. The cumulative costs in environmental damage, and the long-range toll in illness, injury and death may be considerable."

Indeed, as Devaney (1993, p. 8) warns: "Environmental crime is hardly victimless. It is far-reaching and pervasive; its consequences are often concealed for years or even decades. The real victims of environmental crime are our children and our children's children."

According to *Environmental Crime Prosecution: Results of a National Survey* (1994, p. 1): "The most common environmental offenses prosecuted involve illegal waste disposal; the most common substances involved in these offenses are hazardous wastes." This document notes that environmental crime investigation is a new area of specialization that mixes elements of law, public health and science.

Harris (1992, p. 27) notes: "Criminal prosecution of environmental crimes will be to the '90s what savings and loan prosecutions were to the '80s." Harris reports that Congress and administrative agencies are amending environmental laws and regulations to increase punishments for environmental criminal offenses, in many cases making them felonies rather than misdemeanors. Among such acts are the following:

- Comprehensive Environmental Response, Compensation and Liability Act.
- Resource Conservation and Recovery Act.
- Federal Water Pollution Control Act.
- Clean Air Act.

In each of the preceding, amendments were made converting existing misdemeanors to felonies.

Matulewich (1991, pp. 21, 25) notes that environmental crime laws did not exist thirty years ago, but in 1990 the Pollution Prosecution Act was enacted, making enforcement of environmental crimes a new concern for law enforcement. He notes that incidents such as the Love Canal are familiar to most citizens of the United States and that violations of various environmental crime acts call for penalties of up to $25,000 per day for noncompliance or imprisonment up to ten years.

Many of the problems associated with investigating environmental crime are similar to investigating computer-related crime and other crimes which have become more prevalent during the end of the twentieth century. Definitions of environmental crimes vary from state to state. Statistics are not uniformly compiled. The suspects are often otherwise upstanding business people, and they often do not feel they are committing crimes.

Harris (p. 28) suggests one "emerging prosecutorial tool for environmental crimes" as the concept of "conscious avoidance." According to Harris:

The government often employs this principle to present evidence that the defendant deliberately closed his or her eyes to what would have been obvious.

Premeditation or malice are not required to prove an environmental crime. All that must be proved is that some act that violated the law was done knowingly rather than by mistake. For example, the owner of a company makes a conscious decision to dump hazardous materials into a waterway.

Of special concern in environmental crime investigations is the search warrant. Investigators must know what substances may be sought and how such samples should be collected to avoid contamination. Pearsall (1993, p. 2) offers the following observations:

> As the role of the law enforcement community continues to adapt to an ever-changing society, we enter into an era in which the protection of our fragile environment is of primary importance. Although the civil regulatory agencies have been charged with a similar goal, their enforcement powers are limited to civil fines and injunctions. This often is enough; however there are many individuals or entities that violate the environmental protection laws not due to lack of knowledge but by choice. These violations are criminal and need a follow up criminal investigation. . . .

If it seems at this point that we in the law enforcement community could do environmental enforcement on our own, this simply is not the case. Most law enforcement officers have little or no idea of the existence of the complex array of environmental control law with all the exceptions, changes and omissions. We are naive when it comes to the scientific background needed to put together an environmental pollution case. Neither do we understand or have the knowledge to deal safely with the illegal disposal of hazardous waste. Civil regulatory agencies have this knowledge and the resources to document evidence of a violation.

Laska (1996, p. 94) agrees, stating: "Environmental investigations bring together varied professionals and permit each to use his or her unique skills." He suggests: "To the law enforcement officer, these cases are intimidating because of the technical facets involved. By working together with administrative regulators, the technical aspects unique to the investigation can be solved." Laska (p. 96) concludes: "Just as a white collar investigator will call upon an accountant or computer specialist for technical assistance, so will the environmental investigator use the regulator for the technical aspects of the investigation. The skillful investigator will then fit the technical expertise into the developed case, just as in a burglary, drug or murder investigation." Rebovich (1994, p. 22) suggests:

> Special appeals to control environmental crime at the local level are now emanating from low-income, urban areas where illegal dumping of hazardous wastes has been characterized as "environmental racism," exposing vulnerable groups to serious health threats. Through criminal prosecution, local prosecutors serve a crucial function in helping to improve the overall quality of life of these neighborhoods.

In effect, says Rebovich (p. 23): "As the locally based prosecutor of environmental polluters, the district attorney has assumed the role of protector of the public health."

*Read the following articles and imagine yourself as the officer/detective assigned to each case. What elements of the crime are present? What evidence would you need to prosecute the case? Who else might you need to coordinate your efforts with? What is the likelihood of solving each crime?*

## Man arrested on charges of mail fraud

A former Twin Cities man accused of bilking 23 Minnesota and Wisconsin investors out of more than $300,000 was arrested Tuesday in Miami, the U.S. attorney's office said.

Luis Alberto Camus, 32, was charged with 11 counts of mail fraud in a federal grand jury indictment returned June 19 in Minnesota.

Authorities say Camus, doing businesses as Canel Finance Group, sold "slots" in a commodity futures market venture for $16,000. He told prospective investors that they would receive weekly payments of $600 for 52 weeks and that their initial investment would be refunded at the end of the year.

The indictment claims Camus never invested the investors' money but used some of it to pay previous investors.

Authorities say the scheme ended in April 1995, when Camus sent letters to investors in which he said, "Due to the interference of certain government bodies, I am returning everybody their initial investment." The packets also contained a release agreement and post-dated checks. The indictment says investors who tried to cash the checks had them returned because of insufficient funds.

Source: *Star Tribune,* 10 July 1996. Reprinted by permission of the Associated Press.

## Former power co-op employee indicted

MADISON, WIS.—A federal grand jury has accused a former Dairyland Power Cooperative employee of stealing about $264,000 from the La Crosse company.

Darrell H. Lack, 53, of La Crescent, Minn., was indicted Wednesday on charges of mail fraud and interstate transportation of stolen property.

The former La Crescent school board member worked for Dairyland for 15 years before his job was eliminated in June 1995 as part of a reorganization, company spokeswoman Deb Mirasola said. His last position with the company was director of materials management in the finance department.

Assistant U.S. Attorney Grant Johnson said that the indictment accuses Lack of opening an account at M&I Bank in Madison in August 1991 under the name of "Darrell Lack, doing business as Dairyland Power Conversion."

Lack was accused of stealing checks written to Dairyland by various companies that had bought material from the co-op and depositing them into his personal account, Johnson said.

Source: *Star Tribune,* 23 August 1996. Reprinted by permission of the Associated Press.

## Woodbury couple sentenced for fraud

A Woodbury couple were sentenced in federal court in St. Paul Friday for fraudulently concealing assets from the Bankrupt Court.

Richard D. O'Brien, former owner of the now-defunct Carpet Values store in Lakeville, was sentenced to one year in prison and three years of supervised release and was ordered to pay $343,285 in restitution.

He pleaded guilty to submitting false income-tax returns and filing bogus documents to obtain a bank loan.

Karol F. O'Brien was sentenced to five years probation and 300 hours of

*(continued on p. 484)*

*(continued)*

community service and was ordered to pay $47,000 in restitution. She concealed assets from a bankruptcy trustee, the U.S. attorney's office said.

Carpet Values closed in September 1991.

Source: *Star Tribune,* 22 June 1996. Reprinted by permission of the *Star Tribune,* Minneapolis-St. Paul.

## Some thieves can't steal a clue

**By Michael Precker**
*Dallas Morning News*

Did you hear the one about the bank robber who slathered whipped cream on his face so he wouldn't be recognized? His disguise melted, making his life of crime short but sweet.

How about the thief who used a manhole cover to break a jewelry store window, then ran off with the loot—and fell through the manhole? It was all downhill from there.

Police work isn't just the nastiness and tragedy we see on the evening news and reality cop shows. To prove the point, a fellow from Nashville is making a killing by poking fun at dumb crooks.

"People are just dying to laugh at the bad guys instead of being afraid of them," said Daniel Butler, who's crafting a multimedia industry on exactly that premise.

If you agree, check out "America's Dumbest Criminals," (Rutledge Hill, $7.95) a hot-selling paperback book of 100 true vignettes like the two mentioned above. Or wait for the sequel, or the home video or the Web site, all coming soon. Or watch the weekly TV show premiering this fall.

"I think with O.J. and all that, there's a feeling that people are fed up with crime and everybody's getting off," says Butler. "So here are stories about some-

body getting what was coming to him and at his own hand."

The 45-year-old Tennessean, looking sort of official in his "ADC Task Force" cap, is one of three authors of the crook book. As the TV show's designated host, he's on his way to becoming a cross between Bob Saget, who wisecracks his way through "America's Funniest Home Videos," and John Walsh, the oh-so-serious warden of "America's Most Wanted."

"It's going to be the 'Gong Show' of crime," he says. "We were going to offer a reward like "America's Most Wanted," only it was going to be about $14. But none of our guys ever get away with it, so there's no need."

As he juggles book signings, radio interviews and business meetings with show-biz types, Butler is still amazed by the sudden detour in his career. He toiled for years as a writer, actor and comedian, with 22 movie credits and the boast that "I've worked with everybody who's ever come to Nashville."

"If we could show the decision to break the law as just being a dumb idea and that you're going to look dumb and uncool, that was worthwhile," Butler said. "For most people, as soon as you decide to break the law, everything goes downhill. If you have any good sense, you lose it. If you have any luck, you lose it. And there are consequences—you'll get caught."

The idea isn't original. There are several books about laughable lawbreakers out there, including one compiled by Jay Leno. Radio disc jockeys love the subject.

All those, he says, plucked funny stories out of newspapers. He decided to go talk to cops. He packed a credit card and a camera crew into a van and set off for police stations, mostly in the Southeast (closer to home) and mostly in small towns (less bureaucracy).

*(continued on p. 485)*

*(continued)*

Nine months later he had plenty of material: Vending machine thief pays bail in quarters! Convenience store robber chokes on stolen wiener! Goof-balls strap dynamite to coyote, who blows up their truck!

The first printing of "America's Dumbest Criminals" last November sold out in two weeks, and the book is on the New York Times list of best-selling paperbacks.

"All you have to do is say the title and people get the idea," Butler says. "It sounds like a TV show already. People always tell me, 'Yeah, I've seen the show.'"

That's still a little premature. "America's Dumbest Criminals" has been sold to 82 stations, and hits the air this fall. Sight unseen, it has been marketed to a half-dozen countries.

"I think this is kind of enlightening," says Dallas police Sgt. Paul Stanford. "The kind of crime we always think about is murder and rapes and carjackings. There are crimes out there that by their very nature are humorous. But that's not what you usually read about in the paper."

Last week, Sgt. Stanford answered a call from a Western Union office where a man was trying to cash a check made out to Roadway Express, a trucking company. His ID named him as "Roadway V. Express." He was arrested.

More publicity about dumb crooks, Sgt. Stanford says, "might keep somebody else from trying the same thing. All you have to do is think before you do something, and you'd probably keep yourself out of a lot of trouble. I wish the alleged Mr. Express would have sat down and thought, 'Will they really believe I'm Roadway Express?'"

Source: *The Dallas Morning News,* 28 April 1996. Reprinted by permission of the *Dallas Morning News.*

## Hoffenberg sentenced to 20 years for fraud
### *Thousands bilked in investment scam*
Associated Press

NEW YORK—Bill collector Steven Hoffenberg was sent to prison for 20 years Friday by a judge who described the anguish of thousands of defrauded investors, including an 84-year-old retired teacher who must return to work.

U.S. District Judge Robert Sweet said a "whole spectrum of America" was reflected in the hundreds of letters he received before sentencing Hoffenberg.

He quoted a 72-year-old man who lost his savings: "Forgiveness is a great virtue. However, retribution comes to mind."

Assistant U.S. Attorney Amy Millard said Hoffenberg caused "the loss of the dreams, the hopes and the financial security of thousands of victims."

Waitresses, military veterans, nurses, auto mechanics, lawyers and others lost their life savings when Towers Financial Corp., Hoffenberg's bill collection company, collapsed in 1993.

Sweet said the fraud amounted to a pyramid investment scam that lured small, vulnerable investors into buying high interest notes that were paid off with money from investors who joined the scheme later.

In addition to the prison sentence, Sweet ordered Hoffenberg to repay nearly a half billion dollars and imposed a $1 million fine.

Hoffenberg's lawyer, Daniel Meyers, said the restitution order—coupled with an earlier agreement with the Securities and Exchange Commission to pay back nearly a half billion dollars—brings the total debt his destitute client faces to about $1 billion. He called the sentence "excessive and unjust."

*(continued on p. 486)*

Hoffenberg, 52, pleaded guilty April 20, 1995, to conspiracy, mail fraud, conspiracy to obstruct justice, tax evasion and mail and wire fraud. He admitted that he defrauded investors of $460 million.

Sweet rejected pleas by Hoffenberg and his lawyer to knock time off his sentence because he has cooperated with prosecutors and the SEC.

"I put my life at risk doing what they asked me to do," Hoffenberg told the judge.

Sweet did agree to lower the ordered restitution to $462 million, crediting Hoffenberg with $15.69 million he had managed to return.

He said he decided to impose the stiff sentence because Hoffenberg had "demonstrated a capacity to pop up with plans and I suspect he has some even as we speak, whether by selling a story or entering other big schemes even from prison."

Source: *Star Tribune*, 7 March 1997.
Reprinted by permission of Associated Press.

## Summary

Larceny/theft is the unlawful taking, carrying, leading or riding away of property from another's possession. It is synonymous with theft. Both larceny and burglary are crimes against property, but larceny, unlike burglary, does not involve illegally entering a structure. Larceny differs from robbery in that no force or threat of force is involved.

The elements of the crime of larceny/theft are (1) the felonious stealing, taking, carrying, leading or driving away of (2) another's personal goods or property (3) valued above or below a specified amount (4) with the intent to permanently deprive the owner of the property or goods. The two major categories of larceny/theft are grand larceny, a felony based on the value of stolen property (usually more than $100), and petty larceny, a misdemeanor based on the value of the property (usually less than $100). In most states, taking found property with the intent to keep or sell it is also a crime.

Among the common types of larceny are purse-snatching, picking pockets, theft from coin machines, shoplifting, bicycle theft, theft from motor vehicles, theft from buildings, theft of motor vehicle accessories and jewelry theft.

When dealing with shoplifters, remember that altering the price of an item is considered larceny. Also remember that it is not usually required that a shoplifter leave the premises with the stolen item before apprehension.

When investigating jewelry theft, inform the FBI of the theft, even if there is no immediate evidence of interstate operations.

The elements of the offense of receiving stolen goods are (1) receiving, buying or concealing stolen or illegally obtained goods (2) knowing them to be stolen or illegally obtained.

Fraud is intentional deception to cause a person to give up property or some lawful right. It differs from theft in that fraud uses deceit rather than stealth to obtain goods illegally. Fraud is committed in many ways, including the use of checks, credit cards, confidence games and embezzlement. Common types of check fraud are insufficient-fund checks, issuing worthless checks and forgeries.

Elements of the crime of larceny by credit card include (1) possessing credit cards obtained by theft or fraud (2) by which services or goods are obtained

(3) through unauthorized signing of the cardholder's name. Bank embezzlements are investigated jointly by the local police and the FBI.

White-collar or business-related crime includes (1) securities theft and fraud, (2) insurance fraud, (3) credit-card and check fraud, (4) consumer fraud, illegal competition and deceptive practices, (5) bankruptcy fraud, (6) computer-related fraud, (7) embezzlement and pilferage, (8) bribes, kick-backs and pay-offs and (9) receiving stolen property.

## Checklist

### *Larceny*

- What is the name, address and phone number of the complainant or the person reporting the crime?
- What is the name, address and phone number of the victim if not the same person as the complainant?
- Has the victim made previous theft complaints? If so, obtain all details.
- What was the date and time the crime was reported and the date and time the crime was committed if known?
- Who owns the property or has title to it or right of possession?
- Will the owner or person in control or possession sign the complaint?
- Who discovered the loss? Was this the logical person to discover it?
- Where was the item at the time of the theft? Was this the usual place for the item, or had it been recently transferred there?
- When was the item last seen?
- Has the area been searched to determine if the property might have been misplaced?
- What security precautions had been taken? Were these normal?
- Exactly what property was taken? Obtain a complete description of each item, including number, color, size, serial numbers or other identifying marks.
- What was the value of the items? How was the value determined: estimated original price, replacement price or estimated market value?
- How easily could the items be sold? Are there likely markets or buyers?
- Were there any witnesses to the theft or persons who might provide leads?
- Who had access to the property before and during the time of the theft?
- Who were absentee employees?
- Who are possible suspects and why? What might be the motive?

## Application

A cash box was left on top of a desk at the university office. Some students had registered early that day, so there was about $600 in the box. The box was closed but not locked. The office manager went to lunch, leaving a college student in charge. The student took a phone call in the dean's office and the box was out of her sight for about five minutes. Later, she heard a noise in the hallway outside the office. She went out to see what had happened and discovered that a student had been accidentally pushed through a glass door across the hallway from the main office. She observed the scene in the hallway for about five minutes and then went back to the registration office, where she did not notice anything out of order.

After a half-hour, the office manager returned from lunch and helped register two students at the front counter. When she went to the cash box to make change, she found that the $600 was missing. She immediately notified the administrator's office, and a controller was sent over to the registration office. The controller conducted a brief investigation and then notified the police.

You are the investigator arriving at the registration office.

### Questions

1. What procedure would you use upon arrival?
2. What steps would you take immediately?
3. What evidence is likely to be located?
4. What questions would you ask?
5. What is the probability of solving the case?

## Discussion Questions

1. Larceny has been called the most unreported crime in the United States. What factors might account for failure to report larceny? Is there a way to determine how many larcenies actually occur when you consider shoplifting, bicycle thefts and minor thefts of property that victims may regard as simply losing or misplacing things?

2. What are possible motives for committing such larcenies as bicycle theft? Shoplifting? Embezzlement? Thefts from autos? Gasoline thefts? Theft by check or credit card?

3. How does the receiver of stolen goods (fence) fit into the larceny crime problem? Is the fence's role more or less serious than that of the person who initially steals the property?

4. How do petty and grand larceny differ in your state? Do the elements that must be proved for each of these crimes differ in your state?

5. A con artist has bilked a senior citizen in your community out of $2,000. The senior citizen has filed a complaint in the hopes of having his money returned and the perpetrator arrested. What crime has been committed under your state laws, and what is the procedure for following up the complaint?

6. A man has been arrested for shoplifting and taken to the police station for booking. During the search for this offense, the police discover several credit cards that are not issued in the name of the person arrested. What offense is involved? Is there a separate offense from the original offense of shoplifting? Can the person be tried on both offenses? What procedure is necessary to prove the second charge?

7. Embezzlement is most frequently associated with white-collar crime. Has it been a problem in your community?

8. How do the following differ: stealing a suitcase from the baggage claim area at an airport, from an automobile and from a retail store?

9. If a customer knows an article is priced much higher in the store where she is shopping than in another store and can prove it, is it legal for her to change the price on the article?

10. What can the police do to reduce the number of larcenies in a community? Does your community have an antishoplifting program? An antibike-theft program? Do banks send literature to senior citizens concerning con games? What other measures have been initiated in your community? What additional measures might be taken?

Baker, Thomas J. "Combating Art Theft: International Cooperation in Action." *The Police Chief,* October 1996, pp. 19–23.

Biancardi, Raul J. "Corporations Can Defeat Deceit." *Security Management,* November 1992, pp. 72–77.

Burkhard, Bob, and Brad Lantz. "Are Your Computers Safe?" *Talking Business,* October 1996, p. 3.

Clede, Bill. "Cellular Phone Fraud: A Growing Problem." *Law and Order,* June 1993, pp. 87–91.

Dees, Timothy. "Credit Card Fraud." *Police,* March 1994, pp. 44–51.

Devaney, Earl E. "Addressing Environmental Crime." *The Police Chief,* October 1993, p. 8.

*Environmental Crime Prosecution: Results of a National Survey.* Research in Brief. Washington, DC: National Institute of Justice, December 1994.

Frank, Robert W., and Philip A. Serpico. "All That Glitters Becomes a Target." *Security Management,* April 1995, pp. 51–54.

Hammett, Theodore M., and Joel Epstein. *Prosecuting Environmental Crime: Los Angeles County.* Program Focus. Washington, DC: National Institute of Justice, August 1993.

Harman, Alan. "Gypsy Crime." *Law and Order,* May 1996, pp. 97–100.

Harris, Kimberly C. "The Hazards of Environmental Crime." *Security Management,* February 1992, pp. 27–32.

Laska, Paul. "Environmental Investigations: A New Way of Thinking." *Law Enforcement Technology,* October 1996, pp. 94–99.

Lehman, Peter, and Mark Dion. "Stealing Trash: Gray-Collar Crime." *The Police Chief,* August 1996, pp. 39–44.

Masuda, Barry. "Card Fraud: Discover the Possibilities." *Security Management,* December 1992, pp. 71–74.

Matulewich, Vincent. "Environmental Crimes Prosecution: A Law Enforcement Partnership." *FBI Law Enforcement Bulletin,* April 1991, pp. 20–25.

Morrison, Richard. "Dr. Watson I Presume?" *Law Enforcement Technology,* August 1995, pp. 34–36.

———. "New Telephone Technology: A Threat to Law Enforcement?" *Law Enforcement Technology,* October 1992, pp. 48, 50.

Murray, James R. "The Challenges of Financial Investigations." *The Police Chief,* October 1995, pp. 52–59.

"National White Collar Crime Center." *Security Concepts,* January 1996, pp. 11, 17.

Pearsall, James D. *Local Agency Criminal Environmental Investigations: A Place to Start.* Palm Beach County, FL: Environmental Crimes Investigations, 1993.

Rebovich, Donald J. "Expanding the Role of the Local Prosecutor." *Research in Action,* November 1994, pp. 21–24.

Regan, Gregory J. "White Collar Crimes: Today's Financial Crimes Are Something Else Altogether." *The Police Chief,* October 1995, pp. 36–51.

Scott, Lee Brian. "Checks and Balances." *Police,* June 1996, pp. 44–48.

Sharp, Arthur G. "White-Collar Crime: More Resources Needed to Combat Growing Trend." *Law and Order,* July 1994, pp. 91–96.

"Survey of U.S. Retailers." *Security Concepts,* March 1994, pp. 1–2.

Turner, Dana L., and Richard G. Stephenson. "The Lure of White-Collar Crime." *Security Management,* February 1993, pp. 57–58.

# Computer Crime

## DO YOU KNOW

What three key characteristics of computer crime are?

What computer crime can involve?

What types of computer crime are most frequently committed?

What approach is often required in investigating computer crime?

What the characteristics of the "typical" suspect in a computer crime are?

What the most frequent motive is in such crimes?

How evidence of computer crime differs from evidence of other felonies?

What form evidence usually takes in computer crimes?

How an investigator with a search warrant should proceed to execute it
     in a computer crime investigation?

What precautions should be taken when handling computer disks?

How computer disks taken as evidence should be stored?

How computer crimes can be prevented?

## CAN YOU DEFINE

| | | |
|---|---|---|
| computer virus | cyberspace | modem |
| cybercops | hacker | software |
| cyberpunk | hardware | virtual reality |

**Introduction**  TWO COMPUTER PROGRAMMERS FOR AN OIL COMPANY PLANT WHO
were responsible for the company's purchasing files created a fictitious supply
company. They altered the company's computer data base so that the oil
company bought its supplies twice, once from the real supplier and once from
the fictitious supply company, resulting in an embezzlement of several million
dollars over a two-year period. The crime was discovered during a surprise
audit, but the company declined to prosecute, not wanting to publicize how
vulnerable its database was or how long it took to discover the embezzlement.
Ironically, rather than being dismissed, the two embezzlers were promoted
and placed in charge of computer security.

In another instance, a New York bank hired an outside consultant to work with
its computer technicians on transferring funds electronically. In the course of his
work, the consultant observed the access code being used to transfer the funds. He
later used this access code to transfer a large sum of money to his own bank account. When the loss was finally discovered, management insisted that everyone in
the section take a polygraph test, including the consultant. All except the consultant
complied, and all passed. Although management was convinced the consultant had
stolen the money, they did not prosecute. They simply changed their access code.

These cases illustrate three key characteristics of computer crimes.

- Computer crimes are relatively easy to commit and difficult to detect.
- Most computer crimes are committed by "insiders."
- Most computer crimes are not prosecuted.

This chapter begins with a discussion of the scope of the problem of computer crime as well as an explanation of the classification of such crimes and the terminology involved. This is followed by a discussion of the preliminary investigation and the follow-up investigation. Next the subjects of suspects and evidence are presented. The chapter concludes with a discussion of security of police department computers and preventing computer crime.

## The Scope of the Problem

According to Strandberg (1993, p. 22): "New technologies traditionally present new opportunities for crime, and the seemingly harmless home computer is no exception.

A survey ("Survey: Cybercrime . . .," 1995, p. D3) reported the following results from responses of 150 corporate security directors:

- 98.7 percent said their companies had been victims of computer-related crimes. Of those, 43.3 percent said they had been victims at least twenty-five times.
- The most common crimes and misdeeds reported in the survey were credit-card fraud, telecommunications fraud, employee use of computers for personal use, unauthorized access to confidential files and unlawful copying of copyrighted or licensed software.
- Seventy-five to 80 percent of everything happened from inside.

Manning and White (1990, p. 46) point out the "burgeoning amount of computer equipment available to the general public, and the increasing number of people who know how to use it." Likewise, Stites (1990, p. 161) notes:

> It should be no surprise that the hot crime tool for the 90s is the personal computer. Over 33 million PCs have been sold in the United States—for homes, businesses, government offices, and criminal enterprises. The stereotypic criminal who hacked and attacked the main frame computers of corporate America is now a minor player on the field of high technology crime.
>
> Across the United States police are encountering personal computers used in money laundering, narcotics sales and prostitution rings. Child pornographers are using their PCs equipped with telephone modems to exchange facts and photos of victimized children. Political extremist groups use personal computers to conduct campaigns of harassment. Physicians employ PCs to fraudulently bill Medicare for nonexistent patients receiving nondelivered treatments. Sadistic offenders have chronicled and recorded in their word processors the gritty details of their offenses. For the well-trained law enforcement officer, information stored in computers represents a new gold mine of evidence.

According to Nickell (1991, p. 25):

> The average loss to a company through exploitation of computing systems is far greater than the loss from any other form of theft or robbery—by several orders of magnitude. Some estimates place the average insured loss from electronic tampering or exploitation of computer-based systems as high as $500,000.

Figure 15–1 illustrates the extent of losses from electronic crimes compared to other types of crime.

Recent studies indicate that only 1 percent of computer crimes are solved, and of these, only 1 percent are prosecuted.

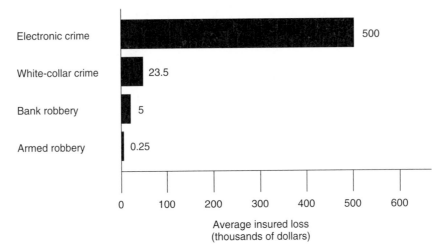

**Figure 15–1  Average Insured Loss from Various Crimes**

Source: "Microcomputer Security." National Computer Security Association, January 1, 1991. p. 5.

In the "1996 Computer Crime and Security Survey" conducted by the Computer Security Institute ("Survey Says Computer Crime Widespread . . .," 1996, p. 15), the following results were reported (N = 428):

- 41 percent had experienced some form of intrusion or other unauthorized use of computer systems within the last twelve months.
- More than half of those who experienced intrusions or attempted probes of their internal systems traced those intrusions to on-board employees.
- Unauthorized probes were also prevalent from remote dial-in sources and Internet connections.
- Altering data in an unauthorized manner (known in the trade as "data diddling") was the most frequent form of attack against medical and financial institutions.

Strandberg (1993, p. 28) observes:

> Computer crimes are growing by leaps and bounds. This is the technology of the present and the future, and the reality is that many people on the front line in law enforcement don't know a hard drive from a floppy disk—and that's dangerous.

According to Kruse (1995, p. 56): "The average computer crime will make between $200,000 to $600,000 with only a two percent chance of the criminal getting caught."

The threat will continue to grow. Manning and White (1990, p. 46) write that "the number of crimes involving computers is increasing dramatically throughout the country. There are documented offenses of every type—theft, fraud, burglary, prostitution, murder, child pornography—in which a computer was used in some way."

It is predicted that the use of computers for home, small and large offices, businesses and government installations will steadily increase; therefore, it can be expected that computer-related crimes will remain a serious police investigative problem.

Students in the lower elementary grades receive computer training; increasingly complex training is given through high school and into college. After graduation, many individuals obtain industrial and governmental jobs that provide not only advanced computer technology training but also training in the systems used by industry and government. In fact, individuals who are not "computer literate" are increasingly perceived as disadvantaged.

## Classification and Terminology

Conly and McEwen (1990, p. 3) define computer crime in this way: "Computer crime today is any illegal act for which knowledge of computer technology is used to commit the offense."

As Martin (1993, p. 92) explains: "Computer crime can be as simple as the unauthorized duplication of a copyrighted software program, or as complex as a corporate manager using his company's computer system to transfer the firm's assets to a dummy corporation."

Enormous sums of money and tremendous quantities of information are transferred electronically by computer throughout the nation daily. These transfers present a unique opportunity for the computer thief. In October 1986, President Reagan signed a bill modernizing the federal wiretap law to protect the privacy of high-tech communications. This bill makes it illegal to eavesdrop on electronic mail, video conference calls, conversations on cellular car phones and computer-to-computer transmissions. Other federal statutes relevant to computer-related crimes include patent laws, espionage and sabotage laws, trade secret laws, the Copyright Act of 1976 and the Financial Privacy Act of 1978.

Rasch (1996, p. 59) notes: "Computer technology has changed the nature of crime. And now legislatures and the courts are racing to catch up." He gives as an example that one of the elements of the crime of larceny requires proof of "taking away" the property, but in the case of computer crime, the stolen data may still be where it was originally. According to Rasch (p. 65): "Every state except Vermont has enacted a computer crime statute."

States address computer crime either by modifying existing statutes such as those pertaining to theft or by adding computer-crime chapters to their criminal codes. For example, some statutes state that disclosing the password of a computer system without the owner's consent is considered "unlawful use of a computer." Additionally, many existing state statutes are applicable to crimes involving computers (see Table 15–1). Well-defined statutes are critical to investigating and prosecuting computer crimes successfully. Conly and McEwen (1990, p. 3) list the following categories of computer crime:

*Internal computer crimes*
- Trojan horses
- Logic bombs
- Viruses

*Telecommunications crimes*
- Phone phreaking
- Hacking
- Illegal bulletin boards
- Misuse of telephone systems

*Computer manipulation crimes*
- Embezzlements
- Frauds

**Table 15–1 Computer Crime and Current Statutes**

| | |
|---|---|
| Arson | Intentionally setting fire to a computer center |
| Burglary | Entering a computer center illegally with the intent to commit a crime therein |
| Extortion/blackmail | Making threats against the operator(s) of a computer center to obtain money |
| Collusion | Working with others to commit a crime |
| Conspiracy | Several persons agreeing to commit an illegal act |
| Counterfeit | Copying or imitating computer documents |
| Embezzlement | Fraudulently converting property to personal use |
| Espionage | Stealing secret documents or information |
| Forgery | Issuing false documents |
| Fraud | Altering accounts or illegally transferring funds |
| Larceny | Theft of computer parts and materials |
| Malicious destruction of property | Destroying computer hardware or software |
| Murder | Tampering with life-sustaining computerized equipment resulting in the death of a patient |
| Receiving stolen property | Accepting any goods or information stolen by computer, knowing they were stolen |
| Sabotage | Intentionally destroying computer information, programs or hardware |
| Theft | Stealing goods or money by use of a computer or stealing computer parts and materials |

*Support of criminal enterprises*
- Data bases to support drug distributions
- Data bases to keep records of client transactions
- Money laundering

*Hardware/software thefts*
- Software piracy
- Thefts of computers
- Thefts of microprocessor chips
- Thefts of trade secrets

Although most of these classifications are self-explanatory, the following explanations may be helpful.

- The Trojan horse uses one computer to reprogram another for illegal purposes.
- The logic bomb secretly attaches another program to a company's computer system. The attached program monitors the input data and waits for some type of error to occur. When this happens, the new program exploits the weakness to steal money or company secrets or to sabotage the system.

In addition, Strandberg (1993, p. 29) offers the following computer terminology:

- **Computer Virus.** A program that attacks computer hardware and either replaces or destroys data.
- **Cyberpunk.** An antiestablishment rebel in the computer universe. Also refers to an entire counterculture existing in thin air.
- **Cyberspace.** The thin air that "exists" between two computers.

- **Hacker.** A computer expert who specializes in unauthorized access into computer networks and other computer systems.
- **Virtual Reality.** An artificial, interactive world created by computer technology (usually involving some kind of immersion system, such as a headset).

Computer viruses are further explained by Forcht (1992, p. 134): "A computer virus is a program created specifically to infect other programs with copies of itself. It may attach itself to other software programs or infiltrate the computer's operating system, affecting the computer's normal operation." These viruses can be transmitted through communication lines or by an infected disk and infect any PC.

According to Craig (1991, p. 65): "Just as biological viruses are spread by organisms coming into contact with it, so are computer viruses spread from program to program, attaching themselves to otherwise useful programs. Viruses can be unintentionally introduced into the system by disks carried between home and work by personnel using home computers."

Nickell (1991, p. 25) suggests that the number of computer viruses is increasing by 47 percent a year. Such viruses can cause disruption, loss of productivity or loss of vital data. A virus can be programmed into software and entered into a computer by anyone with access to that computer. The virus may lay dormant for weeks or months until it is activated by an outside source with access to the computer.

According to the *Washington Post* (1990, p. A7), an advertisement such as the following might be run by the United States Army:

> WANTED: Experienced computer hackers capable of breaking into enemy software systems and destroying secret files. Knowledge of computer viruses a must.

The Army is exploring the use of computer viruses—"a type of unwanted software program that can propagate undetected from one computer to another, thwarting the computer's normal functions and sometimes garbling data." The *Post* reported:

> Incidents of computer sabotage have swept the country in recent months as hackers become increasingly efficient at breaking into the systems of businesses, universities, and research centers. . . .
>
> Myron Cramer, an electronic warfare specialist at Booz, Allen & Hamilton, Inc., in Bethesda, Md., sees a day when viruses could be remotely injected into enemy computers that support air-defense and battlefield-control systems, lurking there covertly until they spring into action.
>
> He even has described an "assassin" virus that would wreak widespread havoc and then erase itself, leaving no trail.

## Nature of the Crimes

---

Computer crimes may involve the input data, the output data, the program, the hardware or computer time.

---

*Input data* may be manipulated. For example, fictitious suppliers may be entered as in the case of the oil company mentioned previously; figures may be changed or data may be removed. Some universities have experienced difficulties with student grades being illegally changed through use of a computer.

*A Michaelangelo computer virus alert.*

*Output data* may be obtained by unauthorized persons through such means as wiretapping, electromagnetic pickup and theft of data sheets. In one case a Charles County, Maryland, teenage hacker used a home PC to access a list of credit card account numbers and then charged $2,000 worth of computer equipment from seven computer firms in California, Georgia, Michigan, Minnesota, New York, Ohio and Wisconsin. The crime was discovered when one computer firm became suspicious of fraud because several orders were received using different names but the same mailing address. The firm contacted the U.S. Secret Service. The youth was subsequently charged with seven counts of theft. Typically, however, output data is misused by an employee, not an outsider.

The *computer program* itself might be tampered with to add costs to purchased items or to establish a double set of records. In one instance, a programmer feared he was about to lose his job, so he altered the computer's payroll program in such a way that if he was not issued a paycheck, the entire payroll records would be scrambled. The *computer hardware,* either the entire machine or some of its components, may be stolen or sabotaged.

*Computer time* may be used for personal use.

---

The most common types of computer crime are misuse of computer services, program abuse and data abuse.

---

Martin (1993, p. 82) states:

The largest area of computer crime is telecommunications fraud—call-selling operations that usually work out of New York, L.A., or Miami. The second largest area where computer crime occurs is in the workplace. Usually it's disgruntled employees who wish to sabotage the system in some way—stealing money, shifting money, causing the computer system to crash.

To deter such crimes, they must be reported to the police, thoroughly investigated and, when the evidence is sufficient, prosecuted.

Too often, however, investigators assigned to computer-related crimes have not been trained to investigate these felonies. Those who commit these crimes are usually more technologically sophisticated than the investigators assigned to the cases. The technological disadvantage of many law enforcement agencies is painfully obvious.

Law enforcement at all levels needs additional training in the following areas: the unique requirements of computer-related crimes; computer evidence; identifying, marking and storing this evidence; the capabilities of present private and state agencies to analyze this evidence; and the procedures for developing teams to conduct investigations of computer-related crimes.

## The Preliminary Investigation

When a report of a possible computer-related crime is received by a police department, the departmental report procedure is followed for the initial information. The officer assigned to the case interviews the reporting person to obtain the information necessary for determining if a crime has been committed.

Overloading of the computer system or a lack of accessibility to records that the system was designed for may indicate illegal use of the computer. This type of crime may occur more frequently in a small computer operation, where greater opportunity exists. However, this makes the investigator's task easier because the number of suspects is reduced.

Employees are a good source of information unless they are suspected of collusion. Internal reporting of this type of crime is the same as for any other crime within an organization. It normally begins at the lowest level and reports upward to the supervisor and then to management. However, supervisory or management persons are conceivably part of the collusion, so care must be used in the initial stages to eliminate those capable of being involved.

Normal or special audit procedures may have brought the crime to the attention of the proper persons, much the same as in embezzlement cases. Because computer operations require contact with other employees in collecting computer-input information, suspicion develops when employees appear to withdraw from other normal relationships.

If a crime is suspected or determined, further interviewing of the complainant and witnesses should continue. It is essential that information be obtained as soon as possible because evidence is easily destroyed. The principles in investigating computer crimes are basically the same as in other felonies. However, the investigator must have personal knowledge of computers or seek the assistance of a computer expert.

### Important Steps at the Crime Scene

Stites (1991, p. 164) offers the following guidelines for the first officers at the scene of a crime involving a computer:*

At the scene of the computer seizure, photographs should be taken of everything in the area of the computer, including the cable connections. DO NOT TOUCH THE KEYBOARD. If the computer is not turned on, do not turn it on. If the computer is on, the screen should be photographed. Only one person should handle

---

*Excerpt used by permission of the publisher.

the computer. If equipped with floppy drives and a disk is in the drive, carefully remove the disk and treat it as evidence. Turn the computer off by removing the plug from the wall. DO NOT USE THE ON/OFF SWITCH. Place a police-owned copy of DOS (Disk Operating System) in Drive A and plug the cord back in the wall. If the computer is equipped with more than one floppy drive, place a police-owned copy of DOS in those drives as well. The computer will boot to Drive A. The hard disk should then be parked. Parking the hard disk is a procedure that protects the hard drive during transportation. A utility program by Paul Mace Software called Park.Exe is recommended.

**Transporting the Computer.** Remove the Park program and place an unformatted disk in the drive and close the door. Seal the disk drive door with evidence tape. Remove the power plug from the wall. Remove the cables from their connections, labeling both with the same notation, i.e., "cable 1" and "connection 1." Be sure to seize everything associated with the computer, to include manuals, printouts, mouse, modem, printer, scanner, monitor, wastebasket contents, discarded printer ribbons, phone books and all floppy disks. Package all contents with care. Place the floppy disks in paper evidence bags and keep them away from magnetic fields. Inspect the entire computer area, looking for labels or notes containing passwords of cryptographic keywords. Criminals also don't want to forget their passwords and have been known to record them near their computers. The computer and components are now ready for transport to the police agency.

At the department, secure the computer where no one, including other officers, can gain access to it.

Martin (1993, p. 83) suggests that the widely held belief that computer crimes are difficult to investigate is nonsense. She contends that the basic tenents of any investigation are used in such crimes. She (p. 84) offers the following step-by-step process for investigating computer crimes:

- Speak with the victim.
- Find out the phone carrier.
- Place a phone-number logger on the phone.
- Obtain affidavits.
- Obtain a search warrant.
- Catch them red-handed.
- Confiscate not only their computer but also their notebook.

## Follow-Up Investigation

Once the initial report has been completed and the general information has been obtained, a plan is made for the remaining investigation. The plan will assist in a directed investigation, even though deviations from the plan may occur because exigencies may not be known at the beginning. The plan should identify the problem, what crime has been committed, areas involved in the crime, people involved, equipment used, internal and external staffing needs, approximate length of time required for the investigation, how evidence will be handled and stored and the assignment of personnel. It is also necessary to determine what federal, state or local laws are applicable to the specific type of computer crime committed.

Sometimes it is necessary to develop an undercover operation within the organization. This operation must be headed by a computer expert and coordinated with the nonsuspects. Lists must be prepared of all persons to be used in the case and the evidence to be obtained. If search warrants are necessary, those arrangements must be made. Motive, opportunity, means of commission, the type of security system bypassed and known bypass techniques must also be ascertained.

Interviewing and interrogating techniques are basically the same as for other felonies, as are search techniques and patterns used. The major difference is in the types of evidence involved.

Investigators will often find that computer-related thefts originate from agencies that already have highly trained computer personnel on their staffs. If the theft is internal, the investigator may confidentially involve personnel of that agency who are not suspect. In internal crimes of this nature, the number of suspects will be necessarily limited, as opposed to a crime such as a residential burglary where the suspect could be local or an outsider. In computer crimes for purposes of theft, supervisory and management personnel may use computers to hide their offenses and thus misdirect the investigative team toward subordinate staff who have committed relatively minor transgressions.

Internal auditing procedures are normally started with the security director involved. If an employee is suspected at this point, management must decide whether it is going to handle the matter internally or proceed with prosecution. If the decision is made to handle the matter internally, then the case is closed. If not, the investigation continues, often involving state or private investigators. Such individuals may have the expertise and anonymity not available to local police departments.

## Data Recovery

Stites (1991, p. 163) cautions: "Data recovery is a forensic science requiring knowledge of the laws of search and seizure, rules of evidence, coupled with an extensive knowledge of computer technology and storage devices." Stites (p. 165) provides some basic rules for data recovery:

■ Develop a plan. Don't hurry and don't allow others to rush you. Lay out a step-by-step plan. Identify the hardware and software tools that will be needed. Pick a site that is quiet and where you will not be interrupted.
■ Use a premium-quality surge protector. Damage occurring to the seized computer or its data during examination, such as the loss of valuable business records, could represent a considerable financial liability to the police.
■ Do not use the original seized disks or hard disk for examination. In processing the seized evidence, make copies of the seized data.
■ Write-protect the diskettes and hard disk.
■ Do not process the data on the seized computer. Because the suspect may have set up a hardware booby trap to destroy data, the hard drive or both, it is dangerous to use his computer for evidence processing.
■ Examine the data using a utility program designed for this purpose.
■ Print all files.
■ Record each step so that the examination can later be reconstructed.

Stites cautions: "Removing data from a seized computer is similar to walking through a mine field. The above steps are absolutely minimal and following them will guide you in avoiding some of the common difficulties. They do not assure the success of your efforts."

# Special Problems in Investigation

Special problems in investigating computer crimes include the scarcity of investigators, attorneys, probation officers and judges who understand computers and computer crimes and the tremendous proliferation of computer crimes and losses. Then there can be problems with determining jurisdiction when the equipment is located in one community and the computer that is illegally electronically entered is in another state.

The major problems in investigating computer-related crimes are the needs to determine the exact nature of the crime and to gather evidence in ways that do not disrupt the organization's operation.

Conly and McEwan (1990, pp. 6–7) note two additional problems:

■ One of the key difficulties is that many victims of computer crime are reluctant to report or press charges.
■ Another problem is the amount of time needed to investigate computer crimes. Estimates range from four months to a year for thorough investigations.

## The Investigative Team

Based on the information received, a plan of action is developed that includes assigning personnel and obtaining specialists for the investigative team. Police agencies that must investigate complex art thefts, bank embezzlements or other types of thefts in which they have had little expertise seek the advice and services of experts. For computer-related crimes, this is also true because the evidence may involve highly technical database systems, operational systems and equipment that are foreign to police officers.

---

Investigating computer crime often requires a team approach.

---

In the majority of computer-related crimes, investigators seek assistance from the victim who owns the equipment, database processing technicians, auditors, highly trained computer experts or programmers and others. If necessary, the team should contact the manufacturer of the equipment, the consulting services of a local university or a private computer-crime investigative agency.

To assist in combating increasing computer-related crimes, government and private businesses have been working toward developing computer crime teams in much the same manner as the FBI developed kidnapping crime teams and the Bureau of Alcohol, Tobacco and Firearms developed arson investigation specialist teams.

The investigative team is responsible for assigning all personnel of the team according to their specialties, including securing outside specialists if necessary; securing the crime scene area; obtaining search warrant applications; determining the specific hardware and software involved; searching for, obtaining, marking, preserving and storing evidence; obtaining necessary disks, printouts and other records; and preparing information for investigative reports.

In the spring of 1990 federal and state authorities completed an eighteen-month investigation of computer crime covering at least twenty-nine locations in thirteen cities. Code-named Operation Sundevil, the investigation culminated in raids in which investigators confiscated 42 computers and 23,000 computer disks, along with telephone test equipment, electronic bulletin boards and other records that might have been used to break into government computers and defraud private companies of millions of dollars in services. According to officials, in one case the amount of stolen services could total $1.7 million (Knight-Ridder News Service, 1990).

Police agencies in many states are forming cooperative groups or associations and are providing training seminars on investigating computer crimes. Such groups are especially helpful for small departments, which are less likely to have the needed expertise in-house.

In Florida, the state's law enforcement agencies can submit computer evidence to the Computer Evidence Recovery (CER) program. The program also provides training to the state's law enforcement agencies on preparing warrants to search computers and procedures to follow when seizing computer-crime evidence.

Icove (1991) describes a threat model for evaluating proposals to combat malicious intrusions, terrorism and other forms of attacks on computer systems being developed by the FBI's National Center for the Analysis of Violent Crime (NCAVC). The model contains all the components needed for combating external and internal attacks on computer centers. Using this model, the NCAVC is developing a handbook to help investigators perform computer threat evaluations.

## Suspects

A major difference in computer crime investigation, other than the involvement with high technology and complex equipment, is the type of person who commits such crimes.

Persons involved in computer crimes are most commonly technical people such as data entry clerks, machine operators, programmers, systems analysts and hackers.

These individuals have the necessary knowledge and access to the computer system. In addition, as Olick (1994, p. 12) cautions: "The 'information superhighway,' aka 'cyberspace,' that is paving the way for rapid exchange of data to all connecting points may also be causing an increase in 'hackers' joy-riding their way right into your top-security computer systems."

Although some computer users may feel they are free to do whatever they please on the computer, a Florida resident learned differently. Although he claimed that it was only a joke when he e-mailed a friend telling him that weasels would rip the flesh off his corpse, he was convicted under the state's stalking laws for threats by computer.

People who commit computer crimes are often regarded as honest, hard-working employees and as respected members of the community. They are not criminal types in the usual sense of the word, nor are they repeat offenders in this or other criminal endeavors. They more than likely have no prior criminal record. Therefore, normal criminal record checks and modus operandi comparisons are not usually useful in determining suspects. Profiling the typical computer criminal poses a special challenge, as it is a very eclectic group.

Research has found four motivations for internal abuse, fairly evenly distributed in frequency.

Frequent motives for computer crimes are ignorance of proper professional conduct, misguided playfulness, personal gain and maliciousness or revenge.

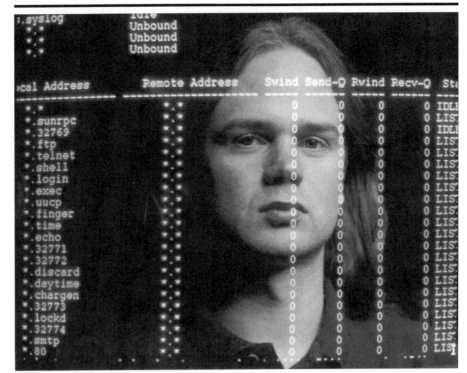

*Professional computer hacker Steve Turcich is shown in this double-exposure photograph. Turcich works for companies that actually pay him to break into their computers, helping them perfect security systems.*

Revenge is a motive where the suspect feels that management has committed injustices or where militants destroy computer centers that deal with controversial issues or products. In contrast, computer hackers gain entrance to computer information simply for the challenge of breaking the code. A number of these types of crimes have been reported nationally in the news media.

The suspect may act alone or in collusion in committing the crime. Commission normally occurs during authorized use or during periods of overtime when the employee is working alone. Developing a suspect's work history assists in locating past opportunities for committing the offense. The suspect's training will provide information about his or her knowledge of computers and computer languages. Comparisons of these factors with the equipment at the crime scene will help determine if the suspect was capable of the crime.

A complete review of all persons within the organization who have access, type of access, technical capability or opportunity greatly assists the investigation if the crime has been committed internally. Check for employees with a prior history of computer crimes.

## Evidence

McEwan (1995, p. 93) explains that **cybercops** is a name given to investigators involved in computer forensics. He stresses: "Successful prosecution may rest upon an evidence technician's ability to adequately secure the system at the crime scene." He offers the following suggestions:*

---

*Excerpt used by permission of the publisher.

1. Prior to executing a search warrant, use intelligence sources to determine the likelihood of encountering computers at the scene. In the document include applicable wording regarding computers and related items to be seized.
2. To secure the site, remove all persons from the computers and prevent further access.
3. Immediately evaluate any possible evidence displayed on the monitor. If possible, photograph the screen and then unplug the system from the wall. Unplug any phone lines leading to the computer. NEVER use the toggle switch to turn off the machine, always unplug from the wall.
4. Photograph the rear of the machine to record the cabling configuration.
5. Label the cabling system (using masking tape and pen) before disconnecting any cables. Label all ports and slots so that proper reconstruction can be done later.
6. If more than one system is seized, keep the components separate. For example, label the monitor from the first system #A1. The monitor from the second system #B1.
7. Collect all operating manuals and software found at the scene, including collections of floppy disks and peripheral components such as printers and keyboards. Pay attention to scraps of paper nearby that may note passwords.
8. In boxing the system for transport, avoid static charges. Do not wrap the unit in plastic and keep the unit away from electromagnetic sources such as a radio transmitter in the trunk of your car. This could cause loss of electronically stored data.
9. The property room should be temperature and climate controlled. Again, keep the unit away from magnetic sources such as stereo speakers.

Procedures for processing and caring for evidence differ from those for the traditional crime scene because of the nature of the evidence, but many of the approaches suggested in Chapter 5 are applicable. Obtaining evidence in computer cases is unique in that the evidence is not as readily discernible as in most other criminal cases. Computer disks, although visible in the physical sense, contain "invisible" information.

---

Computer evidence is often contained on disks, is not readily discernible and also is highly susceptible to destruction.

---

Start the investigation as soon as possible to obtain the physical evidence. Destruction of the program or of information files may be programmed-in so that any attempt to access the information or to print it will cause it to self-destruct. Determine early the computer system used and the types of physical evidence available from this system. Include this information in the application for a search warrant.

In more complex cases, the volume of evidence is significant because large amounts of information can be stored on a single disk. In the majority of felony investigations, the amount of evidence is not a major problem, but in the case of computer crimes, the evidence may involve hundreds of tapes or disks. Copying this amount of evidence can be costly as well as time consuming. In addition, taking equipment into evidence can be a major problem because some equipment is heavy and bulky.

It must be determined if backup copies of existing file materials are available, thus eliminating the necessity of copying or reproducing them. If backup copies are available, it lessens the chance of the same crime being committed against the copies and also permits continued use of the computer during the investigation. Obviously, copying disks must be done according to the rules of evidence specified in Chapter 5. Manning and White (1990, p. 48) warn that "'playing around' with the computer equipment, even with good intentions, could cause irreparable damage to the case." Clede (1991, p. 11) suggests that:

> Handling computer evidence is a lot like handling a booby trapped bomb. It takes a trained bomb technician to go through the proper steps to deactivate a device. It also takes a specially trained computer technician to go through the steps to preserve computer evidence.

### Types of Evidence

Some form of documentation is the most frequent type of computer evidence.

---

Evidence is normally in the form of disks, data reports, programming or other printed information run from information in the computer.

---

In some cases the evidence is the computer equipment, although this is unusual. Also, it may be necessary to keep the equipment operating to continue business. Investigators must work with management to determine how this can best be accomplished. If the evidence cannot be moved from the premises, it may be necessary for management to provide on-premises security by using their own guards or by hiring security temporarily until the evidence can be copied or otherwise secured by court order or by police security.

*Tsutomu Shimomura, computational physicist and computer security expert, helped to break the Kevin Mitnick cybertheft case. Mitnick, until apprehended, was cyberspace's most wanted hacker.*

## Legal Aspects of Obtaining Computer Evidence

Clede (1993, p. 101) cautions: "How a computer is seized could be critical. A federal agency was hit with a $55,000 fine plus legal fees for damaging the electronic data on a citizen's computer."

Also of importance is the fact that often what is stolen is information, which is difficult to value. The question arises as to whether such intangible property *can* be stolen. Investigation is hampered by a lack of precedents or clear definitions in this area.

As in all cases, the evidence must follow the best-evidence rule. Individuals must testify in court to the authenticity of the disks or printouts. It must be proven that the materials introduced are, indeed, the originals or substitutes in accordance with the best-evidence rule. This evidence must be tied to its source by a person qualified to testify about the specific item of evidence. Because computers often use magnetically produced signals, printouts must be made of these signals, and computer experts must verify that the printouts are copies of the original data.

### Search Warrants

It may be necessary to obtain a search warrant to locate the evidence necessary to prosecute successfully. Searches may also be conducted by consent; in other words, the owner of the materials may give voluntary consent for the search. However, if the suspect is unknown, this is not desirable because it could alert the person who committed the crime. In such cases, a search warrant must be obtained. Privacy issues surrounding some or all of the information contained in the computer evidence desired may pose a legal technicality. If the organization involved is the victim of the crime, its management normally grants permission. If it is not the victim, it may be necessary to obtain permission from persons contained in the file, which could be an enormous task. It may be better to take the evidence to a court and obtain court permission if possible.

A sample affidavit and search warrant for a computer-related case involving telecommunications fraud appears in Appendix C.

Investigators may have in their possession both a consent search form and a search warrant, thus avoiding the possibility of destruction of evidence. Consent is better than a search warrant in that it avoids the usual attack by the defense in search-warrant cases.

---

Request the consent initially, and if that fails, use the search warrant—in that order.

---

If the order is reversed, the consent is bastardized because the search warrant was used as a threat in obtaining voluntary consent. The areas of search and the items to be searched for must be specified in the warrant. A person connected with the computer operation in question should assist with the search warrant to provide information to the investigators, and this person should accompany the investigators with the affidavit for warrant in case the judge requires technical explanations that the investigator cannot provide regarding the equipment and the evidence desired.

### Searching for and Processing Physical Evidence

Search techniques and patterns described in Chapter 4 are applicable to computer-related crime searches. The area is sealed, and the search is made according to the type and location of the evidence necessary for prosecution. Avoid pressures to speed up the search because of a desire for continued use of the system, but at the same time, return the equipment as soon as possible.

Despite the time computers have been in use, most investigators, prosecutors and judges have minimal training and experience with computer-related crimes. It is, therefore, important that evidence procedures be followed precisely to avoid dismissal.

Information about the **hardware**—that is, the computer equipment— should include all identification data such as the manufacturer, model, identification numbers and the language(s) used by the system such as Fortran or Cobol. Does it include a **modem,** a device linking the computer to telephone lines so that messages can be exchanged with computers at different locations?

Information about the **software**—the programs used on the computer—is also important. The software must usually be copied or printouts made. Reproducing the material must be done within the rules of evidence. Identification should include case number, date, time and the initials of the person taking the evidence into custody. To mark a metal container, use a carbide metal scribe such as that used in marking items in the Operation Identification program. Use a permanent black-ink marker or felt-tip pen to identify disks. If the evidence is in a container, both the container and the inside disks should be identified in the same way. Marking both identically avoids interchangeability and retains the credibility of the item as evidence. Normal evidence tape may be used to mark containers and to seal them.

---

Avoid contact with recording surfaces of computer tapes and disks. Never write on disk labels with a ballpoint pen or pencil or use paper clips or rubber bands with disks. To do so may destroy the data they contain.

---

Usually printouts must be made of data contained on computer tapes or disks. These printouts should be clearly identified and matched with the software they represent.

Storage problems can arise because of the nature of the evidence in computer-related crimes. Disks can be stored in the manufacturers' containers. All computer evidence should be stored in areas away from strong sources of light. Computers and the information stored in them and on disks are sensitive to temperature extremes and dust. Exposing magnetic media to any magnetic field such as radio waves, motors, degaussers or speakers can alter or destroy data. Disks should be stored vertically, not stacked one on top of another. In addition, plastic bags should not be used to store computer equipment or disks because they can cause static electricity and condensation, both of which can damage electronically stored data.

If possible, obtain from management the procedures normally used for storing their disks and other materials. If this is not possible, contact the manufacturer for this information.

---

Store computer disks vertically, at approximately 70° F and away from strong light, dust and any magnetic field. Do not use plastic bags.

---

### Laboratory Examination of Evidence

Crime laboratories, either public or private, have much of the equipment necessary to examine computer evidence. Computer hardware has individual characteristics, much the same as other items of evidence such as tools. Fingerprints might also be found on the hardware, but frequently the perpetrator's fingerprints are not unusual because he or she has legal access to the hardware. Printers have individual characteristics, much the same as typewriters. Document examinations of printouts can be made, and these printouts can also be analyzed for fingerprints. Fragments of software may be compared.

## Security of the Police Department's Computers

When considering computer crime, law enforcement officers should not overlook the possibility that their own computers may be accessed by criminals. As noted by Craig (1991, p. 63):

> No matter how deeply it may be physically buried within the bowels of a police department, any computer attached to a telephone line is directly accessible by unauthorized persons outside the department. Such a person may be hundreds or even thousands of miles away. . . .
>
> The military's top-secret computers are not connected to phone lines. It was decided that the security of the data was more important than the inconvenience and expense of total isolation.
>
> Organized-crime and special drug enforcement teams should consider this the only way to ensure that confidential data stays that way.

## Preventing Computer Crime

Many managers are unprepared to deal with computer crimes. They may be ignorant, indifferent or both. They also frequently lack control over their information. Without standards to violate, there is no violation.

---

Computer crimes can be prevented by educating top management and employees and by instituting internal security precautions. Top management must make a commitment to defend against computer crime.

---

Management must institute organizationwide policies to safeguard its databases, and it must educate employees in these policies and any security measures that are implemented.

Internal security precautions should also be taken. Data disks should have backup copies and should be kept in locked files.

One of the most important, yet most frequently overlooked, security measures is to use a paper shredder for all sensitive documents once they are no longer needed. Several questions need to be asked when seeking to prevent computer crime. These questions (see Table 15–2) involve both computer security itself and personnel issues.

"Many other areas," say Manning and White (1990, p. 49), "have yet to be fully explored with respect to their impact on law enforcement. Among them are legislative changes, internal computer security procedures, telecommunications system design, new considerations relating to 'high-tech' ethics, computer viruses and increased public awareness of technological crime."

**Table 15–2  Checklist for Evaluating Vulnerability to Computer Crime**

| Computer Security Issues | Personnel Issues |
|---|---|
| Is someone responsible for computer security in the central site? | Are formal reports required for each reported instance of computer penetration? |
| Have standards been developed for designing controls for financial systems? | Are records maintained on the most common methods of computer penetration? |
| Has the confidentiality or sensitivity of each piece of information been identified? | Is one individual accountable for each data processing resource? |
| Have procedures been developed to define who may access the computer facility, as well as how and when that access may occur? | Does management understand the new threats posed by automated applications? |
| Have procedures been developed to handle programs and data at remote sites? | Is management evaluated on its ability to maintain a secure computer facility? |
| Is someone accountable for security at each remote site? | Are the activities of all nonemployees in the computer center monitored? |
| Have security procedures been established for PCs? | Do procedures (such as shredding the program listings, rather than throwing them out in the trash) restrict nonemployees from gaining access to computer program listings and documentation? |
| Has the ownership of microcomputer programs and data been defined by the firm? | Are employees instructed on how to deal with inquiries and requests from nonemployees? |
| Is critical information that is transmitted over common-carrier lines protected (for example, through cryptography)? | Are errors made by the computer department categorized by type and frequency? |
| Have provisions been made for destroying sensitive information controlled by the office system? | Are records maintained on the frequency and type of errors incurred by users of data processing systems? |

SOURCE: W. E. Perry. *Management Strategies for Computer Security.* St. Paul, MN: Butterworth Publishers, 1985. Reprinted by permission of the publisher.

# Summary

Computer crimes are relatively easy to commit and difficult to detect. Most computer crimes are committed by insiders, and few are prosecuted.

Computer crimes may involve input data, output data, the program, the hardware or computer time. The most common types of computer crime are misuse of computer services, program abuse and data abuse. Investigating such crimes often requires a team approach.

Persons involved in computer crimes are usually technical people such as data entry clerks, machine operators, programmers, systems analysts and hackers. Common motivators for such crimes are ignorance, misguided playfulness, personal gain and maliciousness or revenge.

Evidence in computer crimes is often contained on disks, is not readily discernible, and is highly susceptible to destruction. In addition to information on disks, evidence may take the form of data reports, programming or other printed materials based on information from computer files. If investigators possess a search warrant and wish to conduct a search, they should first request permission for the search. If consent is given, the search can proceed right away. If it is not given, then the warrant can be served and the search conducted.

Investigators who handle computer disks should avoid contact with the recording surfaces. They should never write on computer disk labels with a ballpoint pen or pencil and should never use paper clips on or rubber bands around computer disks. To do so may destroy the data they contain. Computer disks taken as evidence should be stored vertically, at approximately 70° F and away from bright light, dust and magnetic fields.

Computer crimes can be prevented by educating top management and employees and by instituting internal security precautions.

*Read the following articles and imagine yourself as the officer/detective assigned to each case. What elements of the crime are present? What evidence would you need to prosecute the case? Who else might you need to coordinate your efforts with? What is the likelihood of solving each crime?*

## Inmates compiled kids' photos for Internet catalog

**Associated Press**

MINNEAPOLIS—When Sandy Baso's children were growing up, they basked in the limelight of Little Eagle Bend, population 524. Her daughter was crowned Snow Day's Queen, and her son took part in spelling bees and the Knowledge Bowl.

As in many small towns, the community newspaper recorded the children's achievements with photographs and articles.

Neighbors were not the only ones watching.

At a prison near Minneapolis, someone was using Baso's hometown newspaper and others to compile a catalog of children, apparently for pedophiles, The New York Times said Monday.

The catalog includes 3,000 children from 67 mostly small towns around northern Minnesota and runs to 52 pages in a computer printout obtained by the Times, the newspaper said.

Source: *Las Vegas Review Journal*, 20 November 1996. Reprinted by permission of Associated Press.

## FBI Isn't laughing

**Associated Press**

ST. LOUIS—They wear FBI logos while holding up banks, use agents' names when buying getaway cars, and write letters to newspapers making fun of the bureau.

The pair of bandits who have hit at least 18 Midwestern banks are playing head games with the FBI.

"They think it's amusing. We do not," said Robert Hawk, FBI spokesman in Cleveland. "We consider this to be a very serious matter. Bank robbery is not funny."

The "Mid-Western Bank Bandits," as they call themselves, are believed to have committed smartly executed bank robberies over the past couple of years in Missouri, Kansas, Iowa, Wisconsin, Nebraska, Ohio and Kentucky.

They are approaching the record of Jesse James, who led about 25 robberies of banks, stage coaches and trains in and around Missouri.

Authorities won't disclose how much money the robbers have gotten, although The (Cleveland) Plain Dealer gave the amount as $226,000.

No one has been hurt, but the bandits have left hints that they're capable of serious harm.

Several newspapers in the Midwest have received at least five taunting letters that appear to have been written by the pair.

Source: *Las Vegas Review Journal*, 14 December 1995. Reprinted by permission of Associated Press.

---

# Checklist

*Computer Crimes*

■ Who is the complainant?

■ Has a crime been committed?

■ What is the specific nature of the crime reported to the police?

■ What statutes are applicable? Can the required elements of the crime be proven?

■ Has the crime been terminated, or is it continuing?

- Is the origin of the crime internal or external?
- Does the reported crime appear to be a cover-up for a larger crime?
- What barriers exist to investigating the crime?
- What are the make, model and identification numbers of the equipment involved? The hardware? The software?
- Is the equipment individually or company owned?
- Is an operations manual available for the hardware?
- Is a flowchart of computer operations available? Is a computer configuration chart available?
- Is documentation for the software available?
- What computer language is involved? What computer programs are involved?
- What is the degree of technicality involved? Simple or complex?
- What are the input and output codes?
- What accounting procedures were used?
- What is the database system? What are the main vulnerabilities of the system?
- Is there a built-in security system? What is it? How was it bypassed?
- What are the present security procedures? How were they bypassed?
- Can the equipment be shut down during the search and investigation or for a sufficient time to investigate the portion essential to obtaining evidence?
- Can the computer records be "dumped" without interfering with the ongoing operations, or must the system be closed down and secured?
- Does the equipment need to be operational to conduct the investigation?
- Does the reporting person desire prosecution or only disciplinary action?
- Are there any suspects? Internal or external?
- If internal, are they presently employed by the reporting organization or person?
- Is a list of current employees and their work histories available? Are all current computer-related job descriptions available?
- What level of employees are involved? Is an organizational table available?
- How can the investigation be carried out without the knowledge of the suspect(s)?
- What is the motive for the crime?
- What competitors might be suspect?
- What types of evidence are needed or likely to be present?
- What external experts are needed as part of the search team?
- Does the evidence available meet the best-evidence requirement?
- What are the main barriers to the continued investigation? How can they be overcome?

## Application

**A.** A local manufacturing company contacts your police department concerning the possible theft of computer customer lists and manufacturing specification information of products manufactured at their plant. The information is being obtained by a hacker using a modem. The hacker is presumed to be in another state. The complainant wants this hacker to be arrested.

### Questions

1. In which jurisdiction is the crime actually committed?
2. How is this type of operation accomplished?

**3.** What crime has been committed?

**4.** What steps would you take to conduct this investigation?

**5.** How would you prepare a search warrant?

**6.** What types of evidence would you look for?

**B.** A local firm contacts your police department concerning theft of customer credit-card and social security numbers from their computer records. This operation and theft is suspected to be internal, so present and past employees are the prime suspects.

*Questions*

**1.** How would you plan to initiate the investigation?

**2.** What statements would you obtain?

**3.** Would you use internal or external assistance?

**4.** What types of evidence would you need?

## Discussion Questions

**1.** What do you perceive to be the differences between investigating computer crime and investigating other felonies?

**2.** What are the differences in interviewing and interrogating individuals involved in a computer crime?

**3.** What are the legal differences between a computer crime investigation and other felony investigations?

**4.** If you were in charge of a team investigating a computer crime, what would you include in your plan?

**5.** Do you have a computer crime law in your municipality?

**6.** Is any person in your police department trained specifically in computer crime investigation? If so, where was this training obtained?

**7.** Do you have a computer? If so, how do you store your information?

**8.** What type of computer security is used in your local police department?

**9.** Of all the various types of computer crime, which do you think is most serious?

**10.** What do you consider the greatest challenge in investigating computer crimes?

## References

Clede, Bill. "Handling Computer Evidence." *Law and Order,* September 1991, p. 11.

———. "Investigating Computer Crimes." *Law and Order,* July 1993, pp. 99–102.

Conly, Catherine H., and J. Thomas McEwen. "Computer Crime." *NIJ Reports* January/February 1990, pp. 2–7.

Craig, David. "Viruses." *Law and Order,* November 1991, pp. 63–65.

Forcht, Karen. "Bolstering Your Computer's Immune System." *Security Management,* September 1992, pp. 134–140.

Icove, David J. "Keeping Computers Safe." *Security Management,* December 1991, pp. 30–32.

Knight-Ridder News Service. "Results of Computer Crime Crackdown Released." *Las Vegas Review Journal,* May 10, 1990.

**Section 4**

**Investigating Crimes against Property**

Kruse, Warren. "How to Make a Million in One Easy Lesson." *Law Enforcement Technology,* October 1995, pp. 54–63.

Manning, Walt W., and Gary H. White. "Data Diddling, Salami Slicing, Trojan Horses . . . Can Your Agency Handle Computer Crimes?" *The Police Chief,* April 1990, pp. 46–49.

Martin, Deirdre. "Fighting Computer Crime." *Law Enforcement Technology,* October 1993, pp. 82–84.

McEwan, Tom. "Cybercops." *Law and Order,* March 1995, pp. 93–94.

Nickell, Daniel B. "Networked for Crime." *Security Management,* December 1991, pp. 25–29.

Olick, M. "Joy-Riding in Cyberspace." *Security Concepts,* April 1994, pp. 12, 20.

Rasch, Mark D. "Legal Lessons in the Computer Age." *Security Management,* April 1996, pp. 59–67.

Stites, Clyde M. "PCs: Personal Computers, or Partners in Crime?" *Law and Order* September 1990, pp. 161–165.

Strandberg, Keith W. "Chief Alfred Olson Pursues Crime in Cyberspace." *Law Enforcement Technology,* October 1993, pp. 22–23.

———. "Thin Blue Line Must Infiltrate On-line Criminals." *Law Enforcement Technology,* November 1993, pp. 28–52.

"Survey: Cybercrime 'Extraordinarily Widespread.'" (Minneapolis/St. Paul) *Star Tribune,* October 25, 1995, p. D3.

"Survey Says Computer Crime Widespread . . . and Many Organizations Unprepared." *Access Control,* August 1996, p. 15.

*Washington Post.* "Army Looking for a Few Good Hackers to Disable Enemy Software." (Minneapolis/St. Paul) *Star Tribune,* May 24, 1990, p. A7.

# Motor Vehicle Theft

## DO YOU KNOW

What a VIN is and why it is important?

What the five major categories of motor vehicle theft are?

What the elements of the crime of unauthorized use of a motor vehicle are?

What types of vehicles are included as "motor vehicles"?

What embezzlement of a motor vehicle is?

What the Dyer Act is and how it assists in motor vehicle theft investigation?

Why false reports of auto theft are sometimes made?

What two agencies can help investigate motor vehicle theft?

How to improve effectiveness in recognizing stolen vehicles?

How to help prevent motor vehicle theft?

## CAN YOU DEFINE

| | | |
|---|---|---|
| chop shop | keyless doors | vehicle identification |
| Dyer Act | motor vehicle | number (VIN) |

**Introduction**

IT IS NOT UNUSUAL FOR AN AMERICAN FAMILY TO FINANCE OR OWN more than $20,000 in motor vehicles. Yet the motor vehicle, even though highly vulnerable, is the least protected of all property subject to theft. The vehicle, its accessories and the property inside are all targets for thieves.

Most people use motor vehicles to travel to work and for pleasure. Thousands of recreational vehicles are also targets for theft and burglary. Aircraft and watercraft thefts add to the problems facing police investigators.

Ruotolo (1992, p. 29) notes: "Every 19 seconds an auto thief steals a vehicle in the United States." According to the FBI *Uniform Crime Reports*, there were 1,472,732 reported motor vehicle thefts in 1995, a 4.3 percent decline from the 1994 figure of 1,539,287 vehicles stolen; 78 percent of vehicles reported in 1995 were passenger cars, and 16 percent trucks and buses. Motor vehicle thefts declined in all regions of the United States. One of every 139 registered vehicles was stolen in 1995 for an estimated total theft value of $7.6 billion; 62 percent of vehicles stolen were recovered. There was a 14 percent motor vehicle clearance rate. The under-eighteen age group was responsible for 24 percent of these thefts. Of the 191,900 arrests made in 1995, 87 percent were males, 59 percent were white, 38 percent were black, and 58 percent of those persons arrested were under 25.

*Instant Evidence* ("Revoking a License . . . ,"1995, p. 6) states that automobile theft costs society at least $8 billion every year.

This chapter begins with an explanation of how motor vehicles are identified and how motor vehicle theft might be classified. This is followed by descriptions of the elements of the crimes of unauthorized use of a motor vehicle, embezzlement and interstate transportation of motor vehicles. Next the chapter describes the preliminary investigation, as well as the problem of insurance fraud and names various agencies that might cooperate in investigating and/or preventing motor vehicle theft. Following this is a discussion of how to recognize a stolen motor vehicle or an unauthorized driver, how to recover an abandoned or stolen motor vehicle and efforts to prevent motor vehicle theft. The chapter concludes with a discussion of thefts of other types of motor vehicles.

## Motor Vehicle Identification

Given the millions of motor vehicles operating on our roads, an identification system is imperative. The most important means of vehicle identification is the **vehicle identification number,** or **VIN.**

> The vehicle identification number (VIN) is the primary nonduplicated, serialized number assigned by the manufacturer to each vehicle made. This number, critical in motor vehicle theft investigation, identifies the specific vehicle in question.

The Motor Vehicle Theft Law Enforcement Act of 1984 requires manufacturers to place the seventeen-digit VIN on fourteen specified component parts including the engine, the transmission, both front fenders, the hood, both front doors, both bumpers, both rear quarter-panels, both rear doors and the deck, lid, tailgate *or* hatchback. Some manufacturers position the labels in plain view; others hide them. Car thieves often attempt to change or replace VINs to conceal vehicles' true identities.

*VINs are often vandalized or altered after a vehicle theft.*

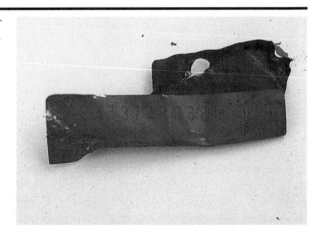

Manufacturers also use numbers to identify engines and vehicle components.

The *engine number (EN)* is an optional, serialized, nonduplicated number the manufacturer assigns to each engine. The EN may or may not be the same as the VIN.

The *engine production code number (EPCN)* is an optional number assigned to groups of engines having identical characteristics produced at a specific plant during a specific production period.

The *unit production code number (unit)* is an optional number assigned to vehicle components such as rear axles or transmissions. Constructed and applied like the EPCN, when used, the name of the feature to which the Production Code Number applies is substituted for the word *unit*.

## Classification of Motor Vehicle Theft

Motor vehicle thefts are often classified by the thief's motive or purpose, recognizing that it is impossible to determine the motive for thefts in which the vehicle is abandoned.

---

Classifications of motor vehicle theft based on the motive of the offender include:
- Joyriding.
- Transportation.
- Stripping for parts and accessories.
- Using to commit another crime.
- Reselling for profit.

---

### Joyriding

The joyrider and the person stealing for transportation are sometimes grouped together, but there is an important distinction between them. The joyrider is generally a younger person who steals for thrills and excitement.

Joyriders look for cars with keys in the ignition that can be started and driven away rapidly. The vehicle is taken for a comparatively short time and then abandoned near the location of the theft or near the destination. A vehicle taken to another community is generally left there. Another vehicle is then stolen for the return trip.

Stolen vehicles are often found where young people congregate: pizza parlors, skating rinks, malls and athletic events. Several vehicle thefts within a short time can follow a pattern, providing clues for investigators. For example, most cars stolen by the same individual or group in a short period are the same make, entered in the same manner and stolen and dropped off in the same general area. Juvenile informants can be extremely helpful in investigating such auto thefts.

Motor vehicle thefts by juveniles are often not regarded seriously by the courts, even though they account for most vehicle thefts and can cause injury or death to others. It is not unusual for juveniles to be involved in up to a hundred car thefts before apprehension. Vehicle theft by juveniles is a serious problem. In fact, in some states joyriding is a separate offense.

### Transportation

Theft of motor vehicle for transportation can involve a joyrider but is more apt to involve a transient, hitchhiker or runaway. The objective is to travel from one point to another at no cost. These offenders are generally older than joyriders. Late fall and winter are peak periods for this type of theft.

A vehicle stolen for transportation is kept longer than one stolen for joyriding. Frequently it is operated until it runs out of gas or stops running. It is then abandoned and another vehicle is stolen. The vehicle is often dumped to avoid suspicion. The license plates may be changed, or a plate may be stolen and put on the rear of the vehicle.

### Stripping for Parts and Accessories

Many vehicles are stolen by juveniles and young adults who strip them for parts and accessories to sell: transmission, rear ends, motors and wheels. Batteries, radiators and heaters are sold to wrecking yards, used car lots and auto repair shops. Expensive accessories such as car phones, stereo tape decks, radios, CBs and CD players also are removed for resale. The stripped vehicle is often crushed for scrap metal. The profit is extremely high.

Sometimes thieves steal specific items for friends, other vehicle owners or themselves. These are often parts that are impossible to buy or that are very expensive.

**Stealing for Chop Shops.**   A **chop shop** is a business, usually a body shop, that disassembles stolen autos and sells the parts. The chop shop deals with car thieves who steal the cars specifically for them, often on demand, stealing the exact make, model and color. The car thief may get $200 for stealing each car. The vehicle may triple in value when sold for parts. There is no waiting period and no tax to the customer. The cars are dismantled, and the parts are cataloged. In some cities it is such big business that network organizations dispose of the stolen parts.

The chop shop may also deal directly with the owner of a vehicle who wants to dispose of it for insurance purposes due to dissatisfaction with its performance. The owner leaves the registration with the chop shop. The shop returns

*This vehicle was dumped by car thieves in Sunset Park, a working-class immigrant neighborhood in Brooklyn. For days, visitors came by to strip parts until the sanitation department arrived to take the skeletal remains away.*

the registration to the owner after the vehicle is dismantled and crushed. The insurance company has no chance of recovery.

## Using To Commit Another Crime

Automobiles are used in most serious crimes. Robberies of banks, bank messengers, payroll offices, businesses and service stations as well as criminal escapes almost always involve a getaway in a stolen vehicle. Vehicles provide both rapid transportation and a means to transport the loot. Other crimes frequently committed while using stolen vehicles include rapes, kidnappings, burglaries, larcenies to obtain gas and assaults of police officers attempting to apprehend a suspect.

A stolen motor vehicle driven by a criminal is 150 to 200 times more likely to be in an accident than one driven by a noncriminal; therefore, regard as suspicious any damaged, abandoned vehicles you observe. Conditions contributing to this high accident rate include operating the vehicle on unfamiliar streets and roads, driving at high speeds in an attempt to escape police pursuit, testing the vehicle's speed, unfamiliarity with the vehicle and the use of drugs.

Records indicate that many habitual criminals have stolen at least one car in their criminal career. Some began as car thieves.

Stolen cars are used in committing other crimes to escape detection at the crime scene and to avoid being identified by witnesses. Therefore, the criminal normally uses the stolen vehicle for only a brief time. In fact, a stolen vehicle report may not yet have been made when the crime is committed. Stolen plates are often used to cause confusion in identification. The vehicle used in committing the crime, the hot car, is usually soon abandoned for a cold car, a vehicle used to escape from the crime scene vicinity.

A criminal apprehended with a stolen vehicle after committing another crime is usually prosecuted only for the major crime, not the auto theft.

## Reselling

Auto thefts are also committed by professional thieves who take an unattended vehicle, with or without the keys, and simply drive it away. They may go to a used car lot, posing as a buyer, and drive the vehicle away on a no-return test drive. Another method is to answer an ad in the paper for a particular car, try it out and then never return it. This gives the thief time to escape because the owner gave permission to take the vehicle—which makes the case one of embezzlement. Cars are also stolen by using bad checks.

Very few vehicles stolen by professional car thieves are recovered. Moreover, such thieves are difficult to detect and prosecute. As specialists in automobiles, the thieves know how to steal cars and how to alter them or the documents needed to make them eligible for resale. The professional is rarely the actual thief; the professional hires others to steal cars and bring them to a specified location, usually a garage, for making the necessary alterations.

Alterations include repainting, changing seat covers, repairing existing damage and altering the engine number. The car is also completely searched to eliminate any items that connect it with the former owner. The VIN is almost always altered or replaced. The most common method of changing the VIN is to buy a similar vehicle from a salvage lot and then remove and replace the entire dash, making the change undetectable. If the VIN is not located on the dash, the car thief has a much more difficult time. In some cases, the VIN plate itself is removed and carefully altered, or embossed tape can be made with a hand-tape numbering device and placed over the regular VIN plate. Unless the inside of the car is investigated, a false VIN plate is not usually detected.

After all number changes on the motor and the VIN plate are completed, the vehicle is prepared for resale by using stolen or forged titles, fictitious bills of sale or titles received with salvage vehicles bought by the thieves. When the mechanical alterations and paperwork are completed, the vehicle is registered through the Department of Motor Vehicles and resold, usually at a public car auction, to a used car dealer or to a private individual.

## Elements of the Crime:
## Unauthorized Use of a Motor Vehicle

Most car thieves are prosecuted not for auto theft but for unauthorized use of a motor vehicle. Prosecution for auto theft requires proof that the thief intended to deprive the owner of the vehicle permanently. This is often difficult or impossible to establish. Therefore, the most common charge is unauthorized use of a motor vehicle.

---

The elements of the crime of unauthorized use of a motor vehicle are:
- Intentionally taking or driving.
- A motor vehicle.
- Without the consent of the owner or the owner's authorized agent.

---

**Intentionally Taking or Driving.**   *Intent* is often described in state laws as "with intent to permanently or temporarily deprive the owner of title or possession" or "with intent to steal." Intent can be inferred from the act of taking or driving, being observed taking or driving or being apprehended while taking or driving. Laws often include any person who voluntarily rides in a vehicle knowing it is stolen.

**A Motor Vehicle.**   **Motor vehicle** is not restricted to automobiles. It includes any self-propelled device for moving people or property or pulling implements, whether operated on land, on water or in the air.

---

Motor vehicles include automobiles, trucks, buses, motorcycles, snowmobiles, vans, self-propelled watercraft and aircraft.

---

Homemade motor vehicles are also included.

**Without the Consent of the Owner or the Owner's Authorized Agent.**   Legitimate ownership of motor vehicles exists when the vehicle is in the factory being manufactured, when it is being sold by an authorized dealership or when it is owned by a private person, company or corporation. *Owner* and *true owner* are not necessarily the same. For example, the true owner can be a lending agency that retains title until the loan is paid.

Usually the owner or the owner's authorized agent reports the theft. Thus, it can be determined immediately if consent was given. Previous consent is not a defense, although it may be considered.

If you stop a suspicious vehicle and the driver does not have proof of ownership, check with the State Department of Motor Vehicle Registration to determine who the legal owner is. If that person is not the driver, check with the legal owner to determine if the driver has permission to use the vehicle.

## Elements of the Crime: Embezzlement

Motor vehicle embezzlement exists if the person who took the vehicle initially had consent and then exceeded the terms of that consent.

This most frequently occurs when a new or used car agency permits a prospective buyer to try out a vehicle for a specific time. The person decides to convert the vehicle to personal use and does not return it. This is fraudulent appropriation of property. Motor vehicle embezzlement can also occur under rental or lease agreements or when private persons let someone try out a vehicle that is for sale.

## Elements of the Crime: Interstate Transportation

In 1919 the need for federal control of motor vehicle theft was recognized, and Congress approved the National Motor Vehicle Theft Act (U.S. Code, Title 18, Sections 2312 and 2313), commonly known as the *Dyer Act*.

The **Dyer Act** made interstate transportation of a stolen motor vehicle a federal crime and allowed for federal help in prosecuting such cases.

The act was amended in 1945 to include aircraft and is now called the *Interstate Transportation of Stolen Motor Vehicles Act.* Since the Dyer Act was passed, more than 300,000 vehicles have been recovered, and more than 100,000 criminals have been convicted in interstate car theft cases.

The elements of the crime of interstate transportation of a motor vehicle are that:

- The motor vehicle was stolen.
- It was transported in interstate commerce or foreign commerce.
- The person transporting or causing it to be transported knew it to be stolen.
- The person receiving, concealing, selling or bartering it knew it to be stolen.

The vehicle thief may be prosecuted in any state through which the stolen vehicle passed. Prosecution is normally in the state where the vehicle was stolen, but sometimes it is in the state where the person was arrested.

Intent is not required. The stolen vehicle could accidently be driven over the state line or could be forced to detour into another state. If the vehicle is transported by train or truck through another state, prosecution is also possible.

The Anti-Car Theft Act of 1992 provides tougher legislation on auto theft, previously a low-profile crime. The penalty for importing or exporting stolen vehicles was increased from five to ten years as was the penalty for interstate transportation of stolen vehicles. The Act provides the U.S. Customs new authority in checking for stolen vehicles and provides funds to states that participate in the National Motor Vehicle Title Information System. It also made armed carjacking a federal offense (Kime, 1993, pp. 25–26).

# The Preliminary Investigation

When a motor vehicle theft is reported, initial information obtained by police includes the time, date and location of the theft; the make, model and color of the vehicle; the state of issue of the license plate; license plate number; direction of travel; description of any suspect; and the complainant's present location.

The complainant is asked to remain at his or her present location, and a police officer is dispatched to obtain further information and to complete the proper complaint form (see Figure 16–1).

---

False motor vehicle theft reports are often filed when the car has been taken by a family member or misplaced in a parking lot, when the driver wants to cover up for an accident or crime committed with the vehicle or to provide an alibi for being late.

---

It is also possible that the vehicle has been reclaimed by a loan company— a civil matter.

A preliminary description is provided to patrol officers, who are told the theft has not been verified; therefore, no all points bulletin is issued. During this time, patrol officers are alerted, but they make no move if they see the stolen vehicle because the report has not been validated. The officer in the field obtains information to determine the validity of the theft charge: the circumstances of the theft, any details of items in the car and any possible suspects. Frequent false reports impair cooperation from other agencies, especially when the errors should have been detected by the investigating officers.

If the vehicle is found later with accident damage, it is necessary to determine if the damage occurred before or after the report. Vehicles involved in a hit-and-run accident are sometimes abandoned by the driver and then reported as stolen. Younger persons sometimes report a car stolen if they have an accident and are afraid to tell their parents.

Auto thieves sometimes use porcelain chips obtained from spark plugs to break the safety glass in vehicle windows. Ferguson (1990, p. 155) explains:

> The properties of the porcelain chip which give it its uniqueness for shattering tempered safety glass are sharpness; its edges, when broken, are razor sharp, and hardness. The porcelain chip is obtained from the spark plugs of vehicles, broken and, depending on the pieces, used in a variety of ways, i.e., on string, wire, taped to blades, or, in a manner that most thieves use, placed between the thumb and forefinger and flicked like a marble at the glass.

Investigators should look for discarded porcelain chips near the scene of a vehicle whose window has been smashed. They should also check suspects' pockets for bits of porcelain.

Computerized police files can assist in searching for suspects. Investigators can enter data concerning past suspects and other individuals in the vehicle, types of vehicles stolen, how they were entered or stolen, types of locations from which they were stolen (apartment complexes, private residences or commercial parking lots, for example), where the vehicles were abandoned and where the vehicles were if the suspects were arrested in them.

| ST. LOUIS PARK POLICE DEPT.<br>MN0272100 | SUPERVISOR<br>APPROVED S/A<br>DATE & TIME REPORT MADE<br>4-5-97    1330 | **MOTOR VEHICLE REPORT**<br>FOR ALL ATTEMPTS AND THEFTS OF<br>MOTOR VEHICLES | PAGE |
|---|---|---|---|

| DATE/TIME COMPLAINT RECEIVED<br>4-5-97    1245 | | | UDC | GRID NO. | COMPLAINT NO. |
|---|---|---|---|---|---|

HOW COMPLAINT RECEIVED    FOUND BY POLICE ☐    RADIO ☐    CITIZEN ☐    STATION ☐    LETTER ☐    PHONE ☒

Date of Theft (DOT)  4-5-97    1115    Time of Theft, Between  4-4-97    and    4-5-97

Owner:  Jerald Combs    Person Reporting  same

Address:  646 13th Street B. City    Address:

Telephone: Res.: 293-2415    Bus.:    Telephone: Res.:    Bus.:

License No. (LIC) AMU 345    State of Issue (LIS)  Minnesota    License Plate Yr.: (LIY)  1994    License Plate Type: (LIT)  P

Vehicle Serial No. (VIN)  643210    Vehicle Year (VYR)  1992    Vehicle Make: (VMA)  Chev    Vehicle Model: (VMO)  4 cyl

Vehicle Style (VST)  4 dr    Vehicle Color (VCO)  Beige    Other Ident. Characteristics (MIS)

Special Equipment:  Spotlight-left side    Odometer Reading  18,000

Damage to Vehicle prior to theft  none    Where?

Personal Property in Vehicle  Little value    Value of Vehicle  7,500

Car was Parked at  646 13th St.    Vehicle Locked  Yes X    No    Location of Keys  in house

Is anyone Permitted to use vehicle?  wife    Under What Conditions?  all times

Do you have Absolute Ownership?  Yes    Name of Finance Co.  none    Name of Insurance Co.  Farmers Life

Will Owner Prosecute?  Yes    Does Owner Suspect Anyone?  No

I Hereby Certify That The Foregoing Statement is True and Correct   X

Date (DOR) Recovered  4-6-97    Time Recovered  2330    Where Recovered  accident-Henderson

Vehicle Impounded At  Henderson PD    Owner Notified By  Boulder City    Date of Notice  4-6-97

Vehicle Recovered By  Henderson PD

Vehicle NCIC Entered into MINCIS  Yes    Date of Entry  4-5-97    NCIC MINCIS No.:  162345

Recovery NCIC Cancelled-MINCIS  Yes    Date of Cancel  4-5-97    NCIC MINCIS No.:  162345

Officer Taking Report:  Milo Prins    Date of Report:  4-6-97    Time of Report:  0015

Case Investigated By:  Det. Thomas Strong,  St. Louis Park PD

DETAILS OF OFFENSE:    Vehicle was parked on street at about 8:30 PM, 4-4-97 and was missing at early morning 4-5-97.  Didn't report until several hours after checking with friends.

DEFENSE CLEARED BY ARREST ☒    EXCEPTIONALLY ☐    CASE UNFOUNDED ☐    INACTIVE (Not Cleared) ☐    OTHER ☐

PERSONS ARRESTED, SUSPECTS, WITNESSES & ADDITIONAL DETAILED REPORT ON SUPPLEMENTARY

Douglas Amherst, 1614 College Street, Henderson, Nevada

**Figure 16–1    Sample Motor Vehicle Report**
Source: Courtesy of the St. Louis Park, Minnesota, Police Department.

# Insurance Fraud

Oliver (1995, p. 44) stresses:

Vehicle insurance fraud is an economic crime of major proportions. It affects every honest premium payer by allowing criminals to reap huge profits that will ultimately push insurance rates up. It also affects law enforcement agencies that must waste valuable resources, time, and money, in pursuing people perpetrating "paper" crimes that are difficult or impossible to solve.

Many police departments actually assist those who perpetrate insurance fraud by allowing car theft reports to be phoned in or taking them "over the counter" at the police station and then never investigating the reports. The primary reason the auto theft is reported is often for insurance purposes.

To avoid this situation, law enforcement agencies should investigate all auto theft reports and should not discount the possibility that the "victim" is actually committing insurance fraud.

For example, a luxury car stolen from a suburban mall parking lot was found four days later on fire on a rural road. The case seemed routine until a detective began an investigation to eliminate the car's reported owner. The detective found that there were three pending lawsuits against the "victim" and that the "victim" had filed for bankruptcy shortly after the lawsuits and months before the car was stolen. He had filed an affidavit claiming he no longer owned the car, that he sold it six months before. Investigation revealed that the buyer was a friend who let the car be transferred into his name so it would not be involved in the bankruptcy proceedings.

This was a "clear case of 'Filing False Information with the Police.'" Further, after a fire investigator and mechanic inspected the car, they reported that the lab tests showed "ongoing engine failure." The "victim" wanted the insurance company to pay for a replacement, a clear case of fraud.

## Cooperating Agencies in Motor Vehicle Theft

Police most frequently use state motor vehicle bureaus to check owners' registrations. They also use driver's license bureaus to compare the driver of a vehicle with the registered owner. When vehicle registration and driver's registration checks are completed, further checks can be made in the FBI's National Crime Information Center files to determine if the vehicle is stolen and if the driver has a criminal record.

---

The FBI and the National Insurance Crime Bureau provide valuable help in investigating motor vehicle thefts.

---

### The FBI

The FBI assists local and state authorities who notify the bureau that a stolen motor vehicle or aircraft has been transported interstate—which places it within the provisions of the Interstate Transportation of Stolen Motor Vehicles Act. The FBI works with local authorities to find the vehicle and the person who stole it. The FBI can also examine suspicious documents relating to false sales or registrations. The Bureau's NCIC contains information on stolen vehicles and stolen auto accessories. Its National Automobile Altered Numbers File is an additional resource.

### The National Insurance Crime Bureau (NICB)

In 1992 the National Auto Theft Bureau was incorporated into the National Insurance Crime Bureau (NICB), a nonprofit organization supported and maintained by hundreds of automobile insurance companies. The organization helps law enforcement agencies reduce and prevent auto thefts and investigate questionable or fraudulent vehicle fires and thefts.

The NICB also disseminates reports on stolen cars to law enforcement agencies and serves as a clearinghouse for information on stolen cars. Computer files are maintained for several million wanted or stolen cars, listed by make, engine number, VIN and component part number. This information is available free on request to law enforcement agencies. The bureau can also trace cars from the factory to the owner. Its staff of specialists and technicians are experts in identifying stolen cars and restoring mutilated, changed or defaced numbers. They also restore altered or obliterated VINs.

The bureau publishes and distributes to police agencies their *Manual for the Identification of Automobiles.* This publication describes the location of identifying numbers, gives license plate reproductions and provides a short legal digest of each state's motor vehicle laws. In an emergency, call the bureau collect. Otherwise, send a letter requesting specific assistance.

## Recognizing a Stolen Motor Vehicle or an Unauthorized Driver

As with other crimes, having a suspicious nature and being alert help an officer to detect motor vehicle thefts. Detection is sometimes improved by an instinct developed through training, observation and experience. Police officers develop individual techniques for recognizing stolen cars. No absolute, single peculiarity identifies a stolen car or its driver, but either one can draw the attention of an observant police officer.

---

To improve your ability to recognize stolen vehicles:
- Keep a list of stolen vehicles in your car.
- Develop a checking system to determine rapidly whether a suspicious vehicle is stolen.
- Learn the common characteristics of stolen vehicles and car thieves.
- Take time to check suspicious persons and vehicles.
- Learn how to question suspicious drivers and occupants.

---

A *potential car thief on foot* usually appears nervous. He or she may be looking into cars on the street or in parking lots, trying door handles and may be carrying some sort of entry tool. Observe such an individual from a distance until an overt act is committed.

*Characteristics of a driver of a stolen vehicle* include sudden jerks or stops, driving without lights or excessively fast or slow, wearing gloves in hot weather and attempting to avoid or outrun a squad car.

*Characteristics of a stolen vehicle* include having one license plate when two are required or two when one is required. Double or triple plates with one on top of the other can indicate lack of time to take off the original plates. A set of old plates with new screws, wired-on plates, altered numbers, dirty plates on a clean car or clean plates on a dirty car, differing front and rear plate numbers, plates bent to conceal a number, upside-down or hanging plates and homemade cardboard plates are all suspicious. Observe whether the trunk lid has been pried or whether side windows or door locks are broken.

When *questioning a driver and any occupants of a car* you have stopped on suspicion of motor vehicle theft, observe their behavior. Watch for signs of nervousness, hesitancy in answers, overpoliteness and indications that the driver does not know the vehicle. Request the driver's license and the vehicle registration papers for identification. Examine the driver's license and ask for the driver's birthdate. The driver will probably not know the correct date unless it is his or her license. Compare the description on the license with the person. Compare the state of issuance of the license with the car's license plates. Ask the driver to sign his or her name and compare the signature with that on the driver's license.

Ask the driver the year, make and model of the car and compare the answers with the registration papers. Ask the mileage. The driver of a stolen car rarely knows the mileage, whereas the owner or regular driver knows within a reasonable number of miles. Ask the driver to describe the contents of the car's trunk and glove compartment.

Check inside the vehicle for an extra set of plates, bullet holes or damage, bloodstains and service stickers showing where and when the car was last serviced. Inspect the VIN plate for alterations. A roll of adhesive tape can indicate it was used to tape windows before breaking them. Wire or coat hangers bent straight to open doors, rubber gloves, jumper cables or tools for breaking into a car are also alerting signals. The common tools used in vehicle theft include car openers, rake and pick guns, tryout keys, impact tools, keyway decoders, modified vice grips, tubular lock picks, hot wires and modified screw drivers.

*Parked cars* may have been stolen if debris under the car indicates it has been in the same place for a long time. Check with neighbors to see how long the vehicle has been parked there. The neighborhood canvass is one of the most effective techniques in investigating abandoned cars. Check for illegal entrance, for open car windows in inclement weather and for dirty vehicles indicating lack of care. A citation under the wiper can indicate when the car was abandoned. Keys left in the ignition and lack of license plates are also grounds for checking.

A warm or running motor and firearms or valuables left in the car may indicate that the thief has temporarily parked the car and intends to return. Stake out stolen vehicles (identified by license number or description) because it is very likely the thief will return. Consider partially immobilizing the vehicle to prevent an attempted escape.

## Recovering an Abandoned or Stolen Motor Vehicle

Most motor vehicle thefts are local problems involving a locally stolen and recovered vehicle. Sixty-nine percent of stolen vehicles are recovered, most within forty-eight hours, especially those stolen by juveniles. Stolen vehicles are recovered when patrol officers observe a vehicle on a hot list, a suspicious vehicle or driver or an apparently abandoned vehicle or when private citizens report an abandoned vehicle.

Although patrol units are responsible for more than 90 percent of the stolen vehicles recovered, investigative personnel have a major role in furnishing information to the uniformed patrol on all areas of motor vehicle theft.

The initial patrol officer at the scene examines recovered and abandoned vehicles unless there is reason to believe the vehicle was involved in a serious crime. Investigators assigned to such a crime may want to look for specific items in the vehicle that might not be known to the patrol officers. In these cases, the vehicle is protected until the specialists arrive.

Once recovery and impound reports have been completed, the car is removed from the hot list, and the owner is notified of the recovery. A vehicle recovery report (see Figure 16–2) should be completed and filed.

If a crime has recently been committed in the area or the vehicle's position and location suggest that the suspect may return, drive by and arrange for a stakeout. If the car is locked and the keys are gone, if heavy rain or fog exists and the windshield wiper marks indicate they were recently used or if no dry spot appears under the car, the vehicle was probably used recently and the driver may return. Round rain spots on the vehicle mean it has been parked for a longer period than if there are elongated rain drops, which indicate recent movement. A quick check of heat remaining on the hood, radiator or exhaust pipe also reveals if the car was recently parked. Consider attempting to apprehend the criminal on return to the vehicle.

On the other hand, if a car has an empty gas tank, a rundown battery or a flat tire, it probably is abandoned and can be immediately processed, either at the scene, the police station or a storage location. Consider the possibility that the vehicle was used in committing another crime such as robbery, burglary, murder, hijacking, abduction or kidnapping. Search the vehicle's exterior first and then the interior as described in Chapter 4. Many car thieves have been located through items left in a vehicle.

If you suspect that the vehicle was used in another crime, take it to a garage or lock and seal it with evidence tape; then notify the proper authorities. After processing, notify the rightful owner.

Technology is making recovery of stolen vehicles much easier. Nilson (1990, p. 36) writes that LoJack, a Massachusetts company, has developed a system that may "revolutionize the way police track down stolen cars and car thieves." The system places a homing device the size of a stick of butter in an obscure

DISTRICT NUMBER | St. Louis Park Police Department | COMPLAINT NUMBER

VEHICLE RECOVERY REPORT

LICENSE ___ STATE ___ YR. ___ SERIAL ___
MAKE ___ YR. ___ TYPE ___ RECOVERED BY ___ DATE ___ TIME ___
WHERE RECOVERED ___ ON STREET - ALLEY - PARKING LOT - GARAGE
RECOVERED ON INFORMATION FROM: RADIO - CITIZEN - FOUND BY POLICE - OTHER
REASON FOR IMPOUNDING: INVOLVED IN ACCIDENT -ARREST - ABANDONED - OTHER
EXTENT OF DAMAGE TO VEHICLE ___
VEHICLE LOCKED? ___ TRUNK LOCKED? ___ WERE KEYS IN CAR? ___
PERSON ARRESTED ___ CHARGE ___
TOW TRUCK ORDERED AT ___ ARRIVED ___ TOW COMPANY ___ DRIVER (SIGNATURE) ___
VEHICLE OWNER ___ ADDRESS ___
VEHICLE DRIVER ___ ADDRESS ___
O.K. TO RELEASE YES ☐ NO ☐ TO OWNER ☐ DRIVER ☐ OTHER ☐

| LIST VEHICLE EQUIPMENT | | | | INVENTORY OF PERSONAL PROPERTY IN VEHICLE |
|---|---|---|---|---|
| | LICENSE PLATES | | BATTERY | |
| | WHEELS | | HEAD LIGHTS | |
| | TIRES | | TAIL LIGHTS | |
| | RADIO | | BUMPERS | |
| | EXPOSED AERIAL | | TAPE PLAYER | |

OTHER EQUIPMENT ___ | DISPOSITION OF PROPERTY: ___
IF RELEASED PRIOR TO VEHICLE, HAVE RECEIVER SIGN HERE:
RELEASED BY ___ RECEIVER ___
DATE ___ TIME ___
REPORT MADE BY ___ DATE ___ TIME ___ REMARKS ___
HOLD ☐ AUTHORITY ___ REASON ___
RELEASED BY ___ | I HEREBY ACKNOWLEDGE RECEIPT OF ABOVE DESCRIBED VEH. & PROP.
DATE ___ TIME ___ | NAME ___
AUTHORIZED BY ___ | ADDRESS ___
CERT. OF REGISTRATION ☐ BILL OF SALE ☐ INS. POLICY ☐ | TELEPHONE ___ DATE ___ TIME ___

**Figure 16–2 Vehicle Recovery Report Form**

Source: Courtesy of the St. Louis Park, Minnesota, Police Department.

place in a vehicle. If the vehicle is reported stolen, the device is activated and a tracker picks up a series of beeps, displayed on a lighted compass and an illuminated strength-meter that tells operators when they are nearing the stolen vehicle. The display also shows the model and color of the car. According to Stern (1990, p. 69), state police in Florida and Massachusetts have reported recovery rates of 95 percent using the LoJack system, with 20 to 30 percent of these recoveries resulting in arrests.

According to Oliver (1995, p. 52):

> Because LoJack maintains a 95 percent recovery rate versus a 64 percent recovery rate for nonequipped cars and a 20 to 25 percent arrest rate for LoJack-equipped vehicles versus only a 5 percent arrest rate for cars without the system, there is little doubt that this technology can be a benefit to the law enforcement community.

The system is not without its drawbacks, however. First, unless police departments across the country install tracking devices in their squad cars, the devices are ineffective. Second, the lag time between a car theft and its report may be hours or even days. Third, there are some dead spots—locations where transmitted radio signals will not be detected. Fourth, some departments hesitate to become a partner with a private company. Finally, some departments worry that the public will perceive them to be focused on preventing car theft from the more affluent members of the community, those who can afford the $600 auto recovery system.

Other systems also are available. Some activate automatically. If someone drives off in the car without deactivating the system, an alarm is sent to the tracking center. Such systems might, however, result in false alarms and pose as great a problem as false burglar alarms pose. Other systems provide a personal alert service that allows motorists to signal authorities in case of emergencies. One system allows controllers to shut off a stolen car's engine by remote control if police tracking the car believe it would be safe to do so.

## Preventing Motor Vehicle Theft

Effective preventive measures could eliminate much of the motor vehicle theft problem. Vehicle theft requires both desire and an opportunity, and often it is difficult to know which comes first. An unlocked automobile with keys in the ignition is a temptation. A parked vehicle with the motor running is also extremely inviting. Many juveniles take cars under such conditions and then boast of their ability to steal.

---

Numerous motor vehicle thefts can be prevented by effective educational campaigns and by installing antitheft devices in vehicles during manufacture.

---

Educate motor vehicle owners about the importance of removing their keys from the ignition and locking their vehicles when parked. Public education campaigns might include distributing dashboard stickers with the reminder "Have you removed your keys from the ignition?" or "Don't forget to take your keys and lock your car."

Automobile manufacturers have helped by installing ignition and door locking devices, as well as buzzer systems that warn the driver that the keys are still in the vehicle. **Keyless doors**—by which the owner enters a combination by pushing numbered pads in a programmed sequence to gain access to the car—may make it harder for thieves to break into vehicles to steal them.

Stern (1990, pp. 65–69) describes several strategies police departments are using to combat rising auto theft levels:

- Establishing auto theft task forces.
- Using computers to check licenses immediately.
- Checking salvage yards to verify the identity of vehicle parts.
- Setting up sting operations; for example, a body shop that purchases stolen vehicles.
- Verifying that the claim is not fraudulent.
- Providing officers with auto theft training.
- Coordinating efforts with the National Insurance Crime Bureau.
- Educating the public on how to minimize their chances for auto theft.
- Coordinating efforts across jurisdictional lines.
- Instituting anti-car-theft campaigns.
- Using high technology to track stolen vehicles.
- Increasing the penalties for stealing vehicles.
- Using a CAT program (discussed next).
- Involving auto manufacturers.

In areas where police have made special efforts to educate the public and to assign extra squads to patrol high auto theft areas, auto theft has been significantly reduced.

New York City has instituted a CAT (Combat Auto Theft) Program that has been highly successful. Participating car owners sign a form indicating they do not normally operate their automobiles between 1 A.M. and 5 A.M., the peak auto theft hours. They also sign a consent form that authorizes the police to stop their vehicle during these hours without probable cause. Owners are given a CAT program decal to affix prominently on the inside of the car's rear window. Hildreth (1990, p. 92) describes these decals as "mobile burglar alarms" that are both distinctive and easy for officers to see. Officers may stop any car having the decal without probable cause if they see it traveling on city streets between 1 A.M. and 5 A.M. According to Hildreth (1990, p. 93), in a three-year period the program registered 37,326 cars, and only 67 of them were stolen.

Minnesota's Help Eliminate Auto Theft (HEAT) program offers up to $5,000 for information leading to the arrest and trial of suspected auto-theft-ring members or chop shop operators. The program's toll-free number is answered by the Minnesota Highway Patrol.

The increased use of alarms and protective devices may, in part, account for the rise in armed carjackings, as explained in Chapter 8. Unwilling to give up their lucrative "trade," car thieves may use force against a vehicle operator to gain control of the vehicle rather than risk being thwarted by antitheft devices.

## Thefts of Other Types of Motor Vehicles

Investigating stolen trucks and trailers, construction vehicles and equipment, recreational vehicles, motorized boats, snowmobiles, motorcycles, motor scooters, mopeds and aircraft is similar to investigating auto thefts.

### Trucks and Trailers

Usually trucks and trailers are stolen by professional thieves, although they are also stolen for parts. A "fingerman" often provides information to the thief. In most cases, the fingerman is an employee of the company that owns the truck.

A "spotter" locates the truck after getting information from the fingerman and then follows the truck to the point where it is to be stolen. A driver experienced in operating the type of vehicle to be stolen then commits the actual theft.

Truck trailers are usually stolen by simply backing up a tractor to the trailer and hauling it away. The trailer's cargo is generally the target.

Stolen trucks and trailers are identified much like passenger vehicles are—by the manufacturer or through the *Commercial Vehicle Identification Manual* published by the National Insurance Crime Bureau.

### Construction Vehicles and Equipment

Expensive construction vehicles whose parts are easily sold are often parked at unprotected construction sites. There is no organized identification system for the numerous types of construction equipment. However, many construction companies have formed protection programs, have identified their equipment with special markings and have offered rewards for information about thefts. Contact the manufacturers or sellers of the equipment for identification information. Local construction firms can also provide information about possible outlets for stolen parts.

### Recreational Vehicles

More than 450 makes and models of recreational vehicles (RVs) are marketed in the United States. Because there are so many makes and models, contact the manufacturer for any special numbers not readily visible. Recreational vehicles are also targets for vehicle burglaries because many contain CB radios, televisions and appliances. Many false theft claims are made because of the high cost of operating these vehicles.

### Motorized Boats

Since 1972 many states have required licensing of boats, including an identification number on the boat's hull. Most such identification numbers are ten to thirteen digits. The first several digits are the manufacturer's number. This is followed by four or five identification numbers and several certification numbers. Because boats also are the objects of many fraudulent insurance claims, determine if the theft claim is legitimate.

### Snowmobiles

Snowmobiles are easy to steal because they can be transported inside vans and trucks. Most of the major snowmobile manufacturers in the United States and Canada use chassis and engine numbers that aid in identification.

### Motorcycles, Motor Scooters and Mopeds

Motorcycles, motor scooters and mopeds are easy to steal because they lack security devices and are often left unprotected. The lock number is easily identified, and substitute keys can be made. These cycles can be driven away, or they can be loaded on trailers or into vans and transported, perhaps several at a time.

Identifying such cycles is difficult because of the many types and the fact that parts are not readily identifiable. However, identification numbers can often be obtained through the National Insurance Crime Bureau, local dealers and manufacturers.

### Aircraft

Aircraft theft, although infrequent, is a high-value theft. Such thefts are jointly investigated with the FBI and the Federal Aviation Administration. Many stolen aircraft are used in narcotics smuggling so that the plane can be sacrificed at no cost if there is danger of apprehension.

Aircraft identification consists of a highly visible *N* identification number painted on the craft. Many aircraft parts, including the engine, radio equipment, landing gear and tires, also have individual serial numbers. Aircraft identification can be verified through the manufacturer.

## Summary

Motor vehicle thefts take much investigative time, but they can provide important information on other crimes under investigation. The vehicle identification number (VIN), critical in motor vehicle theft investigations, identifies the specific vehicle in question. This number is the primary nonduplicated, serialized number assigned by the manufacturer to each vehicle.

Categories for motor vehicle theft based on the offender's motive include (1) joyriding, (2) transportation, (3) stripping for parts and accessories, (4) use in committing another crime and (5) reselling for profit.

Although referred to as "motor vehicle theft," most cases are prosecuted as "unauthorized use of a motor vehicle" because a charge of theft requires proof that the thief intended to deprive the owner of the vehicle permanently, which is often difficult or impossible to establish. The elements of the crime of unauthorized use of a motor vehicle are (1) intentionally taking or driving (2) a motor vehicle (3) without the consent of the owner or the owner's authorized agent. Motor vehicles include automobiles, trucks, buses, motorcycles, motor scooters, mopeds, snowmobiles, vans, self-propelled watercraft and aircraft. Embezzlement of a motor vehicle occurs if the person who took the vehicle had consent initially and then exceeded the terms of that consent.

The Dyer Act made interstate transportation of a stolen motor vehicle a federal crime and allowed for federal help in prosecuting such cases.

False motor vehicle theft reports are often filed because a car has been taken by a family member or misplaced in a parking lot, to cover up for an accident or a crime committed with the vehicle or to provide an alibi for being late.

The FBI and the National Insurance Crime Bureau provide valuable help in investigating motor vehicle theft.

To improve your ability to recognize stolen vehicles, keep a list of stolen vehicles in your car, develop a checking system for rapidly determining if a suspicious vehicle is stolen, learn the common characteristics of stolen vehicles and car thieves, take time to check suspicious persons and vehicles and learn how to question suspicious drivers and occupants.

Numerous motor vehicle thefts can be prevented by effective educational campaigns and by manufacturer-installed security devices.

*Read the following articles and imagine yourself as the officer/detective assigned to each case. What elements of the crime are present? What evidence would you need to prosecute the case? Who else might you need to coordinate your efforts with? What is the likelihood of solving each crime?*

## Nine indicted in car theft operation

**By Sandra Chereb**

*Associated Press*

RENO—Nine people suspected of running an elaborate international car-theft ring have been indicted by a federal grand jury.

The indictments and arrests of five of the defendants cap a two-year investigation into the sophisticated operation that authorities say involved stealing vehicles from Reno car dealers and shipping them to China for sale there.

The indictments, handed up on Wednesday, were sealed until arrest warrants were served, Jerry Hill, a senior FBI agent in Reno, said in a written statement.

Charges include making false statements on loan and credit applications, mail fraud, interstate and foreign transportation of stolen property, aiding and abetting, and attempting to evade financial reporting requirements.

Arrested were Wai Shun Chew, 56; Wai Yuen Cheung, 32; Chung Kwong, 28; and Chi M. Law, 24, all of Reno; and Ming T. Yu, age unknown, of Rosemead, Calif.

The names of the other defendants and the status of their arrests were not immediately available. Hill could not be reached Saturday for comment.

Authorities allege that some of the defendants acted as recruiters, who provided money to others to make down payments on high-priced cars at Reno-area dealerships.

After obtaining financing and insurance, the vehicles were turned over to the recruiter, who took them to the Port of Long Beach in California for shipment to Hong Kong.

Authorities allege the cars were then sold in China for between three and four times the original purchase price.

Once overseas, the defendants who purchased the cars in Reno reported them stolen to police and insurance companies for reimbursement of their losses.

The FBI estimates the scheme may involve total losses of up to $6 million.

An investigation, being conducted by the FBI, U.S. Customs Service, U.S. attorneys office, Reno Police Department and California Department of Insurance, continued.

Source: *Las Vegas Review Journal,* 17 November 1996, Reprinted by permission of the Associated Press.

## Cunanan eludes manhunt*

**By Anne O'Connor and Chris Graves**

*Star Tribune Staff Writers*

MIAMI—As hundreds of law-enforcement agents scoured the nation Wednesday trying to get a step ahead of Andrew Cunanan, prosecutors began gearing up for the possible capture of the elusive suspected serial killer.

The U.S. attorney's office in Newark, N.J., became the second agency to charge Cunanan with murder after authorities in Miami Beach found new evidence in a pickup truck near the scene of the latest killing.

Officials said 16 Florida Department of Law Enforcement officers, 26 FBI agents and 10 Miami Beach police officers were working on the Versace case. The killings began April 27 with the bludgeoning death of Jeffrey Trail, 27, in a loft apartment in Minneapolis' Warehouse District.

The body of architect David Madson, 33, was found in Chisago County

*(continued on p. 531)*

almost a week later. He had been shot in the head with a .40-caliber handgun.

Police then found Madson's missing Jeep Grand Cherokee just outside the Chicago home of a third victim, Lee Miglin, 72, a real-estate developer. He had been tortured and stabbed to death.

Miglin's car, a green Lexus, was missing and showed up at the scene of the next victim. Cemetery caretaker William Reese was shot to death in Pennsville, N.J. In the Lexus was a picture of someone who knows Cunanan, the charges filed Wednesday said.

Missing was Reese's pickup truck, which turned up Tuesday in a Miami Beach parking ramp near Versace's home. In the truck, investigators found Cunanan's passport and a check from Bank of America in his name.

The pickup no longer had New Jersey plates, instead it had a single South Carolina plate. The man who owned the plate didn't report it stolen, but a Florence County officer said that wasn't unusual.

"A lot of people think they just lose them," said Lt. Johnnie Abraham. "Sometimes people's tags just vibrate off. They just go and get another one."

It was unclear how long the truck had been parked at the garage. The manager, Frank Pintado, said the two-part ticket for parking there—one part is kept by the garage and the other by the customer—was left in the truck. It would have the time and the date on it, but Pintado said he didn't see it because everything was sealed from the time police discovered the truck Tuesday morning.

Bloody clothes were found near the truck. It's not known whether any weapons were found.

Source: *Star Tribune*, 17 July 1997. Reprinted with permission of the *Star Tribune*, Minneapolis-St. Paul.

*The manhunt ended in July in Miami Beach, where Cunanan committed suicide aboard a houseboat.

## Checklist

### *Motor Vehicle Theft*

- Description of vehicle: year, make, color, body type.
- Identification of vehicle: VIN, engine number, license number by state and year.
- Registered owner and legal owner, address, telephone number.
- What were the circumstances of the theft: date and time reported stolen, location of theft? Were doors locked? Key in ignition?
- Was the vehicle insured and by whom?
- Was the vehicle mortgaged and by whom? Are payments current?
- Did anyone have permission to use the vehicle? Have these persons been contacted?
- Was owner arrested for another crime or suspected in a crime?
- Was there any motive for owner to falsely report vehicle stolen?
- Was owner involved in hit-and-run accident or driving while intoxicated?
- Did spouse report vehicle missing?
- What method was used to take the vehicle?
- Has vehicle been recovered? Where?
- Were crimes committed in the area where vehicle was stolen or recovered?
- Was anybody seen near where the vehicle was stolen or found? When? How were they dressed? Approximate age?

- Was vehicle seen on the street with suspects in it? Description of the suspects?
- Anything unusual about the vehicle such as color combination or damage?
- Does owner have any suspects?
- Were police field interrogation cards checked for the day of theft and the days after to determine if vehicle had been stopped by police for other reasons?
- Were pawnshops checked for items that were in the vehicle?
- If motorcycle, were motorcycle shops checked?
- If truck, have there been other truck thefts in area or labor problems?
- Is the vehicle suspected of going interstate? Was FBI notified?
- Has check been made with National Insurance Crime Bureau?
- Have junkyards been checked?
- Have known auto thieves been checked to see if they were in the area at the time of theft?
- Was check made with motor vehicle department to determine registered owner?

# Application

**A.** On July 2 an internist finished his shift at a Veterans Administration hospital and went to the hospital parking lot to find that his TR4A was missing. He called the local police, but they refused to come, saying that because the theft occurred on federal property, it was the FBI's problem. The doctor called the FBI, which first said it would not investigate a car theft unless the car was transported out of the state. The doctor's insurance company finally convinced the FBI to investigate the theft, which it did. Two days later, local police in a town 529 miles away discovered the TR4A abandoned in the parking lot at a race track. Because the car had been hot-wired, they assumed it was stolen and made inquiries to the state department of vehicle registration as to its ownership. The car was towed to a local storage garage. When it was learned who owned the TR4A, local police contacted the police in the doctor's city. Because that police department had no record of a stolen TR4A, officers there assumed the message was in error. It was a holiday weekend, they were busy and the matter was dropped. Eight months later the storage garage called the doctor to ask him when he was coming to get his car.

## Questions

1. What mistakes were made in this incident?
2. Who is primarily to blame for the eight-month delay in returning the car to the owner?

**B.** Samuel Paris parked his 1997 Corvette in front of his home shortly after midnight when he and his wife returned from a party. He locked the car and took the keys with him. He discovered the vehicle missing the following morning about 7:45 A.M. when he was leaving for work. He immediately called the police to report an auto theft.

## Questions

1. Were his actions correct?
2. What should the police department do upon receiving the call?
3. What should the officer who is assigned to the case do?

1. How do you identify a stolen vehicle so that you can prove in court that it was in fact stolen?

2. What evidence do you need to charge a suspect with unauthorized use of a motor vehicle? Embezzlement of a vehicle?

3. Where would you start looking for a stolen vehicle that was used in a crime? For joyriding? For transportation? For stripping and sale of parts?

4. How large a problem is auto theft in your community? Are such thefts thoroughly investigated?

5. What agencies besides local police are involved in investigating auto thefts, and under what circumstances can their services be requested? Who would be contacted in your area? What services can they perform?

6. How do juvenile and professional auto thieves differ with regard to motive and type of vehicle stolen? Are there different methods for locating each?

7. A CD player has been taken from a stolen motor vehicle abandoned on a city street. Is this burglary or larceny in your state? Does it make any difference if the car door was closed but unlocked?

8. Does the value of the stolen vehicle affect the charge made? The punishment?

9. What other crimes are frequently committed along with motor vehicle theft?

10. What measures are taken in your community to prevent motor vehicle theft? What else might be done?

# References

Ferguson, Byron E. "Porcelain Chips: An Auto Theft Innovation." *Law and Order,* September 1990, pp. 154–155.

Hildreth, Reed. "The CAT Program." *Law and Order,* May 1990, pp. 92–93.

Kime, Roy C. "Section-by-Section Analysis of the 'Anti-Car Theft Act of 1992.'" *The Police Chief,* 1993, pp. 25–26.

Nilson, Dennis W. "Vehicle Recovery: New Technology Captures Chicago's Attention." *Law and Order,* February 1990, pp. 36–37.

Oliver, Will. "Tracking Stolen Cars with LoJack." *Law Enforcement Technology,* February 1995, pp. 50–52.

"Revoking a License to Steal." *Instant Evidence,* No. 10, Fall 1995, pp. 6–7.

Ruotolo, Andrew K., Jr. "MDTs Aid Auto Theft Task Force." *The Police Chief,* September 1992, pp. 29–34.

Stern, Gary M. "Effective Strategies to Minimize Auto Thefts and Break-Ins." *Law and Order,* July 1990, pp. 65–69.

# Chapter 17

# Arson

## Introduction

ARSON IS ONE OF THE OLDEST CRIMES KNOWN. IT HAS PROBABLY been practiced since soon after fire was discovered. Arson is a major crime that threatens life and causes immense property losses. In October 1978, Congress mandated that the FBI reclassify arson as a Part One Index Crime in its Uniform Crime Reporting Program, effective March 1979.

According to the 1995 FBI *Uniform Crime Reports,* 94,926 arson offenses were reported, a decrease of 4 percent from 1994 figures. Structures were the most frequent target of arsonists, representing 53 percent. Motor vehicles, trailers, crops and timber represented 22 percent. Residential property involved 60 percent of reported offenses. Sixteen percent of arsons were cleared by arrest of 20,000 persons; 47 percent involved persons under 18 years of age; 68 percent were under 25; 84 percent of those arrested were males; 74 percent were white.

**Arson** is the malicious, willful burning of a building or property.

Arson is a combination crime against persons and property. It is difficult to prove because in many fires the evidence is consumed and there are few witnesses. Few police officers or investigators have extensive training in investigating arson, and they are often confused by the complications involved in securing evidence and cooperating with other agencies.

Many sources gather statistics on fires, including the FBI, the National Fire Protection Association, insurance companies, state fire marshals' offices, state crime bureaus, sheriffs' offices and local police and fire departments. Although statistics vary, all reporting agencies agree that arson is a major problem. Woodfork (1990, p. 30) writes that property losses range from $1.5 billion to $5 billion annually and that more than a thousand Americans die in arson fires each year. Slahor (1991, p. 89) cites a Department of Justice study that states: "Arson, next to war, is humanity's costliest act of violence."

This chapter begins with a classification of arson crimes, the elements of the crime of arson and the Model Arson Law. This is followed by a description of the typical arsonist. Then the need for police and fire department cooperation is described, as well as the availability of other sources of assistance in investigating arson incidents. Next is a discussion of the special problems in investigating arson, the preliminary investigation and the types of search warrants that might be required. Challenges presented by investigating vehicle arson and prosecuting arsonists is the next area covered. The chapter concludes with an in-depth look at investigating explosions caused by bombs.

## Classification

Fires are classified as being natural, accidental, criminal (arson), suspicious or of unknown origin.

A *natural fire* is one set intentionally to destroy refuse, weeds or waste products in industrial processes or to provide warmth. It is easy to determine that such fires are natural.

An *accidental fire*, as the name implies, is not intentional. Fires can be accidentally ignited by the heat of the sun's rays, lightning, faulty wiring, leaking gas, a carelessly disposed of cigarette, overheated Christmas tree lights, children playing with matches and many other causes. Arsonists usually try to make their fires appear accidental.

A *criminal fire* (arson) is ignited intentionally and maliciously to destroy property or buildings. Proof must be obtained that the fire was not natural or accidental.

A *suspicious fire* is one suspected to have been arson, even though proof is lacking.

A fire of *unknown origin* is one in which there is no evidence to indicate whether the fire was natural, accidental or criminal. The cause is simply not known.

Fires are presumed natural or accidental unless proven otherwise.

The prosecution has the burden of proving that a fire is not accidental or natural. Because arson cases are hard to prove and require a great deal of work, they are unattractive to prosecutors. Moreover, the prosecutor may feel uneasy with the large amount of expert scientific testimony required.

Exercise caution in investigating fires. The vast majority are not the result of arson. Do not unduly suspect property owners who have already been subjected to fire losses.

## Elements of the Crime: Arson

Under common law, the *crime of arson* was defined as the malicious, willful burning of another's house or outbuilding. It was considered such a serious offense that the penalty was death. Laws have now extended arson to cover other buildings, personal property, crops and the burning of one's own property. As in other crimes, arson laws vary from state to state, but they share some common elements.

---

The elements of the crime of arson include:
- Willful, malicious burning of a building or property.
- Of another, or of one's own to defraud.
- Or causing to be burned, or aiding, counseling or procuring such burning.

---

Attempted arson is also a crime in most states.

**Willful, Malicious Burning of a Building or Property.**   *Willful* means "intentional." If a motive is determined, intent can be proven; therefore, when possible, show motive even if it is not required by law. Merchandise or household goods moved in or out immediately before the fire help to establish motive and intent.

*Malicious* denotes a "spiteful, vindictive desire to harm others." Malice is shown by circumstantial evidence such as statements of ill will, threats against persons or property, a recent increase in insurance coverage or past property burned.

*Burning* is the prime element in the corpus delicti. There must be more than an exposure to heat, although flames need not have been visible nor the property destroyed. Heating to the ignition point is sufficient, even if the fire extinguishes itself.

**Of Another, or of One's Own to Defraud.**   The motive for burning another's property can range from revenge to economic gain. The burning of one's own property, however, is almost always to defraud. Prove the property was insured and show a motive for desiring the insurance money. Copies of the insurance policies obtained from the victim after serving proper notice show if an excessive amount of insurance was taken out, if recent additions or changes were made in the policy or if the insurance was soon to expire. Businesses are sometimes burned because they are failing financially, which can be established by business records or by employee statements.

**Causing to be Burned, or Aiding, Counseling or Procuring the Burning.**   A person who hires a professional ("a torch") to commit arson is also guilty of the crime. Seek evidence connecting this person with the actual arsonist.

*ATF agents search for clues in an arson fire at Mt. Pleasant Baptist Church in Kossuth, Mississippi, 1996.*

### Aggravated and Simple Arson

Some laws categorize arson as either aggravated or simple.

---

**Aggravated arson** is intentionally destroying or damaging a dwelling or other property by means of fire or explosives or other infernal device—creating an imminent danger to life or great bodily harm, which risk was known or reasonably foreseeable to the suspect. **Simple arson** is an intentional destruction by fire or explosives that does not create imminent danger to life or risk of great bodily harm.

---

*Fire* does not require visible burning or an actual flame, but it must involve some extent of burning. *Explosives* include any device, apparatus or equipment that causes damage by combustion or explosion such as time bombs, Molotov cocktails, missiles, plastic explosives, grenades and dynamite.

*Destruction or damage* does not require total destruction or consummation. Damage that affects the value or usefulness of the property is sufficient.

*Creating an imminent danger to life or risk of great bodily harm* is assumed whenever the structure burned is a dwelling or is likely to have people within it. People need not be there at the time. *If the danger or risk was known or reasonably foreseeable* means that even if the suspect did not intend to harm anyone, the risk should have been known or reasonably anticipated. If a person dies in a fire set by an arsonist, the death is first-degree murder, an additional offense to be prosecuted.

### Attempted Arson

The elements of attempted arson are the intent to set a fire and some act toward preparing to commit the crime. The intent is normally specific, and the act must be overt. It must be shown that the fire would have occurred except for some intervening cause. Attempted arson also includes placing any combustible or explosive material or device in or near any property with the intent to set fire, to destroy or to otherwise damage property. Putting materials together at a location where they could not cause a fire does not constitute attempted arson.

### Setting Negligent Fires

Setting a negligent fire consists of causing a fire to burn or to get out of control through culpable negligence, creating an unreasonable risk and the likelihood of damage or injury to persons or property. This charge is often brought against people who leave smoldering campfires that cause forest fires.

## The Model Arson Law

The Model Arson Law was written and promoted in the 1920s by the National Fire Protection Association. The latest revision is included in *The Fire Almanac,* published by the same organization yearly. Many states do not classify fires as aggravated or simple but instead have adopted the Model Arson Law, which specifies four degrees of arson:

---

The Model Arson Law divides arson into the following degrees:
- First-degree: burning of dwellings.
- Second-degree: burning of buildings other than dwellings.
- Third-degree: burning of other property.
- Fourth-degree: attempting to burn buildings or property.

---

The Model Arson Law includes within each degree not only the actual act but also anyone who aids, counsels or procures the act.

## The Arsonist

In arson, unlike other crimes, the victim is often the prime suspect. Motivation, although it need not be proved, has great significance in arson investigations.

### Motivation

Common motives include revenge, spite, jealousy; vandalism and malicious mischief; crime concealment and diversionary tactics; profit and insurance fraud; intimidation, extortion and sabotage; and psychiatric afflictions, pyromania, alcoholism and mental retardation.

*Revenge, spite and jealousy* motivate jilted lovers, feuding neighbors, disgruntled employees, quarreling spouses, people who feel cheated or abused and people who feel racial or religious hostility. In some parts of the country, especially in rural areas, disagreements often result in the burning of homes or barns.

*Vandalism and malicious mischief* are frequent motives for juveniles who burn property merely to relieve boredom or as a general protest against authority. Many fires in schools, abandoned autos, vacant buildings and trash containers are caused by this type of arsonist.

The majority of those arrested for arson are juveniles. Children who set fires usually fall into three categories ("Majority of Those Arrested . . .," 1995, p. 8):

- Those too young to understand the consequences.
- Those who know what fire can do but are curious.
- Those—typically older—who intend to do harm.

*Crime concealment and diversionary tactics* motivate criminals to set fires to destroy evidence of a crime or to destroy evidence connecting them to the crime. In murder cases, arson can be used to attempt to make it impossible to identify the victim. In other cases, people set fires to destroy records containing evidence of embezzlement, forgery or fraud. Arson is also used to divert attention while a criminal commits another crime or covers his or her escape.

*Profit and insurance fraud* are frequent motives for arson. A business person may find him- or herself in financial straits and decide that the easiest way out is to burn the business and collect the insurance. Such financial problems might stem from a large inventory of unsalable seasonal goods, an outmoded plant that needs remodeling, foreclosure of a mortgage, adverse market conditions, poor management or any number of circumstances. Some people overinsure property and then burn it, collecting far more than the property was worth. For example, a St. Louis property owner received more than $415,000 in insurance payments for 54 fires occurring within a two-year period. In large cities, professional arson rings operate to defraud insurance companies of millions of dollars. One such ring included 57 persons who were charged with 186 counts of arson.

Other methods of obtaining profit have used arson to stimulate business, to eliminate business rivals or to secure employment. For example, security guards, firefighters or police officers might set fires to obtain a job.

*Intimidation, extortion and sabotage* are motives of striking workers and employers to apply pressure during a strike. Criminals, especially mobsters, use arson to intimidate witnesses and to extort money.

*Psychiatric afflictions, pyromania, alcoholism and mental retardation* account for many other fires. Pyromaniacs start fires because of an irresistible urge or passion for fire. Some derive sexual satisfaction from watching fires. Arsonists have been known to start fires to help put the fire out, thus becoming heroes. Others become arsonists to show power over their environment or because they believe they are acting with divine guidance.

Several studies reveal the same pattern: revenge is the most common motive. Nonetheless, many arson investigators believe insurance fraud is the most prevalent motive for arson. It may be that arson intended to defraud is often hired out to a professional who is less likely to get caught and who, if apprehended, is more likely to have better legal counsel.

Krzeszowski (1993, pp. 42–47) notes that fire is a tool to accomplish a specific goal and that firesetters' motives fall into two categories, rational and irrational:

### Rational Motives
- Hatred (the most common motive); for example, revenge fires.
- Direct economic gain (the second-most common motive); for example, to collect insurance.
- Indirect economic gain; for example, to sabotage a competitor's business or to break a lease.
- Terrorism; for example, to extort payment from or to intimidate a victim.

■ Vanity; for example, setting a fire so that one can discover and/or extinguish it and thus become a hero.

■ Concealment; for example, to destroy criminal evidence.

### Irrational Motives

■ Pyromania; that is, the uncontrollable urge to light fires.

■ Psychopathology; for example, setting a fire on the instruction of "voices" or for use in a "purification" ritual.

■ Sociopathology; that is, in rebellion against rules and symbols of authority.

■ Fascination with fire; typified by the young child who plays with matches or a cigarette lighter.

The professional "torch," the arsonist for hire, is extremely difficult to identify because such individuals have no apparent link to the fire. Because the majority of arson fires are set with a hate motive, one logical place for investigators to begin is with "enemies" of the victim. Krzeszowski (1993, p. 47) suggests that "the professional torch is a classic sociopath, with strong asocial and antisocial hostilities, who is motivated by financial gain. Among professional torches, fire-setting skills run the gamut from poor to excellent."

Also under suspicion, however, is the victim in many instances. A guilty victim typically has an iron-clad alibi. Also to be considered is the unintentional fire setter, that is, the individual who accidentally sets a fire and then is too embarrassed to admit it or who fears that insurance may not cover the loss if the accident is made known.

Krzeszowski (1993, p. 44) points out: "True pyromaniacs are rare. Nationally, they account for only about 3 percent of all incendiary fires. However, once a pyromaniac moves into an area, he or she may account for up to 90 percent of the fires in that region."

### Serial Arsonists

The National Center for the Analysis of Violent Crime (NCAVC) makes a distinction among three kinds of compulsive firesetters: mass, spree and serial (Icove and Horbert, 1990, pp. 46–47):

*Mass* arson involves one offender who sets three or more fires at the same location during a limited period of time. An example could include an offender who, while confined to a jail, sets several fires in his cell.

A *spree* arsonist sets fires at three or more separate locations with no emotional cooling-off period between them. Examples include arsonists in Detroit, Michigan, who roam the city during "Hell Night" setting numerous fires.

The *serial* arsonist is involved in three or more separate firesetting episodes, with a characteristic cooling-off period between the fires.

Hinds (1994, pp. 31–32) describes how forensic artists helped apprehend Paul Kenneth Keller, one of the worst serial arsonists in United States history. Keller committed arsons over a four-county area in Washington state causing more than $22 million in losses. ATF agents used forensic artists who did composite drawings of the arsonists based on witness information assembled from several fires Keller had started. The artists also sketched physical evidence such as tire tread impressions left at the scene.

Computer software can play a pivotal role in identifying serial arsonists by allowing investigators to organize and manage tips, evidence and other information related to related fires efficiently. Such case management can cut investigations by months ("Managing an Information Overload," 1993, p. 5).

Police and fire agencies work together to study serial-arsonist behavior patterns and motivations through the NCAVC at the FBI Academy. Research is being directed at determining these arsonists' motives, common traits, ignition techniques, most frequent targets, methods of evading detection and any abnormal behavioral characteristics. Until research reveals that special investigative approaches are necessary, the fires set by serial arsonists will continue to be investigated by using the same techniques as for fires set by nonserial arsonists.

### Profiling

Slahor (1991, p. 88) reports that the factors used by the NCAVC program in profiling arsonists include age, gender, race, marital status, intelligence, scholastic achievement, lifestyle, rearing, social adjustment, personality characteristics, demeanor, appearance, emotional adjustment, mental state, occupational history, work habits, socioeconomic status and locational relationship between residence and crime scenes.

Profiling research shows that the majority of arsonists are male. Motive is also important in the profile. According to Slahor (1991, p. 88):

> About 95% of the time vandalism arson is caused by juveniles in groups due to peer pressure. Generally, the juveniles are from lower middle class areas, both parents are at home, and the crime is committed in the morning or early afternoon during the school year. Not much planning or preparation takes place and available materials are used for the fire.

Such fires differ greatly from those committed for revenge. In revenge fires, according to Slahor:

> The perpetrators tend to be adults, the crime targets both people and property, it takes place in the afternoon, evening or early morning hours mainly on weekends and during the autumn and winter seasons. There is a use of flammable liquids and materials on hand, and about half of the perpetrators used drugs or alcohol just before committing the offense.

## Police and Fire Department Cooperation

Arson is investigated by many agencies with joint jurisdiction: state fire marshals, state police, county sheriffs and local police and fire departments. In addition, insurance investigators often become involved.

Lack of trained personnel to investigate arson is a major problem in both police and fire departments, except in large cities that have their own arson investigation squads. Although arson is a crime, police tend to give it low priority, feeling that the fire department should investigate. However, many firefighters are volunteers who are not trained in arson investigation. Many full-time departments do not train their personnel to investigate arson. Rural areas and cities of up to 75,000 in population rely heavily on the state fire marshal's office, which usually does not have enough staff to conduct full investigations throughout the state. State fire marshals' offices can help local police and fire agencies by providing advice, coordinating activities and supplying information on suspect profiles. They cannot, however, assume full responsibility for the investigation. Even fire departments that provide training in arson detection seldom include training on the criminal procedures needed to prosecute arson.

Attitudes about the responsibility for investigating arson vary. Some fire departments feel arson investigation and prosecution are their responsibility; others feel just as strongly that arson is a police matter. Still others feel that fire personnel should investigate the fire and obtain evidence and that the police should conduct the criminal investigation. This approach would seem logical.

---

Logic suggests that the fire department should work to detect arson and determine the fire's point of origin and probable cause, whereas the police department should investigate arson and prepare the case for prosecution.

---

"Fighting Fires with Cooperation" (1995, p. 3) summarizes the strengths law enforcement and the fire department bring to a fire scene investigation:

On the police side, they are the investigators. They know how to interview people. They know how to conduct an investigation and put one together very quickly. They know the streets. As the investigation continues, they are trained to work on it over the long-term and to uncover the motive of a crime. At the fire department, they are the cause and origin people. They're highly trained, skilled and equipped to identify how a fire was set, and to collect the evidence needed to support that theory.

### Fire Department Expertise

Recognizing factors concerning smoke and fire conditions, detecting arson evidence and determining the cause of a fire are specific areas of expertise for the fire department. The fire department investigates many accidental and natural fires. To give this responsibility to the police department would be an unnecessary duplication of skill, especially because only a small number of fires are due to arson.

Trained fire personnel know about buildings, how fires are started and the various components necessary for ignition. Fire marshals also have extralegal powers to summon witnesses, subpoena records and take statements under oath that police officers do not have.

Moreover, fire personnel may enter buildings after a fire without a warrant, a benefit to criminal investigations. They also work closely with insurance companies, and they are apt to recognize persons frequently present at fires.

The fire department's basic role is fire investigation and arson detection, not arson investigation. Once the cause of the fire is determined to be arson, the police are notified and it becomes a joint investigation.

### Police Department Expertise

Police on patrol duty and investigators, through intelligence files, are likely to know possible arson suspects. Field interview cards can include names of persons present in an area where arson fires are being set. Specialized techniques such as interviewing witnesses and interrogating suspects are normal police operations. Moreover, police have contacts with informants and the power of arrest.

### Coordinating Efforts

Regardless of the actual agency assigned to an arson investigation, someone must be in charge of coordinating the efforts of everyone involved. A full-time arson squad has the potential for conducting the best arson investigation. The next-best arrangement is to have a well-trained arson investigator from local jurisdictions or the state fire marshal's office. However, police personnel trained in criminal investigation working with fire personnel trained in arson detection can do an effective job if mutual agreement is reached as to who is in charge.

## Other Sources of Assistance in Investigating Arson

Other sources of assistance in investigating arson are the news media, insurance companies and arson task forces.

### News Media

One source of assistance frequently overlooked is the news media. The media can publish profiles of arsonists and seek the public's help in identifying them. They may also have photographs or videotapes of in-progress fires that can be extremely useful in investigations.

### Insurance Companies

Insurance companies can be very helpful in an arson investigation. According to Goodnight (1990, p. 53): "Conducted properly, the insurance investigation can prove valuable to the criminal investigator since, in many cases, the insurance investigation will develop information not readily available to law enforcement." Insurance companies usually request the insured to sign a release authorizing the company to obtain private records such as income tax returns, financial audits, bank accounts, credit reports, telephone records and utility company records. Without this release, obtaining such records is a long, complex process. Woodfork (1990, p. 33) suggests: "Most insurance companies realize that the flow of information is a 'one-way street,' but they also realize the importance of the information to the success of the criminal investigation and eventual prosecution, which may lead in turn to relief from their civil claims liability."

Private insurance company investigators can assist fire and police efforts in investigating fire losses. Many insurance companies have full-time fire loss investigators, whereas many smaller fire and police agencies do not. The end goal is the same for both—obtaining the truth. For fire and police authorities, the goal is to locate the suspect. If the suspect in a fire-for-profit is arrested, it resolves fire loss problems for the insurance company. In a fire-for-profit investigation, the search for a suspect is limited in most cases to the owner or to individuals in collusion with or under the direction of the owner.

In most criminal cases, on the other hand, locating the suspect is much more difficult. The owner obviously must work with the fire, police and insurance company to collect the insurance money. Consequently, interviewing and interrogating efforts are much enhanced. Background checks, bank and credit inquiries and financial status are also easier to verify.

Insurance investigators have the additional advantage of being able to enter the fire scene without a warrant in their efforts to examine the damage and to determine the cause of the fire.

Further, several index bureaus gather insurance-claim information in attempting to determine if the same claim is being made to more than one company or if a pattern of claims exists. Law enforcement investigators can benefit from information gathered by these bureaus as well. Most states provide limited civil immunity to insurance companies that provide information to law enforcement agencies in their investigations.

### Arson Task Forces

The development of arson task forces made up of fire and police department personnel; community leaders; insurance representatives; city, county and district attorneys; federal agency personnel; and others has a powerful impact on coordinating existing forces and developing new sources for combating arson and arson-related problems in any community, county or state. Arson has the lowest clearance by arrest of the major crimes, primarily due to inadequate training for fire and police department personnel, the difficulty of locating and preserving evidence and a lack of coordination of personnel of the various organizations involved.

## Special Problems in Investigation

---

Special problems in investigating arson include:
- Coordinating efforts with the fire department and others.
- Difficulty in determining if a crime has, in fact, been committed.
- Finding physical evidence, most of which is destroyed by the fire.
- Finding witnesses.
- Determining if the victim is a suspect.

---

Investigating arson often requires even more persistence, thoroughness and attention to minute details than do other crimes. It is a difficult crime to investigate because there are seldom witnesses and because the evidence needed to prove that a crime has been committed is usually consumed in the fire. Moreover, arson is an easy crime to write off without being publicly criticized because the victim and the suspect are often the same person. However, the innocent victim of arson is frequently frustrated by the lack of evidence and witnesses and by the police's inability to prove that a crime was committed.

## The Preliminary Investigation

The fire department, not the police department, usually receives the initial fire call unless the departments have a joint dispatcher or are merged into a public safety department. Fire personnel make out the reports and forward them to the state fire marshal. Insurance companies are also represented, and their efforts are coordinated with those of fire and police personnel.

The scene of a fire is often dirty, messy and complicated, making it difficult to obtain evidence of possible arson. An arson scene may be the most contaminated crime scene you will encounter. As described by the Law Enforcement Assistance Administration:

> No other type of crime scene except bombing is characterized by as much destruction and disorder as arson. Investigators must search through piles of debris and rubble, often on their hands and knees. Ashes, soot, and char make fire scenes filthy and malodorous. . . .
>
> The fire scene search is further aggravated by water and foam remaining from the extinguishment. The scene may be a quagmire, making the rubble wet and heavy to move out of the way. Plaster fallen from walls and ceilings mixes with the water, forming a grey slush retarding the investigator's movements. In cold weather, there is the additional pressure of completing the work before everything freezes and the investigation is severely impeded.
>
> The fire scene may be dangerous to work in because of the imminent collapse of upper parts of the structure. It may be exposed to the elements, making work in foul weather difficult and unpleasant.
>
> In addition to the destruction of the fire, there are further problems caused by firefighter mop-up and salvage operations immediately following the fire. The mop-up process involves finding and eliminating any smoldering spots that might rekindle the fire. This involves tearing open walls, ceilings, roofs, and other partitions, and throwing objects like mattresses and sofas out of the building. The salvage process involves removing any salvageable items, such as furnishings or machinery, to a safe place and covering them from the elements. This process hampers efforts to reconstruct the fire scene and the sequence of events that led to the arson. . . .
>
> The sheer physical effort involved in the investigation is usually much greater for arson than for other crimes, and the number of manhours required is greater. Fire scene searches cannot be avoided, particularly in view of the general lack of witnesses in arson. The investigator must often put together a complex chain of circumstantial evidence to establish arson and implicate a suspect. Any physical evidence may be destroyed by the fire or lost in the debris.
>
> With obstacles such as these, it is little wonder that many fires are never investigated.

Although the fire department is responsible for establishing that arson has occurred, you must verify those findings by understanding what distinguishes an accidental fire from arson and by knowing what evidence and information is available for proving the elements of the crime.

### The Fire Triangle

The fire triangle is a basic concept critical to an arson investigation.

---

The **fire triangle** consists of three elements necessary for a substance to burn: air, fuel and heat. In arson one or more of these elements is usually present in abnormal amounts for the structure.

---

Extra amounts of *air* or oxygen can result from opened windows or doors, pried-open vents or holes knocked in walls. Because firefighters often chop holes in structures, determine whether any such openings were made by the firefighters or by someone else. *Fuel* can be added by piling up newspapers, excelsior or other combustible materials found at or brought to the scene. Gasoline, kerosene and other accelerants add sufficient *heat* to the fire to cause the desired destruction after it has been ignited.

## Arson Indicators

### Accelerants.

---

Evidence of **accelerants,** especially gasoline, is a primary form of physical evidence at an arson scene.

---

Most arson cases involve the use of a flammable liquid, and in 80 percent of these cases, it is gasoline. Other accelerants commonly used are kerosene, charcoal lighter, paint thinner and lacquer solvent. Gasoline is, by far, the most frequently found fire accelerant, perhaps because it is easily obtained and widely known to arsonists or perhaps because its familiar odor makes it easier for investigators to detect.

Look for residues of liquid fire accelerants on floors, carpets and soil because the accelerants, being liquid, run to the lowest level. In addition, these areas often have the lowest temperatures during the fire and may not have enough oxygen to support complete combustion of the accelerant. Accelerants may seep through porous or cracked floors to underlying soil that has excellent retention properties for flammable liquids. Accelerants can also be found on the clothes and shoes of the suspect if apprehended. Fire accelerants can also be identified at the scene either by your own sense of smell or by using portable equipment that detects residues of flammable liquids.

*Olfactory detection,* the sensitivity of the human nose to gasoline vapor, is ineffective if the odor is masked by another strong odor such as that of burned debris. Moreover, it is often inconvenient or impossible to sniff for accelerant odors along floors or in recessed areas.

*Catalytic combustion detectors* are the most common type of flammable vapor detector used by arson investigators. Commonly known as a *sniffer,* a *combustible gas indicator,* an *explosimeter* or a *vapor detector,* this detector is portable, moderately priced and fairly simple to operate. Basically, vapor samples are pumped over a heated, platinum-plated wire coil that causes any combustible gas present to oxidize. The heat from the oxidation raises the coil's electrical resistance, and this change is measured electrically.

Although fire accelerants are the most frequent type of evidence submitted to laboratories for analysis (80 percent), explosives (13 percent) and incendiary devices (4 percent) are also frequently submitted.

**Igniters.** **Igniters** are substances or devices used to start fires. Most common are matches. To be carrying matches is not damaging evidence unless some have been removed from the book or box and the parts found at an arson scene match those found in the suspect's possession.

---

Common igniters include matches; candles; cigars; cigarettes; cigarette lighters; electrical, mechanical and chemical devices; and explosives.

---

Electrical devices left in the "on" position, kerosene-soaked papers in waste baskets, time fuses, shorted light switches, magnifying glasses, matches tied around a lighted cigarette and numerous other igniters have been used to commit arson.

Candles are often used in arsons because they give the suspect time to leave the scene. The average candle burns about 30 to 45 minutes per inch, depending on its size, shape, composition and the amount of air in the room. Tapered candles burn faster at the top and slower toward the base. The arsonist may control the length of time by cutting off part of the candle before lighting it. The candle can be set in a material that will ignite once the candle burns down, or the hot wax may be allowed to drip onto a surface to start a fire. The candle's flame can also be used to ignite other materials in the room.

Regardless of whether arsonists use direct or delayed ignition, they usually plan for the fire to consume the igniter; however, this often does not happen. Moreover, in their haste to leave the scene, arsonists may drop parts of the igniter in an area unaffected by the fire. Any igniter not normally present at the location is evidence.

**Burn Indicators.** **Burn indicators** are visible evidence of the effects of heating or partial burning. They indicate various aspects of a fire such as rate of development, temperature, duration, time of occurrence, presence of flammable liquids and points of origin. Interpreting burn indicators is a primary means of determining the causes of fires.

---

Common burn indicators include alligatoring, crazing, the depth of char, lines of demarcation, sagged furniture springs and spalling.

---

**Alligatoring** is the checking of charred wood that gives it the appearance of alligator skin. Large, rolling blisters indicate rapid, intense heat. Small, flat alligatoring indicates slow, less-intense heat.

**Crazing** is the formation of irregular cracks in glass due to rapid, intense heat, possibly caused by a fire accelerant.

The **depth of char,** or how deeply wood is burned, indicates the length of burn and the fire's point of origin. Use a ruler to measure depth of char.

A **line of demarcation** is a boundary between charred and uncharred material. A puddle-shaped line of demarcation on floors or rugs can indicate the use of a liquid fire accelerant. In a cross-section of wood, a sharp, distinct line of demarcation indicates a rapid, intense fire.

Sagged furniture springs usually occur when a fire originates inside the cushions of upholstered furniture (as from a lighted cigarette rolling behind a cushion) or when a fire is intensified by an accelerant.

**Spalling** is the breaking off of surface pieces of concrete or brick due to intense heat. Brown stains around the spall indicate use of an accelerant.

**Point of Origin.** Knowing the fire's point of origin helps to establish how the fire spread and whether it followed a normal burning pattern. The more extensive the destruction, the more difficult it is to determine the fire's point of origin.

---

The point of origin is established by finding the area with the deepest char, alligatoring and, usually, the greatest destruction. More than one point of origin indicates arson.

---

*Arson investigations are extremely challenging. The alligatoring at this fire scene will provide important information to the investigator.*

Incendiary (igniter) evidence might be discovered at the point of origin. In addition, information from witnesses who saw the fire can establish where the flames began.

### Burning Pattern.

Fires normally burn upward, not outward. They are drawn toward ventilation and follow fuel paths.

Given adequate ventilation, a fire will burn upward. If a door or window is open, it will be drawn toward that opening. If the arsonist places a path of flammable liquid, the fire will follow that path, known as a **trailer.** Such trailers can be made of paper, hay, flammable compounds or any substance that burns readily, and they result in an abnormal pattern. The char marks will follow the trailer's path. Areas of uneven burning can also indicate the presence of an incendiary or that a great amount of flammable material was already at the scene.

### Appearance of Collapsed Walls.
Notice how walls seem to have collapsed, especially if you smell gas. Lighter gases tend to explode walls outward from the top of the room; heavier gases explode walls out from the bottom of the room. Fast-exploding gases such as hydrogen, acetylene or butane give the appearance of the walls caving in. If odors or the walls' appearance suggests gas as the igniter or accelerator, determine if the gas is normally on the premises.

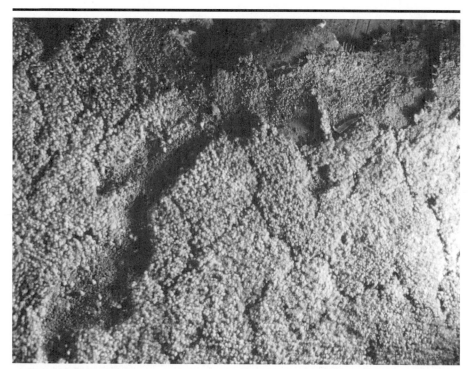

*A photograph of a line of demarcation, seen in this carpet, is important evidence in an arson investigation.*

**Smoke Color.** Generally, blue smoke results from burning alcohol; white smoke from burning vegetable compounds, hay or phosphorous; yellow or brownish yellow smoke from film, nitric acid, sulfur, hydrochloric acid or smokeless gunpowder; and black smoke from petroleum or petroleum products.

Notice the smoke's color if the fire is still in progress. If it has been put out when you arrive, ask the firefighters or witnesses what color the smoke was. Determine if substances likely to produce smoke of that color were on the premises before the fire.

**Summary of Arson Indicators.**

Arson is likely in fires that:
- Have more than one point of origin.
- Deviate from normal burning patterns.
- Show evidence of trailers.
- Show evidence of having been accelerated.
- Produce odors or smoke of a color associated with substances not normally present at the scene.
- Indicate that an abnormal amount of air, fuel or heat was present.
- Reveal evidence of incendiary igniters at the point of origin.

Professional arsonists use a variety of methods to ignite fires, including the following:

Investigating
Crimes against
Property

*Point of origin. This church arson fire was started by two juveniles using altar candles and caused $80,000 damage.*

■ Connecting magnesium rods to timed detonators and placing them in a building's electrical system. The rods burn with extreme intensity and cause a fire that looks as though it was caused by faulty wiring.

■ Connecting a timed explosive charge on one or more barrels of gasoline or other highly flammable liquid. This method is often used when large areas such as warehouses are to be burned.

■ Pouring acid onto key support points in steel-structured buildings to make certain the building will collapse during the fire.

### Photographing and Videotaping an Arson Fire

"A Report From the Smoldering Front Lines" (1995, p. 2) states:

> One of the biggest tools an arson investigator has is photography. Pictures play an important role in recording evidence. They can be helpful in acquiring warrants. And they play an invaluable part in the prosecution of arsonists. . . .
> Many times things we missed in the heat of the investigation are only obvious in retrospect.

Pictures of a fire in progress show the smoke's color and its origination as well as the size of the fire at different points and times. Pictures are especially useful if there appears to be acceleration of the fire at a specific time that would indicate arson or the presence of highly combustible substances. Many fire departments take such in-progress photographs. Smaller departments may seek help from television or newspaper photographers who may take pictures that can be excellent investigative assists. Photographs or videotapes of the fire scene are also ideal to show the judge and jury.

Pictures taken of people at the fire scene might reveal the presence of a known arsonist, or pictures may show an individual who repeatedly appears in photos taken at fires and is, therefore, an arson suspect.

After the fire, take enough pictures to show the entire scene in detail. Start with the outside of the structure, showing all entries and exits. Also show if obstructions were placed in front of windows to prevent seeing inside the building. Persons familiar with the structure can review the pictures for anything out of the ordinary.

Take inside pictures to show the extent of burning. These will prove the corpus delicti. Take close-up pictures of any extra papers, rags, gas cans or other suspicious substances as well as any occurrence of alligatoring and any deep charring. Take pictures at each stage of the search to show the point of origin, the nature of the burning and the direction and speed of the fire's spread.

## Physical Evidence

Preserving evidence is a major problem because much of the evidence is very fragile. Follow carefully the procedures described in Chapter 5. Use disposable cellulose sponges to sop up accelerants for transfer to a container. Use hypodermic or cooking syringes to suck up accelerants between boards or crevices. Sift ashes to detect small objects such as the timing device from an igniter.

Incendiary evidence at the point of origin can be part of a candle, an empty flammable liquid container, excessive amounts of unburned newspaper folded together or a number of unburned matches.

Paper exposed to high temperatures and sufficient air burns with little ash to examine. However, with a limited supply of air, only partial combustion occurs, leaving charred paper evidence that can be collected for laboratory examination. Paper in a fireplace or stove may be only partially burned, even if the building was totally consumed. These papers may provide a motive for the arson. If the paper is not destroyed, the laboratory may be able to recover any messages on it.

Hartnett (1990, p. 20) stresses: "The analysis of physical evidence and the application of the forensic sciences and identification technology are essential to solving bombing and arson cases nationwide." An important step in an arson investigation is identifying potential accelerants at a fire scene. The accepted method of doing so is using gas chromatography with a flame ionization detector (GC-FID). According to Hartnett, GC-FID can make the identification in 95 percent of the cases. He cites the following example (p. 26):

In April 1988, firefighters responded to the scene of a fire at a printing business in Flowood, Mississippi. The origin-and-cause investigation conducted by ATF, the Mississippi State Fire Marshal's Office and the Flowood police and fire departments revealed that the fire was an arson. Samples gathered at the scene were forwarded to the ATF laboratory, where forensic examiners attempted to correctly identify potential accelerants. The chemists took known samples of chemicals used only in the printing process and compared them to accelerants detected in samples of carpet removed from a burn pattern in the building, and found that they matched. As a result of the investigative efforts of the various agencies and the forensic examinations, five defendants pled guilty to committing the arson. A total of $40,000 in fines was levied. In addition, prison sentences ranging from 15 months to 17.5 years were rendered.

### Using K–9s in Arson Investigations

Dogs have been found to be of great assistance in arson investigation. Connecticut's K–9 accelerant-detection program, for example, is the result of collaboration of the ATF, the New Haven County State's Attorney's Office, the State Police Science Laboratory, the Emergency Services Division Canine Unit and the Bureau of the State Fire Marshal. Their first dog, Mattie, was trained to detect extremely small quantities of highly diluted flammable and combustible liquids including paint remover, lacquer thinner, charcoal lighter fluid, paint thinner, kerosene, naphtha, acetone, dry gas, heptone, gasoline, number 2 fuel, diesel fuel, gum turpentine, Heritage lamp oil, transmission fluid, octane and Jet-A-Fuel. As noted by Berluti (1990, p. 41):

> Hydrocarbon detectors are sensitive to gasoline components in the parts-per-million (ppm) range, but the dog demonstrated that her detection limits exceeded that range, consistently locating samples as small in volume as 10 microliters of 87 percent evaporated gasoline.

Mattie is now a lab-certified accelerant-detection canine. She helps detect accelerants at fire scenes and can also search a crowd for possible suspects, search a suspect's clothing and vehicle for the presence of accelerants and search areas for accelerant containers.

### Evidence on the Suspect, at the Residence or in the Vehicle

If you have a suspect, look for any burns he or she may have received while setting the fire. The suspect may have scorched hair, torn clothing, stains, cuts and other injuries, or his or her clothing or shoes may have traces of accelerants. The suspect's residence or vehicle may contain clothes seen at the fire by a witness, objects removed from the scene of the fire or incendiary devices. You may also find insurance documents or business or financial records to provide a motive.

### Observing Unusual Circumstances

Suspicious circumstances implying arson include suddenly emptied premises, the presence of materials not normally part of the business, holes in the plaster or plasterboard that expose the wood, disconnected sprinkler systems, blocked-open interior doors, nailed-open fire doors and any other alterations that would provide more air, heat or fuel to the area.

### Interviewing the Victim, Witnesses and Firefighters

Ask questions such as: How was the fire discovered? Who discovered it? Who were witnesses? What did they see? What color was the smoke and where was it coming from? What direction was the wind? Did the fire appear to suddenly accelerate? Did anything out of the ordinary occur before the fire? Were there any unusual odors? Were the shades up or down? Did any obstructions prevent seeing into the building? Were any suspicious persons or vehicles observed at the scene before, during or after the fire?

Also try to find out who had an opportunity to set the fire and who might benefit from it. Determine who had keys and how the property was normally guarded or protected. Check the victim's financial status and find out how much insurance was carried on the property. Interview the firefighters assigned to the fire and obtain copies of their reports.

## Search Warrants and Fire Investigations

The United States Supreme Court requires a two-step warrant process for investigating fires involving crimes. The initial search may require an **administrative warrant** for searching the premises for cause of fire and origin determination *and* a criminal warrant when evidence of a crime is discovered. Both require probable cause for issuance.

---

An administrative warrant is issued when it is necessary for a government agent to search the premises to determine the cause and origin of the fire. A criminal warrant is issued on probable cause when evidence of a crime is on the premises.

---

Both require an affidavit to be submitted in support of the warrant that states the location and legal description of the property, the purpose (to determine the fire's cause and origin), the area of the search, the time of the search, the use of the building and the measures taken to secure the structure or area of the fire. Searches are limited to the items specified in the warrant. Evidence found may be seized, but once the officers leave after finding the evidence, they must have a criminal warrant to return to the premises for a further search.

As noted by Woods and Wallace (1991, p. 80): "Administrative and criminal law overlap in arson cases due to the nature of the investigation." Administrative warrants are issued to allow civil inspections of private property to determine compliance with city ordinances such as fire codes. The Court has established guidelines for arson investigators. In *Michigan v. Clifford* (1984), the Court held:

If a warrant is necessary, the object of the search determines the type of warrant required. If the primary object is to determine the cause and origin of a fire, an administrative warrant will suffice . . . and if the primary object is to gather evidence of criminal activity, a criminal search warrant may be obtained only on a showing of probable cause to believe that relevant evidence will be found in the place to be searched.

In *Coolidge v. New Hampshire* (1971), the Court held that evidence of criminal activity discovered during a search with a valid administrative warrant may be seized under the plain view doctrine. Any evidence so seized may be used to establish the probable cause needed to obtain a criminal search warrant.

---

Entry to fight a fire requires no warrant. Once in the building, fire officials may remain a reasonable time to investigate the cause of the blaze. After this time, an administrative warrant is needed, as established in *Michigan v. Tyler* (1978).

---

Guidelines on the current legal status of searches conducted during fire investigations include the following:

■ Warrants are not required when an authorized individual consents to the search. The consent must be written and must specify the areas to be searched and the purpose of the search. This consent can be revoked at any time.

■ Warrants are not required when investigators enter under "exigent circumstances," that is, if investigators enter the premises while firefighters are extinguishing the blaze or conducting overhaul. The scope of the search must be limited to determining the cause and origin. If evidence of a crime is discovered, a criminal warrant is required to continue the search.

■ Without consent or an exigency, warrants are required if the premises are subject to a "reasonable expectation of privacy." This includes commercial businesses as well as private residences. Exceptions would be premises that are so utterly devastated by the fire that no expectation of privacy is reasonable or that the property has been abandoned.

■ Evidence of a crime discovered during an administrative search may be seized if in plain view.

■ Once evidence of arson is discovered, the fire's cause and origin are assumed to be known. The scope of the administrative warrant has been exhausted. A criminal warrant is required to continue the search.

When in doubt, obtain a warrant.

## Investigating Vehicle Arson

Although vehicle fires can be caused by accident, vehicles usually do not burn readily. Accelerants are used on many vehicles to accomplish arson. A quart to a half-gallon of flammable liquid is required to cause a major vehicle fire.

---

When investigating vehicle fires, look for evidence of accelerants and determine if the vehicle was insured.

---

Motives for vehicle arson include desire to collect insurance, inability to make needed repairs after an unreported accident, desire to eliminate a loan on the vehicle, desire to cover up another crime committed in or with the vehicle, general dissatisfaction with the vehicle's performance and desire to resolve arguments over the vehicle's use.

A close correlation exists between insurance coverage and vehicle arson; few arsons are committed if there is no insurance coverage. Obtain proof that the vehicle was insured against fire, that the fire was willfully set, that damage resulted and that there was intent to defraud.

## Prosecuting Arsonists

Hartnett (1993, p. 22) reports that some studies indicate that well over 90 percent of all arsonists go unpunished. He notes: "The low arson prosecution and conviction rates are generally attributed to the established reality that arson is a crime of stealth, most often committed without the benefit of witnesses."

The difficulty of investigating arson has been discussed, as has the need for cooperation between law enforcement investigators and firefighters. Equally difficult is prosecution. Cooperative investigation and prosecution are required if the losses from arson are to be stemmed. As noted by Galvin (1990, p. 50):

It is a basic principle of fire science that unless the fire triangle of heat, fuel and oxygen exists, there is no fire. In anti-arson efforts, a variation of the same principle holds true; without the new fire triangle—an investigative trio of police, fire and prosecutor—there is no successful investigation. Creating a comprehensive, cooperative approach to arson investigation in the 1990s will require implementation of this new fire triangle in all of our jurisdictions.

Many prosecutors fail to bring charges because all they have is circumstantial evidence. Hart (1990, p. 35) suggests: "The courts have ruled that circumstantial evidence has the same probative value as direct evidence, but it is up to the investigator to weave the web of circumstantial evidence so tightly that the prosecutor will feel assured in trying the case." Hart offers some examples of circumstantial evidence that often become available during an arson investigation (pp. 34–37):

- Evidence of planning and preknowledge, for example, taking out or increasing insurance coverage, removing items, making off-hand remarks, making unusual changes.
- Evidence of participation, for example, disabling or turning off alarms or sprinkler systems, bringing materials to be used in the arson onto the premises, leaving doors open, rearranging combustibles to provide better fire load.
- Evidence of exclusive access, that is, the owner has the only keys.
- Fire behavior: eliminate accidental or natural causes.
- Evidence of motive.
- False exculpatory statements by the "innocent victim."

Hart (p. 36) points out: "Ninety-nine percent of all arson charges are proved circumstantially."

A specialized area of arson is investigating bombs and bomb threats.

## Bombs and Their Effects

The Bureau of Alcohol, Tobacco and Firearms (ATF) reported that from 1989 to 1993 there were 7,716 bombings, 1,705 attempted bombings, 2,242 incendiary bombings, 4,929 recovered explosives and 2,011 hoax devices in the United States (*Project Response*, no date, p. 3).

As Morris (1996, p. 44) stresses:

For each high-profile incident involving political terrorism, American police officers deal with thousands of bomb incidents each year. From biker gangs and estranged husbands to disgruntled employees and booby-trapped methods, bombs are an ever-present part of law enforcement.

Bombs have become a high-profile—and almost routine—weapon of choice. They generate considerable media attention and are easy, impersonal means of doing a lot of damage without having to be at the scene when terror strikes.

May and Dunn (1996, p. 108) describe how commonplace bombs have become:

On Thursday, October 26, 1995, eight homemade bombs or "grenades" were discovered at St. Xavier High School in Louisville, Kentucky. These bombs were deemed to be well-made, and would have been highly effective had they been detonated.

*A bomb squad robot carries
a pipe bomb out of a house
in Columbus, Ohio, where
Peter Langan, a suspect in a
string of Midwest bank
robberies, was arrested after
a shootout with the FBI and
local police in 1996.*

The students found detailed instructions and components explained and defined on their home computer. Detailed, in-depth instructions are provided to anyone for the fabrication of bombs and explosive devices in clear text on the Internet.

Morris (1996, p. 77) describes the following types of common bombs:*

■ **Dry ice**—All that is involved here is a 2-liter plastic soda bottle, dry ice and some water. Depending on the condition of the bottle, the amount of ice and the weather, the device will explode in three to seven minutes. These dangerous and loud explosions are favorites of youngsters for blowing up trash cans, dumpsters and mailboxes.

■ **Mailbox bomb**—All the bomber needs is a 2-liter bottle of chlorine, a touch of sugar and some water. The somewhat humble explosion can launch an average mailbox 20 feet into the air.

■ **Car bomb**—Traditional bombers have been known to "wire" cars, but according to information on the Internet, a common method of making a car bomb is to wrap a fuse around the car's exhaust manifold. The fuse is ignited by the heat of the manifold, detonating the explosion.

■ **Pipe bomb**—These simple bombs, which are detonated by a spark or some heat source, consist of pipe, end caps and smokeless powder. The pipe bomb that caused two deaths in Atlanta's Centennial Park bombing was laced with nails and other hardware to increase fragmentation.

The bomb, more than any other weapon, makes a person feel vulnerable. Unlike a gun, a bomb doesn't have to be aimed. Unlike poison, it doesn't have to be administered. Bombs are weapons of chance. Victims are simply in the wrong place at the wrong time. Consider: The World Trade Center bombing on Friday, February 26, 1993, in New York resulted in six dead, more than a thousand injured and millions of dollars in property damage ("World Trade Center Bombing," 1993, p. 9).

---

*Reprinted by permission of Bobit Publishing, Redondo Beach, CA.

The April 19, 1995, bombing at the Alfred P. Murrah Federal Building in Oklahoma City claimed 169 lives, caused nearly 500 injuries and resulted in losses totaling $651 million ("Project Response," 1995, p. 18). As noted in "Project Response": "This incident was not just a disaster resulting in mass casualties. Rather, it was a major crime scene—the site of the murder of 169 innocent citizens."

More recently, the pipe bomb that exploded in Atlanta's Centennial Park during the Olympics festivities captured the media's attention.

National attention also has focused on the Unabomber case. After eighteen years of investigation, twenty-three injuries and three deaths, an arrest was made. The trial of the alleged Unabomber, Theodore Kaczynski, is pending as this text goes to press.

## Investigating Explosions Caused by Bombs

From 1940 to 1956 the New York City Police Department was faced with a series of more than thirty bombings by the same individual, who came to be called the "Mad Bomber." The bombings were preceded by written bomb threats that provided extensive information about the bomber. With the help of Dr. James A. Brussel, a New York psychiatrist, three highly trained NYPD investigators were able to identify and apprehend this bomber. Brussel provided the following profile of the Mad Bomber (Chisholm, 1991, p. 42):

> "An unmarried male of Slavic ancestry; well proportioned as to height and weight; between the ages of 40 and 50; a loner who, while not overly antisocial, would be considered reclusive by neighbors; a person with no prior criminal record or reputation; a skilled mechanic with at least a high school education; possibly a resident of Connecticut, who most likely resides with an unmarried female relative; and probably a current or former employee of Consolidated Edison, with a grudge against the company relating to a real or imagined health problem. . . ."

*An ATF agent leans into the crater left by a bomb exploding at the Summer Olympics in Atlanta in 1996. The explosion killed two and injured over 100 people.*

Chisholm continues:

> Police followed a number of leads predicated on Brussel's suggestions and, while several proved to be false trails, within a relatively short time they identified the Mad Bomber as 53-year-old George Metesky, who lived in Waterbury, Connecticut, with his two unmarried sisters.

Neighbors who were interviewed said Metesky was minimally friendly and that they called him "Mr. Think." Meteksy had worked for Consolidated Edison and been injured in an accident on the job. He also suffered from chronic, undiagnosed tuberculosis unrelated to the accident. Psychiatrists who examined him found him to be suffering from acute paranoia. Metesky was committed to a state hospital, where he died in the 1970s.

ATF Special Agent Chisholm (1991, p. 45) notes: "This examination of Dr. Brussel's work in the Metesky case, while dated by time, is not outdated in its concepts. Indeed, it serves as a primer for understanding techniques currently employed on a daily basis by the Arson Bombing Investigative Services (ABIS) sub-unit of the National Center for the Analysis of Violent Crime (NCAVC)."

In July 1989 the small town of Salem, Indiana, received bomb threats that were carried out. Local and federal agents, the state police and the ATF sent officers and agents to help locate the bombs. Ten bombs were found by city residents and search teams during an intensive search, and they were detonated by experts. Chapman (1991, p. 26) contends that if the bombs had exploded, they would have destroyed most of Salem's downtown area.

An intensive investigation was conducted by the Indiana State Police and the ATF. Hundreds of people were interviewed, and two individuals emerged as suspects. The prime suspect was John Hubbard, a factory worker who had vowed revenge against a local agency that had fired him. Three of the bombs found formed a triangle around this agency. The second suspect was Jerry Conrad, a friend and co-worker of Hubbard, who told investigators that he had given Hubbard detailed instructions on making a homemade bomb. The bombs found were identical to those in the instructions. Despite their suspicions, however, the investigators did not have proof until they had a laboratory analyze and compare evidence collected from various sources to the bombs' components.

Under authority of a search warrant based on Conrad's statements, investigators searched both men's homes and vehicles and recovered a large number of tools. They sent these along with the clocks and wiring mechanisms from the bombs to the ATF Laboratory in Washington. As noted by Chapman (1991, p. 28):*

> Using high-powered microscopes, O'Neil [a firearms and toolmark examiner] was able to positively identify two pliers and two wire strippers found in Conrad's workshop as having cut 13 of the wires on eight of the bombs. He was also able to identify these four tools—as well as two more pliers found in Conrad's workshop, a knife found in Hubbard's current residence and a pair of pliers found in Hubbard's former residence—as having the same class characteristics as the tools used to cut wires on nine of the bombs. . . .
>
> Again armed with a search warrant, investigators seized items found in Hubbard's jeep and two trucks belonging to Conrad—clothes, handkerchiefs, caps, papers, etc.—and sent them to the ATF lab, along with acetone swabbings taken from the inside of the vehicles, debris vacuumed from the inside of the vehicles and special vacuum filters containing air samples. . . .

---

*Excerpt used by permission. Copyright held by the International Association of Chiefs of Police, 515 N. Washington St., Alexandria, VA 22314. Further reproduction without express permission from IACP is strictly prohibited.

Ken Snow, a forensic chemist at the ATF lab, extracted vapors from these items and subjected them to a carefully controlled gas chromatographic analysis designed to detect the presence of ethylene glycol dinitrate [found only in commercial dynamite]. . . . The findings showed conclusively that both Hubbard and Conrad had handled commercial dynamite. . . .

The hard scientific evidence provided incontrovertible proof that Conrad's tools had been used to make the bombs and that both men had handled and transported commercial dynamite. . . .

Despite the fact that the entire case hinged on circumstantial evidence, both juries quickly returned verdicts of guilty against Hubbard and Conrad on a total of 29 counts of manufacturing and placing the bombs, and possession of stolen dynamite.

---

When investigating explosions and bombings, pay special attention to any fragments of the explosive device as well as to any powder present at the scene. Determine motive.

---

Laska (1995, p. 59) stresses that bomb-scene investigations must progress logically, with the first step being to determine the parameters of the scene:

As a rule of thumb, the furthest piece of recognizable evidence is located, and a radius established based upon a 50 percent wider field than this item. For example, at Oklahoma City it was reported that the rear axle for the truck was located three blocks from the seat of the blast. If this was the furthest identifiable piece of evidence located, the scene parameters would then be approximately four and a half blocks in all directions.

### Bombings and Drug Trafficking

Use of explosives is frequently connected to drug trafficking. According to Kincaid (1991, p. 68): "For traffickers, explosives have become the second-most preferred weapon in the drug trade. Thus, drug traffickers are continually targeted in ATF explosives investigations." This connection is also affirmed by Higgins (1990, p. 16): "The growth of bombing crimes was most volatile among drug traffickers. ATF has tracked explosives violations by these individuals since 1987. Over three years, bomb crimes linked to drugs escalated more than 1,000 percent."

### Using K–9s in Detecting Explosives

Many agencies are using specially trained K–9s to assist in searching for bombs and in searches for evidence following explosions. As noted by Berluti (1991, p. 59): "Over the past two decades, as bombers have become more sophisticated and bombing incidents more deadly, the use of canines to detect explosive devices has continued to gather momentum. Properly trained, explosives detection dogs are especially valuable in searching inaccessible or cluttered areas." It should be emphasized, however, that such assistance is to supplement specially trained investigators, not to replace them.

### Importance of the Team Approach

As Laska (1995, p. 28) explains:

A bombing requires that responders consider several sometimes divergent aspects at the same time, and interweave them toward the successful culmination of the investigation. The situation that existed at the Federal Office Building in

Oklahoma City required FBI agents, police, fire and medical workers as well as bomb technicians and other experts to all work together as a well-oiled machine.

The teamwork of field investigators and laboratory specialists in investigating bombings is critical. Such teamwork followed a California pipe-bombing incident that killed the driver of the vehicle to which the bomb had been attached. The Rialto Police Department, the San Bernardino Sheriff's Office and the ATF combined efforts in the investigation. They investigated and forwarded evidence found at the scene to the ATF laboratory for examination. Chemists were able to identify the type and brand of powder used in the bomb by examining intact powder particles found in the bomb's end caps. A subsequent search at the suspect's home uncovered a can of smokeless powder identical to the identified powder. Additional evidence obtained during the search provided further links between the suspect and the bombing. The suspect was arrested and charged with murder.

Investigators with technical questions about commercial explosives can receive assistance from the Institute of Makers of Explosives (IME) in Washington, DC. This nonprofit safety organization has thirty-one member-companies and an additional eighty-plus subsidiaries and affiliates, which together produce more than 85 percent of the commercial explosives used in the United States.

Also of help is the ATF National Response Team (NRT), which can be deployed in the "most urgent and difficult bomb cases" (Higgins, 1990, p. 16). Higgins notes:

> Criminals who terrorize with explosives face a new reality in the dawn of the 21st century—that law enforcement officers become better each day at flushing bombers from cover. These officers, agents, scientists and technicians work as a team while preserving jurisdictional integrity. The well-trained team is quick to adapt technological advances that, for example, coax shards of debris to give up their secrets and aid in tracing nondescript bomb components.
>
> The learning curve is moving up for bomb investigators and down for bombers. This will not stop the zealots, but it does influence persons concerned about their fate. Continued success by investigators will lead to a point where a bombing is considered by most would-be lawbreakers to be a crime not worth the risk.

Another source of assistance is the Interpol Explosives Incident System (IEXIS). Thurman (1991, p. 53) reports: "IEXIS's explosives index will ultimately contain complete descriptions—including chemical elements, consistency, color, markings and country and address of manufacture—of all explosives materials manufactured throughout the world." Thurman (p. 56) contends: "IEXIS enables investigators to quickly link a recovered IED [improvised explosive device] with an earlier reported theft of explosives, thus helping to ascertain whether the bombers are using stolen explosives." A primary objective of IEXIS is to determine immediately if a bombing or attempted bombing in one country is significantly similar to bombings in the same or another country. This combination of explosives-theft information, IED componentry and manner of construction, along with modus operandi of the criminal or terrorist groups, should greatly assist in investigating all forms of explosives-related crimes.

## Summary

Arson is the malicious, willful burning of a building or property. Fires are classified as natural, accidental, criminal (arson), suspicious or of unknown origin. They are presumed natural or accidental unless proven otherwise.

The elements of the crime of arson include (1) the willful, malicious burning of a building or property (2) of another, or of one's own to defraud (3) or causing to be burned, or aiding, counseling or procuring such burning. Attempted arson is also a crime. Some states categorize arson as either aggravated or simple. Aggravated arson is intentionally destroying or damaging a dwelling or other property by means of fire or explosives, creating an imminent danger to life or great bodily harm, which risk was known or reasonably foreseeable to the suspect. Simple arson is intentional destruction by fire or explosives that does not create imminent danger to life or risk of great bodily harm. Other states use the Model Arson Law, which divides arson into four degrees: first-degree involves the burning of dwellings; second-degree involves the burning of buildings other than dwellings; third-degree involves the burning of other property; and fourth-degree involves attempts to burn buildings or property.

Logic suggests that the fire department should work to *detect* arson and determine the point of origin and probable cause, whereas the police department should *investigate* arson and prepare the case for prosecution.

Special problems in investigating arson include coordinating efforts with the fire department and others, determining if a crime has been committed, finding physical evidence and witnesses and determining if the victim is a suspect.

Although the fire department is responsible for establishing when arson has occurred, law enforcement investigators must be able to verify such findings. To do so requires understanding what distinguishes an accidental fire from arson. Basic to this understanding is the concept of the fire triangle, which consists of three elements necessary for a substance to burn: air, fuel and heat. In arson, at least one of these elements is usually present in abnormal amounts for the structure. Evidence of accelerants at an arson scene is a primary form of evidence. The most common accelerant used is gasoline. Also important as evidence are igniters. These include matches; candles; cigars and cigarettes; cigarette lighters; electrical, mechanical and chemical devices; and explosives.

Burn indicators that provide important information include alligatoring, crazing, depth of char, lines of demarcation, sagged furniture springs and spalling. The point of origin is established by finding the area with the deepest char, alligatoring and (usually) the greatest destruction. Fires normally burn upward and are drawn toward ventilation and follow fuel. Arson is likely in fires that:

- Have more than one point of origin.
- Deviate from normal burning patterns.
- Show evidence of trailers.
- Show evidence of having been accelerated.
- Produce odors or smoke of a color associated with substances not normally present at the scene.
- Indicate that an abnormal amount of air, fuel or heat was present.
- Reveal evidence of incendiary igniters at the point of origin.

An administrative warrant is issued when it is necessary for the agent to search the premises to determine the cause and origin of the fire. A criminal warrant is issued on probable cause when evidence of a crime is found on the premises. Entry to fight a fire requires no warrant. Once in the building, fire officials may remain a reasonable time to investigate the cause of the blaze.

*Read the following articles and imagine yourself as the officer/detective assigned to each case. What elements of the crime are present? What evidence would you need to prosecute the case? Who else might you need to coordinate your efforts with? What is the likelihood of solving each crime?*

## Officials urge public to think of arson as 'murder by fire,' not just flames

**By Chris Graves**
*Staff Writer*

With the flick of a match or a lighter, an arsonist destroyed Robin Blanchard's life.

She lost virtually everything she owned. The house in which she was raised no longer exists. And her mother, 59-year-old Donna Blanchard, died a week later from injuries she suffered in the blaze.

"This person took my life away, and I can't ever get it back. This person took everything from my past away; took my mom away and it's . . . *Oh God* . . . if I just knew, if I just knew why," said Blanchard, who escaped the January fire in her south Minneapolis home.

Arson is becoming a common weapon, officials said Thursday. They urged citizens to remember that it's not just smoke and flames.

"Arson is more than fraud. It's murder by fire," said Carrye Brown, administrator of the U.S. Fire Administration. "Arson is being used to kill and hurt people more than in any time in the country's history."

Intentionally set fires are reaching "epidemic proportions" in Minnesota, State Fire Marshal Tom Brace said during Thursday's news conference.

Last year the number of reported arson fires—which includes those in dumpsters, trash, grass, vehicles and buildings—increased 16 percent across the state.

The metro area saw a 20-percent increase; numbers grew 10 percent in the rest of the state.

Source: *Star Tribune,* 5 May 1995. Reprinted by permission of the *Star Tribune,* Minneapolis-St. Paul.

## Blaze destroys church
*Officials probe suspicious fire at another black congregation*
*From News Services*

ENID, OKLA.—A lone blackened cross could be seen amid the buckled siding, broken windows and collapsed roof of another church destroyed by fire Thursday, the latest in a string of suspicious fires at black churches around the nation.

Part of the congregation stood bleary-eyed, shaking their heads as they stared at the charred remains of the First Missionary Baptist Church. Others shuddered with the fear that racial hate may have targeted their community.

Source: *Star Tribune,* 14 June 1996. Reprinted by permission of the *Star Tribune,* Minneapolis-St. Paul.

## Bomb threat
*Associated Press*

LOS ANGELES—An auto repair shop owner claiming to have packed his truck with 5,000 pounds of dynamite forced an evacuation at Paramount Studios for nearly 4½ hours Saturday before being taken into custody.

The man, who police said was from Long Beach but wouldn't identify, reportedly demanded to speak to U.S. Attorney General Janet Reno, although details about his motivation were unclear.

Police talked to the man by cellular telephone. He called 911 from his van about 10 a.m., said Lt. Anthony Alba. Shortly before 2:30 p.m., he left the truck, walked across the street and was taken into custody.

Source: *Las Vegas Review Journal,* 26 January 1997, Reprinted by permission of the Associated Press.

*(continued on p. 563)*

(continued)

## After fires on historic street, neighbors worry about safety—and area's renewal

*In Minneapolis' Central neighborhood, residents think there might be a pattern to blazes on holiday weekends.*

**By Steve Brandt**
*Star Tribune Staff Writer*

The tragic thing about the fire at 3201 2nd Av. S., say neighbors of the south Minneapolis lot, was how the flames erased a Victorian treasure that owner Patrick Stenzel was slowly uncovering from layers of asphalt shingles and years of neglect.

But neighbors' sadness turned to suspicion, anxiety and anger as the fire cooled and they noticed a pattern. The fire last Jan. 3 was the third on the block in nine months; all of them happened on holiday weekends.

Now, with the arrival of another holiday weekend, some residents are watching extra carefully, cocking their ears for the sound of a fire siren. "It makes us a little twitchy," said Marjory Holly.

Holly has lived for 31 years in one of the big restored Victorian homes on the 3100 block of 2nd Av. They're a collection known as the Healy block, named after the architect who designed 14 of the homes, which are on the National Register of Historic Places.

The owners of historic houses look for opportunities to match the area's Victorian homes with potential owners willing to take on the years of gritty work needed to restore them. The fires, clearly, have undercut that.

"It was very demoralizing, not just in terms of his individual loss, but it has the potential to sabotage neighborhood efforts," said Craig Anderson, a member of the Central neighborhood's housing committee.

"When someone invests their personal time and resources into turning around a significant property like that, it's not just for their personal benefit. It also helps the neighborhood. It's a collective loss. The impact is beyond the property line."

That's one reason there's anger by some residents over what they view as the failure of investigators to probe more deeply into the 3200 block's pattern of fires. Fire investigators ruled that the cause of the fires at Stenzel's house and a more modern fourplex up the block that burned on Easter weekend last year was undetermined. Another Victorian house on the block burned last Labor Day weekend; that was ruled as arson.

### Security line went dead

Stenzel's fire occurred after he'd spent seven months gutting the house to a skeleton of studs, joints and rafters and uncovering wood siding still in remarkably good condition. He'd installed a security alarm but said the phone line that would have relayed an alarm went dead a day or two before the fire. "I just got a chill up and down my spine," he said.

The night of the fire, Stenzel did structural work until 9 p.m. He was staying down the street at the restored house of friend David Piehl, who'd matched Stenzel with his house. The fire was discovered shortly before 3 a.m.

"You had 110-year-old wood exposed without plaster. It was like a bonfire," Piehl said. The blinds inside a neighbor's windows across a vacant lot melted from the heat.

There was little left standing above the basement. Two days later, city inspectors ordered an immediate demolition for which Stenzel was assessed $13,000—all before an insurance investigator could arrive.

Fire and police arson investigators who examined the block's fires didn't respond to Star Tribune calls. Fire Chief Tom Dickinson said he was not aware of

*(continued on p. 564)*

the block's pattern of holiday fires. His investigators try to determine a cause and origin for a fire, but arson investigations are in the hands of police and must stand up in court, he said.

Stenzel said no investigator talked to him before telling him the investigation was done. "I would think I'd be the first person they'd want to talk to. I was irate," he said. Stenzel said an investigator gave him several possible scenarios for the fire. None made sense to him based on his knowledge of the house's condition.

"I think people were disappointed with the city staff response," said Jana Metge, executive director for the Central Neighborhood Improvement Association. Some residents believe the inner-city location gets shortchanged. Metge believes posting a reward would have turned up a suspect.

Other inner-city areas also have been struck by concentrations of fires. Two blocks in the east side of the Phillips neighborhood have counted 10 buildings destroyed by fire since 1995, including six vacant residential buildings containing 12 dwellings. Lynne Mayo, a block activist, said a police arson supervisor told her he could use twice the number of investigators to handle the caseload.

### Persistence required

Some neighbors along 2nd Av. S. are still hopeful that the other burned house on the 3200 block, an 1892 Queen Anne, might be restored despite extensive damage. They'd lined up a potential buyer before the fire and are talking to another in case it is auctioned for back taxes.

But a buyer needs a strong work ethic: "Every night after work and every weekend. I had no social life," said Stenzel, 28. The house was trashed inside when he bought it, infested with cockroaches, reeking of spoiled food, with boxes of syringes and evidence of prostitution left behind.

Stenzel—who, expecting layoffs from a corporate acquisition, has left his job—says the fire left him too depressed to think about rebuilding for a while. The house had been insured for its mortgage, far short of the replacement cost.

Today, Stenzel's lot holds a carriage house with some salvaged trim and a strong smoke odor. On one corner stands a six-foot black walnut tree. It was moved from his grandfather's farm on the Iowa border to Stenzel's parent's home in Eden Prairie, and last spring Stenzel moved it to his new house.

From a distance, the walnut looks dead. Up close, a few tiny buds show signs of life. It might be a metaphor for what Stenzel has gone through.

His priorities are clear. First, find a job. Then get bids. Then try for financing. He has measurements for many of the house's dimensions.

"I'm going to rebuild that house somewhere. I can visualize every inch."

Source: *Star Tribune,* 24 May 1997.
Reprinted by permission of the *Star Tribune,* Minneapolis-St. Paul.

After this time, an administrative warrant is needed, as established in *Michigan v. Tyler.*

When investigating vehicle fires, look for evidence of accelerants and determine whether the vehicle was insured. It is seldom arson if there is no insurance.

When investigating explosions and bombings, pay special attention to any fragments of the explosive device as well as to any powder present at the scene. Determine motive.

## Arson

- Who first noticed the fire?
- Who notified authorities?
- Who responded from the fire department?
- Did the fire department record the color of the smoke? The color of the flame?
- What was the fire's point of origin? Was there more than one point of origin?
- What material was used to ignite the fire?
- Was there an explosion before the fire? During the fire? After the fire?
- How did the building explode: inward or outward?
- Was the fire's burn time normal? Did it appear to be accelerated?
- Were any accelerants (newspapers, rags, gasoline) found at the scene?
- What was the weather: dry, high wind, snow?
- What property was destroyed that was unusual for the premises?
- Were there any unusual circumstances?
- Was anyone injured or killed? Was an autopsy done to determine if there were other causes for death than fire? Were carbon monoxide tests made of the victim(s) to determine when death occurred—whether before or during the fire?
- Were regular informants checked to determine possible suspects?
- Who had access to the building?
- What appeared to be the motive for the fire? Who would benefit?
- Who owns the property destroyed? For how long?
- Was there insurance and, if so, how much?
- Who was the insurance payable to?
- What is the name of the insurance company? Obtain a copy of the company's report.
- Does the owner have any record of other property destroyed by fire?
- Does the owner have a criminal record for this or other types of crimes?
- Were any suspicious persons or vehicles observed at the scene before, during or after the fire?
- Was the state fire marshal's office notified? Did it send an investigator? If so, obtain a copy of the investigator's report.
- Were photographs or videos taken? Are they available?

# Application

**A.** It is midafternoon on a Sunday. The fire department has just received a call to proceed to the Methodist Church on St. Anthony Boulevard. Smoke has been reported coming out of the church's windows by a nearby resident. When the fire department arrives, the church is engulfed in flames. By the time the fire is brought under control, the church is gutted with damage estimated at $320,000. Suspecting arson, the fire department asks for help from the local police department.

### Questions

**1.** Was the request for assistance justified at this point?

**2.** What are the responsibilities of the investigator(s) assigned to respond to the call?

**B.** (The following account is adapted from "Seattle: Sifting Through the Ashes" by Kevin Krajick, *Police Magazine*, July 1979, pp. 10–11.)

Investigators Bob McDonald and Dennis Fowler spent most of their shifts staked out outside a massage parlor writing down license plate numbers of cars parked nearby. A rash of suspicious fires at the parlors had occurred over the past weeks. McDonald, having spent three of his ten years as a Seattle police detective on the vice squad, was familiar with the parlors; Fowler, a firefighter for eight years, had spent an additional seven years in the fire department's arson and fire investigation unit. They worked together as part of Seattle's special arson task force.

Just before midnight they received three long beeps over the radio and an address from the dispatcher. They arrived two minutes later at a small, one-story frame house, pulling in just behind the first fire rig. Orange flames shot from every window and roared up into the air. "I just hope nobody was in there," said McDonald.

While the firefighters sprayed the house, Fowler and McDonald walked among the bystanders, asking if they had seen anything before the fire, but no one had noticed anything unusual. When the fire had been extinguished and the smoke began to clear, floodlights were extended into the house and McDonald and Fowler began their investigation. They started in the small front room, noticing extensive burning and windows completely blackened from the fire. They continued through a small alcove whose upper portion had been destroyed and then went into what had been the kitchen. The remnants of the glass in a window over the kitchen sink were clear, the glass melted and showing a series of intricate cracks running through each fragment. McDonald and Fowler shoveled out layers of debris and then dragged in a fire hose to wash the floor. They noticed the floor was deeply charred and spongy with water. As they inspected the wooden cabinets around the sink, they found large, rolling blisters.

They checked the electrical hookups and found that the electricity had been disconnected. By the time McDonald had taken several dozen photographs, the owner and his wife arrived. The owner calmly answered their questions. He had been letting an acquaintance, a carpenter, live in the house in exchange for making repairs and fixing it up. But instead the man had stolen all the construction materials as well as much of the furniture and many appliances, so the owner kicked him out. The carpenter threatened to "make him sorry." The owner had no fire insurance, intending not to live in the house but rather to use it as an investment.

After filing their report, the investigators returned to the house at 3 A.M. It had rained heavily the day before, and the mud in the backyard was crisscrossed with footprints. Noticing some boot prints leading from the back door, they took plaster casts of them. As they were doing so, a neighbor walked over and said he had seen a blue van parked in the back of the house with the motor running just before the fire. McDonald photographed all the tire tracks he could find in the dirt alley where the van was reported. The next morning McDonald and Fowler learned that the carpenter, their prime suspect, was in jail when the fire broke out. The blue van belonged to a friend of his, a man who had been arrested for arson once before.

They got a search warrant and executed it that afternoon. The tires of the carpenter's friend's van and his boot soles resembled the impressions found at the fire scene, but the impressions were so spongy it was difficult to be sure. They found no further evidence linking the man to the fire.

*Questions*
1. Where did the fire probably originate? What factors indicate this?
2. What indicators were there that the fire was probably caused by arson?
3. Did the investigators have probable cause to arrest the carpenter's friend? Would the owner also be a possible suspect? Why or why not?
4. What aspects of this case illustrate an effective arson investigation?

## Discussion Questions

1. Do you agree that investigation of arson cases is the joint responsibility of police and fire departments? Which department should be in charge?
2. What are the respective roles of the police and fire departments in your community during an arson investigation?
3. Arson has a low conviction rate. What factors make an arson investigation difficult? What factors make prosecution difficult?
4. Imagine that you are called to the scene of a fire to determine whether it was accidental or of criminal origin. What initial steps would you take in making this determination?
5. What types of evidence are material to the crime of arson? Where do you find such evidence at a fire scene? How do you collect it? Where do you send it for examination in your area?
6. What are common motives for arson? How do these motives help an investigator locate suspects?
7. Arson was added to the Part One Index Crimes in the Uniform Crime Reporting Program. Is arson serious enough to be in this category, along with murder and rape? Are there other reasons it should or should not be a Part One Index Crime?
8. What agencies outside the police and fire departments can assist in an arson investigation? Who would you contact? What services could they provide?
9. What other types of crimes might be involved along with arson?
10. Organized crime has used arson to bring pressure on uncooperative persons and businesses. Why is arson effective for this purpose? Why is it difficult to prosecute such cases?

## References

Berluti, Adam F. "Arson Investigation: Connecticut's Canines." *The Police Chief,* December 1990, pp. 39–45.

———. "Connecticut's Explosives-Detecting Canines." *The Police Chief,* October 1991, pp. 59–65.

Chapman, Linda S. "City under Siege." *The Police Chief,* October 1991, pp. 26–29.

Chisholm, Joseph J. "Targeting Bombers." *The Police Chief,"* October 1991, pp. 42–52.

"Fighting Fires with Cooperation." *Instant Evidence,* Fall 1995, pp. 3–5.

Galvin, Mary. "The New Fire Triangle: Putting the Prosecutor on the Team." *The Police Chief,* December 1990, pp. 50–52.

Goodnight, Kenneth. "Arson for Profit: The Insurance Investigation." *The Police Chief,* December 1990, pp. 53–56.

Hart, Frank. "The Arson Equation: Arson + Circumstantial Evidence = Conviction." *The Police Chief,* December 1990, pp. 34–37.

Hartnett, Daniel M. "Better Arson Courtroom Training: An Idea Whose Time Has Come." *The Police Chief*, April 1993, p. 22.

———. "Bombing and Arson Investigations Enhanced by Advances in ATF Labs." *The Police Chief*, April 1990, pp. 20–28.

Higgins, Stephen E. "Bombs and Bombers: Past and Future." *The Police Chief*, December 1990, p. 16.

Hinds, John D. "Forensic Art: A New Weapon Against Arson." *Law and Order*, November 1994, pp. 31–32.

Icove, David J., and Philip R. Horbert. "Serial Arsonists: An Introduction." *The Police Chief*, December 1990, pp. 46–48.

Kincaid, Donald R. "Drug Trafficking and Explosives: A Means to an End." *The Police Chief*, October 1991, pp. 68–71.

Krzeszowski, Frank E. "What Sets Off an Arsonist." *Security Management*, January 1993, pp. 42–47.

Laska, Paul R. "Investigating a Bomb Scene." *Law Enforcement Technology*, August 1995, pp. 28–30, 58–60.

"Majority of Those Arrested for Arson Are Juveniles." (Minneapolis/St. Paul) *Star Tribune*, January 20, 1995, p. A8.

"Managing an Information Overload." *Law Enforcement News*, April 30, 1993, pp. 5, 16.

May, William A., Jr., and David Dunn. "Terrorists and Bombs." *Law and Order*, March 1996, pp. 108–114.

Morris, Cole. "Explosive Situation." *Police*, September 1996, pp. 44–46, 70–77.

*Project Response: The Oklahoma City Tragedy*. Alexandria, VA: International Association of Chiefs of Police, no date.

"Project Response: The Oklahoma City Tragedy." *The Police Chief*, November 1995, p. 18.

"Report from the Smoldering Front Line." *Instant Evidence*, Fall 1995, pp. 1–2.

Slahor, Stephenie. "Profiling the Arsonist." *Law and Order*, May 1991, pp. 88–89.

Thurman, Joey V. "Interpol Computers Keep Track of Firearms, Explosives." *The Police Chief*, October 1991, pp. 53–58.

Woodfork, Warren G. "Arson: Not Just a Fire Department Problem." *The Police Chief*, December 1990, pp. 30–33.

Woods, Everett K., and Donald H. Wallace. "Investigating Arson: Coping with Constitutional Constraints." *Security Management*, November 1991, pp. 80–84.

"World Trade Center Bombing." *Law Enforcement Technology*, May 1993, pp. 8–9.

# Other Challenges to the Criminal Investigator

The two preceding sections discussed investigating crimes against persons and crimes against property. Many crimes do not fall neatly into one of the eight Part One Index Crimes but involve a combination of illegal acts related to both people and property. Unique investigative challenges are presented by the activities engaged in by members of organized crime, gang-related crime, bias/hate crime and ritualistic crime (Chapter 18) and by drug buyers and sellers (Chapter 19). Investigating the illegal activities related to these groups is more difficult because the elements of the crimes are not neatly spelled out and statistics are not available as they are for the Index Crimes.

Organized crime, gang-related crime, bias/hate crime and ritualistic crime have existed in one form or another for centuries, but not until recently have they had such an impact on law enforcement, straining already limited resources and resulting in what many view literally as "war" on such crimes. A further complication is that the areas overlap; individuals involved in organized crime and drugs and gangs and drugs are often the same individuals—but not necessarily. Although each type of crime is discussed separately, this overlap should always be kept in mind. Further, moral and ethical issues are raised by the activities of these organizations that are not raised by the activities of, say, bicycle thieves, rapists and murderers. Stealing, raping and murdering are clearly wrong in our society. This is not necessarily true for gambling, worshiping Satan or smoking pot.

# Organized Crime, Gang-Related Crime, Bias/Hate Crime and Ritualistic Crime

## DO YOU KNOW

What the distinctive traits of organized crime are?

What organized crime activities are specifically made crimes by law?

What the major activities of organized crime are?

What the investigator's primary role in dealing with the organized crime problem is?

What agencies cooperate in investigating organized crime?

What a street gang is?

What types of crimes gangs typically engage in?

How to identify gang members?

What kinds of records to keep on gangs?

What special problems are involved in investigating illegal activities of gangs?

What two defense strategies are commonly used by gang members' lawyers in court?

What bias crimes are?

What a cult is?

What a ritualistic crime is?

What may be involved in cult or ritualistic crime?

How to identify cult-related or ritualistic crimes?

What special problems are involved in investigating cult-related or ritualistic crimes?

## CAN YOU DEFINE

| | | |
|---|---|---|
| Antichrist | cult | organized crime |
| Beelzebub | gang | pentagram |
| bias crime | graffiti | ritual |
| Black Mass | Hand of Glory | ritualistic crime |
| Bloods | incantation | sabbat |
| bookmaking | loan-sharking | street gang |
| coven | monikers | turf |
| Crips | occult | victimless crime |

Investigations that center around or involve gangs, narcotics sales, fraudulent schemes, and organized crime are not for the faint of heart. The crooks that are associated with these enterprises are frequently wary, intelligent, and sly. They are well-versed in covering their tracks, making false leads for investigators to follow, and hiding their assets so that they can't be seized, even if they are apprehended.

This chapter begins with a discussion of organized crime in the United States, including its characteristics, applicable laws, major activities, role in corruption and its challenge to law enforcement. The discussion then looks at agencies cooperating in investigating organized crime, investigative aids including asset forfeiture and finally an exploration of the current status of organized crime. The discussion on organized crime concludes with a look at a new threat—that of Asian organized crime.

The next major topic to be discussed is gang-related crime, a continuous challenge to law enforcement. The discussion provides some definitions of gangs, a look at their place within society, and their makeup and characteristics, their relationship to drugs, their turf and their graffiti. Next the discussion focuses on ways to identify gang members, the records to keep, how to investigate illegal gang activity and the police responsibility in this important area.

The third major topic presented in the chapter is bias/hate crimes, a type of crime that has only recently been making the headlines and presenting major problems for law enforcement. The last topic addressed in the chapter is ritualistic crime and the police's role in investigating such crimes.

---

## Organized Crime: An Overview

**Organized crime** is most frequently thought of as a highly secretive, sophisticated criminal organization called *the Mafia* or *La Cosa Nostra*. In the early 1960s, Joseph Valachi made public for the first time the awesome power of organized crime and dispelled many misconceptions about it.

First, organized crime is not a single entity controlled by one superpower. Although a large share of organized crime is controlled by the Mafia, other organizations throughout the United States also operate as organized crime syndicates.

Second, organized crime does not exist only in metropolitan areas. Although organized crime operates primarily in larger metropolitan areas, it has associate operations in many smaller cities, towns and rural areas.

Third, organized crime does not involve only such activities as narcotics, prostitution, racketeering and gambling. In fact, organized crime is involved in virtually every area where profits are to be made, including legitimate businesses.

Fourth, citizens are not isolated from organized crime. They are directly affected by it through increased prices of consumer goods controlled by behind-the-scenes activities of organized crime. In addition, citizens who buy items on the black market or who bet through a bookie, take chances on punch boards or participate in other innocent betting operations directly contribute to the financial success of organized crime. Millions of citizens support organized crime by knowingly or unknowingly taking advantage of the goods and services it provides.

# Characteristics of Organized Crime

A number of state laws define organized crime for prosecution purposes. Commonly found definitions include:

- A group of individuals working outside the law for economic gain.
- Any combination or conspiracy to engage in criminal activity as a significant source of income.
- Two or more persons with continuity of purpose, who supply illegal goods or services such as vice or loan-sharking or who commit predatory crimes such as theft or assault.

Even though no agreed on definition of organized crime exists, several characteristics distinguish organized crime from crimes committed by individuals or by unorganized groups.

The *organization* provides direct *control,* leadership and discipline. The leaders are isolated from the general operations through field or area leaders who, in turn, control the everyday activities that bring in the profits. Organized crime deals primarily in *high-profit* crimes that are susceptible to organizational control and that can be developed into larger operations that will provide the continued profit necessary for future existence.

Organized crime functions through many forms of corruption and intimidation to create a *singular control* over specific goods and services that ultimately results in a monopoly. Monopoly provides the opportunity to set higher prices and profits for that product or service. Organized crime flourishes most where there is *protection* from interference and prosecution. The first line of immunity is the indifference of the general public and their knowing or unknowing use of the services or purchase of the goods offered by organized crime. Through such activities, citizens provide the financial power that gives organized crime immunity from legal authorities.

Moreover, organized crime uses enforcement tactics to ensure compliance with its decrees. Paid enforcers intimidate, brutalize and even murder those who fail to obey the dictates of organized crime bosses.

---

Distinctive characteristics of organized crime include:
- Definite organization and control.
- High-profit and continued-profit crimes.
- Singular control.
- Protection.

---

## Applicable Laws

In addition to various state laws, two other distinct groups of laws seek to control organized crime: criminal laws that attack the criminal act itself, and laws that make violations a criminal conspiracy. Charges have also been brought against some types of organized crime through prosecution under the Internal Revenue laws and through initiation of civil lawsuits.

The major federal acts specifically directed against organized crime are the 1946 Hobbs Anti-Racketeering Act, the 1968 Omnibus Crime Control and Safe Streets Act and the Organized Crime Control Act of 1970. These acts make it permissible to use circumstantial rather than direct evidence to enforce conspiracy violations. They also prohibit the use of funds derived from illegal sources to enter into legitimate enterprises (commonly known as *laundering* money). Title 18, U.S. Code, Section 1962, defines three areas that can be prosecuted.

It is a prosecutable conspiracy to:

- Acquire any enterprise with money obtained from illegal activity.
- Acquire, maintain or control any enterprise by illegal means.
- Use any enterprise to conduct illegal activity.

Dahlberg (1994, p. 40) suggests that the Racketeering Influenced and Corrupt Organizations Act (RICO), passed in 1970, has been one of law enforcements favorite legal weapons to prosecute many of the white-collar crimes in which organized crime is involved. Such crimes often involve conspiracy, and the crime scene is often unlike those most investigators are familiar with. Such crimes require use of wiretaps and informants in many cases.

## Major Activities

Organized crime is involved in almost every legal and illegal activity that makes large sums of money with little risk. These include gambling, the drug business (notably cocaine trafficking), pornography, loan-sharking, arson, fraud, organized hijacking rings, armed robbery groups, sale of untaxed cigarettes, credit-card and stock frauds, sale of stolen and counterfeit securities and the manufacture and distribution of counterfeit money. Legitimate businesses are not only infiltrated or manipulated but also taken over. For example, in 1995, state prosecutors charged that a Mafia-dominated cartel used arson and threats to control New York City's commercial garbage business for more than fifty years ("N.Y. Garbage Haulers . . . ," 1995, p. A7). The charges came as the result of a five-year investigation led by an undercover officer posing as a garbage hauler. According to the article, the trade associations that controlled the garbage-hauling industry were dominated by the Genovese and Gambino crime families.

---

Organized crime is heavily involved in gambling, drugs, prostitution, loan-sharking and infiltration of legitimate businesses.

---

Most reports on organized crime indicate that illegal gambling is the backbone of organized crime activities and its largest source of income. **Bookmaking**—soliciting and accepting bets on any type of sporting event—is the most prevalent gambling operation. In addition, various forms of numbers, policy and other lottery games net substantial portions of the financial gain from gambling.

**Loan-sharking** is supported initially by the profits from gambling operations. The hierarchy loans money to persons in lower echelons, charging them 1 to 2 percent interest on large sums of money. These persons, in turn, loan the money to customers at exorbitant rates, usually 20 to 30 percent or more. The most likely customers are people who cannot obtain loans through legitimate sources, often to pay off illegal gambling debts.

*Fencing operations* are used by organized crime figures to dispose of large quantities of stolen goods. Sometimes a business is purchased and operated as a legitimate enterprise, with stolen goods provided along with standard products. The merchandise is stolen on order or acquired through cargo thefts and truck hijackings, or it is taken from semiorganized, smaller criminal groups of shoplifters or burglars.

Be aware of such businesses in the community and be suspicious of delivery vehicles carrying merchandise that does not fit the place of delivery. Be alert to mention of purchases made at ridiculously low prices, which suggests that the items were stolen and sold by persons associated with organized crime.

The relation of organized crime to *street crimes* is not always clear. Some crimes such as prostitution and narcotics selling are initiated in the streets and are organized and directly controlled by organized crime. Other crimes such as burglary or robbery can be committed by amateurs to support narcotics or illegal gambling habits. The stolen goods are often disposed of through fences associated with organized crime.

*Money laundering* is another activity frequently engaged in by organized crime. Karchmer and Ruch (1992, p. 1) describe the motivation behind money laundering and the actual process:

> Drug traffickers and other racketeers who accumulate large cash inventories face serious risks of confiscation and punishment if considerable, unexplained cash hoards are discovered. For these criminals to fully benefit from their illicit activities, they must first convert those cash proceeds to an alternative medium— one that is both easier than cash to use in everyday commerce and that avoids pointing, even indirectly, to the illegal activity that generated it.
>
> "Money laundering" is a term that describes the process of converting illegally earned assets, originating as cash, to one or more alternative forms to conceal such incriminating factors as illegal origin and true ownership. Recently, through heavy colloquial use, the term's meaning has broadened to refer not only to individual acts of laundering, but also to many complex steps of illegal asset conversion, beyond the basic exchange of cash, for less conspicuous and more socially acceptable methods of payment.

Foster (1993b, p. 44) gives a more basic definition: "The term 'money laundering,' in its simplest form, is the process of masking or disguising the origin of funds to permit their use as though they were funds gained from some other source."

Webster and McCampbell (1992, p. 1) report: "According to the U.S. Department of the Treasury, drug traffickers launder an estimated $100 billion each year in this country alone, with much of the activity channeled through financial institutions." They note: "The bank has been called 'the most pervasive money-laundering operation and financial supermarket ever created,' a 'marathon swindle,' and a 'steering service for [Colombian] drug traffickers to deposit hundreds of millions of contraband dollars outside the country.'"

The U.S. Treasury estimates place the amount of money laundering occurring in our nation's financial institutions annually as high as $300 billion (Foster, 1993b, p. 44).

One form of money laundering is *structuring*. As Semesky and Taylor (1995, p. 1) describe it:

> *Structuring* means breaking transactions larger then $10,000 into smaller increments by making multiple deposits or withdrawals or buying cashier's checks, money orders, or other monetary instruments for the express purpose of evading the reporting requirements [of transactions over $10,000]. . . . To be convicted of structuring, an individual must knowingly and willfully transact below the $10,000 threshold level, intending to evade the reporting requirements.

Karchmer and Ruch (1992, pp. 5–6) note: "Investigation of money laundering usually applies white-collar crime investigative techniques including:

- Financial auditing and accounting.
- Undercover operations (perhaps through "sting" operations).
- Electronic surveillance.

Foster (1993b, p. 44) concludes: "Money laundering will continue to increase as a domestic and international enforcement problem."

In recent years, organized crime has become increasingly involved in *legitimate business.* The vast profits from illegal activities are given legitimacy by being invested in legal business. This is another way of "turning dirty money into clean money," or "laundering" it. According to Kouri (1992, p. 31):

> Organized crime bosses long ago realized the potential for controlling and infiltrating legitimate business. While the history of organized crime is filled with bloodshed, violence, and corruption, syndicate figures no longer wield power through the barrel of a Thompson submachine gun. They can touch the very fabric of American society by manipulating the business economy to their benefit.
>
> Today's syndicate figures may be well educated, businesslike, and progressive, but they are still motivated by the prospect of making large profits from illegal activity.
>
> Such crimes as labor racketeering, unwelcome infiltration of unions, fencing stolen property, gambling, loan-sharking, drug trafficking, employment of illegal aliens, and white-collar crimes of all types can signal syndicate involvement.

Kouri (1992, p. 31) presents an example of how organized crime infiltrates legitimate businesses:

> Ms. A is the president of a medium-sized manufacturing company. Business has been bad because of the lagging economy, and she has been unable to get credit extensions from several financial institutions. After serious deliberations, Ms. A decides to borrow money from people she knows have ties to organized crime. The interest rate is 60 percent per week.
>
> Within six months a mob takeover has occurred at Ms. A's company. The new owners keep her on as a figurehead and use her good name to order merchandise worth thousands of dollars with no intention of paying vendors. Within another six months, Ms. A's company files for bankruptcy.

## Organized Crime and Corruption

One of the greatest threats posed by organized crime is the corruption it engenders throughout the entire legal system.

Although the police are interested in any corruption by public officials, they are especially concerned about corruption in their own department. Bribes of police officers can take many forms: outright offers of money, taking care of medical bills, providing free merchandise or providing free vacations. Any police officer offered a bribe must report it immediately to a superior and then attempt to make an arrest that will involve the person making the offer as well as those responsible higher in the organization.

Some officials repay organized crime figures by providing inside information that can be used to manipulate securities or to purchase real estate in areas of future development that can be sold for a much higher price.

## Organized Crime and the Police Officer

Frequently it is difficult for local law enforcement officers to understand their role in investigating or controlling organized crime. But there is a direct relationship between what officers do on assignment and the investigation of organized crime activities. Local law enforcement officers are the first line of defense in the control of all crime, and organized crime is no exception. Because of the highly structured nature of organized crime, law enforcement officers can seldom break into the hierarchy, but they can remain the eyes and ears of the information and intelligence system that is essential in combating organized crime.

---

The daily observations of local law enforcement officers provide vital information for investigating organized crime. Report all suspicious activities and persons possibly associated with organized crime to the appropriate person or agency.

---

Because organized crime is involved in a great number of activities, information can arise from many sources. Thus, your street-level observations can be critical. Every day you observe many conditions related to crime and deal with individuals who are part of the community's activities. Seemingly unimportant details can fit into an overall picture being put together by an intelligence unit. For example, a person suspected of selling drugs may be seen in a certain car, with a specific license number, on a specific date, at a specific time, with the same individuals at the same location for the same length of time. This information could be vital to a current drug investigation.

All information obtained must be provided to the proper authority to be of value. Generally, this is the unit or squad assigned to organized crime, but it may be the chief of police in smaller departments. Information is then analyzed along with other information received from other sources. Action may be taken on the basis of this information alone, or the information may be relayed to a higher authority such as a federal organized crime strike force. Regardless of the ultimate use, local law enforcement officers are a key source of information about almost all types of organized crime.

Ways to become aware of persons and conditions that suggest organized crime activity are provided by the International Association of Chiefs of Police:*

A candy store, grocery store, drug store, or other retail establishment seems to be doing a brisk business—many customers coming and going. But the customers do not remain in the store very long and do not leave with packages or other evidence that purchases were made. The store may have a meager selection of merchandise, which raises the question of how it can attract so many customers day after day. This could indicate the presence of a policy operation at the writer level or the place of business of a bookmaker's commissionman.

At about the same time each day, a package is delivered to a newsstand, bar, or other location. Later the package is picked up by another individual. The location could be a policy drop—the place to which a policy writer sends his slips and/or day's receipts.

A number is chalked on a street lamp pole. The same number is observed in other locations. It might be the winning number for the day's policy play.

You are called to investigate a beating in a bar or at a location near a factory or other place of employment. The incident may occur on a payday or within a couple of days thereafter. The beating may have resulted from the impatience of a loan shark who has not been paid on schedule.

A parked car—often double-parked—is observed daily at the same location and at the same time. The driver remains in the vehicle while a number of "friends" come up to say hello. Such a situation may indicate bet-taking activity.

---

*Reprinted from *Criminal Intelligence,* Training Key #223, with permission of the International Association of Chiefs of Police.

A shopkeeper complains about poor business and notes that as a result he had to borrow money recently. A few comments by the patrol officer about the high interest rates and the shopkeeper might disclose the imposition of an interest above the legal maximum. If so, the shopkeeper may have been dealing with a loan shark. If the shopkeeper advises that he cannot keep up with the payments, the officer might find an opportune time to ask for the identity of the shark. Depending on the desperation and temperament of the victim, the suggestion to cooperate may bring positive results.

After arriving at the scene of an assault, a patrol officer learns that the victim is a union official. This information should be noted because if there have been other similar assaults in the city, the overall total, when analyzed by an organized crime intelligence unit, may strongly indicate an attempt by racketeers to gain control over a local union.

Merchants complain about another price rise by the cartage company that removes their garbage or trash. They also mention that there is either no competitor to deal with or if there is one, it will not accept their business. Not infrequently, this is an indication that an organized crime group is trying to monopolize the cartage business or limit competition through territorial agreements.

A new set of vendors begins to service a business—a restaurant, for example. The linen supplier is new, as are the meat provisioner, fuel oil company, and cartage firm. Perhaps new vending machines or jukeboxes are observed being installed. Some of these suppliers are recognized as enterprises run by organized crime. These are fairly solid indicators that organized crime figures have purchased or have otherwise secured a degree of control in the business being serviced.

A rash of vandalism strikes a number of establishments engaged in the same type of business—such as dry cleaning. Racketeers may be trying to coerce reluctant owners into joining an association or into doing business with mob-controlled vendors.

Appliances are seen being loaded into the storeroom of a sporting goods store. Scams or bankruptcy frauds frequently involve ordering goods (on credit, of course) unrelated to the customary line of the business.

Determining who the bettors are in your area can be as important as knowing who the bookmakers are—indeed, many times the identification of a bettor leads to the identification of a bookie. Patrol officers have identified bettors through conversations with those on their posts—sometimes even by observing who buys racing forms. In some instances, you may even get close enough to a bettor to observe the number dialed when a bet is placed. Observations such as these could trigger an investigation leading to the prosecution of the upper echelon of organized crime's gambling hierarchy.

Just as identification of the bettor is important, so also is identification of addicts and loan shark customers. In two separate incidents, an arrested burglar revealed, under questioning by a patrol officer, that he was stealing to finance his heroin purchases, while another arrested thief said he had to raise money to keep up with his loan shark payments. This information led to the arrest of a pusher in one case and the loan shark in the other.

Make a habit of checking out new businesses that set up shop in the area. If the enterprise is one that requires a license—such as a bar—ask to see it if for no other reason than to observe who the owners are, ascertain the identity of the company which distributes or services the jukeboxes, etc. If, for example, the distributor of the jukeboxes or vending machines is a company controlled by the organized underworld, so also might be the bar in which they are located.

Report in writing all information pertaining to such activities when time permits or immediately if the activity involves an imminent meeting. Report as nearly as possible exact conversations with victims of assaults who are suspected of associating with organized crime members. These conversations can include names or organizations responsible for violence and crime in the community.

# Agencies Cooperating in Investigating Organized Crime

Under the authority of the 1968 Omnibus Crime Control Act, the Safe Streets Act and the Organized Crime Control Act of 1970, the U.S. Justice Department established the Organized Crime and Racketeering Unit. Organized-crime strike forces were formed throughout the country, mostly in major cities.

---

Organized-crime strike forces coordinate all federal organized crime activities and work closely with state, county and municipal law enforcement agencies.

---

Other agencies that play important roles in investigating organized crime are the *Federal Bureau of Investigation,* which often has a member on the strike forces; the *Postal Inspector,* who is in charge of mail fraud, embezzlements and other crimes involving material distributed through the mails; the *United States Secret Service,* which investigates government checks and bonds as well as foreign securities; the *Department of Labor,* which investigates organized crime activities related to labor practices and pension funds; the *Securities and Exchange Commission,* which investigates organized crime activities in the purchase of securities; and the *Internal Revenue Service,* which investigates violations of income tax laws.

In addition to these agencies, the state attorney general's office and the district attorney's office can assist the police in building a case against organized crime figures who violate local and state laws.

The importance of cooperation is illustrated in the investigation of Vincent Rizzo, which the New York County district attorney's office began in 1972. The investigation initially involved the cooperative efforts of the district attorney's office, the New York City Police Department and the FBI. Using both electronic and physical surveillance, the joint investigation discovered that the Rizzo group was involved in, among other things, counterfeiting U.S. currency and importing narcotics. Therefore, the Secret Service and the Bureau of Narcotics and Dangerous Drugs were brought into the investigation.

During the investigation, numerous wiretaps were installed in New York City, Philadelphia, Las Vegas and San Francisco. Through one of the New York wiretaps, investigators learned that Rizzo was going to Munich, Germany, to collect $200,000 that some German businessmen owed for stolen securities Rizzo had delivered to them. The investigators learned when Rizzo would be leaving, on which flight and in what hotel in Munich he would be staying. A New York City detective went to Munich ahead of Rizzo and enlisted the aid of German authorities in wiretapping the phone and installing a bug in Rizzo's hotel room. Rizzo met with two German businessmen in his room and, through the electronic surveillance, investigators learned of a scheme to transport, through interstate and foreign commerce, more than $18 million in stolen and counterfeit securities. At that point it was decided to end the investigation and to begin grand jury proceedings against Rizzo.

## Investigative Aids

Electronic surveillance of suspects is essential in investigating organized crime. Organized crime leaders often avoid direct involvement in criminal acts by planning and coordinating criminal activity over the telephone. Consequently,

**579**

Chapter 18

**Organized Crime,
Gang-Related
Crime, Bias/Hate
Crime and
Ritualistic Crime**

*A federally protected witness testifies at a hearing about mob involvement in the garbage/toxic waste industry as a federal officer keeps watch nearby.*

electronic surveillance can be used to build an effective case based on the criminal's own words while avoiding the risks associated with using informants or undercover agents.

Martin (1993, p. 34) notes: "More liberal surveillance laws and high-tech equipment have given law enforcement an advantage in the campaign against organized crime."

Pen registers also are important in investigating sophisticated criminal networks. Pen registers record the numbers dialed from a telephone by monitoring the electrical impulses of the numbers dialed. In *Smith v. Maryland* (1979) the Supreme Court held that using a pen register does not constitute a search within the meaning of the Fourth Amendment, so neither probable cause nor a warrant is required to use the device. Several state courts, however, have held that using a pen register *is* a search under the respective state statutes and that a warrant supported by probable cause *is* needed. Investigators must be familiar with their state's statutes in this area.

The same situation exists for trap and trace devices. Trap and trace devices reveal the telephone number of the source of all *incoming* calls to a particular number. Their use may or may not require a warrant, depending on the specific state.

## Asset Forfeiture

One effective weapon against organized crime is the asset forfeiture program, which allows law enforcement agencies to seize funds and property associated with criminal activity. This program not only deprives criminals of their illegally gained profits, but it also provides the criminal justice system with resources with which to continue the fight against crime. As noted by the Office of the Attorney General (1992, p. 23): "Asset forfeiture has proven to be an extremely effective law enforcement tool."

Green (1994, p. 14) describes asset forfeiture as follows: "Civil [asset] forfeiture is a legal concept by which property that is illegally used or acquired is seized for forfeiture to the government upon an initial showing of probable cause—without the necessity of a criminal conviction for the underlying crime."

Foster (1993c, p. 57) provides a historical perspective on asset forfeiture:

> The concept of attaching guilt to "things" used in the commission of a crime originated with Greek and Roman law. If, for example, a sword was used to kill a man, then it was deemed to possess an evil quality independent of the killer. The sword would be confiscated and sold, with the proceeds used for good deeds.

Copeland (1993, p. 87) says: "Asset forfeiture is an ancient remedy being employed in a new way." He (p. 86) describes asset forfeiture in this way:

> Asset forfeiture takes the profit out of crime and immobilizes crime syndicates by removing the instrumentalities of crime. Forfeiture is also a means of recovering some of the enormous cost of crime to society.

As Foster (1993a, p. 46) suggests: "This approach [asset forfeiture] can subject criminals to 100 percent tax on their earnings."

## The Decline of Organized Crime?

Martin (1993, p. 34) suggests that from the 1930s through the early 1960s, the Mafia, as depicted in *The Godfather,* pretty much kept to their "code." However, the character of the "mob" has changed as second- and third-generation Italian Americans take their places in the Mafia. Martin (p. 36) contends:

> These new guys didn't care about honor and respect. They wanted to make big bucks fast and the Mafia provided a way for them to do that. . . .
> Couple that with the fact that the older dons were either dying or being sent to prison, and you're left with a Mafia largely headed by inexperienced individuals going up against seasoned law enforcers.

Martin (p. 37) suggests that law enforcement should focus its efforts more on the new internationalism of organized crime: "We're seeing a great increase in the international organized crime movement, which at this point is mainly involved in transporting contraband like drugs and weapons." Martin concludes:

> As long as there are people who are willing to buy what the Mafia is providing, be it drugs or pornography or swag (the goods from a hijacked truck), the Mafia will continue to exist in one form or another.

Law enforcement and the criminal justice system won a significant victory in the battle with organized crime in April 1992 when John Gotti, the country's "most notorious mobster since Al Capone, was found guilty on thirteen counts and sent to prison for life. The news services ("Gotti Is Found Guilty . . . ," 1992, p. A1) reported: "Government officials, giddy with victory over the man known as 'the Teflon Don,' quickly proclaimed the 'death knell' of organized crime in New York." This source also noted:

> Gotti's prosecutors presented a colossal amount of evidence, including six hours of FBI tapes surreptitiously recorded in Gotti's hideaways. They called 38 witnesses, including Gotti's No. 2 man, Salvatore (Sammy Bull) Gravano, one of the highest-ranking turncoats in organized crime.
>
> Rejoicing at what they called the breakup of the 400-member Gambino crime family, FBI officials acknowledged that others would move quickly to acquire the family's lucrative operations.

The rise of Asian, Hispanic and Greek gangs requires the government to re-design the fight against organized crime.

## Asian Organized Crime

"Asian Organized Crime (AOC) groups are becoming increasingly involved in murder, kidnapping, extortion, gambling, drugs and money laundering," says Mosquera (1993, p. 65). Mosquera cautions: "It has been suggested that AOC has the potential to become the number-one law enforcement problem in the United States."

As Young (1995, p. 78) notes: "The so-called 'Mafia of the Future,' Asian organized crime, is often global, transient, well-run, and hard to crack." Young also says:

> With fingers in every criminal activity including narcotics, prostitution, extortion, and illegal-alien smuggling, Asian crime rings have spread beyond urban ghettos to become one of the greatest mainstream crime threats in the U.S.

### Chinese Organized Crime

Triads are the oldest of the Chinese Organized Crime (COC) groups. As Mosquera (1993, p. 65) says: "Most triad societies participate in a wide range of criminal activities, including money laundering, drug trafficking, gambling, extortion, prostitution, loansharking, pornography, alien smuggling and various protection schemes."

### Vietnamese Organized Crime

Vietnamese organized crime groups are generally one of two kinds: roving or local. As the name suggests, roving bands travel from community to community, have a propensity for violence and have no permanent leaders or group loyalty. According to Mosquera (1993, p. 68): "They have few language skills, little or no job skills, and, typically, no nuclear family in the United States."

Local groups, in contrast, tend to band together in a certain area of a specific community and to have a charismatic leader. They also have a propensity for violence and tend to engage in extortion, illegal gambling and robbery.

### Japanese Organized Crime

Japanese Organized Crime is sometimes known as *Boryokudan* but is more commonly known as the *Yakuza*. The term *boryokudan* means "violent ones,"

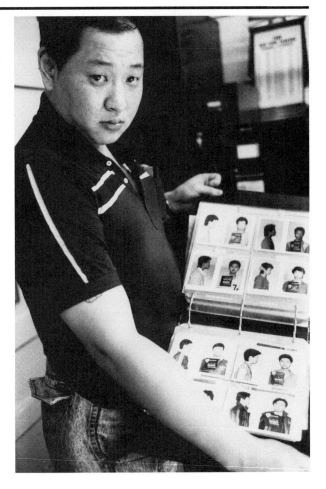

*The Chinese Mafia may be the most secretive in the world. Some organized crime experts believe it is an even greater threat since Hong Kong again became part of China in 1997. Here a police sergeant from New York's 5th precinct task force in Chinatown shows Chinese gang members' mug shots.*

which quite accurately describes these groups. They tend to concentrate on robberies and business extortions.

### The Challenge to Law Enforcement

Mosquera (1993, p. 72) describes some of the unique challenges presented by AOC investigations:

■ Such problems are unique primarily due to cultural and social differences.
■ Many Asians are suspicious of the police.
■ Many Asian citizens are reluctant to deal with the U.S. criminal justice system.
■ Many Asian groups are highly mobile and have family or associates in various parts of the United States.

Mosquera concludes: "Law enforcement must be prepared to face the unique challenge created by these criminal groups. The increasing threats they pose must be dealt with accordingly so that law enforcement and the nation are not suddenly overwhelmed by this new wave of criminal activity."

# Gang-Related Crime: An Overview

Gangs have been of interest and concern to people of all segments of society for centuries. Although a great deal of mysticism, innuendos, rumor, embellishments and concern exist relative to gangs, there is also a need for real involvement of society and law enforcement. Belonging to a gang is *not* illegal; many activities engaged in by gangs, however, are illegal. To investigate such crimes effectively, law enforcement personnel must understand the makeup of these organizations, what types of crimes to expect, how to identify their members and how to deal with the special problems of investigating such crimes.

Johnson et al. (1995, p. 1) note:

> Street gangs have been part of America's urban landscape for most of the country's history and a subject of research since at least the 1920s. . . .
> As the year 2000 approaches, there are many more different types of street gangs. Individual members, gang cliques, or entire gang organizations traffic in drugs; commit shootings, assaults, robbery, extortion and other felonies; and terrorize neighborhoods.

A summit on violence in the United States conducted by the International Association of Chiefs of Police ("Violent Crime in America . . .," 1993, p. 61) noted:

> The rise of gangs has fueled much of the increase in violent crime. What were once loosely knit groups of juveniles and young adults involved in petty crimes have become powerful, organized gangs. There appear to be gangs intent on controlling lucrative drug trade through intimidation and murder, and also street gangs simply claiming "turf." Today, as never before, cities and neighborhoods, even those without long histories of youth gang activity, have been literally overrun by both types of gang violence. While gangs are not new, today's level of gang violence, organization and sophistication is unprecedented.

Bunker cites McBride, Los Angeles County Sheriff's Department, who distinguishes between "conventional" domestic terrorism—a force with a political agenda—and the terrorizing effect of random and pervasive violence:

> I believe if we look at the disconnected violence issues involving the gangs, we are "hip deep" right now in domestic terrorism created by the gangs. Their gang wars and disregard for innocent victims certainly have an effect . . . on the well-being of our citizens.
> Violence perpetrated by street gangs is a principal—if not the major—social affliction affecting American communities today. In the last decade of the twentieth century, gangs exist in virtually every community—suburban, as well as inner-city—in every metropolitan area. Rather than seeking socially acceptable means of achieving influence, gangs use violence, harassment, intimidation, extortion and fear to control a neighborhood (Dart, 1992, p. 96).

Gates and Jackson (1990, pp. 20–21) agree:

> Gang members are no longer limiting their attacks to suspected rivals. In an effort to enhance their own reputations or those of their gangs, gang members are attacking peace officers at an alarming rate. Besides being outgunned by the gang members, police are being subjected to random snipings and planned ambushes.

This was tragically illustrated in September 1992 in Minneapolis when patrol officer Jerome Haaf was purposely shot in the back as he sat in a pizza parlor writing his reports. The murder was attributed to a street gang that wanted to assassinate a police officer.

## Gangs Defined

A **gang** is a number of persons associated together in some way, an organized group of criminals, a group of youths from the same neighborhood banded together for a social reason. Minnesota statutes define a *gang* as "an association of three or more persons, with a common name and established hierarchy, formed to encourage gang members to perpetrate crimes or to provide support to gang members who do commit crime." A gang has the main characteristics of leadership and organization for the purpose of committing illegal acts or crimes, either individually or as a group. Black's Law Dictionary defines a gang as "any company of persons who go about together or act in concert, in modern use, mainly for criminal purposes (*State v. Gaynor*)."

Clay and Aquila (1994, p. 65) define a *gang* as: "A group, often associated with a territory or 'turf,' that shares a common identity and expresses membership through common clothing, symbols, and insignia."

According to Dart (1992, p. 96): "A **street gang** is an association of individuals who exhibit the following characteristics in varying degrees:

1. A gang name and recognizable symbols.
2. A geographic territory.
3. A regular meeting pattern.
4. An organized, continuous course of criminality.

---

A street gang is a group of individuals who form a social allegiance and engage in unlawful or criminal activity.

---

## Gangs and Society

Society sees gangs as undesirable. Many of the defining characteristics of a gang could be applicable to any other organization, however, with the exception of the purpose, which is to engage in antisocial or criminal behavior. Not all gangs engage in criminal behavior, however. Some "gangs" form out of normal relationships in a neighborhood or a school. If they do not engage in antisocial behavior, nothing ever happens that causes them to feel a need to "band together" to protect their group from outside activity or threats. The gang remains a social group or club.

However, when a gang forms for social reasons and then outside activities occur that endanger one or more of the members, the group may "close ranks" and act as a group in their defense. For example, the group may be having a meeting in the park, and an outside group beats up a few of the members. The group may report this to the police, or they may decide to "take things into their own hands" and seek revenge.

Other gangs form for the express purpose of committing antisocial behavior or criminal activities, starting with the manner of initiation into the group, which may require shoplifting or a more serious illegal activity.

Gang membership generally emerges among individuals who live in specific areas of a community. They start out small and grow in relation to the purpose and desire of the group. Most gangs are of limited numbers, sufficient for the entire group to meet and discuss things in person. Incidents that happen to them or that are expressly initiated by them cause them to identify as a group. This normally takes place over a period of time.

Father and son may have been members of the same gang. Gang members who are arrested and sent to prison may be placed with other gang members already in the prison system. When they return to society, they may return to the gang with additional status, although parole requirements may stipulate they must dissociate themselves for a required period.

Valdez (1997, p. 32) provides several reasons for the proliferation of gangs, including the following:

- Increasing academic failure.
- Increasing substance abuse.
- An apathetic society.
- An acceptance of violence as a way to deal with conflict.

## Makeup and Characteristics of Gangs

Gangs range in size from small groups of three to five up to several thousand. Nationally known gangs such as the Crips number in the 50,000 range and the Bloods in the 20,000 to 30,000 range.

Large gangs are normally broken down into smaller groups but are known collectively under one name. It is estimated that more than 90 percent of gangs have between 3 and 100 members, with only 4 percent having more than 100 members. The number of gangs in large cities ranges from 1,200 to 1,500.

Gangs are typically structured around race or nationality. For example, Minneapolis has two Native American street gangs, the Naturals and The Club, with membership estimated at several hundred. This is in addition to black gangs, primarily the Vice Lords and the Disciples, and to Hmong youth gangs. A summary of the characteristic groups of youth gangs is contained in Table 18–1.

The gang establishes its "turf," or area of domination, and then other gangs challenge its reputation and turf. In the past this took the form of gang fights. Today, however, it often takes the form of "drive-by shootings" from a moving vehicle, many of which have killed innocent citizens as well as rival gang members.

Attacks on police officers by snipers or by ambushes using assault weapons have also occurred. A serious development has been the increase of Asian gangs, many of which are committing vicious drug-related crimes. In addition, gangs are heavily involved in drug use, abuse and sales.

### Biker Gangs

One type of gang that has been a problem for decades is the motorcycle gang, typically consisting of older individuals than street gangs. These gangs function throughout the United States. The FBI has recognized the Outlaws gang as being connected with organized crime. Other known motorcycle gangs are the Free-Wheelers, Renegades, Bandidos, Misfits, Hells Angels, Pagans and Dirty Dozen. Some of these gangs are involved in money laundering, narcotics trafficking, murder, extortion, prostitution, rapes and bombings.

**Table 18–1 Characteristic Groups of Youth Gangs**

| | |
|---|---|
| Black Gangs | Origins in Los Angeles, Chicago, New York, Miami and other major urban ghettos. Crips, Bloods, Players, Untouchables and Vice Lords are some of the more prominent gangs. |
| Jamaican Posses | Immigrant Jamaicans in the U.S. with roots in Jamaica. Groups have been identified in New York, Boston, Philadelphia, Washington, D.C., Houston, Atlanta, Detroit, Seattle and Anchorage among other locations. |
| Hispanic Gangs | Origins in Los Angeles, valleys of California, New York (Puerto Rico), Miami (Mariel Cubans, Dominicans), Washington, D.C., and other urban barrios. Tend to use highly stylized graffiti lettering. |
| Asian Gangs | Origins among recent emigres from Vietnam, Hong Kong and Philippines. Activity centered in New York; New Orleans; Los Angeles and Orange County, California; Portland, Oregon; Seattle; San Francisco; and Houston. |
| Pacific Islander Gangs | Primarily Samoans who have migrated to Western urban areas, i.e., Los Angeles, San Francisco, Portland. |
| White "Stoner" Gangs | Caucasian groups identified with Heavy Metal and Punk Rock music preferences and with some British working-class gangs. Sometimes involved with Satanic rites and symbols. |
| Neo-Nazi Gangs | Tend to articulate white supremacy, racism and Nazi symbols. Some call themselves "skinheads" and sport close-cut hair or shaved heads. |
| Motorcycle Gangs | Dominantly Caucasians, branches of Hells Angels and other notorious motorcycle groups. Tend to be heavily involved with the manufacture and sale of methamphetamine. |

SOURCE: Metropolitan Court Judges Committee Report. *Drugs—The American Family Crisis: A Judicial Response: 39 Recommendations,* August 4, 1988.

Trethewy (1993, p. 95) notes: "Street and biker gangs are cousins in crime, but there are some noticeable differences. Street gangs do not have the highly organized structure that most biker gangs have." He (p. 96) also notes: "Bikers use computers, cellular phones, complex surveillance equipment, sophisticated weaponry and pagers."

### Female Gangs

According to Laflin (1996, p. 87): "Gangs consisting of female members, whether it be auxiliary branches of male gangs or fully autonomous female organizations, are fully capable and disposed to commit as many crimes as any male gang."

## Gangs and Drugs

Until the early 1980s, when crack, or rock cocaine, hit the market, gangs here and everywhere supported their criminal lifestyles through burglary, robbery, extortion and car theft. Drug trafficking existed but nowhere near current levels.

Today gangs and drugs exist hand in hand. The sale of illegal drugs such as crack, cocaine, marijuana and PCP generates millions of dollars annually and is the driving force behind the expansion of gangs across the United States (Lamprey, 1990, p. 7).

Economic gain is, indeed, often the reason youths join gangs. It is hard to convince a youth that $4.50 an hour for busing tables is preferable to making $200 for two hours' work as a drug courier.

Gangs often consciously exploit the difference between juvenile and adult law in their drug dealing, using younger gang members whenever possible to avoid adult sanctions. Most states will not allow youths under age 15 to be certified as adults, and most states have statutory restrictions on placing youths under age 18 into adult correctional facilities.

Some law enforcement officials have said that gangs would exist even if the drug problem were to be eliminated. This was the conclusion of Los Angeles County Sheriff Sherman Block at a seminar on gangs: "The general impression put forth by the media today that gangs are fighting each other primarily over drug dealing and turf is really an oversimplification of the problem. Street gangs are really mortal enemies and will not hesitate to kill each other on sight whether drugs are the issue or not."

## Other Criminal Activities of Gangs

Many gang activities are similar to those of other segments of society and are *not* illegal. Gangs gather informally on streets and street corners, in parks, homes, abandoned buildings, vehicles, vacant lots or recreational areas and buildings. Each gang develops its own culture and activities over a period of time. The public often associates drinking and sexual promiscuity with gangs, and this is often the reality. Drinking is associated with becoming an adult. Gangs offer a sense of belonging and importance to their members that society and family do not provide. Gang members gradually dissociate from social conformity and become responsible only to themselves and their group activities. Many are most active at night and sleep during the day.

Most members are weak academically because of the lack of good study habits but are mentally capable. This is an important factor because gangs are essentially self-operated and governed. Some operate by consensus, but the majority have leaders and a subgoverning structure. Leadership may be single or dual. Status is generally obtained by joining the gang, but it does not automatically guarantee equal status within the gang once joined.

Gangs may have a core group and a fringe group. Most of their activity consists of "hanging around" together. The gang provides identification, self-esteem, self-worth, status, reputation, a stable relationship, protection, economic support and emancipation from parental and social control and institutions such as schools and churches.

Most gang members are unemployed or work at part-time jobs. Some stay with their gangs into adulthood, and others may go back to school or gain full-time employment, usually in jobs with very low pay. Many go to prison.

Gangs desire status and recognition, and a major recognition factor seems to be criminal activity. Crime may progress from petty thefts of candy and cigarettes, clothing, electronic equipment, prophylactics and vehicle parts to rolling drunks, mugging, pickpocketing and drug dealing.

The community, the schools and law enforcement each have a somewhat different perspective on gang activity. From the community's view, gang activity includes vandalism in the form of graffiti and the wanton destruction of public and private property. Customers stay away from businesses in gang areas; insurance rates go up; citizens become afraid to leave their homes. In essence, the streets belong to the gangs.

Likewise, in the schools, vandalism and graffiti pose a problem as does violence—including stabbings, shootings and sometimes arson. Teachers and students are intimidated, and learning is disrupted. In fact, if several gang members are in a class, the teacher may be powerless to enforce discipline or to teach. Gang problems in the Clark County, Nevada, school system (much the same as in most other school systems throughout the United States) have caused the Clark County Teachers Union to propose a five-point system for dealing with the problem:

**1.** Permanent expulsion from the school system of hard-core and violent gang members.
**2.** Identification cards for junior and senior high students to keep nonstudent gang members off school grounds.
**3.** Criminal prosecution of students who commit violent acts.
**4.** Adoption of a schoolwide emergency procedure system to be initiated when a violent crime is committed on school grounds.
**5.** Creation of a computerized list of active gang members to be distributed to each school (*Las Vegas Review-Journal,* September 21, 1990).

---

In addition to drug dealing, gang members are often engaged in vandalism, arson, shootings, stabbings, intimidation and other forms of violence.

---

Curry et al. (1994, p. 1) stress: "Gangs and crime committed by gang members are now pervasive in numerous American cities, presenting a challenge to law enforcement."

Figure 18–1 describes the type of gang-related crime by percentage.

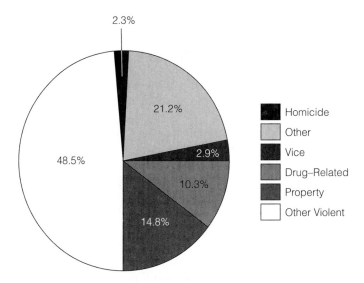

2.3%

21.2%

2.9%

48.5%

10.3%

14.8%

■ Homicide
▨ Other
■ Vice
▨ Drug–Related
▨ Property
□ Other Violent

**Figure 18–1    Gang-Related Crime by Type as Percent of Total Recorded**
Source: NIJ Gang Survey.

## Turf and Graffiti

Gang members establish a specific territory or **turf** that they will defend to the death. The turf includes the schools, businesses, residential areas, streets and alleys in the area, all of it controlled through fear, intimidation and violence.

Gangs identify their turf through **graffiti,** called "throwing a placa." Police officers who deal with gangs can learn much by understanding wall graffiti. The center of a gang's turf will have the most graffiti. It may name members of the gang, often in order of authority, listed in neat rows under the gang's logo. Unchallenged graffiti affirms the gang's control.

Valdez (1996c, p. 30) feels that understanding the messages behind gang graffiti can be of assistance in investigations. Among the messages that might be observed are the following:

- Announce the mere presence of a gang in a certain area or neighborhood.
- Indicate working alliances between gangs.
- Indicate the loss of a homeboy—usually using "RIP" next to the names of "fallen comrades."
- Brag about committed crimes.
- Notify a fellow gang member that disciplinary action is in order.
- Gain recognition or express their identity.
- Intimidate nongang members, particularly on school grounds.

Other gangs may challenge the turf claim by writing over or crossing out the graffiti, replacing it with their own. Such crossouts are usually found at the edge of a gang's territory. Gang members caught in the act of crossing out graffiti in a rival's territory may be killed.

Hispanic graffiti is highly artistic and very detailed. It frequently refers to group or gang power. Black-gang graffiti, in contrast, shows less flair and attention to detail and often is filled with profanity as well as expressions of individual power. The symbolism is more obvious and often includes weapons.

Gang graffiti is a source of frustration and expense to property owners and local governments.

## Identifying Gang Members

The first step in dealing with the gang problem is identifying the gang members. Valdez (1996d, p. 20) suggests: "Photos, jewelry, hairstyles and body piercing are among the obvious physical traits investigators look for when profiling gangs."

Another means of identifying gang members is by their tattoos, sometimes called body art. The most respected tattoos are those earned by serving a prison sentence.

---

Gang members may be identified by their names, symbols (clothing and tattoos) and communication styles, including graffiti and sign language.

---

The **Crips,** for example, are associated with blue or purple bandanas, scarves or rags. The **Bloods** are identified by red or green colors. Some gangs wear jackets and caps identified with professional sports teams, posing a problem for those youth who wear them because of actually loyalty to the particular team. Gang members may also be identified by the hand signals they use.

Valdez (1996e, p. 20) offers suggestions to investigators who are dealing with Southeast Asian gangs:

> Often, the stylized dress, tattoos, graffiti, hand signs, slang, stylized haircuts and jewelry used by other street gangs are also used by their Southeast Asian counterparts. But law enforcement officers have noticed a trend that started among the Southeast Asian gang community—burns and scars on the arms and hands. Displaying these body modifications or inflicting them in the presence of other gang members gives the wearer instant respect among his or her peers. The marks also serve as a kind of silent advertisement to the rest of the population. Without saying a word, a person wearing these marks or tattoos can walk into a cafe or restaurant and intimidate the owner into providing free food or paying for protection.

Valdez also notes that another unique characteristics of Southeast Asian street gangs is that they do not claim turf but rather are very mobile, with informal networks throughout the United States.

Table 18–2 summarizes the criteria for defining gangs used in some jurisdictions.

Police also need to identify the leaders of the gangs and who the "tough guys" are. Reducing the effectiveness of the leaders is important, but this is often difficult and can be accomplished only by having sufficient evidence to convict the leader of a crime that results in being sent to prison. Gangs are similar to other organizations. Take away their leadership and the group loses some of their effectiveness.

## Records to Keep

Information on gangs is an essential tool for law enforcement. The following *gang file* information should be recorded and filed by name separately and alphabetically:

- Number of active and associate members.
- Type of gang it is.
- Ethnic composition.
- Territory.
- Hideouts.
- Type(s) of crime(s) usually committed.
- Method of operation (M.O.).
- Choice of victims.
- Leadership.
- Violent members.

**Table 18–2  Criteria for Defining Gangs**

| Criteria Used | Large Cities* | Smaller Cities* |
|---|---|---|
| Use of Symbols | 93% | 100% |
| Violent Behavior | 81% | 84% |
| Group Organization | 81% | 88% |
| Territory | 74% | 88% |
| Leadership | 59% | 48% |
| Recurrent Interaction | 56% | 60% |

*Of the cities surveyed, 70 (89%) of the large cities and 25 (58%) of the smaller cities indicated the criteria used to define gangs.

SOURCE: 1994 National Institute of Justice Gang Survey (Washington, DC).

*This girl gang, posed in front of a wall of their graffiti, is named "Tiny Diablas of the South Side Grape Street Watts." The gang color is purple, and their hand signal is similar to sign language "g."*

Included within the record system should be a *gang member pointer file* that cross-references the names of suspected gang members with the gang file. This may be a cardex or computerized file.

A *moniker file* connects suspected gang members' street names with their legal names. **Monikers,** or nicknames, are often used during the commission of crimes, and several gangs may have members with the same moniker. Therefore, one card should have on it the moniker and all gang members known by it. A *photograph file* is of great help in preparing to conduct photographic identification sessions. A *gang vehicle file* can be maintained, arranged alphabetically by *make* of the vehicle. Include color, year, body type, license number, distinguishing features, known drivers, where it is usually parked and so on. An *illegal activities file* can also be maintained, arranged alphabetically, listing the gangs known to engage in the activities.

---

Maintain records on gangs, gang members, monikers, photographs, vehicles and illegal activities. The records should be cross-referenced.

---

Quarantiello (1996, p. 36) notes: "Computers are aiding law enforcement by keeping gang members from becoming faces in the crowd." Quarantiello (1996, p. 80) also suggests:

For officers attempting to cope with the ever-increasing number of gang members throughout the country, the ability to execute a computerized records search based on very little known input is a godsend. It is often the difference between a case that remains open and one that is cleared.

*A police map marking the boundaries of South Los Angeles's gang war zone. The officer points
out grid 64, turf of "the Rolling 60s," one of the worst areas in the city.*

## Investigating Illegal Gang Activity

Gang investigations should proceed like most other criminal investigations.
As Valdez (1996a, p. 20) stresses: "Prosecuting the gang case starts with paying
attention to the proper procedures."

Contacts by police with gangs and gang members will occur in much the same
way as with any other criminal activity. Patrol officers are usually the first-line contact. Uniformed officers should establish contacts with the gangs in the community
and become familiar with their size, the names of as many members as possible and
each gang's identifying symbols, colors and graffiti. Uniformed and investigative police personnel need to establish personal contacts with gang members. A mutual
understanding between the police and the gang members can reduce violence.
The police know what gangs do, and the gangs know what police do.

Gangs do not like the police because the police interfere with their unlawful gatherings and criminal activities. Gang members try to avoid the police but
at times engage in open confrontation because of police interference with what
they consider their territory and the criminal activities they carry on.

Some disenchanted gang members may be used by the police as informants.
Children know what is going on among their peers, even though they may not
be gang members themselves. Teachers and school counselors are other sources
of information on youth activities, acceptable and nonacceptable. In addition,
recreation department personnel know what is going on in the youth community and are, therefore, sources of intelligence information.

Police develop information and evidence of gang crimes in much the same
way as for any other crime. Obtaining information from gang members is difficult
because of the unity of gang membership. Obtaining witness information from
nongang members is difficult because they feel threatened by the gang image and
activities and have obvious concerns about their personal security and safety.

**593**

**Chapter 18**

**Organized Crime,
Gang-Related
Crime, Bias/Hate
Crime and
Ritualistic Crime**

According to an NIJ Report, "Victim, Witness Intimidation Rising in Gang Areas" (1995, p. 50): "Intimidation of victims and witnesses by gang members is increasing in some jurisdictions and may be a factor in 75 to 100 percent of violent crimes committed in some gang-dominated neighborhoods."

As Valdez (1996b, p. 20) stresses: "The right approach to witness/victim interviews can make or break a gang investigation."

The same techniques police use to obtain information about organized crime and other serious criminal activity in their communities can be used to gain information about gang activity.

The immediate area in which a crime occurs may offer much information. Any graffiti present indicates which gang is in control of the territory. Crossed-through graffiti, as noted, indicates a contested area. Investigators should keep in mind that gang members do not like to be on foot in a strange area, especially one dominated by their enemies; therefore, commando-type raids on foot are very rare. If a crime suggests that no vehicles were involved, odds are good the suspects are local, possibly members of the same gang as the victim. These crimes generally reflect intragang conflicts involving narcotics, girlfriends or family disputes.

---

Special problems involved in investigating the illegal activities of gangs include the multitude of suspects and the unreliability or fear of witnesses.

---

Illegal activities of gangs usually involve multiple suspects, which makes investigation much more difficult. Evidence may link only a few of the suspects with the crime, and, as with organized crime figures, gang members maintain fierce loyalty to the gang and its members.

A further difficulty in investigating such illegal activities is that many "witnesses" may actually be gang members or people who are at least sympathetic to the gang. Their information is usually unreliable. In addition, other individuals within the neighborhood may have information but may be fearful to become involved. They live in the neighborhood with the gang and may fear for their very lives. They may provide information and then later deny it. For this reason, tape record or videotape all such interviews.

If a house-to-house canvass is conducted and information is obtained, it is critical to continue the canvass. To stop as soon as information is obtained points a finger directly at the inhabitants of that residence as informants. Also, other information may not be obtained simply because the canvass was not completed. People living in the next house down the street may also have important information.

Evidence obtained in gang investigations is processed the same as in other crimes. Graffiti is photographed for later identification. Field interview cards are filed on members, vehicles, territory, locations, crimes committed, drug activities and any other information received. Information can be entered into special card or computer files for easy and immediate retrieval.

Gang members may usually be located within their territory and among gang members, even after they commit a crime, as an individual or as a group—because this is their "home" area. The process of issuing warrants and the arrest procedure is the same as in other crimes.

In January 1992 the FBI announced that it was assigning thirty-nine agents to assist local police in their efforts to combat gang crime. The Associated Press ("FBI Brings Spy-Catching Skills . . . ," 1992, p.A7) noted: "The FBI brings some important tools to the gang front, including broader powers to use wiretaps and seize drug dealers' property; an ability to prosecute under federal laws on extortion, racketeering and interstate crime; and longer prison terms for some crimes."

Throughout the investigation of illegal gang activities, investigators should be aware of the most common defense they may be subjected to in court.

---

The two most often used defense strategies are pleas of diminished capacity and self-defense.

---

Although some states have eliminated "diminished capacity" as a defense, many have not. Therefore, determine if the suspect was under the influence of alcohol or other drugs at the time of the crime. Likewise, establish if the suspect was threatened by the victim and could possibly have been acting in self-defense.

Difficulties in prosecuting gang-related crimes are summarized in Table 18–3. In both large and small jurisdictions, obtaining cooperation of victims and witnesses and intimidation of victims and witnesses presented the most problems.

## Police Responsibility

As reported by Sharp (1996, p. 64): "In a recent poll, 26% of law enforcement administrators said that gangs are more a topic for the media to dwell on rather than a real problem, at least in their communities. Another 13% were not sure. The remaining 61% stated that gangs are real problems." Sharp also notes that gangs and their activities are spreading into small-town America.

Police have the responsibility of investigating gang activities. These activities may involve antisocial behavior resulting in commission of minor crimes such as vandalism or trespassing or more serious felony crimes. In recent years, as noted, a deep involvement in using and selling drugs has developed.

Some police departments have established substations in neighborhoods where the primary purpose of officers assigned to that station is to prevent gang activities, protect the innocent youth of the area and make any necessary arrests. It is a supported form of neighborhood policing. Additionally, the police departments in larger cities may have specialized antigang activity squads that cover the entire city to control gangs and their activities.

Kensic (1992, p. 50) describes how the Los Angeles Police Department targets street gangs. Department personnel classify each individual thought to be affiliated with a gang as a hard-core, secondary or associate gang member and then categorize them by their criminal history.

Pierce and Ramsay (1990, p. 24) describe the approach to the gang problem taken by the Bellingham (Washington) Police Department:

> Volunteers from patrol were used to start a "Gang Enforcement Team" (GET), whose objective was to regulate and mitigate gang activity during peak times. GET consists of two special investigation detectives, including the full-time gang detective, and four patrol officers working on overtime.

This group of officers works to identify gang members, photograph them and gather information about their activities. A tracking system includes a special

**Table 18–3  Prosecution Problems by Size of Jurisdiction**

| Problem | Large Jurisdictions (n = 118) | | | |
| --- | --- | --- | --- | --- |
| | Not a Problem | Minor Problem | Moderate Problem | Major Problem |
| Obtaining cooperation of victims and witnesses | 2.6% | 8.8% | 27.2% | 61.4% |
| Intimidation of victims and witnesses | 1.8% | 17.0% | 30.4% | 50.8% |
| Lack of appropriate sanctions for juvenile gang members who commit crimes | 9.7% | 22.2% | 21.2% | 46.9% |
| Lack of early intervention for youth at risk of gang involvement | 9.7% | 11.5% | 32.8% | 46.0% |
| Lack of resources for witness protection | 6.1% | 20.2% | 31.6% | 42.1% |
| Victim and witness credibility | 6.2% | 16.8% | 46.9% | 30.1% |
| Inadequate police preparation of crime reports | 33.3% | 41.2% | 20.2% | 5.3% |

| Problem | Small Jurisdictions (n = 74) | | | |
| --- | --- | --- | --- | --- |
| | Not a Problem | Minor Problem | Moderate Problem | Major Problem |
| Obtaining cooperation of victims and witnesses | 10.1% | 15.9% | 30.4% | 43.5% |
| Intimidation of victims and witnesses | 13.2% | 19.2% | 25.0% | 42.6% |
| Lack of appropriate sanctions for juvenile gang members who commit crimes | 2.9% | 27.5% | 37.7% | 31.9% |
| Lack of early intervention for youth at risk of gang involvement | 15.7% | 18.6% | 34.3% | 31.4% |
| Lack of resources for witness protection | 7.1% | 27.1% | 37.2% | 28.6% |
| Victim and witness credibility | 1.4% | 30.0% | 41.4% | 27.2% |
| Inadequate police preparation of crime reports | 34.8% | 39.2% | 13.0% | 13.0% |

SOURCE: Claire Johnson, Barbara Webster and Edward Connors. "Prosecuting Gangs: A National Assessment," *National Institute of Justice Research in Brief,* February 1995, pp. 6–7.

gang contact report form designed for all contacts with gang members. Information is entered into the department's computerized records, and a gang intelligence bulletin is disseminated to all departmental units periodically.

Gangs have become a national problem through their activities in drugs and because of the number of crimes they commit. Their activities have created a feeling of fear in the average citizen that restricts normal adult activity and recreation, especially during the night.

Police antidrug programs, such as the Drug Abuse Resistance Education (DARE) program in the schools, may help reduce gang influence by reducing the demand for drugs. Police become involved in prevention, control, arrests and prosecutions and in promoting proper laws to restrict drug and gang activity.

In Chicago and other major cities, laws passed to create "safe school zones" prohibit drug possession or sales on school property and within 1,000 feet of school property. Offenses of these laws were upgraded from misdemeanors and gross misdemeanors to felonies, and sentencing is mandatory. Possession of beepers or pager radios is also prohibited within the "safe school zone" area. Public telephones were removed from some schools because they were being used to make drug contacts and sales during school hours. This restricted telephone calls to the school office, where they could be controlled.

# Gangs of the Future?

McCort (1996, p. 33) describes the evolution of street gangs and their apparent shift toward organized crime:

> Over the past 15 years, street gangs have undergone a swift and dramatic change that has had a significant impact upon America. The problem that was once restricted to large cities is now shared by small suburban and rural communities as well. These gangs have become a driving influence on violent crime, drug trafficking and community stability. . . .
>
> An examination of recent developments in street gang activity . . . reveals an evolutionary process that has been characteristic of ethnic gangs throughout American history. . . .
>
> Where the evolution will lead today's gangs is not completely understood. It is certain, however, that law enforcement must consider the potential emergence of a new organized crime system. . . .
>
> For the most part, street gangs will likely remain loose-knit social entities, involved primarily in street-level crime. However, individuals or elements of the subculture are evolving into a more sophisticated level of organized crime.

Bunker (1996, p. 54) presents a different view of the future of gangs, noting:

> The expanding presence of street gangs in the United States can be linked both to military trends in the non-Western world and to future warfighting concerns— particularly in terms of the disruption of a society's social organization.

## Bias/Hate Crime: An Overview

Bizzack (1991, p. 133) defines a **bias crime** as "a criminal act committed or attempted by a person or group of persons against a person or the property of another person, which in any way constitutes an expression of prejudice toward the victim because of the victim's race, color, religion, or ethnic or national origin." Story (1991, p. 101) suggests this definition of bias, or hate, crimes: "Unlawful actions designed to frighten or harm an individual because of his or her race, religion, ethnicity, or sexual orientation. Such acts range from verbal intimidation and harassment to destruction of property, and even to physical violence."

---

Bias crimes are crimes motivated by bigotry and hatred against a specific group of people.

---

As noted by Lieberman (1994, p. 21): "Hate crimes are designed to intimidate victims and other members of the victim's community in an attempt to leave them feeling isolated, vulnerable and unprotected by the law."

The FBI reported receiving 7,947 reports of hate crimes in 1995 ("FBI Recorded Nearly 8,000 Hate Crimes Last Year," 1996, p. 5). Intimidation was the most commonly reported hate crime, followed by simple or aggravated assaults and then by destruction of property and vandalism.

According to Morris (1997, p. 16), race was the primary motivation with blacks being victimized 61.9 percent of the time. Religious bias was the second most common motivator, followed by the victim's sexual orientation.

Bodinger-deUriate (1991) reports: "The incidence of hate crime is currently occurring at record-breaking rates nationwide. The groups most likely to be victims of hate crime are (in alphabetical order): African-Americans, Arabs, Asians, gay males, Jews, Latinos, lesbians, Native Americans, and white women in interracial relationships" (p. 4). Bodinger-deUriate notes that some characteristics typical of hate-motivated violence are relatively rare in other crimes of violence (p. 2):

- *The relationship of the victim to the perpetrator.* Most assaults involve two people who know each other well. The opposite is true of hate-motivated assaults, which are very likely to be "stranger crimes," where the perpetrator and victim are completely unknown to each other.
- *The number of perpetrators.* The majority of assaults typically involve one victim and one perpetrator or two "mutual combatants." Hate crime generally involves an average of four assailants for each victim, although the ratio varies.
- *The uneven nature of the conflict.* In addition to the frequently unfair dynamic of ganging-up on the victim, hate crime perpetrators often attack younger or weaker victims or arm themselves and attack unarmed victims.
- *The amount of physical damage inflicted.* Hate crime is extremely violent. In fact, victims of hate crime are three times more likely to require hospitalization than normal assault victims.
- *The treatment of property.* In a very large fraction of property crimes something of value is taken. In hate-motivated crimes, it is apparently more likely that something of value is damaged or destroyed.
- *The apparent absence of gain.* Gain is absent in most hate crime. For example, although property may be damaged, it usually is not stolen. In hate crime, no personal score is settled; no profit is made.
- *The places in which hate crimes occur.* Hate crime frequently takes place at churches, synagogues, mosques, cemeteries, monuments, schools, camps and in or around the victim's home.

### Neo-Nazi Groups

Especially troublesome to law enforcement has been the rise of neo-Nazi "skinhead" groups. The skinheads are shaven-headed youths who sport Nazi insignia and preach violence against Blacks, Hispanics, Jews, Asians and homosexuals. Christensen (1990, p. 73) describes the typical skinhead appearance:

The skinheads look like military recruits in basic training. Their clothing adds to the militaristic look. Typically, they wear dark leather jackets or greenish flight jackets. Their pants are either blue or black jeans or camouflage army fatigues. They often wear suspenders, which they call "braces," that are worn over their shoulders or, if they are getting ready to fight, the braces are left hanging down. They roll their pant legs up to show black military boots or the coveted British high-top boots called "Doc Martens," which are black or a reddish tan color.

Their jackets often display patches of American flags, German crosses and swastikas. They may also write on their jackets or pants such expressions as "White Power," "Skins Rule," "KKK" or "WAR."

Their bodies are frequently covered with tattoos depicting skulls, swastikas, or words such as "Skinhead" and "SWP" (Supreme White Power), or any myriad of acronyms representing group affiliations.

The increased number of skinheads has been accompanied by an increase in the number of violent crimes they have committed against members of minority groups, including homicides, shootings, beatings and stabbings.

Some reports indicate that there are more than 3,500 skinhead members in the United States. Police departments find themselves walking a tightrope between protecting the safety and property of citizens and protecting the rights of assembly and free speech. The skinheads have also been linked with drug use and satanism.

### The Police Response

Respond promptly to reports of hate crime, attempt to reduce the victims' fears and to determine the exact type of prejudice involved and then provide follow-up information to the victims. Include in the report the exact words or language used, actions of the perpetrators, symbols, colors, dress or any other identifying characteristics or actions.

Nelson (1994, p. 50) offers the following criteria to determine if a particular act or incident is bias related:

- Is the motivation of the alleged offender known?
- Was the incident known to have been motivated by racial, religious, ethnic or sexual orientation bias?
- Does the victim perceive the offender's action to have been motivated by bias?
- Is there no clear other motivation for the incident?
- Were any remarks reflecting racial, religious, ethnic or sexual orientation bias made by the offender?
- Were there any offensive symbols, words or acts that are known to represent a hate group or other evidence of bias against the victim's group?
- Did the incident occur on a holiday or other day of significance to either the victim's or the offender's group?
- What do the demographics of the area tell you about the incident?

*Some thirty graves scribbled with swastikas and other graffiti in a Jewish cemetery.*

> The most important part of the hate crime equation is the victim. Many hate crimes go unsolved (e.g., graffiti, random racially motivated assault, etc.), so the hate crime units have to concentrate on the needs of the victims, which are different from the victims of other crimes. . . .
>
> People can avoid and/or prepare for other kinds of crimes, but not for hate crimes. Victims are attacked because of who or what they are.

Lieberman (1994, p. 18) suggests: "Law enforcement officials can advance police–community relations by demonstrating a commitment to be both tough on hate crime perpetrators and sensitive to the special needs of hate crime victims."

## Efforts to Combat Bias/Hate Crimes

Nicholl (1994, p. 30) describes the Violent Gang Task Force (VGTF) instituted by the Immigration and Naturalization Service (INS). In an effort to deal with gang members who come here from other countries, this task force has 130 special agents who have conducted a total of 95 criminal investigations since its inception.

According to Walker and Katz (1995, p. 29):

> The creation of bias crime units is part of a national response to the problem of hate-motivated violence that includes state and federal legislation. By 1994 all but four states (Alaska, Nebraska, Utah and Wyoming) had some form of hate crime legislation. . . . The most common elements include:

- Enhanced penalties for common law crimes against persons or property which are motivated by bias based on race, ethnicity, religion, gender, or sexual orientation.
- Criminal penalties for vandalism of religious institutions.
- Collection of data on bias crimes.

### Reporting Bias Crimes

In 1990 the Federal Hate Crime Statistics Act (HCSA) was passed, mandating that the Justice Department collect data on crimes related to religion, race, sexual orientation or ethnicity. Lieberman (1992, p. 33) regards the HCSA as "a powerful new mechanism with which to confront violent bigotry against individuals."

In addition to the federal statute, forty-six states have passed statutes that address prejudicial hate crimes, and eighteen states have established hate-crime data systems. The FBI has also published manuals concerning the types of statistics needed and has established training programs in major cities. It is difficult to establish hate crime records because some hate crimes involve groups rather than individuals. Appendix E contains a sample form for reporting bias crimes.

## Ritualistic Crime: An Overview

Ritualistic crimes are most often associated with cults. For the purposes of this discussion, it is necessary to distinguish between cults and "cults." In general, *cult* refers to a system of religious beliefs and rituals and its body of adherents. As used in this text and in law enforcement, **cult** denotes a group of people whose beliefs and rituals may appear to be similar to those of mainstream society but which the majority of society would view as socially deviant or even violent and destructive. Such cults are commonly connected with the occult, paganism, witchcraft, demonism and satanism or devil worship. Because cults are so varied in organization and purpose, they are difficult to define.

---

A cult is a system of religious beliefs and rituals. It also refers to those who practice such beliefs.

---

One informal definition of a *cult* is "any religion other than your own." The term is often applied to religious or mystical groups that one does not understand. Most cults involve some form of worship—be it individual or group or by principle or philosophy—and followers who are dedicated to the concepts promoted by the leader.

Normally cults have a charismatic leader who develops an idea that attracts persons looking for fulfillment. The leader is normally self-appointed and claims the right of rule because of a supernatural power of appointment. The leaders operate by strict rules established for their own personal power over the followers. Cult membership may include males and females, and there is normally no room for democratic participation. Leadership is most often through fear and mysticism. Charles Manson and Jim Jones are notorious examples of cult leaders.

A cult in Waco, Texas, the "Branch Davidians," headed by David Koresh, clashed with federal agents attempting a raid on February 28, 1993. The raid turned into a gun battle in which four federal agents and at least two cult members were killed. Sixteen agents were wounded. Weapons inside the compound included at least one tripod-mounted .50-caliber machine gun and many semi-automatic weapons. A child who was released from the compound and who had lived with the cult for four years said she had been taught to put a gun into her mouth and told how to commit suicide by taking cyanide.

A fifty-one-day standoff between the federal government and David Koresh's armed cult ended on April 19, 1993, when fire engulfed the compound. The FBI had sent an armored combat vehicle to ram holes into the buildings and pump tear gas into them. The FBI asserted that cultists started the blaze, which killed at least eighty, including women and children. Survivors of the fire, however, insisted the fire was caused by the tank hitting a barrel of propane and tipping over lit camping lanterns. Professor of sociology Ron Enroth "said he sympathized with the frustration law-enforcement officials had in dealing with Koresh and that it was 'a little unfair' to criticize them for the conflagration at the cult's compound, but, he added, 'This points to the need for taking more seriously the psychology of cultism and the theology of cultism'" (Niebuhr, 1993, p. A17). According to Niebuhr:

> Experts on millennial groups (groups who attach special significance to the end of a thousand year period) said if there is a lesson to be learned from Waco, it may be that law-enforcement officials ought to be aware of the potency of millennial beliefs. Throughout the 1990s, interest in end-of-time prophecy will grow, as the current millennium draws to a close.

Over the years a number of terms have been associated with cults. Among the terms law enforcement officers should be familiar with are the following:

**601**

**Chapter 18**

**Organized Crime,
Gang-Related
Crime, Bias/Hate
Crime and
Ritualistic Crime**

*Members of the Montana Freemen, the FBI and Colorado state senator Charles Duke meet at the end of a dirt road near the Freemen compound near Jordan, Montana, in May 1996.*

- **Antichrist**—the son of Satan.
- **Beelzebub**—a powerful demon, right under Satan.
- **Coven**—a group of witches or satanists.
- **Hand of Glory**—the left hand of a person who has died.
- **Incantation**—verbal spells.
- **Occult**—secret knowledge of supernormal powers.
- **Pentagram**—five-pointed star.
- **Ritual**—prescribed form of religious or mystical ceremony.
- **Sabbat**—a gathering of witches.

Symbols commonly associated with satanic and occult groups are illustrated in Figure 18–2.

Among the satanic and occult symbols are the *circle*, which symbolizes totality and wholeness and within which ceremonies are often performed; the *inverted cross*, which mocks the Christian cross; the *goat's head*, symbolizing the devil; the *heart*, symbolizing the center of life; the *hexagram* (six-pointed star), purported to protect and control demons; the *pentagram* (five-pointed star), representing the four elements of the earth surmounted by "the Spirit"; and the *horned hand*, a hand signal of recognition used between those who are members of a cult. This is similar to the hand signals used by street gangs.

Colors also have significance to many cults:

- Black—darkness, night, sorrow, evil, the devil.
- Blue—water, tears, sadness.
- Green—vegetation, nature, restfulness.
- Red—blood, physical life, energy, sexuality.
- White—cleanliness, purity, innocence, virginity.
- Yellow—perfection, wealth, glory, power.

Cults and the occult have created great interest because of recurring stories from children and adults in different areas of the United States concerning

**Figure 18–2   Common Satanic and Occult Symbols**

bizarre satanic rituals and behaviors that involve adults and children. Although some of these may be fantasies, there appears to be some truth, especially regarding the danger to children of the members of satanic groups.

Police, like other members of society, have an interest in the unusual, both as individuals and as police officials. As police officers, however, their concern must be restricted to facts and to incidents that constitute some type of crime.

---

A **ritualistic crime** is an unlawful act committed with or during a ceremony. Investigate the crime, not the belief system.

---

**603**

**Chapter 18**

**Organized Crime,
Gang-Related
Crime, Bias/Hate
Crime and
Ritualistic Crime**

The "Black Masses" of satanism often incorporate religious articles stolen from churches. A **Black Mass** mocks the Christian ritual of communion by substituting blood and urine for the wine, feces for the bread. The cross is usually inverted, and candles and cups may be used in sexual acts. "Hymns" that are either obscene or that praise Satan may be sung, and heavy-metal music may be played.

---

Cult or ritualistic crimes include vandalism, destruction or theft of religious artifacts; desecration of cemeteries; the maiming, torturing or killing of animals or humans; and the sexual abuse of children.

---

The Black Mass frequently involves animal mutilation and sacrifice and sometimes torture and sacrifice of humans, preferably babies or virgins. The sacrifice often incorporates ritualistic incantations. Victims, be they animal or human, are tortured and mutilated because it is believed that while the victim struggles, the life forces given off can be captured and stored for later use. Such sacrifices may be followed by a dance and orgy.

"Stoner" gangs consist of middle-class youths involved in drugs, alcohol and often satanism. Although stoners are not as apt to engage in the violent crimes associated with other street gangs, they may mutilate animals, rob graves and desecrate churches and human remains. Their graffiti frequently depicts satanic symbolism such as inverted crosses and the number *666*.

## Investigating Ritualistic Crimes

Cult and occult reports and activities are investigated much the same way as any other crime. Persons reporting these incidents are interviewed, and reports are prepared concerning any witnesses or alleged victims of any type of activity that constitutes a crime.

Take photos, draw sketches of symbols, describe colors found, take measurements of objects and the distances of objects from each other. Preserve all objects at the scene as evidence. Work from the outside perimeter to the center or the focus point of the site.

Numerous books on the beliefs and rituals of various cults are available. Whether the market is inquisitive minds or followers of satanism is irrelevant; these books sell well. The background contained in such books is beyond the scope of this book, but investigators should be alert to signs that criminal activity may be cult related.

### Signs of Cult-Related Activity

The following articles may be important indicators of satanic or cult activity. If ritualistic crime is suspected, these articles should be listed in any search warrant sought:

■ Altars, stone or metal.
■ Animal parts such as the anus, heart, tongue, ears, front teeth, front legs, genitals.
■ Ashes.
■ Bells.
■ Blood.
■ Body paint.

- Body parts (may be in a freezer).
- Bones used or taken from graves, such as the femur, fibula, index finger, skull and other large bones. The upper right leg and joints of the right-hand fingers are valued.
- Books on satanism.
- Bottles containing blood (may be in refrigerator).
- Bowls with powder, colored salt, drugs or herbs.
- Bullwhips.
- Cages.
- Candles, candle holders or candle drippings. (Candles may be genital-shaped or colored black or white.)
- Cat-o'-nine-tails whips.
- Cauldron for a fire.
- Chalices.
- Circle with a 9-foot diameter (may contain a pentagram).
- Coffin.
- Cords, colored and knotted.
- Crystals.

*Texas Attorney General Jim Mattox (center) views a cauldron of bones found at a ranch where twelve bodies were found buried.*

- Daggers or double-edged short sword.
- Drums.
- Effigylike clay figures, voodoo dolls stuck with pins or otherwise mutilated.
- Flash powder.
- Glove, black satin or velvet, for the right hand.
- Gongs.
- Hoods, hats or helmets.
- Hypodermic needles (for removing blood).
- Incense.
- Inverted crosses.
- Jewelry such as amulets or medallions with satanic symbols.
- Knives.
- Ligatures.
- Martial arts weaponry and clothing.
- Masks.
- Nondiscernible alphabet.
- Occult games.
- Ouija board.
- Painted rocks.
- Parchment (for making contracts).
- Pillow, small red velvet.
- Robes, especially red, white or black.
- Rooms draped in black or red (or nail holes in walls and ceiling indicating that such drapes may have been used).
- Satanic symbols painted on rocks, trees.
- Skulls.
- Smoke bombs.
- Swords.
- Tarot cards.
- Unusual drawings or symbols on walls or floors (hexagrams, pentagrams, horns of death, etc.).
- Vandalized Christian artifacts.
- Wooden stand for altar.

---

Indicators that criminal activity may be cult related include symbols, candles, makeshift altars, bones, cult-related books, swords, daggers and chalices.

---

Mueller (1992, p. 38) expands on this subject by explaining several items commonly found during investigations of ritualistic occult crimes:

*Altars:* May be permanent or entirely portable. Sometimes an occultist will carry his equipment inside a box that also serves as his altar. Such a box may provide drug evidence, serological evidence, and more.

*Black plastic (drop cloth):* Check for blood—plastic drop cloths are reported to be used to catch blood during sacrifices.

*Body parts (or lack of body parts):* Body parts are often used for magical purposes. Some satanists will remove an animal's legs, as they believe the devil uses them to walk around.

*Bones:* Animal bones may yield information as to the type of animal and methods of death. Human bones may also be found. Skulls may or may not have wax on them. Bones may have runic symbols on them.

*Booby traps:* Meant to either frighten intruders and warn occultists or to harm or eliminate law enforcement/intruders. These may consist of trip wires, a board with spikes laid in the footpath, barbed wire, animal traps, etc.

*Book of Shadows:* Can be very simple or very fancy. Basically it is a journal detailing spells, incantations, success/failure of various magick [sic], etc. May provide information of illegal activity.

*Bowls:* May contain salt, water, blood, etc.

*Burnt trees, animals:* Check for accelerants. Identify.

*Cages/stakes:* Sometimes these are found at the scene. Used to secure animals prior to sacrifice.

*Candles:* Although it is rare, some occult literature calls for candles to be made with human baby fat. The colors of candles are always significant, which may get somewhat confusing.

*Chalice:* Check for blood, urine, drugs, etc.

*Circle or triangle:* Magic is often practiced inside a circle or triangle. Note any salt. Note flammable substance.

*Knife/sword:* The ceremonial knife (athame) may be a source of blood. Blood may still be present under or near the handle even if it has been cleaned.

*Mortar/pestle:* May hold evidence of drug use, the use of poisons, or blood.

*Pentagram:* A five-pointed star. Check for presence of salt. Note size and direction. A hexagon (six-pointed star) is also used as a powerful magical symbol.

*Potions:* Check for drugs, poisons. These may also be used to sedate victims pending sacrifice.

*Rune stones:* Cloth bag of 25 "stones," 24 with runic writing. Used as an "oracle." Other oracles include Ouija boards, tarot cards, crystal pendulums, etc.

*Syringe:* Check for drugs, poisons, and blood.

*Unusual signs, symbols, alphabet:* Look for symbols mocking Christianity. Occult alphabets are numerous. They may also be made up by the individual (or group).

If evidence is found to support the commission of a crime, the matter is submitted to the prosecuting attorney's office, as in other crimes. Also as with other crimes, if illegal acts are being committed in the presence of an officer arriving at the scene, an immediate arrest may be executed. However, many authorities on cult activity warn that no one, including a police officer, should ever approach or try to stop an occult ritual alone because in all probability, they would be dealing with mentally deranged people high on drugs.

### Investigating Animal Deaths

Unusual circumstances surrounding animal deaths may be important indicators of satanic or cult activity. The following circumstances connected with dead animals should be noted by police:

- No blood—the blood has been drained from the animal.
- An inverted cross carved on the animal's chest.
- Surgically removed head.
- Intestines or other body organs removed.

If a rash of missing animal reports is experienced, gather information on what kind of animals they are, when they disappeared and from what area.

Look for patterns. Coordinate efforts with the local humane society and veterinarians.

## Investigating Homicides

At the scene of a homicide investigation, the following may suggest a ritualistic death:

- The location and position of the body.
- Missing body parts—heart, genitals, left hand, tongue, index finger.
- Scarring between index finger and thumb or inside the wrist from past rituals involving members' blood.
- Blood drained from body.
- Pentagram drawn on the skin surface or surrounding the area of death.
- Ritualistic symbols associated with satanic worshipers carved on the body.
- Tattoos on armpits or the bottom of feet.
- Wax drippings, oils, incense or powders of ritual on the body.
- Urine on the body.
- Human or animal feces consumed, smeared on body or found in body cavities such as the mouth, eyes, nose.
- Semen inside, on or near body cavities or smeared on the body.
- Victim undressed.
- Body painted or tied up.
- Neck wounds, branding-iron marks or burn marks on body.
- Jewelry missing or near the body, symbolistic jewelry.
- Colored strings near the body.

Cult murders are usually stabbings or cuttings—seldom are they gunshot wounds—and many of the victims are cult members or former members. The person who commits the murder is typically a white male from a middle- to upper-class family with above-average intelligence. Some form of drug use is characteristic.

Guard against reacting emotionally when confronted with ritualistic crime. Such crimes tend to be emotionally and spiritually repulsive. Also, bear in mind that unusual crimes are also committed by individuals with mental problems who are not connected with cults.

During postmortem examination, the stomach contents can be of great importance in determining what occurred just before death.

In many ritualistic homicides the body is not available because it has been burned, leaving no evidence. Further, most juries disbelieve seemingly outlandish charges of satanism and human sacrifice, and most judges do not regard satanism as a real problem. Hence, most cases are dismissed.

## Investigating Satanic Serial Killings

Serial killings may be linked to saticlike rituals in the murder act itself as well as in the killer's behavior following the murder. Serial killings frequently linked to satanism include the following:

Charles Manson had links with the Process, a satanic group. Many of the murders committed by Manson and his followers had ritualistic overtones.

The "Son of Sam" murders involving David Berkowitz are claimed by author Maury Terry in *The Ultimate Evil* to have been a conspiracy among satanic cult members of the Process group.

Some brutal, vicious serial killers find satanism a justification for their bizarre antisocial behavior.

Lucas and Toole, two drifters who claimed to have committed more than 300 murders, were members of a satanic group, the Hand of Death.

"Night Stalker" Richard Ramirez had a pentagram on the palm of his hand, wrote satanic graffiti on the walls of some of his victims' homes and was obsessed with AC/DC's *Highway to Hell* album featuring the song "Night Stalker." Ramirez shouted "Hail, Satan" as he left the courtroom.

### Investigating Youth Suicides

Increasingly, law enforcement has been faced with satanic "overtones" to suicides committed by young people. Lyle Rapacki of Flagstaff, Arizona, has compiled a list of things that might indicate that a youth is involved in cult or occult activities:

- Withdrawal from family and friends.
- Changing of friends and associates.
- Sudden disinterest in church and the Bible.
- "New friends" who are loners, nonacademic, problematic for school officials.
- Change of dress to darker, more subdued color. More jewelry.
- Increased rebellion, depression, aggressive behavior.
- Negative change in moral behavior. Also a change in priorities to a more "I"-centered pattern.
- Drop in grades, disinterest in school, lack of concentration.
- Interest in occult literature. May start their own "Book of Shadows"—a notebook containing personal symbols and rituals, often written in code.
- Magazines focusing on death, violence, secrecy and sexual acting-out.
- Increasing involvement in fantasy role-playing games such as Dungeons and Dragons (D&D).
- Increased viewing of occultic movies and TV.
- Collection of occultic paraphernalia such as bones, skulls, ritual knives, candles.
- Rock, punk and heavy-metal music.
- Nightmares. Shades drawn during the day.
- Preoccupation with death, destruction or harming things.
- Sudden missing pets or animals in neighborhood.

Investigators dealing with youth suicides that they suspect may be occult related should inquire into the kind of music the youths listened to—hard rock, acid rock, punk rock, new wave; the kinds of games they played; whether they had Ouija boards or tarot cards; and whether they dabbled in astrology or seances.

### Special Problems Involved

Just as law enforcement officers may have a difficult time relating to gang members and not reacting negatively to them because of their gang associations, they may also have difficulty relating to individuals who engage in ritualistic activity outside what is considered normal. This is also true of the general public and the media, which frequently sensationalize cases involving ritualistic or cult-related crimes, particularly sexual abuse of children and homicides.

**609**

Chapter 18

**Organized Crime,
Gang-Related
Crime, Bias/Hate
Crime and
Ritualistic Crime**

Special problems involved in investigating ritualistic or cult-related crimes include separating the belief system from the illegal acts, the sensationalism frequently accompanying such crimes and the "abnormal" personalities of some victims and suspects.

Frequently the "victims" of occult-related crimes are former participants in the cult. Many have been or are currently undergoing psychological counseling, which makes their testimony less than credible to some people. Likewise, many of the suspects are outside what most would consider to be normal and, consequently, may be treated differently because of how they look and what they believe rather than because of their actions.

## Summary

Distinctive characteristics of organized crime include definite organization and control, high-profit and continued-profit crimes, singular control and protection. It is a prosecutable conspiracy to acquire any enterprise with money obtained from illegal activity; to acquire, maintain or control any enterprise by illegal means; or to use any enterprise to conduct illegal activity. Organized crime is continuously attempting to do all of the preceding with money obtained through its heavy involvement in gambling, drugs, prostitution and loan-sharking.

The daily observations of local law enforcement officers provide vital information for investigating organized crime. All suspicious activities and persons possibly associated with organized crime must be reported to the appropriate person or agency. Organized-crime strike forces coordinate all federal organized crime activities and work closely with state, county and municipal law enforcement agencies.

Belonging to a gang is not illegal; however, the activities of gang members frequently *are* illegal. A street gang is a group of people that form an allegiance for a common purpose and engage in unlawful or criminal activity. In addition to drug dealing, gang members often engage in vandalism, arson, shootings, stabbings, intimidation and other forms of violence. Gang members may be identified by their names, symbols (clothing and tattoos) and communication styles, including graffiti and sign language. Maintain records on gangs, gang members, monikers, photographs, vehicles and illegal activities. The records should be cross-referenced.

Special problems involved in investigating the illegal activities of gangs include the multitude of suspects, and the unreliability or fear of witnesses. The two most often used defense strategies are pleas of diminished capacity and self-defense.

Bias crimes are crimes motivated by bigotry and hatred against a specific group of people.

A cult is a system of religious beliefs and rituals and those who practice them. A ritualistic crime is an unlawful act committed within the context of a ceremony. Investigate the crime, not the belief system.

Ritualistic crimes are known to have included vandalism; destruction and theft of religious artifacts; desecration of cemeteries; the maiming, torturing and killing of animals or humans; and the sexual abuse of children. Indicators that criminal activity may be cult related include symbols, candles, makeshift alters, bones, cult-related books, swords, daggers and chalices.

*Read the following articles and imagine yourself as the officer/detective assigned to each case. What elements of the crime are present? What evidence would you need to prosecute the case? Who else might you need to coordinate your efforts with? What is the likelihood of solving each crime?*

## New police unit to wage war on gang crimes
### St. Paul, Ramsey County join to get 'the real bad guys'
**By Kevin Duchschere**
*Star Tribune Staff Writer*

Hard-core gang members—the thugs who cheat, steal, shoot and deal drugs as a daily routine—are the targets of a new inter-departmental police unit that will combine St. Paul and Ramsey County resources to wage a coordinate war on gang-related crime in the East Metro Area.

Source: *Star Tribune,* 2 August 1996. Reprinted by permission of the *Star Tribune,* Minneapolis-St. Paul.

## Teen gangs 'swarming'
**By Michael Badger**
*Review Journal*

Las Vegas police Lt. Wayne Petersen has watched the tape probably 50 times, but it still amazes him.

The grainy surveillance video, taken Sept. 16, shows more than 40 teenagers flooding into the tiny Carey Mini Market, 1504 W. Carey Ave.

Three of the youths jump the counter and rob the cashier at gunpoint while the others swarm to coolers at the back of the store. A human traffic jam clogs the entrance as teenagers rush out carrying cases of beer and handfuls of food.

The whole thing takes less than 1 1/2 minutes, and at the end the cashier is left alone, cowering behind his counter.

For Petersen, who heads the Metropolitan Police Department's robbery division the scene is becoming too familiar. In the past two months, groups of teen-age thieves have used their numbers and an I-dare-you-to-stop-me attitude to overwhelm at least four stores in the Las Vegas area.

Police call the technique "swarming."

"It seems to be a very recent phenomena here in Las Vegas," Petersen said. "We're very concerned this doesn't become a trend."

On Oct. 7 a group of as many as 25 teens filtered into The Wherehouse music store at 320 S. Decatur Blvd. When some of them tried to walk out with cassettes and compact discs, clerk Lorraine Mosca got in their way.

Source: *Las Vegas Review Journal.* 21 October 1995. Reprinted by permission of the *Las Vegas Review Journal.*

## Police arrest reputed mob boss, staff in murder, racketeering
*Associated Press*

PHILADELPHIA—Law enforcers struck a major blow against one of the nation's most violent Mafia families Thursday, arresting its reputed boss and 11 underpins after months of bloody warfare.

Teams fanned out across Philadelphia and southern New Jersey to make the arrests before dawn, a day after the indictments of 24 people. Three men—all allegedly low-level—remained fugitives; the others were either already in prison or surrendered.

The indictment alleges that reputed mob boss John Stanfa ordered the others to commit murders, attempted murders, kidnapping, extortions, loan sharking, gambling and arson.

During the past 15 months, the struggle for control of a multimillion dollar crime business stretching from Philadelphia to Atlantic City has escalated into street warfare between factions loyal to Stanfa and those aligned with Joseph "Skinny Joey" Merlino and a group called the Young Turks. At least five men have been killed and five others wounded.

*(continued on p. 611)*

*(continued)*

"This is a tremendous blow to the organization," said Joel M. Friedman, chief of the organized crime division of the U.S. Attorney's Office.

The indictment named all the top men in the mob family, plus six "soldiers," and 11 others who carry out mob work but have not been inducted into the family.

Source: *Las Vegas Review Journal,* 18 March 1994. Reprinted by permission of Associated Press.

## Gang membership led to fatal shooting, Minneapolis police say

Sixteen-year-old Gerado Lopez Rios shot and killed another teenage boy who gave the wrong answer when asked which gang he was in, a complaint filed Friday said.

The first-degree murder complaint said the victim, Juan Antonio Inga, 17, died from three bullet wounds.

Inga was walking Sunday afternoon with another man away from a laundromat at 28th St. and Nicollet Av. S. in Minneapolis, according to the complaint. Inga bent down to tie his shoe and three males came up and asked: "Who do you hang with, Bishops or Vatos Locos?"

When Inga said the Bishops, Rios shot him several times, the complaint said.

Rios, a student at Southwest High School in Minneapolis, is also known as Jose Jimenez Rios, Gerado Lopez, Pedro Rosas Rios and Gerado Rios Lopez. When police searched his home in the 3900 block of Portland Av. S., they found a piece of wood with the words "Bishop Killer" on it, the search warrant said.

He is being held in lieu of $1 million bail at the Hennepin County jail.

**Anne O'Connor**

Source: *Star Tribune,* 8 March 1997. Reprinted by permission of the *Star Tribune,* Minneapolis–St. Paul.

Special problems involved in investigating ritualistic or cult-related crimes include separating the belief system from the illegal acts, the sensationalism frequently accompanying such crimes and the "abnormal" personalities sometimes found in both victims and suspects.

## Checklist

### *Organized Crime*

■ Have persons recently moved into the city and purchased businesses that obviously could not support their standard of living?

■ Do any public officials appear to live beyond their means?

■ Does a public official continuously vote in favor of a business that is suspected of being connected with organized crime?

■ Have business owners complained of pressure to use a specific truck delivery service or of threats to close the business if certain persons are not hired?

■ Does a business have high-level executives with police records?

■ Have there been complaints of someone on the premises operating as a bookie?

■ Have families complained about loss of wages paid to a loan shark?

■ Have union officials suddenly been replaced by new, nonlocal persons?

■ Has there been damage or injury to property during union problems?

■ Are goods being received at a store that do not fit in with merchandise sold there?

■ Has a discount store suddenly appeared without a clear indication of true ownership?

■ Has arson suddenly increased?

■ Do nonemployees hang around manufacturing plants or nonstudents hang around a school? (This could indicate a bookie operation or narcotics sales.)

■ Is a pay telephone being used by the same person at the same time each day?

■ Is evidence of betting operations being left in public wastebaskets or trash containers on the streets?

■ When assaults occur, what are the motives? Could they be a result of gambling debts owed to a loan shark?

■ Are persons seen going into and out of certain businesses with which they are not ordinarily associated?

■ Are known gamblers or persons with other criminal records repeatedly seen in a specific location?

### Gangs

■ What illegal activities have been committed?

■ Who reported the activities?

■ What evidence is there?

■ Who are the suspects?

■ What signs tend to implicate a specific gang?

■ Who are leaders of this gang?

■ What records exist on this gang?

■ Who might provide additional information?

### Cults

■ What type of activity brought the cult to the attention of the police?

■ Is the activity illegal?

■ What statutes or ordinances are applicable?

■ Who reported the activity? What is their connection to the cult?

■ What evidence is there that the illegal activity is part of a ritual?

■ Who are suspected members of the cult?

■ What records exist on the cult?

■ Who might provide additional information?

## Application

**A.** Determine how each of these situations might indicate organized crime activity.*

> You note pickets outside one or two stores in the same line of business. The picketing may be a perfectly legitimate tactic.
>
> A cheap hotel appears to be doing a reasonably brisk business. Its patrons travel light—many do not carry luggage. A bar has a reputation for being a clip joint; charges of watered-down liquor are frequent.

---

*Reprinted from *Criminal Intelligence*, Training Key #223, with permission of the International Association of Chiefs of Police.

**613**

Chapter 18

**Organized Crime,
Gang-Related
Crime, Bias/Hate
Crime and
Ritualistic Crime**

A truck is loaded at a location other than a depot or shipping dock. Goods are transferred from a truck of a well-known company to an unmarked truck or vehicle. A warehouse that is almost always empty is now full. Unusual activity at an unusual time occurs in a warehouse area. Merchandise is transferred from a truck to the garage of a residence.

A group begins to congregate at a certain street location at certain times during each day.

A business establishment suspected of being mob-controlled burns to the ground.

Certain individuals always seem to frequent a certain bar although none of them live in the neighborhood.

A club shuts down at irregular times—sometimes early in the afternoon, other times at midevening. Do these times coincide with the completion of racing or when the results of other sporting events become available?

A known racketeer frequently meets with certain unidentified individuals.

**B.** Graffiti has suddenly appeared in increasing amounts in specific areas on walls, public buildings, telephone poles and street lights in your community. Some are in blue paints and some are in red. Groups in the local park have been seen wearing blue bandanas, while in another park they are wearing red kerchiefs. Some of them have been seen flashing particular hand signals to each other. Some of the graffiti symbols represent animals and insects. A blue word *Crips* has the letter *C* crossed out with a red *X*.

*Question*

If graffiti is truly the "newspaper of the street gangs," what information should the above description give to a police officer?

**C.** While looking for a stolen safe in a wooded area, the police discover a circular open area about 200 feet in diameter with candles placed around the circumference. A rough altar has been constructed with a cross. A fire has been burned beneath the cross. A five-pointed star is scratched in the dirt, and the word *NATAS* is scrawled on several trees and on the cross. The number *6* also appears on several trees. What appears to be bones are found in the ashes of the fire below the altar.

*Question*

What do these findings suggest? Is this something the police should investigate further? Why or why not?

## Discussion Questions

**1.** Most experts believe organized crime can flourish only in areas where it has corrupted local officials. Do you agree?

**2.** What is your perception of the prevalence of organized crime in your community? Your state? The country?

**3.** Has organized crime become more or less of a problem for police in the past decade?

**4.** How would you define *gang? Cult?* What is the difference between them?

**5.** Are there any gangs in your community? If so, in what activities are they engaged?

**6.** What are the symptoms of occult influence among teenagers?

**7.** What can parent groups do about community gangs? Cults?

**8.** What does gang membership provide for its members that society does not?

**9.** What is the police responsibility with regard to investigating gang activity? Cult activity?

**10.** Is there any evidence of cult or ritualistic crime in your community? Your state?

# References

Bizzack, John. *Criminal Investigation: Managing for Results.* Lexington, KY: Autumn House Publishing, 1991.

Bodinger-deUriate, Cristina. *Hate Crime: The Rise of Hate Crime on School Campuses.* Bloomington, IN: Phi Delta Kappa, 1991.

Bunker, Robert J. "Street Gangs—Future Paramilitary Groups?" *The Police Chief,* June 1996, pp. 54–59.

Christensen, Loren W. "Hate Warriors." *Law and Order,* September 1990, pp. 73–76.

Clay, Douglas A., and Frank D. Aquila. "Gangs and America's Schools." *Phi Delta Kappan,* September 1994, pp. 65–68.

Copeland, Cary H. "National Code of Professional Conduct for Asset Forfeiture." *The Police Chief,* October 1993, pp. 86–88.

*Criminal Intelligence.* Training Key #223. International Association of Chiefs of Police, p. 19.

Curry, G. David, Richard A. Ball and Robert J. Fos. *"Gang Crime and Law Enforcement Recordkeeping."* Research in Brief. Washington, DC: National Institute of Justice, August 1994.

Dahlberg, Thomas. "White Collar Criminals—Beware of RICO." *Police,* February 1994, p. 40.

Dart, Robert W. "Chicago's 'Flying Squad' Tackles Street Gangs." *The Police Chief,* October 1992, pp. 96–104.

Dees, Timothy M. "Managing Complex Investigations with Watson." *Law Enforcement Technology,* November 1996, pp. 41–44.

"FBI Brings Spy Catching Skills into War against Gangs." (Minneapolis/St. Paul) *Star Tribune,* January 16, 1992, p. A7.

"FBI Recorded Nearly 8,000 Hate Crimes Last Year." *Criminal Justice Newsletter,* November 15, 1996, p. 5.

Foster, James A. "Cleaning Up Money Laundering." *Law Enforcement Technology,* November 1993a, pp. 44–46.

———. "The Paper Trail: How Criminals Ensure Crime *Does* Pay Through Money Laundering." *Law Enforcement Technology,* October 1993b, pp. 44–45.

———. "The Seizing and Sharing of Assets." *Law Enforcement Technology,* April 1993c, pp. 57–62.

Gates, Daryl F., and Robert K. Jackson. "Gang Violence in L.A." *The Police Chief,* November 1990, pp. 20–22.

"Gotti Is Found Guilty on All 13 Counts." (Mineapolis/St. Paul) *Star Tribune,* April 3, 1992, pp. A1, A12.

Green, Stephen H. "Changing Trends in Asset Forfeiture." *The Police Chief,* January 1994, pp. 14–22.

Johnson, Claire, Barbara Webster and Edward Connors. *Prosecuting Gangs: A National Assessment.* Research in Brief. Washington, DC: National Institute of Justice, February 1995.

Karchmer, Clifford, and Douglas Ruch. *State and Local Money Laundering Control Strategies.* Research in Brief. Washington, DC: National Institute of Justice, October 1992.

Kensic, Richard F. "Targeting a Los Angeles Street Gang." *The Police Chief,* March 1992, pp. 50–51.

**615**

Chapter 18

**Organized Crime,
Gang-Related
Crime, Bias/Hate
Crime and
Ritualistic Crime**

Kouri, James J. "Keeping the Mob at Bay." *Securtiy Management,* June 1992, pp. 31–33.

Laflin, Melanie. "Girl Gangs." *Law and Order,* March 1996, pp. 87–89.

Lamprey, Melinda. *Las Vegas Review-Journal,* February 1990, p. 7.

Lieberman, Michael. "Enforcing Hate Crime Laws: Defusing Intergroup Tensions." *The Police Chief,* October 1994, pp. 18–28.

Lieberman, Michael. "Preventing Hate Crime: New Tools, New Expectations for Law Enforcement." *The Police Chief,* June 1992, pp. 33–35.

Martin, Deirdre. "The Menace of the Mob: High Tech Versus Organized Crime." *Law Enforcement Technology,* August 1993, pp. 34–37.

McCort, Michael C. "The Evolution of Street Gangs: A Shift Toward Organized Crime." *The Police Chief,* June 1996, pp. 33–38, 51–52.

Morris, Cole. "FBI Releases Hate Crime Stats." *Police,* January 1997, p. 16.

Mosquera, Richard. "Asian Organized Crime." *The Police Chief,* October 1993, pp. 65–72.

Mueller, Leo E. "Occult Crime Scene Technology." *Law and Order,* November 1992, pp. 35–38.

Nelson, Marshall W. "A Multifaceted Approach." *The Police Chief,* October 1994, pp. 49–50.

"N.Y. Garbage Haulers Indicted; Mafia Link Alleged." (Minneapolis/St. Paul) *Star Tribune,* June 23, 1995, p. 7A.

Nicholl, Bruce J. "The Violent Gang Task Force." *The Police Chief,* June 1994, pp. 30–35.

Niebuhr, Gustav. "Standoff Fit Scenario of Apocalyptic Prophet." *Washington Post,* reported in (Minneapolis/St. Paul) *Star Tribune,* April 21, 1993, pp. A1, A17.

Office of the Attorney General. *Combatting Violent Crime: 24 Recommendations to Strengthen Criminal Justice.* Washington, DC: U.S. Government Printing Office, July 1992.

Pierce, Donald, and Todd G. Ramsay. "Gang Violence . . . Not Just a Big-City Problem." *The Police Chief,* November 1990, pp. 24–25.

Quarantiello, Laura E. "Gang Tracking: War on Gangs Hi-Tech." *Police,* December 1996, pp. 36–38, 69.

———. "Tracking the Homeboys." *Law and Order,* June 1996, pp. 80–82.

Semesky, Donald C., and Christine M. Taylor. *Money Laundering Forfeitures—Landmark Structuring Case Provides Guidance.* BJA Bulletin. Washington, DC: Bureau of Justice Statistics, August 1995.

Sharp, Arthur G. "A Sad Fact of Life." *Law and Order,* July 1996, pp. 64–66.

Story, Donald W. "Hate/Bias Crimes: The Need for a Planned Reaction." *Law and Order,* August 1991, p. 101.

Strandberg, Keith W. "Hate Crime: Strategies Used by Bias Crime Units." *Law Enforcement Technology,* September 1992, pp. 40–46.

Trethewy, Steve. "Biker Gang Update: Street and Biker Gangs Are Cousins in Crime." *Law and Order,* September 1993, pp. 95–98.

Valdez, Al. "Back to Basics Approach to Gang Investigations." *Police,* May 1996a, pp. 20–21.

———. "Conducting Effective Witness Interviews." *Police,* December 1996b, pp. 20–21.

———. "Decoding the Secret Messages on the Wall." *Police,* April 1996c, pp. 30–31, 85.

———. "Easing Investigations on the Gang Battlefield." *Police,* March 1996d, pp. 20–21.

———. "A New Gang Threat Rears Its Ugly Head." *Police,* July 1996e, pp. 20–21.

"Victim, Witness Intimidation Rising in Gang Areas." *NCJA Justice Research,* September/October 1995, pp. 5, 7–8.

"Violent Crime in America: Recommendations of the IACP Summit." *The Police Chief,* June 1993, pp. 59–62.

Walker, Samuel, and Charles M. Katz. "Less than Meets the Eye: Police Department Bias-Crime Units." *American Journal of Police,* Vol. XIV, No. 1, 1995, pp. 29–48.

Webster, Babara, and Michael S. McCampbell. *International Money Laundering: Research and Investigation Join Forces.* Research in Brief. Washington, DC: National Institute of Justice, September 1992.

Young, Betsy Showstack. "The International Asian Organized Crime Conference." *Law and Order,* November 1995, pp. 78–80.

# Drug Buyers and Sellers

## DO YOU KNOW

How drugs are commonly classified?

What drugs are most commonly observed on the street, in possession of users and seized in drug raids, and what the most frequent drug arrest is?

How to recognize a drug addict? What the common symptoms are?

When it is illegal to use or sell narcotics or dangerous drugs and what physical evidence can prove these offenses?

What the major legal evidence in prosecuting drug sale cases is?

When an on-sight arrest can be made for a drug buy?

What precautions to take in undercover drug buys and how to avoid a charge of entrapment?

What hazards exist in raiding a clandestine drug laboratory?

What agency provides unified leadership in combating illegal drug activities and what its primary emphasis is?

## CAN YOU DEFINE

| | | |
|---|---|---|
| crack | drug addict | ice |
| depressant | entrapment | narcotic |
| designer drugs | flashroll | sinsemilla |
| drug abuse | hallucinogen | stimulant |

THE FEDERAL DRUG ENFORCEMENT AGENCY (FDEA) HAS ESTIMATED that 5 percent of the population, or nearly 10 million Americans, are involved in drug abuse of some sort. The seriousness of the drug problem is highlighted by Strandberg (1995, p. 26): **Introduction**

> No matter who you talk to about drugs in America, the answer is the same: the future of our country hangs in the balance. Law enforcement is extremely concerned about this problem, and the people on the front line acknowledge that many of society's ills, from poverty to violent crime, end up squarely upon the drug problem's doorstep.

Walchak (1996, p. 6), likewise, underscores the seriousness of the problem:

> When crack cocaine was introduced in the United States in the mid-1980s, violent crime rates began to soar. In fact, much of the violent crime in America is linked to drug trafficking and drug abuse. Over one-third of all violent acts and almost half of all homicides are drug-related. According to a recent report from DEA, the two causes most frequently cited for the growth of violent crime are drug lords protecting and expanding their drug turf, and drug users seeking to obtain money for drugs.

The violence inspired by drug-related activities translates into murders, arsons, drive-by shootings, car bombs and other random acts that threaten and terrorize a community. Drug gangs have turned many communities into virtual war zones. Sometimes these acts are gang reprisals or witness intimidation; others are designed simply to frighten innocent citizens enough to ensure that they refrain from calling the police.

Strandberg (1997, p. 28) states: "The experts agree that drugs, guns, and youth crime are inexorably interconnected." He continues: "Youths get involved with the drug trade, and soon they are carrying guns for protection; then they are using guns for violent crimes. It's a natural progression, and one that is seen by law enforcement every single day."

According to Blumstein (1996, p. 1): "The surge in violent juvenile crime [has] coincided with an increase in drug arrests, which rose particularly among nonwhites in urban areas."

Cushing (1994, p. 58) notes: "Numerous studies confirm that a relationship exists between drugs and crime. . . . Cocaine, the predominant drug found at street level in many major urban areas, has a particularly high correlation with crime."

A study by the University of Southern California's Graduate School of Business ("Justice by the Numbers. . . ," 1993, p. 27) puts the cost to the U.S. economy—in treatment, prevention and enforcement expenses as well as productivity losses—due to drug abuse at $76 billion.

Law enforcement agencies have encountered all types of technology used by drug sellers, ranging from two-way radios and cellular phones to robot planes. One seller of two-way radios stated that drug dealers were his biggest customers. If a radio was confiscated in an arrest, another was immediately purchased.

Drug dealers are reported to use personal computers, sophisticated encryption systems that even federal agencies have difficulty deciphering, night vision equipment, police frequency jamming equipment, scanners and networking systems. The main advantages drug dealers have over government in using technology are the availability of almost unlimited funds and a lack of bureaucratic approval systems.

Law enforcement officers must understand the drug problem, know when drugs are being used, recognize a wide variety of drugs by sight and know the procedures for seizing drug evidence and making an arrest. Local officers have a responsibility not only to their community but also to other jurisdictions and to agents of other levels of government that enforce drug laws.

Street officers have an important responsibility, even in large departments that have special narcotic units. Drugs are a major problem because users often commit crimes to support their habit. Law enforcement personnel are required to attempt to minimize the flow of drugs and to control their sale and use. Unquestionably, drugs and illicit drug trafficking are intertwined with the general crime problem. Many criminals who formerly confined their activities to other crimes turn to the higher profits available from drug sales. Others commit crimes simply to support a drug habit. Lyman (1990, p. 143) cautions:

> The business of criminal investigation presents ever-changing challenges for law enforcement professionals, and change is most dramatic in the area of drug enforcement. This is evidenced, in part, by the fluctuating forms of popular street drugs such as crack and ice, the spreading technology in clandestine laboratories which manufacture such drugs as methamphetamine and PCP, the emerging

drug gangs and foreign criminals which occupy many major U.S. cities, and the increased use of fully automatic weapons by drug dealers at all levels.

This chapter begins with an explanation of the classification of controlled drugs, followed by investigating illegal possession or use of controlled substances. Next the chapter discusses investigating the illegal sale and distribution of controlled substances. Then, investigative aides and the hazards involved in investigating clandestine drug laboratories are presented. This is followed by a look at agency cooperation and the role of drug asset forfeitures in combating the drug problem. The chapter concludes with an exploration of where efforts might be concentrated in the 1990s.

## Classification of Controlled Drugs

A major problem for law enforcement officers is to recognize drugs found in a suspect's possession. Because of the many different types, colors, sizes, trade names and strengths of commercial drugs, many officers use a pharmaceutical reference book. The *Physicians' Desk Reference* (PDR), used widely by health-care providers, is the basis for PDR I.D., a drug identification tool used by criminal investigators. The portable, easy-to-use "fan-deck" of cards contains colored, actual-size photographs of 1,700 capsules and tablets and gives information about each drug (see Figure 19–1). Street drugs, on the other hand, can be identified by using a field test kit to provide probable cause for the officer to arrest and then be sent to a laboratory for comprehensive testing.

Seven categories of drugs are frequently used:

Central nervous system depressants (alcohol, barbiturates, tranquilizers)

Central nervous system stimulants (cocaine, amphetamines, methamphetamines)

Narcotic analgesics (heroin, codeine, Demerol, methadone)

Hallucinogens (LSD, peyote, psilocybin)

Phencyclidine (PCP and its analogs)

Cannabis (marijuana, hashish, hash oil)

Inhibitants (model airplane glue, aerosols)

---

Drugs can be classified as depressants, stimulants, narcotics, hallucinogens, phencyclidine, cannabis or inhibitants.

---

Stimulants and depressants are controlled under the Drug Abuse Control Amendments to the Federal Food, Drug and Cosmetic Act (United States Code Title 21).

---

The most commonly observed drugs on the street, in possession of users and seized in drug raids are cocaine, codeine, crack, heroin, marijuana, morphine and opium. Arrest for possession or use of marijuana is the most frequent drug arrest.

---

Larger cities experience a broad spectrum of drug sales, use and abuse. A particular drug will seem to achieve popularity over other drugs for a time and

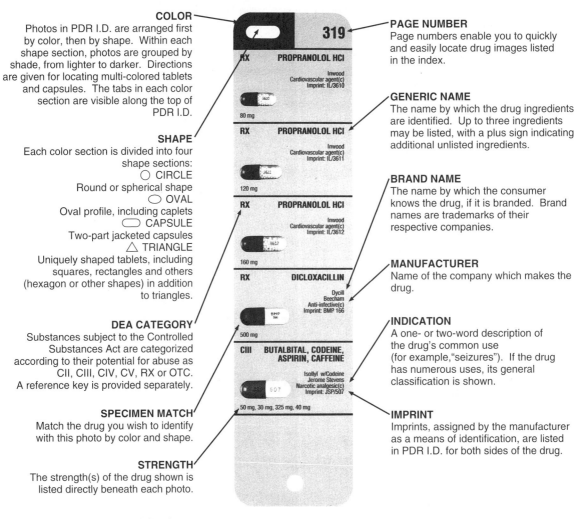

**COLOR**
Photos in PDR I.D. are arranged first by color, then by shape. Within each shape section, photos are grouped by shade, from lighter to darker. Directions are given for locating multi-colored tablets and capsules. The tabs in each color section are visible along the top of PDR I.D.

**SHAPE**
Each color section is divided into four shape sections:
○ CIRCLE
Round or spherical shape
○ OVAL
Oval profile, including caplets
⊂⊃ CAPSULE
Two-part jacketed capsules
△ TRIANGLE
Uniquely shaped tablets, including squares, rectangles and others (hexagon or other shapes) in addition to triangles.

**DEA CATEGORY**
Substances subject to the Controlled Substances Act are categorized according to their potential for abuse as CII, CIII, CIV, CV, RX or OTC. A reference key is provided separately.

**SPECIMEN MATCH**
Match the drug you wish to identify with this photo by color and shape.

**STRENGTH**
The strength(s) of the drug shown is listed directly beneath each photo.

**PAGE NUMBER**
Page numbers enable you to quickly and easily locate drug images listed in the index.

**GENERIC NAME**
The name by which the drug ingredients are identified. Up to three ingredients may be listed, with a plus sign indicating additional unlisted ingredients.

**BRAND NAME**
The name by which the consumer knows the drug, if it is branded. Brand names are trademarks of their respective companies.

**MANUFACTURER**
Name of the company which makes the drug.

**INDICATION**
A one- or two-word description of the drug's common use (for example, "seizures"). If the drug has numerous uses, its general classification is shown.

**IMPRINT**
Imprints, assigned by the manufacturer as a means of identification, are listed in PDR I.D. for both sides of the drug.

**Figure 19–1 "PDR I.D." Card**
Source: Reprinted by permission of *Medical Economics Data*.

then to lose popularity because it becomes difficult to obtain, is found to produce ill effects or increases in cost. The drug may then return to a lower level of use or go into disuse. At different times opium or its derivatives, LSD, cocaine and crack have been heavily used drugs. However, marijuana has always been the most frequently used drug because of its lower cost, ease in using and lesser effects.

### Cocaine and Crack

Cocaine and its derivative, crack, are major problems for law enforcement officers. **Crack**, also called *rock* or *crack rock,* is produced by mixing cocaine with baking soda and water, heating the solution in a pan and then drying and splitting the substance into pellet-size bits or chunks. These are put into small plastic vials and sold for $10 to $25 per vial, substantially less expensive than cocaine which, in similar amounts, would sell for $100 or more.

Crack is smoked in glass pipes and has ten times the impact of cocaine. The user experiences a rapid high because the drug is absorbed through the lungs

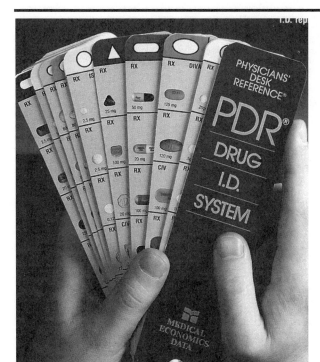

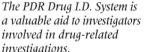

*The PDR Drug I.D. System is a valuable aid to investigators involved in drug-related investigations.*

and travels directly to the brain within seconds. It is described as "cocaine intensified or amplified" in terms of its effects on the human body. These effects include the following:

■ Brain—creates craving for the drug, irritability, euphoria followed by severe depression, convulsions, sleeplessness, inability to feel normal pleasures, paranoia, psychosis and a tendency to suicide.
■ Heart—increases the heart rate and blood pressure, which can result in arrhythmia or heart attack. Death can result from heart failure.
■ Lungs—causes damage similar to emphysema and may cause respiratory arrest or death.
■ Throat—causes sore throat and hoarseness.
■ Skin—creates the sensation of bugs crawling on the skin.
■ Appetite—reduces the desire for food, which can result in malnutrition.

The intense high produced by crack is usually followed by a severe depression or "crash" and a deep craving for more of the drug. It is more addictive than cocaine, at a much earlier stage of use, sometimes after the first use.

Some users "space base" the drug; that is, lace it with PCP or other drugs. PCP causes out-of-control behavior, an added hazard to the already dangerous effects of crack itself. Moreover, the buyer of crack cannot visually determine if the crack purchased has been laced with PCP because PCP is colorless. Thus the user runs a much increased risk of physical, emotional and mental damage.

Warshaw and Daly (1996, p. 18) state that during the past fifteen years the cocaine supply in this country has been controlled by the Medellin and Cali mafias.

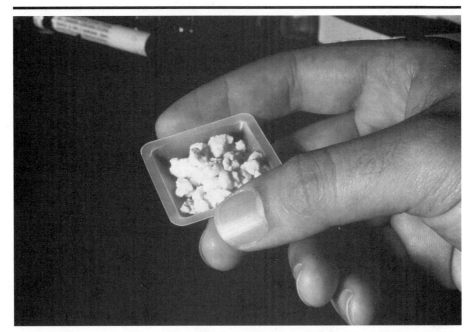

*A container of rock cocaine, more commonly known as* crack. *Crack is much less expensive than cocaine and has 10 times the impact.*

### Heroin

Heroin, a commonly abused narcotic, is synthesized from morphine and is up to ten times more powerful in its effects. Heroin is physically addictive and expensive. It may cause an easing of fears, followed by euphoria and finally stupor.

According to Warshaw and Daly (1996, p. 19): "Heroin available in the United States is produced in four source areas: Southeast Asia (principally Burma), Southwest Asia/Middle East (Turkey, Pakistan, Lebanon), Mexico and South America (Colombia)."

### Marijuana

According to Peoples and Hahn (1991, p. 119): "The drug of choice among abusers since the 1960s, marijuana is currently used by approximately 10 million Americans, making it the most abused drug in the country." Marijuana is variously classified as a **narcotic,** a **depressant** and a **hallucinogen** and is the most controversial of the dangerous drugs. Its use was outlawed by the Federal Marijuana Tax Act of 1927.

A wide spectrum of opinions exist regarding the harmfulness of marijuana. Some feel it should be legalized; others feel it is a very dangerous drug. Many surveys document *psychological* addiction from continued use of marijuana, as is true for most drugs. Like alcohol, marijuana is used socially. Although research does not indicate that marijuana is *physically* addictive, some users claim withdrawal symptoms similar to those resulting from discontinuance of hard narcotics.

Whether marijuana abusers progress to hard narcotics or other controlled substances has not been totally researched. The vast majority of hard-narcotics users once used marijuana, but how many marijuana users proceed to hard drugs is unknown. Marijuana is frequently used with alcohol, barbiturates and amphetamines. The marijuana user may be more susceptible to experimenting with other drugs while under the influence of marijuana.

Although research does not clearly establish or disclaim harmful results from continued use, marijuana is an illegal drug in all states except Alaska, making its use or sale a violation of the law.

The wide availability of marijuana makes it less costly, but the potency ("quality") of the drug varies greatly depending on the area where it is grown and the methods used. Much marijuana is now grown by hydroponic methods indoors, often in abandoned barns or other buildings in rural areas. Such controlled cultivation practices increase its potency—by three to ten times—which increases its value and thus the growers' profits.

Known as **sinsemilla,** homegrown marijuana has become extremely popular. According to Peoples and Hahn (1991, p. 119): "As the popularity of sinsemilla increases, so do the number and sophistication of illegal entrepreneurs who domestically cultivate it."

One good indication of indoor marijuana growing operations is excessive use of electricity. The plants need lots of light and, obviously, cannot be placed near windows, so artificial light is required. In one case, police were alerted to a residence that had been using ten times the normal amount of electricity. Based on this information and observations of the type and amount of traffic to and from the house, police were able to obtain a search warrant and to break up a large marijuana-growing operation.

Griffith (1995, p. 80) describes one valuable source for finding targets for indoor marijuana-cultivation investigations—the Green Merchant List: "This is a document produced by the USDEA showing recipients of cultivation materials sold by and shipped from retailers who advertise in *High Times* magazine, what was ordered, the date of delivery, and the weight and cost of the items."

### Other Narcotics and Drugs

**Designer drugs** are so named because they can be created by adding to or taking something away from an existing drug. In many instances the primary drug is not illegal. The drugs are called *analogs* of the drug from which they are created, for example, meperidine analog or mescaline analog. These drugs may cause the muscles to stiffen and give the appearance of someone suffering from Parkinson's disease. Because designer drugs are difficult for amateurs to manufacture, they are high-profit drugs for dealers. Due to their complex natures, these drugs must be submitted to a laboratory for analysis.

Smokable methamphetamine, known as **ice,** is another problem drug. According to Pennell (1990, p. 12), ice was first noted in Hawaii and has become that state's greatest drug problem:

> Ice has the same properties as the stimulant methamphetamine (the most common form of amphetamine available on the street), but through a recrystalization process, the rock-like crystals can be smoked like rock (crack) cocaine. Methamphetamine is more potent when smoked and can be highly addictive.

Some narcotics agents note that ice has been around since the 1970s and feel that promoting it as a "super drug" is simply a gimmick used by dealers to create interest in it. Doane and Marshall (1996, p. 24) describe the threat of methamphetamine in the United States:

The domestic production, trafficking and distribution of methamphetamine are becoming the fastest-growing drug threat to the United States. Even now within the United States, methamphetamine is the number-one clandestinely produced drug product . . . 92 percent of all labs seized in the United States manufactured methamphetamine as their primary product.

Doane and Marshall (1996, p. 28) contend: "The domestic production in clandestine drug laboratories of methamphetamine and, to a much lesser degree, LSD and PCP, is perhaps the most complex emerging drug problem faced by the United States today."

Fisk (1996, p. 56) cautions: "Tracking the methamphetamine trail is a multifaceted problem with no easy solution." He suggests that the great majority of methamphetamine is produced in California and that much of it is related to outlaw biker gangs.

## Prescription Drugs

Beary et al. (1996, p. 33) suggest: "One-third of the drug abuse problem in the United States can be linked to prescription controlled drugs." They list the following drugs as frequently being involved in prescription fraud: narcotics, stimulants, barbiturates, benzodiazepines, tranquilizers and other psychoactive substances manufactured for use in legitimate medical treatment.

Beary et al. (1996, p. 34) state: "Law enforcement officers are discovering that a substantial portion of their time is spent investigating cases involving prescription fraud, many of which involve insurance, Medicare or Medicaid fraud as well."

Table 19–1 summarizes the various narcotics and dangerous drugs. As you study it, pay special attention to each drug's effects. This information is important in investigating the sale and use of drugs.

Many narcotics and dangerous drugs can be legally obtained with a prescription from a physician and legally sold or distributed by licensed manufacturers and pharmacies.

---

It is illegal to possess or use narcotics or dangerous drugs without a prescription and to sell or distribute them without a license.

---

Most narcotics laws prohibit possessing, transporting, selling, furnishing or giving away narcotics. Possession of controlled substances is probably the most frequent charge in narcotics arrests. Actual or constructive possession and knowledge by the suspect that the drug was illegal must be shown. If the evidence is not on the person, it must be shown to be under the suspect's control.

## Legal Definitions and Problems

The legal definitions of *narcotics* and *controlled substances* as stated in local, state and federal laws are lengthy and technical. The laws define the terms used to describe the drugs, the various categories and the agencies responsible for enforcement.

Laws generally categorize drugs into five Schedules of Controlled Substances, arranged by the degree of danger associated with the drug. The five schedules contain the official, common, usual, trade and chemical names of the drugs. The laws also establish prohibited acts concerning the controlled substances. Basically, these laws state that no person, firm or corporation may manufacture, sell, give away, barter or deliver, exchange, distribute or possess these substances with intent to do any of the prohibited acts. The schedules establish penalties in ratio to the drug's danger, with Schedule I drugs being the most dangerous. Possessing a small amount of marijuana is a felony in some states, a misdemeanor in others and not a crime at all in a few states.

## Investigating Illegal Possession or Use of Controlled Substances

If you observe an individual using a narcotic or other dangerous drug, you may arrest the person and seize the drugs as evidence. The arrested person may be searched incidental to the arrest. If a vehicle is involved, but the suspect was not in the vehicle, post a guard at the vehicle or impound it. Drugs found on a person during a legally conducted search for other crimes may also be seized and additional charges may be made.

Take the suspect into custody quickly. Then make sure the suspect does not dispose of the drugs by swallowing them, putting them between car seat cushions or placing them in other convenient hiding places. While in custody, the suspect may experience withdrawal pains and other bodily ills that can create special problems for the arresting officers.

### Recognizing the Drug Addict

In drug crimes, the victims are implicated; thus, they usually avoid contact with the police, conspiring with the sellers to remain undetected. If apprehended and faced with charges, however, the drug addict may be willing to work with the police. Therefore, many drug investigations involve identifying those who buy drugs illegally and who can thus provide information about sources of supply.

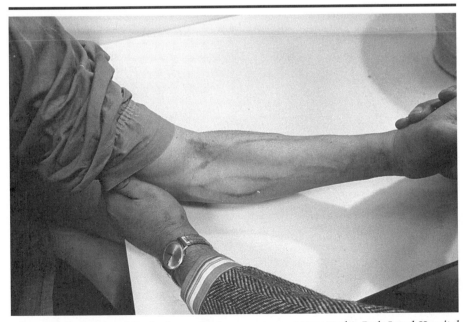

*The arm of a heroin addict in the methadone program at New York's Beth Israel Hospital shows the track marks of needles.*

**Table 19–1 Summary of Controlled Substances**

| Drug | Trade or Other Names | Methods of Usual Administration |
|------|---------------------|-------------------------------|
| *Narcotics* | | |
| Opium | Dover's powder, paregoric, Parepectolin | Oral, smoked |
| Morphine | morphine, pectoral syrup | Oral, smoked, injected |
| Codeine | Tylenol with Codeine, Empirin Compound with Codeine, Robitussan A–C | Oral, injected |
| Heroin | diacetylmorphine, horse, smack | Injected, sniffed, smoked |
| Hydromorphone | Dilaudid | Oral, injected |
| Meperidine (pethidine) | Demerol, Merpergan | Oral, injected |
| Methadone | Dolophine, methadone, Methadose | Oral, injected |
| Other narcotics | LAAM, Leritine, Numorphan, Percodan, Tussionex, Fentanyl, Darvon, Talwin, Lomotil* | Oral, Injected |
| | | |
| *Depressants* | | |
| Chloral hydrate | Noctec, Somnos | Oral |
| Barbiturates | phenobarbital, Tuinal, Amytal, Nembutal, Seconal, Lotusate | Oral |
| Benzodiazepines | Ativan, Azene, Clonopin, Dalmane, diazepam, Librium, Xanax, Serax, Tranxene, Valium, Verstran, Halcion, Paxipam, Restoril | Oral |
| Methaqualone | Quaalude | Oral |
| Gluethimide | Doriden | Oral |
| Other depressants | Equanil, Miltown, Noludar, Placidyl, Valmid | Oral |
| *Stimulants* | | |
| Cocaine** | coke, flake, snow | Sniffed, smoked, injected |
| Amphetamines | Biphetamine, Delcobese, Desoxyn, Dexedrine, Mediatric | Oral, injected |
| Phenmetrazine | Preludin | Oral, injected |
| Methylphenidate | Ritalin | Oral, injected |
| Other stimulants | Adipex, Bacarate, Cylert, Didrex, Ionamin, Plegine, Pre-Sate, Sanorex, Tenuate, Tepanil, Voranil | Oral, injected |
| *Hallucinogens* | | |
| LSD | acid, microdot | Oral |
| Mescaline and peyote | mesc, buttons, cactus | Oral |
| Amphetamine variants | 2,5–DMA, PMA, STP, MDA, MDMA, TMA, DOM, DOB | Oral, injected |
| Phencyclidine | PCP, angel dust, hog | Smoked, oral, injected |
| Phencyclidine analogs | PCE, PCP, TCP | Smoked, oral, injected |
| Other hallucinogens | Bufotenine, Ibogaine, DMT, DET, psilocybin, Psilocyn | Oral, injected, smoked, sniffed |
| *Cannabis* | | |
| Marijuana | pot, Acapulco gold, grass, reefer, sinsemilla, Thai sticks | Smoked, oral |
| Tetrahydrocannabinol | THC | Smoked, oral |
| Hashish | hash | Smoked, oral |
| Hashish oil | hash oil | Smoked, oral |

*Not designated a narcotic under the CSA (Controlled Substance Act)
**Designated a narcotic under the CSA

**Table 19–1  (continued)**

| Possible Effects | Effects of Overdose | Withdrawal Syndrome |
|---|---|---|
| Euphoria, drowsiness, respiratory depression, constricted pupils, nausea | Slow and shallow breathing, clammy skin, convulsions, coma, possible death | Watery eyes, runny nose, yawning, loss of appetite, irritability, tremors, panic, chills and sweating, cramps, nausea |
| Slurred speech, disorientation, drunken behavior without odor of alcohol | Shallow respiration, clammy skin, dilated pupils, weak and rapid pulse, coma, possible death | Anxiety, insomnia, tremors, delirium, convulsions, possible death |
| Increased alertness, excitation, euphoria, increased pulse rate and blood pressure, insomnia, loss of appetite | Agitation, increase in body temperature, hallucinations, convulsions, possible death | Apathy, long periods of sleep, irritability, depression, disorientation |
| Illusions and hallucinations, poor perception of time and distance | Longer, more-intense 'trip' episodes, psychosis, possible death | Withdrawal syndrome not reported |
| Euphoria, relaxed inhibitions, increased appetite, disoriented behavior | Fatigue, paranoia, possible psychosis | Insomnia, hyperactivity and decreased appetite occasionally reported |

Congress has defined a **drug addict** as "any person who habitually uses any habit-forming narcotic drug so as to endanger the public morals, health, safety or welfare, or who is or has been so far addicted to the use of habit-forming narcotic drugs as to have lost the power of self-control with reference to the addiction."

Drug addiction is a progressive disease. The victim moves to using increased amounts of the same drug or harder drugs. Each increase has a corresponding cost increase—thus the frequent "necessity" for committing crime. In addition, as the addiction increases, the ability to control the habit decreases. Drug addicts become unfit for employment as their mental, emotional and physical condition deteriorates.

---

Common symptoms of **drug abuse** include:
- Sudden, dramatic changes in discipline and job performance.
- Unusual degree of activity or inactivity.
- Sudden, irrational outbursts.
- Significant deterioration in personal appearance.
- Dilated pupils or wearing sunglasses at inappropriate times or places.
- Needle marks or razor cuts or constant wearing of long sleeves to hide such marks.
- Sudden attempts to borrow money or to steal.
- Frequent association with known drug abusers or dealers.

---

The addict generally is unkempt, appears drowsy, does not feel well, has copious quantities of tears or mucus in eyes and nose and suffers from alternate chills and fever. Needle marks resembling tattoos may be present in the curve of the arm at the elbow or, after prolonged drug use, in other areas of the body. Because addicts often help each other obtain drugs, exercise extreme caution when addicts are in jail to prevent visitors getting drugs to them.

Once addicted, it is extremely difficult to quit using drugs without special assistance. Drugs preoccupy the addict; nothing and nobody else matters. Institutional rehabilitation of drug addicts has not had much long-term success because the drugs have such a powerful influence over the individual's mental, emotional and physical being. A high percentage of addicts eventually return to their drug habit, their familiar setting and their old associates in drug abuse.

### Drug Recognition Experts

Police officers are adept at recognizing and legally charging individuals who are under the influence of alcohol, especially if they are driving. They are not so able to recognize the drug-impaired individual. However, a Drug Recognition Projects Unit has an impressive 97 percent conviction rate.

Officers begin by using the standard field sobriety tests. If impairment is noticeable, the subject is given a breath test. If the blood alcohol reading is inconsistent with the perceived impairment, a drug recognition expert (DRE) is called in to evaluate the individual. The evaluation uses "a totality of the subject's appearance, performance on psychological tests, eye exams and vital signs."

The initial interview includes questions about the subject's behavior; response to being stopped; attitude and demeanor; speech patterns; and possible injury, sickness or physical problems. Physical evidence such as smoking paraphernalia, injection-related material and needle marks on the subject is sought.

The physical examination includes an eye examination, an improved Walk and Turn test, the Rhomberg Standing Balance test and the One-Leg Stand Test, as well as the Finger-to-Nose test. Also tested are vital signs (blood pressure, pulse rate and temperature) and muscle rigidity. If warranted, a toxicological examination is also conducted.

According to Bocklet (1989, p. 109): "The DRE program is scientifically founded on two controlled studies. . . . The DREs correctly identified those who were impaired by drugs in 98.7% of the evaluations. Of those subjects who had not received a drug, 95% were correctly identified as such by the officers."

### Physical Evidence of Possession or Use of Controlled Substances

The suspect's clothing may conceal drugs. Drugs have been found in neckties, shirt collars, coat and pants linings and seams, shoe tongues, soles of shoes or slippers, hat or cap bands and naturally, in pockets. Suspects are usually strip-searched because drugs can be concealed in any body opening including the rectum or vagina, in the hair, behind the ears and between the toes. Drugs can also be attached to the body with tape.

Objects in the suspect's possession also can contain drugs, depending on the suspect's ingenuity. Cigarette cases, lighters, holders and packages as well as chewing gum wrappers, fountain pens, jewelry, glasses cases, lockets, pencil erasers and many other objects can conceal illegal drugs.

Vehicles have innumerable hiding places, including under seat covers, behind cushions or seats, in heater pipes, hubcaps, glove compartments, under floor mats, in false auto batteries and oil filters, as well as secret compartments devised for great amounts of smuggled drugs. Put the vehicle on a hoist and examine the undercarriage.

In a residence or building, do not give the suspect a chance to flush the toilet or turn on the water in a sink to destroy evidence. Look for drugs in drawer bottoms, fuse boxes, bedposts, behind pictures, in tissue boxes, in overhead light fixtures, under rugs and carpets, in and under furniture and in holes in walls. If evidence is found, attempt to locate the owner of the property and inform him or her of the arrest. Gather all correspondence addressed to the person arrested if it is not in a mailbox. Obtain rent receipts, utility bills and other evidence that establishes that the suspect resides at that location.

One initial problem is identifying the suspected substance. As noted earlier, pharmaceutical manuals and physicians' desk manuals provide information needed to identify various drugs. Field tests can be conducted to serve as the basis for a search warrant, but such tests must always be verified by laboratory examination.

A recently developed residue detection swab can be used to test surfaces for traces of cocaine. Investigators simply wipe the swab across the area to be tested. If cocaine residue is present, the swab instantly turns color. Individually wrapped in foil packaging, such swabs are easy to carry and to use, and they have a relatively long shelf life.

If evidence of narcotics or other dangerous drugs is found on an arrested suspect, as a result of a search of the premises or even by accident, immediately place it in a container, label it and send it to the laboratory. If it is already in a container, leave it there and process the container for fingerprints. Package uncontained drug evidence carefully to avoid any challenge to its integrity as evidence. Use special precautions for drugs to avoid contaminating or altering them by exposure to humidity, light or chemicals.

Physical evidence of possession or use of controlled substances includes the actual drugs, apparatus associated with their use, the suspect's appearance and behavior and urine and blood tests.

Often found along with drugs are various types of pipes, syringes, cotton, spoons, medicine droppers, safety pins, razor blades, hypodermic needles and the like—common components of a drug addict's "outfit."

The suspect's general appearance and such signs as dilated pupils, needle marks or razor cuts in the veins, confusion, aggressiveness, watery eyes, runny nose and profuse perspiration provide additional evidence of drug use. Table 19–2 lists some indicators of drug abuse. To establish that a person arrested is under the influence of drugs, a urine and blood test, a medical examination and a report of personal observations are used along with an alcoholic or drug influence test form.

## Characteristics of Drug-Dealing Locations

A study of 189 drug-dealing locations and their neighborhoods by the Police Executive Research Forum (1992) found that:

■ The type of building used for dealing tends to vary by drug type. For example, sales of marijuana and methamphetamines were more likely to be made from single-family homes than were sales of cocaine powder, crack or heroin.
■ There did not seem to be a distinct preference by drug dealers for apartments over single-family homes.
■ Dealers seem to prefer smaller apartment buildings (less than nine units).
■ The presence of resident managers in apartment buildings seems to have no impact on dealers' choices of location.

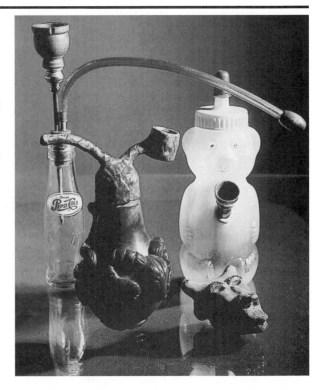

*Some of the drug paraphernalia collected by Sharry Heckt-Deszo, an anti-drug activist. Nearly all of this equipment was confiscated from teenagers. Heckt-Deszo uses the real-life props for "The Bong Show," a show-and-tell program about drug abuse reserved for adults-only audiences of parents and teachers.*

■ Dealers seem to prefer apartment buildings that have tight physical security.
■ Dealers tend to locate in buildings (apartments and single-family houses) that have access to paths and alleys as well as to streets.

These findings "suggest that dealers choose their locations based on whether there is easy access to customers and opportunities to watch for police."

### In-Custody Deaths

One serious problem that may be encountered in dealing with drug users is what Benner and Isaacs (1996, p. 20) call "excited delirium," a term used to describe the "manifestations of extreme drug abuse." They note that such a condition may be related to the sudden, seemingly inexplicable deaths of some suspects being held in police custody. They also note: "A not-uncommon cause of sudden death in police custody is cocaine toxicity." Benner and Isaacs (p. 21) cite the following "published symptoms attributed to 'excited delirium'":

■ Bizarre and/or aggressive behavior.
■ Violence toward others.
■ Shouting.
■ Unexpected physical strength.
■ Paranoia.
■ Sudden tranquility.
■ Panic.

Reak and Gunta (1996, p. 10) note that hog-tying an individual under the influence of cocaine might result in Toxic Reaction to Cocaine (TRTC). They suggest that individuals who ingest cocaine and then engage in bizzare, violent behavior are at high risk of dying in the custody of police if they are restrained.

**Table 19–2 Indicators of Drug Abuse**

| Drug | Physical Evidence | Observable Conditions |
|---|---|---|
| Morphine | Burning spoon, candle, hypodermic needle, actual substance | Needle marks, euphoria |
| Heroin | Burning spoon, candle, hypodermic needle, razor blade, eyedropper, actual substance | Needle marks or razor cuts, euphoria, starry look, constricted pupils, profuse perspiration |
| Cocaine | White or colorless crystalline powder, hypodermic needle, pipe | Needle marks, dilated pupils, increased heart rate, convulsing |
| Crack | Pellets, glass pipes, plastic bottle | Depression, euphoria, convulsions |
| Stimulants | Pills of various shapes and sizes | Restlessness, nervousness, hand tremor, dilated pupils, dry mouth, excessive perspiration |
| Depressants | Pills of various shapes and sizes | Symptoms resemble those of drunkenness: slurred, indistinct speech and loss of physical coordination |
| Hallucinogens | Hypodermic needle, eyedropper, spoon, bottle caps, tourniquets, cotton balls, actual substances | Needle marks on inner elbow, extreme emotionalism, noticeable dilation of pupils, often causing persons to wear dark glasses even at night |
| Marijuana | Roach holder, pipe with a fine screen placed halfway down the bowl, actual substance | Sweet smoke odor; symptoms resemble those of mild intoxication: staring off into space, glassy eyes, semiconsciousness, drowsiness |

# Investigating Illegal Sale and Distribution of Controlled Substances

Because addiction depends on drug availability, drug control must be directed toward the supplier. This is often a joint effort among law enforcement agencies at all levels. Drug users and sellers know the local police, so it is difficult to operate locally. Outsiders are frequently brought in by the police to make buys and arrests. However, local patrol officers are still responsible for investigating drug offenses because they see the users and sometimes observe drug sales. Actions they take against users can put pressure on sellers because their market is hurt when users are arrested and jailed.

Moreover, drug users often become sellers to support their habit. Many such individuals, called mules, sell or transport drugs for a regular dealer in return for being assured of a personal drug supply. Whereas some remain in small operations that are sufficient to support their needs, others see the profit to be made in large operations and go into business on a larger scale. Further, many drug pushers become users—an occupational hazard. This sometimes occurs accidently as the result of having to test the quality of the merchandise over an extended period.

Investigating illegal sale and distribution of drugs requires all the basic techniques used for other crimes, plus special investigative skills related to the behavior of drug users and sellers, both of whom can be dangerous and unpredictable. The wide variety of drugs makes it difficult to identify them under street conditions, and special types of searches are required to locate minute amounts of drugs that may be hidden ingeniously.

Special problems are also encountered in finding drugs that are smuggled across national borders in a variety of ways and in identifying those who transport and distribute them. It takes much time and expense to develop informants and to make a purchase or otherwise discover and confiscate drugs while ensuring that the evidence will stand up in court.

Harris (1995, p. 48) notes that: "The problem with making drug cases is not a lack of desire but a lack of knowledge on what can and cannot be done, what can and cannot be searched." For example, investigators must know the different types of possession that might be involved in a drug case. As Samaha (1993, p. 109) explains:

> *Constructive possession* is not physical or *actual possession;* it is legal possession or custody. An owner has custody over a home but does not physically possess the cocaine that a weekend guest keeps in the host's closet. One who buys cocaine in order to use it has *knowing possession* of the cocaine. One who does a friend a favor by carrying a brown paper bag without knowing that the bag contains stolen money has what the law designates as *mere possession* of the money.

---

The actual transfer of drugs from the seller to the buyer is the major legal evidence in prosecuting drug sale cases.

---

The transfer may be seen by chance by a patrol officer, or it may be observed after long surveillance or when an undercover officer makes a planned buy. Some transfers are quite intricate. In one case, a drug seller put drugs on a dog's back, and the dog brought them to the buyer and then returned to the seller with the payment. Even though the seller did not personally hand the drugs to

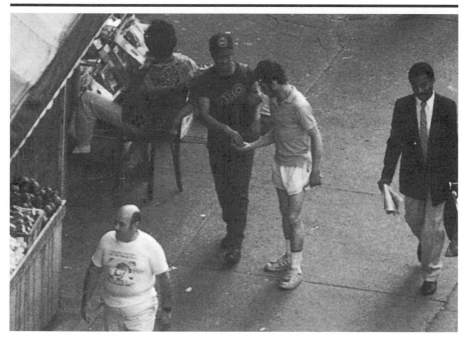

*Crack and cocaine dealers in action.*

the seller, there was a sale. In other cases, the seller leaves drugs at a predetermined location and picks up payment at another location. Such subterfuge is countered by personal testimony.

If either the buyer or seller throws the drugs away to avoid being caught with drugs in possession, the property can be recovered as abandoned property and taken into custody. If the suspect was seen discarding the drugs, they can be used as evidence.

Narcotics cases begin with a report of suspicious drug activity, a search warrant obtained on information from a reliable informant or an on-sight observation of a drug buy. Undercover officers and informants then become central figures in obtaining evidence.

### On-Sight Arrests

Patrol officers witnessing a suspected drug buy should obtain as complete a description as possible of the persons and vehicles involved. There is usually no urgency in making a drug arrest because the seller and buyer continue to meet over time.

---

If you observe what appears to be a drug buy, you can make a warrantless arrest if you have probable cause. Often, however, it is better to simply observe and gather information.

---

Probable cause is established through knowledge of the suspect's criminal record, by observing other persons making contact with the suspect and finding drugs on them, by knowing of the suspect's past relationships with other drug users or sellers and through observing actions of the suspect that indicate a drug buy. The courts usually give weight to officers' experience and to their information about the suspect and the circumstances of the arrest, including any actions by the suspect before the arrest that are commonly associated with drug selling.

If probable cause is based on information supplied by an informant, check the information for accuracy against intelligence files. If no prior intelligence information exists, add the facts provided to the file. Check the informant's reliability by asking about other suspects in drug cases. Are these suspects already in the files? Has the informant helped before? How many arrests or convictions were based on the information? You might ask the informant to obtain a small amount of the drug if possible.

### Surveillance

As noted, it is frequently best simply to watch and obtain information if a drug buy is witnessed. The suspected seller or the location of the buy can then be put under surveillance, an especially important technique in narcotics investigations. Surveillance can provide protection for planned buys, protect the money put up to make the buy, provide credibility for the buyer, provide information regarding the seller's contacts and provide information to establish probable cause for an arrest or search warrant. It is not necessary to make an arrest on the first surveillance. In fact, it is generally advisable to make several surveillances to gather evidence.

Surveillance officers must have patience because many planned drug buys necessitate a long period of surveillance before the actual sale, or bust, is made. The drug dealer is concentrating on making the sale. No sale, no profit. At the same time the dealer is trying to avoid being "busted." It is essentially a cat-and-mouse game. Drug dealers often feel they are being observed when they are not, and surveillance officers often feel they have been "burned" when they have not. Prearranged signals and communications between surveillance officers and undercover officers are needed to prevent untimely drug busts. A detailed plan of action is mandatory. The surveillance team must be prepared with adequate equipment, food and drink for the estimated period of surveillance. Surveillance officers should have specialized training and detailed briefing prior to actual assignment.

### Planned Buys

Planned buys are usually made by working an undercover agent into the group that is selling or buying drugs or by having an informant make the buy. Before using an informant to buy drugs, determine why the person is involved and keep a strict log of his or her activities. Use care in working with drug users as buyers because they are known by the courts to be chronic liars.

Sclabassi (1995, p. 82) says that it has become common to assign female officers to undercover drug units: "A lot of times women tend to be more believable than the male officers—especially here by the border where a lot of the street women buying drugs are dancers and prostitutes. The officers can use that as their cover, and it works well."

Caron (1992, p. 90) suggests: "The least confrontational and most cost-effective approach to eliminate the open street distribution [of drugs] would be through undercover purchases by police officers." Nonetheless, the enormous number of drug buys by undercover agents and informants have made drug sellers wary of new customers. Informants are often used as introductions to the undercover officer. Informants are often involved in criminal narcotics as users or sellers and are "turned" by the police for providing information in exchange for lesser charges. The decision to use an informant in this manner is usually made by the prosecutor's office. Most people who are arrested for dealing drugs and who are given the option of either going to jail or becoming an informant choose the latter. Police departments should have written policies on the use of informants.

Undercover agents are usually police officers of the investigating agency (in large cities) or of cooperative agencies on the same level of government in some sort of exchange operation. Kaminski (1992, p. 73) describes the exchange program instituted in Illinois between the Evanston Police Department and the Waukegan Police Department: "The exchange program took the form of a mutual-aid agreement providing for an exchange of narcotics officers trained to conduct undercover drug operations. . . . This first exchange, lasting several months, resulted in 115 charges and netted 82 defendants."

If working undercover, be thoroughly conversant with the language of the user and the seller, know the street prices of drugs and have a tight cover. Talk little and listen much. Observe without being noticed. Also, devise some excuse to avoid using the drugs. Attempt to work within the seller's system. Drug pushers, like other criminals, tend to develop certain methods for making their sales. Asking them to change their method can cause suspicion, whereas going along with the system establishes your credibility for subsequent buys. Avoid dangerous situations by insisting that you do not want to get into a situation where you could be ripped off, injured or killed.

---

Undercover drug buys are carefully planned, witnessed and conducted so that no charge of **entrapment** can be made.

---

Make careful plans before a drug buy. Select a surveillance group and fully brief them on the signals to use and their specific assignments. Small transmitters are important communications devices for members of the surveillance team. Have alternative plans in case the original plan does not work.

Careful preparation includes searching the buyer immediately before the transaction to avoid the defense that drugs were planted on the suspect. Any items on the buyer other than the money are retained at the police station or with other police officers until after the buy.

Prepare the buy money in advance—marked, identified, counted and recorded by serial number, date, time and denomination. This procedure is witnessed by one or more persons. The money is not given to the buyer until immediately before the buy. Fluorescent powders can be used, but some drug sellers check money for such powders before making a transaction. All buys should be observed from a location where the movements of both the seller and the buyer can be seen by the surveillance team.

At the meeting to buy drugs, record the seller's description, the vehicles used, telephone numbers called to set up the buy and observations about the seller's personal statements and habits. If the informant and the undercover officer are both present, the officer makes the buy to protect the informant's identity if an arrest is planned. If no arrest is planned, both the undercover officer and the informant make buys, providing additional evidence.

If several buys are made from the seller over a period of time, the seller may relax security and include other persons higher in the organization. Even if this is not the case, the seller usually visits his or her source of drugs frequently. The route to or the actual location of the drug supplier can then be put under surveillance. Such an opportunity seldom arises on the first contact because sellers usually devise very clever ruses to cover their tracks.

Lyman (1990, p. 146) notes some risk variables in undercover drug work:

- Lack of uniform investigative procedures for law enforcement agencies in different jurisdictions.
- Increased use of automatic weapons by drug dealers.
- Increased use of violence by foreign nationals involved in drug trafficking.
- New emerging types of drugs which alter the mental state of drug suspects.
- Inexperienced or untrained drug enforcement personnel.
- High enforcement personnel attrition—job turnover.
- Reinventing the wheel—agents failing to learn from the mistakes of other law enforcement agencies.
- Job-related stress in undercover work.
- The expansion of drug-dealing gangs and the criminal sophistication of such groups throughout the United States.
- Working undercover in any capacity.
- Handling informants whose allegiances may be confused.
- Participating in raids.
- Big-money drug deals.

Harmon (1992, pp. 85–86) suggests five major factors that lead to successful undercover drug buys:

1. Teamwork.
2. Excellent evidence for courts.
3. Numerous safety precautions.
4. The element of surprise.
5. Special training.

He also offers some do's and don'ts when making an undercover drug buy (p. 85):

- *Don't* go into gangways, residences or garages to do your deal. Not only is this very dangerous, but it cuts the arrest team's evidence-gathering ability to zero, severely limits its ability to reach the officer if necessary and gives the suspect a better chance to escape.
- *Do* control the buy. Tell the suspect what you want, where the deal will take place, etc. Keep talking to keep the suspect off guard.
- *Don't* front your money, as many times the suspect will not return it. Tell him you have been robbed before and you want to keep the money.
- *Do* make copies of buy money in advance. Each day, make a new copy indicating a new date.
- *Don't* drive the suspect to another location to buy the product. Rolling surveillance is difficult and puts the officer in a dangerous position.
- *Do* have back-up signals to let the team know how the deal is going in the event the equipment doesn't work. Taking off a hat or flashing a car's lights are good signals.
- When the deal is done, *do* leave the area and inform the team by radio that you are out of danger.

- *Do* dress down in dirty clothes to look like a junkie. *Don't* wear any jewelry, as this may invite a robbery.
- If you are on the arrest team, *do* wear your police identification jacket during all arrests.
- If you are the purchasing officer, *don't* give chase to a suspect if the suspect runs. This does no good.
- If you have any doubts about the deal, *don't* do it. Follow your instincts. There are plenty of other deals around.
- *Don't* enter a residence as a member of the arrest team unless you are in foot pursuit.
- *Don't* linger in the target area.

The FBI's Drug Enforcement Administration (DEA) has adapted the traditional triangle used in tactical training to illustrate the dynamic balance between the drug dealer and the police officer; see Figure 19–2.

The three things valued by the dealer are the drugs, the money the drugs can bring and his or her freedom to do business. In the middle of the triangle is the officer. When both the money—that is, the **flashroll**—and the drugs are present at the same time, the undercover officer faces the greatest danger. Moriarty (1990, p. 51) offers these axioms of flashroll management:

**1.** Never flash the money twice unless absolutely necessary. If it is unavoidable, do not flash it the same way the second time, because it will no longer be a surprise.
**2.** Always move the flashroll as soon as possible after it has been displayed, thereby severely limiting the subject's access to the money.
**3.** Never move to a second location with the flashroll in your possession—no matter what enticement is offered by the dealer.
**4.** Take pains to ensure that the dealer is not inadvertently tipped that the money will be flashed. It is better to remove all doubt by telling the dealer directly, "I won't have the money with me. I will show it to you another time."

The ability to negotiate is essential for an undercover officer. Almost everything is negotiable in a drug deal. Remaining cool and collected during the actual buy is absolutely necessary. If the situation does not look right or appears to be too dangerous, the officer should walk away from the deal; there is always another time and place in this business. Because of the prevalence of weapons in drug trafficking, Moriarty (1990, p. 44) points out that the undercover officer "is literally negotiating for his own life, and he is usually alone with his adversary at the time."

If the buy is successful, an arrest can be made immediately, or a search warrant can be obtained on the basis of the buyer's observation of other drugs on

**Figure 19–2   Drug Dealer–Officer Dynamics**

the premises. After the buy, the buyer is searched again and the exact amount of money and drugs on the buyer recorded.

---

Make two or more buys to avoid the charge of entrapment.

---

Although police are responsible for investigating narcotics offenses and arresting violators, they are equally responsible for making every reasonable effort to avoid arresting an innocent person. The illegal act involved in the sale should be voluntary, without special urging or persuasion. An agent who knows that a seller is in business and merely asks for, pays for and receives drugs is not using entrapment. But continued requests for drugs from a person who does not ordinarily sell them is entrapment. If there has been more than one voluntary drug transaction, no basis exists for a defense of entrapment.

### Narcotics Raids

Surveillance frequently provides enough information for obtaining a no-knock search or arrest warrant. Successful narcotics raids are rarely spontaneous; they are planned on the basis of information obtained over an extended period. They can be designed to occur in two, three or more places simultaneously, not only in the same community but in other communities and even in other states.

Narcotics raids are often dangerous; therefore, before the raid, gather information about the persons involved and the premises where the drugs are located. Also determine how many police officers are needed, the types of weapons needed and the location of evidence, as discussed in Chapter 7.

The raid itself must be carried out forcefully and swiftly because drugs can easily be destroyed in seconds. All drugs confiscated are taken to the laboratory for examination. Disposition of confiscated drugs is carefully controlled to avoid tainting the integrity of the police.

## Investigative Aids

According to Uchida (1990, p. 8), the National Institute of Justice has funded the development of a computerized Drug Market Analysis Program (DMAP) to aid in drug investigations. This sophisticated information and mapping system will help law enforcement target retail drug sellers:

> The Drug Market Analysis Program (DMAP) will focus on where users go to buy drugs. It will collect drug arrest data, crime and incident reports, and calls for service, combining information from police and citizens and entering it into a computer so that it can be quickly retrieved by narcotics and patrol officers.

Figure 19–3 illustrates the automated pin map used in the program.

Finding secret compartments that might contain drugs is now easier with a special high-accuracy laser rangefinder developed for the U.S. Customs Service. Investigators use the unit to measure the interior dimensions of cargo containers in their search for hidden compartments in which drugs may be smuggled. The small laser beam allows measurements of loaded containers in which physical access to the rear wall is limited. The hand-held, battery-operated, laser rangefinder measures distances from 6 to 85 feet with an accuracy of 1 inch.

The use of dogs to detect drugs has been common for decades. Their keen sense of smell enables them to detect minute traces of illicit drugs. More re-

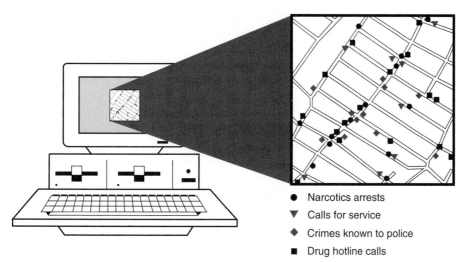

● Narcotics arrests

▼ Calls for service

◆ Crimes known to police

■ Drug hotline calls

**Figure 19–3  DMAP's Automated Pin Map**

The automated pin map allows narcotics and patrol officers to use computers to zoom to particular neighborhoods—and even particular streets—to get an up-to-date picture of drug trafficking activity. Information about narcotics arrests, calls for service, crimes known to police and drug hotline calls is consolidated onto one map.

Source: Courtesy of the National Institute of Justice.

cently, drug-sniffing pigs also have been used. As reported in *Law Enforcement News* ("These Narcs Bring Home the Bacon," 1992):

> Nowadays, a handful of law enforcement agencies are discovering that pot-bellied pigs—the four-legged, Vietnamese variety—offer a new, albeit unlikely weapon against drug trafficking.
>
> According to trainers interviewed by *LEN,* the porcine drug agents have a keen sense of smell that is rivaled only by bloodhounds, are the third-smartest land mammals behind humans and apes, and can be trained much more quickly than dogs. . . .
>
> Their relatively small size—for pigs—allows them to muscle into small areas that dogs can't reach and they are friendly enough to strangers to take home . . . as a pet.

Burke (1993, pp. 104–105) lists the following advantages of using pot-bellied pigs to detect narcotics rather than using K–9s:

■ Pigs are smarter than dogs.
■ Pigs are cost-effective.
■ They are easily housebroken.
■ They do not shed.
■ They are less likely to have physical problems.

Another investigative aid of recent origin is the Internet. Although communicating information about drugs on the Internet can pose a problem for law enforcement, it can also be a source of assistance. As Sclabassi (1996, p. 62) notes: "Trading drug information is nothing new, but keeping this illegal business off the Internet is tough to tackle." She (p. 63) notes: "Everything from the side effects of using a particular drug to how to best grow marijuana plants indoors can be discussed on the Internet by drug users and dealers." Sclabassi suggests that rather than trying to stop these communications, investigators can use the information to their advantage.

## Hazards Existing in Clandestine Drug Laboratories

An increase in clandestine drug laboratories has occurred as more emphasis has been placed on reducing illegal foreign drug imports into the United States. These laboratories pose serious health hazards to law enforcement agencies conducting raids on the premises.

Heiskell (1996, p. 32) cautions: "Clandestine drug labs can be deadly chemical time bombs if you do not take appropriate and immediate precautions." He states (p. 33): "Knowledge of clandestine drug lab hazards and safety procedures could mean the difference between life and death." In fact, according to Heiskell: "Clandestine laboratories are considered the largest single source of on-the-job injuries to narcotics officers."

Several hazards may exist in clandestine drug laboratories:

■ *Physical Hazards.* Improper ventilation, few access routes, poor lighting, booby traps, potential for explosions and fire and potential for assaults from attack dogs or gun-wielding suspects.
■ *Chemical Hazards.* Many of the substances are explosive and extremely flammable. They often are unidentified or misidentified.
■ *Toxic Hazards.* Irritants and corrosives, asphyxiants and nerve toxins may be encountered.

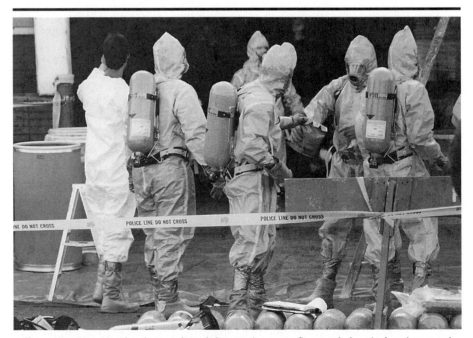

*Officers investigating clandestine drug laboratories wear fire- and chemical-resistant suits, gloves and boots and use self-contained breathing devices for protection.*

Clandestine drug laboratories present physical, chemical and toxic hazards to law enforcement officers engaged in raids on the premises.

Hermann (1994, p. 93) suggests the following "rules" to be followed when encountering a drug lab or its components:

- Request fire department or hazardous-materials-team assistance.
- Avoid using matches, lighters or items that could ignite fumes.
- Do not turn switches on or off; they could produce sparks or be booby trapped.
- Do not taste, smell or touch any substance.
- Do not smoke, eat or drink in the area.
- Decontaminate yourself, clothing and equipment if you touched any substances or contaminated containers.
- Check for booby traps before moving or touching containers.

A safety program developed by the DEA and the California Bureau of Narcotics Enforcement following OSHA and NIOSH recommendations has four basic elements:

- Policies and procedures.
- Equipment and protective clothing.
- Training.
- Medical monitoring.

*Policies and procedures* are aimed at ensuring officer safety through a certification process. Only certified individuals are allowed to seize, process and dispose of clandestine laboratories. Their procedure for conducting a raid has five stages: planning, entry, assessment, processing and exit. During the planning stage, certified agents and chemists identify the chemicals that may be present and arrange for the proper safety *equipment and protective clothing*.

Entry has the most "potential for danger. The entry team faces the possibility of armed resistance by owners and operators, booby traps, and exposure to hazardous chemicals." Still, the entry team wears the least protection because the gear limits mobility, dexterity, vision and voice communications.

Once entry has been successful, the assessment team—an agent and a chemist—enter the site to deal with any immediate hazards, to ventilate the site and to segregate incompatible chemicals to halt reactions. Assessment team members wear fire-protective, chemical-resistant suits, gloves and boots. They also use self-contained breathing devices for respiratory protection. This team determines what safety equipment and clothing the processing team will need.

The processing team then enters and identifies and collects evidence. They photograph and videotape the site and collect samples of the various chemicals. The final step involves removing and disposing of hazardous materials, decontaminating and posting the site.

*Training* involves forty hours of classroom instruction followed by a twenty-four-hour in-service training course at the field level. *Medical monitoring* has two stages: medical screening of potential team members and annual monitoring to learn if any team members have "developed any adverse health effects as a result of working with hazardous chemicals." Guidelines and training for clandestine drug laboratory investigations are available through the National Sheriffs Association.

## Agency Cooperation

Investigating illegal drug activities requires the cooperation of all law enforcement agencies, including the exchange of suspect car lists and descriptions of sellers and buyers. Local police assist state and federal narcotics investigators by sharing their knowledge of drug users and sellers in their community. In addition, many narcotics officers exchange vehicles and personnel with other agencies to have less-identifiable operators and equipment.

Hinkle (1990, p. 151) describes an interagency drug task force formed by sheriffs of five counties in eastern Virginia:

> Every sheriff in the Task Force pointed to the drug problem as his number one priority. (Estimates vary, but a figure repeatedly suggested is 75 percent of all crime in the Northern Neck and Middle Peninsula can be attributed either directly or indirectly to drugs.) They agreed that their single overriding problem was manpower, with equipment a close second. They agreed further that the only way to effectively address the problem was to combine resources—to share manpower, equipment, specialists and, above all, intelligence.

The federal government has mobilized an all-out attack on illegal drug activities.

---

The Federal Drug Enforcement Administration (FDEA) provides unified leadership in attacking narcotics trafficking and drug abuse. Its emphasis is on the source and distribution of illicit drugs rather than on arresting abusers.

---

Before 1973 several federal agencies were involved in investigating illegal drug activities. These included the Bureau of Narcotics and Dangerous Drugs (BNDD), the Office for Drug Abuse Law Enforcement, the Office of National Narcotics Intelligence, the drug investigative and intelligence units of the Bureau of Customs and the drug enforcement sections of the Office of Science and Technology. In 1973, all these agencies were merged into the Federal Drug Enforcement Administration (FDEA), often called simply the DEA.

The FDEA's emphasis is on stopping the flow of drugs at their foreign sources, disrupting illicit domestic commerce at the highest levels of distribution and helping state and local police to prevent the entry of illegal drugs into their communities. According to Bocklet (1991, p. 272):

> The Drug Enforcement Administration provides national leadership culminating in the arrest, conviction and incarceration of important narcotics traffickers. Their actions disrupt major drug operations and add deterrence to others. The bulwark of such effective drug enforcement efforts is smooth-running interagency and intergovernmental cooperation including many police departments nationwide. Increasingly, these local law enforcement entities are reaping numerous benefits from working with federal forces, especially in task force operations.

Quinn (1996, p. 36) describes the Drug Enforcement Administration's Mobile Enforcement Team (MET) established in 1995. He notes that 20 teams, or more than 200 agents, have been deployed across the nation to help in the "drug war." Bocklet (p. 279) notes that: "One of the greatest benefits of working with a DEA State Local Task Force is shared forfeiture revenues."

## Drug Asset Forfeitures

The asset-forfeiture program was introduced in the preceding chapter as it relates to the seizing of assets of organized crime figures. This program is also operative in drug-related cases. The Federal Comprehensive Crime Control Act of 1983 initiated procedures for asset forfeitures as a result of drug arrests. Confiscating drug dealers' cash and property has proven to be effective in reducing drug trafficking and is providing local, state and federal law enforcement agencies with assets they need for their fight against drugs.

The asset forfeiture laws provide for the confiscation of cash and other property in possession of the drug dealer at the time of the arrest. Precise recording of all proceedings is necessary to avoid allegations of abuse or misuse of these funds. Because of the required legal and judicial proceedings regarding these confiscations, it is often six months or longer after an arrest before the assets are available for police agency use.

Forfeiture proceedings may be initiated by the United States District Attorney's office, state attorney generals' offices or local county or municipal legal counsel. All expenses involved with the forfeiture may be taken from the confiscated assets. For example, if there are liens against the confiscated property, they must be paid. Police agencies must emphasize to the public that the asset forfeitures benefit the agency and the community. Forfeited vehicles, boats or airplanes may be used directly by the agency or sold at auction to generate funds. Monetary assets may be used to purchase police equipment, to hire additional law enforcement personnel or for training in drug investigation.

Investigators should be aware of a common defense to asset seizure: the Innocent Owner Defense. As noted by Foster (1993, pp. 60–61):

> The interests of an owner who was without knowledge of the prohibited activity, either act or omission, is not subject to forfeiture when evidence is established by that owner. . . .
>
> Landlords who allow criminal activity to occur on their property can be liable for forfeiture of their property, particularly if they have been warned previously by the police. . . .
>
> Remember, the property being seized should be connected, it must be documented, and probable cause must exist.

Ison (1991, p. A1) notes: "The Justice Department is seizing cash, cars, boats, jewelry—even golf courses and race horses—from drug traffickers and other criminals at astonishing rates. . . . The government's take [in 1990] totaled nearly $500 million nationally. That's a 20-fold increase since the criminal forfeiture program started in 1985."

According to Warchol and Johnson (1996, p. 49): "While arrest, prosecution and incarceration can incapacitate drug dealers, forfeiture can destroy their illegal organizations by undermining their economic foundation. Forfeiture has also been used successfully to eliminate crack houses, money-laundering facilitates and clandestine drug labs." They (p. 53) conclude: "Used equitably, it [asset forfeiture] is an effective method of destroying criminal organizations and deterring aspiring criminals, while providing much-needed revenue to fight drug trafficking."

The program has not been without problems and misunderstandings. The confiscated funds may be used only for police department efforts to increase their fight against drugs. Police budgets cannot be reduced because of the availability of the asset-forfeiture funds.

## Focus of the 1990s

Tremendous national, state and local efforts are being directed to meeting the challenges of drug use and abuse in the United States. A national drug czar serves at the direction of the president, and many states appoint people to similar positions to direct state and local efforts. Federal funding is available through state agencies. Federal, state and local agencies with roles in the drug war coordinate their efforts. Thousands of volunteers, groups and agencies have joined the fight against illegal drugs. For example, Operation Weed and Seed is a national initiative for marshaling the resources of a number of federal agencies to strengthen law enforcement and revitalize communities. It is a comprehensive, coordinated approach to controlling drugs and crime in targeted high-crime neighborhoods. The Bush administration committed funding of $500 million in fiscal year 1993 to be used by the Justice Department's Weed and Seed anticrime plan ("Justice by the Numbers," 1993, p. 27).

Many communities have adopted communitywide programs for dealing with drug abuse, guided by people who represent community organizations and agencies. An example of such community change is the adoption of drug-free zones around schools. Any person committing drug violations within this zone—typically defined as a 1,000-foot radius—may be charged with a felony. Public telephones have been removed from some schools, and many no longer allow students to carry pagers or radios on the school grounds.

The International Association of Chiefs of Police, in conjunction with the Drug Enforcement Administration, a division of the U.S. Department of Justice, has published a manual for police chiefs and sheriffs, *Reducing Crime by Reducing Drug Abuse.*

Anti-illegal-drug programs must be a total national, state and local government effort, combined with local community programs. Law enforcement interdiction efforts must combine with these drug reduction efforts. This requires leadership, cooperation and coordination at all levels to succeed.

## Summary

Drugs can be classified as depressants, stimulants, narcotics, hallucinogens, phencyclidine, cannabis or inhibitants. The most common drugs on the street, in possession of users and seized in drug raids are heroin, opium, morphine, codeine, cocaine, crack and marijuana. Arrest for possession or use of marijuana is the most frequent drug arrest.

It is illegal to possess or use narcotics or other dangerous drugs without a prescription; it is illegal to sell or distribute them without a license. Investigators learn to recognize drug addicts by being aware of common symptoms of drug abuse, such as sudden, dramatic changes in discipline or job performance; unusual degrees of activity or inactivity; sudden, irrational outbursts; significant de-

*Read the following articles and imagine yourself as the officer/detective assigned to each case. What elements of the crime are present? What evidence would you need to prosecute the case? Who else might you need to coordinate your efforts with? What is the likelihood of solving each crime?*

## Police suspicions led to arrest of 2 women, both 68

*A Brooklyn Park woman and her friend have been charged with smuggling drugs from Mexico*

**By Dennis Cassano**
*Star Tribune Staff Writer*

Jacqueline Homa looked at her friend Gloria Slopek and told her to give the cop the keys to the trunk.

"It's over," Homa said, as a night of gambling and excitement for the two grandmothers ended at dawn Wednesday along an Arizona highway, authorities said.

Friday morning, 68-year-old Slopek, who lives with her daughter and grandchildren in Brooklyn Park, was ushered into a federal courtroom in Tucson wearing a dark green prison uniform and with her hands shackled behind her back, said Homa's attorney, Jeffrey Marks.

Charged with possessing nearly 400 pounds of marijuana valued at almost $320,000, Slopek cried as she promised the magistrate she would commit no crimes if he released her while a grand jury considers indicting her and her friend.

Homa had been released earlier. Her 68th birthday was Thursday. They left the courthouse together Friday and returned to Homa's rural Tucson home, where Slopek has been visiting since January. Marks said the two women are certain to be indicted by a grand jury within 30 days.

According to Rob Daniels, a border patrol spokesman, agents stopped the women's car Wednesday morning and spotted a large package of marijuana on the floor of the back seat. He said the package wrapped in cellophane and duct tape was "about half the size of a bale of hay."

The agents asked if they could look into the truck. Slopek, who was driving, at first said yes, but then hesitated. She turned the keys over at Homa's urging and the agents found 16 more packages of marijuana.

"This is a bigger load than most," Daniels said.

### One jackpot to another

The women told the agents that Slopek had won $4,000 playing video poker at a casino near Tucson late Tuesday or early Wednesday.

Soon after, they said, a man approached them and asked if they wanted to increase their winnings. They said they didn't know his name and had never talked with him before but that he was a nodding acquaintance from the casino. They said they didn't know if he was an employee or a customer.

They allegedly agreed to leave right away for Mexico, pick up the marijuana and drive it back to Tucson. They were given directions to drive down a small desert road, where they would be flagged down. The car was loaded and they were allegedly told to drive to a parking lot in Tucson, where they would be paid $2,000.

They never got there.

Daniels said police agencies have noticed a new tactic by drug dealers: having older people smuggle drugs for them because they're unlikely suspects. Just last week, Daniels said, a 70-year-old woman was arrested by Arizona police for smuggling marijuana.

He said Slopek and Homa "don't look like criminals. They look like women you would see in a bingo parlor."

Another thing that arouses agents' suspicion is rental cars. Daniels said smugglers like to use them because authorities can't confiscate them as they can privately owned vehicles.

*(continued on p. 646)*

One reason the agents stopped Slopek and Homa was that a license check showed that the 1997 Lincoln Town Car belonged to a rental agency. When agents heard the women's story, they assumed that the drug dealer had supplied the car.

But Slopek had rented it herself a week earlier because Homa's car was being repaired, Marks said.

Homa's husband died recently, he said. Slopek's husband died of cancer two years ago, said Mary Engels, who bought Slopek's townhouse shortly afterward.

The women met in Minneapolis in 1951 when their children were playing on a swing set. Homa's son was hurt and Slopek's child caused the accident, Marks said. They've been friends ever since, even after Homa moved to Arizona in the 1970s.

While the women await indictment, Marks said, they have some consolation: The authorities returned their $4,000 jackpot.

Source: *Star Tribune*, 28 June 1997. Reprinted by permission of the *Star Tribune*, Minneapolis-St. Paul.

terioration in personal appearance; dilated pupils or wearing sunglasses at inappropriate times or places; needle marks, razor cuts or constant wearing of long sleeves to hide such marks; sudden attempts to borrow money or to steal; and frequent associations with known drug abusers or pushers.

Physical evidence of possession or use of controlled substances includes the actual drugs, apparatus associated with their use, the suspect's appearance and behavior and urine and blood tests.

Evidence of the actual transfer of drugs from the seller to the buyer is the major legal evidence required for prosecuting drug sale cases. If you observe what appears to be a drug buy, you can make a warrantless arrest if you have probable cause. Often, however, it is better simply to observe and gather information. Undercover drug buys are carefully planned, witnessed and conducted so that no charge of entrapment can be made. Two or more buys are made to avoid the charge of entrapment.

Clandestine drug laboratories present physical, chemical and toxic hazards to law enforcement officers engaged in raids on the premises.

The Federal Drug Enforcement Administration (FDEA) provides unified leadership in attacking narcotics trafficking and drug abuse. The FDEA's emphasis is on the source and distribution of illicit drugs rather than on arresting abusers.

## Checklist

### Drugs and Controlled Substances

■ How did the complaint originate? Police? Victim? Informant? Neighbor?
■ What is the specific nature of the complaint? Selling? Using? Possessing? Overdose? Are all required elements present?
■ What type of narcotics are suspect?
■ Is there enough evidence of sale to justify planning a buy?
■ Were obtained drugs tested with a department drug-detection kit?
■ Has the evidence been properly collected, identified and preserved?

- Has the evidence been sent to a laboratory for examination?
- Has it been determined that the drug is a controlled substance?
- Have all persons involved been interviewed or interrogated?
- Do persons involved have prior arrests for similar offenses?
- Is surveillance necessary to obtain evidence for an arrest and/or a search warrant?
- Is a raid called for? (If so, review the checklist for raids.)
- Have cooperating agencies been alerted?

## Application

**A.** *The Narc**

It is dark as the five men emerge from the plane. They haul out their luggage and walk to the parking lot of the tiny, one-strip airport. The pilot enters a white shack that is trimmed in red.

When the pilot leaves, the others gather around a young man who has driven out to meet them. His name is Bruce Preece, and he looks like an outdoorsman. Bearded, he wears a suede hat and red plaid jacket.

Moments later, a camper occupied by two more men pulls into the parking lot, and most of the group piles into the back. Seated with troops along foam-rubber benches, they are dim in the shadows as the camper moves through the empty town.

"That guy sure was an inquisitive one," the pilot remarks, referring to the man in the shack. "He knew we were here last week and he wanted to know what we were up to."

"Tourists," someone else replies, his head silhouetted against a window. Everyone looks like a visitor—a hunter, perhaps, or a fisherman. They carry small bags and wear down jackets and jeans.

The clothing is deceptive.

Half of the men are narcotics agents, or *narcs,* from the Minnesota Bureau of Criminal Apprehension. Like Preece, most are stationed in northern Minnesota towns. The others represent the Federal Drug Enforcement Administration; most are based in Minneapolis.

They're in this little town on business.

One of two men they're after lives a few miles east of town with his wife and six small children. He works for a chemical firm in town. They suspect that at home, in his spare time, he is manufacturing illegal drugs in a clandestine laboratory. The agents call him "No. 1."

The other lives north of town. He is married and appears to be unemployed. They suspect that he is getting illegal drugs and distributing them in nearby towns. The agents call him "No. 2."

No. 1 came under suspicion when a chemical supply company in Connecticut notified the feds that someone in this little town was ordering chemicals that are often used to make illegal substances.

No. 2's activities were noticed in a more direct manner. He is said to have told a local deputy sheriff that the deputy would be paid $2,000 if No. 2 were notified of any state or federal narcotics investigations.

---

*David Peterson wrote this account of an actual narcotics investigation. Reprinted from the *Minneapolis Star,* December 9, 1978.

The two men have been under surveillance for several weeks. No. 1's house, beside a creek, is surrounded by trees. Agents have watched him from the woods, from a boat on the creek while pretending to fish and from cars in town.

Preece has even been inside the house. He did that by taking a shipment of chemicals from the Connecticut firm and making what's called a "controlled delivery"—that is, he pretended to be the mailman and hauled the heavy boxes inside the house.

The agents have noticed a pattern: On Wednesdays, when No. 1's wife goes into town to play bingo, No. 2 stops by.

It is Wednesday night. The plan is to watch No. 2 enter and leave the house and to arrest him before he reaches his car. Assuming that he is carrying illegal drugs, the agents will arrest No. 1 as well, search his home and seize the contents of the lab. Both men are known to be armed.

By 7 P.M. surveillance has begun in earnest. Eight of us are waiting for something to happen.

Two agents are sitting in an unmarked car along the highway that leads to the house. Two more are in the woods, within view of the house.

The rest of us are in the camper, which is parked just off the highway. Among us is a young state agent named Stan Leach, a tall, muscular extrovert with dark curly hair and glasses whose home base is Bemidji.

He unsnaps his overalls and drapes a heavy black flak vest over his torso. "This thing is so uncomfortable," he says. "But if anything's going down, I don't want to be without it."

Even from inside, the camper looks entirely normal. But its cabinets contain an array of radios, cameras, lenses, firearms and other gear.

From the camper's bathroom, Leach takes out a telephoto lens the size of a small wastebasket. He says that on another such mission, in Chisolm, he was half a mile from a house but could, with the lens, read the initials on the door.

He attaches the lens to a smaller device called a "night scope," which is designed to allow the user to see in the dark. He places the apparatus on a bed above the cab. He will spend the night with his eyes to the scope, watching for No. 2's car.

At about 7:15, the radio crackles. "The broad's coming," someone says. And, a couple of minutes later: "The broad's leaving."

That means that a female friend of No. 1's wife has picked her up and driven into town to play bingo.

"Good," Leach says to us. "That excites me." The stage is set.

But wait: Has she left, or was it another car? Two driveways are close together; it's tough to be sure in the dark. "How come it never goes like it goes in the movies, y'know?" Leach says. "This never happens to Starsky and Hutch."

Each of the three groups of men has a radio. The problem is, No. 1 is believed to have a police scanner, which would allow him to monitor their conversation.

So they speak in a rough sort of code, as though they were squad cars checking for speeders. "I'm in position," a voice says, "so let me know if you get a hot one going on the radar."

Preece climbs into the camper along with the top-ranking federal agent on this trip, an older man named Dave. They arrange a code with Leach—"401," for example, will mean that No. 2 has arrived. They exchange some nervous jokes.

"Stanley? Stanley?" Bruce implores as he steps out of the camper. "Let's make this thing go, OK?"

"I got a good feeling, Bruce," Leach replies. Neither of them has any control over what the two suspects will do tonight. They can only watch and wait.

That's what they do, for an hour. The camper is getting chilly. At least, there's music from the tape deck.

Another hour. None of us has eaten since noon. A bag of Halloween-sized Snickers bars goes around. They start telling narc stories.

"Tim goes to this town, undercover, right? And less than a year later, he comes back to the same town—he's changed his appearance a lot, with a beard and what-not—and he's sitting with some dopers and they're warning him to avoid this narc. And they're talking about him! They're doing a perfect job of describing Shanley, to Shanley! So Shanley says, 'Well, was he a good-looking guy?'"

By 9:30, Leach is getting impatient. "Puh-leeeeeze, No. 2!" he says. At 10, a sober, low voice over the radio. "You may have three visitors shortly."

Leach fishes for his mike and says, "Is it Halloween?"

"It may as well be," the voice responds.

A few minutes later, Preece, Dave and the boyish deputy (who's wearing a "Cat diesel power" baseball cap) climb into the camper, shivering.

"He's busy in there," says Preece, who has been watching No. 1 through his kitchen window with binoculars. "He's pouring stuff, and he's running some-thing, like a tableting machine."

Preece and the others know in their guts that if they could just bust into that house, they'd find a guilty man surrounded by evidence.

## Questions

1. Do the investigators have probable cause to conduct a raid at this time?
2. Could they seize the materials No. 1 is working with as plain view evi-dence? Why or why not?
3. What aspects of the surveillance illustrate effective investigation?
4. Have the officers made any mistakes?
5. What should be the next step for these officers?
6. Is there likely to be a link between the suspects and organized crime? Why or why not?

**B.** The 1992 *LET* Challenge*
**The Investigation**
INTERIOR ANYTOWN (SOUTH FLORIDA) POLICE DEPARTMENT—DAY ONE. You are the detective lieutenant in charge of a large drug operation, the largest you've ever conducted. In the 12 years you've been on the force you've worked in patrol, then as a detective assigned routine burglaries, car thefts and an oc-casional homicide case. But last year, because your jurisdiction is rife with drug dealers, orders came from the top for you to handle the major narcotics caseload.

It is up to you to make all the right calls, make sure all the evidence is there, plan the complete operation, organize the surveillance and orchestrate the tac-tical operation.

At the end of the operation, if you do everything correctly, the result will be a huge drug bust and seizure, all the officers involved will come out safely and you will put a major drug supplier behind bars.
CUT TO: INTERIOR YOUR OFFICE—SAME DAY
[*ESTABLISHING SHOT OF MESSY DESK, CLUTTERED BOOKSHELVES AND DIRTY FLOOR.*] It's your office, and you call it home. As you are sitting behind your

---

*Reprinted by permission from *Law Enforcement Technology*, July, August and September 1992.

desk, Rogers, the undercover officer whom you have assigned to this case *enters* without knocking. You look up and shout in mock anger:

**You:** You ever knock, Rogers?

Rogers shrugs and sits down heavily in the only chair in your office not piled high with junk.

**Rogers:** It's all set, boss. The buy is happening this weekend.

Rogers goes on to fill in the details about the buy, set up by an informant that your department arrested previously. Introduced by this informant, Rogers has been able to set up the buy, and now all you have to do is supply the necessary "show money"—$100,000—100 big ones that your department definitely does not have in its budget!

*Questions*

*1.1.* Where should you obtain the needed money?
A. The Department of Justice
B. The DEA
C. The State
D. None of the above
E. All of the above

Putting together this investigation has definitely been a great deal of work, and your stomach has seen a great deal of greasy Chinese "take-out." As you lean back in your worn desk chair, its leather splitting at the seams, you think back on what you had to do to proceed thus far:

You knew that your informant had proven unreliable in the past, so you decided to run all known information about the principals involved through your department's new computer system. Entering the key subject's alias and the strange tattoo on his shoulder into the data base, the computer returned with the following information about the subject and the group he travels with:

■ The subject has three prior convictions for drug dealing and distribution.
■ The group has a propensity for violence, particularly with high-powered automatic weapons.
■ They regularly make trips to drug distribution cities.

Your undercover officer, Rogers, has already set up the buy, so you headed to the D.A.'s office to arrange the warrant.

*1.2.* Do you have enough to obtain a search warrant?
A. Yes  B. No

Next, you requested and received from Rogers a building plan of the apartment complex in question, the "Longwood Gardens Housing Project." Shown [in Figure 19–4] is a map of the project, the layout of the apartments, the street, and various sundry information relevant to the operation. Study it carefully.

After his trip to town hall for the blueprints, Rogers found out this about the location:

■ The exact apartment in which the buy is going down—on the 3rd floor
■ Steel apartment doors
■ Windows open out

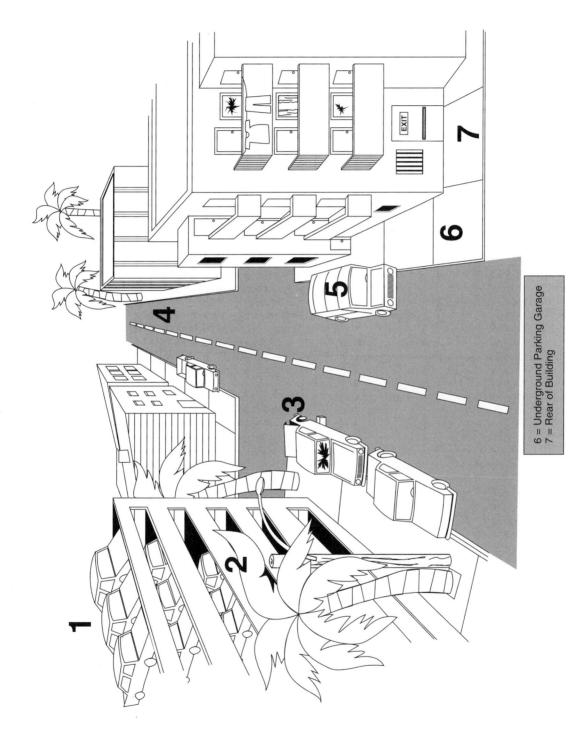

6 = Underground Parking Garage
7 = Rear of Building

**Figure 19–4   Map of the Longwood Gardens Housing Project**

- Sewer system bypass information
- No fire escapes; stairways on exterior with private entrances
- Exits (front exit; one on each side; rear exit; one from the underground garage)

*1.3.* Do you also need a search warrant for the apartment next door?
A. Yes   B. No
*1.4.* Should you set up a phone tap for the apartment in which the deal is going down?
A. Yes   B. No
*1.5.* Would you need a separate warrant to tap the phone?
A. Yes   B. No

The week before the actual buy, the sellers contacted Rogers and demanded a "flashroll" (pre-buy)—they wanted to see the money, to make sure that Rogers is serious. What should you do?

*1.6.* Do you agree to the "flashroll"?
A. Yes   B. No

If you answered "yes" to the above question, please answer the following two questions. If you answered "no," skip questions 1.7 and 1.8.

*1.7.* Do you take the entire $100,000 to the "flashroll"?
A. Yes   B. No
*1.8.* Where should the pre-buy be held?
A.  A public place
B.  The apartment in question

### The Surveillance

EXTERIOR APARTMENT BUILDING—MORNING [*ESTABLISHING SHOT OF THE APARTMENT BUILDING. It is open to the air, the hallways and doorways of the building exposed.*] You arrive at the scene of the impending drug bust with your response team of 9 officers, making a total of 10 people including yourself. Using the map [Figure 19–4], it is up to you to place your 3 surveillance officers in strategic points so that all the exits are covered and you are faced with no surprises.

*2.1.* There are five (5) exits: where do you place your 3 officers? (Use the numbers on the map.)
A.  #3, 6, and 7
B.  #2, 5, and 6
C.  #4, 5, and 7
D.  #1, 4, and 6

You have separate officers to operate the surveillance/command center. Select a strategic position for the command center.

*2.2.* Where is the best place for the command center?
A.  #1
B.  #2
C.  #4
D.  #5

Being the early morning, there is little activity in the apartment building. As the sun rises higher in the South Florida sky, the day doesn't just get hotter, the activity increases.

Kids start to come out into the open hallway/balconies, and people are mingling in the stairwells and the hallways themselves. Sight lines are being obstructed as the balconies fill up, and telling the good guys from the bad guys is becoming increasingly difficult.

*2.3.* You should clear the building.
A. True   B. False
*2.4.* You should cut off electricity to restrict movement of those living in the apartment.
A. True   B. False
*2.5.* You should mark the apartment door.
A. True   B. False
*2.6.* You should disable the sewage system.
A. True   B. False
*2.7.* Please eliminate the one unnecessary piece of knowledge from the following list:
A. Which way the windows open (in or out)
B. Where the stairways are located
C. Where the fire escapes are
D. The number of people inside the apartment building
E. What weapons the sellers have
*2.8.* You need to arrange a battering ram or hydraulic tool to get through the apartment door.
A. True   B. False
*2.9.* Here are some ways to find out more about the apartment in question. Which answer does not belong?
A. Get blueprints of the building
B. Wiretaps
C. Surveillance on the building
D. Send Rogers in before the buy to check it out
E. Talk to the apartment manager

Your communications system finally indicates a caller from the command center.

*2.10.* Your mode of communication should be:
A. Cellular phone   B. Radio

You switch it on to hear the following:

**Voice:** Rogers is going in.

**You:** He's wired, right?

**Voice:** Affirmative! Rogers is wired.

**You:** OK! Stay frosty and wait for his signal.

You sign off and review your surveillance choices as you wait for the signal that everything is in place and your team is ready to go in.

**The Bust**

OUTSIDE THE APARTMENT BUILDING—SAME DAY

[*ESTABLISHING SHOT OF APARTMENT BUILDING.*] The officers in your command are in place on the walkway around the corner of the building, waiting for the drug bust to go down. Your communication system signals to you and you hear:

**Voice:** Take 'em!

Using three of your officers for backup, decide how many of your six officers to place into the following teams.

*3.1.* Divide your six (6) officers into the following teams:
Entry:
Arrest:
Evidence:
Evidence/entry:

*3.2.* What equipment should your team be carrying? Of the following list, eliminate two (2) items your team would not need:
A. Shields
B. Bullet-resistant vests
C. Diversionary devices (flash bangs, etc.)
D. Tear gas
E. Dogs
F. Evidence kits

You give the order to go in, and your entry team, backed up by the evidence team, is heading for the door. Just as they turn the final corner to the apartment door, three small children come walking up the open hallway, laughing and singing.

Seeing the team and their guns, the children *freeze,* right in front of the apartment door. They are ready to scream.

*3.3.* What do you do with the kids?
A. Yell for them to "get down" and storm the door?
B. Have a member of the entry team take them away?
C. Have a member of the evidence team take them away?
D. Ignore them and hope for the best?

The kids are taken care of, and your team goes up to the door. If you had chosen a battering ram to get through the door, you'd be in trouble, as you are faced with a thick steel door. Luckily, you had already arranged for a master key, which you pull from your pocket and slip into the lock.

The door opens easily, and you are inside the apartment.

CUT TO: INTERIOR APARTMENT—SAME DAY

[*ESTABLISHING SHOT OF THE APARTMENT INTERIOR.*] There are six (6) people inside, including the informant and your officer, and a pregnant woman. They are all huddled in the center of the room, leaning over a table.

They freeze for a second when "flash bang" explodes as you open the door, but they break and scatter quickly. Drugs are in evidence everywhere, as is a pile of weapons.

*3.4.* It is correct to use either tear gas or pepper mixture to incapacitate the occupants of the apartment.
A. True   B. False

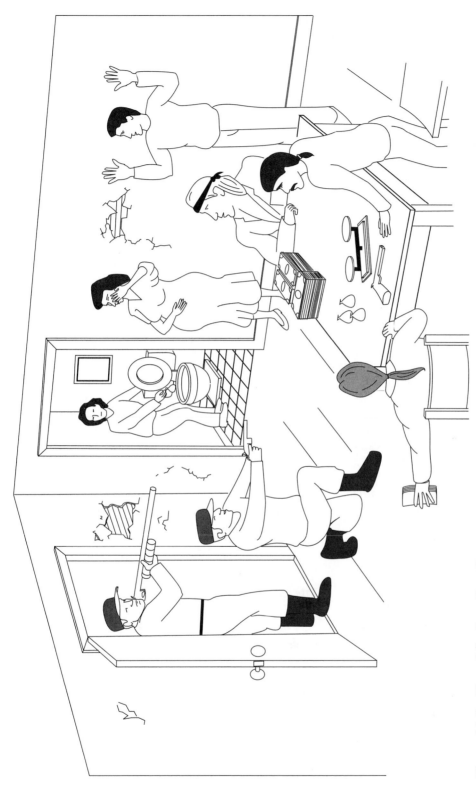

**Figure 19–5   Map of the Drug Bust Room**

As your team enters, they shout loudly for everyone to get down and stay down. Some comply, while others are *screaming* and *yelling* at your team. *PANDEMO-NIUM REIGNS SUPREME.*

In the midst of the confusion of the entry, your team fans out to cover the room, and one of the entry team heads for the bathroom.

*3.5.* Place your officers strategically within the room so that all possible eventualities are covered.
(Use map of room [Figure 19–5].)
A. #1, 2, 4, and 5
B. #1, 2, 5, and 6
C. #2, 4, and 6
D. #1, 5, and 6

**Team Leader:** POLICE OFFICERS! EVERYBODY DOWN! RIGHT NOW!

*3.6.* Is it reasonable to place a pregnant woman on the floor?
A. Yes   B. No

One of the bad guys gets to the bathroom first, and you hear the sound of the toilet flushing.

Luckily, during the previous section, you chose to divert the sewage system, so all that he is flushing down the drain is going straight to your evidence people.

Finally, the chaos in the room calms down and the arrest team goes to work, cuffing the occupants and reading them their rights.

*3.7.* Your team should treat the undercover officer and the informant as just two of the arrestees.
A. True   B. False

Your arrest team takes the bad guys out of the apartment, while the evidence team collects all the drugs and the money, including the $100,000 you have to return. It's been a good day all around, and you and your officers share a smile.

## Discussion Questions

**1.** How serious do you feel the drug problem is nationally? Statewide?
**2.** Would legalizing drugs be a feasible solution to the problem?
**3.** Why should alcohol abuse be considered an illness and drug abuse a crime?
**4.** Does your high school have a drug awareness program?
**5.** How are drug raids treated by the media in your community?
**6.** Do you know anyone with a drug abuse problem? How has it affected that individual's life?
**7.** To what extent are drugs used in your community? What types are most prevalent? Are they used primarily by adults or juveniles? (You may also want to consider legally prescribed drugs, alcohol and tobacco in this discussion.)
**8.** Should the penalty for use of marijuana be reduced to a misdemeanor as it has been in some states? Should it be legalized, or should it remain a felony? In what amounts should the determination be made?

**9.** Is the drug abuse problem too large for the police to handle? Has it reached a status of social acceptance such that drug laws should not be enforced? Who makes this determination?

**10.** What effect do educational campaigns have in reducing or controlling drug abuse? Do you have such a campaign in your community? How successful is it?

# References

Beary, Kevin, John P. Mudri and Linda Dorsch. "Countering Prescription Fraud." *The Police Chief*, March 1996, pp. 33–35.

Benner, Alan W., and S. Marshall Isaacs. "'Excited Delirium': A Two-Fold Problem." *The Police Chief*, June 1996, pp. 20–22.

Blumstein, Alfred. *Youth Violence, Guns, and Illicit Drug Markets*. Research Preview. Washington, DC: National Institute of Justice, June 1996.

Bocklet, Richard. "DEA—State and Local Task Forces: A Body for Law Enforcement." *Law and Order*, January 1991, pp. 272–279.

————. "Drug Recognition Experts." *Law and Order*, September 1989, pp. 105–112.

Burke, Tod. "Pot Bellied Pigs." *Law and Order*, September 1993, pp. 104–106.

Caron, Patrick E. "Combating Urban Drug Distribution." *The Police Chief*, October 1992, pp. 88–94.

Cushing, Michael A. "Reducing Crime Through Street-Level Drug Enforcement." *The Police Chief*, September 1994, pp. 58–59.

Doane, George, and Donnie Marshall. "Methamphetamine: A Growing Domestic Threat." *The Police Chief*, March 1996, pp. 24–28.

Fisk, Irwin W. "The Meth Connection." *Police*, September 1996, pp. 56–63.

Foster, James A. "The Seizing and Sharing of Assets." *Law Enforcement Technology*, April 1993, pp. 57–62.

Griffith, James A. "Indoor Marijuana Cultivation." *Law and Order*, 1995, pp. 79–82.

Harmon, Clarence. "SCAT: Drawing the Community into the Fight against Drugs." *The Police Chief*, October 1992, pp. 80–87.

Harris, Wesley. "Improving Your Drug Enforcement Efforts." *Law and Order*, May 1995, pp. 46–50.

Heiskell, Lawrence E. "Danger: Clandestine Drug Labs." *Police*, September 1996, pp. 32–35, 73.

Hermann, Stephen L. "Clandestine Drug Laboratory Hazards." *Law and Order*, May 1994, pp. 93–94.

Hinkle, Douglas P. "A Drug Task Force." *Law and Order*, September 1990, pp. 149–152.

Ison, Chris. "Turned Tables: U.S. Government Uses Criminals' Assets to Finance War against Drugs." (Minneapolis/St. Paul) *Star Tribune*, July 29, 1991, pp. A1, A12.

Justice by the Numbers." *Law Enforcement News*, January 15/31, 1993, p. 27

Kaminski, Frank. "Narcotics Officer Exchange Program: Do More with Less. . .,"*Law and Order*, April 1992, pp. 73–74.

Lyman, Michael D. "Minimizing Danger in Drug Enforcement." *Law and Order*, September 1990, pp. 143–147.

Moriarty, Mortimer D. "Undercover Negotiating: Dealing for Your Life." *The Police Chief*, November 1990, pp. 44–47.

Pennell, Susan. "'Ice': DUF Interview Results from San Diego." *NIJ Reports: Research in Action*, September 1990, pp. 12–13.

Peoples, John T., and Larry M. Hahn. "Indoor Cannabis Cultivation: Marijuana in the '90s." *The Police Chief,* October 1991, pp. 119–120.

Police Executive Research Forum (PERF). "Drug Market Analysis Finds Dealers Like High-Security Buildings." *Subject to Debate,* May/June 1992, pp. 4, 11.

Quinn, Steve. "DEA: Metropolitan Enforcement Teams." *Police,* September 1996, pp. 36–38, 79–82.

Reak, Keven P., and S.C. Gunta. "Cocaine, Restraints and Sudden Death." *The Police Chief,* June 1996, p. 10.

Samaha, Joel. *Criminal Law,* 4th ed. St. Paul: West Publishing Company, 1993.

Sclabassi, Mary A. "A Class Act." *Police,* November 1995, pp. 32–36, 82.

———. "Drug Users on the Net." *Police,* December 1996, pp. 62–70.

Strandberg, Keith W. "Drugs, Guns and Youth Crime." *Law Enforcement Technology,* January 1997, pp. 28–30.

———. "Drugs in America." *Law Enforcement Technology,* May 1995, pp. 26–35.

"These Narcs Bring Home the Bacon: Drug-Sniffing Pigs Offer Police an Unlikely Ally." *Law Enforcement News,* November 20, 1992, p. 4.

Uchida, Craig. "NIJ Sponsors System to Speed Information to Police on Drug Hotspots." *NIJ Reports: Research in Action,* September 1990, pp. 8–9.

Walchak, David G. "Drugs and Violent Crime." *The Police Chief,* March 1996, p. 6.

Warchol, Greg L., and Brian R. Johnson. "Ensuring the Future of Asset Fortfeiture Programs." *The Police Chief,* March 1996, pp. 49–53.

Warshaw, Bob, and Paul Daly. "Drug Trafficking in the United States." *The Police Chief,* March 1996, pp. 18–23.

# The Investigator's Role in the Judicial Process

**T**he ultimate goal of a criminal investigation is determining the truth—the facts that will establish the innocence or guilt of people related to a crime. Here, as in all other phases of criminal investigation, objectivity, accuracy and thoroughness are essential.

Investigators are responsible for preparing cases for court and presenting testimony in court. Their role is critical in the quest for justice. From the receipt of the initial complaint to the court appearance, investigators play a key role in the criminal justice system.

# Preparing for and Presenting Cases in Court

## DO YOU KNOW

Why some cases are not prosecuted?

What steps are taken in preparing a case for court?

What to concentrate on when reviewing a case?

What is included in the final report?

Why the quality of the content and the writing are important in the final report?

What occurs during the pretrial conference?

What the usual sequence in a criminal trial is?

What direct examination is? What cross-examination is?

What kinds of statements are inadmissible in court?

How to testify most effectively?

When to use notes while testifying?

What nonverbal elements can influence courtroom testimony positively and negatively?

What strategies can make testifying in court more effective?

What defense attorney tactics to anticipate?

## CAN YOU DEFINE

cross-examination
direct examination
expert
judge

## Introduction

MOST CRIMINAL CASES ARE RESOLVED WITHOUT A TRIAL. THE explanation may be an excellent investigation that causes the defendant to plead guilty, the desire of the defendant to plead guilty without going through a trial, the plea-bargaining process or some other factor.

Police training seldom devotes enough time to the subject of trial testimony. Most officers receive on-the-job experience with all its anxieties and frustrations. Morrison (1992, p. 86) notes that although: "Courtroom techniques are taught in police academies, . . . most of them fall short of what is necessary for an officer to survive an intense cross-examination and be left with his dignity." He goes on to point out: "Most veteran officers know the procedure. Anything—and everything—the defense attorney can do to discredit, confuse or otherwise destroy a police officer's testimony will be utilized." Morrison also suggests that officers should attend court when off duty to "observe the battlefield tactics used by those who were taught in a law school."

Willingham (1993, p. 45) stresses: "Conventional wisdom says a job is not finished until the paperwork is done. In law enforcement, the job is not finished until the testimony is done—in court." He suggests four areas of concern for being a good witness:

- The quality and completeness of your original notes and report.
- The pretrial conference and deposition.
- Courthouse behavior.
- Personal appearance and demeanor.

Willingham cautions: "These four areas all speak directly to the key elements in courtroom testimony—to be impressive."

In addition, law enforcement should consider using some of the new technology currently being used in corporate presentations. As Strandberg (1996, p. 34) suggests:

> Justice may be blind, but she doesn't have to be technologically impaired. . . . Lawyers, judges and law enforcement alike will have to alter the way their jobs are done in . . . a virtual courtroom, but the task of the jury may be made easier by the advantage of reviewing exactly what happened in any given case. Justice may prevail, even better than it did before.

This final chapter begins with a discussion of why some cases do not go to court and how a case might be closed by arrest and prosecution. This is followed by a detailed explanation of how to prepare a case for prosecution. Next the chapter describes the trial and the typical sequence of events. Then suggestions are provided regarding testifying under direct examination, strategies for excelling as a witness and testifying under cross-examination. The chapter ends with a discussion on concluding your testimony.

## Nonprosecution

A criminal case can be closed without prosecution for several valid reasons.

Cases are not prosecuted if:
- The complaint is invalid.
- The prosecutor declines after reviewing the case.
- The complainant refuses to prosecute.
- The offender dies.
- The offender is in prison or out of the country and cannot be returned.
- No evidence or leads exist.

### Invalid Complaints

Some complaints turn out to be unfounded. For example, investigation may reveal that property claimed stolen was lost, misplaced and later found; that damage was caused by other than a criminal act; or that the complainant is senile, habitually intoxicated, mentally incapacitated or for some other reason incapable of providing a valid crime report.

### Exceptional Clearance

Some cases cannot be prosecuted because of circumstances beyond the investigating officer's control. Despite ample evidence, prosecution may be impossible

**662**

Section 6

**The
Investigator's
Role in the
Judicial Process**

because the complainant refuses to prosecute and withdraws the complaint, the suspect dies or the offender is identified but is in prison or out of the state or country and cannot be returned for prosecution.

### Lack of Evidence or Leads

Administrative policy closes other cases to further investigation. Specific criteria are established for these decisions. The caseload of investigative personnel has grown so large that cases with little probability of successful prosecution must be closed as a matter of maintaining priorities.

Many police departments have incorporated such criteria into their crime report forms. If enough criteria are met, the case is closed to further investigation and the complainant is notified of the decision. This often happens when the complainant files a report "only because my insurance company requires me to report the loss to the police." The loss may have occurred many days before the report, or there may be no leads. In some cases there are insufficient facts to support the complaint, but the victim insists on filing a complaint and has the right to do so.

In other cases, there is a valid report, but investigation reveals that witnesses have left the area or that no physical evidence remains at the crime scene. Without physical evidence, witnesses, identifiable leads or information to follow up, it is unwise to use investigative time to pursue the case when many other cases need investigation. Such cases are placed in an inactive file and are reopened only if time is available or new information is received. Occasionally, such cases are cleared by the admission or confession of a suspect who is arrested for another crime. The case is then reopened and cleared by exceptional clearance.

## Closing a Case by Arrest and Prosecution

If sufficient evidence exists to continue the investigation or if a person is already in custody for the offense, pursue the case for all possible information and evidence to prove innocence or guilt. If no arrest has been made, consider all information and evidence to determine whether a crime was committed, whether evidence is sufficient to prosecute and whether the suspect should be arrested. Make such decisions after consulting with the prosecuting attorney's office.

The prosecutor is your legal adviser throughout the process—during the investigation, the pretrial conference and the court presentation. Follow the prosecutor's advice, even if you disagree. It is best to try to work out the issues of the case together. Jealousy and animosity must not impede the end goal: justice. Tell the prosecutor the facts of the case, and then listen to and learn from the prosecutor.

The decision to charge or to arrest is made by the investigator alone or jointly with the prosecuting attorney's office. If the suspect was at the scene of the crime, you probably made an immediate arrest. Otherwise, consult the prosecuting attorney's office to obtain an arrest warrant.

## Preparing a Case for Prosecution

Once the decision is made to prosecute a case, more than "probable cause" is required. The prosecution must prove the case *beyond a reasonable doubt—*

the degree of proof necessary to obtain a conviction. To do so, the prosecution must know what evidence can be introduced, what witnesses will testify, the strengths and weaknesses of the case and the type of testimony police investigators can supply.

To prepare a case for court:
- Review and evaluate all evidence, positive and negative.
- Review all reports on the case.
- Prepare witnesses.
- Write the final report.
- Hold a pretrial conference with the prosecutor.

### Review and Evaluate Evidence

Each crime consists of one or more elements that must be proven. The statutes and ordinances of the particular jurisdiction define these elements.

Concentrate on proving the elements of the crime and on establishing the offender's identity.

Review physical evidence to ensure that it has been properly gathered, identified, transported and safeguarded between the time it was obtained and the time of the trial. Make sure the evidence is available for the trial and that it is taken to the courtroom and turned over to the prosecuting attorney. Arrange for trained laboratory technicians' testimony if necessary. Select evidence that is material,

*Confessed murderer William Flynn is confronted with the murder weapon during his testimony on the killing of Gregory Smart.*

**664**

Section 6

The
Investigator's
Role in the
Judicial Process

relevant and competent and that helps to establish the corpus delicti: what happened and who was responsible.

Review and evaluate witnesses' statements for credibility. If a witness claims to have seen a specific act, determine if the light was sufficient and if the witness has good eyesight and was in a position to see the act clearly. Also assess the witness's relationship to the suspect and the victim.

Establish the identity of the suspect by eyewitness testimony, transfer evidence and supporting evidence such as motive, prior knowledge, opportunity and known modus operandi.

Videotapes are being used increasingly in court, especially in child abuse and sex crimes. Expert witnesses with heavy time commitments may be allowed to testify by videotape, saving the time and expense of a trip to the city where the trial is taking place. Videotapes have also been made of witnesses who are severely injured and cannot appear in court. In addition, videotapes of suspects' confessions are invaluable as are videotapes of crime scenes (Giacoppo, 1991, pp. 1–4).

Rereviewing every aspect of the case before entering the courtroom is excellent preparation for testifying at the trial. Do not memorize answers to imagined questions, but be prepared and then think briefly before you give your statement in answer to direct or indirect questions.

### Review Reports

Review written reports of everything done during the investigation. This includes the preliminary report, memorandums, summary reports, progress reports, evidence records and receipts, photographs and sketches, medical examiner's reports, emergency squad records, laboratory test reports on evidence, statements of witnesses (positive and negative) and any other reports on actions taken during the investigation.

### Prepare Witnesses

Reinterview witnesses to refresh their memories. Read their previous statements to them and ask if this is the evidence they will present in court. Such a review also helps allay any fears witnesses have about giving testimony in court. Describe trial procedures to the witnesses so that they understand what will occur. Explain that they can only testify to facts from their own personal knowledge or from common knowledge. Emphasize that they must tell the truth and present the facts as they know them. Explain the importance of remaining calm, having a clean appearance and remaining impartial.

By experience, police officers know of the many delays in court proceedings and of the waits in the courtroom or in the hall outside the courtroom before they can testify. This also should be explained to witnesses who may be testifying for the first time so that they can make flexible arrangements for the day. In addition, the complainants should be prepared for the delays and continuances that may be part of the defense's strategy to wear them down so that they will drop the charges.

### Prepare the Final Report

The final, or prosecution, report contains all essential information for prosecution. Submit the entire case file along with the prosecution report. The final decision about what evidence is to be used is made by the prosecutor who will try the case in court.

The report presents the facts of the case, a criminal history of the person charged, the types of evidence available and who can support such evidence by testimony in court, names of people the prosecutor can talk to for further information and a chronological account of the crime and subsequent investigation.

---

The final report contains (1) the complaint; (2) the preliminary investigation report; (3) all follow-up reports; (4) statements, admissions and confessions; (5) laboratory reports; (6) photographs, sketches and drawings; and (7) a summary of all negative evidence.

---

Prepare the report after a careful review of all information. Organize the facts logically.

**The Complaint.**    Include a copy of the original complaint received by the police dispatcher and complaint desk. This should include the date and time of the complaint, location of the incident, brief details, times when officers were dispatched and the names of the officers assigned to the initial call.

**The Preliminary Investigation Report.**    The report of the officer's initial investigation at the crime scene provides essential information on time of arrival, lighting and weather conditions, what was observed at the scene and immediate and subsequent actions taken by officers responding to the call.

**Follow-Up Reports.**    Assemble each contact and follow-up report in chronological order, presenting the sequence of the investigation and the pattern used to follow leads. These reports contain the essential information that was gathered in proving the elements of the crime and in linking the crime to the suspect. The reports can be in the form of progress notes.

**Statements, Admissions and Confessions.**    Include the statements of all witnesses interviewed during the investigation. If written statements were not obtained, report the results of oral interviews with witnesses. Assemble all statements, admissions or confessions by suspects in a separate part of the report. Include the reports of all polygraphs or other examinations used to determine the truth of statements, admissions or confessions.

**Laboratory Reports.**    Assemble laboratory results in one segment of the final report. Make recommendations on how these results relate to other areas of the report.

**Photographs, Sketches and Drawings.**    Include photographs, sketches and drawings of the crime scene to show conditions when officers arrived and what evidence was available.

**Summary of Negative Evidence.**    Include a summary of all negative evidence developed during the investigation. Statements of witnesses claiming that the suspect was elsewhere at the time of the crime are sometimes proved false, but the prosecution must consider such statements and develop a defense. If information exists that the crime was committed by the suspect but that it was done in self-defense or accidentally, state this in the report. Include all recognizable weaknesses in proving the corpus delicti or the offender's identity.

**666**

Section 6

The
Investigator's
Role in the
Judicial Process

Write the report clearly and accurately, following the guidelines presented in Chapter 3.

---

The quality of the final report influences its credibility.

---

Arrange the material in a logical sequence and a convenient format. A binder or loose-leaf notebook is well suited for this, as it allows the various units of information to be separated, with a labeled, tabbed divider for each unit.

### Pretrial Conference

Before testifying in court and after you have made the final case preparation and final report, arrange for a pretrial conference with the prosecuting attorney. Organize the facts and evidence and prepare a summary of the investigation. Include in this summary the focal points and main issues of the case, an envelope containing copies of all reports and all other relevant documents.

---

At the pretrial conference with the prosecutor:
- Review all the evidence.
- Discuss the strengths and weaknesses of the case.
- Discuss the probable line of questioning by the prosecutor and the defense.

---

Discuss complicated or detailed information fully to avoid misunderstanding. Discuss any legal questions concerning admissibility of evidence or testimony.

Sometimes witnesses are included in the pretrial conference. If so, listen carefully to what each witness says to the prosecuting attorney and the prosecuting attorney's responses. During the trial, the judge may exclude all witnesses from the courtroom except the one who is testifying. Therefore, you may have no opportunity to hear the testimony of other witnesses or the approach used by the prosecuting attorney.

It is also a good idea to review the case with other officers who are going to testify. You may not hear their actual testimony, and it will help you if you know in advance what they are going to say.

### Final Preparations

Shortly before the trial, again review your notes and your final report. Take with you only those notes you want to use in testifying. Check to be certain that the physical evidence is being taken to the courtroom and will be available for the prosecuting attorney when needed. Also make sure that laboratory technicians are available to appear when they are required.

Vail (1992, p. 97) suggests the following steps before entering the courthouse:

1. Know which courtroom you'll be testifying in. If you are unfamiliar with the particular courthouse or courtroom, check it out before the trial so that you will know your way around.
2. Do not discuss anything about the case in public or where your conversation may be overheard. Anyone could be a juror or defense witness!
3. Treat people with respect, as if they are the judge, or a juror in your cases going to trial. Your professionalism, politeness, and courtesy will be noted and remembered—especially by those who do see you in court in an official capacity.

4. Do not discuss your personal life, official business, biases, prejudices, likes and dislikes, or controversial subjects in public for the same reasons as above. You might impress a judge, juror, defense counsel, or witness the wrong way.

5. Judges and attorneys have little patience with officers appearing in court late, so be on time. Know when you will be expected to be called to testify.

6. Dress appropriately. Look businesslike and official. If in uniform, it should be clean, neat, and complete. If not in uniform, a sport coat and slacks are as appropriate as a business suit (male and female officers alike).

7. Avoid contact with the defense counsel and any defense witnesses before the trial. Assume that they will try to get you to say something about the case, to their advantage.

## The Trial

The main participants in the trial are the judge, jury members, attorneys, the defendant and witnesses. The **judge** presides over the trial, rules on the admissibility of the evidence and procedures, keeps order in the court, interprets the law for the jurors and passes sentence if the defendant is found guilty.

The *jurors* hear and weigh the testimony of all witnesses. Jurors consider many factors other than the words spoken. The attitude and behavior of witnesses, suspects and attorneys are constantly under the jury's scrutiny. Jurors notice how witnesses respond to questions and their attitudes toward the prosecution and the defense. They reach their verdict based on what they see, hear and feel during the trial. Typical jurors will have had limited or no experience with the criminal justice system outside of what they have read in the newspaper and seen on television.

*Legal counsel* presents the prosecution and defense evidence before the court and jury. Lawyers act as checks against each other and present the case as required by court procedure and the rulings of the presiding judge.

*Defendants* may or may not take the witness stand. If they do so, they must answer all questions put to them. They may not use the Fifth Amendment as a reason for not answering.

*Witnesses* present the facts personally known to them. Police officers are witnesses for the prosecution. Most police departments have regulations regarding attire when appearing in court. Usually, these specify that officers should appear in uniform. A weapon may not be worn into the courtroom without special permission. If one is worn, it should not be visible. Do not wear dark or deeply tinted glasses when appearing in court.

If street clothes are worn, dress conservatively. Avoid bright colors and large plaids. Do not overdo on the accessories, and avoid bizarre haircuts. Your personal appearance reflects your attitude and your professionalism and has a definite effect on the jury.

Each time a law enforcement witness enters a courtroom is a challenge. It is fraught with danger to the prosecution's case because it is always they who have to establish the burden of proof beyond a reasonable doubt.

## Sequence of a Criminal Trial

The trial begins with the case being called from the court docket. If both the prosecution and the defense are ready, the case is presented before the court.

**668**

Section 6

The
Investigator's
Role in the
Judicial Process

The sequence in a criminal trial is as follows:
- Jury selection.
- Opening statements by the prosecution and the defense.
- Presentation of the prosecution's case.
- Presentation of the defense's case.
- Closing statements by the prosecution and the defense.
- Instructions to the jury.
- Jury deliberation to reach a verdict.
- Reading of the verdict.
- Acquittal or passing of sentence.

If the trial is before a judge *without a jury*, the prosecution and the defense make their opening statements directly to the court. The opening statements are brief summaries of what the prosecution plans to prove against the defendant and what the defense plans to do to challenge the prosecution's allegations. In a *jury trial*, the jury is selected and then the opening statements are made by both counsels before the judge and jury.

The prosecution presents its case first. Witnesses for the prosecution are sworn in by the court, and the testimony of each is taken by direct examination through questions asked by the prosecuting attorney. At the conclusion of each witness's testimony, the defense attorney may cross-examine the witness. After the cross-examination, the prosecuting attorney may redirect examine, and the defense attorney may re-cross-examine.

**Direct examination** is the initial questioning of a witness or defendant by the lawyer who is using the person's testimony to further his or her case. **Cross-examination** is questioning by the opposing side for the purpose of assessing the validity of the testimony.

After the prosecutor has completed direct examination of all prosecution witnesses, the defense presents its case. After the direct examination of each defense witness, the prosecutor may cross-examine, the defense counsel may redirect examine and the prosecutor may re-cross-examine.

After each side has presented its regular witnesses, both sides may present *rebuttal* and *surrebuttal* witnesses. When the entire case has been presented, prosecution and defense counsel present their closing arguments to the jury. In these arguments, the lawyers review the trial evidence of both sides and then tell the jury why the defendant should be convicted or acquitted. Sometimes the lawyers also make recommendations for penalty.

The judge instructs the jury on the laws applicable to the case and on how they are to arrive at a decision. The jury then retires to the jury room to deliberate and arrive at a verdict. When the verdict is reached, court is reconvened and the verdict is read. If the verdict is for acquittal, the defendant is released. If the verdict is guilty, the judge passes sentence or sets a time and date for sentencing.

## Testifying under Direct Examination

You are on trial, too—your credibility, your professionalism, your knowledge, your competence, your judgment, your conduct in the field, your use of force, your adherence to official policies, your observance of the defendant's rights—they're all on trial.

—Devallis Rutledge

First impressions are critical. Know what you are doing when you enter the courtroom. Go to the courtroom ahead of time and familiarize yourself with the layout of the room.

When your name is called, answer "Here" or "Present" and move directly to the front of the courtroom. Do not go between the prosecutor and the judge; go behind the attorneys. Walk confidently; the jurors are there to hear the facts from you. If your investigation has been thorough and properly conducted, the jury will give a great deal of weight to your testimony.

If you have notes or a report, have them contained in a clean manila file folder carried in your left hand so your right hand is free for taking the oath.

Taking the oath in court is basically the same as taking your oath of office. Stand straight and face the clerk of court, holding the palm of your hand toward the clerk. Use a clear, firm voice to answer "I do" to the question: "Do you promise to tell the truth, the whole truth and nothing but the truth, so help you God?" Do not look at the judge, either legal counsel or the jury. Do not raise your hand and take your oath on the way from your seat in the courtroom. Wait until you are directly in front of the clerk.

Sit with your back straight but in a comfortable position, usually with your hands folded in your lap or held on the arms of the chair. Do not move the chair around or fidget in the chair because this distracts from your testimony. The witness chair in all courtrooms is positioned so that you can turn to face the judge, legal counsel, jury or the audience, depending on to whom your answers are directed. Hold notes and other reports in your lap.

The prosecutor will ask you to state your name, department and position. As you respond to these questions, keep in mind the types of statements that are not admissible.

*A witness at the 1996 trial of accused subway firebomber Edward Leary points to photographs of his burned shoes as she testifies that when Leary took a subway seat next to her, she began "to smell gasoline." Leary, an unemployed computer programmer, was charged with forty-five counts of attempted murder for two 1994 subway firebombings.*

**670**

Section 6

The
Investigator's
Role in the
Judicial Process

Inadmissible statements include:
- Opinion (unless the witness is qualified as an expert).
- Hearsay.
- Privileged communication.
- Statements about character and reputation, including the defendant's past criminal record.

Testify only to what you actually saw, heard or did, not what you believe, heard from others or were told about. You can testify to what a defendant told you directly, but any other statements must be testified to by the person making them. Opinions and conclusions also are inadmissible unless you are qualified as an expert. You cannot testify about criminal offenses the defendant committed before the present case.

Proper preparation is the key to being a good witness. After a review of your personal notes and all relevant reports, you will be familiar with the case and can "tell it like it is," which will come across well to the jury and establish your credibility. Vail (1992, p. 96) stresses: "Testifying in court is as important as using a weapon: you don't do it often, but when you do, you had better be correct and accurate."

Guidelines for effective testimony:
- Speak clearly, firmly and with expression.
- Answer questions directly. Do not volunteer information.
- Pause briefly before answering.
- Refer to your notes if you do not recall exact details.
- Admit calmly when you do not know an answer.
- Admit any mistakes you make in testifying.
- Avoid police jargon, sarcasm and humor.
- Tell the complete truth as you know it.

How you speak is often as important as what you say. Talk slowly, deliberately and loudly enough to be heard by everyone. Never use obscenity or vulgarity unless the court requests a suspect or victim's exact words and they include it. In such cases, inform the court that the answer requested includes obscenity or vulgarity. Vail points out (p. 96): "It is said that an audience remembers 7 percent of what you say, 38 percent of how you sound, and 55 percent of how you look. In other words, 93 percent of the strength of your testimony lies in your presentation—how you sound and look."

Ignore the courtroom's atmosphere. Devote your entire attention to giving truthful answers to questions. Answer all questions directly and politely with "Yes," or "No," unless asked to relate an action taken, an observation made or information told to you directly by the defendant. Refer to the judge as "Your honor" and to the defendant as "the defendant." Do not volunteer information. Instead, let the prosecution decide whether to go into a particular line of questioning.

Take a few seconds after hearing the question to form your answer. If the counsel or the court objects to a question, wait until instructed to proceed. If it takes some time for the objection to be ruled on, ask to have the question repeated.

Refer to your notes if you are uncertain of specific facts, but do not rely on them excessively.

Reviewing the case thoroughly before your courtroom appearance does not mean you should memorize specific dates, addresses or spellings of names and places. Memorization can lead to confusion. Instead, use notes to help avoid contradictions and inconsistencies in testimony. An extemporaneous answer is better received by the judge and jury than one that sounds pat.

Using notes too much detracts from your testimony, weakens the strength of your presentation and gives the impression that you have not adequately prepared for the case. It can also lead to having your notes introduced into the record. If as you refer to your notes you discover that you have given erroneous testimony such as an incorrect date or time, notify the court immediately. Do not try to cover up the discrepancy. Everyone makes mistakes; if they are professionally admitted, little harm results. Do not hesitate to admit that you do not know the answer to a question or that you do not understand a question. Never bluff or attempt to fake your way through an answer.

In addition, be aware of certain phrases that may leave a negative impression on the jury. Phrases such as "I believe" or "to the best of my recollection" will not impress a jury.

Do not argue or use sarcasm, witticism or smart answers. Be direct, firm and positive in your answers. Be courteous whether the question is from the prosecutor or an objection from the defense or the judge. Do not hesitate to give information favorable to the defendant. Your primary responsibility is to state what you know about the case.

### Nonverbal Factors

Don't underestimate the power of nonverbal factors as you testify.

Important nonverbal elements include dress, eye contact, posture, gestures, distance, mannerisms, rate of speech and tone of voice.

Some nonverbal messages such as dress, posture, rate of speech and tone of voice have already been stressed. How you appear *is* crucial.

Vail (1992, p. 99) notes: "In order to win cases in court, you must always appear to be self-confident and in control of yourself and the situation."

Actions associated with deception include putting the hand over the mouth, rubbing the nose, preening, straightening the hair, buttoning up a coat, picking lint off clothing or tugging at a shirt or a pant leg.

## Strategies for Excelling as a Witness

Vail (1995, p. 23) suggests: "Learning the rudiments in two areas will give officers an edge in court: self-confidence and techniques of public speaking." He stresses: "Knowing, understanding and practicing the basic elements of self-confidence and techniques of public speaking will have a marked improvement on the officer's chance of winning in court under any circumstances." Investments in courses in these two areas would be time and money well spent.

**672**

**Section 6**

**The
Investigator's
Role in the
Judicial Process**

Hope (1992, pp. 56–60) has compiled the following "Ten Commandments of Courtroom Testimony":

    **I.** Relax and be yourself.
    **II.** Answer only questions that are before you.
    **III.** Refer to your report only when allowed.
    **IV.** Paint the scene just as it was.
    **V.** Be ready to explain why you are remembering details in court if they are not in your report.
    **VI.** Avoid jargon or unduly difficult language.
    **VII.** Avoid sarcasm.
    **VIII.** Maintain your detachment.
    **IX.** You don't need to explain the law.
    **X.** Explanation of what you said is possible on rebuttal.

The quotation at the beginning of the previous section is by Devallis Rutledge, a former police officer, presently a prosecutor. His book *Courtroom Survival: The Officer's Guide to Better Testimony* (1987) contains more than 180 pages of practical, commonsense, vital advice for courtroom testimony and many examples of courtroom dialogue.

---

Rutledge's strategies for testifying in court include the following: (1) set yourself up, (2) provoke the defense into giving you a chance to explain, (3) be unconditional and (4) don't stall.

---

- Get into the habit of thinking ahead to the trial while you're still out in the field. What if they ask me this in court?
- The rules of court severely restrict you in answering questions. No defense attorney in his right mind is ever going to give you a chance to explain anything. So, if you're ever going to get the chance to explain yourself before the jury's impression of you gets set in their heads, you've got to know how to provoke the defense attorney into giving you a chance to explain. Some of these provokers are: *definitely; certainly; certainly not; naturally; naturally not;* and one that always does the trick: *Yes, and no.*
- Be unconditional. Some cops seem to like the sound of the conditional word *would.* When I'm prosecuting a case, I cringe at the sound of it. It's too indefinite:
  Example:
  Q: Who was your partner?
  A: That would be Officer Hill.
- Don't stall. Don't repeat the question back to the attorney.
  Example:
  Q: Were you holding a flashlight?
  A: Was I holding a flashlight? Yes, I was.

### Expert Testimony

Officers who qualify as experts in an area are allowed to give opinions and conclusions, but the prosecution must qualify the officer as an expert on the stand. It must be established that the person has special knowledge that persons of moderate education or experience in the same field do not possess. To qualify as an **expert** witness, one must have:

- Present or prior employment in the specific field.
- Active membership in a professional group in the field.
- Research work in the field.
- An educational degree directly related to the field.
- Direct experience with the subject if not employed in the field.
- Papers, treatises or books published on the subject or teaching experience in it.

Police officers can become experts on sounds, firearms, distances, lengths of time, visibility problems and the like simply by years of experience in police work. Other areas, such as firearms identification, fingerprint classification and handwriting analysis, require specialized training.

White (1992, p. 32) stresses three basic precepts for law enforcement witnesses: "Be exceptionally well prepared, be truthful, and possess the ability to withstand tough cross-examination." According to White: "A well-prepared officer will be able to deliver convincing testimony, even under the unpredictable pressure of cross-examination."

## Testifying under Cross-Examination

As Vail (1995, p. 23) notes: "It might be a bit upsetting to know that attorneys are willing to spend $375-plus to learn professional acting techniques in order to defend criminals in court—while making you, a professional police officer, look as inept and stupid as possible."

Cross-examination is usually the most difficult part of testifying. The defense attorney will attempt to cast doubt on your direct testimony in an effort to win an acquittal for the defendant. Know the methods of attack for cross-examination to avoid being trapped.

---

During cross-examination the defense attorney might:
- Be disarmingly friendly or intimidatingly rude.
- Attack your credibility and impartiality.
- Attack your investigative skill.
- Attempt to force contradictions or inconsistencies.
- Ask leading questions or deliberately misquote you.
- Ask for a simple answer to a complex question.
- Use rapid-fire questioning.
- Use the silent treatment.

---

The defense attorney can be extremely friendly, hoping to put you off-guard by making the questioning appear to be nothing more than a friendly chat. The attorney might praise your skill in investigation and lead you into boasting or a show of self-glorification that will leave a very bad impression on the jury. The friendly defense attorney might also try to lead you into giving testimony about evidence of which you have no personal knowledge. This error will be immediately exposed and your testimony tainted, if not completely discredited.

At the opposite extreme is the defense attorney who appears outraged by statements you make and goes on the attack immediately. This kind of attorney appears very excited and acts as though a travesty of justice is being presented in the courtroom. A natural reaction to such an approach is to overreact by exaggerating your testimony or by losing your temper, which is exactly what the

**674**

Section 6

**The
Investigator's
Role in the
Judicial Process**

defense attorney wants. If you show anger, the jury might believe you are too concerned about the case and are more interested in obtaining a conviction than in determining the truth. It is often hard for a jury to believe that the well-dressed, meek-appearing defendant in court is the person who was armed with a gun and robbed a store. Maintain dignity and impartiality, and show concern only for the facts.

The credibility of your testimony can be attacked in many ways. The defense may attempt to show that you are prejudiced, have poor character or are interested only in seeing your arrest stick. If asked, "Do you want to see the defendant convicted?" reply that you are there to present the facts you know and that you will abide by the court's decision.

The defense may also try to show that your testimony itself is erroneous because you are incompetent, lack information, are confused, have forgotten facts or could not have had personal knowledge of the facts testified to. Do not respond to such criticism. Let your testimony speak for itself. If the defense criticizes your reference to notes, state that you simply want to be completely accurate. Be patient. If the defense counsel becomes excessively offensive, the prosecutor will intervene. Alternatively, the prosecutor may see that the defense is hurting its own case by such behavior and will allow the defense attorney to proceed.

The defense attorney may also try to force contradictions or inconsistencies by incessantly repeating questions using slightly different wording. Repeat your previous answer. If the defense claims that your testimony does not agree with that of other officers, do not change your testimony. Whether your testimony is alike or different is irrelevant. The defense will attack it either way. If it is exactly alike, the defense will allege collusion. If it is slightly different, the defense will exaggerate this in an attempt to make the jury believe the differences are so great that the officers are not even testifying about the same circumstances.

The defense counsel may use an accusatory tone in asking whether you talked with others about the case and what they told you about how to testify. To inexperienced officers, such accusations may produce guilt because the officers know they have talked about the case with many people. Because the accusing tone implies this was legally incorrect, the officers may reply that they talked to no one. Such a response is a mistake because there is nothing wrong with discussing the case before testifying. Simply state that you have discussed the case with several persons in an official capacity, but that none of them has told you how to testify.

If defense counsel asks whether you have refreshed your memory before testifying, do not hesitate to say "yes." You would be a poor witness if you had not done so. Discussions with the prosecution, officers and witnesses and a review of notes and reports are entirely proper. They assist you in telling the truth, the main purpose of testimony.

Another defense tactic is to use leading questions. For example, defense counsel may ask, "When did you first strike the defendant?" This assumes you did, in fact, strike the defendant. Defense attorneys also like to ask questions that presume you have already testified to something when in fact you may have said no such thing. If you are misquoted, call it to the counsel's attention and then repeat the facts you testified to. If you do not remember your exact testimony, have it read from the court record.

In addition, defense counsel may ask complicated questions and then say, "Please answer 'yes' or 'no.'" Obviously, some questions cannot be answered that simply. Ask to have the question broken down. No rule requires a specific answer. If the court does not grant the request, answer the question as directed and let the prosecutor bring out the information through redirect examination.

Yet another tactic used by defense attorneys is rapid-fire questioning in the hope of provoking unconsidered answers. Do not let the attorney's pace rush you. Take time to consider your responses.

Do not be taken in by the "silent treatment." The defense attorney may remain silent for what seems like many seconds after you answer a question. If you have given a complete answer, wait patiently. Do *not* attempt to fill the silence by saying things such as, "At least that's how I remember it," or "It was something very close to that."

Another tactic frequently used by defense attorneys is to mispronounce officers' names intentionally or address them by the wrong rank. This is an attempt to cause the officer to lose concentration.

Regardless of how your testimony is attacked, treat the defense counsel as respectfully as you do the prosecutor. Do not regard the defense counsel as your enemy. You are in court to state the facts and tell the truth. There should be no personal prejudice or animosity in your testimony, no reason to become excited or provoked at the defense counsel. Be professional.

Few officers are prepared for the rigor of testifying in court, even if they have received training in this area. Until officers have actually testified in court, they cannot understand how difficult it is. Because police officers are usually the main and most damaging witnesses in a criminal case, defense attorneys know they must attempt to confuse, discredit or destroy the officers' testimony.

The best testimony is accurate, truthful and in accordance with the facts. Every word an officer says is recorded and may be played back or used by the defense.

## Handling Objections

Rutledge (1987, pp. 99–115) gives the following suggestions for handling objections:*

There are at least 44 standard trial objections in most states. We're only going to talk about the two that account for upwards of 90 percent of the problems a testifying officer will have: that your answer is a conclusion, or that it is non-responsive.

■ How to avoid conclusions. One way is to listen to the form of the question. You know the attorney is asking you to speculate when he starts his questions with these loaded phrases:
Would you assume . . .?
Do you suppose . . .?
Don't you think that . . .?
Couldn't it be that . . .?
Do you imagine . . .?
Wouldn't it be fair to presume . . .?
Isn't it strange that . . .?
And the one you're likely to hear most often:
Isn't it possible that . . .?
■ Another major area of conclusionary testimony is what I call mindreading. You can't get inside someone else's brain. That means you don't know for a

---

*Reprinted by permission of the publisher.

**676**

**Section 6**

**The
Investigator's
Role in the
Judicial Process**

fact—so you can't testify—as to what someone else sees, hears, feels, thinks or wants; and you don't know for a fact what somebody is trying to do, or is able to do, or whether he is nervous, excited, angry, scared, happy, upset, disturbed, or in any of the other emotional states that can only be labeled with a conclusion.

■ How to give "responsive" answers. You have to answer just the question that you're asked—no more, no less. That means you have to pay attention to how the question is framed. You answer a yes-or-no question with a "yes" or "no."
Q: Did he perform the alphabet test?
A: Yes, twice—but he only went to "G."
Everything after the "yes" is non-responsive. The officer anticipated the next three questions and volunteered the answers. He should have limited each answer to one question:
Q: Did he perform the alphabet test?
A: Yes.
Q: How many times?
A: Twice.
Q: How far did he go correctly the first time?
A: To the letter "G."

---

Avoid conclusions and nonresponsive answers. Answer yes-or-no questions with "yes" or "no."

---

The defense lawyer's most important task is to destroy your credibility— to make you look like you're either an incompetent bungler, or a liar, or both. How does he do that? He attacks you. He tricks you. He outsmarts you. He confuses you. He frustrates you. He annoys you. He probes for your most vulnerable characteristics.

Willingham (1993, p. 48) suggests the following:

The formula for successful courtroom testimony is: be brief, politely; be aggressive, smilingly; be emphatic, pleasantly; be positive, diplomatically; and be right, graciously.

## Concluding Your Testimony

Do not leave the stand until instructed to do so by the counsel or the court. As you leave the stand, do not pay special attention to the prosecution, defense counsel, defendant or jury. Return immediately to your seat in the courtroom or leave the room if you have been sequestered. If you are told you may be needed for further testimony, remain available. If told you are no longer needed, leave the courtroom and resume your normal activities. To remain gives the impression you have a special interest in the case.

If you are in the courtroom at the time of the verdict, show neither approval nor disapproval at the outcome. The complainant should be notified of the disposition of the case. A form such as the one shown in Figure 20–1 is frequently used.

Morrison (1992, p. 88) concludes: "When the system works, it is because an arresting officer and the prosecutor do the things to make it happen. It's not an accident. It's the American way."

CASE DISPOSITION REPORT

Date Disposition Made: ___4-25-97___          D.R. #: ___97-1002___
Date of Incident: ___2-10-97___          Type of Incident: ___Burglary___

DISPOSITION:
(X) Case Clearance
(X) Property Recovered
( ) Disposition of Property: (X) Owner ( ) Police Evidence
( ) Other
If Other, specify type: _____

VICTIM: (If Runaway Juvenile or Missing Adult, disregard this section)
Name ___Jerome Slater___          Address ___3041 Harding, Edina, Minnesota___

SUSPECT(S):
NO. 1: ___John Toben___          Arrested? ___Yes___          BCPD I.D. # 20146
NO. 2: ___William Moss___          Arrested? ___Yes___          BCPD I.D. # 20147
NO. 3: _____          Arrested? _____          BCPD I.D. # _____

PROPERTY RECOVERED:
Item No. 1: _One Car Radio, Sears_          Value ___$87.00___
Item No. 2: _One car battery, Sears_          Value ___60.00___
Item No. 3: _Micro Wave Oven-GE_          Value ___250.00___
Item No. 4: _One 17"-Sears Solid State_          Value ___350.00___
Recovering Agency: _Edina Police Department_     Total Value Recovered Property: _$747.00_

CANCELLATIONS: (Specify date, time, agency and officer receiving cancellation and
                officer making cancellation)

NCIC: _____
Other Agencies: _Hennepin County Sheriffs Office_____
Other Agencies: _____

OFFICER MAKING DISPOSITION: _____
SUPERVISOR APPROVING: _____
DETAILS: _Full recovery of property_____

**Figure 20–1   Case Disposition Notice**

# Summary

To prosecute or not to prosecute is often a question. Some cases are never prosecuted because the complaint is invalid, it is exceptionally cleared, or no evidence or leads exist. If the decision is made to prosecute, thorough preparation is required. To prepare a case for court: (1) review and evaluate all evidence, positive and negative; (2) review all reports on the case; (3) prepare witnesses; (4) write the final report; and (5) hold a pretrial conference with the prosecutor. Concentrate on proving the elements of the crime and on establishing the offender's identity.

The final report contains (1) the complaint; (2) the preliminary investigation report; (3) all follow-up and progress reports; (4) statements, admissions

**678**

Section 6

The
Investigator's
Role in the
Judicial Process

and confessions; (5) laboratory reports; (6) photographs, sketches and drawings; and (7) a summary of all negative evidence. The quality of the content and writing of the final report influences its credibility.

Before the trial, hold a conference with the prosecutor to review all the evidence, to discuss the strengths and weaknesses of the case and to discuss the probable line of the prosecutor and defense attorney's questioning.

A criminal trial begins with the jury selection. When court convenes, prosecution and defense make their opening statements. The prosecution then presents its case, followed by presentation of the defense's case. After closing statements by the prosecution and the defense, the judge instructs the jury, which then retires to deliberate its verdict. When a verdict is reached, court is reconvened and the verdict read. If the defendant is found guilty, the judge passes sentence or sets a sentencing date.

Direct examination is the initial questioning of a witness or defendant by the lawyer who is using the person's testimony to further his or her case. Cross-examination is questioning by the opposing side with the intent of assessing the validity of the testimony.

Certain types of statements are inadmissible in court, including opinions, hearsay, privileged communications and statements about the defendant's character and reputation. To present testimony effectively: speak clearly, firmly and with expression; answer questions directly, and do not volunteer information; pause briefly before answering; refer to your notes if you do not recall exact details; admit calmly when you do not know an answer; admit any mistakes you make in testifying; avoid police jargon, sarcasm and humor; and above all, tell the complete truth as you know it. Refer to your notes if you are uncertain of specific facts, but do not rely on them excessively; this would give the impression that you are not prepared for the case and thus weaken your testimony. Important nonverbal elements include dress, eye contact, posture, gestures, distance, mannerisms, rate of speech and tone of voice.

Strategies for testifying in court include (1) setting yourself up, (2) provoking the defense into giving you a chance to explain, (3) being unconditional and (4) not stalling.

Anticipate the tactics commonly used by defense attorneys during cross-examination. They may be disarmingly friendly or intimidatingly rude; attack your credibility and impartiality; attack your investigative skill; attempt to force contradictions or inconsistencies; ask leading questions or deliberately misquote you; request a "yes" or "no" answer to complex questions; use rapid-fire questioning; or use the "silent treatment."

Avoid conclusions and nonresponsive answers. Answer yes-or-no questions with "yes" or "no."

If you are well prepared, know the facts and present them truthfully and professionally, you have done your part in furthering the cause of justice. The disposition of a case should be made known to the complainant.

## Checklist

*Presenting the Case in Court*
- Have all reports been reviewed?
- Have all reports been organized for presentation to the prosecutor?
- Has all evidence been located and made available for court presentation?

- Has all evidence been examined by competent laboratories and the results obtained? Are copies of the reports available?
- Have all known leads been developed?
- Have both negative and positive information been submitted to the prosecuting attorney?
- Has all arrest information been submitted?
- Has a list of witnesses been prepared? Addresses? Telephone numbers?
- Has the final report been assembled? Are there copies of investigators' reports? Photographs? Sketches? Evidence? Lab reports? Medical examiner reports? Statements? Confessions? Maps? All other pertinent information?
- Has a pretrial conference been held with the prosecutor's office?
- Have all witnesses been reinterviewed? Notified of the date and time of the trial?
- Have all expert witnesses been notified of the date and time of the trial?
- Have arrangements been made to have the evidence taken to court?
- Have notes needed for testimony been removed from your notebook?
- Is your personal appearance professional?

## Application

Read these three examples of courtroom testimony and evaluate the officer's performance in each instance.*

**A.**
**Defense Attorney:** Is it fair to say your job is to arrest people who have committed a crime?

**Officer Dodd:** Yup, that's right.

**D.A.:** You don't go around arresting innocent people, do you?

**O.D.:** Never.

**D.A.:** Do you arrest only guilty people?

**O.D.:** Yup.

**D.A.:** Isn't it fair to say, then, that when you arrest someone, you believe he or she is guilty?

**O.D.:** Sure.

**D.A.:** Do you believe guilty people should be punished?

**O.D.:** Sure do.

**D.A.:** Do you believe your job is to see that they are punished?

**O.D.:** Sure do.

**D.A.:** Do you believe you should do everything you can to see that they are punished?

**O.D.:** Yup.

---

*From Henry Wrobleski and Kären M. Hess. *Introduction to Law Enforcement and Criminal Justice*, 2d ed. St. Paul, MN: West Publishing Co., 1986, pp. 440–442. Reprinted by permission.

**D.A.:** Isn't part of your job to come to the courtroom and offer testimony?

**O.D.:** Sure is.

**D.A.:** When you came into this courtroom today, did you believe that Mr. Johnson, the defendant, was guilty?

**O.D.:** Definitely.

**D.A.:** You want Mr. Johnson convicted?

**O.D.:** Definitely.

**D.A.:** And you'll do everything you can to see that happen?

**O.D.:** Right.

**B.**

**Defense Attorney:** Officer, you testified on direct examination that when you left the store, walked out of the door, and found the sack, you followed a trail of bloodstains. Do you recall that specifically?

**Officer Troy:** Yes, sir.

**D.A.:** Did you make a test to determine the nature of these stains?

**O.T.:** No, not me.

**D.A.:** You made no chemical analysis?

**O.T.:** No.

**D.A.:** Did anyone report to you that they made a chemical analysis?

**O.T.:** No.

**D.A.:** Then, as a matter of fact, you do *not* know now, nor did you know then, that those stains were actually blood.

**O.T.:** Well, I know what blood looks like.

**D.A.:** What does blood look like?

**O.T.:** When it's dried, it's kind of rusty-looking.

**D.A.:** Are there other things that are rusty-looking when they are dried?

**O.T.:** I suppose there are.

**D.A.:** How about candle wax from a rust-colored candle?

**O.T.:** Could be.

**D.A.:** We've all seen movies where the prop used is ketchup or something else that resembles blood. Many substances are rusty-looking when dried, aren't they?

**O.T.:** Not this; this was blood.

**D.A.:** On what scientific basis do you draw that conclusion? I'll withdraw the question. Officer, it is fair to say that you make assumptions from time to time, isn't it?

**O.T.:** Yes.

**D.A.:** And that in this particular case you saw a stain that looked sort of rusty and was dried, and you assumed it was blood?

**O.T.:** No. It *was* blood.

**C.**
**Defense Attorney:** Officer Bell, what type of test did you conduct to determine whether or not the defendant understood you when you advised her of her rights.

**Officer Bell:** I asked her if she understood the rights as I read them from the card to her.

**D.A.:** And what was her response?

**O.B.:** She said she did.

**D.A.:** Well, what tests did you make to determine whether or not she actually understood each of those rights?

**O.B.:** I asked if she understood what I read to her.

**D.A.:** Do you know the defendant's I.Q.?

**O.B.:** No, but from my personal observation and conversation with her, she seemed to be reasonably intelligent.

**D.A.:** Do you know whether or not she can read?

**O.B.:** She said she could.

1. What errors did the officers make in their testimony?
2. Which officer's testimony was the most effective?
3. What tactics were used by each defense attorney?

## Discussion Questions

1. Plea bargaining has become very controversial in many states, and some states have eliminated it as a part of the prosecution process. Is plea bargaining good or bad?
2. The news media can affect jury and court decisions by publicizing information about a criminal case before it goes to trial. May police refuse to give information to the press if doing so might jeopardize the case in court? How significantly does such publicity affect the later trial?
3. Are you familiar with cases where outside judges have had to be brought in to try a case or where the trial has had to be moved to another jurisdiction because of advance publicity?
4. Should criminal trials be televised? What are the advantages and disadvantages?
5. What is the investigator's role in preparing a case for court? How does the investigator cooperate with the prosecutor to make a better courtroom presentation?
6. What are the necessary steps in preparing to testify in a criminal trial? What materials may be brought into the courtroom?

**682**

Section 6

The
Investigator's
Role in the
Judicial Process

**7.** Imagine that you are preparing a final report for the prosecutor. What materials should you include? How should they be organized to show the continuity of your investigation and how you gathered evidence related to the elements of the offense charged?

**8.** If you were accused of a crime, would you prefer a trial with a jury or without a jury?

**9.** Is there a better system than the jury system?

**10.** Does an acquittal mean the investigator failed?

# References

Giacoppo, Michael. "The Expanded Role of Videotape in Court." *FBI Law Enforcement Bulletin,* November 1991, pp. 1–4.

Hope, George. "Ten Commandments of Courtroom Testimony." *Minnesota Police Journal,* April 1992, pp. 55–60.

Morrison, Richard D. "You Survived the Street: Now Can You Survive Cross Examination?" *Law and Order,* March 1992, pp. 86–87.

Rutledge, Devallis. *Courtroom Survival: The Officer's Guide to Better Testimony.* Incline Village, NV: Copperhouse Publishing Company, 1987.

Strandberg, Keith W. "The Courtroom of the Future." *Law Enforcement Technology,* June 1996, pp. 34–39.

Vail, Christopher. "Combating Courtroom Butterflies." *Law and Order,* September 1995, pp. 23–26.

———. "Presenting Winning Testimony in Court." *Law and Order,* June 1992, pp. 96–99.

White, Maxine Aldridge. "Testifying in Criminal Court: A Training Program for Law Enforcement Officers." *The Police Chief,* November 1991, pp. 32–34.

Willingham, Mark. "The Importance of Being an Impressive Witness." *Law and Order,* February 1993, pp. 45–48.

# Self-Assessment Guide for Police Response to Child-Abuse Calls

# A

This self-assessment guide was developed to assist police departments in examining their response to child abuse. It is unlikely that any department will employ or be characterized by each item; some of them may even be inappropriate to the particular locality. Nevertheless, the list is designed to encourage agencies to review their policies and practices.

## A. Departmental Commitment

**1.** Has the chief or sheriff made a serious commitment to address the problem of child abuse?

**2.** Has the chief or sheriff communicated this commitment to the relevant personnel?

**3.** Has the chief or sheriff provided adequate resources to those responsible for dealing with child abuse?

**4.** Has the chief, sheriff or a high-ranking designee participated in the development of interagency cooperative efforts to address child abuse in the community?

## B. Specialized Investigative Unit

**1.** Does the agency have at least one investigator or a unit of investigators specifically assigned to child-abuse cases?

**2.** Have all child-abuse specialists received specialized training in interviewing children? In identifying signs and symptoms of child abuse?

**3.** Do child-abuse investigators have responsibility for both sexual and physical abuse of children?

**4.** Are one or more investigators trained to conduct and responsible for carrying out proactive investigations of exploitation and child-pornography cases? Is the child-abuse unit responsible for these investigations?

**5.** Is the unit administratively located in a juvenile/youth unit or a criminal investigation division?

Source: Susan E. Martin and Douglas J. Besharov. *Police and Child Abuse: New Policies for Expanded Responsibilities.* Washington, DC: U.S. Department of Justice, National Institute of Justice, 1991, pp. 45–49.

**6.** Is someone in the unit responsible for reviewing and screening all cases referred by child protective workers and patrol officers?

**7.** Do child-abuse specialists investigate a high proportion of the cases reported and referred to the unit?

**8.** Do the personnel in the investigative unit reflect the community with respect to race, ethnicity, sex and language?

## C. Investigative Capabilities

**1.** Do investigators follow a well-developed interviewing protocol?

**2.** Are there clear intra-agency mechanisms for promptly notifying the child-abuse unit of all reports and investigations of child abuse by other units in the department?

**3.** Do homicide detectives involve child-abuse investigators in investigations of deaths of children where abuse is a possible factor?

**4.** Are there sufficient investigative personnel in the unit to handle the caseload?

**5.** What is the unit's turnover rate?

**6.** Is participation in this unit a clearly valued assignment?

**7.** Are unit selection procedures designed to attract and retain supervisors and investigators knowledgeable in psychology and human development?

**8.** Is there an informal support system, or are there other procedures to minimize investigator burnout?

**9.** Is a trained investigator available (either on duty or on call) to respond to child-abuse cases during the evening and on weekends?

**10.** Is a victim–witness coordinator available to provide support, referrals and continued contact with the victim throughout processing of a court case?

**11.** Is videotape equipment available? Is it used selectively? Are taped victim interviews also used for investigator training and obtaining perpetrator confessions?

**12.** Do investigators have a suitable place to interview child victims?

**13.** Are there detailed procedures guiding the use of anatomical dolls and drawings in interviews with young children?

**14.** Are cases kept open until all leads are exhausted (as opposed to being exceptionally cleared to attain a high closure rate)?

**15.** How frequently do investigators obtain confessions from perpetrators?

## D. Role of Patrol

**1.** Have policy and training materials emphasized the role of patrol officers in identifying cases?

**2.** Has the role of patrol in investigating cases been reduced by having the child protective agency refer calls directly to police specialists and by having patrol officers refer cases to those specialists (or to investigators in a larger agency with which the department has an interagency agreement) once they identify probable abuse?

## E. Relations with Prosecutors

**1.** Is there frequent informal consultation about cases with prosecutors?

**2.** Do prosecutors usually file charges when investigators request that they do so (either by signing arrest warrants, seeking indictments or filing criminal information)?

**1.** Does preservice training include at least four hours of instruction on handling child abuse?

**2.** Does the preservice training include instruction by child-abuse specialists and child protection personnel?

**3.** Is there in-service training for patrol officers that periodically reviews their reporting responsibilities and the indicators of abuse?

**4.** Do newly assigned investigators receive at least twenty hours of training in child development and child-abuse investigation?

**5.** Do investigators receive at least twenty hours per year of specialized in-service training related to child abuse?

**6.** Is child-abuse-investigator training interdisciplinary in substance (that is, does it include material related to forensic, mental health, child development and community resource issues)? Are instructional personnel and class participants also drawn from several agencies?

## G. Written Policies

**1.** Does the agency have a written policy covering child abuse and neglect?

**2.** Has the policy been developed or reviewed in the past two years?

**3.** Does the policy clearly specify the roles and responsibilities for case identification and investigations of dispatchers, patrol officers and investigators?

**4.** Does the agency have a written procedure for dealing with difficult or large-scale cases such as those with multiple victims or those occurring in institutional settings like day-care centers?

**5.** Does the written policy include the following elements:

- A statement that interagency coordination is essential for dealing with child abuse effectively?
- Procedures for notifying the child protective agency?
- Guidelines for identifying cases of child abuse?
- Procedures for initial investigation?
- Guidelines for when to take a child into protective custody?
- Procedures for how to place a child into protective custody?
- Guidelines for when to make an arrest?

**6.** Does agency policy on domestic disturbances or spouse-abuse investigations include a directive to assess the safety of abused children in the home?

## H. Interagency Agreements

**1.** Does the agency have a written interagency cooperative agreement for handling investigations with:

- Child protective service agencies?
- Other local law enforcement agencies?
- The local prosecutor?
- Medical and mental health agencies?
- Schools?
- Criminal or juvenile courts?
- Other public or private agencies?

**2.** Does the agreement clearly specify the responsibilities of personnel of each of the agencies with respect to:

- Reporting?
- Notification procedures?
- Investigations?
- Protective custody?
- Review of problem cases?

**3.** Does the agreement specify when a joint investigation is to be conducted?

**4.** Does the agreement provide a mechanism for team review of problem cases?

**5.** Does the agreement include a procedure for resolving conflicts among agency personnel?

**6.** Do participants in the agreement (or the members of the multidisciplinary team) share a physical location?

**7.** Does the agreement provide for a staff coordinator?

**8.** Does the agreement include a procedure for evaluating its effectiveness and, if appropriate, modifying its provisions?

**9.** Does the agreement provide for joint interdisciplinary training of team members?

**10.** Does the agreement include an abuse prevention program in which law enforcement officers play an active role?

# Death Scene Checklist

This form is to be used as a supplementary source sheet for readily available information and is not intended to replace conventional reports. Copies should be distributed to investigating officers and medical examiners.

---

**Name of deceased:**

First                Middle                        Last

**Address:**

**Age:**        **Race:**  White   Black   Hispanic   Asian   Native American   Unknown

**Sex:**    Male    Female

**Telephone number:**

**Marital status:**   S    M    W    D    Separated    Unknown

**Next-of-kin:**

Name:

Address:

Telephone number:

**Police notified by:**

Date:                    Time:

Name:

Address:

Telephone number:

Relationship to deceased:

**Deceased found:**

Date:                    Time:

Address: (if different from above)

Location: Apartment     House     Townhouse     Other (describe)

Entrance by: Key Cutting chain Forcing door Other (describe)

Type of lock on door:

Condition of other doors and windows: Open    Closed    Locked    Unlocked

**Body found:**

Living Room    Dining Room    Bedroom    Kitchen    Attic    Basement Other (describe)

Location in room:

Position of body: On back    Face down    Other:

**Condition of body:**

Fully clothed     Partially clothed     Unclothed

Preservation:     Well preserved     Decomposed

Estimated Rigor:     Complete     Head     Arms     Legs

Livor: Front     Back     Localized

Color:

Blood: Absent     Present     Location

Ligatures: Yes     No

---

**Apparent wounds:** None     Gunshot     Stab     Blunt force
Number:

Location: Head     Neck     Chest     Abdomen     Extremities

Hanging: Yes     No     Means:

---

**Weapon(s) present:** Gun (estimate caliber)
Type:

Knife:

Other (describe)

---

**Condition of surroundings:** Orderly     Untidy     Disarray

Odors: Decomposition     Other

---

**Evidence of last food preparation:**
Where:

Type:

---

**Dated material:**
Mail:

Newspapers:

TV guide:

Liquor bottles:

---

**Last contact with deceased:**
Date:

Type of contact:

Name of contact:

---

**Evidence of robbery:** Yes     No     Not determined

---

**Identification of deceased:** Yes     No
If yes, how accomplished:

If no, how is it to be accomplished:

---

**Evidence of drug use:** (prescription and nonprescription)     Yes     No
If drugs present, collect them and send with body.

---

**Evidence of drug paraphernalia:** Yes     No
Type:

---

**Evidence of sexually deviant practices:** Yes     No
Type: (collect and send with body)

Name and telephone number of investigating officer:

---

Source: James C. Beger, M.D., and William F. Enos, M.D. *FBI Law Enforcement Bulletin*. August 1981, pp. 16–18. Reprinted by permission of the FBI.

# Public and Private Associations that Provide Support in Investigating Computer-Related Crimes

Appendix

# C

## Public-Sector Associations

**COLORADO ASSOCIATION OF COMPUTER CRIME INVESTIGATORS**
c/o Larry Scheideman
Lakewood Police Dept.
Lakewood, CO 80226-3105
303-987-7370

Founded 1986. A professional association including federal, state and local law enforcement personnel and those persons from the private sector concerned with computer crime. The association assists law enforcement agencies with resource allocation and intelligence/investigation of computer-related crimes. The association also provides training on an individual basis.

**ECONOMIC CRIME INVESTIGATOR'S ASSOCIATION (ECIA)**
Glendale Police Department
7119 North 57 Drive
Glendale, AZ 85301
602-931-5511
Wayne Cerow

Members include law enforcement and regulatory personnel. The association focuses on economic crime, including computer-related crimes. The association holds a yearly training seminar in order to exchange information, ideas and data on new technological advances.

**FEDERAL COMPUTER INVESTIGATIONS COMMITTEE (FCIC)**
c/o U.S. Secret Service Fraud Division, Room 942
1800 G Street, N.W.
Washington, DC 20223
202-535-5850
Steve Purdy

This committee has been in existence for about three years. It is comprised of representatives from federal, military and civilian law enforcement agencies. The organization meets three times a year for the purpose of enhancing techniques to investigate computer-related crimes. The committee strives to develop universal guidelines for these types of investigations. Membership is diverse (U.S. Secret Service, IRS, FBI, Department of Defense, CID, AFOSI, NIS, Department of Labor and others), which contributes to a broad-based forum for developing techniques and guidelines. Participating agencies and private industry provide specialized training for members. Nonvoting members from state and local governments also participate in association meetings.

### HIGH-TECH CRIME INVESTIGATORS' ASSOCIATION (HTCIA)
c/o L.A. County Sheriff's Dept. (Forgery/Fraud Detail)
11515 South Colima Road, Room M104
Whittier, CA 90604
213-946-7212
Jim Black, President

Members include federal, state and local law enforcement personnel as well as security managers from private industry. The association brings together private industry and law enforcement officials in order to communicate and educate each other about computer-related crimes.

### INTERNATIONAL ASSOCIATION OF CREDIT CARD INVESTIGATORS (IACCI)
1620 Grant Avenue
Novato, CA 94945
415-897-8800
D. D. Drummond, Executive Director

Founded 1968; 2,700 members. Special agents, investigators and investigation supervisors who investigate criminal violations of credit-card laws and prosecute offenders; law enforcement officers, prosecutors or related officials who investigate, apprehend and prosecute credit-card offenders; employees of card-issuing institutions who are responsible for credit-card security and investigations. The association's objective is to aid in the establishment of effective credit-card security programs, to suppress fraudulent use of credit cards and to detect and proceed with the apprehension of credit-card thieves. Provides workshops, training conferences and seminars to acquaint law enforcement and the membership with technological advances in the industry.

### LAW ENFORCEMENT ELECTRONIC TECHNOLOGY ASSISTANCE COMMITTEE (LEETAC)
Office of the State Attorney
700 South Park Avenue
Titusville, FL 32781
407-269-8112
Jim Graham

The organization is comprised of ten prosecutors from the State Attorney's office, thirteen officers representing each municipality in the county, two representatives from the sheriff's department and Nassau. The organization provides technical expertise to law enforcement regarding computer crimes.

## COMMUNICATIONS FRAUD CONTROL ASSOCIATION (CFCA)

P.O. Box 23891
Washington, DC 20026
703-848-9760
Rami Abuhamdeh, Executive Director

A security organization involved in investigations of telecommunications fraud. Membership includes individual and corporate, associate individual and vendor members.

## COMPUTER LAW ASSOCIATION, INC. (CLA)

8303 Arlington Boulevard, Suite 210
Fairfax, VA 22031
703-560-7747
Barbara Fieser, Executive Director

Founded 1973; 1,200 members. Lawyers, law students and others interested in legal problems related to computer communications technology. The association sponsors continuing legal education on computer law. CLA also publishes a reference manual that lists organizations involved with computer law.

## COMPUTER VIRUS INDUSTRY ASSOCIATION

4423 Cheeney Street
Santa Clara, CA 95054
408-988-3832
John McAfee, Executive Director

Founded 1987. The association's objective is to help identify and cure computer viruses. The association has worked with state and local law enforcement agencies in the investigation and detection of computer and computer-related crimes.

## INFORMATION SYSTEMS SECURITY ASSOCIATION (ISSA)

P.O. Box 71926
Los Angeles, CA 90071
714-863-5583
Carl B. Jackson

Founded 1982; 300 members. Computer security practitioners whose primary responsibility is to ensure protection of information assets on a hands-on basis. Members include banking, retail, insurance, aerospace and publishing industries. The association's objective is to increase knowledge about information security. ISSA sponsors educational programs, research, discussion and dissemination of information. The association has regional and state chapters.

## INSTITUTE OF INTERNAL AUDITORS (IIA)

249 Maitland Avenue
Altamonte Springs, FL 32701
407-830-7600

Founded 1941; 30,000 members; 74 staff; local group: 183 members. Professional organization of internal auditors, comptrollers, accountants, educators and computer specialists. IIA holds an annual conference that offers training and education on detection of computer-related crimes. IIA does research in the areas of whistle blowing, fraud, ethics and technology. Individual members have assisted state and local police with investigations involving computer-related crimes.

## MIS TRAINING INSTITUTE
Information Security Division
498 Concord Street
Framingham, MA 01701
508-879-7999

Information security seminars for information security professionals, EDP auditors and data processing management. The institute provides both training and consulting services and has assisted local police in investigations of computer-related crimes.

## NATIONAL CENTER FOR COMPUTER CRIME DATA (NCCD)
2700 North Cahuenga Boulevard
Los Angeles, CA 90068
213-874-8233
Jay Bloom Becker, Director

Founded 1978. The center disseminates data and documents to facilitate the prevention, investigation and prosecution of computer crime. The center sponsors speakers and seminars, conducts research and compiles statistics.

## SRI INTERNATIONAL
Information Security Program
333 Ravenswood Avenue
Menlo Park, CA 94025
415-859-2378
Donn B. Parker

Founded 1947. A staff of senior consultants and computer scientists perform research on computer crime and security and provide consulting to private and government clients worldwide. A case file of more than 2,500 computer abuses since 1958 has been collected and analyzed. It is available for use by criminal justice agencies and students free of charge. An electronic bulletin board called Risks Forum is operated and sponsored by the Association for Computing Machinery to collect and disseminate information about risks in using computers.

# Sample Affidavit and Search Warrant for Computer-Related Crime Cases

**DISTRICT COURT**
**FOR**
**BALTIMORE COUNTY**

**Application and Affidavit for Search and Seizure Warrant***

To the Honorable Judge _____ of the District Court of Maryland, for Baltimore, County your affiants, DETECTIVE CALVIN L. LANE and DETECTIVE FRANK K. SIMMONS, members of the Baltimore County Police Department, being duly sworn depose and say that they have reason to believe that on the premises known as 6958 MARYSUE Drive, Apt 2D, Pikesville, Maryland 21215, more particularly described as a three-story brick apartment building with the numbers 6958 on the front, there is an open foyer inside with teal-color doors on the apartments. Apartment 2D is located on the uppermost floor. In the foyer area are mailboxes, one of which is designated 2D with the name TERRAPIN on same. The apartment is located in an area known as the MILBROOK APARTMENTS. There are items subject to seizure, such as computers, keyboards, central processing units, external drives and/or internal drives, internal and/or external storage devices such as magnetic tapes and/or disks, terminals and/or video display units and/or receiving devices and peripheral equipment such as, but not limited to, printers, automatic dialers, modems, acoustical couplers and/or direct line couplers, peripheral interface boards and connecting cables and/or ribbons, customer listings, diaries, logs and other records, correspondence, journals, ledgers, memoranda, telephone and communications service billing information, computer software, programs and source documentation, computer logs used in the obtaining, maintenance, and dissemination and/or sale of confidential information obtained from official files and computers of the MCA Telecommunications Corporation and other evidence of the offense. Also any papers which would tend to show occupancy and/or ownership, such as utility bills, rent/lease contracts, etc., for 6958 Marysue Drive, Apt. 2D, Pikesville, Maryland 21215. Further, any papers, logs, disks, files on any media which would tend to show who may be the custodian, user, owner, or have interest in the above-stated hardware, software, or files. And, that facts tending to establish grounds for issuance of a Search Warrant are set forth and the basis for the probable cause is as follows:

Your affiant, DETECTIVE CALVIN L. LANE, has been a member of the Baltimore County Police Department in excess of 19 years, currently assigned to the Computer Crime Unit of the Criminal Investigation Division. During this time your affiant DETECTIVE CALVIN L. LANE has been a detective in excess of 14 years working in various specialized areas of investigation. During this fourteen-year period your affiant DETECTIVE CALVIN L. LANE has been the affiant of eighteen (18) court-ordered wiretaps. Also has worked on several court-ordered wiretaps as monitor over and above the above-stated 18. Also your affiant DETECTIVE CALVIN L. LANE has established several Dialed Number Recorders as an electronic surveillance tool to monitor the activity of a telephone line. During the course of the above investigation it was required to do analysis of the information provided by the DNR paper recording tape. As a result of these investigations and DNR analysis, in excess of 50 search and seizure warrants have been issued to search for various evidence. As a result of the search and seizure warrants, arrests were made and convictions obtained. Your affiant Lane has also established a basis of expertise in the area of computer crime and investigations. Your affiant has completed several college courses of study in this area to include four computer languages and a one-semester course on computer crime at a local community college. A two-week course conducted at the Federal Law Enforcement Training Center,

---

*Used with permission.

Glynco, Ga., for computer crime investigations. An 80-hour instruction period conducted by the Baltimore Gas & Electric Company in the area of computer-related security. Further your affiant Lane has completed an internship with the Baltimore County Data Processing Section as a programmer. Your affiant Lane has also owned a personal computer for in excess of five years and is familiar with its use and jargon used by the personal computer community. While assigned to the Baltimore County Narcotic Section, your affiant Lane was charged with the setup and design of the computer system used there, to include all aspects of its operation.

Your affiant DETECTIVE FRANK K. SIMMONS has been a member of the Baltimore County Police Department in excess of 18 years and is currently assigned to the Computer Crime Unit of the Criminal Investigation Division. Your affiant Simmons has worked as a detective for over nine (9) years in various assignments, specializing in the area of fraud investigations. During this period your affiant Simmons has been the affiant on five previous warrants that have led to the arrest and convictions of suspects in fraud/drug related investigations. Your affiant Simmons has investigated hundreds of felony fraud cases of all types leading to the arrest and conviction of suspects. One of these previous investigations was directly related to the theft of services from a public utility. In the area of computer related investigations, your affiant has attended a two-week course of study conducted at the Federal Law Enforcement Training Center, Glynco, Ga., dealing with the investigation of computer-related crime. Also your affiant attended an 80-hour period of instruction on computer operations and security conducted by the Baltimore Gas & Electric Company.

Further, your affiants Lane and Simmons have as members of the Computer Crime Unit executed in excess of nine search and seizure warrants. These warrants were directly related to computer seizures and their use in the violations of Maryland law. All of these cases have led to successful prosecution of the persons involved with one pending court action.

Mr. John Jones has been an employee of the Chesapeake and Potato Telephone Company, State of Confusion, since July 9, 1970. During this period Mr. Jones has been a Service Representative, specifically working with billing, i.e. toll investigations and order processing. As of March 1, 1980, Mr. Jones has been assigned to the security division. Mr. Jones has received 13 weeks of Basic Programmers training and initial service representative training; of that 13 weeks toll fraud investigations was included. In the area of toll fraud, the use of the Dialed Number Recorders (DNR) and the analysis of the printed data produced by the DNR was covered in detail. During Mr. Jones's tenure as security investigator, he has had occasion to do in excess of 5 DNR-related investigations. These investigations required the analysis of the paper DNR activity reports. Further, Mr. Jones has been awarded a B.A. in criminology from the University of Orlando and completed a four-month internship with the campus police there. Mr. Jones has also received additional college credits in computer-related studies.

Within the recent past the computer and information services industry has been plagued with a high-tech intruder and thief. The term "Hacker" is most generally used to describe this individual and can be defined as someone who makes unauthorized attempts to access a host database (computer) most generally from a remote location, often by circumventing access controls. The Hacker will use impersonation, or masquerading as an authorized user, to gain access to the host computer. In some instances the Hacker will in fact be an authorized user to the system and be making access attempts into unauthorized areas of the computer. The motive of the Hacker could be to browse or steal information that would offer a personal gain for the Hacker. The term "Passive wiretapping" could also be applied to the Hacker's activity. By gaining access to the host computer the Hacker can monitor data transmissions of records, memos, or any other information being sent across communication links. Another technique used by the Hacker is scavenging of information left in unsecured areas of the computer. The computer may contain common work areas used by several people, with the intent of the information being destroyed after the job has been completed. In other instances the Hacker's only intent is to cause disruptions or deny access to the rightful owners. The Hacker may insert or modify records, making the owner aware of his past presence in the system.

In this present illegal scheme the Hacker is accessing the computer system of the MCA Telecommunications Corporation located at #1 Investigation Place, Towson, Maryland, in Baltimore County. The Hacker will use a computer and a device known as a modem to communicate with computers of the MCA Telecommunication Corporation. The purpose of the modem is to act as the link or interface between the two computers. The modem will translate the computer language of digital signals into aural tones that can be sent across telephone communication lines. A modem on the receiving system will then accept the aural tones and convert them back into digital signals the computer can understand.

The host computer may, as in the case of MCA Telecommunication Corp. have a dial-in access telephone number. The access number authorizes the subscriber to communicate with the MCA computer. In the case of MCA, the authorized subscriber does not need a computer to use their system in a legitimate manner. The authorized subscriber will dial the access number, enter a five digit account code and then dial the telephone number of the person to whom they wish to call. The fact that the authorized user is using a computer is transparent to them; it is only seen as a long series of numbers being dialed.

In this illegal scheme the Hacker is using the computer to dial the access code for them and then sequentially trying five digit account codes with a terminating number following the code. The terminating number is another computer system. The terminating number is the telephone number of a dialup line of a computer system in this specific instance. In order to instruct the Hacker's computer on what action to take given a variety of circumstances, a set of coded instructions in the form of software known as a "Demon Dialer," "War Dialer," or "Hacker" is used. The reason the Hacker uses the computer is to allow for automation and record keeping to be done unattended. The Hacker's computer will then keep track of the account codes that have been tried and the ones that have been rejected as invalid codes and the ones that have been accepted as valid. If the random code has been accepted by the MCA computer as valid, the call is then forwarded to the terminating number selected by the Hacker. In this case the termination number is another computer. This number was verified by your affiant DETECTIVE FRANK K. SIMMONS as a computer. Again the reason is for automation. With a valid account code and completed call, the Hacker's computer knows that it has in fact selected a valid account code. The Hacker's computer will then terminate the call to the terminating number and start the process over again. The valid code will then be recorded on the printer or to a magnetic disk file for later use. If the random code is rejected by the MCA computer, the Hacker's computer will disregard the rejected account code and again starts over. Now armed with a list of valid account codes, the Hacker uses these account numbers to make long-distance telephone calls or for communication with other computers outside his general area, thus avoiding any payment to the utility for the service.

On 3/24/88 at approximately 0100 hrs., the switch (computer) operator for the MCA Telecommunications Corporation observed what he believed to be unusual activity on their computer-based telephone-switching equipment. Based on his experience and computer-generated reports at that time, the activity was that of a Hacker attacking their system. The Hacker continued this activity for a period of 38 hours, making 3000 attempts to obtain customer billing codes. This is one attempt every 45.6 seconds. During this period legitimate codes were compromised. Mr. Luis Abad, MCA supervisor of the Towson switch, caused a check to be made through the Chesapeake and Potato Telephone Company in an attempt to identify the source of the hacking activity. It was determined that the activity was coming from 6958 Apt 2D, Marysue Drive, aforementioned and described.

Mr. Smith forwarded this information to the MCA Telecommunication Corp. Security Director, Ms. Helen Brooks. Ms. Brooks initiated an investigation and made a complaint to the Baltimore County Police Department and your affiants. As part of the MCA investigative procedure, Ms. Brooks also contacted the Chesapeake and Potato Telephone Company, State of Maryland, Mr. John Jones. Based on agreements and contracts with MCA, Telecommunication Corporation installed a Dialed Number Recorded (DNR) on telephone number (301) 555-1212 list to Ann TERRAPIN at the suspect address described above, on 3/26/88.

A dialed number recorder (DNR) is an electronic device used to monitor line activations initiated by the opening and closing of a telephone line. When the receiver of a telephone is removed from the cradle, the DNR is activated. In this case, when the Hacker's computer opens the dial tone circuit via the modem, these activations are recorded on roll paper with the date and time the line was activated. The DNR will also record any numbers that are dialed when the line is open. When the line is again closed by placing the receiver on the cradle or by the modem, this time also is recorded on the DNR paper. With this record of activity as recorded by the DNR, an analysis can be done to determine hacking patterns and line activation indicative of calls. The DNR does not allow for oral communication to be monitored. Therefore, completed calls are determined based on the training, knowledge, and experience of your affiants, Detectives Lane and Simmons, and Mr. John Jones of the Chesapeake and Potato Telephone Company, State of Maryland.

On 4/7/88 your affiants Lane and Simmons went to the area of 6958 Marysue Drive, Apt. 2D, Pikesville, Maryland 21215. It was learned through covert interviews that a young male lived at the above address and was a student at the University of Maryland. Because of another ongoing investigation with MCA concerning the University, your affiants contacted the campus police in an attempt to identify Mr. TERRAPIN. It was learned that there was a student Gregory (nmn) TERRAPIN of 6958 Marysue Drive, Apt. 2D, Pikesville, Maryland 21215, telephone (301) 555-1212, D.O.B. 11/12/67. Ms. Brooks of MCA advised your affiant that MCA has been experiencing a serious code abuse problem at this campus, although Mr. TERRAPIN had not been identified, as of this date, as a targeted abuser.

As a result of the DNR being placed on the suspect line at 6958 Marysue Drive, Apt. 2D, Pikesville, Maryland 21215, a close monitoring of the activity could be done. The DNR showed hacking activity directed at the MCA computer on several occasions.

3/26/88 1,302 attempts were made to obtain MCA billing codes.
3/27/88 926 attempts
3/28/88 988 attempts

During his period of hacking activity, 73 valid MCA customer codes were compromised. These codes when used would be billed to their rightful owners. Experience has shown that these stolen codes and subsequent bills have caused their owners great anxiety. A case in point is that your affiants picked one specific code that shows abuse in this illegal scheme. A check with MCA security revealed that the customer had a maximum bill of $55.00 prior to this hacker. The most recent bill sent out for billing period March is $461, an increase of $406.00 over the customer's past highest bill.

This hacking activity has been ongoing, with thousands of attempts to steal codes. Also, these stolen codes have been used, which are billed to their rightful owners. The most recent DNR tape being analyzed was dated up to and including 4/13/88. On 4/13/88 hacking activity extended from 0025 Hrs. to 0625 Hrs., six hours. It is the belief of your affiants based on past experience and the pattern of activity in this specific illegal scheme, that it will continue until action is taken by law enforcement.

Therefore, your affiants believe, based on their training, knowledge and experience, that evidence of theft, unlawful access to a computer, and a device to avoid telephone charges is located on the premises known as 6958 Marysue Drive, Apt. 2D, Pikesville, Maryland 21215, described above. Past experience has proven that hackers will maintain records of their activity for long periods of time. It is not unusual for these records to be kept for eight to ten months. This information is traded amongst hackers. Information is the "coin of the realm" to be exchanged. The hacker with the most information is held in esteem. Codes tried and failed are also valuable, so as not to repeat past mistakes.

Therefore, your affiants pray that a Search and Seizure warrant be issued, authorizing that any Police Officer with authority in this jurisdiction, with the necessary and proper assistance to enter and search the aforementioned and described location and to search for and seize all contraband, evidence, fruits of the crime, and instrumentalities of the crime, which are subject to seizure and are in violation of, or evidence of, the violation of, the Laws of Maryland pertaining to illegal Access to a Computer Article 27 Section 146, Theft Article 27 Section 340-342, and Device to avoid Telephone Charges Article 27 Section 557A.

———————————————
Signature of Affiant

———————————————
Signature of Affiant

SWORN to before Me and subscribed to in my presence this        day of        1988.

———————————————
JUDGE

1. *Justification for seizing hardware, etc. (where appropriate)*

Affiant interviewed _____ , employed as a _____ in the _____ office. _____ informed affiant that in connection with his employment, he uses computer systems as well as conducting computer-related investigations. In the past two years, _____ has supervised or participated in several executions of search warrants for computer-stored records and evidence. _____ informed affiant that conducting a search of a computer system, documenting the search, and making evidentiary and discovery copies is a lengthy process. It is necessary to determine that no security devices are in place which could cause the destruction of evidence during the search; in some cases it is impossible even to conduct the search without expert technical assistance. Since computer evidence is extremely vulnerable to tampering or to destruction through error, electrical outages, and other causes, removal of the system from the premises will assist in retrieving the records authorized to be seized, while avoiding accidental destruction or deliberate alteration of the records. It would be extremely difficult to secure the system on the premises during the entire period of the search. _____ also stated that whether records are stored on floppy disks or on a hard drive, even when they purportedly have been erased or deleted, they may still be retrievable. _____ is familiar with the methods of restoring "lost" data commonly employed by computer users, and has used those methods himself. _____ has also obtained the assistance of a computer expert in several cases, in order to obtain the contents of computer-stored evidence, where normal methods were unsuccessful. He stated that should such data retrieval be necessary, it is time-consuming, and would add to the difficulty of securing the system on the premises during the search.

_____ stated that the accompanying software must also be seized, since it would be impossible without examination to determine that it is standard, commercially available software: it is necessary to have the software used to create data files and records in order to read the files and records. In addition, without examination, it is impossible to determine that the diskette purporting to contain a standard commercially available software program has not been used to store records instead.

_____ informed affiant that the system documentation, instruction manuals, and software manuals are also necessary to properly operate that specific system in order to accurately obtain the records authorized to be seized.

2. *Dialed number recorder (DNR)/pen register*

A dialed number recorder captures the electronic impulses travelling over a telephone line as the numbers on a telephone are dialed or pushed. The device records the numbers dialed or pushed on a paper tape (NB: not always! newer ones may include magnetic-media storage) for review, but does not record the content of the communication. A dialed number recorder, in addition, records any transmission of the special signalling tones which are used to control communications networks and their associated automatic billing systems (see below).

3. *Tone generator ("blue box" or "blue computer")*

_____ from the _____ Telephone Company advised that special signalling tones are used to control communications networks and their associated automatic billing systems. The special signalling tones can be generated by an electronic tone-generating device known as a "blue box," or by a personal computer and software programs which enable the computer to generate the tone signal through a communications device (a modem or acoustic coupler) connecting the computer to the telephone line. In his past investigations, _____ has frequently found that persons stealing communications services have possessed a personal computer and the necessary software which would allow them to manipulate communications networks by means of the special signalling tones.

4. *Packet-switched networks*

_____ , an employee of the ____Net informed affiant that the ____Net is a packet-switching common carrier providing facilities for the transmission of data, rather than voice communications, for its subscribers. ____Net maintains high-speed communications lines which are used to transmit "packets" of data throughout the United States. At various places on the network, ____Net maintains communications handling devices (or switches), some of which are accessed by telephones using commercial telephone lines. A subscriber may gain access to the network by dialing its local telephone number, connecting the subscriber to the switch. When the connection is complete, the subscriber hears an audible tone and connects his telephone receiver to his modem or accoustic coupler, connected to his computer. (This step is omitted with an automatic modem connecting the computer directly with the telephone line.)

Once the communication link has been established, the caller must enter certain fixed-format information which identifies the "address" of the subscriber computer system with which he wishes to communicate. The caller must then enter certain fixed-format information, including a password and/or user identification number, which are known only to authorized users and are registered in the computer system.

A similar communications network operating in Canada is _____Pac; communications between American _____Net and Canadian _____Pac subscribers can be routed through the "Gateway," a communications facility in Canada, allowing subscribers of each network to send communications to subscribers of the other.

5. *"Voice-mail" systems*

The _____ voice-mail system allows authorized _____ employees to obtain a "voice mailbox" which is capable of performing several functions. Among these are the ability to receive and store messages from callers, to send messages to other boxes on the system, and to send messages to a preselected group of boxes. These functions are achieved by pushing the appropriate numerical commands on a telephone keypad for the desired function.

To leave a message, the caller dials the company's "800" telephone number, and hears a greeting identifying the system as the _____ voice-message system, along with instructions for leaving a message. The caller can exercise several options, one of which is to leave a message after the tone. In this respect, the voice-mail system operates much like a telephone answering machine. Rather than being recorded on audio tape, however, the message is stored in digitized form by the computer system. The entire voice-message system is actually a computer system accessible through the company's telephone lines. The dictated messages are stored on large-capacity computer disks.

An outside caller needs to know only the assigned box number (the same as the telephone extension number) in order to leave a message for a _____ employee. In order to retrieve the messages or to delete them from the system, however, the person to whom the box is assigned must know both the box number and a confidential password—-the password ensures privacy of the communications by acting as a "key" to "unlock" the box and reveal its contents. The employee to whom the box has been assigned also has the ability to change his password, thereby preventing access to the box contents by anyone who may have learned his password.

Since _____, 198___ , authorized users of the _____ voice-mail system have been reporting abuse of the system, including the "taking over" of numerous boxes by unknown persons who somehow obtained the passwords, gained access to the boxes, then changed the passwords to deny access to the assigned users. _____ also reported a significant increase in use of the system, and in incoming 800-line calls, during this period. While _____ does not yet know the full extent of its losses, the company pays the charges for calls made on their 800-line, and the unauthorized users have interrupted service to _____ employees and customers. The unauthorized users have occupied a significant portion of the system's disk capacity, necessitating the purchase and installation of an additional disk, at a cost of $_____ , in order to avoid further damage to the company's communication system.

# DISTRICT COURT
## FOR
## BALTIMORE COUNTY

**Search and Seizure Warrant***

To: Any Police Officer of Baltimore County

Affidavit having been made before me by Detective Calvin Lane and Detective Frank Simmons, members of the Baltimore County Police Department, that they have reason to believe that on the premises known as 6958 MARYSUE DRIVE, Apt 2D, Pikesville, Maryland 21215 more particularly described as a three-story brick apartment building with the numbers 6958 on the front, there is an open foyer inside with teal-color doors on the apartments. Apartment 2D is located on the uppermost floor. In the foyer area are mailboxes, one of which is designated 2D with the name TERRAPIN on same. The apartment is located in an area known as the MILBROOK APARTMENTS.

In the County of Baltimore, there is now property subject to seizure, such as computers, keyboards, central processing units, external and/or internal drives, internal and/or external storage devices such as magnetic tapes and/or disks, terminals and/or video display units and/or receiving devices, and peripheral equipment such as, but not limited to, printers, automatic dialers, modems, acoustic couplers and/or direct line couplers, peripheral interface boards and connecting cables and/or ribbons, diaries, logs, and other records, correspondence, journals, ledgers, memoranda, computer software, programs and source documentation, computer logs, magnetic audio tapes and recorders used in the obtaining, maintenance, and/or dissemination of information obtained from the official files and computers of MCI Telecommunications, Inc., and other evidence of the offense. Also, any papers which would tend to show occupancy or ownership for the residence of 6958 MARYSUE DRIVE, Apt 2D, Pikesville, Maryland 21215, such as utility bills, rent and/or lease agreements, etc. Further, any papers, logs, disks or files on any media which would tend to show who may be the custodian, user, owner or interest in the above stated hardware, software, or files, which are in violation of, or evidence of the violation of, the Laws of Maryland pertaining to Article 27 Section 340, theft, Article 27 Section 146, Unauthorized access to a computer, Article 27 Section 557 A, Device to avoid telephone charges, and I am satisfied that there is probable cause to believe that the property so described is on the premises above described and that the grounds for the issuance of the search warrant exist, being those grounds as stated on the application and affidavit attached hereto and incorporated herein by reference.

You are, therefore, hereby commanded with the necessary and proper assistance, to search forthwith the premises herein above described for the property herein above specified, executing this warrant and making the search; and if the property be found there, to seize it; leaving a copy of said warrant, Application/Affidavit therefore with an inventory of the property seized and returning a copy of said warrant, Application/Affidavit and inventory, if any, to me within ten (10) days after the execution of this warrant; or if not served, to return this warrant and Application/Affidavit to me within five (5) working days after its expiration, as required by law.

Dated this        day of        , 1988

Signed _____
Judge

# Excerpts from Computer Search Warrants

*ITEMS TO BE SEARCHED FOR AND SEIZED:*

1. Electronic data processing and storage devices, computers, and computer systems including central processing units; internal and peripheral storage devices such as fixed disks, external hard disks, floppy disk drives and diskettes, tape drives and tapes, optical storage devices or other memory storage devices; peripheral input/output devices such as keyboards, printers, video display monitors, optical readers, and related communications devices such as modems; together with system documentation, operating logs and documentation, software, and instruction manuals.

_____

*Used with permission.

*Note:* this type of language applies to the situation in which the presence of a personal or small-business computer is suspected (a large drug operation) or probable (a computer hacker), but where it has been impossible to determine in advance what kind of system it is. Ideally, investigation prior to execution of the warrant has produced specific information about the system, and those specifics should then be included in the description of items to be seized.

2. [Description of specific records to be seized] All of the above records, whether stored on paper, on magnetic media such as tape, cassette, disk, diskette, or on memory-storage devices such as optical disks, programmable instruments such as telephones, "electronic address books," calculators, or any other storage media, together with indicia of use, ownership, possession, or control of such records.

*Note:* if the search warrant is properly specific as to the nature and content of records to be seized, the *form* in which the record is found should be irrelevant. However, to avoid challenges to the seizure of computer diskettes, etc., not mentioned in a traditional "books and records" warrant, some language such as this should be included in situations in which it is not absolutely known that all the records sought are on paper. Of course, the search team can always obtain a supplemental warrant if there is any doubt that records found in unexpected "hardware" form, such as a programmable electronic telephone directory, are authorized to be seized.

# Sample Form for Reporting Bias Crimes

PS-21410-01 (9/92)

## BIAS OFFENSE REPORT*

AGENCY IDENTIFIER (ORI)_____

MONTH AND YEAR_____        AGENCY NAME_____

This form is to be used to report any bias motivated crimes in violation of Minnesota State Statute 626.5531. The chief law enforcement officer for an agency must complete form and return to the Department of Public Safety, Office of Information Systems Management, 314 Transportation Building, 395 John Ireland Blvd., St. Paul, Minnesota 55155 within 30 days (Laws of Minnesota, 1996, Chapter 643).

### A. GENERAL OFFENSE INFORMATION

1) Agency Case Number: _____        2) Date of Offense:_____

3) Bias offense based on:  ☐ Officer's belief        ☐ Victim's belief

4) *Description of Offense: _____        5) *Disposition:_____

6) *Type of Bias and Description: _____ / _____
                              Type Code                          Description Code or Literal

7) *Target: _____        8) *Place of Occurrence: _____

### B. VICTIM/OFFENDER INFORMATION

| 9) VICTIMS | | | | 10) OFFENDERS | | | 11) *RELATIONSHIP TO VICTIM | 12) AFFILIATION (if any) |
|---|---|---|---|---|---|---|---|---|
| # | Age | Sex | Race | Age | Sex | Race | | |
| 1 | | | | | | | | |
| 2 | | | | | | | | |
| 3 | | | | | | | | |
| 4 | | | | | | | | |
| 5 | | | | | | | | |
| 6 | | | | | | | | |
| 7 | | | | | | | | |
| 8 | | | | | | | | |
| 9 | | | | | | | | |
| 10 | | | | | | | | |
| 11 | | | | | | | | |
| 12 | | | | | | | | |
| 13 | | | | | | | | |
| 14 | | | | | | | | |
| 15 | | | | | | | | |

COMMENTS:_____
_____
_____

*Use code tables on reverse

Return to: DPS/OISM
314 DOT Building
395 John Ireland Blvd.
St. Paul, MN 55155

_____

*Reprinted by permission of the Minnesota Bureau of Criminal Apprehension.

4) DESCRIPTION of OFFENSE:

To be used in further identifying offense

01–Cross Burning
02–Swastika
03–Bombing
04–Hanging in Effigy
05–Disturbing Public Meeting
06–Graffiti
07–Spitting
08–Letter
09–Verbal Abuse (Person to Person)
10–Telephone
11–Homicide
12–Criminal Sexual Conduct
13–Robbery
14–Burglary
15–Aggravated Assault
16–Arson
17–Larceny Theft
18–Disturbing the Peace
19–Property Damage
20–Simple Assault
00–Other (Describe)

5) DISPOSITION: Based on CJRS Reporting
System—-Major Offenses

A–Arrest of Adult and/or Adult & Juvenile
J–Arrest of Juvenile
E–Exceptionally Cleared
U–Unfounded
P–Pending

6) TYPE of BIAS and DESCRIPTION:

| Type | Description |
|---|---|
| 01–Racial | W–White |
| | H–White/Hispanic Origin |
| | N–Negro/Black |
| | B–Black/Hispanic Origin |
| | I–Indian or Alaskan Native |
| | M–Indian w/Hispanic Origin |
| | O–Asian or Pacific Islander |
| | A–Asian or Pacific Islander w/Hispanic Origin |
| 02–Religious | 01–Catholic |
| | 02–Hindu/Buddhist |
| | 03–Islamic/Moslem |
| | 04–Jewish |
| | 05–Protestant |
| | 06–Fundamentalist |
| | 07–Other (Describe) |
| 03–National Origin | Specify |
| 04–Sex | M–Male |
| | F–Female |
| 05–Age | Specify age(s) |
| 06–Disability | Specify disability |
| 07–Sexual Orientation | 01–Homosexual Male |
| | 02–Homosexual Female |
| | 03–Heterosexual Male |
| | 04–Heterosexual Female |

7) TARGET CODES:
01–Person
02–Private Property
03–Public Property

8) PLACE of OCCURRENCE:
01–Residence
02–Hotel, Motel or Other Commercial
Short-Term Residence
03–Parking Lot Areas
04–Business
05–Vehicle
06–Street/Sidewalk
07–Highway/Freeway
08–Park/School Ground
09–Vacant Lot
10–Jail
11–Rural Area/Country Road
12–Cemetery
13–Religious Building
14–Government Building
15–School Building
16–Private Club
17–Other (Describe)

11) RELATIONSHIP of OFFENDER to VICTIM:
01–Family Member
02–Neighbor
03–Acquaintance
04–Boyfriend/Ex-Boyfriend
05–Girlfriend/Ex-Girlfriend
06–Ex-Husband
07–Ex-Wife
08–Employee
09–Employer
10–Friend
11–Homosexual Relation
12–Other–Known to Victim
13–Stranger
14–Gang Member
15–Peace Officer Related
16–Unknown
17–Other (Describe)

# Glossary

*Number in parentheses is the chapter(s) in which the term is discussed.*

**ABANDONMENT** the act of parents deserting their children. (11)

**ACCELERANTS** substances that cause fires to burn faster and hotter. (17)

**ACCESSORY** anyone except a husband, wife or member of the offender's family who knows the offender has committed a felony or is liable to arrest and yet harbors, conceals or helps the offender avoid or escape arrest, trial, conviction or punishment.

**ACTIVE VOICE** the subject performs the action of the sentence. In contrast to passive voice. (3)

**ADIPOCERE** soapy appearance of a dead body left for weeks in a hot, moist location. (12)

**ADMINISTRATIVE WARRANT** official permission to inspect a given property to determine compliance with city regulations; for example, compliance with fire codes. (17)

**ADMISSION** statement containing some information concerning the elements of a crime, but falling short of a full confession. (6)

**AGGRAVATED ARSON** intentionally destroying or damaging a dwelling or other property, real or personal, by means of fire or explosives, creating an imminent danger to life or great bodily harm, which risk was known or reasonably foreseeable to the suspect. (17)

**AGGRAVATED ASSAULT (FELONIOUS ASSAULT)** an unlawful attack by one person on another to inflict severe bodily injury. (9)

**ALLIGATORING** checking of charred wood giving the appearance of alligator skin. Large, rolling blisters indicate rapid, intense heat; small, flat blisters indicate long, low heat. (17)

**AMPHETAMINE** a stimulant. (19)

**ANTICHRIST** the son of Satan. (18)

**ARREST** taking a person into custody in the manner authorized by law. (7)

**ARSON** the malicious, willful burning of a building or property. *See also* **AGGRAVATED ARSON.** (17)

**ASPHYXIATION** death or unconsciousness resulting from insufficient oxygen to support the red blood cells reaching the body tissues and the brain. (12)

**ASSAULT** unlawfully threatening to harm another person, actually harming another person or attempting to do so. Formerly referred to threats of or attempts to cause bodily harm, but now usually includes *battery*. (9)

**ASSOCIATIVE EVIDENCE** evidence that links a suspect with a crime. (5)

**AUTOEROTIC ASPHYXIATION** accidental death from suffocation, strangulation or chemical asphyxia resulting from a combination of ritualistic behavior, oxygen deprivation, danger and fantasy for sexual gratification. (12)

**AUTOMATED FINGERPRINT IDENTIFICATION SYSTEM** a computerized system of reviewing and mapping fingerprints. (5)

**BACKING** marking photographs on their back with a felt-tip pen or label to indicate the photographer's initials, date photo was taken, brief description of what it depicts and the direction of north. Evidence can be circled on the back of the photo in the same way. (2)

**BAIT MONEY** currency whose serial numbers are recorded and which is placed so it can be added to any robbery loot. (8)

**BARBITURATE** a depressant drug. (19)

**BARCODES** identification symbols affixed to an item that can be scanned into a computer; now being used in property control systems. (5)

**BASELINE PLOTTING METHOD** establishes a straight line from one fixed point to another from which measurements are taken at right angles. (2)

**BEELZEBUB** a powerful demon, right below Satan, according to satanists. (18)

**BEST EVIDENCE** the original object, or the highest available degree of proof that can be produced (*Cheadle v. Bardwell*). (3)

**BIAS CRIME** a crime motivated by bigotry and hatred against a specific group of people. (18)

**BIGAMY** marrying another person when one or both of the parties are already married. (10)

**BIOMETRICS** the statistical study of biological data such as fingerprints. (5)

**BLACK MASS** diabolical communion ritual performed by satanists that mocks and desecrates the Christian mass. (18)

**BLOODS** a black gang; associated with the colors red and green. (18)

**BLOWING A SAFE** opening a safe using cotton, primer cap, copper wire and nitroglycerine. (13)

**BOOKMAKING** soliciting and accepting bets on any type of sporting event. (18)

**BUGGING** using a machine to record conversations within a room without the consent of those involved. (7)

**BURGLARY** the unlawful entry of a structure to commit a felony or theft. (13)

**BURN INDICATORS** visible evidence of the effects of heating or partial burning. (17)

**BURNING A SAFE** opening a safe using a burn bar or an oxy-acetylene tank, a hose and a torch. (13)

**CADAVERIC SPASM** a condition occurring in certain muscle groups that can indicate suicide. It usually occurs when the victim is holding something at the time of death and the hand closes tightly around the object due to the stress and tension of dying. Does not disappear as rigor mortis does. (12)

**CARJACKING** taking of a motor vehicle from a person by force or the threat of force. A new category of robbery. (8)

*CARROLL* **DECISION** established that vehicles may be searched without a warrant if there is probable cause for the search and if the vehicle would be gone before a search warrant could be obtained. (4)

**CAST** to make an impression using plaster of Paris or a similar substance. Also, the physical reproduction of such an impression. (5)

**CHAIN OF EVIDENCE** establishes each person having custody of evidence. (5)

**CHICKENHAWK** an online pedophile. Use chatlines and member profiles to locate potential victims. (11)

**CHILD MOLESTATION** the violation of a child by lewd or lascivious acts, indecent exposure, incest or rape. Usually a felony. (10)

**CHILD SEXUAL ABUSE** includes sexually molesting a child, performing sexual acts with a child and statutory rape and seduction. (11)

*CHIMEL* **DECISION** established that in a search incidental to a lawful arrest, the search must be made simultaneously with the arrest and must be confined to the area within the suspect's immediate control. (4)

**CHOP SHOP** an auto body shop that disassembles stolen vehicles and sells the parts. (16)

**CHOPPING A SAFE** opening a safe by chopping a hole in it. (13)

**CHRONOLOGICAL ORDER** in time sequence. (3)

**CIRCLE SEARCH PATTERN** begins at the center of the crime scene and then spreads out in ever-widening concentric circles. (4)

**CIRCUMSTANTIAL EVIDENCE** a fact or event that tends to incriminate a person in a crime; e.g., being seen running from a crime scene. (5)

**CIVIL LIABILITY** a person's risk of being sued. Any person acting under the authority of law who violates another person's constitutional rights can be sued. (1)

**CLASS CHARACTERISTICS** features that place an item into a specific category; e.g., the size and shape of a tool. (5)

**CLOSE TAIL** moving surveillance by which the subject is kept constantly within view. Also called a *tight tail*. (7)

**COGNITIVE INTERVIEW** interviewing technique that helps victims or witnesses to put themselves mentally at the scene of the crime. (6)

**COMMERCIAL EXPLOITATION** having as a direct or indirect goal monetary or other material gain. (11)

**COMPASS-POINT PLOTTING METHOD** measures the angles between two lines. (2)

**COMPETENT EVIDENCE** evidence that has been properly collected, identified, filed and continuously secured. (5)

**COMPETENT PHOTOGRAPH** a photograph that accurately represents what it purports to represent, is properly identified and is properly placed in the chain of evidence and secured until court presentation. (2)

**COMPLAINANT** the person who requests an investigation or that action be taken. Is often the victim of a crime. (6)

**COMPUTER VIRUS** a computer program created specifically to "infect" other programs with copies of itself. (15)

**CONCLUSIONARY LANGUAGE** nonfactual; drawing inferences; for example, "The man was *nervous.*" To be avoided in police reports. (3)

**CONFESSION** information supporting the elements of a crime that is provided and attested to by any person involved in committing the crime. Can be oral or written. (6)

**CORPUS DELICTI** the elements of a specific crime. Evidence establishing that a specific crime has been committed. (5)

**CORPUS DELICTI EVIDENCE** all evidence establishing that a crime was committed. (5)

**COVEN** a group of witches or satanists. (18)

**COVER** assumed identity used while on an undercover assignment. (7)

**CRACK** cocaine mixed with baking soda and water, heated in a pan and then dried and split into pellet-size bits or chunks, which are smoked to produce effects reportedly ten times greater than cocaine at a tenth the cost. (19)

**CRAZING** formation of irregular cracks in glass due to rapid, intense heat. It can indicate arson or the use of an accelerant. (17)

**CREDIT CARD** any credit plate, charge plate, courtesy card or other identification or device used to obtain a cash advance, a loan or credit or to purchase or lease property or services on the issuer's or holder's credit. (14)

**CRIME** an act or omission forbidden by law and punishable by a fine, imprisonment or even death. Crimes and their penalties are established and defined by state and federal statutes and local ordinances. (1)

**CRIMINAL HOMICIDE** includes murder and manslaughter and is a felony. (12)

**CRIMINAL INTENT** performing an unlawful act on purpose, knowing the act to be illegal. (1)

**CRIMINAL INVESTIGATION** seeking all facts associated with a crime to determine the truth: what happened and who is responsible. (1)

**CRIMINAL NEGLIGENCE** acts of commission or omission creating situations resulting in unreasonable risk of death or great bodily harm. (12)

**CRIMINAL STATUTE** legislative act relating to crime and its punishment. (1)

**CRIMINALISTICS** *see* **FORENSIC SCIENCE.** (1)

**CRIPS** a black gang; associated with the colors blue and purple. (18)

**CROSS-EXAMINATION** questioning by the opposite side in a trial that attempts to assess the validity of testimony given under direct examination. (20)

**CROSS-PROJECTION SKETCH** a sketch that presents the floor and walls of a room on the same surface. (2)

**CULT** a system of religious beliefs and rituals and its body of adherents. (18)

**CUNNILINGUS** sexual activity involving oral contact with the female genitals. (10)

**CURTILAGE** the portion of the residence that is not open to the public and is reserved for private owner or family use—in contrast to sidewalks and alleys which are used by the public. (4)

**CUSTODIAL ARREST** *see* **IN CUSTODY.** (6)

**CUSTODIAL INTERROGATION** questioning by law enforcement officers after a person has been taken into custody or otherwise deprived of freedom in a significant way. Requires that the Miranda warning be given. (6)

**CYBERCOPS** name given to investigators involved in computer forensics. (15)

**CYBERPUNK** an anti-establishment rebel in the computer universe. Also refers to an entire counter-culture existing in thin air. (15)

**CYBERSPACE** the thin air that "exists" between two computers. (15)

**DANGEROUS WEAPON** any firearm, loaded or unloaded; any device designed as a weapon and capable of producing great bodily harm or death; or any other device or instrument that is used or intended to be used in a way likely to produce great bodily harm or death.

**DEFENSE WOUNDS** nonfatal wounds incurred by victims as they attempt to ward off attackers. Indicative of murder. (12)

**DEPRESSANT** drug that reduces restlessness and emotional tension and induces sleep; most common are the barbiturates. (19)

**DEPTH OF CHAR** how deeply wood is burned. (17)

**DESIGNER DRUGS** substances created by adding to or taking something away from an existing drug. (19)

**DIRECT EVIDENCE** *see* **PRIMA FACIE EVIDENCE.** (5)

**DIRECT EXAMINATION** the initial questioning of a witness or defendant during a trial by the lawyer who is using the person's testimony to further his or her case. (20)

**DIRECT QUESTION** a question that is to the point with little chance of misinterpretation, for example, "What time did you leave?" (6)

**DNA** deoxyribonucleic acid. An organic substance found in the nucleus of living cells that provides the genetic code determining a person's individual characteristics. (5)

**DNA PROFILING** analysis of blood, hair, saliva, semen or cells from almost any part of the body to determine a person's identity. (5)

**DRAGGING A SAFE** *see* **PULLING.** (13)

**DRUG ABUSE** use of illegal drugs. (19)

**DRUG ADDICT** a person who habitually uses habit-forming narcotic drugs and thus endangers the public morals, health, safety or welfare; or who is or has been so far addicted to habit-forming narcotic drugs as to have lost self-control. (19)

**DYER ACT** made interstate transportation of a stolen motor vehicle a federal crime and allowed for federal assistance in prosecuting such cases. (16)

**ELDER ABUSE** the physical or mental mistreatment of a senior citizen. May include fraud as well as assault, battery and even murder. (9)

**ELECTRONIC SURVEILLANCE** using wiretapping and/or bugging to obtain information. (7)

**ELEMENTS OF THE CRIME** conditions that must exist and be proven to exist for an act to be called a specific kind of crime. (1)

**"ELEPHANT IN A MATCHBOX" DOCTRINE** doctrine requiring that searchers consider the probable size and shape of evidence they seek; e.g., large objects cannot be concealed in tiny areas. (4)

**ELIMINATION PRINTS** inked fingerprints taken of all persons whose prints are likely to be found at the crime scene but who are *not* suspects. (5)

**EMBEZZLEMENT** fraudulent appropriation of property by a person to whom it was entrusted. (14)

**EMERGENCIES** a dangerous suspect at or near a crime scene and/or a gravely injured person at the scene. (1)

**EMOTIONAL ABUSE (CHILDREN)** causing fear or feelings of unworthiness in children by such means as locking them in closets, ignoring them or constantly belittling them. (11)

**ENTRAPMENT** tricking someone into committing a crime that they would not normally commit. (7,19)

**EVIDENCE** anything that helps to establish the facts related to a crime. (5)

**EXCLUSIONARY RULE** established that the courts cannot accept evidence obtained by unreasonable searches and seizures, regardless of its relevance to the case (*Weeks v. United States*). (4)

**EXCULPATORY EVIDENCE** physical evidence that would clear one of blame, for example, having a blood type different from that found at a homicide. (5)

**EXCUSABLE HOMICIDE** unintentional, truly accidental killing of another person. (12)

**EXHIBITIONIST** a person who gains sexual satisfaction by exposing himself or herself. (10)

**EXPERT** a person having special knowledge not known to persons of moderate education and/or experience in the same field. (20)

**EXPLOITATION** taking unfair advantage of people or using them illegally. (11)

**FACT** something known to be true. (1)

**FELLATIO** sexual activity involving oral contact with the male genitals. (10)

**FELONIOUS ASSAULT** *see* **AGGRAVATED ASSAULT.** (9)

**FELONY** a major crime such as homicide, aggravated assault or robbery. Usually carries a penalty of imprisonment in a state penitentiary or death. (1)

**FIELD IDENTIFICATION** on-the-scene identification of a suspect by the victim of or witnesses to a crime, conducted within minutes of the commission of the crime. (7)

**FINISHED SCALE DRAWING** *see* **SCALE DRAWING.** (2)

**FIRE TRIANGLE** the three elements necessary for a substance to burn: heat, fuel and air. (17)

**FIRST PERSON** the use of *I, me, we* and *us* in speaking and writing. This is in contrast to the second person (*you*) and the third person (*he* or this *officer*). (3)

**FIRST-DEGREE MURDER** premeditated killing of another person or killing someone while committing or attempting to commit a felony. (12)

**FIXED SURVEILLANCE** *see* **STATIONARY SURVEILLANCE.** (7)

**FLASHROLL** money used in an undercover drug buy. (19)

**FLOOR-RELEASE LIMIT** maximum dollar amount that may be paid with a check or credit card without authorization from the central office. (14)

**FORCIBLE RAPE** sexual intercourse against a person's will by use or threat of force. (10)

**FORENSIC SCIENCE (CRIMINALISTICS)** application of the physical sciences and their technology to examining physical evidence of crimes. (1)

**FORGERY** signing someone else's name to a document or altering the name or amount on a check or document with the intent to defraud. (14)

**FRAUD** intentional deception to cause a person to give up property or some lawful right. (14)

**FRISK** an external search of an individual's clothing. Also called a **PATDOWN**. (4)

**FRUIT OF THE POISONOUS TREE DOCTRINE** the doctrine that evidence obtained as a result of an earlier illegality must be excluded from trial. (4)

**GANG** a group of people who form an allegiance for a common purpose and engage in unlawful or criminal activity. (18)

**GENETIC FINGERPRINT** using DNA analysis to identify a person. (5)

**GOOD FAITH DOCTRINE** a doctrine stating that illegally obtained evidence may be admitted into trial if the police were truly not aware that they were violating the suspect's Fourth Amendment rights. (4)

**GOODS** property, including anything that is tangible and has value; e.g., gas, clothing, money, food. (14)

**GRAFFITI** wall writing; sometimes called the "newspaper of the street." (18)

**GRAND LARCENY** a felony based on the substantial value of the property stolen. (14)

**GRID SEARCH PATTERN** adaptation of the lane search pattern in which the lanes are traversed and then cross-traversed. *See also* **LANE SEARCH PATTERN.** (4)

**HACKER** a computer buff. (15)

**HALLUCINOGEN** a mind-expanding drug; e.g., LSD, DMT and PCP or angel dust. (19)

**HAND OF GLORY** the left hand of a person who has died. (18)

**HARDWARE (COMPUTER)** computer equipment, including the keyboard, monitor and printer. (15)

**HEAT OF PASSION** extremely volatile emotional condition. (12)

**HEBEPHILE** a person who selects high-school-age youths as sex victims. (11)

**HESITATION WOUNDS** less severe cutting marks caused by an individual's attempts to build up courage before making a fatal cutting wound. Indicates suicide. (12)

**HOLDER** person to whom a credit card is issued. (14)

**HOMICIDE** the killing of one person by another. (12)

**HYPNOSIS** a trancelike condition psychically induced where the person loses consciousness but responds to the hypnotist's suggestions. (6)

**ICE** smokable methamphetamine. (19)

**IDENTIFYING FEATURES** *see* **INDIVIDUAL CHARACTERISTICS.** (5)

**IGNITERS** substances or devices used to start a fire. (17)

**IMMEDIATE CONTROL** within a person's reach. (4)

**IN CUSTODY (CUSTODIAL ARREST)** that point when an officer has decided a suspect is not free to leave, there has been considerable deprivation of the suspect's liberty or the officer has, in fact, arrested the suspect. (6)

**IN LOCO PARENTIS** having the authority to take the place of the parent. Teachers usually have this right. (9)

**INCANTATION** verbal spells. (18)

**INCEST** sexual intercourse with another person known to be nearer of kin than first cousin. (10,11)

**INDECENT EXPOSURE** revealing oneself to such an extent as to shock others' sense of decency. (10,11)

**INDIRECT QUESTION** question that skirts the issue, for example, "How do you and the victim get along?" Should be used sparingly if at all. (6)

**INDIVIDUAL CHARACTERISTICS** features that set one item apart from others of the same type. Also called *identifying characteristics*. (5)

**INEVITABLE DISCOVERY DOCTRINE** the doctrine that if the evidence would in all likelihood eventually be discovered anyway, it may be used even if it was obtained illegally. (4)

**INFERENCE** a judgment based on reasoning. (1)

**INFORMANT** any individual who can provide information related to a case and who is not a complainant, witness, victim or suspect. (6)

**INFORMATION AGE** period of time driven by information rather than by agriculture or industry as in the past. (6)

**INFRARED ENERGY** the invisible energy beyond the red end of the color spectrum. Used in photography to see through a haze, to read smeared or deteriorated writings and erasures and to distinguish among inks, dyes and other pigments. (5)

**INKLESS FINGERPRINTS** a fingerprinting procedure that uses pretreated or special card stock or standard cards to retain nonsmearable, nonerasable fingerprints that can be read by a computer. (5)

**INTEGRITY OF EVIDENCE** referring to the requirement that any item introduced in court must be in the same condition as when it was found at the crime scene. (5)

**INTERROGATION** questioning persons suspected of direct or indirect involvement in the crime being investigated. (6)

**INTERVIEW** a questioning of persons not suspected of being involved in a crime but who know about the crime or the individuals involved in it. (6)

**INTIMATE PARTS** usually refers to the primary genital areas, groin, inner thighs, buttocks and breasts. (10)

**INTUITION** the "time of knowing" without any conscious reasoning or apparent logic. Based on knowledge and experience or what is commonly called "street sense." An intangible urge; a "gut feeling" developed by experience. (1)

**INVESTIGATE** to observe or study closely; to inquire into something systematically in a search for truthful information. (1)

**INVISIBLE FINGERPRINTS** fingerprints that are not readily seen but that can be developed through powders or chemicals. (5)

**INVOLUNTARY MANSLAUGHTER** killing someone through extreme, culpable negligence. Unintentional homicide. (12)

**JUDGE** any official authorized to hold or preside over a court of record. (20)

**JUSTIFIABLE HOMICIDE** killing another person under authorization of the law. (12)

**KEYLESS DOORS** doors that are unlocked by entering a set combination by pushing numbered pads in a programmed sequence. Used on some newer automobiles. (16)

**KIDNAPPING** taking a person to another location by force, often for ransom. (11)

**KLEPTOMANIACS** compulsive thieves. (14)

**LANE SEARCH PATTERN** a search pattern that divides a crime scene into lanes by using stakes and strings or by having officers walk shoulder to shoulder or at arm's length. (4)

**LARCENY/THEFT** the unlawful taking, carrying, leading or riding away of property from another's possession. (14)

**LASER-BEAM PHOTOGRAPHY** a photographic process that reveals evidence indiscernible to the naked eye, such as a footprint in a carpet. (2)

**LATENT FINGERPRINTS** fingerprint impressions caused by perspiration on the ridges of the fingers being transferred to a surface or occurring as residues of oil, dirt or grease. (5)

**LAWFUL AUTHORITY** any person who owns, leases or controls property by an act of the courts or the person who owns the property. (14)

**LEGEND** that part of a crime scene sketch containing the case number, name of victim or complainant, location, date, time, investigator, person(s) assisting, scale, direction of north and any other identifying information required by the department. (2)

**LEWDNESS (WITH MINOR)** touching a minor so as to arouse, appeal to or gratify the perpetrator's sexual desires; the touching may be done by the perpetrator or by the minor under the perpetrator's direction. (11)

**LINE OF DEMARCATION (FIRE)** a boundary between charred and uncharred material. (17)

**LINEUP IDENTIFICATION** having victims or witnesses identify suspects from among at least five individuals presented before them. Used when the suspect is in custody. (7)

**LIVIDITY** *see* **POSTMORTEM LIVIDITY.** (12)

**LOAN-SHARKING** the loaning of money at exorbitant rates. (18)

**LONG-CON GAMES** schemes in which the victims are sent for whatever money they can raise. (14)

**LOOSE TAIL** moving surveillance in which it does not matter if the subject is temporarily lost. (7)

**MACROPHOTOGRAPHY** photographic enlargement of a subject to show details of evidence such as fingerprints or toolmarks. (2)

**MALICIOUS INTENT (MALICE)** ill will, wickedness, cruelty or recklessness; an evil intent, wish or design to annoy or injure another person. Can be inferred from an act done in willful disregard for the rights of another, an act done without just cause or excuse or an omission of a duty by willful disregard. (12)

**MANSLAUGHTER** unlawful killing of another person with no prior malice. Can be voluntary or involuntary. (12)

**MARKER (PHOTOGRAPHIC)** an item included in a photograph to show accurate or relative size. (2)

**MATERIAL EVIDENCE** evidence that is relevant to the specific case and forms a substantive part of the case presented or that has a legitimate and effective influence on the decision of the case (*Porter v. Valentine*). (5)

**MATERIAL PHOTOGRAPH** a photograph that relates to the specific case and the subject being discussed. (2)

**METALLURGY** the study of metals and alloys. Frequently used in police laboratories in analyzing metallic materials. (5)

**MICROPHOTOGRAPHY** taking pictures through a microscope to help identify minute particles of evidence (e.g., hair or fiber). (2)

**MIRANDA WARNING** informs suspects of their right to remain silent, to have counsel present and to have the state appoint and pay counsel if they cannot afford one. It also warns suspects that anything they say can be used against them in court. (6)

**MISDEMEANOR** a minor crime such as shoplifting or pilferage. Usually carries a fine or a short sentence in a county or municipal jail. (1)

**MISOPED** a person who hates children, has sex with them and then brutally destroys them. (11)

**MODEM** a device linking a computer to telephone lines so that messages can be sent between computers at different locations. (15)

**MODUS OPERANDI (M.O.)** the characteristic way a criminal commits a specific type of crime. (1)

**MOLESTATION (SEXUAL)** acts motivated by unnatural or abnormal sexual interest in another person that would reasonably be expected to disturb, irritate or offend the victim. No touching of the victim is necessary. (11)

**MONIKERS** street names; nicknames. (18)

**MOTOR VEHICLE** any self-propelled device for moving persons or property or pulling implements, whether operated on land, water or air. Includes automobiles, trucks, buses, motorcycles, snowmobiles, vans, construction equipment, self-propelled watercraft and aircraft. (16)

**MOVING SURVEILLANCE** following persons or vehicles on foot or in a vehicle to observe their actions or destinations. Also called *tailing*. (7)

**MUG SHOTS** photographs of those who have been taken into custody and booked. (2)

**MUMMIFICATION** complete dehydration of all body tissues that occurs when a cadaver is left in an extremely dry, hot area. (12)

**MUNCHHAUSEN SYNDROME** involves self-induced or self-inflicted injuries. (11)

**MUNCHHAUSEN SYNDROME BY PROXY (MSBP)** a form of child abuse where the parent or adult caregiver deliberately stimulates or causes medical distress in a child. (11)

**MURDER** *see* **FIRST-, SECOND-** and **THIRD-DEGREE MURDER.** (12)

**NARCOTIC** a drug that is physically and psychologically addicting; examples include heroin, morphine, codeine and cocaine. (19)

**NATIONAL CRIME INFORMATION CENTER (NCIC)** the FBI clearinghouse for criminal fingerprint records and information on wanted criminals, stolen property and vehicle information. (7)

**NEGLECT** failure to properly care for a child, property or one's actions. (11)

**NETWORK** relationships, links between people, and between people and their beliefs. (6)

**NIGHTCAP PROVISION** provision that an arrest or search warrant may be carried out at night. (7)

**NO-KNOCK WARRANTS** search warrants that contain a special provision permitting officers to execute the warrant without first announcing themselves. (4)

**NONCRIMINAL HOMICIDE** classification that includes excusable and justifiable homicide. (12)

**NONVERBAL COMMUNICATION** messages conveyed by dress, eye contact, posture, gestures, distance, mannerisms, rate of speech and tone of voice. (6)

**OCCULT** secret knowledge of supernormal powers. Many cults claim to have such knowledge. (18)

**OPINION** a personal belief. (1)

**ORAL COPULATION** the act of joining the mouth of one person with the sexual organ of another person. *See* **CUNNILINGUS** and **FELLATIO.** (10)

**ORDINANCE** an act of the legislative body of a municipality relating to all the rules governing the municipality, inclusive of misdemeanor crimes (*Bills v. Goshen*). (1)

**ORGANIZED CRIME** two or more persons conspiring to commit crimes for profit and using fear and corruption to obtain immunity from the law. (18)

**OVERLAPPING** a photographic technique whereby the entire scene is photographed in a clockwise direction with the picture so that a specific object is on the right side of the first photograph, on the next photo the same object is on the left side of the photo and so on until the entire scene is photographed. (2)

**PAST TENSE** use of verbs that indicate that the action has already occurred, for example, *lived* rather than *lives*. (3)

**PATDOWN** *see* **FRISK.** (4)

**PEDOPHILE** a person who is sexually attracted to young children. (10,11)

**PEELING A SAFE** opening a safe using a breast drill, a set of graduate drills and a jimmy. (13)

**PENETRATION** *see* **SEXUAL PENETRATION.** (10)

**PENTAGRAM** five-pointed star. (18)

**PERSON** legally includes not only individuals, but any corporation or joint stock association or any state, government or country that can lawfully own property. (14)

**PETTY (PETIT) LARCENY** a misdemeanor based on the value of the property stolen. (14)

**PHARMACOLOGY** the study of drugs. Applied in analyzing and identifying drugs submitted as evidence. (5)

**PHOTOGRAPHIC IDENTIFICATION** having victims or witnesses identify suspects from among pictures of people of comparable general description. Used when a suspect is not in custody or when a fair lineup cannot be conducted. (7)

**PHYSICAL ABUSE** beating, whipping, burning or otherwise inflicting physical harm. (11)

**PHYSICAL EVIDENCE** anything real—that has substance—and helps to establish the facts of a case. (5)

**PLAIN VIEW EVIDENCE** unconcealed evidence that is seen by an officer engaged in a lawful activity. (4)

**PLANT** *see* **STATIONARY SURVEILLANCE.** (7)

**PLASTIC FINGERPRINTS** impressions left in soft substances such as putty, grease, tar, butter or soft soap. *See also* **VISIBLE PRINTS.** (5)

**PLOTTING METHODS** systematic methods for finding the exact location of objects by using fixed points, including rectangular coordinates, base lines, triangulation and compass points. (2)

**POLYGRAPH** lie detector. Scientifically measures respiration and depth of breathing, changes in the skin's electrical resistance and blood pressure and pulse. (6)

**POSTMORTEM LIVIDITY** dark blue or purple discoloration of the body where blood has drained to the lowest level after death. Also called simply *lividity*. (12)

**PREMEDITATION** considering, planning or preparing for an act, no matter how briefly, before committing it. (12)

**PRIMA FACIE EVIDENCE** evidence that is made so by law; e.g., the blood alcohol level for intoxication. Also called *direct evidence*. (5)

**PRINCIPAL** every person involved in committing a crime, whether directly committing the act constituting the offense or aiding in its commission, whether present or absent. It includes every person who directly or indirectly advises, encourages, pays, commands or otherwise induces another to commit a felony.

**PROBABLE CAUSE** evidence that warrants a person of reasonable caution to believe that a crime has been committed. (4)

**PROBATIVE EVIDENCE** evidence that is vital for the investigation or prosecution of a case. Tending to prove or actually proving guilt or innocence. (5)

**PROCESSING EVIDENCE** includes discovering, recognizing and examining it; collecting, recording and identifying it; packaging, conveying and storing it; exhibiting it in court; and disposing of it when the case is closed. (5)

**PROFILING** *see* **PSYCHOLOGICAL PROFILING.**

**PROPERTY** all forms of tangible property, real and personal, including valuable documents, electricity, gas, water, heat and animals. (14)

**PROSTITUTION** soliciting sexual intercourse for pay. (10)

**PSYCHOLOGICAL PROFILING** indicates the type of person most likely to have committed a crime having certain unique characteristics. Also called simply *profiling*. (7)

**PUBLIC SAFETY EXCEPTION** ruling that police may interrogate a suspect without first giving the Miranda warning if a public threat exists that might be removed by having the suspect talk. (6)

**PULLING (DRAGGING) A SAFE** opening a safe with a heavy plate of steel by using a V-cut and drilling holes in the corners in which to insert bolts. (13)

**PUNCHING A SAFE** opening a safe with a short-handled sledge, a steel chisel and a drift pin. (13)

**RAID** a planned, organized invasion that uses the element of surprise to recover stolen property, seize evidence and/or arrest a suspect. (7)

**RAPE** having sexual intercourse with a person against his or her will. (10)

**RAPPORT** a harmonious relationship between individuals created by genuine interest and concern. (6)

**REASONABLE FORCE** the amount of force a prudent person would use in similar circumstances. (7)

**RECTANGULAR-COORDINATE PLOTTING METHOD** uses two adjacent walls of a room as fixed points from which distances are measured at right angles from each wall. (2)

**RELEVANT EVIDENCE** evidence that applies to the matter in question (*Barnett v. State*). (5)

**RELEVANT PHOTOGRAPH** a photograph that assists or explains testimony regarding the matter in question. (2)

**RES GESTAE STATEMENTS** spontaneous statements made at the time a crime is committed. Considered more truthful than planned responses. (1)

**RIGOR MORTIS** a stiffening of portions of the body after death, presumably due to enzyme breakdown. (12)

**RITUAL** prescribed form of religious or mystical ceremony. (18)

**RITUALISTIC CRIME** an unlawful act committed with or during a ceremony. (18)

**ROBBERY** the felonious taking of another's property, either directly from the person or in the person's presence, through force or intimidation. (8)

**ROGUES' GALLERY** mug shots gathered in files and displayed in groups. (2)

**ROUGH SKETCH** the first, pencil-drawn outline of the crime scene, which shows the location of objects and evidence. Basis for the finished *scale drawing*. (2)

**ROUGH TAIL** moving surveillance in which it does not matter if the surveillant is detected. (7)

**SABBAT** a gathering of witches. (18)

**SADIST** person who receives sexual gratification from causing pain to others, often through mutilation. (10)

**SADOMASOCHISTIC ABUSE** fettering, binding or otherwise physically restraining, whipping or torturing for sexual gratification. (10)

**SAFE** semiportable strongbox with combination lock. (13)

**SCALE DRAWING (FINISHED DRAWING)** the final drawing, drawn to scale using exact measurements, done in ink and usually on a better grade paper. (2)

**SEARCH** an examination of a person's house or other buildings or premises or of the person for the purpose of discovering contraband, illicit or stolen property or some evidence of guilt to be used in prosecuting a criminal action with which the person is charged (*Elliot v. State*). (4)

**SEARCH PATTERNS** systematic approaches to seeking evidence at a crime scene; e.g., by using lanes, concentric circles or zones. (4)

**SECOND-DEGREE MURDER** intent to cause the death of another, but without premeditation. (12)

**SECTOR SEARCH PATTERN** *see* **ZONE SEARCH PATTERN.** (4)

**SERIAL MURDER** the killing of three or more victims with emotional time breaks between the killings. (12)

**SERVICES** as an economic term, includes labor, professional services, hotel and restaurant services, entertainment, gas, electricity, water and transportation. (14)

**SEXUAL CONTACT (ILLEGAL)** any sexual act committed without the complainant's consent for the suspect's sexual or aggressive satisfaction. (10)

**SEXUAL EXPLOITATION (OF MINOR)** to employ, use, persuade, induce, entice or coerce a minor to engage or assist in engaging in any sexually explicit conduct; e.g., prostitution and pornography. (11)

**SEXUAL PENETRATION** includes sexual intercourse, cunnilingus, fellatio, anal intercourse or any other intrusion, no matter how slight, into the victim's genital, oral or anal openings by the suspect's body or by an object. An emission of semen is not required. (10)

**SEXUAL SEDUCTION (OF MINOR)** ordinary sexual intercourse, anal intercourse, cunnilingus or fellatio committed by a nonminor with a consenting minor. (11)

**SEXUALLY EXPLICIT CONDUCT** general term referring to any type of sexual intercourse between persons of the same or opposite sex, bestiality, sadomasochistic abuse, lewd exhibition or masturbation. (10, 11)

**SHOPLIFTING** taking an item from a retail store without paying for it. (14)

**SHORT-CON GAMES** victims are taken for whatever money they have on their person at the time of the swindle. (14)

**SHYLOCKING** *see* **LOAN-SHARKING.** (18)

**SIMPLE ARSON** intentional destruction by fire or explosives that does not create imminent danger to life or risk of great bodily harm. (17)

**SIMPLE ASSAULT** intentionally causing another person to fear immediate bodily harm or death or intentionally inflicting or attempting to inflict bodily harm on another. Usually a misdemeanor. (9)

**SINSEMILLA** homegrown marijuana. (19)

**SKETCH** a drawing. May be a rough or a finished sketch. (2)

**SODOMY** any form of unnatural sex. (10)

**SOFTWARE (COMPUTER)** the programs run by a computer. (15)

**SOURCES OF INFORMATION FILE** a file that contains the name and location of persons, organizations and records that can assist in a criminal investigation. (6)

**SPALLING** the breaking off of surface pieces of concrete, cement or brick due to intense heat. (17)

**SPECTROGRAPHIC ANALYSIS** using a laboratory instrument that rapidly analyzes color and coloring agents in small samples of material to determine what elements they contain. (5)

**STAKEOUT** *see* **STATIONARY SURVEILLANCE.** (7)

**STALKER** a person who intentionally and repeatedly follows, attempts to contact, harasses and/or intimidates another person. (9)

**STANDARD OF COMPARISON** an object, measure or model with which evidence is compared to determine whether both originated from the same source. (5)

**STATEMENT** a legal narrative description of events related to a crime. (6)

**STATIONARY SURVEILLANCE** observing a location from a fixed location. Also called *fixed surveillance, plant* and *stakeout*. (7)

**STATUTORY RAPE** sexual intercourse with a minor, with or without consent. (10)

**STIMULANT** drug that peps people up; the most common is the *amphetamine*. (19)

**STREET GANG** a group of individuals who form a social allegiance and engage in unlawful or criminal activity. (18)

**STRIP SEARCH PATTERN** an adaptation of the lane search pattern that is used when only one officer is available to search. (4)

**SUBJECT** what is observed during surveillance; e.g., a person, place, property, vehicle, group of persons, organization, object. (7)

**SUICIDE** intentionally taking one's own life. (12)

**SURVEILLANCE** the covert, discrete observation of people, places or objects. (7)

**SURVEILLANT** an investigator assigned to surveillance. (7)

**SUSPECT** person considered to be directly or indirectly connected with a crime, either by overt act or by planning and/or directing it. If charged and brought to trial, is called a *defendant.* (6)

**TAIL** *see* **MOVING SURVEILLANCE.** (7)

**TEMPLATE** a pattern, often used by architects and drafters. (3)

**TEMPORARY CUSTODY WITHOUT HEARING** removing a child from the custody of parents or guardians for a brief period, usually forty-eight hours. (11)

**TERRY DECISION** established that a patdown or frisk is a protective search for weapons and, as such, must be confined to a scope reasonably designed to discover guns, knives, clubs and other hidden instruments for the assault of a police officer or others.

**THEFT** *see* **LARCENY.** (14)

**THIRD DEGREE** the use of physical force, threats of force or other physical, mental or psychological abuse to get a suspect to confess. (6)

**THIRD-DEGREE MURDER** death that results from an imminently dangerous act but does not involve premeditation or intent. (12)

**TIGHT TAIL** *see* **CLOSE TAIL.** (7)

**TOOLMARK** an impression left by a tool on a surface. (5)

**TOXICOLOGY** the study of poisons. Toxicologists are consulted if food or drink poisoning is suspected. (12)

**TRACE EVIDENCE** extremely small physical matter. (5)

**TRAILER** a path, consisting of paper, hay, flammable compounds or any other substance that burns, that is set down for a fire to follow. Indicates arson. (17)

**TRAP PHOTOGRAPHY** also called *surveillance photography.* (2)

**TRIANGULATION PLOTTING METHOD** uses straight line measurements from two fixed objects to the location of the evidence, creating a triangle. The evidence is in the angle formed by the two straight lines. (2)

**TRUE (UNCONTAMINATED) SCENE** crime scene where no evidence has been introduced or removed except by the person(s) committing the crime. (4)

**TRUTH SERUMS** fast-acting barbiturates used to produce sleep at the approximate level of surgical anesthesia for the purpose of releasing a person's inhibitions so that he or she will give information not available otherwise. Most commonly used are sodium amytol and sodium pentathol. (6)

**TURF** geographic area claimed by a gang. Often marked by graffiti. (18)

**ULTRAVIOLET LIGHT** the invisible energy at the violet end of the color spectrum that causes substances to emit visible light. Commonly called *fluorescence.* Used to detect secret inks, invisible laundry marks, seminal fluid stains, marked buy money or extortion packages. (5)

**ULTRAVIOLET-LIGHT PHOTOGRAPHY** uses the low end of the color spectrum, which is invisible to human sight, to make visible impressions of bruises and injuries long after their occurrence. In addition, the type of weapon used can often be determined by examining its impression developed using ultraviolet light. (2)

**UNCONTAMINATED SCENE** *see* **TRUE SCENE.** (4)

**UNDERCOVER** using an assumed identity to obtain information and/or evidence. (7)

**VAULT** stationary security chamber of reinforced concrete, often steel-lined, with a combination lock. (13)

**VEHICLE IDENTIFICATION NUMBER** *see* **VIN** (16)

**VICTIM** the person injured by a crime. (6)

**VICTIMLESS CRIME** crime in which the victim is a willing participant in the illegal activity; e.g., a person who bets. (18)

**VIN (VEHICLE IDENTIFICATION NUMBER)** the primary nonduplicated, serialized number assigned by the manufacturer to each vehicle manufactured. Formerly called *serial number* or *motor vehicle identification number.* (16)

**VIRTUAL REALITY** an artificial, interactive world created by computer technology (usually involving some kind of immersion system such as a headset). (15)

**VIRUS, COMPUTER** a program created specifically to infect other programs with copies of itself. (15)

**VISIBLE FINGERPRINTS** prints made when fingers are dirty or stained when they leave their impression on a soft substance. (5)

**VISUAL MEDIUM** also called **VISUAL PRINT**; any film, photograph, negative, slide, book, magazine or other visual medium. (11)

**VOICEPRINT** graphic record of an individual's voice characteristics made by a sound spectrograph that records energy patterns emitted by speech. (5)

**VOLUNTARY MANSLAUGHTER** intentionally causing the death of another person in the heat of passion. (12)

**VOYEURISM** window peeking; Peeping Tomism. (10)

**WAIVER** giving up of certain rights. (6)

**WHITE-COLLAR CRIME** business-related or occupational crime; e.g., embezzlement, computer crimes, bribery, pilferage. (14)

**WIRETAPPING** intercepting and recording telephone conversations by a mechanical device without the consent of either party in the conversation. (7)

**WITNESS** a person who saw a crime or some part of it being committed or who has relevant information. (6)

**X-RAY DIFFRACTION** laboratory instrument that compares unknown crystalline substances and mixtures of crystals. (5)

**ZERO FLOOR RELEASE** the requirement that all transactions by credit card be authorized. (14)

**ZONE (SECTOR) SEARCH PATTERN** search pattern in which an area is divided into equal squares and numbered and then each square is searched individually. (4)

# Author Index

# Subject Index

**718**

## Photo Credits